# ISC

# Information Systems & Controls

CPA Exam Review

**2025**
Edition

# Permissions

The following items are utilized in this program, and are copyright property of the American Institute of Certified Public Accountants, Inc. (AICPA), all rights reserved:

- Uniform CPA Examination and Questions and Unofficial Answers, Copyright © 1991 – 2025
- Audit and Accounting Guides, Auditing Procedure Studies, Risk Alerts, Statements of Position, and Code of Professional Conduct
- Statements on Auditing Standards
- Statements on Standards for Accounting and Review Services
- Statements on Quality Control Standards
- Statements on Standards for Attestation Engagements
- Accounting Research Bulletins, APB Opinions
- Uniform CPA Examination Blueprints
- Independence Standards Board (ISB) Standards

Portions of various FASB and GASB documents, copyright property of the Financial Accounting Foundation, 401 Merritt 7, PO Box 5116, Norwalk, CT 06856-5116, are utilized with permission. Complete copies of these documents are available from the Financial Accounting Foundation. These selections include the following:

*Financial Accounting Standards Board (FASB)*

- The FASB Accounting Standards Codification™
- Statements of Financial Accounting Concepts
- FASB Statements, Interpretations, and Technical Bulletins

*Governmental Accounting Standards Board (GASB)*

- GASB Codification of Governmental Accounting and Financial Reporting Standards and GASB Statements
- GASB Concepts Statements
- GASB Interpretations and Technical Bulletins

Published by UWorld
9111 Cypress Waters Blvd.
Suite 300
Dallas, TX 75019
accounting.uworld.com/cpa-review



Printed in English, in the United States of America.

## Acknowledgments

Keeping the course materials updated and accurate would not be possible without the contribution of our team of content experts. Our team includes academics and professionals who have expertise and experience in their respective fields; several have had experience at the Big Four or have PhDs in areas related to the exam. All are passionate about helping candidates pass the exam and about UWorld's dedication to creating the highest quality materials.

# Information Systems & Controls

# Introduction

# Introduction

# Introduction

## How to Best Use Your Course

Welcome to the UWorld CPA Review course! Our expert team is passionate about helping you succeed and has developed an award-winning program that is proven to yield results. Before you get started, please read through this guide on how to best use your course so that you can master all of the topics laid out for you in the AICPA Blueprints and ultimately pass the CPA Exam. At UWorld, our passion is to make the hard stuff easy to learn and understand.

### Plan Your Studies

When preparing for the CPA Exam, half the battle is setting yourself up for success with a solid plan from the get go. This includes establishing short- and long-term goals to ensure you're staying on track.

To get started, use the Study Plan in your course. Start your plan by setting the beginning and ending dates for your schedule. Then select your pace (Fast Track vs Customize) and set the number of hours per day you will study. The system will create your plan based on your choices. It is important to follow your plan steadily so that you can ensure you hit your goals. If you miss a day, make it up!

**Tip!**

Download the app! This gives you access to everything your course offers while on the go.

### Master the Concepts through Active Learning

With this program, you will build your foundational knowledge and mastery of core exam topics through **active learning**. This evidence-based learning methodology centers around the principle that students retain information best when they actively participate in answering questions.

- **Begin with the Representative Task.** Read through each representative task carefully. (The Representative Tasks are from the AICPA Blueprints and are presented in our books and videos to guide you through the materials.) Pay particular attention to the words at the beginning of the task; they provide guidance on level and focus
- **Scan the book chapter.** Do you feel confident with the material? If you do, you might want to move directly to the questions and begin to practice. If you find that you are hesitant about an area, read the book or watch the video to solidify your understanding before you practice on some questions
- **Watch the videos.** If you prefer to absorb material on video rather than by reading the book, you will notice that the videos are deliberately set up in small segments. Our team created these segments so you can review what you need, either as part of the whole topic or for specific review of a smaller area
- **Practice the questions.** In our question bank (our QBank) we have taken great care to provide you with very high-quality questions and explanations. Each explanation not only tells you why the concept tested is important to understand but also teaches you why the answer is correct and why the other answer choices are not correct. Images, tables, and links to definitions also help fill in gaps as you use the questions and explanations to learn by doing

## Track Your Progress and Performance

As you complete each chapter, track your progress and performance using our signature **SmartPath Predictive Technology™**. SmartPath is a data-driven platform that provides recommended targets based on previous students who have passed the CPA Exam. This is an important tool to help you study efficiently and gauge whether you are *exam-ready*. Your goal is to hit both your progress target (Questions Attempted) and performance target (Score) for each chapter.

As you work through the material, don't worry about hitting your "Score" target right away and focus your efforts on hitting the "Questions Attempted" target first. This approach may feel uncomfortable, but trust that you are building your knowledge as you absorb the answer explanations.

Once you've completed all the topics in a chapter, you can go back and focus your efforts on hitting the "Score" target. If you are falling short, drill down in the Performance tab to see which topics need extra attention.

**Tip!**

Don't over-study. **SmartPath™** helps determine when you can move on to the next topic.

## Solidify the Concepts

Need extra help mastering the concept? Take advantage of the additional learning tools that are integrated into your course. For example, you could be working through a difficult question and find you need further explanation. No problem! There's a link to the supporting lecture right there in the question. Want to remember something for later review? Easily transfer content directly from the question to a digital flashcard. These are just a few ways we make it easy to navigate to and access the right tools you need at the right time.

These additional tools are designed to enhance your studies—**you do not necessarily need to read or watch all of this material!** Rather, use these tools as a means to improve on weak areas:

- **Video Lectures** – From the Lectures tab or directly integrated in the link at the bottom of each practice question, you have access to the profession's most motivating and effective lecturers. Lectures break down difficult topics into simplified concepts and provide helpful memory aids. These are especially recommended for visual and auditory learners
- **Textbooks** – Digital eTextbooks are accessible side by side with the video lectures or in a printed format with some of our course packages. These can be used as a reference if you need further explanation of a concept. Many students also find it beneficial to follow along in the textbook while watching the lectures and either take notes directly in the physical books or by using the Notes feature and highlighting tool in the platform
- **Digital Flashcards** – Create custom flashcards directly from your practice questions by clicking on the lightning bolt symbol. Depending on your program package, your course may also be pre-loaded with an "Expert Deck" of flashcards covering the most heavily tested topics. You can review all your cards in Study Mode or using our **Spaced-Repetition Technology**. This is an evidence-based learning method that presents cards you've marked as *difficult* more frequently and cards you've marked as *easy* less frequently. The spacing of how and when the flashcards are introduced has been proven to increase retention and strengthen memory recall

## Get Exam-Ready

The final days leading up to the exam are a critical time in which you're going to want to review your SmartPath data and ask, "Am I *exam-ready*?" If you have hit all the targets, you are in a really good spot. However, if any areas are still marked "Needs Improvement," now is the time to focus your efforts on meeting those targets.

Finally, we recommend you **take at least one full practice exam before exam day** (click on the "Exam Sim" tab in the QBank). This allows you to hone your test-taking skills in an exam-like environment that follows the same 5-testlet, 4-hour structure as the exam.

## AICPA Blueprints

The UWorld CPA Review course is based on the AICPA Blueprints, which show candidates what skills and content topics will be tested on the CPA Exam. You don't have to make tough decisions about what concepts to focus on. If you follow our methodology, you will be well on your way to passing the exam.

Let's take a look at what we mean by starting with the AICPA Blueprints. The Blueprints have four levels:

- Area
- Group
- Topic
- Representative Task

Each Representative Task also has a Skill level.

- Remembering & Understanding
- Application
- Analysis
- Evaluation (used only in AUD)

Here is a snapshot of a Blueprint with the levels and skills marked.

Area I – Business Analysis (40–50%)

| | Skill | | | | |
|---|---|---|---|---|---|
| Content group/topic | Remembering & Understanding | Application | Analysis | Evaluation | Representative Task |
| A. Current period/historical analysis, including the use of data | | | | | |
| 1. Financial statement analysis | | ✓ | | | Determine attribute structures, format, and sources of data needed to prepare financial statement analysis. |
| | | | ✓ | | Compare current period financial statement accounts to prior periods or budget and explain variances. |
| | | | ✓ | | Interpret financial statement fluctuations and ratios (eg, profitability, liquidity, solvency, performance). |
| | | | ✓ | | Use outputs (eg, reports, visualizations) from data analytic techniques to identify patterns, trends, and correlations to explain an entity's results. |
| | | | ✓ | | Derive the impact of transactions on the financial statements and notes to the financial statements. |

BAR
Area I: Business Analysis
Group A: Current Period/Historical Analysis
Topic 1: Financial Statement Analysis

The Table of Contents of the BAR book shows how each UWorld textbook is set up to follow the order of the AICPA Blueprints, with

- Area
- Group
- Topic

## Business Analysis & Reporting



In the pages of each book, we provide the Representative Tasks from the AICPA Blueprints. We did that to make a direct connection between the exam and our content. Our team deliberately focused on what the Tasks say and wrote study materials that match with the Task. There is no closer connection between what will be tested and what you are studying.

# 1.01 Financial Statement Analysis

## Overview

A company appraises the past, present, and future execution of goals and economic fitness by performing **financial statement analysis** on its results from operations in a given period. Refer to the financial ratios used in the FAR exam for this section.

The results are viewed in relation to prior periods, budgets, and key performance indicators (ie, benchmarks). Companies **make informed decisions** using this analysis. The analysis is often presented using summaries and visualizations that present the financial data in an easy-to-understand, meaningful report.

## Attribute Structures, Format, and Sources of Data

**Representative Task (Application):** Determine attribute structures, format, and sources of data needed to prepare financial statement analysis.

Beyond connecting to the topics of the AICPA Blueprints, our team also differentiated the textbook content to match the skill levels of the Tasks.

- **Remembering & Understanding** tasks require you to understand the definitions and fundamentals of the topic. We have presented the information in these areas with an eye to creating clear explanations of the topics
- **Application** tasks are more about using your knowledge in scenarios to indicate that you understand the concepts. Our authors have therefore provided examples that show you how to apply your knowledge in specific situations. Many of these examples are similar to questions that you will find on the exam
- **Analysis** tasks require a higher level of thinking, many times leading you to choose one outcome over another or to make a decision. On the exam, these tasks will always be addressed in Task-Based Simulations, or TBSs. The AICPA intentionally makes these more challenging to determine if you really know the material and can work with it as a professional. In our materials, our authors often guide you through the critical thinking required to work with TBSs
- **Evaluation** tasks are only in the AUD section of the exam and are at the highest level of thinking. They go a step further than the Analysis level and require you to evaluate or judge different approaches or outcomes

## The CPA Exam

Within the AICPA Blueprints, there is information about how much time candidates have for each section and how many questions by question type each section contains. Question types include Multiple-Choice Questions (MCQs) and Task-Based Simulations (TBSs).

| Section | Section Time | Multiple-Choice Questions (MCQs) | Task-Based Simulations (TBSs) |
|---|---|---|---|
| AUD – Core | 4 hours | 78 | 7 |
| FAR – Core | 4 hours | 50 | 7 |
| REG – Core | 4 hours | 72 | 8 |
| BAR – Discipline | 4 hours | 50 | 7 |
| ISC – Discipline | 4 hours | 82 | 6 |
| TCP – Discipline | 4 hours | 68 | 7 |

## Scoring Weight by Exam Section

The AICPA also shows candidates how the question types for each section are weighted and account for their overall score.

| | Score Weighting | |
|---|---|---|
| **Section** | **Multiple-Choice Questions (MCQs)** | **Task-Based Simulations (TBSs)** |
| AUD – Core | 50% | 50% |
| FAR – Core | 50% | 50% |
| REG – Core | 50% | 50% |
| BAR – Discipline | 50% | 50% |
| ISC – Discipline | 60% | 40% |
| TCP – Discipline | 50% | 50% |

## Skill Allocations

As mentioned earlier, each Representative Task is tested at a specific Skill Level, and each part of the exam has its own weighting of the Skill Levels, as seen here.

| Section | Remembering & Understanding | Application | Analysis | Evaluation |
|---|---|---|---|---|
| AUD – Core | 30–40% | 30–40% | 15–25% | 5–15% |
| FAR – Core | 5–15% | 45–55% | 35–45% | – |
| REG – Core | 25–35% | 35–45% | 25–35% | – |
| BAR – Discipline | 10–20% | 45–55% | 30–40% | – |
| ISC – Discipline | 55–65% | 20–30% | 10–20% | – |
| TCP – Discipline | 5–15% | 55–65% | 25–35% | – |

## Content Allocations

The AICPA Blueprints address how coverage of the various content areas is allocated in each exam. Using the UWorld system that ties directly to the Blueprint structure, it is easy to see which topics are covered to what extent.

### AUD

| Content Area | | Allocation |
|---|---|---|
| Area I | Ethics, Professional Responsibilities, and General Principles | 15–25% |
| Area II | Assessing Risk and Developing a Planned Response | 25–35% |
| Area III | Performing Further Procedures and Obtaining Evidence | 30–40% |
| Area IV | Forming Conclusions and Reporting | 10–20% |

### FAR

| Content Area | | Allocation |
|---|---|---|
| Area I | Financial Reporting | 30–40% |
| Area II | Select Balance Sheet Accounts | 30–40% |
| Area III | Select Transactions | 25–35% |

### REG

| Content Area | | Allocation |
|---|---|---|
| Area I | Ethics, Professional Responsibilities, and Federal Tax Procedures | 10–20% |
| Area II | Business Law | 15–25% |
| Area III | Federal Taxation of Property Transactions | 5–15% |
| Area IV | Federal Taxation of Individuals | 22–32% |
| Area V | Federal Taxation of Entities (including tax preparation) | 23–33% |

### BAR

| Content Area | | Allocation |
|---|---|---|
| Area I | Business Analysis | 40–50% |
| Area II | Technical Accounting and Reporting | 35–45% |
| Area III | State and Local Governments | 10–20% |

### ISC

| Content Area | | Allocation |
|---|---|---|
| Area I | Information Systems and Data Management | 35–45% |
| Area II | Security, Confidentiality, and Privacy | 35–45% |
| Area III | Considerations for System and Organization Controls (SOC) Engagements | 15–25% |

### TCP

| Content Area | | Allocation |
|---|---|---|
| Area I | Tax Compliance and Planning for Individuals and Personal Financial Planning | 30–40% |
| Area II | Entity Tax Compliance | 30–40% |
| Area III | Entity Tax Planning | 10–20% |
| Area IV | Property Transactions (disposition of assets) | 10–20% |

## Exam Testlets

Each section of the exam is divided into five testlets. Two testlets cover MCQs, and three testlets cover TBSs. Not all sections have an equal number of MCQs and TBSs, as the following chart shows.

| | Testlet | | | | | Total | |
|---|---|---|---|---|---|---|---|
| | 1 | 2 | 3 | 4 | 5 | | |
| Section | MCQ | MCQ | TBS | TBS | TBS | MCQ | TBS |
| AUD - Core | 39 | 39 | 2 | 3 | 2 | 78 | 7 |
| FAR - Core | 25 | 25 | 2 | 3 | 2 | 50 | 7 |
| REG - Core | 36 | 36 | 2 | 3 | 3 | 72 | 8 |
| BAR - Discipline | 25 | 25 | 2 | 3 | 2 | 50 | 7 |
| ISC - Discipline | 41 | 41 | 1 | 3 | 2 | 82 | 6 |
| TCP - Discipline | 34 | 34 | 2 | 3 | 2 | 68 | 7 |

Finally, to manage your time effectively in the exam, we recommend that you:

- Use 75 seconds per multiple-choice question as a benchmark,
- Allocate 15-20 minutes per task-based simulation, depending on complexity, and
- Take the standard 15-minute break after the third testlet; it doesn't count against your time.

To see the full AICPA Blueprints, visit
https://www.aicpa.org/becomeacpa/cpaexam/examinationcontent

Above all, start the study process with confidence! As Roger always says, "You do not have to be a genius to pass the CPA Exam. If you study, you will pass!" You've got this.

# ISC

## Considerations for System and Organization Controls (SOC) Engagements

# ISC 1
# SOC Planning and Performing

# ISC 1: SOC Planning and Performing

# 1.01 Introduction to SOC Engagements

## SOC Suite of Services

**We present blueprint Area III at the beginning of this book as the content is important to understanding the representative tasks in blueprint Areas I and II. Area III's representative tasks cover planning, performing, and reporting on System and Organization Controls (SOC) examinations. Areas I and II require the application of SOC knowledge.**

### SOC Report Categories

The AICPA's SOC Suite of Services offers three categories of engagements:

**AICPA SOC Suite of Services**

| SOC for Service Organizations | SOC for Cybersecurity | SOC for Supply Chain |
|---|---|---|

- **SOC for Service Organizations (SOC 1®, SOC 2®, SOC 3®):** System-level controls at a service organization supplying outsourced services.
- **SOC for Cybersecurity:** An entity's cybersecurity risk management program.
- **SOC for Supply Chain:** System-level controls at an entity that produces, manufactures, or distributes products.

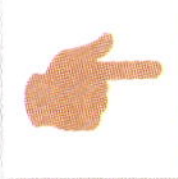

Most of Area III's representative tasks focus on SOC for Service Organizations because those examinations are performed most often. Appendix B and C present examples of SOC 1® and SOC 2® reports. Reading those reports prior to, during, and after this chapter is recommended.

Each of the SOC offerings is unique, with different answers to the following questions:

- Who are the intended report users?
- What standards and guidance apply?
- What subject matter is being examined?
- Which criteria are suitable?
- What information does the report include?

## Attestation Standards

**The SOC Suite of Services comprises attestation engagements performed according to the AICPA's *Statements on Standards for Attestation Engagements* (SSAE Nos. 18, 20, and 21).**

The relevant attestation standards are AT-C 105, AT-C 205, and AT-C 320. While AT-C 320 is specific to SOC 1®, parts of its guidance may also be helpful in other SOC examinations.

SOC engagements are **assertion-based examinations**. AT-C 105 provides that:

- An assertion is a declaration about whether a subject matter complies with criteria.
- In an assertion-based examination, a responsible party measures or evaluates a subject matter against criteria and provides an assertion about the outcome.
- A CPA expresses an opinion in a written report about whether:
  - The subject matter is in accordance with the criteria, or
  - The responsible party's assertion is fairly stated, in all material respects.

Therefore, the basic concept underlying all SOC examinations is the following:

The ***responsible party*** measures or evaluates the ***subject matter*** against ***criteria*** and provides an assertion about the outcome.

- **Responsible party:** Normally management or those charged with governance of the entity under examination, but must be a party who:
  - Takes responsibility for the subject matter and
  - Has a reasonable basis for making an assertion.
- **Subject matter:** An identifiable topic that can be:
  - Consistently measured or evaluated by applying criteria, and
  - Subjected to procedures to obtain evidence.
- **Criteria:** Benchmarks against which the subject matter can be measured or evaluated.

AT-C 205 states that a CPA's role in an assertion-based examination is to:

- **Obtain reasonable assurance** about whether the subject matter is free from material misstatement when measured or evaluated against criteria.
- **Express an opinion in a written report** about whether:
  - The subject matter is in accordance with (or based on) the criteria, in all material respects, or
  - The responsible party's assertion is fairly stated, in all material respects.

## COSO Internal Control–Integrated Framework

**Representative Task (Remembering and Understanding):** Explain the purpose of the Trust Services Criteria and its organization (eg, alignment with the COSO Internal Control–Integrated Framework, supplemental criteria, common criteria, and additional specific criteria).

The subject matter of a SOC examination includes two parts:

- Management's **description of the system** (or program), which is measured or evaluated against suitable **description criteria**.
- The entity's **controls,** which are measured or evaluated against suitable control criteria.

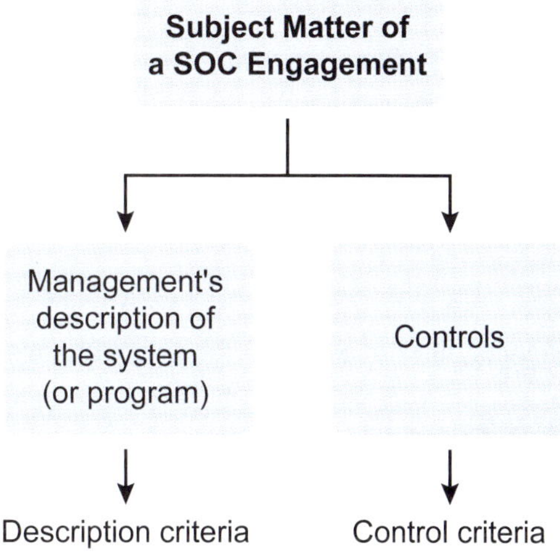


Both sets of criteria relate to the COSO Internal Control–Integrated Framework. COSO defines **internal control** as:

> *"A process, effected by an entity's board of directors, management, and other personnel, designed to provide reasonable assurance regarding the achievement of* ***objectives*** *related to operations, reporting, and compliance."*

COSO further defines **risk** as "the possibility that an event will occur and adversely affect the achievement of objectives."

Objectives represent the aim of an entity's governance activities. Controls mitigate risk and provide **reasonable assurance** of achieving objectives.

**Remembering SOC Terminology**

Terms vary among the SOC examinations, reflecting different subject matters. For example, in a SOC 1®, objectives are "control objectives." However, in a SOC 2®, objectives are "principal service commitments and system requirements."

Remembering the correct terms makes it easier to recognize the type of SOC examination that a CPA exam question refers to.

A section of the description criteria includes management's discussion of COSO's five components of internal control:

**COSO Internal Control Components and Principles**

| Internal Control Component | Principles |
|---|---|
| Control Environment | 1. Demonstrates commitment to integrity and values<br>2. Demonstrates independence and exercises oversight responsibility<br>3. Establishes structure, authority, and responsibility<br>4. Demonstrates commitment to attracting, developing, and retaining competent staff<br>5. Enforces accountability |
| Risk Assessment | 6. Specifies suitable, specific objectives<br>7. Identifies and analyzes risks<br>8. Assesses fraud risk<br>9. Identifies and analyzes significant changes |
| Control Activities | 10. Selects and develops control activities that help mitigate risks<br>11. Selects and develops general controls over technology<br>12. Bases controls on thorough policies and procedures |
| Information and Communication | 13. Uses relevant, high-quality information<br>14. Communicates internally to support controls<br>15. Communicates externally |
| Monitoring | 16. Conducts ongoing and/or separate evaluations<br>17. Evaluates and communicates deficiencies |

There are two primary control criteria that apply to SOC engagements:

- **AT-C 320:** Lists the minimum control criteria for SOC 1® examinations.
- **Trust services criteria:** Control criteria for examinations related to the **trust services categories** (security, availability, processing integrity, confidentiality, or privacy). All SOC engagements may use the trust services criteria, except SOC 1®.

  There are three series of trust services criteria: common, supplemental, and additional category specific:

  - **Common criteria:** Align to the 17 COSO principles.
  - **Supplemental criteria:** Expand COSO Principle 12, control activities.
  - **Additional criteria:** Criteria specific to the availability, processing integrity, confidentiality, and privacy trust services categories. (There are no additional criteria specific to the security category.)

**"Management's Planning Responsibilities," in Lecture 1.03 Engagement Planning, further explains the trust services criteria.**

# SOC for Service Organizations

**Representative Task (Remembering and Understanding):** Recall the types of subject matter a practitioner may be engaged to report on using the trust services criteria.

**Representative Task (Remembering and Understanding):** Identify management assertions specific to the different categories and types (type 1 and type 2) of SOC engagements (SOC 1®, SOC 2®, SOC 3®).

**Representative Task (Remembering and Understanding):** Recall the purpose and intended users of SOC 1®, SOC 2®, SOC 3® and SOC for Cybersecurity reports.

## Overview

**In outsourcing, a user entity (buyer) hires a service organization (seller) to supply services using the service organization's personnel, expertise, equipment, or technology.**

User entity management must assess third-party risks and monitor the service organization's activities. The service organization may be contractually obligated to provide a SOC for Service Organization report to the user entity every six months or annually.

The primary intentions of a SOC for Service Organization report are the following:

| Give report users information needed to understand the service organization's system and controls. | Get an independent CPA's opinion about whether the service organization has<br>• Completely and accurately described its system and controls based on the criteria.<br>• Suitably designed its controls based on the criteria.<br>• Designed controls that operate effectively when included in the engagement. |
|---|---|

## SOC 1®

**SOC 1® reports give assurance about systems and controls relevant to user entities' internal control over financial reporting (ICFR).**

User entities and their auditors (ie, **user auditors**) use SOC 1® reports in a financial statement audit. User auditors are required to obtain an understanding of the service organization's system and evaluate how it affects the user entity. A SOC 1® type 2 report is the most practical way to provide the user auditor with evidence regarding the services provided and whether controls are suitably designed and implemented and have operated effectively. Without the SOC report, the user auditor would need to evaluate the controls by auditing the service organization directly.

**Examples of Service Organizations That May Need a SOC 1® Report**

- Transaction, payment, and payroll processors
- Investment custodian or trust service providers
- Retirement and employee benefit plan processors
- Health insurance claim processors
- Loan or mortgage servicers
- SaaS, PaaS, and IaaS cloud service providers

SOC 1® is a **restricted report**. **Intended users** include the service organization, user entities, and user entity auditors. An **engaging party** selects an independent CPA firm (**service auditor**) to examine the service organization and express an opinion. The engaging party may be the service organization, a user entity, or another interested party.

Based on the AT-C 105 basic attestation concept, a SOC 1® examination has the following characteristics:

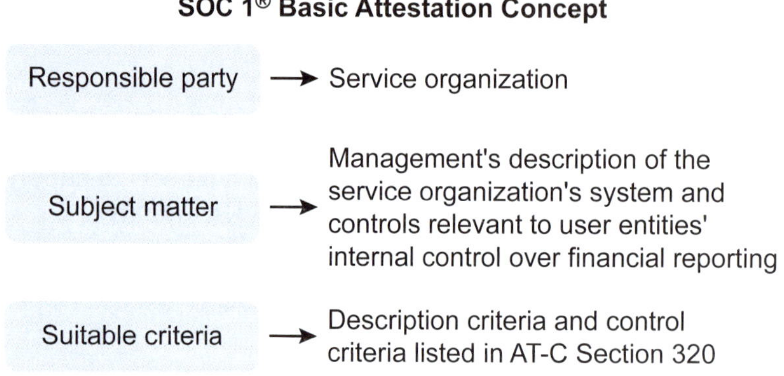


Thus, in a SOC 1® examination:

The ***service organization*** measures or evaluates ***the description of its system and controls relevant to user entities' internal controls over financial reporting*** against ***the criteria listed in AT-C Section 320*** and provides an assertion about the outcome.

The following definitions from AT-C 320 apply to SOC 1® engagements:

- **Management's assertions:** Management's claims about whether the description of the service organization's system and related controls are in accordance with (or based on) the criteria
- **Management's description of the system:** Management's narrative describing the following:
  - Service organization's system
  - Control objectives
  - Criteria and related controls
- **Service organization's system:** The policies, procedures, and technology used to provide services to user entities
- **Control objectives:** The goals a service organization wants to achieve through controls
- **Controls at a service organization:** Controls relevant to user entities' internal controls over financial reporting, which provide reasonable assurance of achieving control objectives

SOC 1® and SOC 2® reports can be a **type 1** or **type 2**:

| | Type 1 | Type 2 |
|---|---|---|
| **Examination scope** → | As of a specified date | Throughout a period |
| **Service organization management describes the system and asserts...** → | Controls were suitably designed | Controls were suitably designed and operated effectively |
| **Service auditor evaluates...** → | Description of system and suitability of design of controls | Description of system, suitability of design of controls, and operating effectiveness of controls |

Management's assertions and a service auditor's report in both SOC 1® type 1 and type 2 examinations include the following:

**SOC 1® Type 1 vs. Type 2: Management Assertion and Examination Scope**

| | **Type 1** | **Type 2** |
|---|---|---|
| | *As of specified date* | *Throughout a period* |
| Management's description of the system and related controls | ✓ | ✓ |
| Management's written assertion that description fairly presents system | ✓ | ✓ |
| Management's written assertion that the controls related to the control objectives stated in management's description of the system were suitably designed | ✓ | ✓ |
| Report expressing an opinion on management's description of the system and suitability of the design of controls | ✓ | ✓ |
| Management's written assertion that the controls related to the control objectives stated in management's description of the system operated effectively | | ✓ |
| Report expressing an opinion on management's description of the system, the suitability of the design of controls, and the operating effectiveness of controls | | ✓ |
| A description of the auditor's tests of controls and the results thereof | | ✓ |

AT-C 320 states that the service auditor's role in a SOC 1® examination is to:

- **Obtain reasonable assurance about whether, in all material respects, based on the criteria**
  - Management's description of the service organization's system fairly presents the service organization's system that was designed and implemented throughout the specified period (or, in a type 1 report, as of a specified date).
  - The controls related to the control objectives stated in management's description of the service organization's system were suitably designed to provide reasonable assurance that the control objectives would be achieved if the controls operated effectively throughout the specified period (or, in a type 1 report, as of a specified date).
  - In a type 2 engagement, the controls operated effectively to provide reasonable assurance that the control objectives stated in management's description of the service organization's system were achieved throughout the specified period.
- **Express an opinion in a written report** about the matters above.

## SOC 2®

**SOC 2® reports give assurance about systems and controls relevant to security, availability, processing integrity, confidentiality, or privacy.**

SOC 2® reports help user entities understand a service organization's system and controls. Shared data and networked systems may expose user entities to regulatory, operational, or financial risks. A SOC 2® report helps the user entity fulfill its oversight responsibilities. Prospective user entities may request a SOC 2® report prior to signing an agreement with a service organization.

**Examples of Service Organizations That May Need a SOC 2® Report**

| | | |
|---|---|---|
| Customer support | Data centers | IT management and support services |
| Health insurance claim processors | Financial technology services (FinTech) | SaaS, PaaS, and IaaS cloud service providers |

SOC 2® is a **restricted report**. Intended users must have a relationship with the service organization and **sufficient knowledge to understand** the report. The organization's relationships may include user entities and user auditors, business partners and their auditors, prospective user entities and business partners, as well as regulators.

The AICPA SOC 2® Guide *Reporting on an Examination of Controls at a Service Organization Relevant to Security, Availability, Processing Integrity, Confidentiality, or Privacy* describes sufficient knowledge as the ability to understand:

- The type of services offered by the service organization
- How the service organization's control system affects user entities, business partners, subservice organizations, and other parties
- The limitations of internal controls
- The effect of complementary user entity controls (CUECs) and complementary subservice organization controls (CSOCs)
- Risks that may interfere with the service organization's commitments and related controls

A **subservice organization** is a third party or affiliate that fulfills part of the service organization's services or provides components of its system. A **business partner** is a third party or affiliate that allows the service organization to use its technology or patents when providing services to user entities.

Service organizations may design their systems with the assumption that certain controls will be implemented by a subservice organization. Under the **inclusive method**, the subservice organization's objectives and controls are *included* in the service organization's SOC examination. In the **carve-out method**, the subservice organization's objectives and controls are *excluded*.

**Complementary controls** assumed in the design of the service organization's system must be disclosed. Such controls may stem from both carved-out subservice organizations and user entities. AT-C 320 defines complementary controls as:

- **Complementary subservice organization controls (CSOCs):** Controls that the service organization's management has assumed, in the design of the system, would be implemented by subservice organizations and are necessary, in combination with controls at the service organization, to provide reasonable assurance that the service organization's objectives would be achieved. When using the carve-out method, the service organization's system description would identify the types of CSOCs that the subservice organization is assumed to have implemented.
- **Complementary user entity controls (CUECs):** Controls that the service organization's management has assumed, in the design of the system, would be implemented by user entities and are necessary, in combination with controls at the service organization, to provide reasonable assurance that the service organization's objectives would be achieved.

**Subservice organizations and complementary controls are further explained under "Management's Responsibilities" in Lecture 1.03 Engagement Planning.**

Based on the AT-C 105 basic attestation concept, a SOC 2® examination has the following characteristics:

**SOC 2® Basic Attestation Concept**

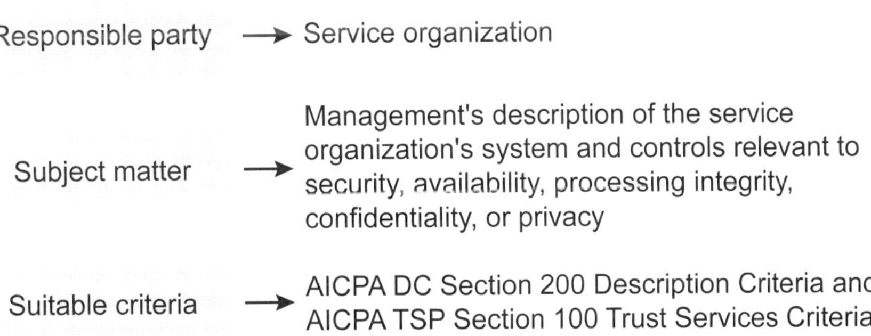


So, in a SOC 2® examination:

The ***service organization*** measures or evaluates ***the description of its system and controls relevant to security, availability, processing integrity, confidentiality, or privacy*** against ***the AICPA's DC Section 200 Description Criteria and Trust Services Criteria*** and provides an assertion about the outcome.

The engaging party selects the trust services categories for the examination. The categories must include the **security** category at a minimum but could include other trust services categories. Additional criteria, such as compliance with HIPAA regulations, may also be examined simultaneously in a SOC 2® examination. These dual-purpose engagements are commonly known as "**SOC 2®+**" (ie, SOC 2® plus).

The following definitions from the AICPA's SOC 2® Guide apply:

- **Management's assertions:** Management's claims about whether the description of the service organization's system and related controls are in accordance with (or based on) the criteria.
- **Management's description of the system:** Management's narrative describing the following:
  - Service organization's system
  - Principal service commitments and system requirements
  - Criteria and related controls
- **Service organization's system:** The infrastructure, software, people, procedures, and data designed, implemented, and operated to achieve the service organization's principal service commitments and system requirements
- **Principal service commitments and system requirements:** Promises the service organization makes to user entities about its services and how its system will operate
- **Controls at a service organization:** The policies and procedures applicable to security, availability, processing integrity, confidentiality, or privacy that provide reasonable assurance of achieving the principal service commitments and system requirements

Note how the service organization's objectives in a SOC 2® differ from a SOC 1®:

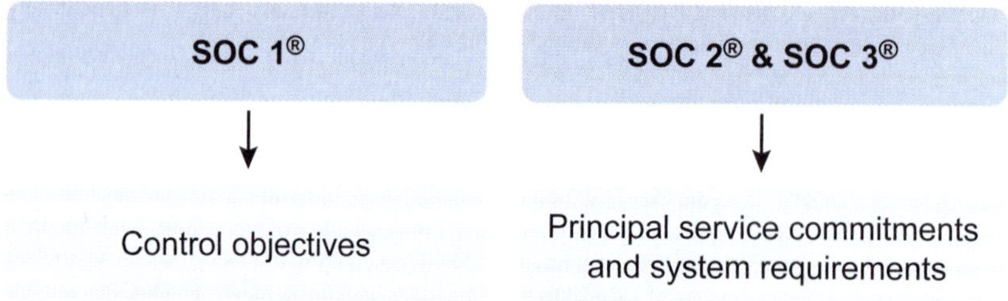

The engaging party may choose a type 1 or type 2 report. Management's assertions and the examination scope are the following:

**SOC 2® Type 1 vs. Type 2: Management Assertion and Examination Scope**

| | **Type 1** | **Type 2** |
|---|---|---|
| | *As of specified date* | *Throughout a period* |
| Management's description of the system and related controls | ✓ | ✓ |
| Management's written assertion that description fairly presents system | ✓ | ✓ |
| Management's written assertion that the controls related to the principal service commitments and system requirements stated in management's description of the system were suitably designed | ✓ | ✓ |
| Report expressing an opinion on management's description of the system and suitability of the design of controls | ✓ | ✓ |
| Management's written assertion that the controls related to the principal service commitments and system requirements stated in management's description of the system operated effectively | | ✓ |
| Report expressing an opinion on management's description of the system, the suitability of the design of controls, and the operating effectiveness of controls | | ✓ |
| A description of the auditor's tests of controls and the results thereof | | ✓ |

AT-C 205 and the AICPA's SOC 2® Guide state that the service auditor's role in a SOC 2® examination is to:

- **Obtain reasonable assurance about whether, in all material respects, based on the criteria**
  - Management's description of the service organization's system fairly presents the service organization's system that was designed and implemented throughout the specified period (or, in a type 1 report, as of a specified date).
  - The controls stated in management's description of the service organization's system were suitably designed to provide reasonable assurance that the principal service commitments and system requirements would be achieved if the controls operated effectively throughout the specified period (or, in a type 1 report, as of a specified date).
  - In a type 2 engagement, the controls stated in management's description operated effectively to provide reasonable assurance that the principal service commitments and system requirements were achieved, based on the applicable trust services, throughout the specified period.
- **Express an opinion in a written report** about the preceding matters.

## SOC 3®

**SOC 3® reports provide assurance about the effectiveness of controls relevant to security, availability, processing integrity, confidentiality, or privacy. The subject matter is the same as a SOC 2® report. However, a SOC 3® is a general use report that can be shared publicly.**

The public does not have sufficient knowledge to understand, or a specific need for, the detailed information in a SOC 2® report. SOC 3® removes parts of the SOC 2® type 2 report so the service organization can distribute it freely.

SOC 3® reports include the following:

**SOC 3®: Management Assertion and Examination Scope**

| | *Throughout a period* |
|---|---|
| Management's description of the boundaries of the system, principal service commitments, and system requirements | ✓ |
| Management's written assertion that the controls related to the principal service commitments and system requirements stated in management's description of the system operated effectively based on the trust services criteria | ✓ |
| Report expressing an opinion on management's assertion that controls operated effectively to achieve the principal service commitments and system requirements based on the trust services criteria | ✓ |

## Comparison: SOC 1®, SOC 2®, and SOC 3®

**Comparison of SOC 1®, SOC 2®, and SOC 3® Reports**

| | SOC 1® | SOC 2® | SOC 3® |
|---|---|---|---|
| **Intended Users** | Service organization management, user entities and their auditors, and other specified parties who have a need for the report and sufficient knowledge to understand it | Service organization management, user entities and their auditors, business partners and their auditors, and other specified parties who have a need for the report and sufficient knowledge to understand it | General public |
| **Subject Matter of Management's Assertions** | Description of the service organization's system and controls relevant to a user entity's controls over financial reporting | Description of the service organization's system and controls relevant to security, availability, processing integrity, confidentiality, or privacy | Boundaries of the service organization's system and operating effectiveness of controls relevant to security, availability, processing integrity, confidentiality, or privacy |

**Comparison of SOC 1®, SOC 2®, and SOC 3® Reports**

| | SOC 1® | SOC 2® | SOC 3® |
|---|---|---|---|
| **Description Criteria** | AT-C Section 320 | DC Section 200, *Description Criteria for a Description of a Service Organization's System in a SOC 2® Report* | DC Section 200, *Description Criteria for a Description of a Service Organization's System in a SOC 2® Report* |
| **Control Criteria** | AT-C Section 320 | TSP Section 100 *Trust Services Criteria* | TSP Section 100 *Trust Services Criteria* |
| **AICPA Guidance** | AT-C Section 105<br>AT-C Section 205<br>AT-C Section 320<br>SOC 1® Guide: *Reporting on an Examination of Controls at a Service Organization Relevant to User Entities' Internal Control Over Financial Reporting* | AT-C Section 105<br>AT-C Section 205<br>SOC 2® Guide: *Reporting on an Examination of Controls at a Service Organization Relevant to Security, Availability, Processing Integrity, Confidentiality, or Privacy* | AT-C Section 105<br>AT-C Section 205<br>SOC 2® Guide: *Reporting on an Examination of Controls at a Service Organization Relevant to Security, Availability, Processing Integrity, Confidentiality, or Privacy* |

## SOC for Cybersecurity

**A SOC for Cybersecurity report discloses information about an entity's cybersecurity risk management program. SOC for Cybersecurity is a general-use report that can be shared publicly.**

Management, boards, investors, customers, and business partners may need assurance that an entity is managing cybersecurity threats. An independent CPA may be engaged to express an opinion on the entity's description of its **cybersecurity risk management program** and the effectiveness of controls.

Based on the AT-C 105 basic attestation concept, a SOC for Cybersecurity examination has the following characteristics:

**SOC for Cybersecurity Basic Attestation Concept**

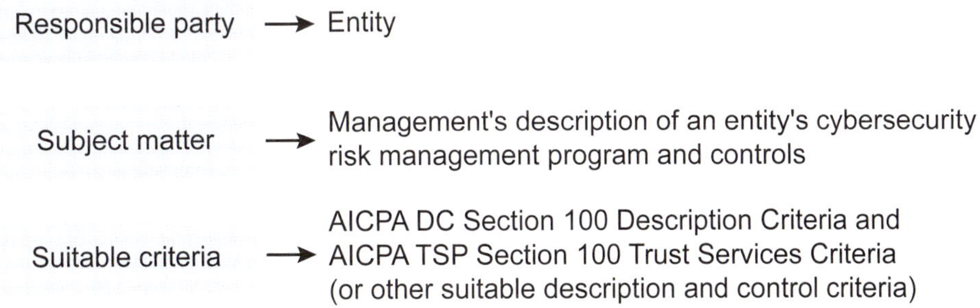

Thus, in a SOC for Cybersecurity examination,

An ***entity*** measures or evaluates ***the description of its cybersecurity risk management program and controls*** against ***the AICPA's DC Section 100 Description Criteria and Trust Services Criteria*** and provides an assertion about the outcome.

The following definitions pertain to SOC for Cybersecurity examinations:

- **Management's assertions:** Management's claims about whether the description of the entity's cybersecurity risk management program is in accordance with (or based on) the criteria, as well as the operating effectiveness of controls
- **Management's description of the entity's cybersecurity risk management program:** Management's narrative describing the following:
    - Nature of the entity's business operations
    - Types of sensitive information created, collected, transmitted, used, or stored
    - Cybersecurity objectives
    - Criteria and related controls
- **Cybersecurity risk management program:** From the AICPA's Attestation Guide: *Reporting on an Entity's Cybersecurity Risk Management Program and Controls:* "the set of policies, processes, and controls designed to protect information and systems from security events that could compromise the achievement of an entity's cybersecurity objectives and to detect, respond to, mitigate, and recover from security events"
- **Cybersecurity objectives:** The goals an entity expects to achieve through its cybersecurity risk management program
- **Cybersecurity controls:** The policies and procedures that provide reasonable assurance of achieving cybersecurity objectives

Management's assertions and the CPA's report include the following:

| SOC for Cybersecurity Management Assertion and Examination Scope | |
|---|---|
| | *Throughout a period* |
| Management's description of the entity's cybersecurity risk management program | ✓ |
| Management's written assertion that the description of the entity's cybersecurity risk management program was presented in accordance with the description criteria | ✓ |
| Management's written assertion that the controls related to the cybersecurity objectives stated in management's description of the cybersecurity risk management program operated effectively based on the control criteria | ✓ |
| Report expressing an opinion about whether the description of the entity's cybersecurity risk management program was presented in accordance with the description criteria and the controls within that program were effective in achieving the entity's cybersecurity objectives based on the control criteria | ✓ |

## SOC for Supply Chain

**SOC for Supply Chain applies to entities that produce, manufacture, or distribute products. This report provides assurance about the entity's system and controls relevant to security, availability, processing integrity, confidentiality, or privacy.**

Business customers and partners use a SOC for Supply Chain report to assess risks within their supplier and distribution networks. Customers and partners may have a formal **supply chain risk management program** or have contractual language specifying performance, quality, or delivery commitments. The entity may also wish to give the SOC for Supply Chain report to prospective customers and partners.

**Examples of Entities That May Need a SOC for Supply Chain Report**

| | | |
|---|---|---|
| Oil, gas, and mineral producers | Food, grain, and fiber farming | Commercial software developers |
| Manufacturers and contract manufacturers | Freight and warehousing companies | Order fulfillment and logistics companies |

SOC for Supply Chain is a **restricted report** intended for only the entity's management and users who have sufficient knowledge and understanding of the entity and its system. Users are normally business customers and their auditors, business partners and their auditors, and prospective business partners or customers.

Sufficient knowledge includes understanding:

- The nature of the goods produced, manufactured, or distributed
- Internal control and inherent limitations
- Applicable criteria
- Risks that may threaten the achievement of the entity's principal system objectives and how controls address those risks.

Based on the AT-C 105 basic attestation concept, a SOC for Supply Chain examination has the following characteristics:

**SOC for Supply Chain Basic Attestation Concept**

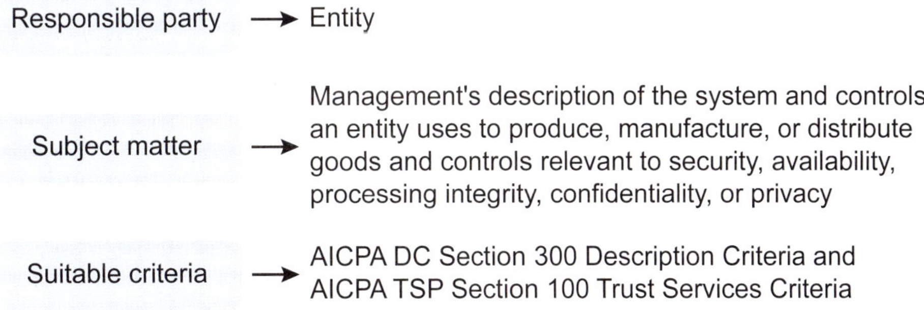

Thus, in a SOC for Supply Chain examination:

An ***entity*** measures or evaluates ***the description of the system it uses to produce, manufacture, or distribute goods and controls relevant to security, availability, processing integrity, confidentiality, or privacy*** against ***the AICPA's DC Section 300 Description Criteria and Trust Services Criteria*** and provides an assertion about the outcome.

The following definitions pertain to SOC for Supply Chain engagements:

- **Management's assertions:** Management's claims about whether the entity's system and related controls are in accordance with (or based on) the criteria.
- **Management's description of the system:** Management's narrative explaining the following:
  - Nature of the entity's business
  - Principal system objectives
  - Criteria and related controls
- **Principal system objectives:** Promises the entity makes to business customers and partners about producing, manufacturing, or distributing goods and how its system fulfills operational and compliance commitments
- **Controls at an entity that produces, manufactures, or distributes goods:** Policies and procedures applicable to security, availability, processing integrity, confidentiality, or privacy that provide reasonable assurance of achieving the principal system objectives

Management's assertions and the CPA's report include the following:

**SOC for Supply Chain Management Assertion and Examination Scope**

| | *Throughout a period* |
|---|---|
| Management's description of the entity's system for producing, manufacturing, or distributing products | ✓ |
| Management's written assertion that the description of the entity's system was presented in accordance with the description criteria | ✓ |
| Management's written assertion that the controls related to the principal system objectives stated in management's description of the system operated effectively based on the trust services criteria | ✓ |
| Report expressing an opinion about whether the description of the entity's system was presented in accordance with the description criteria and the controls within the system description were effective in achieving the entity's principal system objectives based on the trust services criteria | ✓ |

## SOC-Related Consulting Engagements

CPAs may use the trust services criteria when performing consulting services. These engagements do not fall under the attestation standards but follow CS 100, *Consulting Services*. In a consulting service, the CPA's role is to help management perform its duties. For example, a CPA may assist management in IT systems design or implementation.

**Consulting Engagements Performed by CPAs**

**Consultations**
Counseling a client on a specific subject, such as suggesting computer software.

**Transaction services**
Assisting the client with a specific transaction. Examples include litigation and valuation services, obtaining financing, or mergers.

**Implementation services**
Putting a client's plan into action, such as installing a computer system and providing support.

**Product services**
Selling a product to the client and providing support. Products may include training systems or computer software.

**Staff and support services**
Acting as a service organization by providing personnel to perform client's tasks. Services may include controllership, computer programming, data processing, or facilities management.

**Advisory services**
Developing findings, conclusions, and recommendations for a client's consideration, (for example, analyzing regulatory compliance or performing IT security risk assessments).

Often companies, especially those that are new to SOC reporting, will hire a CPA firm or IT consultant to perform a **SOC Readiness Assessment** to evaluate and provide recommendations for remediating their controls prior to a SOC 2® examination. The entity's existing controls and processes are evaluated against the trust services criteria to identify gaps and provide remediation recommendations. A CPA firm cannot implement the recommendations or function as management of the service organization and still perform a SOC 2® examination; this would create an independence issue. Thus, in a consulting engagement, the firm should only **suggest recommendations** for management's consideration.

A SOC 2® readiness assessment typically consists of the following steps:

**SOC Readiness Assessment**

Determine scope and trust services categories → Control description and gap assessment → Recommend steps to remediate control gaps → Readiness testing → Evaluate effectiveness of controls | **SOC audit begins**

Readiness assessment

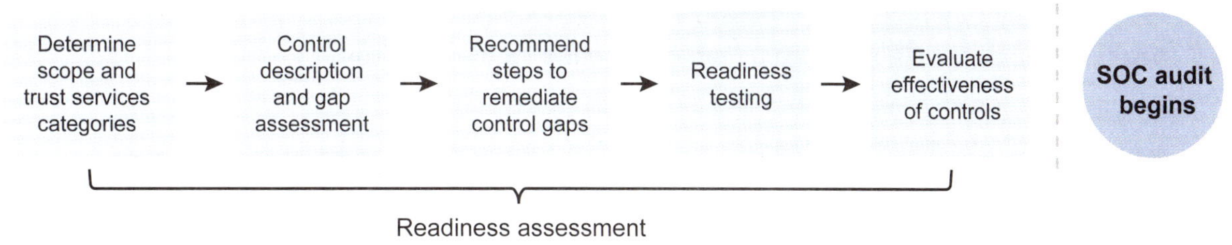

# 1.02 SOC Engagement Acceptance

## Engagement Acceptance

**The CPA, responsible party, and engaging party must fulfill specific duties prior to a SOC examination.**

### Preconditions

The general attestation preconditions as outlined in AT-C 105 include:

- CPA must be independent of the responsible party.
- Engagement team must meet ethical and quality standards.
- Responsible party (management) acknowledges its responsibility for the subject matter.
- Engagement has the following qualities:
  - Subject matter is appropriate.
  - Criteria are suitable and available to report users.
  - CPA has unrestricted access to evidence, such as information and personnel.
  - CPA will express an opinion in a written report.

AT-C 205 and AT-C 320 add the following preconditions for SOC engagements:

- Management will not limit the engagement scope to the point that it will not be helpful to report users.
- Management takes responsibility for the following:
  - Preparing a description of the service organization's system in accordance with the *description criteria*
  - Stating the service organization's *objectives* in the description
  - Preparing an assertion and having a reasonable basis for the assertion
  - Selecting the *control criteria* and stating them in the assertion
  - Identifying the risks that threaten the achievement of the service organization's *objectives*
  - Suitability of the design and operating effectiveness of controls to provide reasonable assurance that the service organization's *objectives* were achieved

| | SOC 1® | SOC 2®, SOC 3® | SOC for Cybersecurity | SOC for Supply Chain |
|---|---|---|---|---|
| **Description Criteria** | Suitable description criteria | DC Section 200 Description Criteria | DC Section 100 Description Criteria | DC Section 300 Description Criteria |
| **Objectives** | Control objectives | Principal service commitments and system requirements | Cybersecurity objectives | Principal system objectives |
| **Control Criteria** | Suitable control criteria | Trust services criteria | Trust services criteria or other suitable criteria | Trust services criteria |

## Independence

**Representative Task (Remembering and Understanding):** Summarize the independence considerations between the service auditor, service organization, and subservice organizations.

**CPAs offering SOC examination services must adhere to professional and ethical standards, such as the AICPA Code of Professional Conduct and AICPA Quality Control Standards. External peer review is required for any CPA firm providing attestation services.**

CPAs must be **independent**, in both fact and appearance, when performing a SOC examination. They should be free from conflict of interest, able to be neutral and fair. Prior to accepting an engagement, the engagement partner should do an **independence assessment**. The assessment includes reviewing financial or familial ties that could undermine independence.

Service auditors must be independent of the service organization and any included subservice organizations. However, service auditors do *not* need to be independent of user entities or carved-out subservice organizations.

The **AICPA Code of Professional Conduct** general Independence Rule, found in ET Section 1.200.001, states that CPAs must be independent as prescribed by the Code. Two other independence rules are of note in SOC engagements:

- **ET Section 1.210 Conceptual Framework Approach:** The service auditor must consider whether a third party would believe that there is a threat to independence.
- **ET Section 1.297 Independence Standards for Engagements Performed in Accordance with Statements on Standards for Attestation Engagements:** The service auditor must be independent of the responsible party, which includes the service organization and any subservice organizations for which the *inclusive method* is selected.

**Threats to Service Auditor Independence**
**AICPA Code of Professional Conduct ET Section 1.210.010**

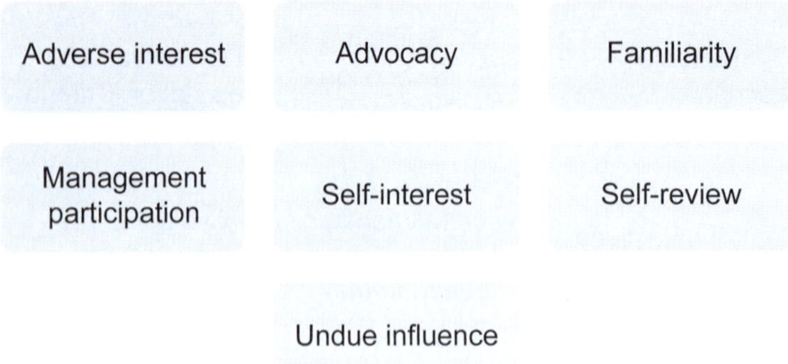


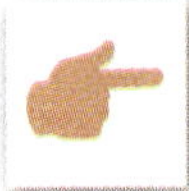

**Under the Independence Rule, may a service auditor help a service organization prepare for a SOC examination?**

Under the Independence Rule, a management participation threat exists when a CPA performs management responsibilities for an attest client. Management responsibilities include "designing, implementing, or maintaining internal controls" and "performing ongoing evaluations of internal control as part of its monitoring activities."

A self-review threat is the concern that a CPA "will not appropriately evaluate the results of a previous judgment made or service performed or supervised by the member or an individual in the member's firm and that the member will rely on that service in forming a judgment as part of an attest engagement."

A service auditor may perform a SOC readiness assessment and offer remediation suggestions. However, the service auditor should not take part in:

- Management's decision-making
- Designing, implementing, or maintaining internal controls
- Ongoing monitoring
- Preparing source documents

## Ethical and Quality Standards

AT-C 105 links the attestation standards and quality control standards. Attestation standards relate to conduct on individual engagements, while QC 10 *A Firm's System of Quality Control* addresses a firm's full **quality control system**, including:

- Policies that provide reasonable assurance that the firm and its staff adhere to professional codes, as well as legal and regulatory requirements
- Procedures to carry out quality control policies and monitor compliance

**Firm's Quality Control System: Policies and Procedures**

| Leadership tone | Ethical requirements | Client relationships |
| --- | --- | --- |
| Human resources | Engagement performance | Monitoring compliance |

The engagement partner should follow the firm's client relationship procedures and make appropriate decisions. A firm should accept a SOC engagement only when it can show that the firm and staff:

- Are competent to perform the engagement
- Have the expected time and resources
- Can comply with professional standards and legal and ethical requirements
- Believe that the client's integrity is satisfactory
- Consider the service organization's expectations to be realistic

**What skills does a SOC engagement team member need?**

Competence to perform a SOC engagement means having the skills to understand the service organization's:

- System
- Industry and business
- Business processes and controls
- IT systems and technology
- IT processes and controls
- Suitability of design and operating effectiveness of controls
- Professional skepticism and judgment
- Legal and regulatory requirements

## Appropriate Subject Matter

The subject matter of an examination is appropriate when it can be:

| Identified and consistently measured or evaluated | Subjected to procedures for obtaining sufficient appropriate evidence to support an opinion |
| --- | --- |

## Suitable and Available Criteria

A service auditor should assess whether management has used suitable and available criteria when:

- Evaluating the description of the system
- Evaluating whether the controls were suitably designed to achieve the objectives stated in the description
- In a type 2 report, evaluating whether the controls operated effectively to achieve the objectives stated in the description

AT-C 105 states that criteria are **suitable** when they possess all the following qualities:

| | |
|---|---|
| **Relevance** | Criteria are relevant to the subject matter |
| **Objectivity** | Criteria are free from bias |
| **Measurability** | Criteria allow for consistent measurement of the subject matter |
| **Completeness** | Criteria do not omit relevant factors about the subject matter |

The AICPA considers criteria suitable those criteria come from:

- Laws or regulations
- Authorized or recognized bodies of experts that follow a transparent process (eg, AICPA, COSO)

For criteria developed by any party other than the above, the CPA needs to decide if the criteria are suitable, using the four qualities. Either the responsible party or the engaging party may choose the criteria, but the engaging party must determine if the criteria are appropriate for its purpose.

The criteria must be available to report users so they can understand how the subject matter was measured or evaluated. Examples include criteria that are publicly available, circulated through industry associations, or contained in either the CPA's report or the presentation of the subject matter.

## Agreeing on the Terms of the Engagement

The service auditor and engaging party should agree on the terms of the SOC examination. AT-C 205 states that a **written engagement letter** signed by both parties should spell out:

- The objective and scope of the engagement
- The CPA's responsibilities
- A statement that the CPA will perform the engagement in accordance with the AICPA's attestation standards
- The responsibilities of the responsible party (ie, management) and engaging party, if different
- A statement about the inherent limitations of an examination
- The description and control criteria that the CPA should use to evaluate the subject matter
- That the engaging party must supply a representation letter at the end of the engagement

# 1.03 SOC Engagement Planning

## Planning

After satisfying preconditions and agreeing on terms with the service organization's management, the service auditor's planning responsibilities are to:

- Form an overall engagement strategy, including scope, timing, and direction
- Create a comprehensive engagement plan that includes the consideration of materiality and identification of the risks of material misstatement
- Obtain an understanding of the service organization's system and controls
- Obtain an understanding of the service organization's service commitments and system requirements that define the engagement (ie, relevant contractual terms between the user entity and the service organization), as well as an understanding of the relevant contractual terms between the service organization and any subservice organizations
- Perform procedures to assess the risk of material misstatement
- Request a written assertion from management

### Engagement Plan

An **engagement plan** is a step-by-step checklist of all **risk assessment procedures** and and **further procedures** that the engagement team will perform during an examination. Firms typically have a standard plan for each type of SOC examination, which the engagement team can alter as needed.

According to AT-C 205, the engagement plan should address the following:

- Scope of the engagement based on management's decisions
- Timing and nature of communications
- Materiality considerations
- Understanding of the service organization's system and the risks of misstatement
- Attestation risk considerations
- Sources for sufficient appropriate evidence
- Needs of user entities and other report users
- Risk of fraud
- Use of the service organization's internal audit department and/or external specialists
- Resources and staff needed to complete the engagement
- Prior period findings

Planning is **continuous** throughout the engagement, as unforeseen issues could require a different approach. For example, obtaining contradictory evidence can force a change in the nature, timing, or extent of procedures.

## Materiality

**Representative Task (Remembering and Understanding):** Explain how materiality is determined and used in performing a SOC® engagement (SOC 1®, SOC 2®).

Service auditors express an opinion about whether a subject matter is in accordance with criteria, **in all material respects**. AT-C 205 requires the service auditor to consider **materiality** during the planning, performing, and reporting phases of an examination.

Materiality is the service auditor's professional judgment about:

- Misstatements, including omissions, which may influence report users
- Circumstances, nature, size, and extent of misstatements
- Qualitative and quantitative factors

Misstatements can be unintentional (error) or intentional (fraud), qualitative or quantitative, and may include omissions. AT-C 105 defines a **misstatement** as the difference between:

- The service organization's measurement or evaluation of the subject matter, and
- The proper measurement or evaluation based on the criteria.

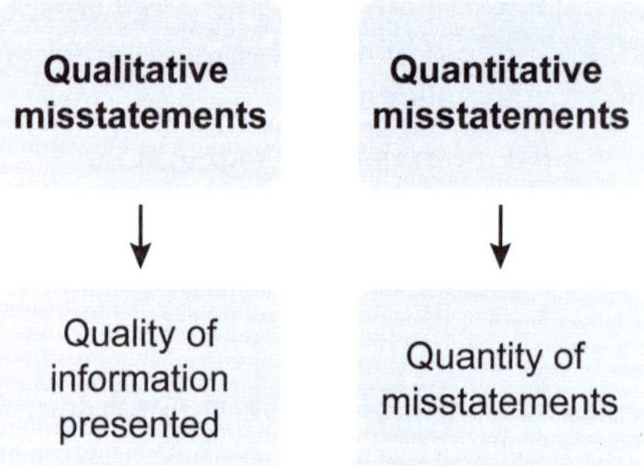


Qualitative misstatements in narratives involve the following:

- Omission of disclosures required by criteria
- Factual misstatements
- Unjustified changes to disclosures

**Qualitative vs. Quantitative Misstatements:**

- **Qualitative:** In a SOC 2® examination of a data center, a service auditor performed tests of controls to decide if security-related service commitments were achieved. The service auditor found that the data center did not fairly describe how the organization restricts unauthorized access to its facility.
- **Quantitative:** In a SOC 1® examination of a payroll service provider, a service auditor performed procedures for the control objective of processing transactions completely and accurately. The service auditor found 20 deviations in which controls did not operate effectively.

The AICPA refers to the following terms to describe **misstatements** in SOC engagements:

| **Description misstatement** | **Deficiency** | **Deviation** |
|---|---|---|
| Differences between (or omissions in) management's description and the criteria in management's assertion | Misstatements related to controls that were not suitably designed | Misstatements resulting from the failure of a control to operate effectively in a single instance |

Misstatements might be immaterial individually but material when combined with other misstatements. For this reason, the service auditor should prepare a **summary of misstatements** to keep track of all findings.

The primary concern is whether a misstatement is significant enough to influence or mislead intended report users. To decide if a misstatement is **material**, the service auditor should consider:

- The results of procedures compared with quantitative materiality thresholds
- Whether misstatements are significant enough to suggest a failure to meet specific criteria
- Qualitative factors
- The effect on the subject matter
- The aggregated effect of uncorrected misstatements

Once misstatements reach the threshold of materiality, the service auditor should decide if their effect is **pervasive**. Materiality and pervasiveness affect the type of opinion that the service auditor should issue. Pervasive effects on the subject matter are those that have the following characteristics:

- They are *not* confined to a specific aspect of the subject matter.
- If confined, they affect a sizable part of the subject matter.
- They are important to report users' understanding of the subject matter.

**Type of Opinion Based on Materiality and Pervasiveness of Misstatements**

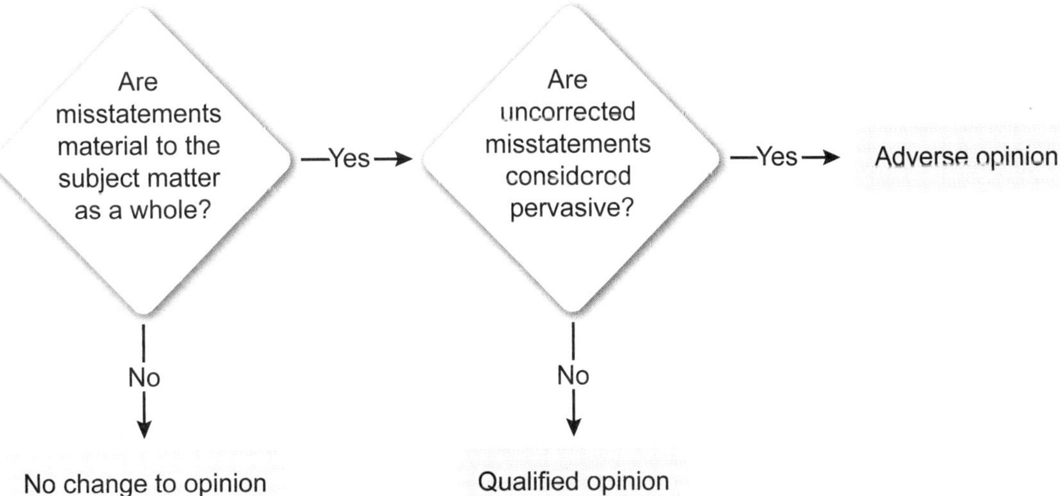

## Understanding the Service Organization's System

**Representative Task (Application):** Obtain an understanding of the system addressed by a SOC 2® examination, including the clear identification of boundaries of the system as defined by the service organization.

**Representative Task (Application):** Perform procedures to obtain an understanding of how a service organization provides its personnel and external users information on how to report failures, incidents, concerns, and other complaints related to a system subject to a SOC 2® engagement.

AT-C 205 requires service auditors to obtain an understanding of the subject matter of an examination, including related controls. Their understanding must be sufficient to:

- Identify risks and assess the risk of material misstatement
- Design and perform procedures to assess the risks
- Obtain reasonable assurance to support their opinion

### Identify and Assess Risk

- Establish materiality levels
- Assess the risk of material misstatement
- Design and perform procedures to respond to assessed risks

### Understand Description of System

- Identify the processes and procedures within the system
- Understand how the system interfaces with other systems
- Assess whether the description meets suitable description criteria

### Understand Controls

- Assess whether controls meet suitable control criteria
- Understand complementary user entity controls (CUECs) and complementary subservice organization controls (CSOCs)
- In a type 2, evaluate the operating effectiveness of controls

### Form an Opinion

- Evaluate evidence
- Consider misstatements, deficiencies, deviations, and fraud
- Support the service auditor's opinion

AT-C 205 further explains that obtaining an understanding of the subject matter requires the service auditor to:

- Perform procedures to understand how the service organization:
  - Prepares the description of its system
  - Prepares objectives (principal service commitments and system requirements in a SOC 2®)
  - Identifies controls that provide reasonable assurance of achieving the objectives (principal service commitments and system requirements in a SOC 2®)
  - In a type 2, assesses the operating effectiveness of controls
- If the service organization has an internal audit function, obtain an understanding of the internal audit function's:
  - Responsibilities
  - Position in the overall organizational structure

A service auditor **obtains an understanding** of the subject matter and related controls by performing one or more of the following **risk assessment procedures:**

**Risk Assessment Procedures**

| **Reperformance** | **Inquiry** |
| --- | --- |
| Evaluating a process, procedure, or control by performing it and then comparing the result with that of the service organization | Asking service organization personnel to answer questions verbally or on a questionnaire |
| **Inspection** | **Observation** |
| Reviewing documentation of the service organization's risk assessment, policies, procedures, monitoring, internal audit evaluations, contracts with user entities and business partners, and reports from regulators | Watching the service organization's personnel perform procedures |

Risk assessment procedures may also include a **walkthrough**. In walkthroughs, service auditors obtain an understanding of all the steps in a process by performing a combination of procedures. For example, the service auditor may inquire about a process, inspect documents, and then observe a process. The observed process is then compared with the documented process (eg, policies and procedures manual).

### Perform Procedures to Obtain an Understanding of a Service Organization's Objectives and Related Controls in a SOC 2® Examination

Principle 14 of the COSO Internal Control–Integrated Framework states:

*"The entity internally communicates information, including objectives and responsibilities for internal control, necessary to support the functioning of internal control."*

Each COSO principle has certain points of focus, which are expanded upon when using the trust services criteria. One point of focus under COSO Principle 14/Trust Services Criterion CC2.2 is:

***"Communicates Information on Reporting Failures, Incidents, Concerns, and Other Matters:*** *Entity personnel are provided with information on how to report systems failures, incidents, concerns, and other complaints."*

During planning, the service auditor performs risk assessment procedures to obtain an understanding of the system and controls. Controls should provide reasonable assurance of achieving the service organization's principal service commitments and system requirements in a SOC 2® examination.

To obtain an understanding of how a service organization provides its personnel and external users with information about reporting failures, incidents, concerns, and other complaints, procedures may include the following:

- **Inquiry:** Ask management and other personnel:
  - How are incident response plans, policies, and procedures communicated internally and externally?
  - How do internal and external users receive security awareness training?
  - What are the prescribed communication methods and time frames?
  - What forms and records do they maintain to log reported failures, incidents, concerns, and complaints? Is there a ticketing system in place?
  - What is required under contracts with user entities or by laws and regulations?
  - How long has a reporting process been in place? Is it fully implemented? Have there been any changes?
- **Inspection:** Obtain and review the following documents:
  - Management's description of the system
  - Incident response plans, policies, and procedures
  - Security awareness training slides, handouts, and attendance records
  - Internal employee handbooks, posted notices, paper and electronic communications
  - Reported issue tickets and records
  - Contracts and communications with external parties
  - Contracts with user entities or service-level agreements
  - Laws and regulations to which the service organization is subject
- **Observation:** If possible, be present at security awareness training sessions.
- **Walkthrough:** Perform all the above procedures and document the internal and external incident reporting and security awareness training process in a narrative, flowchart, or diagram.

The extent of risk assessment procedures depends on:

- The type of report to be issued
- Whether the service organization selects the inclusive method for any subservice organizations

A type 2 report requires the service auditor to examine the service organization's description and controls throughout a period. The service auditor also performs additional procedures to express an opinion on the operating effectiveness of controls. Thus, a type 2 report carries far more attestation risk than a type 1 report. **Attestation risk** is the probability that the service auditor will express an *inappropriate* opinion when the subject matter is materially misstated.

The service auditor must also perform risk assessment procedures on subservice organizations treated under the inclusive method. When the **carve-out method** is used, the service auditor's risk assessment procedure would be to read the subservice organization's SOC report and identify the relevant complementary subservice organization controls.

## Obtaining an Understanding of the System in a SOC 2® Examination

A service auditor might obtain an understanding of the system by performing inquiry and inspection procedures to figure out how the service organization:

| Prepares the system description | Identifies the boundaries of the system | Assesses risk | Monitors controls |
|---|---|---|---|

- How does the service organization prepare its system description?

  Each service organization has a unique method for preparing its system description. Smaller businesses may use an informal process, while larger companies may have a formal process. Understanding how a service organization prepares its system description according to the DC 200 Description Criteria in a SOC 2® examination may help a service auditor:

  - Identify sources of description misstatements
  - Determine the likelihood of description misstatements
  - Design procedures to determine if the description is in accordance with the description criteria

Compare the risk of misstatement in an organization that struggles to prepare the description internally with that of a service organization that hires a SOC consultant to prepare the description.

The service auditor may have more confidence in the description if a qualified consultant helped prepare it. This, of course, does not relieve the service auditor of the duty to perform risk assessment procedures.

The service auditor may inquire about who prepared the description and whether key executives reviewed it. A service auditor who concludes the process was flawed may be concerned about the description's accuracy and completeness. Such issues would increase the likelihood of a description misstatement, and the service auditor would respond by increasing procedures or advising the service organization about how to improve the description.

- **What are the boundaries of the service organization's system?**

  The service organization's description should include only the components used to provide the relevant services to user entities. It should not include parts of the service organization's system that are not necessary to provide the relevant services for user entities.

  The boundaries of the system include the following components when necessary to provide services to user entities:

  - **Infrastructure:** Physical and virtual IT hardware, facilities, servers, storage, environmental monitoring, data storage and media, mobile devices, internal networks, external networks
  - **Software:** Application programs, operating systems, middleware, utilities, databases, external web-facing applications, mobile applications, in-house development
  - **People:** Governance, management, operations, security, system users, third parties
  - **Procedures:** Automated and manual processes showing how services are initialized, authorized, performed, delivered, and reported; includes the technical aspects of a system's process
  - **Data:** Types of data used by the system, transaction streams, files, tables, inputs, outputs
  - When the examination relates to **confidentiality or privacy**, the boundaries of the system also include the following:
    - Types of data created, collected, processed, transmitted, used, or stored
    - Methods to collect, retain, disclose, dispose of, or anonymize data
    - Personal and third-party information that requires security, data protection, or breach disclosures by laws or service commitments

When the service organization provides multiple services, each service may have different system boundaries. Some components may not be relevant to the examination for a specific trust service category. It is important to clearly describe the **boundaries** of the service organization's **system** so report users understand the **scope** of the service auditor's **examination**.

The service auditor must specify the boundaries of the system during risk assessment. Identifying the boundaries helps the service auditor determine the components that pose a risk of description misstatement. In addition, the service auditor should understand how the service organization's system interfaces with other systems, such as those of user entities or subservice organizations.

**Boundaries of the System**

A hospital uses a collection agency to negotiate outstanding patient balances and report delinquencies to credit reporting agencies. The collection agency is considered a service organization.

The contract requires the collection agency to supply a SOC 2® report covering the security trust service category. The boundaries of the system include any infrastructure, software, people, data, and procedures that the collection agency uses to perform collection services for the hospital.

The service auditor would perform risk assessment procedures and walkthroughs to determine how the collection agency:

- Prepared its system description
- Assesses risks that threaten the achievement of its principal service commitments and system requirements
- Designs, implements, documents, and monitors controls

- **What is the service organization's internal risk assessment process?**

  If a service organization has a formal process for internal risk assessment, the service auditor may inspect its documentation. For example, a service organization may assess risk through its internal auditors or other governance, risk, and compliance (GRC) professionals. Inspecting internal risk assessment documents may help the service auditor identify misstatements or determine whether all the controls in the applicable trust services criteria were evaluated.

  If a service organization does not have a formal process to assess risks associated with the trust services criteria, the likelihood of misstatement would be greater. The service auditor would respond by increasing procedures.

- **How does the service organization monitor controls?**

  The service auditor would inquire about the techniques the service organization uses to monitor controls, including documentation. For example, the service auditor may inspect any reports from vulnerability scans or penetration tests and inquire about responses to identified issues. The service auditor may also review internal audit reports.

  Performing procedures such as reperformance, inquiry, inspection, or observation may give the service auditor insight into the suitability of controls and their operating effectiveness. The service auditor can adjust the plan for procedures depending on the findings.

# Risk Assessment

**Representative Task (Remembering and Understanding):** Identify the risk assessment requirements for a service organization and the service auditor.

## Service Organization

One precondition to engagement acceptance is that management takes responsibility for identifying the risks that threaten the achievement of objectives stated in its system description. Management's **risk assessment** process may be formal or informal. While there is no prescribed method, ideally, the service organization's risk assessment process would encompass:

- Estimating the significance of risks
- Assessing the likelihood and frequency of occurrence of risks
- Taking steps to mitigate risks

The service organization may perform its risk assessment either internally or as part of an externally assisted **SOC Readiness Assessment**. If existing controls do not address the identified risks, the SOC readiness team may offer suggestions and a remediation plan.

Risks may be identified by reviewing internal documentation, such as contracts, organizational structures, policies and procedures, processes, and changes. A formal **Risk Control Self-Assessment (RCSA)** might include the following steps:

**Service Organization Internal Risk Assessment Process**

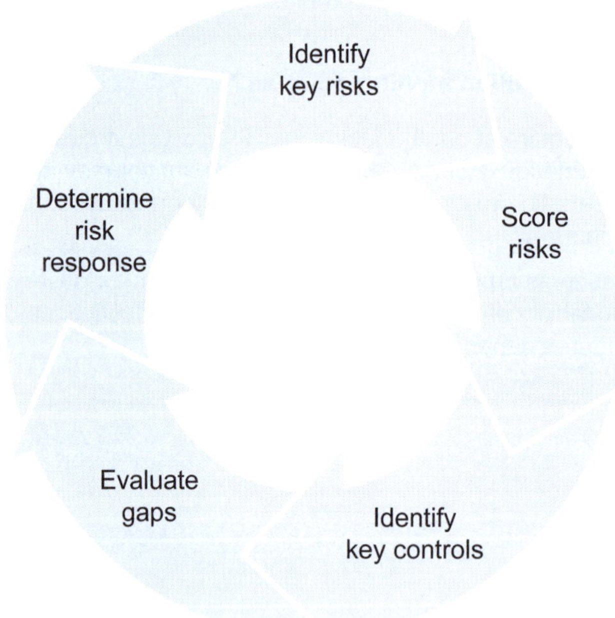


Risk stems from both internal and external factors. **Internal risks** may be related to improperly designed controls that do not prevent, detect, or correct misstatements or controls that do not align with suitable criteria. **External risks** may arise from relationships with customers, vendors, subservice organizations, business partners, and regulatory bodies. Use of a framework, such as the COSO Internal Control–Integrated Framework, helps management identify key risk areas and necessary controls.

**Key risks** are those that are significant enough to interfere with achieving the service organization's objectives. When identifying risks, it is best to take a cost-benefit approach. Service organizations should decide which risks pose the most significant threat or vulnerability.

Management should also determine the extent to which controls do not mitigate key risks. **Control risk** is the risk that the service organization's controls are not suitably designed or do not operate effectively. Control risk directly results from management's decision-making and actions.

**Inherent risks** are those that exist naturally before management puts controls in place. The effectiveness of controls may be limited or undermined by human error or fraudulent activities, such as collusion and management override.

Total risk – Inherent risk = Control risk

A formal risk assessment might look like this:

**Risk Control Self Assessment (RCSA)**

| Criteria | | | Controls | | |
|---|---|---|---|---|---|
| **Trust Services Criteria Number** | **Trust Services Criteria** | **Point of Focus** | **Risk** | **Current Control** | **Current Control Documentation Reference** |
| CC6.1 | Logical and physical access controls | Restricts logical access | Unauthorized access to systems | Passwords must be changed every 90 days | Access control policy |

| Risk Score | | | | Risk Assessment | | |
|---|---|---|---|---|---|---|
| **Total Risk (1–10)** | **Inherent Risk (1–10)** | **Control Risk (1–10)** | **Risk Tolerance Level** | **Likelihood** | **Impact** | **RCSA Level** |
| 10 | 4 | 6 | Low | E | C | Medium |

| Risk Likelihood | | | Risk Impact | | |
|---|---|---|---|---|---|
| A | Unanticipated | More than 100 years | A | Minimal | Negligible impact |
| B | Very rare | 25–100 years | B | Low | Acceptable, but monitor periodically |
| C | Rare | 5–25 years | C | Medium | Mitigation potential; monitor regularly |
| D | Moderate | 1–5 years | D | Significant | Material impact at department level; department continuous monitoring |
| E | Frequent | Month–Year | E | Very high | Material impact at a business segment level; requires management attention |
| F | Regular | At least monthly | F | Catastrophic | Material impact on entire entity; requires management attention |

The RCSA documentation provides evidence of management's risk assessment, control identification, and deficiency disclosure. Service organizations must share documents with the service auditor, who may use them to obtain an understanding of the system and plan further procedures.

Management must disclose the following deficiencies to the service auditor when known:

- Deficiencies in the design or operating effectiveness of controls
- Noncompliance with laws or regulations
- Actual, suspected, or alleged fraudulent acts
- Uncorrected misstatements
- System incidents that thwarted control objectives or service commitments and system requirements
- Subsequent events: those that happen after the reporting period but prior to issuing the service auditor's report

Service organizations or their advisers may use a commercially available SOC tool (software) to prepare for an examination. SOC tools help management evaluate risks, match controls to suitable criteria, and prepare documentation for the service auditor.

Regardless of the use of SOC tools, management is always responsible for the completeness and accuracy of the information it presents. Service auditors should consider the risks associated with a service organization's use of SOC tools, especially if the service auditor uses the same tool or has a relationship with the same software developer.

## Service Auditor

AT-C 205 defines the **risk of material misstatement** as:

> *"The risk that the subject matter is **not** in accordance with (or based on) the criteria in all material respects or that the assertion is **not** fairly stated, in all material respects."*

Identifying and assessing the risk of material misstatement is crucial to designing and performing further procedures. The evidence obtained through procedures provides reasonable assurance that the subject matter is in accordance with the criteria. In a SOC examination, risks of material misstatement are based on the service auditor's understanding of the subject matter, materiality, and the assessed risk that:

| Management's description does ***not*** fairly present the system | Controls were ***not*** suitably designed or implemented | In a type 2 report, controls did ***not*** operate effectively |
|---|---|---|

The service auditor's consideration of the risk of material misstatement should also consider the risk of material misstatement because of both **errors** (unintentional) and **fraud** (intentional). Fraud risks may include management override of controls, misappropriation of the user entity's or business partner's assets, and creation of misleading records or documents.

AT-C 105 requires the service auditor to use professional judgment and professional skepticism when planning and performing an attestation engagement. **Professional judgment** includes all the service auditor's knowledge, training, and experience that are relied on to make informed decisions and take appropriate actions during the engagement. **Professional skepticism** is having an attitude to question issues that may cause misstatements because of error or fraud. The service auditor should be alert to unusual circumstances that could increase the risk of misstatement.

**Internal and External Factors That Might Increase the Risk of Material Misstatement**

- Industry or market factors
- Organizational structure
- Nature of operations
- Data collection and storage methods
- Advanced technology
- New service offerings
- Changes to system operations or controls
- Changes to personnel
- Legal or regulatory matters

## Risk Assessment Documentation

The service auditor's **workpapers** should include documentation of the risk assessment procedures performed and the findings. A CPA with no knowledge of the engagement should be able to understand the service auditor's work and agree with the conclusions.

At a minimum, the documentation of risk assessment should include:

- Principal elements of the service auditor's understanding of the subject matter and controls
- Sources of information and the risk assessment procedures performed
- Identified risks of material misstatement and the related controls
- Decisions made by the engagement team, including explanations

Workpapers might contain the following risk assessment documents:

## Requesting Management Assertion Letter

A CPA performing a SOC examination should request that the responsible party provide a **written assertion** about measuring or evaluating the subject matter against criteria. The assertions depend on:

- The type of SOC engagement
- Whether management requested a type 1 or type 2 report
- Whether the service organization chooses the inclusive or carve-out method for subservice organizations

Under the inclusive method, a subservice organization is also a responsible party. The included subservice organization's management also needs to supply a written assertion. If a service organization (or a subservice organization treated under the inclusive method) refuses to supply a written assertion, the service auditor should **withdraw** from the engagement.

# Management's Responsibilities

## Overview of Management's Responsibilities

The service organization management's responsibilities during the planning, performing, and reporting phases of the examination are as follows:

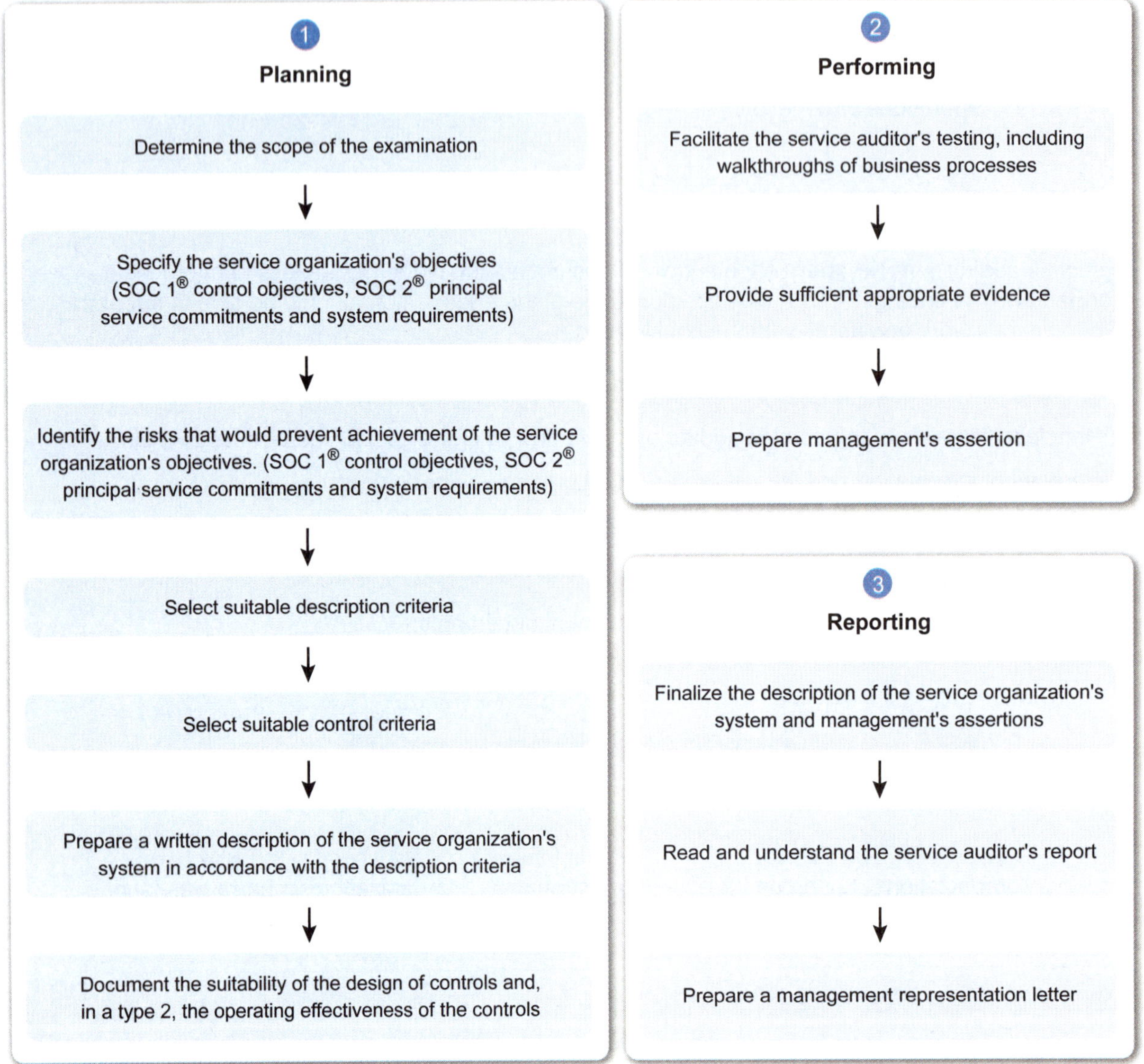


## Scope of the Examination

The scope of a SOC examination is based on a service organization's services and system, as well as certain decisions made by its management. Management determines:

- The type of engagement (ie, type 1 or type 2)
- The length of time covered by the examination (type 1 "as of" date, type 2 throughout a period)
- In a SOC 1®, the control objectives and suitable criteria
- In a SOC 2®, the trust services categories and related criteria included in the examination

- Boundaries of the service organization's system
- Which vendors are subservice organizations
- Whether to report subservice organizations using the inclusive method or carve-out method

Management determines if the engagement will be a **type 1** or **type 2** and the date(s) covered. The type of report affects management's assertions and the extent of the service auditor's work. To recall from earlier:

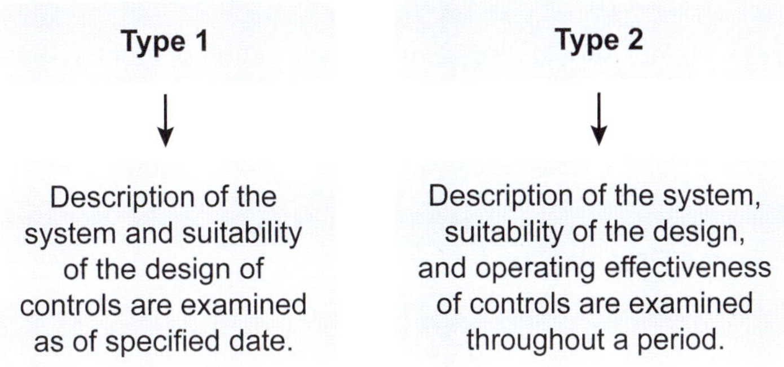


## Subservice Organizations

**Representative Task (Remembering and Understanding):** Summarize the criteria for a vendor to be considered a subservice organization.

Management should determine which vendors to classify as subservice organizations. This decision should be based on whether all the following factors are present:

- The vendor's services affect the delivery of the services to user entities,
- The vendor's services are important to user entities' understanding of the service organization's system, and
- The vendor's controls must be combined with the service organization's controls to provide reasonable assurance of achieving the service organization's:
  - Control objectives if a SOC 1® examination
  - Principal service commitments and system requirements if a SOC 2® examination

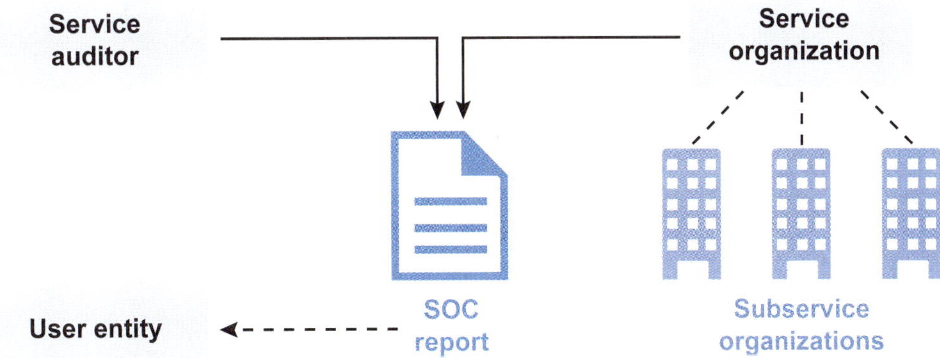

If the service organization's controls are sufficient by themselves (ie, not dependent on the vendor's controls), the vendor is not a subservice organization. Management may, but does not need to, explain the vendor's services in its system description. The service auditor would not refer to the vendor in the report.

A common example of a subservice organization is when a service organization relies on **cloud services providers** for its IT infrastructure (IaaS) or platform (PaaS). The cloud services can affect the service organization's delivery of services to user entities and are important to the user entities' understanding of the service organization's system. In addition, the cloud hosting provider's controls may be integral to the service organization's overall control environment.

Management and the service auditor should discuss the classification of vendors as subservice organizations. That decision affects the description of the service organization's system, management's assertions, and the scope of the service auditor's work.

**Vendor or Subservice Organization?**

When determining if a vendor is a subservice organization, all the facts must be considered.

**SaaS Application**

An online retailer uses a service organization to warehouse inventory and fulfill customer orders. During a SOC 2® examination, the service organization discloses that it uses another vendor's cloud-based software to print labels, track shipments, and notify the user entity's customers of delivery status.

The shipping software would be relevant to the provision of services and the retailer's understanding of the service organization's system. The service organization should classify the software vendor as a subservice organization if it relies on the vendor's controls to ensure that the labels, tracking, and customer notifications are complete, accurate, and timely. If the service organization retains responsibility for controls and monitors the software vendor's activities, the vendor would not be considered a subservice organization.

**Utilities**

A service organization providing services that affect a user entity's internal controls over financial reporting needs a SOC 1® report. The service organization pays its local government for water and sewer utilities. While necessary for business operations, the utilities do not relate to the user entity's internal controls over financial reports. Thus, the utility company is considered a normal vendor, not a subservice organization.

## Inclusive vs. Carve-Out Method

**Representative Task (Remembering and Understanding):** Explain the considerations for deciding between, and use of, the inclusive and carve-out method for subservice organizations and complementary subservice organization controls (CSOCs).

If one or more vendors are classified by management as subservice organizations, management must then decide whether to include them in its system description. Management makes this decision for each subservice organization separately.

As previously discussed, the two different methods of reporting on subservice organizations are the inclusive method and the carve-out method:

- **Inclusive method:** Include the following in the service organization's description of the system:
  - Nature of subservice organization's services
  - Subservice organization's system
  - Subservice organization's objectives and controls

  The inclusive method is appropriate when the subservice organization's services and controls have a **pervasive effect** and the subservice organization does not have its own SOC report. The inclusive method provides the most information to report users but complicates the examination for the following reasons:
    - The subservice organization is also a *responsible party*. The subservice organization's management must comply with the same rules as the service organization regarding providing written assertions and representations.
    - The subservice organization must provide a description of its system and necessary disclosures.
    - The service auditor must coordinate planning, communication, and evidence gathering with both the service organization and the subservice organization.
    - If the service organization uses multiple subservice organizations, the system description should clearly present which of them are included versus carved out.

**Factors to Determine if a Subservice Organization's Services and Controls Have a Pervasive Effect on the Service Organization's System**

| Significance of system functions | Complexity of services and controls | Service commitments and requirements |
|---|---|---|
| Number and extent of criteria affected | Contractual obligations and needs of intended users | |

- **Carve-Out Method:** The body of management's description of the system explains the nature of the subservice organization's services but excludes its controls. Any complementary subservice organization controls (CSOCs) are disclosed in a separate section, distinct from the service organization's description of the system.

Carved-out subservice organizations are not responsible parties. They do not make an assertion. The service auditor does not perform any procedures on any carved-out subservice organizations.

The carve-out method is used more often than the inclusive method. When choosing the carve-out method, it is important to ensure that the exclusion does not severely limit the usefulness of the service organization's report.

The carve-out method is appropriate in the following situations:

- The subservice organization's services and controls are not pervasive.

- It is too difficult or impractical to use the inclusive method.
- There is an independence-related conflict between the service auditor and the subservice organization.
- The subservice organization already has a SOC report covering the same period under examination.
- The subservice organization is not willing or not contractually required to take part in the service organization's SOC engagement.
- The subservice organization's management refuses to provide written assertions and representations.

Management must disclose CSOCs when using the carve-out method so report users can understand the full set of controls that are in place and who implements them. The service organization can obtain information about the subservice organization's controls in its SOC report if one is available. The service organization may also make inquiries, review internal subservice organization documents, or make site visits if its contract allows. The service organization should also monitor any CSOCs it relies on.

**Complementary Subservice Organization Controls**

A property insurance company contracts with an independent adjusting firm to estimate damages and make claim payments to policyholders. The adjusting firm stores claims data using third-party software.

The adjusting firm considers the software company to be a subservice organization and relies on that company's controls to provide reasonable assurance of meeting the data security commitments and system requirements of the contract with the insurance company. The adjusting firm management has elected to use the carve-out method because the software company can provide its own SOC 2® report.

The adjusting firm management would disclose the software company CSOCs it depends on, such as logical access controls. It may obtain this information by reviewing the software company's SOC 2® report and internal documents, as well as making inquiries and site visits.

The adjusting firm's system description would describe the type of services performed by the software company, the CSOCs, and the adjusting firm's controls that monitor the software company.

The service auditor would obtain an understanding of the CSOCs and how they relate to the criteria being examined.

## Objectives

**Representative Task (Remembering and Understanding):** Define service commitments and system requirements in a SOC 2® engagement and how they correspond to an entity's objectives referred to in the trust services criteria.

As discussed earlier, the COSO Internal Control–Integrated Framework describes **objectives** as management's goals. Risks threaten the achievement of objectives. **Controls** mitigate those **risks**. Management must describe its objectives and controls so report users can understand how their business relationship with the entity is affected by them.

In a SOC examination, management is responsible for the following:

- Specifying the service organization's objectives
- Identifying the risks that would prevent the achievement of the objectives

- Designing, implementing, and documenting controls that provide reasonable assurance of achieving objectives
- Describing the objectives and related controls in the description of the service organization's system, including whether any complementary user entity controls (CUECs) or complementary subservice organization controls (CSOCs) are necessary to achieve the objectives

Since each type of SOC examination has its own subject matter, the objectives are different:

| | SOC 1® | SOC 2®, SOC 3® | SOC for Cybersecurity | SOC for Supply Chain |
|---|---|---|---|---|
| **Objectives** → | Control objectives | Principal service commitments and system requirements | Cybersecurity objectives | Principal system objectives |
| **Definition of Objective** → | The aim or purpose for the service organization's controls; addresses the risks that controls are intended to mitigate | Promises the service organization makes to user entities about services and how its system will fulfill service commitments | The goals an entity expects to achieve through its cybersecurity risk management program | Promises the entity makes to business customers and partners about producing, manufacturing, or distributing goods and how its system fulfills operational and compliance commitments |
| **Control Criteria** → | Suitable control criteria | Trust services criteria | Trust services criteria or other suitable criteria | Trust services criteria |

Both management and the external CPA measure or evaluate controls against suitable control criteria. For example, a user entity may require a SOC 2® report from a service organization. The user's purpose for obtaining the report is to ensure that the service organization meets the agreed-to service commitments and system requirements.

When selling services, the service organization makes certain representations or promises to its user entities about how it will provide those services. These representations, referred to as **service commitments**, may cover a wide range of topics, such as how algorithms perform calculations, hours of availability (ie, uptime), standards for passwords, encryption levels, etc.

Service commitments can be outlined in contracts, in service-level agreements (SLAs), or through published statements (eg, annual notice of privacy practices). They may be related to the achievement of specific trust services criteria and may extend beyond the user entity. For example, a service organization may pledge that it will not transfer a user entity's customer data without each customer's consent. The service organization may also have to comply with service commitments to business partners.

**System requirements** specify how the service organization's system will operate to fulfill service commitments, comply with laws or industry guidelines, and meet the trust services criteria. Documentation of system requirements may be found in:

- Service organization internal policies and procedures documents
- System design documents such as source code and instruction manuals

- Contracts with user entities and business partners
- Government regulations

**Service Commitment and System Requirements**

A data center was awarded a contract to provide secure cloud services to the U.S. federal government. One of the principal service commitments required by the contract is that the data center will hire only U.S. citizens who pass an extensive background check.

The data center, a service organization, undergoes a SOC 2®+ examination with an additional subject matter of meeting the criteria set forth in the federal regulations. The data center's system requirements would be found in a combination of its internal employment policies and procedures, the federal contract, and applicable federal law.

It is important to understand the relationship between objectives, risks, controls, and the trust services criteria. Objectives are the goals that the service organization wants to achieve. Risks threaten the achievement of objectives. Controls respond to risks by trying to mitigate them. In a SOC 2® engagement, the outcome of controls is benchmarked against the trust services criteria.

Criteria benchmark the outcome of controls

Controls respond to risks

Risks threaten the achievement of objectives

**Objectives are the service organization's goals**

## Description Criteria

**Representative Task (Remembering and Understanding):** Explain the purpose and common sections of a system description subject to SOC 1® or SOC 2® engagements.

**Representative Task (Remembering and Understanding):** Explain the purpose of complementary user entity controls (CUECs) identified by the service organization management in their system description.

Management must prepare the description of the service organization's system according to the **description criteria** that correspond to the type of SOC examination. Description criteria are a **benchmark** that lists the **minimum information** management should include. The service auditor also uses the description criteria to evaluate whether management stated the description fairly. A **fair** description is complete and accurate.

Suitable description criteria for each SOC examination are the following:

| | SOC 1® | SOC 2®, SOC 3® | SOC for Cybersecurity | SOC for Supply Chain |
|---|---|---|---|---|
| **Description Criteria** → | Suitable description criteria | DC Section 200 Description Criteria | DC Section 100 Description Criteria | DC Section 300 Description Criteria |

### SOC 1®

AT-C 320 defines a **service organization's system** in a SOC 1® examination as:

> *"The policies and procedures designed, implemented, and documented by management of the service organization to provide user entities with the services covered by the service auditor's report. Management's description of the service organization's system identifies the services covered, the period to which the description relates (or in the case of a type 1 report, the date to which the description relates), the control objectives specified by management or an outside party, the party specifying the control objectives (if not specified by management), and the related controls."*
>
> *"The policies and procedures referred to in the definition of service organization's system refer to the guidelines and activities for providing transaction processing and other services to user entities and include the infrastructure, software, people, and data that support the policies and procedures."*

The body of management's description explains the service organization's control objectives along with the five components of the COSO Internal Control–Integrated Framework. Disclosing the components of the internal control framework helps report users understand the identification and assessment of risks. While there is no prescribed format, management's description in a SOC 1® report ordinarily includes the following common sections:

| | |
|---|---|
| **Service Organization Overview** | • Company name, location, and background<br>• Services provided to user entities<br>• Customer and transaction types |
| **Scope of the Description** | • Type 1 or type 2<br>• Time covered by the examination<br>• Boundaries of service organization's system<br>• Subservice organization identification<br>• Subservice organization, inclusive vs. carve out |
| **Internal Control Framework** | • Control environment<br>• Risk assessment process<br>• Control activities<br>• Information and communication<br>• Monitoring activities<br>• Changes to system during examination period (type 2 only) |
| **Complementary Subservice Organization Controls (CSOCs)** | • Controls performed by each carved-out subservice organization |
| **Complementary User Entity Controls (CUECs)** | • Controls performed by user entities |
| **Control Objectives and Related Controls** | • Control objectives<br>• Controls |

The system description is presented in a narrative but may include flowcharts, tables, diagrams, or other graphics. Regardless of form, user entities and user entity auditors should be able to assess:

- How the services affect the user entity's financial statements
- The flow of transactions or information
- Processes and controls
- Complementary subservice organization controls (CSOCs)
- Complementary user entity controls (CUECs)

Management separately describes complementary subservice organization controls when using the carve-out method. The subservice organization's services would still be included in the narrative describing the service organization's system. Management should also describe its monitoring activities over subservice organizations. Monitoring activities may include:

- Reviewing and reconciling the subservice organization's reporting outputs
- Discussions with the subservice organization's management
- Site visits to the subservice organization's facilities
- Evaluating the subservice organization's controls through the service organization's internal audit function
- Reviewing the subservice organization's SOC reports
- Reviewing external communications, such as customer complaints

Likewise, management must describe CUECs so user entities and their auditors can understand what controls the user entity is responsible for. Only those CUECs that pertain to the service organization's objectives need to be described.

**Complementary User Entity Controls (CUECs)**

A service organization provides outsourced security camera monitoring to banks. The cameras, backup recording equipment, and backup media storage are located inside the user entity banks' facilities.

One of the service organization's security objectives relates to restricting physical access to its equipment. The service organization must rely on each bank's controls to restrict physical access within its facility. This CUEC would be disclosed in the service organization's system description so report users can understand all the controls in place.

## SOC 2®

The AICPA's SOC 2® Guide defines a service organization's system as:

> *"A system includes the infrastructure, software, procedures, and data that are designed, implemented, and operated by people to achieve one or more of the organization's specific business objectives (for example, delivery of services or production of goods) in accordance with management-specified requirements."*

In a SOC 2® examination, management's description must be prepared and evaluated in accordance with the AICPA's DC 200, *Description Criteria for a Description of a Service Organization's System in a SOC 2® Report*. The purpose of management's description in a SOC 2® report is to help intended users (eg, user entities, business partners) understand how the service organization's system achieves the principal service commitments and system requirements.

It is important to understand that the description criteria are benchmarks for management's description of the system, whereas the trust services criteria are benchmarks for the outcome of *controls*. Management and the service auditor use the two sets of criteria for different purposes:

| Description Criteria (DC 200) | Trust Services Criteria |
|---|---|
| **Management's Purpose** | **Management's Purpose** |
| To prepare the description of the service organization's system for a SOC 2® examination | As a guide to design, implement, and operate appropriate controls |
| **Service Auditor's Purpose** | **Service Auditor's Purpose** |
| To evaluate if management's description of the service organization's system is fairly presented in a SOC 2® examination | To evaluate whether controls were suitably designed to provide reasonable assurance that the service organization's service commitments and system requirements were achieved |

The DC 200 *Description Criteria* include **implementation guidance** on what type of information management should disclose for each criterion. The disclosures require judgment based on the service organization's services and operating environment.

| | |
|---|---|
| **Service Organization Overview** | • Company name, location, and background<br>• Services provided to user entities<br>• Customer types<br>• Type 1 or type 2; examination date or period<br>• Trust services categories under examination<br>• Boundaries of service organization's system<br>• Subservice organization identification; inclusive vs. carve out |
| **Principal Service Commitments and System Requirements** | • Service commitments relevant to the trust service categories under examination<br>• Service commitments made in service-level agreements and contracts<br>• Compliance with laws and regulations<br>• Adherence to industry guidelines |
| **Components of the System Used to Provide Services** | • Infrastructure<br>• Software<br>• People<br>• Procedures<br>• Data<br>• Third-party access |
| **Identified System Incidents** | • Whether public disclosure was required by cybersecurity regulations or resulted in a financial statement disclosure filing<br>• Whether any sanctions were issued by a legal or regulatory authority<br>• Whether the incident resulted in the withdrawal from material markets or cancellation of material contracts |
| **Internal Control Framework** | • Control environment<br>• Risk assessment process<br>• Control activities<br>• Information and communication<br>• Monitoring activities<br>• Changes to system during examination period (type 2 only) |
| **Complementary Subservice Organization Controls (CSOCs)** | • Controls performed by each carved-out subservice organization |
| **Complementary User Entity Controls (CUECs)** | • Controls performed by user entities |
| **Trust Services Criteria and Related Controls** | • Trust services criteria<br>• Controls |

There is no prescribed format or required organizational structure for the description of the system in a SOC 2® report. While the description is mostly narrative, it can include flowcharts, tables, and other graphics.

## SOC for Cybersecurity

The benchmarks for preparing and evaluating management's description of an entity's cybersecurity risk management can be found in the AICPA's DC 100 *Description Criteria for Management's Description of the Entity's Cybersecurity Risk Management Program*. That document defines an entity's cybersecurity risk management program as:

> *"The set of policies, processes, and controls designed to protect information and systems from security events that could compromise the achievement of the entity's cybersecurity objectives."*

The DC 100 *Description Criteria* may be used for both SOC for Cybersecurity examination engagements and consulting engagements. In all such engagements, management may select alternate criteria (eg, NIST Cybersecurity Framework) if they are more suitable or contractually required. Recall that a SOC for Cybersecurity examination results in a report that can be distributed to the public. Examples of this report are easily obtained on the Internet.

The DC 100 *Description Criteria* also include **implementation guidance** on what type of information management should disclose for each criterion. The disclosures require judgment based on the entity's business and risks.

| | |
|---|---|
| **Entity Overview** | • Company name and location<br>• Company background<br>• Products or services sold, including distribution methods<br>• Principal markets<br>• Geographic locations |
| **Nature of Information at Risk** | • Principal types of sensitive information created, transmitted, used, or stored<br>• Information regarding individuals that is protected by law, commitment, or reasonable expectation of confidentiality (such as personally identifiable information (PII), protected health information (PHI), and payment card data)<br>• Third-party information that is protected by law, commitment, or reasonable expectation or confidentiality, availability, and integrity<br>• Trade secrets, corporate strategy, and financial and operational data important to the entity's objectives |
| **Cybersecurity Objectives** | • Cybersecurity objectives related to availability, confidentiality, integrity of data, and processing integrity<br>• Commitments made to customers, vendors, and business partners related to the security and availability of information systems<br>• Laws and regulations<br>• Government certifications and authorization processes<br>• Industry standards<br>• Process for establishing, maintaining, and approving cybersecurity objectives |

| | |
|---|---|
| **Factors That Affect Cybersecurity Risk** | • Technologies, connection types, use of service providers, and delivery channels such as cloud computing, IT hosted services, mobile devices, network architecture, applications, infrastructure, data storage, external access, and web applications<br>• Organizational and user characteristics such as IT structure, user groups, risk assessment, responsibilities between business functions, separated IT systems<br>• Environmental, technological, or organizational changes made during the period<br>• Security incidents during the period that resulted in disclosure or impairment of cybersecurity objectives |
| **Cybersecurity Risk Management Program** | • Control environment<br>• Risk assessment process<br>• Control activities<br>• Information and communication<br>• Monitoring activities |

Note how an entity's description of its cybersecurity risk management also contains information that aligns with the five components of the COSO Internal Control–Integrated Framework. The intent of the DC 100 *Description Criteria* is to provide report users with the information necessary to understand their interactions with the entity.

## Control Criteria

Management's description of the system includes detailed information about objectives and related controls. Management asserts that it has designed, implemented, and documented controls that provide reasonable assurance of meeting the service organization's objectives. The suitability of the design of controls is determined by measuring or evaluating them against criteria (ie, benchmarks).

The following are suitable control criteria for each type of SOC examination:

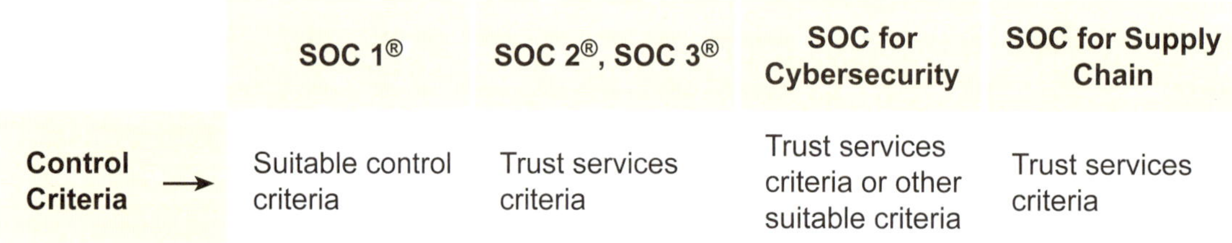

| | SOC 1® | SOC 2®, SOC 3® | SOC for Cybersecurity | SOC for Supply Chain |
|---|---|---|---|---|
| **Control Criteria** → | Suitable control criteria | Trust services criteria | Trust services criteria or other suitable criteria | Trust services criteria |

### SOC 1®: Suitable Criteria

SOC 1® reports give assurance about controls relevant to user entities' internal control over financial reporting (ICFR). Management's description of the system presents the service organization's governance structure in terms of the COSO Internal Control–Integrated Framework. It also outlines all the control objectives and related controls.

Unlike other SOC examinations, there is no list of specific control criteria to be used as a benchmark. Management's control objectives are the criteria used to determine if controls are suitably designed and operating effectively. The control criteria selected by management in a SOC 1® examination must simply be "suitable," which means that management's control objectives must have the following characteristics:

Suitable Criteria

| **Relevant** | **Objective** |
|---|---|
| Control objectives are relevant to the subject matter | Control objectives are free from bias |
| **Measurable** | **Complete** |
| Control objectives provide a reasonably consistent measurement of the subject matter | Control objectives do not omit factors that are important to report users' decision-making |

Meeting the suitability requirements requires management to be specific in the wording of its control objectives. For example, it is not sufficient to have a control objective stating, "Controls provide reasonable assurance that physical access to data centers is adequate." The word "adequate" is not measurable. A suitable objective might say, "Controls provide reasonable assurance that physical access to data centers is limited to authorized personnel who have passed a background check."

While there are no requirements for the manner of presentation, control objectives and related controls might appear in the description in a table or matrix. In a type 1 examination, only the control objectives and related controls are presented. In a type 2 examination, the matrix would include the control objectives and related controls, the service auditor's tests of controls, and the results of the service auditor's tests of controls.

## All Other SOC Examinations: Trust Services Criteria

In all other SOC examinations, the TSP 100, *2017 Trust Services Criteria for Security, Availability, Processing Integrity, Confidentiality, or Privacy* serve as suitable control criteria.

In its system description, management lists the controls that provide reasonable assurance of meeting objectives. The trust services criteria are benchmarks used to measure and evaluate whether controls are **suitably designed**.

The SOC examination must address one or more of the five trust services categories, and it must, at minimum, include security. The details of each category relate to representative tasks in blueprint Areas I and II. The five categories are:

- **Security:** Systems and information are protected from unauthorized access, disclosure, and damage.
- **Availability:** Information is accessible for operational, monitoring, and maintenance purposes.
- **Processing Integrity:** System processing is complete, accurate, timely, and authorized.
- **Confidentiality:** Sensitive information is protected from the point of creation through disposal.
- **Privacy:** Personal information is protected from the point of creation through disposal.

The trust services criteria align with the 17 principles of the 2013 COSO Internal Control–Integrated Framework. There are three categories of trust services criteria:

- **Common criteria:** Linked to the five COSO components and applicable to all engagements using the trust services criteria (CC1–5)
- **Supplemental criteria:** Expand COSO component 12, deploying control activities; the supplemental criteria apply to all engagements using the trust services criteria (CC6–9)
- **Additional category-specific criteria:** Only apply if relevant to the trust services category that is included in the examination; all trust service categories except security have additional criteria (A, C, PI, P)

The trust services criteria are numbered and each has a heading describing the primary principle. Each criterion has correlating **points of focus**. The points of focus may help management and the engaged CPA in evaluating whether the controls are suitably designed; however, use of the criteria does not require management or the practitioner to separately assess whether points of focus are addressed. The points of focus are the specific detailed benchmarks used to measure and evaluate whether management's controls provide reasonable assurance of achieving objectives.

**Appendix A** includes a summary of all the criteria found in the AICPA's TSP Section 100 2017 *Trust Services Criteria for Security, Availability, Processing Integrity, Confidentiality, and Privacy (with Revised Points of Focus – 2022).* An example of the trust services criteria is as follows:

## Trust Services Criteria and Points of Focus

**CC1.1 COSO Principle 1: The entity demonstrates a commitment to integrity and ethical values.**

### COSO Framework

- Sets tone at the top
- Establishes standards of conduct
- Evaluates adherence to standards of conduct
- Addresses deviations in a timely manner

### Modification for Trust Service Engagements

- Considers contractors and vendor employees in demonstrating commitment

The general organization of the trust services criteria and their alignment to the COSO Internal Control–Integrated Framework is as follows:

| Criteria Type | TSC Series | TSC Category | TSC Criteria | COSO Component | COSO Principles |
|---|---|---|---|---|---|
| Common | CC1 | All | Control Environment | Control Environment | 1–5 |
| Common | CC2 | All | Communication and Information | Information and Communication | 13–15 |
| Common | CC3 | All | Risk Assessment | Risk Assessment | 6–9 |
| Common | CC4 | All | Monitoring of Controls | Monitoring Activities | 16–17 |
| Common | CC5 | All | Control Activities | Control Activities | 10–12 |
| Supplemental | CC6 | All | Logical and Physical Access Controls | Control Activities | 12 |
| Supplemental | CC7 | All | System Operations | Control Activities | 12 |
| Supplemental | CC8 | All | Change Management | Control Activities | 12 |
| Supplemental | CC9 | All | Risk Mitigation | Control Activities | 12 |
| Additional | A | Specific | Availability | | |
| Additional | C | Specific | Confidentiality | | |
| Additional | PI | Specific | Processing Integrity | | |
| Additional | P | Specific | Privacy | | |

# 1.04 Performing Further Procedures in a SOC Engagement

## Performing Further Procedures

Engagement acceptance → Planning → **Performing** → Reporting

### Responding to Assessed Risks and Obtaining Evidence

AT-C 205 requires the service auditor to:

- Design and implement an overall response addressing the assessed risks of material misstatement
- Design and implement further procedures whose nature, timing, and extent are based on, and responsive to, the assessed risks of material misstatement
- Obtain sufficient appropriate evidence to reduce attestation risk to an acceptable low level and provide reasonable assurance of conclusions from which to form an opinion

A service auditor's procedures vary based on whether a type 1 or type 2 report will be issued. In a type 2, the service auditor performs tests of controls to determine the operating effectiveness of controls. A type 2 report is also performed throughout a period. Thus, the service auditor's procedures are more extensive in a type 2 examination.

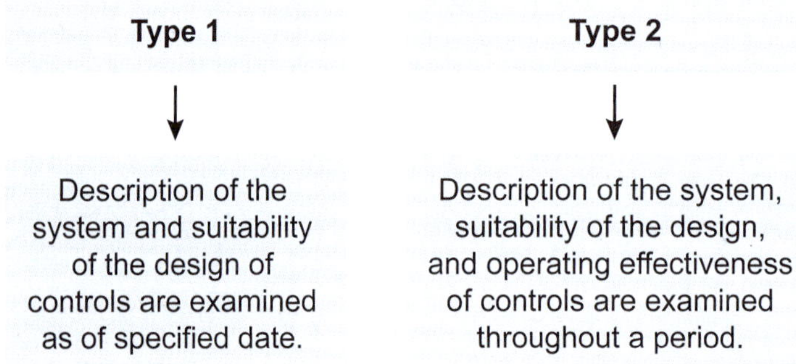


#### Overall Response to Risks of Material Misstatement

The engaged CPA firm must design and implement a structure for the engagement. The engagement team should include properly supervised staff who can maintain professional judgment and skepticism.

## Nature, Timing, and Extent of Procedures

The selection and timing of the procedures should be **unpredictable**. This ensures that the service auditor performs procedures in a live environment, rather than in one manipulated by the service organization.

When designing and performing further procedures, the service auditor should consider assessed risk. This includes evaluating the likelihood of a material misstatement and whether controls can be relied on. The greater the assessed risk, the more persuasive evidence the service auditor needs to reach a level of reasonable assurance. If there is a high probability of a material misstatement, the service auditor may increase procedures. If the service auditor feels that controls can be relied on, the service auditor may decrease procedures.

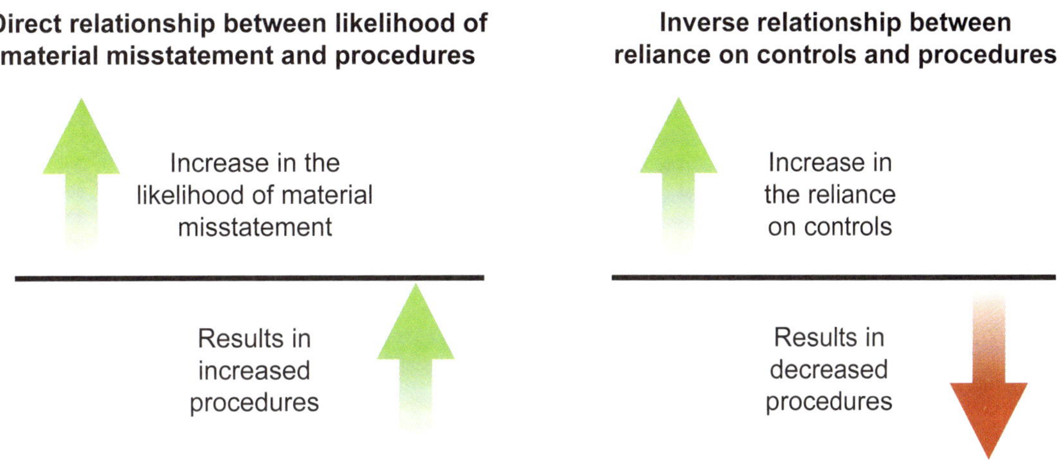


The engagement team should balance the efficiency and effectiveness of its procedures. For example, a service auditor testing role-based access controls might not examine every employee's user permissions. The service auditor could use sampling techniques to provide reasonable assurance.

Sampling involves the following steps:

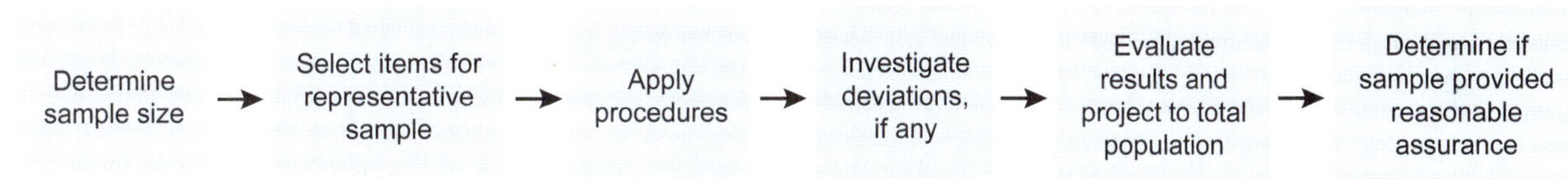


## Sufficient Appropriate Evidence

The purpose of performing further procedures is to obtain **sufficient appropriate evidence**. Evidence reduces attestation risk to a low level and provides reasonable assurance for the service auditor's opinion. **Attestation risk** is the probability that the service auditor will issue an incorrect opinion because their procedures did not detect an existing material misstatement.

**Attestation risk** is similar to the **audit risk model** and is expressed mathematically as:

$$\text{Attestation risk} = \text{Risk of Material Misstatement} \times \text{Detection Risk}$$

$$\text{Risk of Material Misstatement} = \text{Inherent Risk} \times \text{Control Risk}$$

Inherent risk and control risk are the same concepts as discussed in the service organization risk assessment. **Detection risk** is the amount of risk the service auditor is willing to accept that the examination procedures do not uncover material misstatements. It is the only risk directly affected by the auditor's decisions and actions.

The service auditor's willingness to accept detection risk is based on its assessment of the **risk of material misstatement**. The higher the assessed risk of material misstatement, the less detection risk the service auditor will accept; the auditor would respond by increasing procedures and/or sample sizes. On the other hand, the lower the risk of material misstatement, the more detection risk the service auditor can accept; the auditor could feel comfortable enough to reduce the number of procedures and/or sample sizes.

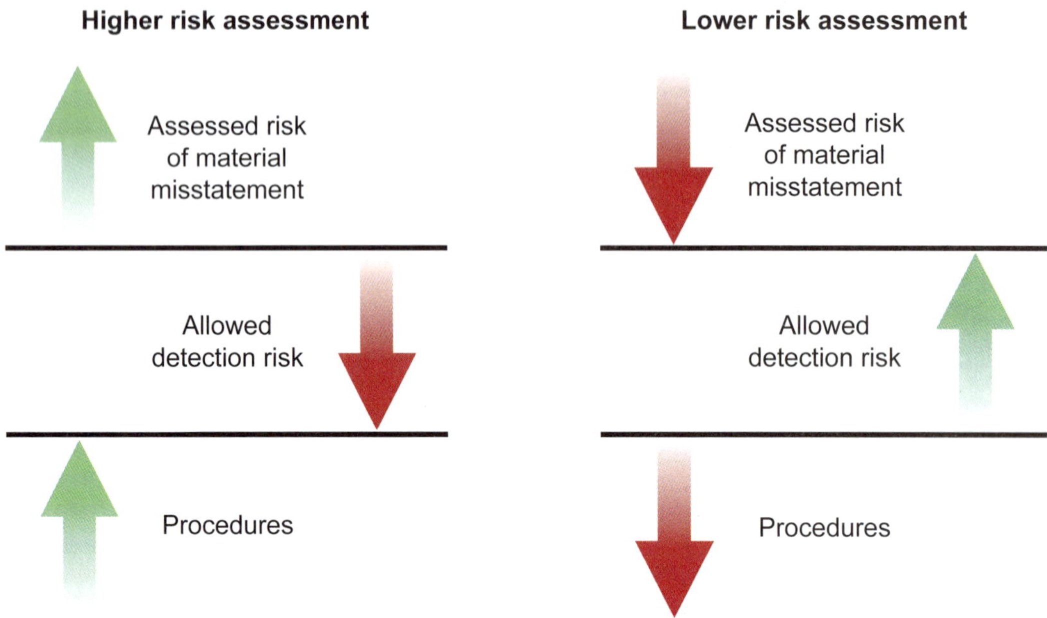


Sufficient appropriate evidence either supports (ie, corroborates) or contradicts management's written assertions.

- **Sufficiency** measures the *quantity* of audit evidence. The necessary quantity of evidence is a matter of the service auditor's professional judgment about the assessed risk of material misstatement and the appropriateness of evidence.
- **Appropriateness** refers to the *quality* of audit evidence, that is, its relevance and reliability in supporting the conclusions on which the auditor's opinion is based.
  - Evidence is **relevant** if it pertains to management's assertions.
  - Evidence is **reliable** if it is complete, accurate, and sufficiently precise and detailed.

Reliability depends on the source of information, the method of acquisition, and its format. Evidence obtained directly by the service auditor through procedures is the most dependable. **Information provided by the entity (IPE)** (ie, the service organization) is the least dependable.

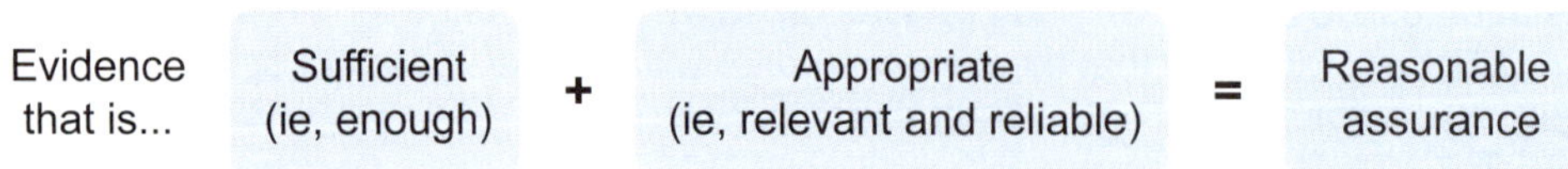

## Obtaining Evidence: Management's Description of the System, Type 1 and Type 2

**Representative Task (Application):** Prepare a comparison of management's system description to suitable criteria in a SOC 1® engagement or to the description criteria in a SOC 2® engagement.

Service auditors must determine if the description of the system is **fairly stated, in all material respects, based on the criteria** in management's assertion and the scope of the engagement. Fairly stated means that management's description:

- Is based on suitable criteria;
- States reasonable objectives;
- Includes only controls that have been implemented;
- Adequately describes complementary subservice organization controls and complementary user entity controls; and
- Adequately describes the services performed by subservice organizations, including whether the inclusive or carve-out method was used.

The following procedures may be performed to obtain evidence about management's description of the system:

**Further Procedures**

**Reperformance**

Evaluating a process, procedure, or control by performing it and then comparing the result with that of the service organization

**Inquiry**

Asking service organization personnel to answer questions verbally or on a questionnaire

**Inspection**

Reviewing documentation of the service organization's risk assessment, policies, procedures, monitoring, internal audit evaluations, contracts with user entities and business partners, and reports from regulators

**Observation**

Watching the service organization's personnel perform procedures

A service auditor may also perform a walkthrough to determine if a process is carried out in a manner that is consistent with the documented process. Walkthroughs normally involve performing a combination of procedures such as reperforming calculations, asking questions, reading procedure manuals, and observing a process from initiation to reporting. The service auditor may also inquire about instances when controls or processes did not operate as designed.

Typical procedures to obtain evidence about management's description include:

### Inquiry

- Ask personnel about the content of the description

### Inspection

- Read contracts and service-level agreements
- Read the service organization's annual financial report
- Read documents that show how the service organization assesses and mitigates risk
- Read board minutes and organizational charts
- Read policies and procedures related to the scope of the engagement
  - SOC 1®: How transactions are processed and reported
  - SOC 2®: Communications about the trust service categories included in the examination (security, availablity, and processing integrity of the system; confidentiality and privacy of information)
- Read system documentation, flowcharts, hardware asset management records
- Review security awareness and training programs and read code of conduct, employee handbook, information security policies, and incident notification procedures
- Read internal audit reports, third-party assessments, audit committee presentations
- Read about laws, regulations, or industry standards relevant to the service organization
- Read SOC reports from subservice organizations

### Observation

- Visit facilities
- Watch processes being performed by service organization personnel

### Reperformance

- Recalculate any figures or statistics in the description

### Walkthroughs

- Perform inquiries, inspections, and observation to understand a process from start to finish

The extent of the service auditor's procedures depends on assessed risk and materiality. Since management's description is mostly narrative, **materiality** is based on **qualitative factors** such as completeness, reasonableness, and accuracy. For example, does the description include enough information for report users to understand changes to the system during the period? Are the controls stated in the description complete, objective, and measurable? Is any information omitted or distorted that might mislead report users?

The service auditor should document the procedures performed and evidence obtained. The evidence, along with the service auditor's understanding of the system, serves as the basis for a comparison of management's system description to suitable criteria. For example, the service auditor may prepare a **mapping** of management's description to the description criteria. Such a comparison helps the service auditor find **material description misstatements**.

If a description misstatement exists, the service auditor may ask management to amend its description. If management refuses, circumstances may require a **modification** to the service auditor's report as a **separate paragraph**. The separate paragraph serves to inform report users that in the service auditor's opinion, management's description of the system is *not* fairly presented.

**Material Description Misstatements in a SOC Examination**

**Inappropriately included**

- Controls that are not reasonable
- Controls that were not implemented
- Information that is not measurable
- Information that is not relevant to the service organization's objectives
- Information that is not consistent with management's written assertion
- Information that is not relevant to the period under examination

**Inappropriately omitted**

- Relevant controls
- Information relevant to the service organization's objectives
- Information about CSOCs and CUECs
- Information about subservice organizations and whether the inclusive or carved-out method is used
- Changes during the period under examination (type 2 reports only)

## SOC 1®

The following factors are important to the fair presentation of the description in a SOC 1® examination (bold items highlight differences between a SOC 1® and SOC 2® examination):

**SOC 1®: Evaluation of the Fair Presentation of Management's Description of the System**

| | | |
|---|---|---|
| **Description is based on suitable criteria** | **Control objectives are reasonable** | Identified controls were implemented and disclosed with sufficient detail |
| System incidents were disclosed with sufficient detail | CUECs and user entity responsibilities are adequately described | CSOCs are adequately described |
| Subservice organizations, and the method used, are adequately described (inclusive or carved out) | Changes to the system during the period are adequately described (type 2) | **The needs of user entities and user auditors are considered** |

Management's description should contain enough detail for the service auditor, user entities, and user auditors to understand:

- The boundaries of the service organization's system
- The types of services provided, including classes of transactions
- The automated and manual procedures used to provide services, explaining how transactions are initiated, authorized, recorded, processed, corrected (if needed), and transferred to reports given to the user entity
- The types of electronic and paper-based information used to perform procedures, including accounting records
- How the service organization's system captures significant events other than transactions
- The processes used to prepare reports
- COSO's five components of internal control relevant to the services provided: control environment, risk assessment, control activities, information and communication, and monitoring activities
- How the control objectives relate to the types of assertions in user entity's financial statements

**Comparison: Management's System Description to Suitable Criteria—SOC 1®**

Management of a payroll processing service organization asserted that the description of its system is fairly stated. One of the criteria listed in the assertion is that the description explains how the system was designed and implemented, including the automated and manual procedures through which transactions are processed.

Management's description discussed the monitoring activities component of its internal control framework. The description further contained the following control objective and related control:

**Control objective:** *"Controls provide reasonable assurance that payroll tax computations are complete and accurate."*

**Control:** *"Automated payroll tax calculations are updated and monitored for accuracy by personnel."*

The service auditor assessed the criteria to be suitable. When performing further procedures, the service auditor inquired about the service organization's process for updating automated payroll tax calculations for IRS revisions to withholding tables. Service organization personnel stated they did not monitor payroll tax calculations for accuracy after updating withholding calculations.

The service auditor obtained a sample of payroll withholding calculations made after the IRS tables were revised. The calculations were not correct in 5 of the 25 payroll withholdings sampled.

The service auditor concluded that the control activity failed and thus resulted in a qualification of the control objective.

**Description Compared to Suitable Criteria—SOC 1®**

| Management's Description of the System | Suitable Criteria | Service Auditor's Procedures | Results of Service Auditor's Tests |
|---|---|---|---|
| Management describes a control in which service organization personnel monitor the accuracy of automated payroll withholding calculations | Management's description presents how the system was designed and implemented, including specified control objectives and controls to achieve those objectives | Inquiry of service organization personnel and reperformance of calculations | Exception noted. Calculations were not correct in 5 of the 25 payroll withholdings sampled |

## SOC 2®

The following factors are important to the fair presentation of the service organization's system in a SOC 2® examination (bold items highlight differences between a SOC 2® examination and a SOC 1® examination):

**SOC 2®: Evaluation of the Fair Presentation of Management's Description of the System**

| | | |
|---|---|---|
| **Description is based on the DC-200 Description Criteria** | **Service commitments and system requirements are disclosed and appropriate** | Identified controls were implemented and disclosed with sufficient detail |
| System incidents were disclosed with sufficient detail | CUECs and user entity responsibilities are adequately described | CSOCs are adequately described |
| Subservice organizations, and the method used, are adequately described (inclusive or carved out) | Changes to the system during the period are adequately described (type 2) | **The needs of user entities, business partners, and other report users are considered** |

When evaluating whether the description is in accordance with the DC Section 200 *Description Criteria*, the service auditor should consider the following characteristics:

- Factors that indicate the description is in accordance with DC 200 *Description Criteria*:
  - Includes significant components of the system designed and implemented by the service organization
  - Describes the service organization's services and controls that have been implemented
  - Describes the service organization's principal service commitments and system requirements and related controls
  - Includes the trust services categories included in the scope of the examination
  - Matches controls to the trust services criteria included in the scope of the examination
  - Does not omit or distort information important to report users' decisions
  - Provides sufficient information relevant to each of the DC 200 *Description Criteria* and related implementation guidance
  - Information can be measured or evaluated against the description criteria
  - Format is clear and understandable
- Factors that indicate the description is *not* in accordance with DC 200 *Description Criteria*:
  - Implies facts that are not true, such as including components that do not exist or stating that certain frameworks are followed when they are not
  - States that processes or controls have been implemented when they have not
  - Omits or distorts information relevant to report users' decisions
  - Contains statements that cannot be evaluated (eg, advertising statements such as "world's best")
  - Information is summarized too much or presented too generally for users to make decisions
  - Format is confusing or obscure

**Comparison: Management's System Description to Suitable Criteria—SOC 2®**

A service auditor performs a SOC 2® type 2 examination of a service organization that provides learning management system software to educational institutions. To determine if management's description was prepared in line with the DC 200 *Description Criteria*, the service auditor inspected the following documents:

- Management's description of the system
- Board minutes
- System manuals and flowcharts
- Hardware asset records

The service auditor noticed that the board minutes referenced a third-party cloud services vendor. In addition, system manuals had been changed, and asset records revealed that hardware was disposed of during the period under examination. A review of management's description found that it was the same as the prior examination.

Additional inquiries were performed. Service organization personnel stated that there had been a flood, damaging a significant amount of equipment. The board decided to start moving data storage to the cloud.

The service auditor did not find any reference to the new subservice organization, complementary subservice organization controls, or the flooding incident disclosed in management's description. After a discussion, management agreed to obtain a SOC 2® report from the cloud service provider and amend the description.

**Description Compared to DC-200 Description Criteria—SOC 2®**

| Management's Description of the System | Suitable Criteria | Service Auditor's Procedures | Service Auditor's Results |
|---|---|---|---|
| Did not describe:<br>• New subservice organization<br>• Complementary subservice organization controls<br>• Flood damage<br>• Changes to the system during the period | DC200: Management's description should include disclosure of subservice organization controls, complementary subservice organization controls, significant incidents, and changes that occurred during the period under review | Inquiry of service organization personnel and document inspections | Exception noted. Management did not describe material changes to its system, subservice organizations, or CSOCs in its system description |

## Obtaining Evidence: Design of Controls, Type 1 and Type 2

Two of the preconditions to a SOC examination are that management takes responsibility for:

- Identifying the risks that threaten the achievement of the service organization's objectives
- Suitability of the design and operating effectiveness of controls (only in a type 2 examination) to provide reasonable assurance that the service organization's objectives were achieved

The service auditor should consider risks identified by management and through its own risk assessment procedures. Controls should be suitably designed to prevent these risks from thwarting the service organization's objectives.

Controls may be suitably designed either individually or when combined with other controls. For example, a control may need to be combined with other service organization controls, complementary user entity controls (CUECs), or complementary subservice organization controls (CSOCs).

A service auditor assesses the suitability of the design of controls by performing procedures to:

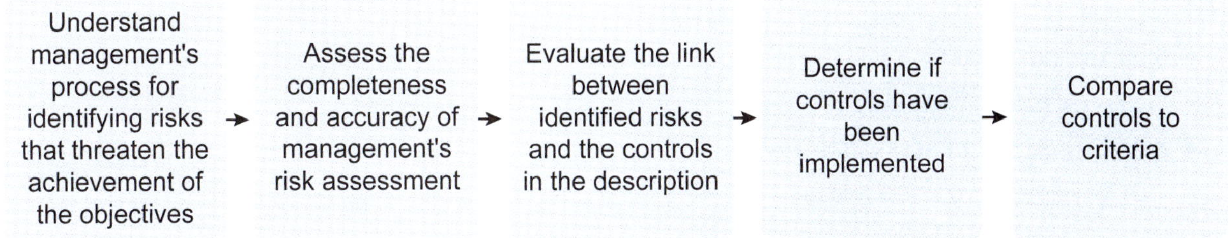


Procedures to evaluate the suitability of the design of controls include:

- **Inquiry:** Ask questions of management or personnel, either verbally or through questionnaires. For example, the questions may regard risk assessment, the design and operation of controls, and system incidents.
- **Inspection:** Review documents related to management's identification of risks and their linkage to controls. Review evidence gathered by the service auditor (eg, from system documentation) while obtaining an understanding of the system and determining whether the description is fairly stated.
- **Observation:** Watch service organization personnel perform tasks.
- **Reperformance:** Perform the same tasks as the service organization personnel (ie, recalculate totals or determine if IT application controls are working).
- **Walkthroughs:** Understand and document the control process.

**Subservice Organizations under the Inclusive Method**

If the inclusive method is used, the service auditor must perform procedures on the subservice organization as well.

A deficiency in the suitability of the design of a control happens when a control:

- Is missing, or
- Exists but would not achieve the service organization's objective even if performed as designed.

If, in the service auditor's opinion, a control is not suitably designed, a separate paragraph should be added to the report. A separate paragraph is a form of a report modification. Modifications are discussed in Lecture 2.01 "Reporting on a SOC Engagement."

**Representative Tasks Related to the Suitability of Design and Operating Effectiveness of Controls**

The following lectures include Analysis representative tasks about performing procedures to detect deficiencies in the suitability or design and deviations in the operation of controls in a SOC 2® type 2 examination:

- 6.03 Testing: Security
- 3.03 Availability: Availability
- 3.02 ERP/AIS: Processing Integrity
- 7.01 Confidentiality and Privacy

## SOC 1® Considerations

AT-C 320 states that the minimum criteria for determining if controls are suitably designed include the following:

- Management has identified the risks that threaten the achievement of the control objectives stated in the description of the system.
- If the controls listed in the description of the system operated effectively, the identified risks would not prevent the achievement of management's control objectives.

In a SOC 1® examination, risks relate to transactions and information technology that affect user entities' controls over financial reporting. The service auditor should consider risks that stem from both unintentional (error) and intentional (fraud) acts. When evaluating the **suitability** of a control's design, **materiality** is primarily based on **qualitative factors**.

The service organization's **control objectives** should correspond with **user entities' financial statement assertions**. A user auditor's concern is whether the service organization's controls are designed to prevent, detect, or correct misstatements in the user entity's financial statements.

The following table shows example connections between a user entity's financial statement assertions and a service organization's control objectives. Management's financial statement assertions are discussed in the Auditing (AUD) book.

**Service Organization Processes Transactions and Records Events for User Entities**

| User Entity Financial Statement Assertion | Service Organization Control Objective | Risks That Threaten Control Objectives |
|---|---|---|
| **Completeness** | Transactions are reported completely. | Reports don't include all transactions. |
| **Cutoff** | Transactions are processed in a timely manner. | Transaction is recorded in a different period. |
| **Accuracy** | Transactions are entered accurately. | Application makes incorrect calculations. |
| **Classification** | Transactions are recorded in the proper accounts. | Ineffective IT application controls result in posting to wrong account. |
| **Occurrence** | Transactions are received only from authorized sources. | Manual transactions are not properly authorized. |

Control objectives would also include **IT general controls** related to a user entity's financial statements. The following table includes examples:

| IT General Control | Service Organization Control Objective | Risks That Threaten Control Objectives |
|---|---|---|
| **Information Security** | Logical access to data is restricted to authorized users. | Unauthorized users gain access and modify data. |
| | Physical access to computers is restricted to authorized personnel. | Unauthorized physical access is granted, and media is taken. |
| **Change Management** | Changes to applications are authorized, tested, documented, approved, and implemented to result in complete, accurate, and timely processing of user entities' transactions. | Application does not function as specified. |
| **Computer Operations** | System processing errors are recorded, tracked, and resolved in a timely manner. | System processing errors are not detected. |
| | Data transmissions between the service organization and user entities are complete. | Data is corrupted in transit. |

A service auditor cannot determine what would cause a misstatement for every user entity. From the service auditor's standpoint, a **control** is **suitably designed** if it provides **reasonable assurance** of **achieving** the **control objectives** stated in management's description. Multiple controls may be needed. Service auditors can use flowcharts, diagrams, and tables to visualize how a series of controls work together.

Understanding control objectives and identified risks, a service auditor should assess the **linkage** between the **risk** and **controls**. A suitably designed control should include all the following elements:

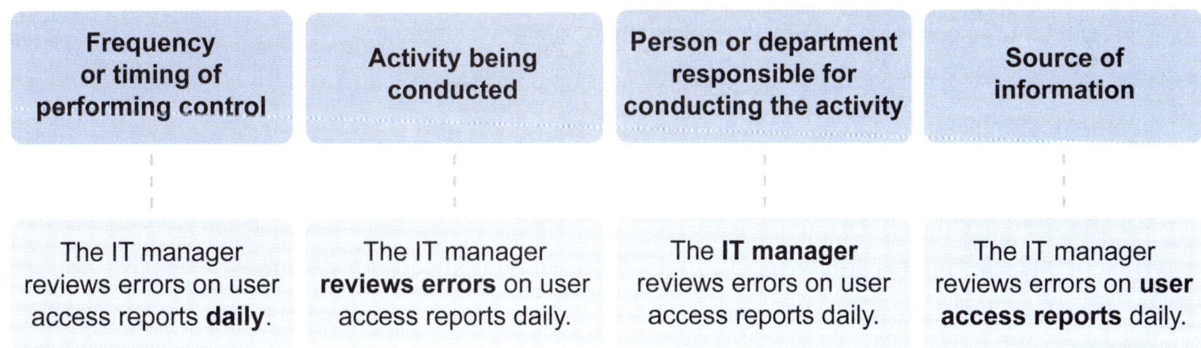


## SOC 2® Considerations

In a SOC 2® examination, suitably designed controls provide reasonable assurance of achieving the service organization's principal service commitments and system requirements *based on the trust services criteria* (if those controls are implemented and capable of operating effectively). To recall, the service auditor's process to evaluate the suitability of the design of controls includes:

- Obtaining an understanding of the service organization's risk assessment process and linkage to controls

- Evaluating whether controls are suitably designed and implemented

The service auditor obtains an understanding of the service organization's risk assessment process by considering how the service organization:

- Identifies principal service commitments and system requirements
- Identifies information used by the system to provide services to user entities
- Identifies threats to the achievement of principal service commitments and system requirements
- Identifies threats to the components of the system
- Evaluates the likelihood and severity of risks
- Incorporates information from monitoring activities and events
- Evaluates deficiencies caused by a flaw in the design of controls
- Uses an appropriate security framework (eg, NIST CSF) for managing its system processes and controls
- Assesses the risk of fraud
- Selects the inclusive method or carve-out method for subservice organizations

To evaluate the suitability of the design of controls, the service auditor compares the following:

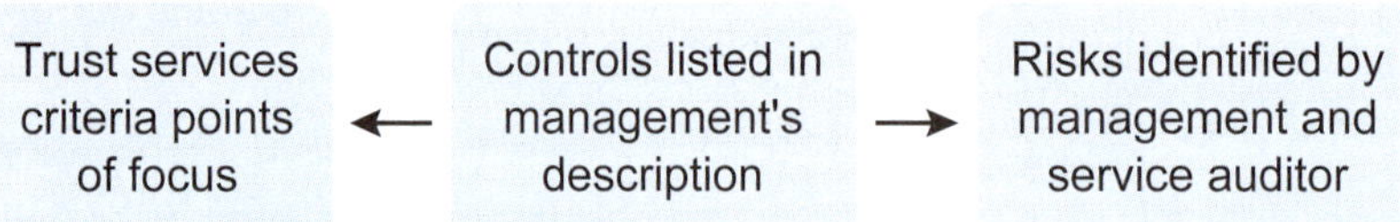


The service auditor may consider the following additional factors:

- Frequency and timing of the control
- Authority and competence of the person performing the control
- Tasks within the control
- Evidence that the control is not functioning, such as system incidents
- Whether the control mitigates risks to principal service commitments and system requirements
- Whether information used in the control is dependable
- Whether controls are updated for new threats
- Likelihood and extent of risk
- Whether multiple controls are necessary to address risk or trust services criteria
- Whether threats and vulnerabilities listed by public organizations, such the US Computer Emergency Readiness Team (US-CERT), have been addressed.

## Obtaining Evidence: Operating Effectiveness of Controls, Type 2 Only

**Service auditors perform procedures to assess the operating effectiveness of controls only when a type 2 report is requested.**

AT-C 205 states that tests of controls to obtain sufficient appropriate evidence about the **operating effectiveness** of relevant controls are appropriate when the **subject matter** is **internal control**. Recall that in a type 2 examination, management asserts that controls are suitably designed and operating effectively **throughout a period**. The service auditor performs **tests of controls** and includes the **results** in the report.

The difference between a deficiency in the suitability of the design of a control and a **deviation in the operating effectiveness of a control** is as follows:

| Deficiency in Design | Deviation in Operating Effectiveness |
|---|---|
| Control is missing | Suitably designed control does not operate as expected |
| Control would not achieve objectives even if operated as designed | Person performing the control does not have the necessary authority or competence |
| To correct: redesign control | To correct: determine why control isn't working as designed |

In a SOC 2® examination, a control in management's description operates effectively if it provides reasonable assurance that the principal service commitments and system requirements are achieved based on the trust services criteria. By including controls in the description, management indicates that they are part of the system. The same applies to any subservice organizations for which the inclusive method is selected.

Principal service commitments and system requirements can be achieved through a single control or a group of controls operating together. A service auditor's consideration of materiality is in terms of both quantitative and qualitative factors.

Tests of controls should be performed on those controls that management identifies in its description of the system as needed to achieve principal service commitments and system requirements. Service auditors normally only test controls that management has implemented and that are suitably designed. By definition, a deficiency in the design of a control prevents achievement of the service organization's principal service commitments and system requirements.

To recall, in both a SOC 1® and SOC 2® examination, management's description of the system includes a narrative of COSO's five components of internal control. These include:

| Control environment | Risk assessment | Control activities | Information and communication | Monitoring activities |
|---|---|---|---|---|

The controls within each of COSO's components may enhance other controls or mitigate other deficiencies. When the COSO components themselves do not operate effectively, the service auditor must perform further procedures. Factors that the service auditor should consider when designing further procedures include:

- Type of misstatements a control is designed to prevent, detect, or correct
- Materiality, quantitative and qualitative
- History of operating deficiencies
- Effectiveness of monitoring activities
- Nature of the control and how frequently it is expected to be performed

A service auditor's opinion that a control operates effectively requires more evidence than opining that one does *not*. It cannot be assumed that controls that operated effectively in prior periods are effective in the current examination. The service auditor must still perform full procedures in the current period. Knowledge of deficiencies in prior periods may, however, lead to increased testing.

The following procedures are performed to evaluate the operating effectiveness of controls:

### Reperformance, Inquiry, Inspection, Observation

- Was the control performed as designed?
- Was the control applied consistently throughout the period?
- By whom or by what means was the control applied?
  - Manual versus automated
  - Competency of personnel performing the control

### Do the Controls Depend on Other Controls?

- Does the service auditor have evidence the other controls operated effectively?

### Is the Information Produced by the Service Organization Reliable?

- Accurate and complete?
- Sufficiently precise and detailed?

### How Will Items for Testing be Selected?

- Sampling
- 100% of population

Inquiry alone is not enough to determine that a control operated effectively. It must be combined with other procedures such as inspection or observation. When using information produced by the service organization (**IPE**), the service auditor must determine if the information is **sufficiently reliable**. This may include:

- Obtaining evidence to determine the accuracy and completeness of the information or data
- Evaluating whether the information is sufficiently precise and detailed for the service auditor's purposes

There are three general types of information supplied by the service organization when testing the operating effectiveness of controls:

| Information produced in response to ad hoc requests from the service auditor | Information used to perform a control | Information prepared for user entities |
|---|---|---|
| *Example:* Population list of all users with access to the service organization's application | *Example:* Reports from the service organization's internal access monitoring | *Example:* Reports listing user entity employee's access activity throughout a period |

Service auditors should perform additional **procedures** to **test the reliability of information** produced by the service organization. Those procedures may include:

- Inspecting the source of information provided by the service organization
- Inspecting the query, script, or parameters used to generate the information
- Observing service organization personnel inputting the query, script, or parameter
- Comparing data from the source to the output of a query, script, or parameter
- Inspecting the information for gaps in timing or sequence
- Testing the IT general and application controls related to the information
- Inspecting the change log or change tickets for changes to the query, script, or parameters throughout the SOC period (for a type 2)
- Inspecting the permissions of users who make changes to the query, script, or parameters in order to verify they have appropriate authority to do so

## Subsequent Events and Subsequently Discovered Facts

**Representative Task (Application):** Determine the effect of subsequent events in a SOC 1® or SOC 2® engagement.

**Representative Task (Remembering and Understanding):** Recall the impact of subsequently discovered facts on the SOC engagement (SOC 1®, SOC 2®).

### Subsequent Events

AT-C 205 requires the service auditor to ask the responsible party or the engaging party, if different, whether any **subsequent events** occurred *after the examination but up to the date of the report*. **Failure to disclose** a significant event that occurs prior to the issuance of the service auditor's report may **mislead report users**.

Besides inquiry, the service auditor may perform other procedures to determine if there were any subsequent events. These additional procedures would cover only the period after the examination and may include:

- Reading minutes of meetings of the board of directors and other committees occurring after the examination to determine if there is discussion of subsequent events
- Making inquiries of the service organization's legal counsel to determine if there were any lawsuits, claims, or assessments arising or settled after the examination
- Reading interim reports prepared by management, internal audit, other CPAs, or regulatory bodies
- Reviewing the service organization's website and recent press releases

Subsequent events that have a significant impact on the subject matter, controls, or assertions may require disclosure or changes to the assertions. If a subsequent event becomes known, the service auditor should perform additional procedures or obtain additional evidence, as necessary.

If the responsible party refuses to disclose the subsequent event or allow additional procedures, the service auditor may:

- Disclose the event in the report and modify their opinion, or
- Withdraw from the engagement.

Subsequent events that would *not* have affected the examination but are significant may also be disclosed in management's assertions or the service auditor's report. Examples of such events might include the service organization being acquired after the examination, a natural disaster, or a change in a subservice organization.

**Subsequent Events**

**SOC 1®**

A service auditor performed a SOC 1® type 2 engagement on a real estate management company. The management company provides administrative services for corporations that own apartment complexes paid for with federal and state low-income housing deferred payment loans. The loan programs set upper rental rate limits, which must be reported on a regular basis.

The service auditor conducted the SOC 1® examination and then performed the following procedures to determine if any significant subsequent events occurred:

**Inquiry:** The service auditor asked if any compliance audits were performed by any regulatory bodies after the SOC 1® examination. Management responded that a state authority had performed an audit and determined that rental rate limits were exceeded in one subsidized community. The outcome was unknown but might result in owner sanctions.

**Inspection:** The service auditor obtained a copy of the government audit report. The noncompliance was related to a data entry error in the real estate management company's system. The service auditor's tests of controls did not uncover any deficiencies with the suitability of design or operating effectiveness of controls.

This scenario presents two issues: a significant subsequent event and the service auditor learning that the examination procedures did not detect a deficiency. The engagement team would review its workpapers to determine why its procedures failed to uncover a problem. Additional tests of controls would be performed, and the management company would need to amend its description. If the management company refused to amend the description or allow additional procedures, the service auditor could modify their opinion or withdraw from the engagement.

**SOC 2®**

A service auditor performed a SOC 2® type 1 examination of a FinTech SaaS provider for the security trust services category. After the examination, the service auditor performed the following procedures to determine if there were any significant subsequent events:

**Inquiry:** Asked management questions verbally and in a questionnaire.

**Inspection:** Read board minutes and internal audit reports.

The service auditor learned that the SaaS provider made plans to migrate to a new cloud service provider prior to the next SOC 2® examination. Thus, there was no effect on the current examination.

The service auditor and management agreed that this change was significant enough to disclose in management's assertion. Management could also add information to the end of the SOC 2® report in Section 5 as "Other Information Provided by the Service Organization," which is not included in the examination or subjected to testing by the service auditor.

## Subsequently Discovered Facts

The service auditor has no responsibility to perform any procedures regarding the subject matter or assertion after the date of the report. **Subsequently discovered facts** are those that existed during the time covered by the examination and could have resulted in a revision but did not become known to the service auditor until *after the report date*. Such facts may be related to an event involving the service organization or an error later discovered in the service auditor's work.

AT-C 205 requires the service auditor to determine if the facts existed as of the report date and, if so, to determine which report users might be misled so that the service auditor can respond appropriately. The course of action depends on the circumstances. The service auditor should consider the time elapsed since the report was issued and whether a new report will be issued imminently.

If a new report is not imminent, the service auditor may seek the service organization's cooperation in performing additional procedures and revising the report. If the report has been distributed, the service organization should notify users, *not* the service auditor. If the service organization refuses to cooperate regarding subsequently discovered facts that would have resulted in a revision, the service auditor should seek legal advice and maintain confidentiality until otherwise directed.

## Forming an Opinion

AT-C 205 states that, after completing all procedures, including those for subsequent events, the service auditor should form an opinion about whether the subject matter (or assertion) is based on the criteria in all material respects. The opinion is the culmination of all the service auditor's planning, risk assessment, evidence gathering, and testing results.

To form an opinion, the service auditor should use professional judgment and skepticism to evaluate the following:

| Sufficiency and appropriateness of evidence | Materiality of uncorrected misstatements | Presentation of the subject matter |
|---|---|---|

When judging the sufficiency and appropriateness of evidence, the service auditor should answer the following questions:

- Are potential misstatements material, either individually or in combination with other misstatements?
- Is management's response to known risks effective?
- What are the results of the procedures performed?
- What is the source of evidence, and is it dependable?
- Is the evidence persuasive?
- Does the evidence support the understanding of the system?

The service auditor should also consider whether the presentation of the subject matter is misleading. If areas need explanation, added disclosures may be necessary. The presentation should be detailed enough to **meet the needs of a broad range of users** without ambiguity.

## Management Representations

**Representative Task (Remembering and Understanding):** Recall requirements about obtaining management's written representations in a SOC engagement (SOC 1®, SOC 2®).

AT-C 205 requires all responsible parties (ie, service organization and included subservice organizations) to prepare a written letter containing certain representations. The service auditor should also request a representation letter from the engaging party, if different. Representation letters are prepared at the **end of an engagement**. They should be dated the same date as the service auditor's report.

The purpose of the representation letter is for the responsible party (parties) and the engaging party to accept responsibility for their decisions, as well as for the information provided. Should there be an issue with the SOC report later, it is important to reaffirm what each party, including the service auditor, may be legally or financially accountable for. This is particularly necessary for information obtained through oral inquiries.

Management's representation should do the following, according to AT-C 205:

- Include management's assertion about the subject matter based on criteria
- State that all relevant matters have been included in the measurement or evaluation of the subject matter or assertion
- State that all known matters contradicting or having a material effect on the subject matter were disclosed, including subsequent events
- State that all known communications from regulatory agencies or others were disclosed, including subsequent events
- Acknowledge responsibility for:
  - The subject matter and responsible party's assertion
  - Selecting the criteria
  - Determining that the criteria are suitable, available to report users, and appropriate for the purpose of the engagement
- State that management has disclosed the following to the service auditor:
  - All relevant internal control deficiencies that the responsible party is aware of
  - Knowledge of any actual, suspected, or alleged fraud
  - Knowledge of any actual, suspected, or alleged noncompliance with laws and regulations
  - Other matters deemed appropriate by the service auditor
- State that management has provided the service auditor with access to all relevant information
- State that management believes that the effects of any uncorrected misstatements are immaterial, individually and in the aggregate

AT-C 205 also states that when the engaging party is not the responsible party, the engaging party should make the following additional representations in the form of a letter:

- Acknowledge that the responsible party is responsible for its assertions and for making sure the subject matter is based on the criteria
- Acknowledge that the engaging party is responsible for selecting the criteria
- Acknowledge that the engaging party is responsible for ensuring that the criteria are suitable, available to report users, and appropriate for the purpose of the engagement
- State that the engaging party is not aware of any material misstatements in the subject matter information or assertion
- State that the engaging party has disclosed all known subsequent events to the service auditor

The service auditor should evaluate the representations for reasonableness and consistency with the evidence obtained. This includes determining if those who make the representations are well informed. If the representations are not provided or are not considered reliable, the service auditor should seek further information and consider the effect on its opinion.

# ISC 2
# SOC Reporting

# ISC 2: SOC Reporting

# 2.01 Reporting on a SOC Engagement

Engagement acceptance | Planning | Performing | Reporting

## Overview

**Representative Task (Remembering and Understanding):** Summarize the carve-out vs. the inclusive method of reporting on CSOCs.

**Representative Task (Remembering and Understanding):** Explain the effect of CUECs on the SOC report (SOC 1®, SOC 2®).

The last step in the SOC engagement process is to prepare the **service auditor's report** and compile the entire SOC report package. AT-C 205 requires the service auditor's report to be **in writing**. A **licensed CPA**, normally the engagement partner, must **sign** the report.

AT-C 205 provides the general standards for reporting on an assertion-based examination. AT-C 320 outlines the reporting standards specific to a SOC 1® examination. Because there are no official standards specific to a SOC 2® examination, the service auditor should follow the general standard found in AT-C 205, although the general format outlined in AT-C 320 is helpful.

While there is no required standardized format, service auditors typically arrange **SOC report packages** in sections and subsections. The contents of a report package depend on the following factors:

- The type of SOC engagement (ie, SOC 1®, SOC 2®, etc.)
- The type of report (ie, type 1 or type 2)
- The method used to report subservice organizations (ie, inclusive or carved-out)
- The need to report complementary subservice organization controls (CSOCs)
- The need to report complementary user entity controls (CUECs)
- Information the service organization wants to attach to the report that was not part of the examination

### Subservice Organization Controls: Inclusive Method

Under the inclusive method, the subservice organization's assertion is typically placed immediately behind the service organization's assertion. The subservice organization's services, system components, objectives, and controls are included in the service organization's description.

The service auditor's report should make the following clear:

- That the service organization uses a subservice organization
- The types of service provided by the subservice organization
- That the subservice organization's objectives and controls have been evaluated by the service auditor

### Subservice Organization Controls: Carve-Out Method

When the service organization selects the carve-out method, only the subservice organization's services are included in the description. Any **complementary subservice organization controls (CSOCs)** are detailed in a **separate** subsection of the description. The service organization would include in its description any controls implemented to monitor the subservice organization.

The service auditor's report should specify:

- Complementary subservice organization controls, along with the service organization's controls, that are necessary to achieve objectives.
- The description presents the service organization's controls and any complementary subservice organization controls assumed in the design of the service organization's controls.
- That the service auditor did not evaluate the suitability or operating effectiveness of complementary subservice organization controls.

### Complementary User Entity Controls

When the service organization's system relies on user entity controls, the service organization includes a list of **complementary user entity controls (CUECs)** in a **separate** subsection of the description. The service auditor's report should specify:

- Complementary user entity controls that are necessary, along with the service organization's controls, to achieve the service organization's objectives.
- The description presents the service organization's controls and any complementary user entity controls assumed in the design of the service organization's controls.
- That the service auditor did not evaluate the suitability or operating effectiveness of complementary user entity controls.

## Common Sections of SOC 1® and SOC 2® Report Packages

The following tables present the common sections and subsections of SOC 1® and SOC 2® report packages, respectively. Each table is broken down by report type and the method used to report subservice organizations.

## SOC 1® Report Package — Customary, Not Prescribed

| | | Type 1 | | Type 2 | |
|---|---|---|---|---|---|
| | | Inclusive | Carved-Out | Inclusive | Carved-Out |
| Section 1 | Independent service auditor's report | Yes | Yes | Yes | Yes |
| Section 2 | Service organization management's assertion | Yes | Yes | Yes | Yes |
| | Subservice organization management's assertion | Yes | No | Yes | No |
| Section 3 | Service organization management's description of the system | | | | |
| | • Service organization's services | Yes | Yes | Yes | Yes |
| | • Subservice organization's services | Yes | Yes | Yes | Yes |
| | • Service organization's description scope | Yes | Yes | Yes | Yes |
| | • Subservice organization's description scope | Yes | No | Yes | No |
| | • Internal control framework | Yes | Yes | Yes | Yes |
| | • Service organization's control objectives and related controls | Yes | Yes | Yes | Yes |
| | • Subservice organization's control objectives and related controls | Yes | No | Yes | No |
| | • Complementary subservice organization controls* | No | Yes | No | Yes |
| | • Complementary user entity controls* | Yes | Yes | Yes | Yes |
| Section 4 | Service organization control objectives and related controls | Yes | Yes | Yes | Yes |
| | Service auditor's tests of controls | No | No | Yes | Yes |
| Section 5 | Other information provided by service organization not included in service auditor's report* | Yes | Yes | Yes | Yes |

**Only when applicable*

**SOC 2® Report Package — Customary, Not Prescribed**

| | | Type 1 | | Type 2 | |
|---|---|---|---|---|---|
| | | Inclusive | Carved-Out | Inclusive | Carved-Out |
| Section 1 | Service organization management's assertion | Yes | Yes | Yes | Yes |
| | Subservice organization management's assertion | Yes | No | Yes | No |
| Section 2 | Independent service auditor's opinion | Yes | Yes | Yes | Yes |
| Section 3 | Service organization management's description of the system | | | | |
| | • Service organization's services | Yes | Yes | Yes | Yes |
| | • Subservice organization's services | Yes | Yes | Yes | Yes |
| | • Service organization's service commitments and system requirements | Yes | Yes | Yes | Yes |
| | • Service organization's system components | Yes | Yes | Yes | Yes |
| | • Subservice organization's system components | Yes | No | Yes | No |
| | • Identified incidents* | Yes | Yes | Yes | Yes |
| | • Internal control framework | Yes | Yes | Yes | Yes |
| | • Complementary subservice organization controls* | No | Yes | No | Yes |
| | • Complementary user entity organization controls* | Yes | Yes | Yes | Yes |
| Section 4 | Trust services category, criteria, related controls | Yes | Yes | Yes | Yes |
| | Service auditor's tests of controls | No | No | Yes | Yes |
| Section 5 | Other information provided by service organization not included in service auditor's report* | Yes | Yes | Yes | Yes |

**Only when applicable*

# Independent Service Auditor's Report

**Representative Task (Application):** Determine the appropriate form and content of a report on the examination of controls at a service organization (SOC 1®, SOC 2®).

Both AT-C 205 and AT-C 320 outline the elements included in a service auditor's report. AT-C 320 has two lists, one for a type 1 report and another for a type 2 report. While the basic elements are the same, SOC 1® and SOC 2® reports do not use the same language because the subject matter is different. The language will also differ between a type 1 and type 2 report because the time and scope of the engagement are not the same.

**The independent service auditor's report** should contain the following information according to AT-C 205, AT-C 320, the AICPA's *SOC 1® Guide*, and the AICPA's *SOC 2® Guide:*

- **Title:** SOC reports must contain the word "independent" (for example, "Independent service auditor's report).
- **Addressee:** The service auditor should address the report to the *engaging party*.
- **Identification of the service organization's system:** Describe the *subject matter* or *assertion* being reported on, including the point in time (type 1) or period (type 2) that was evaluated. This identification should also state that the objectives and controls included in the description are only those that management believes are likely to be relevant to user entities.
    - **Type 1:** Description of the service organization's system and controls as of a *specified date*
    - **Type 2:** Description of the service organization's system and controls *throughout a period*
    - **Subservice organizations, inclusive:** Description includes the subservice organization's services, system components, objectives, and controls; the service auditor would include a statement that it performed procedures on the included subservice organization's system description and controls.
    - **Subservice organizations, carve-out:** Description includes the subservice organization's services and complementary subservice organization controls; the service auditor would include a statement clarifying that the complementary subservice organization controls were not a part of the examination, but may be necessary to achieve some of the service organization's objectives.
- **Criteria:** Identify the criteria that the service auditor's measurement or evaluation is based on.
- **Responsible party and responsibilities:** Service organization management is responsible for the following:
    - Preparing the objectives
    - Identifying risks that may threaten the achievement of objectives
    - Designing, implementing, and operating effective controls to provide reasonable assurance of achieving objectives
    - Providing an assertion about the description of the system, suitability of the design of controls, and—in a type 2 engagement—the operating effectiveness of controls
    - Preparing the description of the system and management's assertion
    - Presenting the assertion and system description completely and accurately
    - Providing the services covered by the description
    - Selecting the criteria and stating the objectives with related controls in the description
- **Service auditor's responsibility for expressing opinion:** The service auditor expresses an opinion on the subject matter or management's assertion.

- **Examination conducted in accordance with AICPA attestation standards:** The service auditor's report should state, "Attestation standards require that the practitioner plan and perform the examination to obtain reasonable assurance about whether the subject matter is in accordance with (or based on) the criteria, in all material respects, or the responsible party's assertion is fairly stated, in all material respects. The practitioner believes that the evidence the practitioner obtained is sufficient and appropriate to provide a reasonable basis for the practitioner's opinion."
- **Nature of examination engagement:** A SOC examination involves:
  - Performing procedures to obtain evidence about the fairness of the presentation of management's description of the system, the suitability of the design of controls, and—in a type 2 engagement—the operating effectiveness of the controls
  - Assessing the risk that management's description is not fairly presented and that the controls were not suitably designed or, in a type 2 engagement, did not operate effectively
  - Testing the operating effectiveness of controls in a type 2 examination
  - Evaluating the overall presentation of management's description, the suitability of the objectives stated in the description, and the suitability of the criteria
- **Inherent limitations:** Examinations provide "reasonable assurance," not absolute assurance.
  - Management's description should meet the common needs of a broad range of users and may not contain all the information needed by an individual user entity
  - Internal controls can be overridden accidentally by human error or intentionally circumvented
  - Controls may not be effective in the future if conditions change
- **Control testing:**
  - **Type 1 report:** Service auditor did not perform tests of controls and does not express an opinion on the operating effectiveness of controls
  - **Type 2 report:** Reference to the service auditor's tests of controls and results, which describes the following:
    - The controls that were tested
    - The tests performed
    - Deviations in the operating effectiveness of controls identified by the service auditor
    - A discussion of any work performed by the service organization's internal auditors
- **Service auditor's opinion:** A statement expressing the service auditor's opinion about the following, in all material respects:
  - Whether management's description fairly presents the system and is in accordance with the applicable description criteria
  - Whether controls were suitably designed and provide reasonable assurance of achieving objectives
  - In a type 2 engagement, whether controls operated effectively
  - Whether complementary subservice organization controls and complementary user entity controls are necessary to provide reasonable assurance of achieving objectives
- **Restricted use:** A statement that the report may be used by the service organization management, as well as the following:
  - **SOC 1®:** User entities and user auditors
  - **SOC 2®:** User entities and user auditors, business partners and business partner auditors, regulators, prospective user entities, prospective business partners, and others who have the knowledge to understand:
    - The type of services offered by the service organization

- How the service organization's control system relates to user entities, business partners, subservice organizations, and other parties
- The limitations of internal controls
- The effect of complementary user entity controls and complementary subservice organization controls
- User entity responsibilities and the impact on the effectiveness of a service organization
- Risks that may interfere with the service organization's commitments and related controls

- **Signature of service auditor firm:** The signature may be manual or printed.
- **Service auditor city and state:** State the location where the service auditor practices.
- **Date of service auditor's report:** Report should be dated no earlier than the date on which the service auditor has obtained sufficient appropriate evidence on which to base an opinion, including evidence of the following:
  - The attestation engagement documentation has been reviewed
  - Management's description of the system has been prepared
  - Management has provided a written assertion and representation letter, both typically signed and dated the same date as the service auditor's report

## Types of Service Auditor Opinions

**Representative Task (Remembering and Understanding):** Explain the types of opinions and report modifications when deficiencies have been identified.

Service auditors may issue an **unmodified opinion** or a **modified opinion**. An unmodified opinion (ie, unqualified opinion) is appropriate when the service auditor did not find any material problems with the service organization's description of the system, the suitability of controls, or, in a type 2 engagement, the operating effectiveness of controls.

AT-C 205 and AT-C 320 explain that the service auditor should issue a modified opinion when either of the following conditions exist and the effect is material:

| The service auditor cannot obtain sufficient appropriate evidence to conclude that the subject matter is in accordance with the criteria. | **or** | Based on the evidence obtained, the service auditor concludes that the subject matter is not in accordance with the criteria. |
|---|---|---|

In a modified opinion, the service auditor's report should include a **separate paragraph** describing the **specific reasons** for the modification. Detailing the reasons allows report users or their auditors the ability to determine how the service auditor's findings affect their own risk assessment.

Applying the general criteria, the following conditions would give rise to a modification:

- The description *does not* fairly present the system.
- The controls *are not* suitably designed to provide reasonable assurance of achieving objectives based on the applicable criteria.
- In a type 2 report, the controls *did not* operate effectively.
- The service auditor *could not* obtain sufficient appropriate evidence.

If a modified opinion is necessary, the service auditor should determine which type of opinion modification is appropriate under the circumstances. A modification may be a **qualified opinion**, **adverse opinion**, or **disclaimer of opinion**.

The service auditor's decision would be based on the **materiality** and **pervasiveness** of the following:

- Description misstatements (and omissions)
- Deficiencies in the suitability of design of controls
- Deviations in the operating effectiveness of controls (type 2 only)

Materiality is a matter of professional judgment about whether misstatements, deviations, and deficiencies are beyond what the service auditor believes is tolerable. Pervasiveness is a measure of the extent to which material misstatements, deviations, and deficiencies affect the description of the system, suitability of design, or operating effectiveness of controls (type 2 only).

**Type of Opinion Based on Materiality and Pervasiveness of Misstatements**

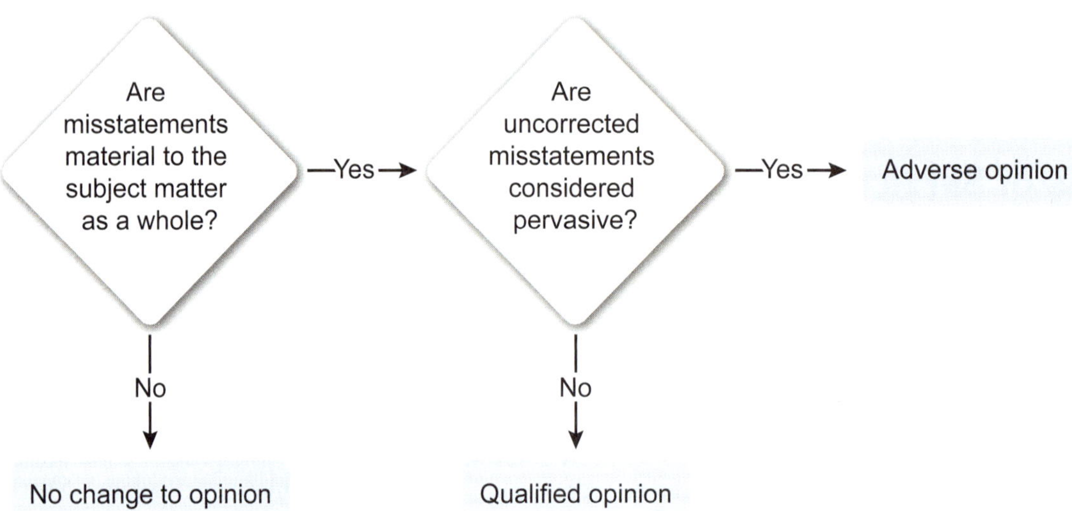


## Qualified Opinion

According to AT-C 205, the service auditor should issue a qualified opinion when, based on sufficient appropriate evidence, the detected misstatements (either individually or combined) are material but not pervasive. A qualified opinion may also be appropriate when there is a scope limitation that is not pervasive. A **scope limitation** means that the service auditor could not obtain sufficient appropriate evidence. A qualified opinion is appropriate when the service auditor believes that considering the scope limitation, there may be undetected material misstatements, but they are not pervasive.

## Adverse Opinion

An adverse opinion would be appropriate when the service auditor obtained sufficient appropriate evidence but identified misstatements that are *both* material and pervasive. An adverse opinion indicates that management did not present the subject matter in accordance with the criteria. To issue an adverse opinion, the service auditor must have evidence of misstatements that are so significant that the service organization did not achieve its objectives.

## Disclaimer of Opinion

A service auditor should disclaim an opinion when the potential effects of a scope limitation could be both material and pervasive. A disclaimer means that the service auditor does not express an opinion due to a lack of sufficient appropriate evidence.

The following table summarizes the appropriate circumstances for each report modification:

| | Type of Modified Opinion | |
|---|---|---|
| **Reason for Modification** | **Material but not Pervasive** | **Material and Pervasive** |
| Scope limitation | Qualified opinion | Disclaimer of opinion |
| Description misstatement | Qualified opinion | Adverse opinion |
| Deficiencies or deviations in the suitability of design of controls | Qualified opinion | Adverse opinion |
| Deficiencies or deviations in the operating effectiveness of controls *(type 2 only)* | Qualified opinion | Adverse opinion |

## Service Auditor's Tests of Controls and Results

**Representative Task (Application):** Prepare results of testing of controls to be included in the SOC 2® report of the test of a control, including where there was an exception identified by the test.

The report on a **type 2** examination includes a detailed list of the **service auditor's procedures** to obtain evidence about the operating effectiveness of controls. The **results** of those procedures are also included, indicating any and all deviations (ie, exceptions). Disclosure of the service auditor's tests of controls and results helps report users assess management's assertion that controls operated effectively throughout the period. It also supports the service auditor's opinion.

While there is no prescribed format, testing and results are normally presented in a two-table format. The first table lists the applicable trust services criteria with reference to a second table containing the service organization's controls. For example:

| Trust Services Criteria # | Trust Services Criteria | Service Organization Control #'s |
|---|---|---|
| CC2.2 - Communications and Information | The entity internally communicates the information necessary to support the functioning of internal control, including objectives and responsibilities. | CI-3 |

| Service Organization Control | Test Procedures Performed | Results of Tests |
|---|---|---|
| CI-3 - Entity personnel are provided with information on how to report systems failures, incidents, concerns, and complaints. | For a sample of employees, inspected attendance records evidencing participation in incident response and security awareness training. | No exceptions noted. |

The AICPA's SOC 2® Guide contains a list of the items that should be included when describing tests of controls and results. Note that the service auditor must describe additional information when deviations (ie, exceptions) are found through tests of controls. Materiality does not apply to disclosing testing exceptions, so the service auditor should **describe all deviations**.

| Information to Be Described | No Deviations Identified | Deviations Identified |
|---|---|---|
| Controls tested | Yes | Yes |
| Tests performed on full population or sample | Yes | Yes |
| Nature of tests performed (with enough detail to allow report users to determine the effect of the tests on their risk assessments) | Yes | Yes |
| Number of items tested | No | Yes |
| Number and nature of deviations | N/A | Yes |
| Causative factors | N/A | Optional |
| Test performed by service organization internal audit function and service auditor's work | Optional | Optional |

The description of tests of controls should provide enough detail for report users to understand the effects on their own risk assessment. The following information is relevant to describing tests of controls:

- Nature of tests performed (reperformance, inquiry, inspection, observation, walkthroughs)
- Document or electronic file that was observed or inspected as the source of the service auditor's evidence
- Extent of testing, including whether the entire population was tested or a sample
- Titles and roles of the service organization personnel who answered inquiries
- Documents, files, or other sources from which the tested items were selected
- Testing performed on information supplied by the service organization
- Procedures performed when management's design of the control allows for a tolerable threshold of deviations

When deviations are identified, report users will want information about them even if the service auditor concludes that the control still provided reasonable assurance of achieving principal service commitments and system requirements based on the trust services criteria. If management has a response to the deviations found by the service auditor, management's explanation may be included in Section 4 of the SOC report under the Results of Tests or in Section 5, Other Information Provided by the Service Organization. The service auditor must perform additional procedures to evaluate any response management includes in Section 4, but has discretion with respect to evaluating any information in Section 5.

The following tables present an example of the description of tests of controls when the service auditor found deviations:

| Trust Services Criteria # | Trust Services Criteria | Service Organization Control #'s |
|---|---|---|
| CC2.2 - Communications and Information | The entity internally communicates the information necessary to support the functioning of internal control, including objectives and responsibilities. | CI-3 |

| Service Organization Control | Test Procedures Performed | Results of Tests |
|---|---|---|
| CI-3 - Entity personnel are provided with information on how to report systems failures, incidents, concerns, and complaints. | For a sample of employees, inspected attendance records evidencing participation in incident response and security awareness training. | Three employees in an initial sample of 100 did not attend incident response and security awareness training within 365 days of their last completed training. Subsequently tested an additional 50 employees and found no further exceptions. |

# ISC

## Information Systems and Data Management

# ISC 3
# Information Systems

# ISC 3: Information Systems

# 3.01 IT Infrastructure

## IT Architecture

**Representative Task (Remembering and Understanding):** Explain the purpose of IT architecture and recognize its key components (eg, operating systems, servers, network infrastructure, end-user devices)

IT architecture is part of the overall **system** management designs to support an organization's business operations, security, and strategies. As discussed in the System and Organization Controls (SOC) chapter, systems include infrastructure (hardware), software, data, people, and procedures.

**IT System Components**

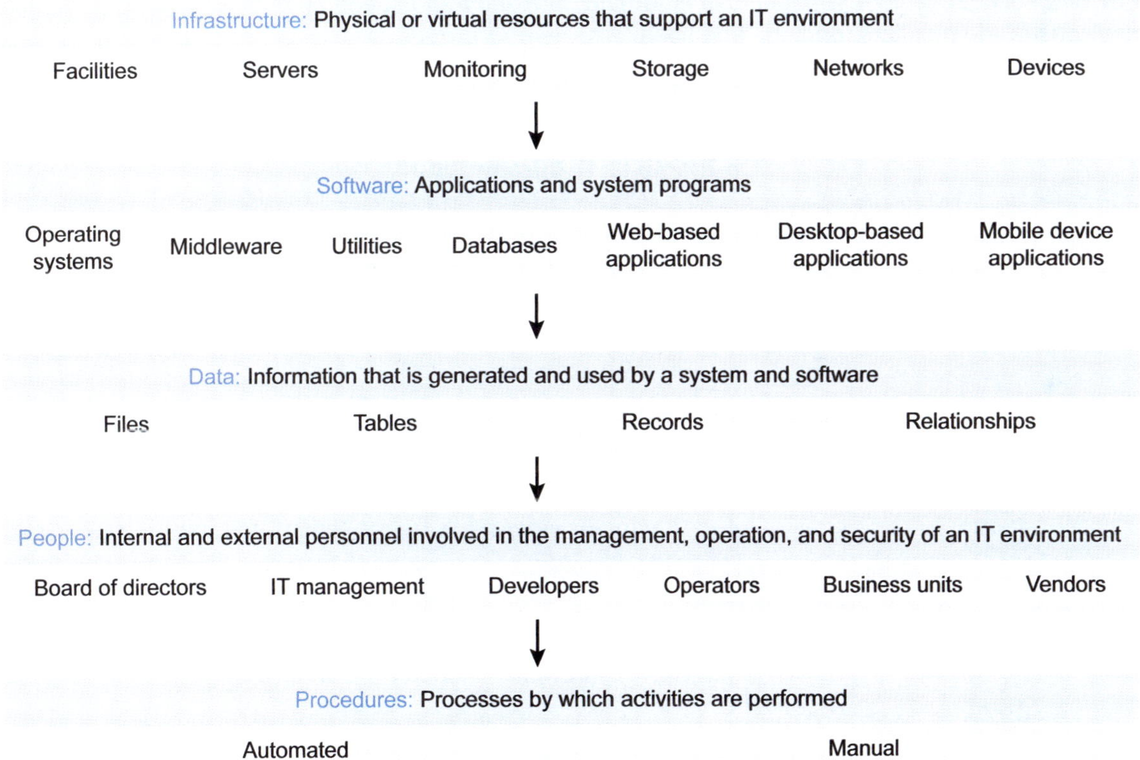


### Infrastructure

Infrastructure is the collection of physical or virtual resources that supports an overall IT environment. Organizations may use infrastructure housed at their own facility (**on premises**) or at another facility connected by the Internet (cloud). Organizations may manage their cloud services directly or outsource them to external vendors.

Common infrastructure components include:

- **Facilities:** The physical building where IT infrastructure is housed, including systems for security and environmental monitoring. Organizations may keep IT infrastructure at one or more facilities owned by the organization or an external vendor. Security guards and cameras monitor facilities to detect unauthorized access or disasters, such as fires.
- **Server:** Servers are powerful computers that store, process, and manage data for multiple users and devices. They may be physical or virtual. Organizations may use multiple servers dedicated to performing distinct functions. For example, servers can run databases, host websites, manage email, or store files.
- **Internal storage:** Hardware within a computer system that stores data inside the device for later use. Common examples include hard drives (HDDs) and solid-state drives (SSDs).
- **External storage devices:** Organizations may use external storage devices and cloud storage for operational and backup purposes. Magnetic tape, flash drives, network-attached storage, and external hard drives are some devices used for saving data outside of computers and servers.
- **Networking equipment:** Networking equipment manages communications between devices, wired local area networks (LANs) or wireless local area networks (WLANs), and the Internet. Such equipment includes routers, switches, firewalls, wiring, and other security protection systems.
- **End-user devices:** Hardware that allows the intended end user to interact with software and data. End-user devices include desktop computers, laptops, tablets, and even smartphones. For example, employees can access their email through laptops or tablets.
- **Input and output devices:** These devices allow for communication between the computers and/or users. Basic input devices include a scanner, keyboard, and light pen (ie, a stylus). Certain input devices, such as barcode readers, can automate data entry and speed up business processes. Output devices include monitors, printers, and speakers.

A simple, **on-premises IT infrastructure** may include the following components:

**On-Premises IT Infrastructure**

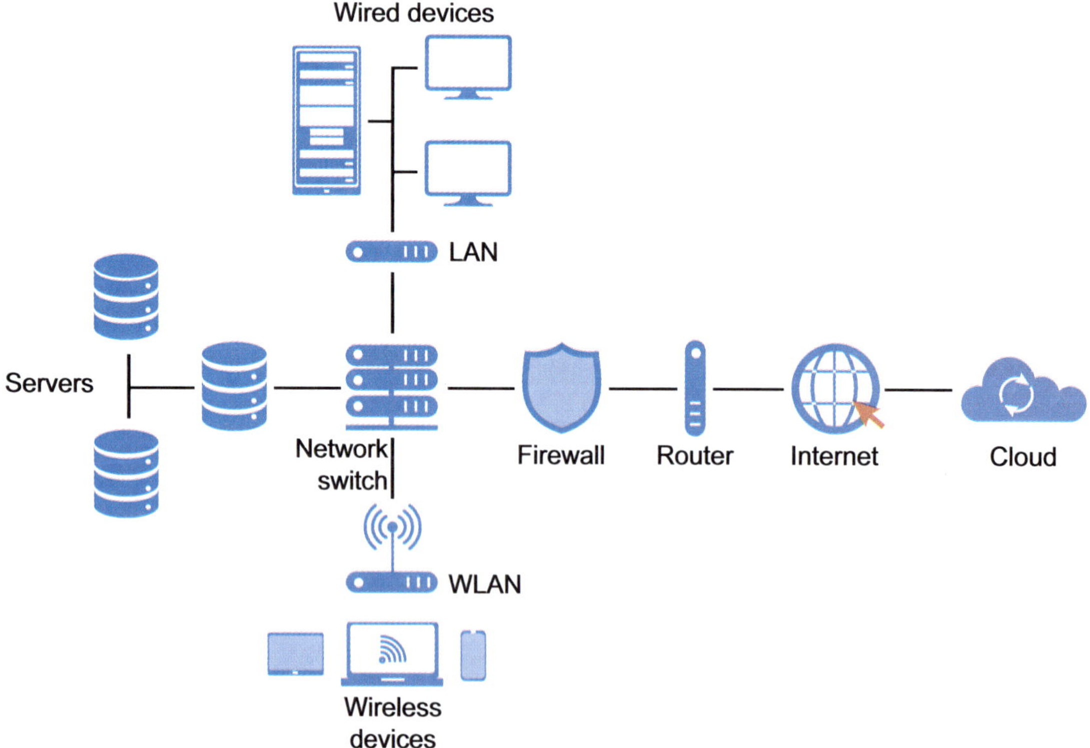

**IT Infrastructure Used in Purchasing Process**

An employee's job duties include entering new purchase orders. The employee accesses the organization's purchasing system from an office desktop computer (end-user device), which is connected to a wired network (network equipment). The purchasing software resides on an application server, using information stored on a database server. The employee uses a keyboard (input device) to type the purchase order and a printer (output device) to generate a paper (hard) copy. Every night, changes made to the database, including new purchase orders, are saved to magnetic tape (external storage) at a backup facility.

## Software

Software refers to computer programs that run hardware, process data, and execute tasks. While hardware is a physical component, software includes instructions written in code. **Source code** is written in a **programming language**, which is a set of commands, instructions, and other syntax.

Software programs may be categorized as:

- **Application software:** Computer programs that perform end-user functions. Applications are desktop based (ie, installed locally), web based, or cloud based. Examples include management systems, security software, enterprise resource planning (ERP) systems, accounting information systems (AIS), data analysis programs, and software to create documents or spreadsheets. Organizations may develop applications in house or purchase software made by external parties.
- **System software** includes programs that run the system and direct its operations. System software, along with the supporting hardware, is used to create a computing platform. Despite being a vital component of the computer system, system software runs in the background and is often unnoticed by the end user. The two major categories of system software are:
  - **Operating system (OS):** System software that regulates a computer's basic operations. The OS manages an application's use of computer hardware, as well as how users interact with their computers. Microsoft Windows is a well-known OS.
  - **Utility programs** support and improve the efficiency of a computer system.

**System Utility Software**

| Middleware | Runtime | Database management system (DBMS) | Antivirus and antimalware |
|---|---|---|---|
| Helps different software programs communicate with each other | Enables the execution of applications by managing memory, system resources, and input/output operations | Creates, reads, updates, and deletes information in a database | Protects computer systems from malicious software such as viruses, worms, and Trojans |
| **Backup software** | **System monitoring and diagnostic tools** | **Password managers** | **Automation software** |
| Creates and manages backups to prevent data loss | Monitors the performance of a computer system, including detecting and correcting problems | Stores and manages passwords so users do not have to remember them | Automates repetitive tasks to increase productivity |

**Interaction Between Application and System Software**

An organization's ERP system runs on the Windows OS. End users log in to Windows first and then open the ERP application. The ERP system was developed using the Java programming language, which exists on the application server. Runtime software executes the program. As the end user saves information, raw data is stored on a database server using a DBMS. Middleware enables communication between the Windows OS and the ERP application.

## Networks

A computer network is a group of connected computers, servers, network devices, or other devices that share resources. Networks can vary in size from two devices (as with home networks) to devices around the world. The Internet is a worldwide network that allows any computer system to link to it through an electronic gateway.

**Types of Networks**

| Local Area Network (LAN) | Wireless Area Network (WLAN) | Virtual Private Network (VPN) |
|---|---|---|
| Connects devices in a building or geographical area through hardwiring, such as Ethernet cables | Connects devices using wireless technology such as Wi-Fi and Bluetooth | Connects devices to the Internet through secure encryption |

The following hardware is necessary to create and connect to a network:

- **Network switch:** Connects the devices on an entity's local network by moving data between the devices.
- **Gateway:** A device on a network that serves as an entrance to another network. For example, to connect to the Internet, a device must first connect to a gateway computer at the Internet service provider (ISP). This computer serves as the first router, connecting to the rest of the Internet. Common gateways include:
  - **Routers:** Specialized devices that receive data packets from one network and send them toward a destination network, using the best path. For example, a router may transmit data packets between a LAN or WLAN and an ISP.

    The Internet consists primarily of a series of routers used to transmit information between all the computers connected to the Internet. For example, when a computer in California connects to a website in Australia, there might be 10 computers between them acting as intermediary routers. When parts of the Internet go down, most people never notice because the routers find another way (route) to get the information to its destination.
  - **Firewall:** A computer program (software) or physical device (hardware) that prevents unauthorized users from accessing a system, thus limiting the transmission of media. The concept of a firewall is like living in a gated community: When entering, a homeowner must scan their badge to gain access to the neighborhood. In the same way, a firewall blocks unauthorized access to a company's network.

# Introduction to Cloud Computing

**Representative Task (Remembering and Understanding):** Explain cloud computing, including cloud computing models (infrastructure as a service [IaaS], platform as a service [PaaS], and software as a service ([SaaS]) as well as deployment models (eg, public, private, hybrid).

## Overview

**Cloud computing** is a method of accessing on-demand computer resources and applications over the Internet. It allows organizations to use distributed computing and storage for applications, data processing, and infrastructure services. Organizations that use cloud computing may manage the cloud service themselves, pay a third party **cloud service provider (CSP)** to supply services (infrastructure, applications, networking), or combine those two approaches.

- **Traditional (on-premises) infrastructure** involves using IT components within a physical **data center** or computing facility owned by the organization. This setup may be preferable when it is necessary to keep full control over infrastructure and security. Another benefit of traditional infrastructure is that the organization has access to the data in case of network issues or Internet outages. On-premises infrastructure is more expensive than the cloud as it requires organizations to maintain physical space, support staff, and technology components.
- **Cloud computing IT infrastructure** has the same components as an on-premises setup; however, the organization accesses them virtually through an Internet connection. In cloud computing, hardware that would normally be physically on-site is made accessible online through a process called virtualization. **Virtualization** allows the creation of **virtual machines** that clients can access on a single physical server. For example, one physical server could host multiple virtual servers.

**Traditional vs. Cloud Computing**

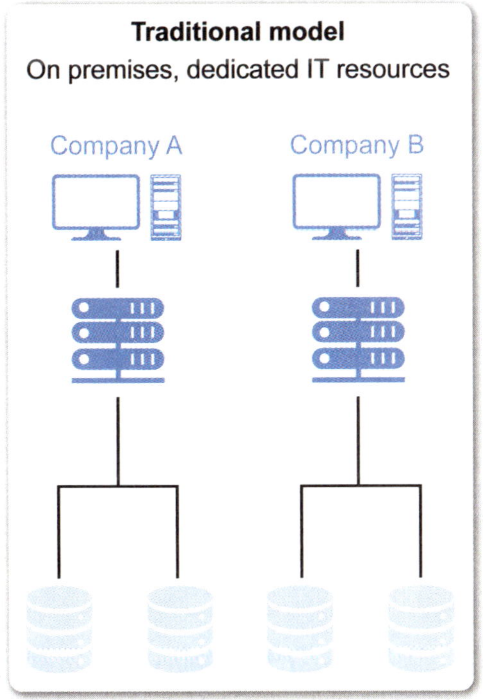


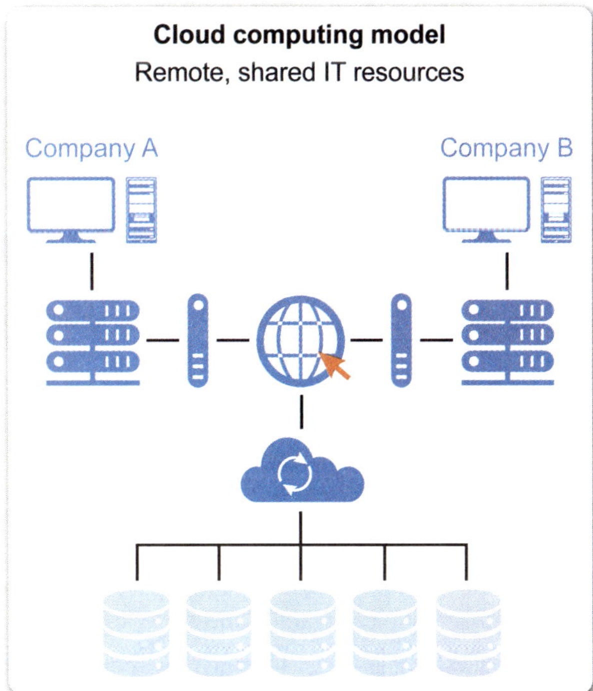

Making the decision to use a third party service provider for cloud computing services requires weighing the advantages and disadvantages. The advantages of using a cloud service provider (CSP) include:

- **Cost savings:** Cloud computing allows the organization to save money by not having to buy and support the same infrastructure and staff needed for an on-premises model. In addition, the organization pays only for the resources used. Cloud computing also results in tax savings because the associated costs are expensed instead of capitalized.

  The cost of cloud computing and applications is lower in a **multitenant architecture**, where a single instance of software runs on shared servers. Multitenancy is common with cloud-based applications sold by developers to end users. However, shared resources increase the risk of data leakage. **Single tenant architecture**, in which a single instance of software runs on a dedicated server, is more secure but higher in cost.

| Single Tenant | Multitenant |
|---|---|
| Hardware and software that serve one customer | Hardware and software that serve multiple customers |
| Customer can control or configure | Customer cannot control or configure |
| Stronger security | Reduced cost |
| More reliable | Less maintenance |
| Easier to backup and restore | Efficient use of resources |

- **Accessibility:** Cloud resources can be made available to a variety of end-user devices and locations, so employees no longer need to be in the office to access work resources.
- **Reliability:** Because CSPs have multiple clients using their cloud services, they must keep the cloud up and running so that it is available whenever their customers need it.
- **Scalability:** Cloud computing allows customers to expand or reduce their services based on changes in the business environment. It also allows for faster implementation of those services.

Despite the advantages, there are potential disadvantages that need to be considered before using a CSP:

- **Downtime or outages:** When a CSP experiences downtime, outages, or technical issues, users of the cloud services might not be able to perform business processes or access company information that depends on IT resources. However, CSPs typically offer a "guaranteed uptime" with credits to compensate for lack of **availability**.
- **Security threats:** Cloud services are high-value targets for cyberattacks such as breaches and unauthorized access by external parties. Potential users should review the contract and **service level agreement (SLA)**, along with the CSP's **System and Organization Controls (SOC)** and other compliance reports, in order to understand its system and controls.
- **Limited control:** Organizations have less control over contracted cloud services than traditional IT elements that would be under their domain. An action that would take an organization a few hours to complete may take the CSP several days or weeks, depending on the issue. Even a **cloud latency**—the delay between a user organization's request and the CSP's response—can harm the organization. In addition, the setup and data migration associated with cloud computing can take extensive amounts of time and limit the company's access to its data.
- **Vendor Lock-in:** Cloud users must pay special attention to contracts and SLAs with cloud service providers. Data transfer costs and the use of cloud-specific technologies can lock users in with a specific cloud provider. Cloud users should carefully evaluate the agreement and develop a withdrawal plan when negotiating a contract.

Consider an organization that uses a cloud-based accounting software such as QuickBooks. Over the years, the organization accumulates a significant amount of data within that application. Because migration to a new system could be time-consuming and/or difficult, the organization might be forced to stay with an accounting program they have outgrown.

## Cloud Computing Models

Cloud computing varies based on the type of infrastructure, software, and services the CSP offers. There are three general delivery models:

**Cloud Computing Service Delivery Models**

| Infrastructure as a Service (IaaS) | Platform as a Service (PaaS) | Software as a Service (SaaS) |
|---|---|---|

- **Infrastructure as a Service (IaaS):** With IaaS, the CSP supplies infrastructure capabilities, which include hosting the data center, servers, network devices, and storage devices. Companies using this service maintain their systems remotely through the cloud, still managing their applications and operating systems while the third party CSP provides the infrastructure. Thus, IaaS allows organizations to control their infrastructure without having to buy and support the hardware on premises. A popular IaaS provider is Amazon Web Services (AWS).
- **Platform as a Service (PaaS):** Organizations often use PaaS cloud services to support activities related to software development, analytics, or business intelligence. Besides providing the infrastructure services of IaaS, PaaS includes operating system and data management tools hosted on the cloud.

  Companies interested in developing software may choose PaaS services so that the development team can focus on building and testing applications without having to worry about the supporting infrastructure, operating systems, and development environment.
- **Software as a Service (SaaS):** SaaS is used to supply cloud-based application access to end users. It encompasses the same services that an organization would have with a traditional on-premises solution. The CSP manages application deployment, maintenance, configuration, and the underlying IT support structures. A commonly used SaaS accounting application is NetSuite; end users access NetSuite via the Internet instead of having to download the application on a computer. **Business Process as a Service (BPaaS)**, an extension of SaaS, involves outsourcing an entire business process, such as payroll, to a third party provider offering cloud services.

**Difference between Cloud Computing Service Delivery Models**

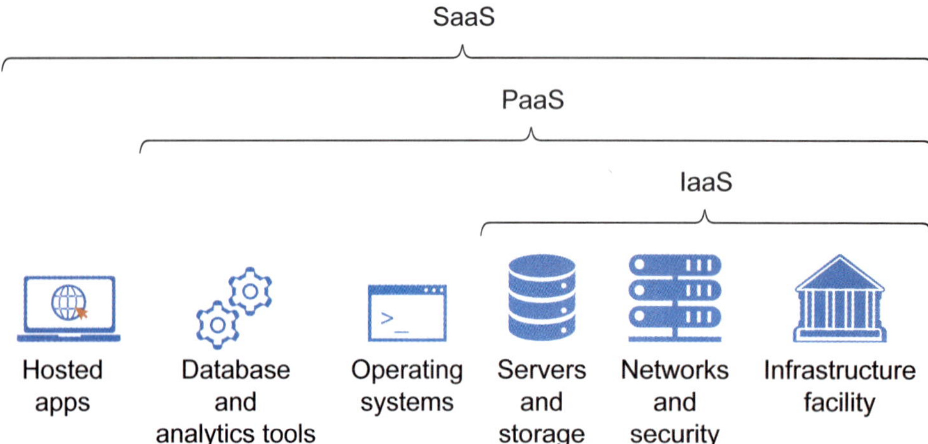


Management may not have direct access to the systems and subsystems hosted by a third party on the cloud and must rely on that CSP to keep a strong control environment. Therefore, management may require a **SOC** report that describes the CSP's system and controls.

## Cloud Deployment Models

Cloud deployment models describe the ways cloud computing resources may be provided (ie, set up and configured). Each model offers a different level of service, cloud-hosting responsibilities, and ownership.

**Cloud Deployment Models**

Public cloud | Private cloud | Community cloud | Hybrid cloud

- **Public cloud:** In the public cloud deployment model, a third party service provider owns and manages computing resources and allows multiple public users to share access to those resources via the Internet. Multitenancy associated with public cloud deployment results in cost savings, scalability, and efficiency. Popular public cloud services include Google's Cloud Platform Services, Microsoft Azure, and Amazon Web Services.
- **Private cloud:** A private cloud configuration is set up for use by a single organization or single tenant. It can be managed by the organization itself or by a third-party service provider. Because only a single organization can access the resources for its internal use, private cloud deployment reduces the security risks associated with the public cloud. The private cloud owner manages the controls over data and data privacy. The costs of a private cloud are much higher than those of a public cloud.
- **Community cloud:** A specific group of organizations with a common purpose may use a community cloud, with one of the members or a third party managing the cloud resources. For example, organizations in the health care industry might use a community cloud to share patient information; because of stringent health care legal requirements, they could configure the community cloud to ensure compliance with privacy laws specific to that business sector.
- **Hybrid cloud:** Hybrid cloud deployment uses a combination of the public, private, and/or community models to fulfill specific data or processing requirements while taking advantage of the benefits of each model. For example, a company may use a public cloud service for nonsensitive data while using a private cloud for sensitive data.

# Cloud Service Providers: Roles & Responsibilities

**Representative Task (Remembering and Understanding):** Summarize the role and responsibilities of cloud service providers.

CSPs perform functions that allow for the delivery of services according to the terms of their contracts and service level agreements (SLAs). Both the service provider and the businesses using its services must understand the CSP's roles and responsibilities. The CSP performs five major activities:

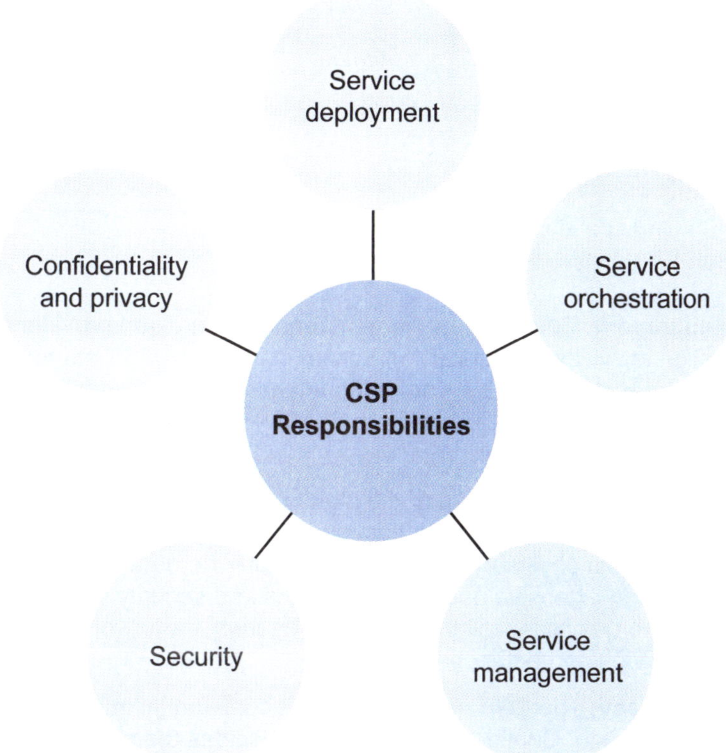


- **Service deployment:** The cloud provider delivers cloud services (IaaS, PaaS, and SaaS) through one of the deployment models (public, private, hybrid, or community).
- **Service orchestration:** Service orchestration refers to setting up, organizing, and running the cloud infrastructure to meet the CSP's service commitments and system requirements. The CSP's responsibilities for components will vary depending on the service model used:

**CSP vs. Customer Responsibilities**

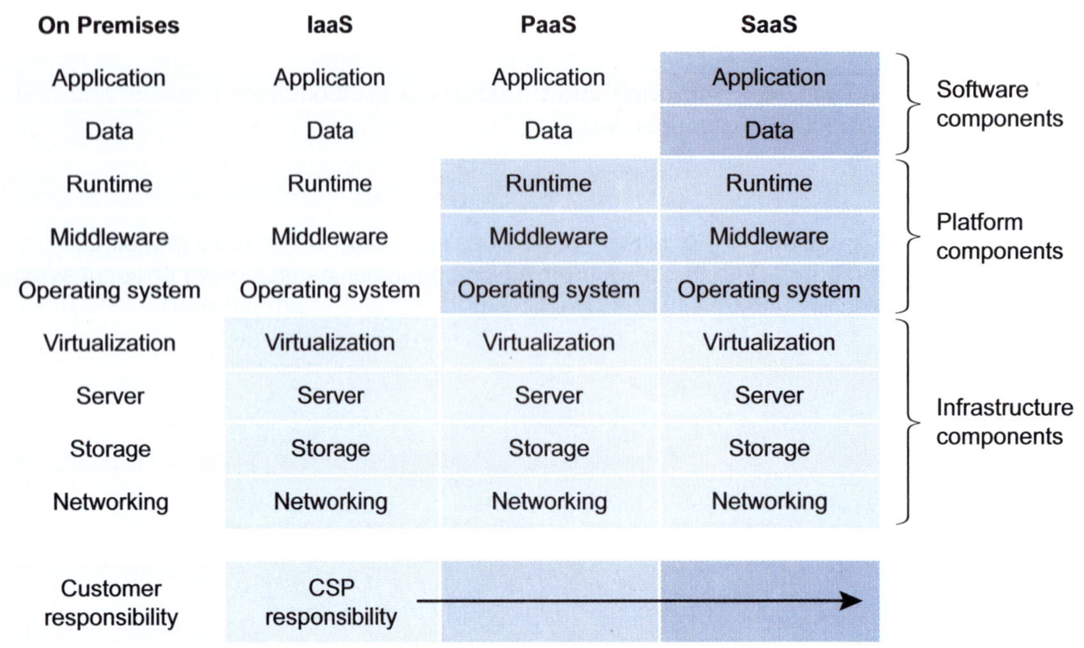

| On Premises | IaaS | PaaS | SaaS | |
|---|---|---|---|---|
| Application | Application | Application | Application | Software components |
| Data | Data | Data | Data | |
| Runtime | Runtime | Runtime | Runtime | Platform components |
| Middleware | Middleware | Middleware | Middleware | |
| Operating system | Operating system | Operating system | Operating system | |
| Virtualization | Virtualization | Virtualization | Virtualization | Infrastructure components |
| Server | Server | Server | Server | |
| Storage | Storage | Storage | Storage | |
| Networking | Networking | Networking | Networking | |

Customer responsibility | CSP responsibility →

- **Cloud service management:** Service management requires the cloud provider to perform the business administration activities associated with cloud computing. CSP management performs activities such as customer management, contract management, pricing, billing, reporting, and auditing. Service management also includes internally driven activities like governance, performance monitoring, and following the SLA terms.
- **Security:** Cloud security involves all layers of the cloud computing environment, from physical security to application software security. Keeping the cloud secured is a responsibility shared by the CSP and the users. CSPs maintain physical resources and secure the data center facility. Data center employees must go through extensive background checks and security awareness training. In addition, the cloud provider stays in compliance with the various security frameworks and regulations, which may differ between countries and authorities.
- **Confidentiality and privacy:** The CSP must ensure that confidential and private information is not accessed without authorization. Confidential information includes the proprietary information of cloud users, such as an organization's financial statements. Private information is any data that can reveal a person's identity, also known as personally identifiable information (PII); PII includes names, Social Security numbers, driver's license numbers, or even biometrics, like fingerprint or retinal scans.

CSPs must meet their service commitments, including regulatory compliance and certifications. To offer independent assurance, a CSP typically must undergo annual examinations, including those within the SOC Suite of Services, and compliance or certification audits, such as those required by the Health Insurance Portability and Accountability Act (HIPAA). Larger CPA firms offer these engagements, which require staff who are knowledgeable of information systems and controls.

# COSO Cloud Computing Governance

**Representative Task (Remembering and Understanding):** Explain how the COSO framework addresses cloud computing governance.

The COSO *Enterprise Risk Management–Integrated Framework* outlines a voluntary method for organizations to assess risks and develop strategies that respond to those risks. The same principles outlined in the ERM framework can apply to identifying, monitoring, and mitigating the risks associated with cloud computing. To supply specific guidance, COSO issued a separate publication, *Enterprise Risk Management for Cloud Computing.*

## Cloud Computing Opportunities and Risks

COSO outlines the opportunities and risks of cloud computing, which organizations should consider prior to making operational changes or implementing modern technologies. Potential benefits include:

**Benefits of Cloud Computing**

### Cost Savings

- Instead of buying or leasing equipment, multitenant cloud customers pay only for the computing resources they use
- Requires less physical space, staff, and utilities
- Cost is expensed rather than capitalized and amortized

### Speed of Deployment

- CSPs can provide IT resources faster than internal purchasing processes
- CSPs may provide onboarding assistance to reduce confusion and speed migration

### Scalability and Alignment of Technology

- Resources can be scaled up or down easily as needs require
- Organizations can start small and add on over time instead of purchasing equipment that exceeds or does not meet current needs

### Easier IT Management

- Cloud services normally have standardized, prebuilt functionality and support
- Because the CSP specializes in cloud computing, the organization's IT staff does not have to "reinvent the wheel"

### Environmental Benefits

- Having data centers in shared facilities instead of private facilities reduces needs related to physical space, power consumption, and emissions

In the **ERM–Integrated Framework**, COSO defines risk as *"the possibility that an event will occur and adversely affect the achievement of objectives."* Overall, the risks of cloud computing are like those of on-premises systems. Organizations need to be concerned with security, integrity, availability, and performance issues. As cloud computing is adopted, organizations must gauge their own risk appetite to decide how and when cloud computing fits into their strategies.

COSO recommends that organizations perform an assessment, considering the following risks:

**Cloud Computing Risks**

| Disruptive force | New dependency relationships | Lack of transparency | Reliability and performance issues | Vendor lock-in |
|---|---|---|---|---|
| Security and compliance concerns | High-value cyberattack target | Risk of data leakage | IT organizational changes | CSP viability |

- **Disruptive force:** The lower cost of cloud computing, as well as its lack of barriers to entry and speed of implementation, may be disruptive to an industry if it enables new or existing competitors to be faster at making changes or bringing new ideas to market. Organizations may need to adopt the same cloud computing resources to meet customer expectations.
- **New dependency relationships:** Using a CSP has legal and operational implications, especially in case of security incidents and breaches. Although a CSP and its clients are separate organizations, a security failure caused by the CSP's lack of controls could cause legal exposure for the clients. For example, a client organization's customer data might be breached while stored at the CSP's data center. Regardless of the relationship, the client organization is still responsible for governance over the CSP. Therefore, it is essential to read SOC and other compliance examination reports to obtain an understanding of the CSP's system and controls.
- **Lack of transparency:** Even with a SOC report, the client may not receive detailed information about the CSP's operations. The CSP may use subservice organizations to perform critical functions. When subservice organizations are carved out of the SOC report, too little information may be supplied for the client to understand the CSP's system and controls.
- **Reliability and performance issues:** An organization using a CSP must have faith that the system will be available and perform within the metrics in the SLA. However, there is no guarantee that everything will go smoothly, and dependence on the CSP to fix a problem quickly could result in a major disruption for the organization and its customers.
- **Vendor lock-in:** Development and application tools offered by a CSP may be proprietary. The more these tools are used and the more data is stored by the CSP, the harder it is to change vendors.
- **Security and compliance concerns:** When a CSP is used, an organization's data is outside of its control. However, the organization is still responsible for following laws and regulations, and a security incident can have legal, financial, and reputational consequences. Contracts and SLAs must be clear about the CSP's responsibilities and require independent SOC or compliance examinations. Another possibility is for the organization to audit the CSP directly.
- **High-value cyber targets:** Unauthorized access to a CSP's systems provides an attacker with an efficient, attractive path to gain access to the data of multiple organizations.
- **Risk of data leakage:** Multitenant cloud deployment models have a higher risk for data leakage than dedicated servers, due to the sharing of resources and applications.

- **IT organizational changes:** When cloud computing is adopted, an organization needs fewer internal IT personnel. IT personnel may need to be trained for use of the cloud and integration with other systems.
- **CSP viability:** Because cloud offerings are relatively new, the long-term sustainability and profitability of an individual CSP may be unknown. An unstable CSP may not meet performance metrics or may eventually be merged with another CSP. Disruptions or changes to services could adversely affect client organizations.

Organizations should also consider the inherent risks of the various cloud computing delivery and deployment models. Inherent risk is highest when an organization has the least amount of direct control. The more control the CSP has, the more risk to the organization. For example, the delivery and deployment model with the lowest inherent risk is a private IaaS solution, while a public SaaS solution has the highest risk. An organization's risk appetite should guide decisions about what delivery and deployment models are most suitable.

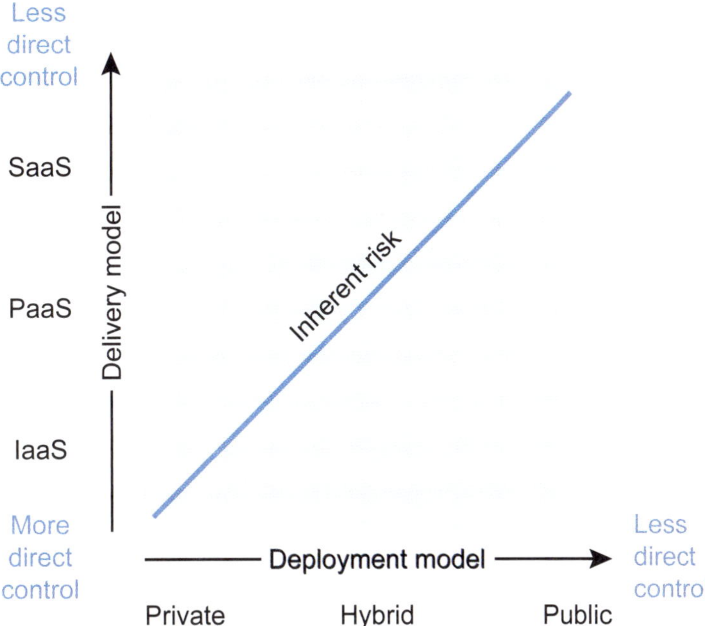


## Cloud Computing ERM

To find the ideal cloud solution, organizations should consider which delivery and deployment model fits their business processes. Each cloud possibility, whether new or existing, should be evaluated in terms of the COSO ERM components and principles. Doing so helps management assess risks and develop mitigation strategies.

The COSO *ERM–Integrated Framework* has 20 principles that organizations can apply to cloud computing:

| Governance and Culture | Strategy and Objective Setting | Performance | Review and Revision | Information, Communication, and Reporting |
|---|---|---|---|---|
| **Mission, Vision, and Core Values** | **Strategy Development** | **Business Objective Formulation** | **Implementation and Performance** | **Enhanced Value** |
| 1. Exercises board risk oversight<br>2. Establishes operating structures<br>3. Defines desired culture<br>4. Demonstrates commitment to core values<br>5. Attracts, develops, and retains capable individuals | 6. Analyzes business context<br>7. Defines risk appetite<br>8. Evaluates alternative strategies<br>9. Formulates business objectives | 10. Identifies risks<br>11. Assesses severity of risks<br>12. Prioritizes risks<br>13. Implements risk responses<br>14. Develops portfolio view | 15. Assesses substantial change<br>16. Reviews risk and performance<br>17. Pursues improvement in ERM | 18. Leverages information systems<br>19. Communicates risk information<br>20. Reports on risk, culture, and performance |

## Governance and Culture

**COSO Cloud Computing ERM: Governance and Culture Principles**

### Exercises Board Risk Oversight

**ERM:** Board provides oversight of management strategies and objectives

**Cloud ERM:** Board understands cloud computing risks, trends, and impact on the organization

### Establishes Operating Structures

**ERM:** Organization has operating structures to pursue its strategies and objectives

**Cloud ERM:** A cloud computing steering committee oversees the migration and implementation of cloud computing

### Defines Desired Cultures

**ERM:** Organization defines behaviors that characterize desired culture

**Cloud ERM:** Organization defines its cloud usage culture and how that culture is used to support strategies and objectives

## COSO Cloud Computing ERM: Governance and Culture Principles

### Demonstrates Commitment to Core Values

**ERM:** Organization demonstrates commitment to core values

**Cloud ERM:** Cloud computing steering committee promotes cloud governance

### Attracts, Develops, and Retains Capable Individuals

**ERM:** Organization is committed to building human capital

**Cloud ERM:** Organization retains talent necessary for cloud computing environment

- **Exercises board risk oversight:** Governance is the "tone at the top," which means the board of directors and management demonstrate the importance of **oversight** responsibilities through their actions. **Culture** relates to an organization's values, including its risk appetite. Because board members must oversee management's objectives and strategies, they need a broad knowledge of the technology used in the organization's industry in order to answer the following questions:
  - How can technology help achieve organizational objectives?
  - Does technology increase or decrease risk?
  - What is the impact of depending on third parties?
  - What are the trends in the industry?
  - What is the impact of retiring on-premises infrastructure and moving to the cloud?
  - How do the CSP's risk assessment and mitigation strategies align with the organization?
  - How does the organization compare with competitors or industry benchmarks?
- **Establishes operating structures:** Before migration to the cloud, an organization should set up a governance framework and operating structures that support its business objectives. A **cloud computing steering committee** may be formed to determine which processes, applications, and data should be migrated to the cloud. Policies, procedures, and personnel structures will need to be amended.

An assignment matrix helps define internal roles and responsibilities based on cloud computing:

**Internal Cloud Computing Roles and Responsibilities**

| Roles | Responsibilities |
|---|---|
| **Board of Directors** | • Be aware of cloud computing trends<br>• Understand the impact of cloud computing on the industry and business<br>• Have oversight over cloud services<br>• Understand how risks are balanced with cloud service and deployment models<br>• Use internal audit to perform IT audits |
| **Chief Executive Officer (CEO)** | • Define how cloud computing supports business strategies<br>• Define policies for outsourcing cloud services<br>• Understand where and how the organization uses cloud services |
| **Chief Financial Officer (CFO)** | • Provide financial reporting disclosures about cloud usage<br>• Evaluate cost of cloud services and internal IT personnel<br>• Evaluate tax benefits or costs of cloud service and deployment models<br>• Implement purchasing policies over cloud services<br>• Monitor the financial health of CSPs<br>• Participate in cloud governance |
| **Chief Legal Officer (CLO)** | • Ensure cloud activities comply with laws and regulations<br>• Review cloud services contracts and service level agreements<br>• Understand implications of cloud services for operations in different countries |
| **Chief Compliance Officer** | • Work with Chief Legal Officer to monitor changes for compliance needs<br>• Establish plans and monitor cloud services for compliance<br>• Participate in external examinations such as SOC, HIPAA, Payment Card Industry Data Security Standard (PCI-DSS), GDPR<br>• Monitor CSPs for compliance |

**Internal Cloud Computing Roles and Responsibilities**

| Roles | Responsibilities |
|---|---|
| **Chief Information Officer (CIO)** | • Establish strategy and oversight to secure cloud infrastructure, applications, and data<br>• Establish and oversee change management processes<br>• Monitor cloud services security<br>• Perform cybersecurity assessments, such as penetration testing<br>• Review CSP cybersecurity assessments, SOC, and compliance reports<br>• Determine whether CSPs meet availability metrics in service level agreements |
| **Chief Audit Executive** | • Perform risk-based audits to evaluate the design and effectiveness of controls and processes shared with the CSP<br>• Perform audits or review CSP examination reports for SOC, HIPAA, PCI-DSS, GDPR, or other regulatory audits<br>• Perform audits to verify compliance with data classification policies<br>• Perform audits on cloud service spending and adherence to contracts |
| **Privacy Officer** | • Maintain the organization's privacy policies and procedures<br>• Review data classification policies and understand what data is in the cloud<br>• Monitor the CSP for privacy compliance |
| **Cloud Computing Steering Committee** | • Oversee the cloud migration process<br>• Monitor the organization to ensure cloud governance is part of its processes |
| **Purchasing** | • Define requirements for cloud computing vendors through coordination with business process owners<br>• Maintain a list of approved cloud vendors<br>• Evaluate CSPs |
| **Vendor Risk Management** | • Define CSP vendor management policies<br>• Monitor CSP service level agreements |
| **Technology Architect** | • Implement and maintain overall IT environment<br>• Design the overall technology strategy, including cloud services |

**Internal Cloud Computing Roles and Responsibilities**

| Roles | Responsibilities |
|---|---|
| **Network Engineer** | • Design network architecture to ensure availability of systems, including those in the cloud<br>• Maintain IaaS or PaaS cloud infrastructure<br>• Optimize network software<br>• Implement communication and hardware connections in and out of the cloud |
| **Security Engineer** | • Design a security strategy and implement tools to protect the security, availability, processing integrity, confidentiality, and privacy of cloud services<br>• Monitor the cloud environment for threats<br>• Manage the organization's incident response<br>• Coordinate incident response with the CSP |
| **DevOps Engineer** | • Maintain processes for cloud development operations<br>• Create cloud-based applications |
| **Quality Assurance (QA) Engineer** | • Test cloud-based systems and application changes<br>• Prepare data for business continuity planning |
| **System/Application Administrator** | • User administration and security<br>• Manage system configuration<br>• Monitor managed services for cloud services<br>• Manage cloud system maintenance |
| **End Users** | • Attend security awareness and incident response training<br>• Understand data privacy practices<br>• Secure use of cloud applications and tools |

- **Defines desired culture and demonstrates commitment to core values:** The organization should have a cloud-aware culture. Management sets the tone for data usage, privacy, security, and cybersecurity by communicating policies and procedures. Personnel should receive training on security awareness, incident response, and data privacy. This training should also be provided to the CSP personnel, and management should monitor the CSP's culture to ensure that its values align with the organization's.
- **Attracts, develops, and retains capable individuals:** Management should identify the skills needed by internal personnel to manage cloud services. Employees should receive proper training to ensure a suitable level of knowledge.

## Strategy and Objective Setting

**COSO Cloud Computing ERM: Strategy and Objective-Setting Principles**

### Analyzes Business Context

**ERM:** Organization considers effect of business context on risk profile

**Cloud ERM:** Organization assesses the effects of different cloud service and deployment models on the achievement of business strategies and objectives

### Defines Risk Appetite

**ERM:** Organization defines risk appetite

**Cloud ERM:** Organization defines risk appetite for cloud risks such as data privacy, access, reliability, compliance, and cybersecurity

### Evaluates Alternative Strategies

**ERM:** Organization evaluates alternative strategies and risks

**Cloud ERM:** Organization considers different cloud service options and impact on business objectives

### Formulates Business Objectives

**ERM:** Organization considers risk while establishing business objectives

**Cloud ERM:** Organization defines cloud objectives that support its business objectives

- **Analyzes business context:** Prior to cloud migration, the organization should define its cloud computing strategy and objectives. **Business context** includes trends, events, relationships, or other factors that may influence or change the organization. IT personnel should coordinate with business process owners to ensure that cloud computing aligns with their needs. Business context may focus on factors such as user interfaces, customization options, deployment speed, scalability, maintenance, and cost savings.
- **Defines risk appetite:** Cloud computing strategies should be assessed for risks based on different delivery and deployment models. The organization's **risk appetite**, or the amount of risk it will accept, dictates cloud preferences. For example, an organization with sensitive data subject to regulatory compliance may not have the appetite for the higher risk associated with public SaaS offerings. Risk appetite may vary among business processes depending on the type of data, availability requirements, or needed recovery time.
- **Evaluates alternative strategies:** Cloud alternatives should be evaluated based on risk and the organization's business objectives, such as growth, productivity, or efficiency. The cost of alternative systems should be estimated, not only in terms of upfront costs and maintenance, but also potential lost opportunity when a system is old (ie, technology debt).

  **Technology debt** may come from using customized systems that are hard to update, short-term solutions, or obsolete technology. These factors should be weighed against options like cloud computing, which may end the problems stemming from technology debt. For example, when considering migrating to the cloud from a traditional on-premises system, weigh the potential improvements against the difficulty of making the change.
- **Formulates business objectives:** Once a strategy is defined, cloud objectives (ie, goals) should support business objectives such as security and data privacy. Cloud objectives should be updated in response to changes in the organization's business or industry, as well as changes in risk appetite.

## Performance

**COSO Cloud Computing ERM: Performance Principles**

### Identifies Risk

**ERM:** Organization identifies risks that threaten achievement of strategies and business objectives

**Cloud ERM:** Organization analyzes internal and external factors to identify cloud computing risks

### Assesses Severity of Risk

**ERM:** Organization asesses the severity of risks

**Cloud ERM:** Organization considers the impact and likelihood of cloud computing risks

### Prioritizes Risk

**ERM:** Risks are prioritized to select the most important risk responses

**Cloud ERM:** Cloud computing risks and risk responses are prioritized

### Implements Risk Responses

**ERM:** Risk responses are selected based on priority

**Cloud ERM:** Organization designs and implements cloud computing controls to respond to risks

### Develops Portfolio View

**ERM:** Risk is evaluated based on a portfolio view

**Cloud ERM:** Cloud computing risks are viewed in terms of strategic, financial, operational, reporting, and compliance objectives

- **Identifies risk:** Cloud computing risks can come from both **internal and external factors**. One of the greatest risks of cloud computing is outsourcing control to third-party vendors. The organization's board and management are still responsible for governance, including the choice to outsource. Thus, they must identify risks and have mitigation plans based on an understanding of which party will design and implement certain controls. **Shared responsibility** becomes more complicated when CSPs rely on external subvendors. For example, an organization may use a software vendor's SaaS application, which relies on a subvendor's PaaS service.

### Comparison of Responsibilities under Cloud Service and Deployment Models

| | On Premises | Private IaaS | Public IaaS | Public PaaS | Public SaaS | Public Saas with Subvendor IaaS | Public Saas with Subvendor PaaS |
|---|---|---|---|---|---|---|---|
| Data Accountability | | | | | | | |
| Client & Endpoint Protection | | | | | | | |
| Account & Access Management | | | | | | | |
| Identity Management | | | | Shared | Shared | Shared | Shared |
| Application Controls & Configuration | | | | Shared | Shared | Shared | Shared |
| Application Source Code | | | | Shared | | | |
| Platform Controls | | Shared | Shared | | | Shared | |
| Operating System and Database | | Shared | Shared | | | Shared | |
| Virtualization | | Shared | Shared | | | Shared | |
| Physical | | Shared | | | | | |

Customer responsibility | CSP responsibility | CSP subvendor responsibility

- **Assesses severity of risk:** Cloud computing risks should be assessed for severity by estimating their **impact** and **likelihood**. Risk assessments may be made based on qualitative or quantitative factors. Cloud delivery and deployment model types should be considered, as the risk may vary based on the type of data or application.
- **Prioritizes risks:** After an assessment, the most severe risks (ie, those with the highest impact or likelihood) should be prioritized. Because risk assessment and prioritization occur before a CSP is selected, additional assessment and prioritization will need to be performed once specific information is known.
- **Implements risk responses:** Organizations must decide how to respond to the risks they have identified as priorities. There are five primary risk responses. **Reduction** (ie, increasing governance and monitoring) controls are often used in cloud computing. Organizations may design their controls using the COSO *Internal Control–Integrated Framework*, regulations, or other accepted cybersecurity frameworks.

**Risk Response Options**

 **Accept**

Organizations may consent to a certain level of risk to receive benefits, especially if there are no other options.

 **Avoid**

When the consequences may exceed the benefits, organizations may choose not to use a particular cloud solution.

 **Pursue**

Migrating to the cloud may offer additional opportunities for innovation and increased efficiency despite risks.

 **Reduce**

Most often, cloud computing risks can be reduced by adding governance and monitoring controls.

 **Share**

Cloud computing risks can be shared through contractual agreements with CSPs or by purchasing cyber insurance.

## Risk Reduction Responses

**Risk: reliability and vulnerability**

Organizations should choose CSPs with high reliability. Reliability is the CSP's ability to run for a given period without failure. An organization's risk response should include monitoring the CSP for performance and uptime.

The CSP should perform security and vulnerability assessments. Reports should be shared with the organization and the independent service auditors performing SOC examinations. The CSP should have an incident response plan and a method for the organization to report incidents.

Common reliability and vulnerability risk responses include:

- Vendor selection due diligence
- Performance monitoring
- Security monitoring
- Incident response plans

**Risk: data classification, data destruction, and security**

The risk of data leakage is higher for public, multitenant cloud services. Classifying the data by type allows an organization to determine what type of cloud computing model and applications to use. Data loss prevention (DLP) controls help the organization safeguard sensitive data by storing it in the best environment.

Organizations should also have a data destruction policy, especially for confidential and private information. Keeping excessive or outdated data exposes the organization to unnecessary risks. A formal destruction method supports security.

Data security can also be increased by using secure networks, threat protection, and strong network access protocols. Data should be secure both in transit and at rest.

Common data classification, data destruction, and security risk responses include:

- Data classification policies
- Data destruction policies
- Security processes

**Risk: single point of failure**

All cloud computing traffic must pass through the Internet, which represents a single point of failure. Organizations should choose Internet service providers and CSPs that offer redundancy options to reroute traffic if there is a problem. Because potential failure of a component or system is always a concern, organizations should have plans for business continuity and incident response, as well as recovery backups (ie, data redundancy).

Common risk responses related to single points of failure include:

- Data redundancy
- Internet redundancy
- Business continuity plans
- Incident response plans

**Risk: compliance**

Organizations need to watch the external environment for changes in regulations such as HIPAA or the General Data Protection Regulation (GDPR). Internal changes may also require efforts to stay compliant. In addition, the organization must monitor the CSP's compliance, which can be done through internal monitoring and/or independent examinations performed by CPAs.

Common compliance risk responses include:

- External compliance monitoring
- Internal compliance monitoring
- Vendor monitoring

**Risk: cyberattacks**

Cybersecurity threats are prevalent in both on-premises and cloud-based solutions. There is an increased risk with public, multitenant cloud services. Multitenant environments are a high-value target because attackers can gain access to multiple organizations through one point of access. The organization should understand the CSP's cybersecurity controls and have a method to report incidents. Common cyberattack risk responses include:

- Security monitoring
- Incident response plans

**Risk: shadow IT**

Organizations should have policies and procedures to prevent shadow (ie, unauthorized) cloud activities. The policies should specify when cloud computing is allowed, which vendors are acceptable, who may contract with a CSP, and what data can be moved to the cloud. Technology such as data loss prevention tools may keep data from being accessible outside the organization. Firewalls, proxy servers, and web filters may prevent potentially harmful websites from being accessed through the organization's network.

Common shadow IT risk responses include:

- Cloud computing policies
- Data loss prevention
- Security monitoring

- **Develops portfolio view:** Cloud computing is just one part of an organization's overall IT portfolio. Organizations must look at the "big picture" and understand how cloud computing helps different units achieve business objectives. Cloud computing may make sense for one business process but not for another. Risks related to cybersecurity should be mitigated by organization-wide data classification policies that help determine whether data can be safely moved to the cloud and which delivery and deployment model is appropriate.

## Review and Revision

**COSO Cloud Computing ERM: Review and Revision Principles**

### Assesses Substantial Change

**ERM:** Organization identifies and assesses changes that may substantially affect strategies and business objectives

**Cloud ERM:** Organization assesses internal and external changes that impact cloud computing and determines how cloud computing can supply infrastructure to achieve business strategies and objectives

### Reviews Risk and Performance

**ERM:** Organization reviews performance and considers risk

**Cloud ERM:** Organization reviews cloud governance and CSPs for performance and risk

### Pursues Improvement in ERM

**ERM:** Organization improves enterprise risk management

**Cloud ERM:** Organization assesses cloud improvements as part of an overall enterprise risk management program

- **Assesses substantial change:** Enterprise risk management (ERM) is an ongoing process that is part of an organization's daily operations. Management should evaluate risk whenever there are significant changes to the environment, organization, business processes, or the CSP. External changes, such as regulatory compliance, technology advancements, or cyber threats, must also be monitored.

Organizations should have formal **change management** processes to manage and keep track of all IT changes, including those related to cloud computing.

- **Reviews risk and performance:** Cloud computing processes should be reviewed to determine if improvements can be made. The performance of CSPs should also be reviewed to evaluate whether they are providing the agreed-upon level of service and performance. Organizations should review the SOC and compliance examination reports of all outsourced vendors, including CSPs.
- **Pursues improvement in ERM:** Risk and performance reviews provide insight on how to improve ERM processes and controls. Such reviews may indicate improvements to not only cloud computing but the organization's overall response to risk.

## Information, Communication, and Reporting

**COSO Cloud Computing ERM: Information, Communication, and Reporting Principles**

### Leverages Information Technology

**ERM:** Organization leverages information and technology to support ERM

**Cloud ERM:** Organization uses cloud computing and data to support ERM

### Communicates Risk Information

**ERM:** Organization uses communication channels to support ERM

**Cloud ERM:** Organization uses cloud computing communication channels to support ERM

### Reports on Risk, Culture, and Performance

**ERM:** Organization reports on risk, culture, and performance across the entire entity

**Cloud ERM:** Organization reports on cloud computing risk, culture, and performance across the entire entity

- **Leverages information and technology:** Technology should support identifying, communicating, and responding to cloud computing risks as part of the overall ERM function. The monitoring of cloud computing relies on various sources, including monitoring applications, internal audits and assessments, vendor management systems, and compliance tools. External examinations and security ratings also provide insight regarding a CSP's systems and controls.
- **Communicates risk information:** Clear communication and reporting are essential to ERM. Without current and correct information, good decisions cannot be made. Risk awareness information should be shared with end users who understand how to report concerns or problems. Employee roles and responsibilities for cloud computing must be communicated throughout the organization. Communication with CSPs is important for daily operations, as well as incident management.
- **Reports on risk, culture, and performance:** The board of directors should receive reports that help them understand whether cloud computing strategies are achieving the organization's business objectives or changes are needed.

# 3.02 Enterprise and Accounting Information Systems

## Enterprise and Accounting Information Systems

**Representative Task (Remembering and Understanding):** Summarize enterprise resource planning (ERP) and accounting information systems, what they encompass, and how they interact.

### Enterprise Resource Planning (ERP)

An enterprise resource planning (ERP) system is a group of **software modules** that manage and automate business operations. ERP systems are ordinarily prebuilt (ie, packaged, off the shelf), residing **on premises** or in the **cloud**. Cloud offerings range from full web-based software-as-a-service (SaaS) applications to those that only host data.

Popular ERP applications include Oracle NetSuite, Sage, Microsoft Dynamics, SAP, and Oracle JD Edwards. Each vendor offers various modules that an organization can buy and add on, based on their needs and budget.

Common ERP modules include:

Each module connects to a single **relational database**, which has a uniform data structure. A single, well-defined data structure provides a framework for standardization and data integrity throughout the organization. Relationships (associations) between **resources, events, and agents (REA)** create give-and-take (debit-and-credit) workflows that span ERP modules. **Unified Modeling Language (UML)** diagrams make it easier to visualize the connections between database tables; these diagrams may also be called **entity relationship diagrams (ERD).**

**Example of ERP Database Relationships: UML Diagram**

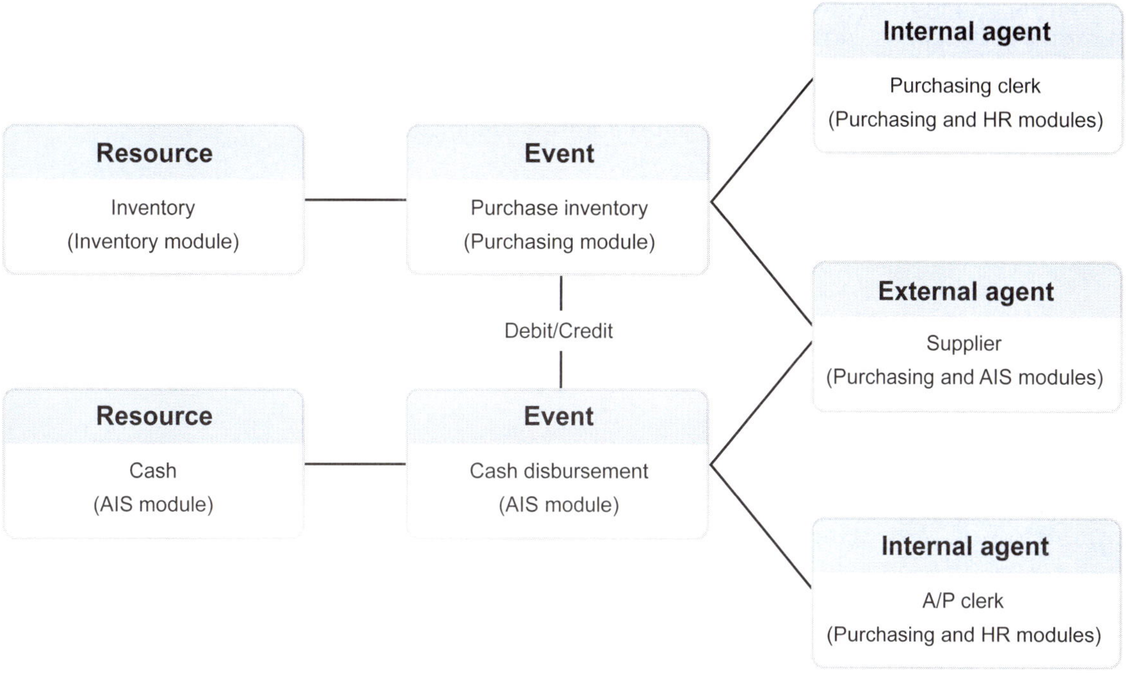

Shared data enables the exchange of information between ERP modules while preventing duplication and errors (ie, one fact, one place). Every individual within the company can access the same data from a **single source of truth**. The central collection of data for widespread use is a **fundamental ERP principle**. A single source of truth improves business insight (eg, real-time reports, dashboards), collaboration, and efficiency while lowering operational costs.

Risks of ERP systems include:

- **Implementation risks:** Implementation of a new ERP system may disrupt operations because of its pervasiveness and complexity.
- **Improper segregation of duties:** A unified ERP system that joins business functions can cause an improper segregation of duties, decreasing internal controls that mitigate the risk of loss.
- **Data management risks:** Complex data structures (eg, tables, relationships) used within an ERP can inhibit access to data or make changes difficult.
- **Business process risks:** Use of packaged ERP software may require changes to business processes. This can increase process interdependence risk, where one business process becomes a single point of failure for the entire system.
- **Financial reporting risks:** ERP systems record transactions and events that flow to financial statements. Management must ensure the software includes internal controls to prevent, detect, and correct material misstatements.
- **Security, availability, and processing integrity risks:** Unauthorized access, as well as unavailable or incorrect data, threaten the integrity of an ERP system.
- **Confidentiality and privacy risks:** Disclosure of sensitive or personal information can have legal and regulatory consequences, such as lawsuits or fines.

## Accounting Information Systems (AIS)

An information system is a formal process for gathering data, converting it into information, and distributing that information to users. An **accounting information system (AIS)** collects, stores, and processes financial data. AIS outputs include reports that managers and other stakeholders (investors, lenders, managers, auditors, and regulators) use to make business decisions.

Accounting information systems serve three main purposes:

1. **Gathering and storing information** about financial activities. This includes extracting transaction data from source documents and posting entries to ledgers or journals.
2. **Supplying data to make decisions**, such as generating financial statements and managerial reports.
3. **Ensuring system-level and IT application controls** are in place.

**Accounting Information System Functions**

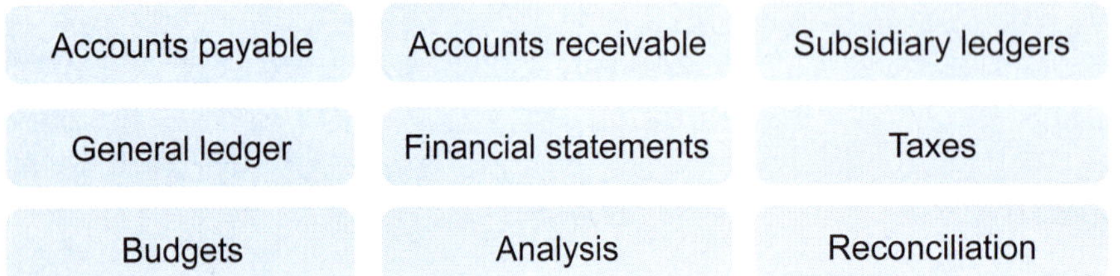


## ERP and AIS Interface

An AIS may be a module in an ERP system or a standalone application. **Data interfaces** (interactions) between different modules of ERP systems are ordinarily seamless, with minimal risk of transmission errors. When an AIS interacts with other systems, there is a substantial risk of incomplete and inaccurate transmission. Data can be transferred between two systems manually through download and upload. More often, data is transferred between two applications using **middleware software**.

To mitigate risks, a company using multiple systems from different vendors should implement **data interface controls**. Data interface controls are communication rules to ensure that transmission is timely, accurate, and complete.

**Data Interface**

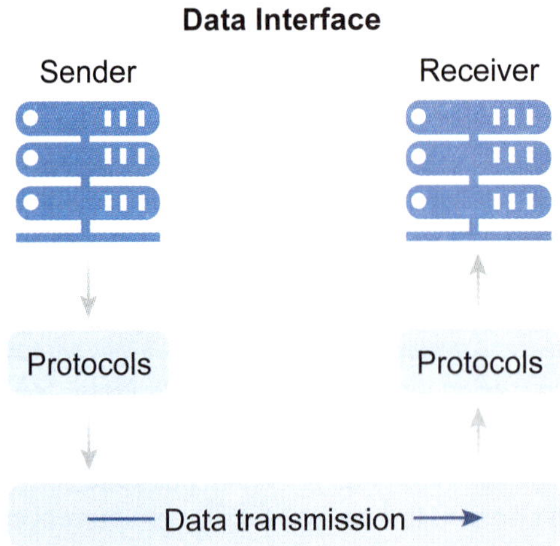

Such controls should address:

- Access to different application and network layers
- Management of communication sessions
- Hardware, software, and network protocols
- Extraction of information from databases
- Security methods for protecting data during transit

# COSO Internal Control and Blockchain

**Representative Task (Remembering and Understanding):** Explain how the COSO internal control framework can be used to evaluate risks related to the use of blockchain in the context of financial reporting and to design and implement controls to address such risks.

## Blockchain

According to the document *Blockchain and Internal Control: The COSO Perspective*, a **blockchain** is:

> *"An append-only ledger, a sequential database maintained by a decentralized network of users responsible for agreeing upon additions to the chain and secured through cryptography."*

**Cryptography** uses **encryption** to secure network communications about blockchain transactions. Another cryptographic method, **hashing**, creates a unique identifier that links each block with the prior block on the chain. The purpose of cryptography is to make the blockchain resistant to data modification.

A blockchain primarily trades and tracks assets in a business network. An asset may be tangible (eg, products, property) or intangible (eg, intellectual property, patents, copyrights). Blockchains also record **digital assets**, such as cryptocurrency. Digital assets can be exchanged, put up as collateral, or used for financing.

**Key Elements of Blockchain**

| Distributed ledger | Validated | Anonymous |
|---|---|---|
| All network participants have a copy of the ledger for transparency | Legitimacy of new transactions is confirmed by a consensus of network computers (nodes) | Identity of network participants is hidden (eg, use of pseudonyms) |
| **Immutable** | **Time stamped** | **Programmable** |
| Validated records are encrypted and cannot be changed | The time of a transaction is recorded in a block | Blockchain activities can be automated (ie, smart contracts) |

Some blockchain-related terms include:

- **Distributed ledger technology:** The distributed ledger and its immutable record of transactions are available to all network users. Transactions are recorded only once in a shared ledger, thus preventing the duplication of effort present in conventional corporate networks.
- **Nodes:** Nodes are computers on a blockchain network that validate new blocks (ie, transactions).

- **Immutable records:** No participant may alter or interfere with a transaction recorded on a shared ledger. Errors can only be corrected by entering an adjusting transaction. Some blockchains may allow a rollback in which a limited number of blocks can be reversed to correct an error. Rollbacks must be heavily scrutinized because they diminish the blockchain's immutability.
- **Smart contracts:** Smart contracts are blockchain-based algorithms that execute upon meeting predefined criteria, thus automating the implementation of an agreement. All parties can be certain of the conclusion right away, without an intermediary or other delay. Workflows are automated such that when criteria are met, the action is executed.

### How Does Blockchain Work?

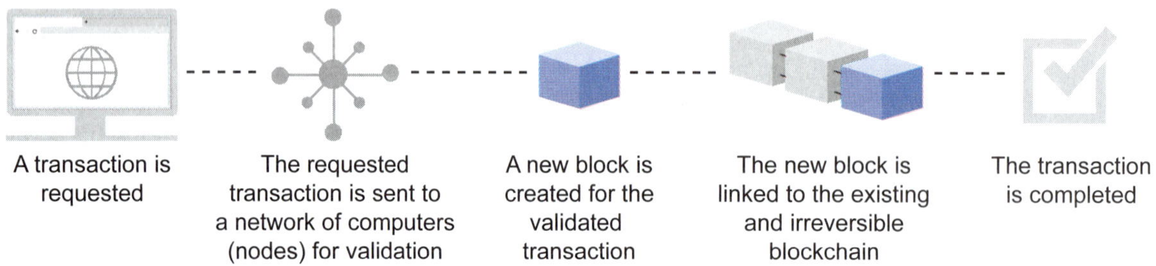


- **Transaction requests are sent to the network for validation:** Before a new block is created, validators must first allow it to be included, thus ensuring that the block is legitimate. A majority of the nodes (ie, network computers) must agree to each transaction block. Validators are third parties who are paid a fee, normally in cryptocurrency.
- **Each transaction, as it occurs, is recorded as a "block" of data:** The transactions depict how an asset has been exchanged. The information of choice (eg, who, what, when, where, and how much) can be recorded in the **data block**.
- **Each block is linked to the blocks that come before and after it:** As an asset moves from one location to another or ownership changes, the blocks form a data chain. The blocks confirm the exact time and sequence of transactions, and they are **securely linked** to prevent any block from being altered or inserted between two existing blocks.
- **Transactions are linked in an irreversible chain (ie, blockchain):** Every new block reinforces the prior block's verification and, by extension, the entire blockchain. This gives the blockchain its crucial strength of **immutability** and makes it tamper-evident.

## COSO Internal Control–Integrated Framework and Blockchain

Blockchain-enhanced tools can increase operational efficiency, reporting accuracy, and regulatory compliance. They also introduce unique risks, which require more controls.

**Blockchain Financial Reporting Considerations**

| | | |
|---|---|---|
| Controls are delegated to the blockchain platform | Audit trails may include both on-chain and off-chain sources | Vendor approval and transaction processes may be different |
| Traditional AIS systems may not accommodate digital assets | Digital assets may be hard to value | Data from blockchains may not be in a usable format |

The **COSO Internal Control–Integrated Framework** provides an effective approach to designing and implementing controls to mitigate blockchain risks. The **five components** of COSO's Internal Control–Integrated Framework are:

| Control environment | Risk assessment | Control activities | Information and communication | Monitoring activities |
|---|---|---|---|---|

## Control Environment

Blockchain may provide an effective control environment (eg, by documenting transactions with minimal human interaction). However, many of this component's principles relate to human behavior, such as management supporting integrity and ethics, which the blockchain cannot analyze. The control environment can be difficult to manage when an entity is intertwined with other participants.

| Risk | Mitigation |
|---|---|
| Anonymous and permissionless blockchains can be used for unethical activities | • Code of conduct<br>• Noncompliance guidelines<br>• Governance processes |
| Lack of oversight and accountability | • Transaction partner criteria<br>• Blockchain access criteria<br>• Due diligence procedures<br>• Know-your-customer (KYC) procedures<br>• Anti-money-laundering (AML) procedures<br>• SOC examinations<br>• Dispute resolution processes |
| Reputational risks from participating in a technology many people view as negative | • Effective communication |
| Lack of adoption by employees | • Reporting lines<br>• Cross-disciplinary teams |
| Lack of expertise and competence | • Segregation of duties<br>• Ongoing training<br>• Outsourced specialist services |

## Risk Assessment

Blockchain helps to mitigate existing risks by promoting accountability, supporting record integrity, and providing an irrefutable record. Blockchain also creates an agile business environment in which real-time reporting is provided to management, the board, and external parties; this helps to identify and assess the achievement of entity objectives (eg, operations, reporting, compliance). However, blockchain also introduces risks.

| Risk | Mitigation |
|---|---|
| Network partners are willing to take on unacceptable risks | • Blockchain use objectives<br>• Transaction partner criteria |
| Vulnerability to new types of fraud | • Risk assessment processes<br>• Outsourced specialist services |
| Lack of data governance and data overload | • Information transfer controls |
| Lack of sufficient appropriate evidence to support transactions in a financial statement audit | • Defined accounting policies |
| Self-executing smart contracts that are difficult to stop and result in significant loss | • Transaction authorization controls |
| Digital assets are new, have volatile market values, lack proper controls, and are prone to cybersecurity risks | • Change management processes<br>• Incident response plans<br>• Segregation of duties<br>• Cybersecurity mitigation technology |
| Difficulty integrating blockchain with legacy systems | • Outsourced specialist services<br>• Change management processes |
| Uncertainty in regulatory requirements | • Legal counsel<br>• Regulatory monitoring |

## Control Activities

Blockchain can serve as a tool for facilitating control activities. Smart contracts can help organizations do business around the world effectively (eg, by reducing the chance of human error and fraud). However, the collaborative aspects of blockchain introduce complexity, especially when the technology is decentralized and there is no single party accountable for internal controls over financial reporting (ICFR).

| Risk | Mitigation |
|---|---|
| Blockchain is poorly implemented or there is a lack of controls | • Change management controls<br>• Exception reports<br>• Data verification<br>• Internal audits<br>• External examinations |
| Lack of recourse for automatic execution and recording of invalid transactions | • Smart contract input control<br>• Increased number of validating nodes<br>• Tests of node validations<br>• Node validation tracking<br>• Incentives for proper node validations |
| Lack of controls over access to private keys and transaction initiation | • Key access control<br>• Third-party custodian<br>• Split key access<br>• Multiple required signatures<br>• Segregation of duties |
| Improper consensus protocol leads to the recording of invalid transactions | • Periodic evaluation<br>• Authorized node participation<br>• Effective protocol controls<br>• Incentives for protocol compliance<br>• Penalties for protocol noncompliance |
| Altered transactions due to chain rollbacks | • Change tracking<br>• Change alerts |
| Off-chain transactions cannot be reconciled with on-chain transactions | • Audit trails |

## Information and Communication

Blockchain's intrinsic qualities improve transaction visibility and data availability, allowing management to communicate financial information to important stakeholders more quickly and effectively. Management should consider whether there is enough information to support financial records that are in an auditable form.

| Risk | Mitigation |
|---|---|
| False sense that blockchain information is always correct | • Stakeholder education<br>• Governance oversight<br>• Communication of changes<br>• Whistleblower hotline |
| Obtained data requires transformation | • Data analytic software and procedures |
| Lack of sufficient appropriate evidence to support financial statement assertions about digital assets | • Information standards<br>• Coordination with internal and external auditors |

## Monitoring Activities

The ability of blockchain to provide more frequent, comprehensive, and detailed monitoring could significantly alter current processes.

| Risk | Mitigation |
|---|---|
| Difficulty monitoring data overload | • Computerized continuous monitoring |
| Lack of competent monitoring workers | • Segregation of duties<br>• Ongoing training<br>• Outsourced specialist services<br>• Monitoring controls<br>• Evaluation of monitoring activities |
| Difficulty staying current with frequent technology and regulatory changes | • Legal counsel<br>• Regulatory monitoring |
| No one is responsible for executing monitoring controls | • Independent examinations |

When an organization evaluates the potential use of blockchain through the COSO perspective, the board of directors and senior executives gain a better understanding of the context and can make more informed assessments of the technology's potential and applicability for internal control. This enables others within the organization to perform a detailed risk analysis and design suitable controls to mitigate risks, which facilitates effective adoption and use of blockchain.

# Business Process Improvements

**Representative Task (Application):** Determine potential changes to business processes to improve the performance of an accounting information system (eg, robotic process automation, outsourcing, system changes).

Businesses constantly face competitive threats, demanding consumer expectations, regulatory compliance issues, and increasing costs. These burdens can be partially mitigated through business process changes, such as using automation software, outsourcing, or making system changes. Implementing these modifications may improve the performance of an AIS but are not without risk.

## Automation

Advancements in **robotic process automation (RPA)**, **artificial intelligence (AI)**, and **machine learning (ML)** have increased the efficiency of business processes. Using these technologies reduces repetitive tasks, such as data entry and calculations, improving performance and reducing errors.

RPA uses rule-based software technology to build, deploy, and manage "bots" that automate manual tasks. The **bot** is a script that instructs applications to replicate the same actions or the clicks that a human would make. When combined with AI and ML, RPA can expand into "thinking" and "learning." AI and ML train algorithms to recognize data patterns, so that the software can perform tasks faster.

| Accounting Automation Considerations | |
|---|---|
| **Advantages** | **Disadvantages** |
| • Time and cost savings | • Complexity |
| • Accuracy | • Prolonged training |
| • Speed of data retrieval | • Technical issues |
| • Improved data analysis | • Data migration errors |
| • Enhanced security | • Regulatory noncompliance |

### Advantages of Accounting Automation Include:

- **Saving time:** Accounting automation saves time and effort, thus providing scale. It eliminates time spent on repetitive, manual accounting tasks like data entry and reconciliation. This process improvement shortens the financial reporting and analysis cycle and frees the accounting department's time for strategic decision-making.
- **Improving data accuracy:** Data accuracy is critical to accounting operations. Even the most meticulous professionals can occasionally overlook minor details or enter incorrect data. An error could be as simple as transposing a number or forgetting a decimal point, but it may have wide implications. Accounting automation helps to prevent input errors.
- **Reducing cost:** Accounting automation software reduces tedious clerical tasks, allowing a company to process more documents in less time and for less money. This reduces workforce size and associated costs.

- **Comprehensive analysis:** Accountants and analysts need relevant and correct data to analyze trends, detect fraud, and generate metrics. Reports, dashboards, and other data visualizations can be automated to provide real-time insights.
- **Faster data retrieval:** Automation simplifies data retrieval. To find a document, one can search by file name, owner name, or meta tags. Automated accounting systems also make data archiving cheaper.
- **Better security:** Securing financial data in basic computer applications is risky. Hackers target small businesses every year, putting customers, employees, and sensitive data at risk. Manually filing paper documents is even less secure because it is easy to misplace documents. A password-protected computer is harder to access than a cabinet holding vital client data in paper form.

### Disadvantages of Accounting Automation Include:

- **Complex software interface:** Automated accounting software may be too complex to understand and navigate.
- **Prolonged training period:** When implementing automated accounting, employees need adequate training in how to use the system. Training time may vary from person to person, delaying the implementation of the solution.
- **Technical problems:** Operating systems and software bugs can cause errors, requiring IT support. Though infrequent, system downtime slows operations and increases workload.
- **Data migration/integration difficulties:** Accounting software may misread the existing database or skip parts of it, creating discrepancies in the freshly created database. In addition, the accounting software may not easily interface to share data with the existing ERP system.
- **Compliance issues:** If there is an accounting software error, the auto-generated regulatory reports may be inaccurate, resulting in fines and sanctions.

**Commonly Automated Accounting Functions**

| | |
|---|---|
| Payroll | Purchasing |
| Finance and tax | Employee expense management |
| Accounts payable and accounts receivable | Cash management and forecasting |

Automation may improve the performance of an AIS. Using modern technology may require changes to business processes or systems. CPAs can help management in designing business processes and controls around automated workflows. Often, CPAs will provide their clients with the software, packaged with implementation, consulting, and training. For example, small and medium business clients primarily use QuickBooks or Xero; both platforms offer integrations with other applications to expand capabilities and data sharing.

## Examples of Automated Business Processes Include:

- **Payroll:** Manual processing of payroll is labor intensive, especially when performed weekly or biweekly. It is important to pay employees as promised and file employment taxes on time to comply with laws and regulations.

  Payroll automation saves time by:

  - Synchronizing hours or salaries with time and attendance software
  - Creating time approval workflows
  - Calculating pay, including overtime, and deductions for taxes or benefits
  - Processing paper checks or direct deposits (ie, Automated Clearing House [ACH] payments)
  - Preparing tax filings and workers' compensation reports

  Automation reduces calculation errors, improves the timeliness of paycheck distribution, and ensures tax filings are correct. Businesses may use on-premises or cloud-based software to automate payroll or outsource the process to a third-party service, such as ADP.

  An automated process requires the employer to set up payroll policies and schedules, input employee data, and set up routings for approvals. For hourly employees, supervisors must confirm the time worked prior to a payroll run. Once approved, the software will perform the calculations, issue payments, and generate reports.

**Payroll Example**

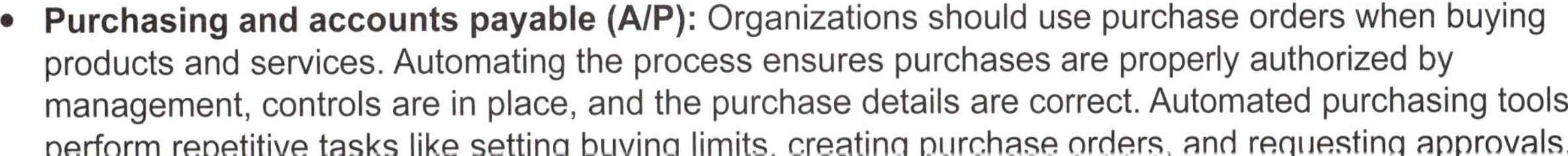


- **Purchasing and accounts payable (A/P):** Organizations should use purchase orders when buying products and services. Automating the process ensures purchases are properly authorized by management, controls are in place, and the purchase details are correct. Automated purchasing tools perform repetitive tasks like setting buying limits, creating purchase orders, and requesting approvals.

  Purchases normally begin with a **requisition** (ie, written request). Requisitions arise from a specific request or an automated ordering system. Ordinarily, purchases are related to capital outlays, supplies, or inventory. **Automated inventory ordering software** monitors quantity on hand and triggers a requisition at a designated **reorder point**. Requisitions automatically flow to the proper approver.

  Once approved, the requisition is routed by the software to the purchasing department for conversion to a **purchase order**. The purchasing department may send the purchase order to a vendor electronically or enter it directly into the vendor's web-based system. Item numbers, descriptions, and agreed-upon prices are preloaded into the software to avoid errors or overcharges.

  When the vendor delivers the order, the **receiving** department checks the item description against a blind copy of the purchase order and counts the items received. To require the receiving department to physically count the delivered items, a **blind purchase order** does not list the quantity purchased. The software automatically updates inventory levels when the receiving department enters the receipt of goods.

Upon receiving the vendor's invoice (either in the mail or electronically), the **accounts payable** department matches the invoice with the purchase order and the receiving documents (**three-way match**). If everything agrees, accounts payable requests a cash disbursement through the software.

**Purchasing and Accounts Payable Example**

| Requisition | Purchase order | Receiving | Accounts payable |
|---|---|---|---|
| • Specifically requested or automatically generated based on inventory reorder points<br>• Automatically flows to requisition approver | • Approved requisition is routed to purchasing department<br>• Purchase order is sent electronically to vendor or directly entered into vendor's web based system | • Items received are counted and checked against a blind purchase order without quantities<br>• Inventory level automatically updates upon confirmation of receipt | • A/P clerks perform three-way match between purchase order, receiving document, and vendor invoice<br>• Cash disbursement is requested for approved vendor invoices |

Another modern, automated approach to purchasing is the use of **procurement cards (ie, P-cards)**. Employees can use P-cards to make corporate purchases, rather than going through the purchase order process. When a purchase is requested, management allows a set spending limit at a specific vendor. The employee makes the purchase on a P-card and attaches the receipt electronically. Accounts payable reviews the P-card activity prior to payment. Management and internal auditors also use reports to monitor P-card activity.

- **Employee expense reimbursement:** Collecting expense reports and receipts from employees can be challenging under traditional systems. Automated reimbursement simplifies receipt collection, approval, and disbursement.

  Employee expenses are normally associated with business travel, education, conferences, and supplies. Employees may pay for such expenses using their personal credit card or a corporate credit card. Corporate credit cards automatically track expenses. Employees can use smartphones to take pictures of paper receipts; the images are then uploaded into software that "reads" them using **optical character recognition (OCR)**. Once the employee's supervisor approves the expenses, accounts payable sends an electronic payment to the employee's bank account or issues a paper check.

- **Sales and accounts receivable (A/R):** An organization's **cash flow** highly depends on receivable collections. Working capital issues result when companies do not effectively manage high-risk customers who pay late or do not pay at all. The longer a balance is overdue, the greater the risk of nonpayment.

  To maximize cash flows from receivables, organizations should set up sound **credit-granting policies** and reasonable **payment terms**. Invoices should be accurate to prevent payment delays because of disputes. **Accounts receivable aging reports** help to identify high-risk customers, who constitute a collection priority.

  Many accounts receivable activities can be automated using software. When sales originate from purchase orders, online systems, or other communications, delivery of the items automatically triggers invoice generation and ledger/journal entries. Organizations may send invoices to customers in the mail or electronically. After a period, the software automatically sends payment reminders, a process known as **auto dunning**.

The accounts receivable department should match each customer's payment to the correct invoice. The software automatically updates the customer's subsidiary ledger. Customers may send payments through ACH transfers, credit cards, P-cards, or paper checks. When payments are past due, accounts receivable personnel receive a notification to seek collection or refer to an external third-party debt collector. **Dashboards** also provide management with real-time reports to monitor accounts receivable balances and collection.

**Sales and Accounts Receivable Example**

| Sale | Credit granting | Delivery/Billing | Collection |
|---|---|---|---|
| • Customer orders products online via purchase order or other verbal or written contracts/ agreements | • Make a credit granting decision for new A/R customers after checking their credit history through a credit reporting agency such as Dun & Bradstreet<br>• If customer is buying on account, check to make sure the purchase is not over customer's credit limit | • Items are shipped or picked up by customer. Inventory levels are adjusted.<br>• Delivery triggers a sales invoice. If sold on account, invoice is sent to customer electronically or through the mail.<br>• Sale is posted to customer's A/R subsidiary ledger | • Payments received are matched to sales invoices and posted to customer subsidiary ledger and cash journals<br>• If payment is not received, auto dunning sends customer reminders<br>• Review A/R aging and contact delinquent accounts |

- **Cash visibility and forecasting:** Finance and accounting (F&A) professionals work with vital data and influence strategic decisions; thus, it is crucial that they accurately collect and present this data to the leadership teams. Strategic investment decisions depend on high cash visibility. F&A teams can use ERP or AIS data to estimate cash flows, generate trend reports, and track critical metrics like account aging, sales forecasts, and expenses. Such software quickly gathers data from multiple sources for comprehensive reporting.

## Outsourcing

Outsourcing involves contracting with a vendor or independent contractor to complete functions that have traditionally been performed in house. The vendor may supply personnel, equipment, or technology. Organizations that outsource remain responsible for governance and monitoring of the vendor's activities.

**Outsourcing Considerations**

| Advantages | Disadvantages |
|---|---|
| • Might be cost effective | • Delegate internal control |
| • Provides additional resources | • Requires additional monitoring |
| • Flexible | • Changes to business processes |
| • Focus on core operations | • Hidden costs/scope creep |
| • Specialized compliance knowledge | • Cultural and time differences |

## Advantages of Outsourcing Include:

**Cost effective:** Outsourcing accounting functions may be less expensive than hiring employees for on-premises work. By contracting with a third party, businesses can reduce overhead costs, such as equipment maintenance, taxes, and employee benefits.

**Provides additional resources:** Many businesses, especially those that are small- to medium-sized, lack the personnel to perform certain tasks. An outsourced vendor may have knowledge and technology that the organization does not have internally.

**Flexibility:** Rather than hiring year-round employees or buying special equipment, outsourcing to a vendor can fill temporary workforce or technology needs.

**Focus on core operations:** Paying an external party to perform tasks frees up time and energy to concentrate on core business operations.

**Compliance:** Hiring an external company that specializes in an area reduces the risk of noncompliance and incorrect financial statements, especially for smaller startups.

## Disadvantages of Outsourcing Include:

**Delegation of internal control:** The organization sacrifices control when it outsources tasks to vendors who design and implement the related internal controls. This can affect the organization's internal controls over financial reporting (ICFR), as well as security, availability, processing integrity, confidentiality, or privacy. The organization may need to rely on SOC 1® or SOC 2® reports to understand the vendor's system and controls.

**Changes to business processes:** Delegating tasks to a vendor ordinarily requires changes to internal processes. Outsourcing may also require reassigning employees to other tasks or reducing the workforce. If not effectively managed, such changes can cause confusion or tension. To oversee the vendor's work, the organization may also have to design new monitoring controls, including requiring independent examinations for compliance with standards, laws, or regulations.

**Hidden costs and scope creep:** An outsourced vendor will typically require a signed contractual agreement that may provide for extra charges. Scope creep, a situation where one task leads to the necessity of other tasks, can increase costs. Setting clear expectations and a formal approval process for changes can prevent unauthorized scope creep.

**Cultural and time differences:** Having staff on site to answer questions right away is preferable in most organizations. Outsourced teams may not respond promptly, and their communication style may not fit the overall company culture. In a global economy, time zone differences may also present communication problems.

## Examples of Outsourced Accounting Functions Include:

### Business Process Outsourcing

- Payroll
- Accounts payable
- Accounts receivable
- Collections

### Specialty Accounting Outsourcing

- Employee benefit administration
- Sales and use tax
- Real estate and construction
- Data analytics

### Technology

- Cloud data hosting
- SaaS software
- ACH payment processing

### Outsourced CFO

- Entire accounting function
- Specialty reporting
- Advisory services
- Training

### Outsourced Internal Audit

- Entire internal audit function
- Co-sourced internal audit
- Specialty internal audit

## System Changes

System changes refer to any alteration of IT architecture, software, or business processes. These can include major changes, such as switching ERP/AIS applications or moving from an on-premises solution to the cloud. Other changes may include adding modules to an ERP, connecting to third-party applications, adding new hardware, software patches, or making code upgrades.

Business needs should drive all system changes. While there can be many reasons for change, they commonly include:

- Accommodating new business structures, processes, or products
- Acquiring another organization that uses a different system

- Overcoming frequent bottlenecks or errors
- Streamlining or automating workflows
- Adding advanced features
- Smoothing the financial close process
- Meeting accounting or industry standards
- Strengthening contractual or regulatory compliance
- Implementing or bolstering controls
- Enhancing data detail, reporting, metrics, analytics, and forecasting
- Creating data connections to vendors, customers, or business partners
- Integrating data and reporting with outsourced service providers
- Using modern technology, such as robotic process automation, artificial intelligence, or machine learning
- Supporting remote workforces
- Improving security, confidentiality, and privacy

System changes should be managed through a formal **change management process** to ensure proper approvals, planning, implementation, testing, and documentation. For example, a system change may affect several or all business units across an organization. All stakeholders should be involved in the process because the change may alter the way people work. Often, personnel may be resistant to change, derailing a project from achieving its intended purpose.

Testing is a crucial step in any change as the transition may not go smoothly (eg, data transfers may be incomplete or wrong). Organizations may choose a stepped approach, where changes occur in smaller increments, are test-piloted, or made while continuing to run the older system. The advantage of a gradual approach to implementing changes is that problems can be found and corrected without causing a major disruption to business operations.

## Accounting Information Systems: Business Processes

**Representative Task (Analysis):** Reconcile the actual sequence of steps and the information, documents, tools, and technology used in a key business process of an accounting information system (eg, sales, cash collections, purchasing, disbursements, human resources, payroll, production, treasury, fixed assets, general ledger, reporting) to the documented process (eg, flowchart, business process diagram, narrative).

When performing an internal audit or an external consulting or attest engagement, CPAs may need to understand and document a business process. For example, in a **walkthrough procedure**, the CPA compares an actual process to the documented process. This is done by obtaining an understanding of a process by performing **inquiries**, **inspecting** policy and procedure documentation, and **observing** the process. Walkthroughs may also include **reperformance** (eg, recalculating a computer-calculated figure).

**Reconciling** the **sequence of steps** to the **documented process** helps the CPA understand the related workflows or data flows and technology use, as well as the system of internal control. Based on this understanding, the CPA may evaluate whether internal controls are suitably designed and operate effectively. In other engagements, the CPA may need to figure out if a system has been described fairly or meets contractual and regulatory requirements. The CPA may also offer advice about how to improve processes, technology, or controls.

Thus, the CPA's work includes two separate activities:

- Documenting the sequence of a business process from beginning to end *as actually performed*, and
- Comparing the actual sequence of steps to the documented process.

Policy manuals may list the procedures and their order; however, such documentation does not ensure the policy will be followed in actual situations. One role of the CPA is to **find** any **differences** and **ask for an explanation** of each difference. Differences may occur because policies have not been communicated effectively, personnel find workarounds or shortcuts, or the procedures have changed but the written policy has not been updated.

CPAs should first document their understanding of the process, either through **written narratives** or process diagrams. Process diagrams, such as **flowcharts** and **Business Process Model and Notation (BPMN)** graphics, use a standardized set of symbols to depict a process from start to finish.

Flowcharts, diagrams, and narratives perform the same function in that they all:

- Describe each procedural step in a cycle in sequence
- Name the department responsible for performing the procedure, the process owner, or the control owner
- Identify the documentation and technology that relate to the cycle, including how many copies of the documents are created and how those copies are distributed
- Show the key controls performed for each process

## Written Narratives

Written narratives are the part of a CPA's workpapers that explain processes and internal control through text rather than diagrams. In written narratives, the CPA may also discuss control deficiencies, inquiries with personnel, or client-provided documentation. In an external engagement, these narratives are private documents belonging to the CPA firm and are not shared with the client.

The advantage of written narratives over diagrams, besides format, is the amount of detail. Diagrams include only symbols and brief text, while narratives have extensive text. This format may supply more information than conveyed in a diagram, although diagrams may also be embedded within a written narrative. The disadvantage of written narratives is that they take longer to read and may have so many details that the process steps and control deficiencies cannot be envisioned as easily as in a diagram.

Consider the following revenue cycle example:

**Written Narrative for Revenue Cycle**

On March 31, Year 1, we performed a walkthrough of Roger Wholesale Distributors, Inc. to obtain an understanding of the client's revenue cycle, including the information, documents, tools, and technology used. The client uses an ERP system with AIS, order management, and customer relationship management (CRM) modules.

The walkthrough included the following procedures:

- **Inquiry:** Met with the managers of the sales, warehouse, and accounting departments. Asked each manager to explain the steps their department takes, respectively, to get a customer and create a sales order, fulfill the sales order, and account for sales, accounts receivable, and payments.
- **Inspection:** Reviewed policy and procedure manuals, as well as internal audit reports pertinent to the revenue cycle functions.

- **Observation:** Shadowed client's personnel as they performed each stage of the workflow, noting inputs and outputs. Obtained the name and job title of each observed employee to figure out if there is a proper segregation of duties.
- Compared the observed procedures to the written policies and procedures and verbal information provided by the managers.

**Inquiry**

- **Sales Manager:** Explained that the company uses a CRM application for sales force automation. Leads could come from a marketing cold call, inbound telephone call, emailed purchase order, or website contact. For each potential customer, a lead record is created. Lead records are then filtered into territories and assigned to the right sales representative. When leads are provided with a written estimate, their status is changed to Prospect.

  Prior to an actual sale, a prospect and estimate must be approved for credit. New customers receive a credit check, and existing customers are checked to make sure their outstanding balance is not too old and that the new order will not exceed their current credit limit. When approved, a sales order is created, and the status is changed to Customer. The statuses help the Sales Manager generate reports that show where potential customers are in the pipeline. He uses this information to keep track of workloads and whether sales representatives are effective at quickly converting potential customers into actual sales.

- **Warehouse Manager:** When a sales order is approved, the order management module creates a fulfillment request. The fulfillment request is automatically routed to the right warehouse, from which the sold items can be shipped. Each warehouse has a kiosk and tablets that receive fulfillment requests via a mobile app. The mobile app allows the warehouse to:
  - See if the customer has multiple orders that can be shipped at the same time
  - See which items have already been picked and shipped
  - See the weight of the picked items in a shipment
  - Print carton labels, bills of lading, and packing lists
  - Print shipping manifests

  The order management module automatically updates the sales order status from Picking to Shipped.

- **Accounting Manager:** The accounting department receives a notice when an order is partially or fully shipped to the customer. The act of shipping the order triggers the accounting module to create a journal entry, increasing cost of goods sold and decreasing inventory. To record the sale, an electronic invoice is automatically created and emailed to the customer. When the invoice is created, the sale is recorded in a sales journal and the customer's accounts receivable balance is updated. In the general ledger, accounts receivable is debited and sales is credited.

  Customers can pay their invoices using a check, credit card, or ACH transfer. The printed invoice includes a remittance form at the bottom. Payments are received by the accounts receivable department and a clerk applies the receipt to the correct invoice. Payments can be in full or only partial payment. The payments are recorded in the cash receipts journal, and the customer's outstanding balance is decreased. An entry in the general ledger debits cash and credits accounts receivable. The Accounting Manager's dashboard includes an accounts receivable aging that is updated in real time as invoices are created and payments are applied. The software emails payment reminder notices to customers at certain escalation points, using the auto dunning feature. An allowance is made to estimate bad debts as part of the monthly close.

### Inspection

Policy and procedure manuals were read to find out if the process described by the managers was the same as written directives. In addition, internal audit reports were read to determine if the internal auditors have documented the process, found any deviations, and made any recommendations.

Noted that the process described by the managers matched the manuals and internal auditor reports except for the way customer payments are received. The manuals describe a mailroom and cashier function where an employee receives check and credit card payments. This information is recorded in the cash receipts journal. An accountant is supposed to review the bank statements and record ACH payments in the cash receipts journal daily. However, the Accounting Manager stated these duties are performed by an accounts receivable clerk.

The internal audit department also brought up this issue and recommended changing the process to be the same as the written policy and procedure manual. The internal audit report contained the following BPMN diagram to document the process of receiving and recording customer payments as written in the policy and procedure manual:

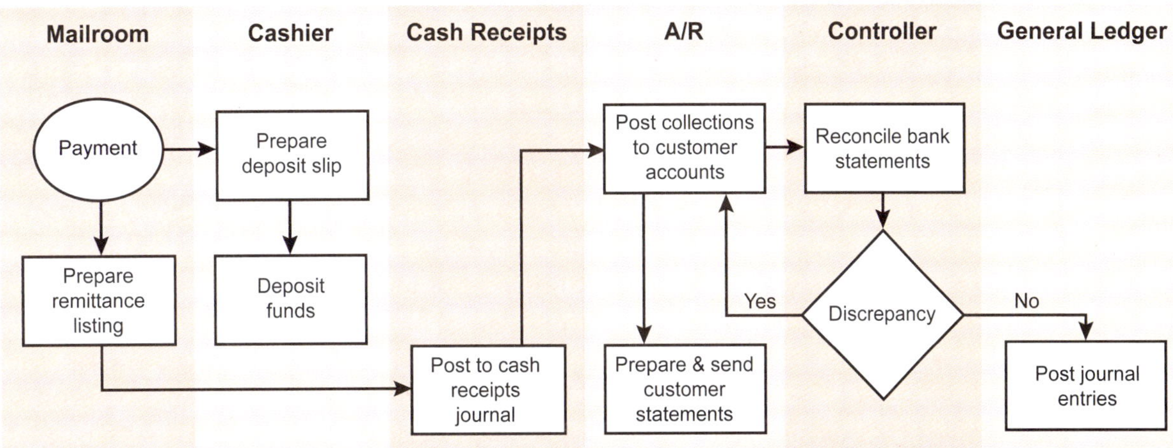


### Observation

Because there appeared to be a difference noted through inquiry and inspection procedures, we observed each stage of the process to find out what is actually taking place. All policies and procedures appeared to be operating as verbally reported by the managers, not according to the manual. Cash payments were received and applied by the accounts receivable clerk. This creates a segregation of duties problem in which one employee has both a custody and recording responsibility. Such a problem with segregation of duties could lead to fraud.

Echoed the internal auditor's recommendation that the process be changed to reflect written policies and procedures. Suggested further procedures to figure out if there were any discrepancies with the receipt and posting of customer payments. In addition, further procedures should be performed to evaluate IT logical access and application controls.

## Flowcharts

A flowchart is a **diagram** that shows the **sequential steps** in a business process or system. It may depict document flows, processing tasks, and internal control. Flowcharts are drawn from top to bottom or left to right, with flow lines connecting symbols.

Flowcharts should show:

- Separation of duties
- Internal controls
- Comments and explanations
- Document sources
- Document dispositions
- Flowlines

Flowcharts use a **standardized set of symbols** to signify specific types of documents, storage, decisions, and tasks. The American National Standards Institute (ANSI) and the International Organization for Standardization (ISO) have issued guidelines to standardize the use of flowchart symbols. Common symbols include:

**Flowcharts & Business Process Diagrams**

| Symbol | Description | Symbol | Description |
|---|---|---|---|
| 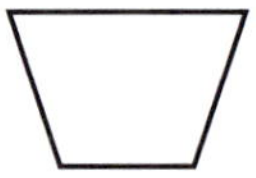 | Manual operation (prepare, compare, or match) | 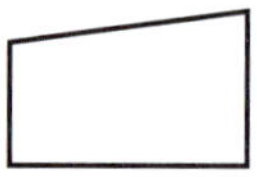 | Manual input (keyboard) |
| 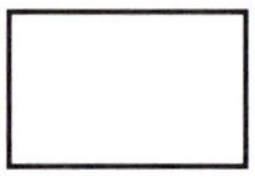 | Computer operation or process (print PO) | 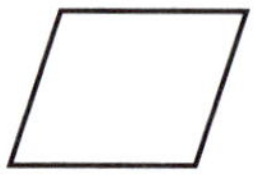 | Input or output (general ledger) |
|  | Document (invoice, PO, error listing) |  | Magnetic tape (sequential access storage) |
| 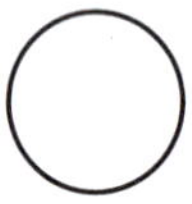 | On-page connector (to connect to another location without a connecting line) |  | Off-page connector (eg, from customer) |
|  | A decision (granting credit, if/then/else) |  | Offline storage (file by name, date, order number) |
| 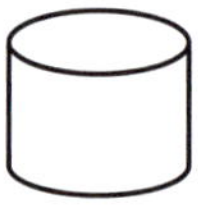 | Magnetic disc storage (database) |  | Online storage (disc, drum) |
| 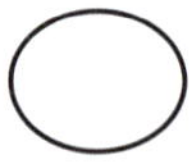 | Start/finish |  | Direct access storage |

When reconciling the actual business process to the documented policy, a CPA must first perform procedures such as inquiry, inspection, and observation to obtain an understanding of the actual process and documented policies. Any differences should be investigated to find the reason.

Consider the following payroll example:

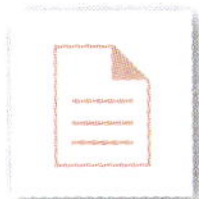

**Flowchart: Payroll**

A service auditor performed a SOC 1® engagement on an outsourced payroll provider named Outsourced Payroll Solutions (OPS). To obtain an understanding of the system and to determine if management's description is fairly stated, the service auditor made flowcharts for a portion of the system after observing OPS's personnel performing the procedures. The flowcharts were then compared with management's description.

### Service auditor flowcharts

**New Client Implementation**



**QTD** = Quarter to Date; **YTD** = Year to Date.

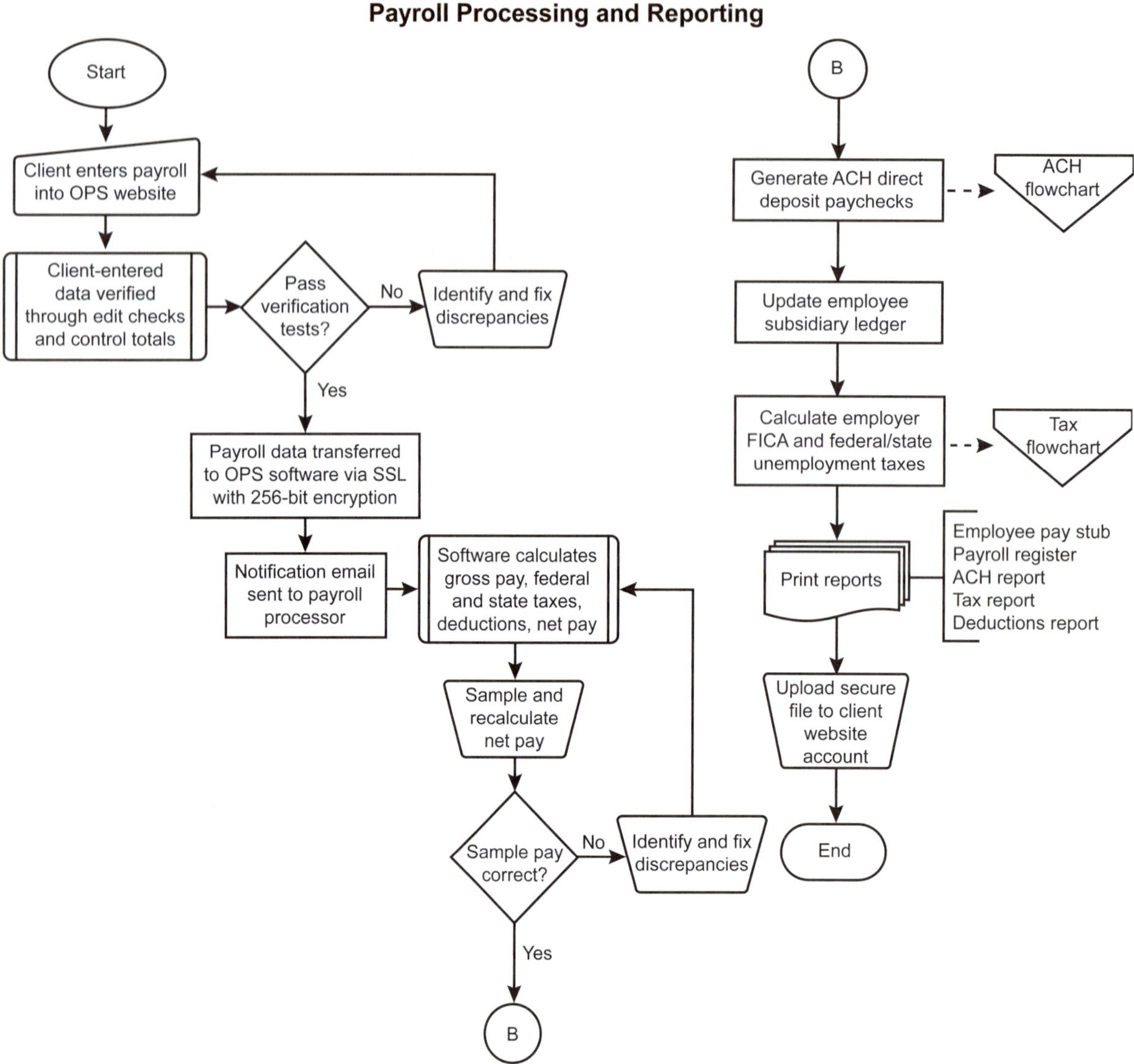


## Management's Description

### Payroll Processing Controls

OPS uses an in-house developed software application to process user entities' payroll. Features of the software include processing payroll payments and reporting. All payroll payments to employees must be made through ACH direct deposit.

User entities submit their employee information and pay data online through OPS's website, which gives each user entity control of its employee information, pay data, and reports. OPS calculates payroll and processes direct deposits. Tax reports are uploaded to the website. The client is responsible for filing federal and state employment tax returns and submitting tax payments.

### New Client Implementation

New clients are provided an implementation checklist. Depending on the size and/or complexity of the client, an implementation team may meet with the client at the client's location or through remote video. New client setup is critical to accurate payroll processing. The following information is needed to set up a new client:

- Company name
- Authorized contacts
- Federal ID#
- Payroll processing and payment dates
- Tax information
- ACH banking information
- Employee payroll data for the current year

Once the information is received from the client, the OPS implementation team sets up the client in the software and runs an installation test payroll to ensure that all beginning information (eg, quarter to date, year to date) totals are correct. The implementation team samples enough employees to be confident that the employee data has been transferred correctly.

### Payroll Processing

The OPS team includes dedicated payroll processing personnel who work with clients to ensure each client's payroll is processed accurately and on time. Clients enter their pay data online through OPS's website. Each client contact has a unique login and password. Two-factor authentication is required because the data is sensitive. The client enters their payroll information, and it is transferred to the OPS software through secure socket layer (SSL) technology with 256-bit encryption. To ensure account security and data accuracy, clients are required to go through a multistep verification process that includes edit check and control totals. When a client submits payroll to be processed, an email is automatically sent to the OPS payroll processors. Payroll processing includes the following tasks:

- Calculate gross pay
- Calculate federal, state, and FICA (Social Security and Medicare) withholdings
- Calculate employee deductions for benefits and garnishments
- Calculate net pay
- Sample employee checks and manually recalculate to ensure accuracy
- Generate ACH direct deposits to employees
- Update employee subsidiary ledger
- Calculate employer's FICA match, federal, and state unemployment taxes

### Reporting

When payroll is processed for a client, an encrypted and password-protected file is uploaded to the OPS website with reports. It can be opened only by a user who has been authorized and two-factor authenticated. Standard reports include:

- Employee Pay Stubs/Statements
- Payroll Register
- ACH Deposit Report
- Tax Liability Report
- Deductions Report

### Service Auditor Analysis

After preparing the flowcharts, the service auditor read management's description again. The service auditor also inspected OPS's policy and procedures manuals and verbally confirmed the accuracy of the flowcharts through client inquiries. No discrepancies were found.

## BPMN Diagrams

The **Business Process Model and Notation (BPMN)** diagram also depicts **workflows** and is part of the ISO standards. Like a flowchart, the BPMN shows the steps in a workflow. However, the steps are divided into "pools" and "swim lanes" to show the internal or external party who performs each task. The symbols in a BPMN are also different from a flowchart.

BPMNs are meant to be simple enough that all business users can understand them. A **pool** shows the coordination between *multiple parties* and a **lane** includes *individual or department level* responsibilities. Normally, **internal and external parties** are shown in **different pools** so that the user will understand there are two separate entities involved.

The BPMN diagram can be vertical or horizontal. Its symbols include:

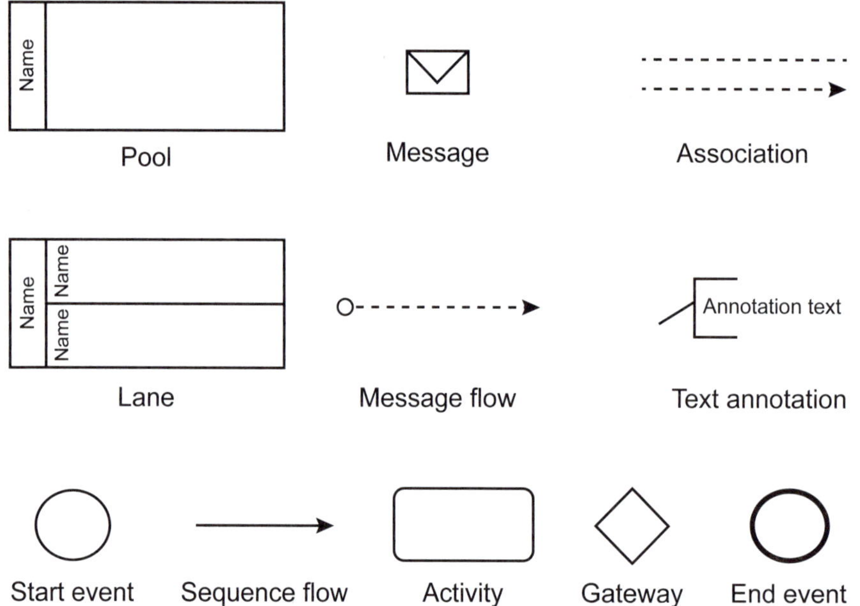


The **start event** is the beginning of the process. This event's symbol is the same as an end event; however, the start event symbol is not bold while the one for the end event is. The **sequence flow** takes the user along a guided path in order of the steps, from left to right. An **activity** shows the task performed and is the most widely used BPMN symbol. A **gateway** is like a decision symbol in a flowchart. It shows branching and forking, where a different path can be taken depending on some variable or the answer to a question. **Message flows** show one- or two-way communication. **Annotations** supply added explanations. An **end event** stops the process. **Associations** show the information relationships in a system.

Consider the following BPMN diagram of the purchasing process:

**Business Process Model and Notation (BPMN) Diagram**

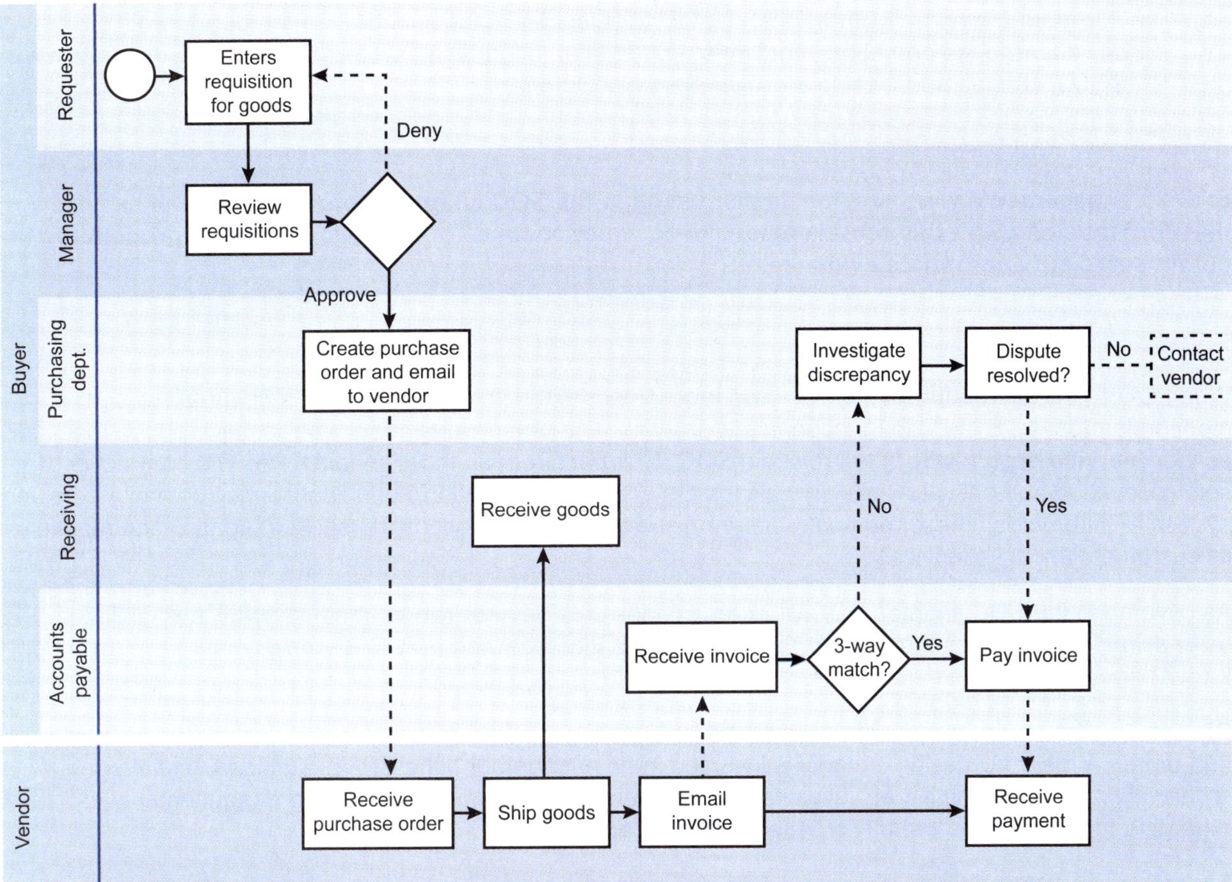


As with the earlier examples, the CPA performing an internal audit, external attest, or consulting engagement would compare the BPMN diagram to information received through oral or written inquiries, document inspections, and observations. These procedures may be combined in a walkthrough, which helps the CPA obtain an understanding of the process. Any discrepancies should be noted and discussed with the client.

# SOC 2® Examination Procedures: Processing Integrity

**Representative Task (Analysis):** Detect deficiencies in the suitability of the design and deviations in the operation of controls related to an information system's processing integrity in a SOC 2® engagement using the Trust Services Criteria.

**SOC 2® engagements were previously discussed in the SOC chapter. It would be helpful to review that content along with this representative task, which focuses on a service auditor's procedures to obtain sufficient appropriate evidence.**

## Overview

When an organization **outsources** business functions or technology, it must have a governance and monitoring process in place to manage third-party risk. The organization may contractually require the vendor **(service organization)** to provide a **SOC 2® report** from an independent CPA. The contract or service level agreement (SLA) usually outlines the service organization's principal service commitments and system requirements. These represent the promises and representations the service organization makes to its customers about its services.

As covered in the SOC chapter, SOC 2® examinations provide **assurance** about security, availability, *processing integrity*, confidentiality, or privacy. A user entity receiving a SOC 2® report must have **sufficient knowledge** to understand and assess its contents.

**Processing integrity** refers to the ability to process and store data in a way that is **complete**, **accurate**, and **timely**. When processing integrity is included in an engagement, the CPA examines the service organization to determine if it achieves its principal service commitments and system requirements regarding the processing integrity **trust services category**.

Examples of services that may require a SOC 2® report for the processing integrity trust services category include any services related to transactions, such as:

**Examples of Service Organizations That May Need SOC2® Report for Processing Integrity**

| | | |
|---|---|---|
| ERP and AIS SaaS developers | Blockchain platforms | ACH payment processors |
| Payroll processors | Cloud data hosting | Data analysis services |

## Management's Controls

Service organization management designs and implements controls to mitigate risks and achieve the organization's objectives. In a SOC 2® engagement, those objectives are the **principal service commitments and system requirements** promised to user entities through contracts or SLAs. The service auditor benchmarks the outcome of management's controls against the **trust services criteria**.

Controls are *preventive, detective, or corrective*. Preventive controls attempt to stop errors and fraud before they occur. Detective controls find problems after the fact. Corrective controls fix errors or fraud when found.

In a SOC 2® engagement, controls can be separated into two broad categories: general internal controls and IT-specific controls.

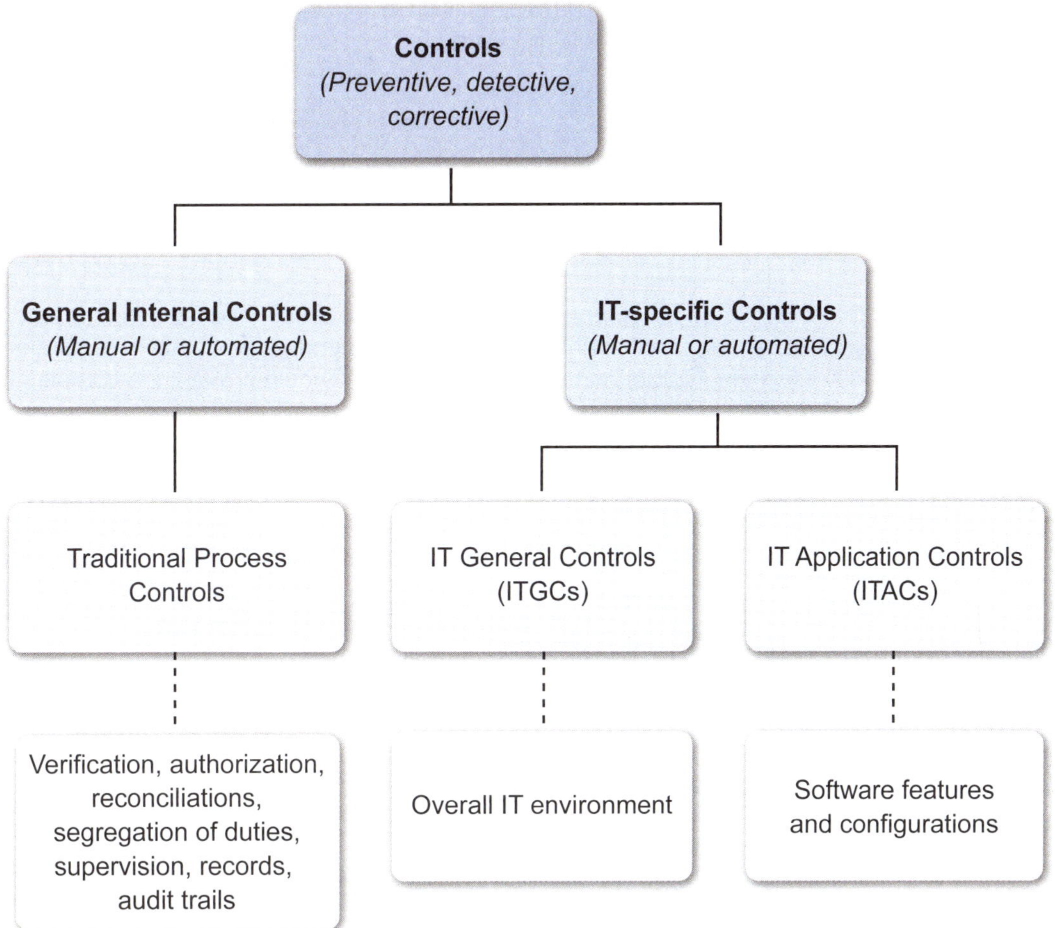


## General Internal Controls

In a SOC 2® examination, management describes the service organization's system in terms of the five components of the COSO Internal Control–Integrated Framework. System-level controls (ie, traditional business process controls) related to processing integrity may include:

- **Control environment:** The control environment sets the tone of an organization, influencing consciousness and ethical behavior. It provides discipline and structure, acting as the foundation for all other components of internal control. The control environment should ensure that management:
    - Demonstrates commitment to integrity and ethical values
    - Exercises its oversight responsibility
    - Establishes structure, authority, and responsibility
    - Demonstrates a commitment to competence
    - Enforces accountability

**Examples of Controls in the Control Environment**

- Established code of conduct for employees and vendors
- Board of Directors has independent oversight
- Organization charts and formal job descriptions
- Employee training and defined job competencies
- Performance evaluations

- **Risk assessment:** In a SOC 2® engagement, management must assess the risks that threaten the achievement of the service organization's principal service commitments and system requirements. Processing integrity risks include internal and external factors that would prevent the completeness, accuracy, or timeliness of data input, processing, output, or storage.

  Regarding processing integrity, risk assessment controls should ensure that management:
  - Specifies processing integrity objectives
  - Assesses risks that threaten processing integrity service commitments and system requirements
  - Identifies threats and vulnerabilities
  - Considers compliance with laws and the potential for fraud
- **Control activities:** Control activities are policies and procedures that help ensure management directives are carried out. They show that management:
  - Mitigates risk through automated and manual controls
  - Segregates duties
  - Selects and develops general and application controls over technology
  - Implements controls through policies and procedures
  - Assesses controls and takes corrective action when necessary

**Examples of Control Activities**

- Performance reviews comparisons, and metrics
- Controls that prevent processing until criteria are met
- Controls that limit access or count physical assets
- Segregation of duties (separate authorization, recording, custody, and comparison functions)

- **Information and communication:** Information and communication relates to how the service organization captures and processes data, and how it communicates information internally or externally. These controls ensure that management:
  - Captures internal and external data
  - Processes data
  - Maintains data quality
  - Communicates processing objectives and internal control, internally and externally
  - Communicates how to report incidents internally and externally

- **Monitoring:** Monitoring relates to activities undertaken to ensure that controls are operating effectively and deficiencies are communicated in time to take corrective action. These activities ensure that management:
  - Performs a mix of continuous and separate evaluations to detect errors and fraud, including internal audits, penetration testing, vulnerability testing, and independent evaluation or certification
  - Assesses the results of monitoring activities in a timely manner and takes corrective action when needed

## IT-specific Controls

Both IT general and application controls are relevant to processing integrity. Service organization management is responsible for designing and implementing controls that prevent, detect, and correct errors and fraud during data input, processing, output, and storage.

- **IT general controls (ITGCs):** Controls that relate to the overall integrity of an information system. There are three categories of ITGCs:

**IT General Controls**

| Access controls | Change controls | Operations controls |
|---|---|---|

  - **Logical access controls:** Controls that prevent, detect, and correct unauthorized access to systems, networks, and data. Examples of logical access controls include limited permissions, access logs, firewalls, antivirus software, user authentication, encryption, vulnerability scans, penetration testing, and intrusion detection.
  - **Change controls:** Controls that prevent, detect, and correct unauthorized changes to systems, applications, configurations, and data.
  - **Operations controls:** Controls that relate to specific aspects of protecting an IT environment, including:
    - Physical security: Controls that prevent, detect, and correct the loss, corruption, destruction, or deterioration of system records because of threats such as burglaries, electrical surges and fires, humidity, or natural disasters.
    - Processing/job scheduling: Controls that ensure the complete, accurate, and authorized processing of data.
    - Backup and recovery: Policies and procedures for securely archiving and storing data and recovering it in case of loss.
    - Incident management: Management's response plans for situations that could threaten or cause loss to system records. Incident response plans include requiring awareness training so that personnel understand how to recognize and report problems or concerns, such as cybersecurity incidents.
    - Business continuity/disaster recovery: Policies and procedures for continuing or restoring operations if a disaster or other event hinders the use of information systems.

| Risks/Threats: Overall Computer Environment | IT General Controls |
|---|---|
| **Not Meeting IT Objectives** | **IT Governance** |
| • Misalignment of IT strategy with business strategy<br>• IT doesn't deliver the value it should | • Strategic guidance<br>• Direction (setting policies & procedures)<br>• Monitoring |
| **Unauthorized Access** | **Logical Access Controls & Cybersecurity** |
| • Cyberattacks<br>• Theft, alteration, or destruction of data<br>• Malicious code<br>• Social engineering<br>• Misuse of data by employees<br>• Incompatible functions (fraud/error) | • Firewalls & user authentication (lockout after 3 unsuccessful attempts)<br>• Encryption of sensitive data<br>• Antivirus software<br>• Security awareness training<br>• Authorization controls |
| **Computer Facility Vulnerabilities** | **Physical Security** |
| • Unauthorized access<br>• Theft, physical destruction of IT assets<br>• Environmental hazards<br>• Fire, heat, humidity, electrical outages | • Locks, ID badges, cameras, etc.<br>• Fire protection (no sprinklers)<br>• Uninterruptible power supply (ie, battery backup) and emergency power supply (ie, generators) |
| **Change Risk** | **Change Controls** |
| • Disruption of operations<br>• Unauthorized or incorrect system alterations<br>• Uninformed IT staff | • Systems development life cycle (SDLC)<br>• Change management<br>• Systems documentation |
| **Disruption of Operations** | **Business Resilience Planning** |
| • Accidental/intentional destruction or unauthorized alteration<br>• Natural disasters | • Back up controls<br>• Disaster recovery planning<br>• Incident response planning<br>• IT risk assessment & mitigation |

- **IT application controls:** Controls related to processes within a specific application. These controls ensure a program performs properly, accepts authorized input, processes that input correctly, and generates output that is relevant and complete. IT application controls related to processing integrity include:

**IT Application Controls**

Input controls | Processing controls | Output controls

  - **Input controls:** Controls that ensure only authorized personnel enter data into the system and that it is done in a complete, accurate, and timely manner. Management designs and implements controls to prevent, detect, and correct errors and fraud within the data input process. Examples of input controls include logic tests and edit checks, such as input formatting rules, field checks, validity checks, limit checks, and check digits.
  - **Processing controls:** Controls that ensure data processing is complete, accurate, and timely, without omission or duplication. Management designs and implements controls to prevent, detect, and correct errors and fraud while data is being processed. Examples of processing controls include transaction or event logs, auto-generated tracking numbers, sequence checks, automated calculations, and error testing.
  - **Output controls:** Controls that ensure outputs are delivered or made available only to authorized personnel, in a complete, accurate, and timely manner. Management designs and implements controls to prevent, detect, and correct errors and fraud while outputs are delivered or stored. Examples of output controls include audit trails, error lists, records of delivery and viewing, data sharing permissions, and archive policies.

| Risks/Threats: Specific Programs | Application Controls | |
|---|---|---|
| **Inappropriate Inputs** | **Input Controls** | |
| • Invalid data<br>• Poor data quality<br>• Incomplete data<br>• Inaccurate data | • Check digit<br>• Validity check<br>• Edit test<br>• Limit test | • Financial total<br>• Record counts<br>• Hash total<br>• Nonfinancial totals |
| **Compromised Processing Integrity** | **Processing Controls** | |
| • Invalid data<br>• Incomplete data<br>• Inaccurate data<br>• Redundant data | • Run-to-run totals<br>• Transaction logs<br>• Prenumbered documents | • Sequence checks<br>• Concurrency control<br>• Periodic system testing |
| **Ineffective Outputs** | **Output Controls** | |
| • Inaccurate and/or incomplete data<br>• Improper disposal<br>• Improper distribution of information | • System testing<br>• Shredders<br>• Distribution lists | |

## Detect Deficiencies in the Suitability of the Design of Controls

In all SOC 2® examinations, a service auditor must obtain evidence that the service organization's controls were suitably designed based on the **trust services criteria**. A service auditor evaluates the suitability of the design in all SOC 2® examinations, but the operating effectiveness of those controls are tested only in a type 2 examination.

When evaluating whether controls are suitably designed, the service auditor may consider each control individually or in combination with other controls. To assess control design in a SOC 2® examination, service auditors must:

- Understand management's process for identifying risks that threaten the achievement of the service organization's principal service commitments and system requirements
- Assess the completeness and accuracy of management's risk assessment
- Perform their own risk assessment
- Evaluate the link between the identified risks and the controls stated in management's description of its system
- Determine whether the controls have been implemented

**Procedures** to evaluate the suitability of the design of controls normally include **reperformance**, **inquiries**, **inspection**, **observation**, **and walkthroughs**. When evaluating the suitability of the design, the service auditor should use professional judgment, **comparing management's controls against identified risks** and the **trust services criteria**. Risks include both those identified by management and the service auditor. The trust services criteria serve as a benchmark for the outcome of controls.

When examining the processing integrity trust services category, the service auditor should consider all relevant **common** and **supplemental criteria**, as well as **additional criteria** specific to processing integrity.

See the Trust Services Criteria exhibit in the Appendix for the detailed common and supplemental criteria. Those criteria are discussed further in the Security chapter.

- Common Criteria
  - **CC1 Control Environment**
  - **CC2 Communication and Information**
  - **CC3 Risk Assessment**
  - **CC4 Monitoring**
  - **CC5 Control Activities**
- Supplemental Criteria
  - **CC6 Logical and Physical Access Controls**
  - **CC7 System Operations**
  - **CC8 Change Management**
  - **CC9 Risk Mitigation**
- Additional Category-Specific Criteria for Processing Integrity
  - **PI1.1** Obtains/generates, uses, and communicates processing objectives.
    - Identifies and communicates functional and nonfunctional system processing requirements and information specifications.

- Defines the data necessary to support a product or service:
  - Definition and purpose of data is available to data users.
  - Definition of data includes:
    - Population of events or instances included in the data set
    - Nature of each element (ie, field)
    - Sources of data
    - Units of measurement for data elements
    - Accuracy, correctness, or precision of measurement
    - Uncertainty or confidence interval inherent in each data element and in the population of those elements
  - Data definition is relevant and complete.
  - Data description identifies the information necessary to understand each data element consistent with both its definition and the intended purpose (ie, metadata) that has not been included in the data.

- **PI1.2** Implements policies and procedures over system inputs, including controls over completeness and accuracy.
  - Defines the characteristics of processing inputs.
  - Inputs are evaluated for compliance with data input requirements.
  - Records of system input activities are created and maintained completely, accurately, and in a timely manner.
- **PI1.3** Implements system processing policies and procedures to achieve objectives (ie, principal service commitments and system requirements in a SOC 2® report).
  - Defines processing specifications.
  - Defines processing activities.
  - Processing errors are detected and corrected in a timely manner.
  - System processing activities are recorded completely, accurately, and in a timely manner.
  - Inputs are complete, accurate, and timely.
- **PI1.4** Implements policies and procedures for delivering output to achieve objectives (ie, principal service commitments and system requirements in a SOC 2® report).
  - Output is protected when stored or delivered to prevent theft, destruction, corruption, or deterioration.
  - Output is distributed or made available only to intended parties.
  - Procedures are in place to ensure output is complete, accurate, and timely.
  - System output activities are recorded and maintained.
- **PI1.5** Implements policies and procedures to store inputs, items in processing, and outputs completely, accurately, and in a timely manner in accordance with system specifications to meet objectives (ie, principal service commitments and system requirements in a SOC 2® report).
  - Stored items are protected to prevent theft, destruction, corruption, or deterioration.
  - Stored records are archived, and archives are protected to prevent theft, destruction, corruption, or deterioration.
  - Procedures are in place to support the complete, accurate, and timely storage of data.
  - System storage activities are recorded and maintained.

In a SOC 2® engagement, a **deficiency in the suitability of the design of controls** means that a control would not achieve the service organization's principal service commitments and system requirements because the control either does not exist or the design is flawed. The only way to correct a deficiency is to change (or add) the control. For this reason, material deficiencies result in a **report modification**, such as a separate paragraph.

**A Deficiency in the Suitability of the Design of a Control Exists When...**

| The control does not exist | The control exists but would not achieve objectives even if performed as designed |
|---|---|

**Detect Deficiencies in the Suitability of the Design of Controls**

User entities require an ERP SaaS developer (service organization) to provide an annual SOC 2® report for the security and processing integrity trust services categories. The ERP system comprises different modules, including an AIS. One of the service organization's principal service commitments and system requirements is that the developed system ensures that only authorized personnel can make additions or deletions to the chart of accounts.

Risk assessments performed by both management and the service auditor identify a risk that *"the AIS module does not prevent unauthorized additions or deletions from the chart of accounts."* Unauthorized changes to the chart of accounts could cause the improper processing of transactions.

The service auditor performs the following procedures to determine if controls are suitably designed to achieve the developer's service commitments and system requirements based, in part, on the processing integrity trust services criteria:

- **Inquiry:** The service auditor asks the developer's coders to explain the built-in controls limiting the personnel who may add or delete accounts. The coders are also asked whether the system generates a report or sends a notification when accounts are added or deleted.
- **Inspection:** The service auditor obtains and reads the AIS module documentation and asks for an example of any reports or notifications that would be generated when an account is added or deleted.

Upon inquiry, the service organization coders state that user entities can select role-based permissions, which would prevent an unauthorized person from changing the chart of accounts. However, the developed system does not generate any reports or notifications when changes are made. The service auditor could not find reference to any system-generated reports within the system documentation.

In this scenario, the service auditor's opinion would include a separate paragraph explaining that some controls regarding inputs are missing. One point of focus under trust services criterion PI1.2 states that records of system inputs should be created and maintained in a complete, accurate, and timely manner. While the AIS system has controls to limit who may change the chart of accounts, there is no report or notification sent when a change is made. Thus, incorrect or unauthorized changes could occur without a monitoring method to detect or correct problems.

## Detect Deviations in the Operating Effectiveness of Controls

In a SOC 2®, type 2 examination, the service auditor performs tests of controls to determine whether the controls operated effectively to achieve the service organization's principal service commitments and system requirements throughout a period. The service auditor's tests of controls and results are included in the report.

Note that a service auditor must first determine whether a control is suitably designed. By definition, a control that is not suitably designed cannot operate effectively.

**A Deviation in the Operating Effectiveness of a Control Exists When...**

| The control is suitably designed but does not operate as expected | The person performing the control does not have authority or is not competent |
| --- | --- |

Evaluating the operating effectiveness of controls requires the service auditor to determine whether:

- The control operated effectively, and
- The evidence provided by the service organization is reliable.

Tests of controls include reperformance, inquiry, inspection, and observation. Walkthroughs may also be performed. The service auditor must use professional judgment to decide whether to test a sample or the entire population. Evidence is reliable if it is accurate, complete, precise, and detailed.

### Detect Deviations in the Operating Effectiveness of Controls

A third-party administrator (TPA) processes workers' compensation medical payments for a large employer. The employer contractually requires the TPA to provide a SOC 2®, type 2 report for the security and processing integrity trust services categories.

In its description, the service organization's management lists the following control to meet the principal service commitments and system requirements:

*"User entity employee's medical invoices that are mailed to the TPA are processed within 10 business days."*

The service auditor performs the following procedures to evaluate the operating effectiveness of the control:

- **Inquiry:** The service auditor asks TPA management how medical invoices are processed when received by mail. In addition, the service auditor inquires whether the TPA has ever been unable to process these invoices within 10 business days.
- **Inspection:** The service auditor asks TPA personnel to run a query showing the date when a medical invoice was received in the mail, the date it was processed, and a calculation of the number of days in between. The service auditor inspects a printout of this query to determine whether the report was complete and accurate. In addition, for a sample of the population, the service auditor inspects the source documents to verify the dates.
- **Reperformance:** For a sample of the population, the service auditor recalculates the number of business days it took the TPA to process the mailed-in medical invoices.

No deviations in the operating effectiveness of controls are found during the tests of controls. The service auditor describes the tests of controls and the results, stating, "No exceptions noted." An unmodified opinion is issued.

# 3.03 Availability

## Business Continuity and Resilience Planning

**Representative Task (Remembering and Understanding):** Recall the scope, purpose, and key considerations for business resiliency, disaster recovery, and business continuity plans.

### Business Continuity

The term "business continuity" refers to a company's ability to keep providing products and services at acceptable levels despite an unexpected disruption. **Business continuity management** is a risk mitigation activity in which management:

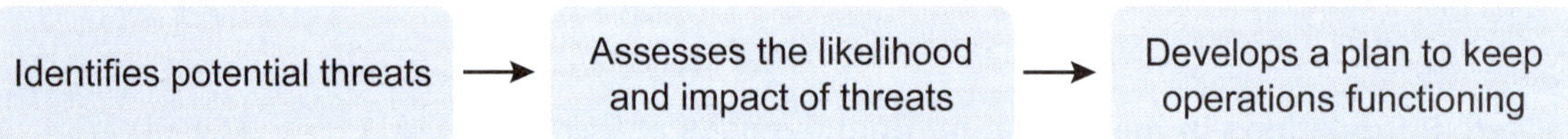


Management should assess the likelihood of and impact of threats by performing the following processes:

- **Risk assessment:** Determine the risks that threaten the entity's objectives. Threats to business operations can come from a range of sources, including government emergency orders, cyberattacks, labor strikes, riots, wars, fires, and natural disasters.
- **Business impact analysis (BIA):** Quantify the impact on time-sensitive business operations, assets, customers, locations, technologies, and suppliers.

A business continuity planning document outlines **critical business operations** and management's predetermined decisions about how to ensure their continuance in an **emergency**. An overall business continuity plan includes the development of **strategies** to respond to different **contingencies**:

**Type of Business Continuity Plans**

| | | |
|---|---|---|
| Disaster recovery | Incident response | Emergency operations |
| Crisis management | Communications | Damage assessment |

**Business Continuity Planning for Natural Disasters**

Coastal regions have a higher incidence of natural disasters, such as hurricanes. While forecasting has improved, the exact landfall location is normally not known until hours before a weather event. There are many steps that should be taken when an organization is under threat of a catastrophe.

Planning begins with traditional risk management strategies, including purchasing insurance to cover physical damage to buildings and other property, as well as loss of income and additional expenses. Purchasing the right amounts and types of insurance is critical to recovery.

Next, internal plans are needed so that personnel understand how to communicate, especially during power outages and interruptions in cell phone or Internet service. Plans should be made to decide who will be responsible for important tasks, both before and after an event. For example, if a hurricane is approaching, what should the IT department be doing to protect assets, networks, and data? What information should the risk management department have on hand? How will the business access the substantial amounts of cash needed to implement plans?

Imagine the worst-case scenario: the business's roof is off, windows are blown out, wires are dangling, and all IT equipment is wet. The business needs to contact its employees, get money from the insurance company, find an alternate work site, purchase new equipment, and reestablish business operations as fast as possible, all while being in a disaster zone.

Without business continuity planning, it would be very difficult and chaotic for a business to spring to action under such circumstances. Identifying key risks and planning far ahead of time could make the difference between business survival and failure.

Management should integrate business continuity planning into every aspect of the organization on an ongoing basis. For IT systems, a business continuity plan should include:

- Written plan
- Insurance
- Teams with assigned roles for both before and after an event
- Team training and awareness programs
- Communication plans
- Alternate facilities, including IT equipment, power, security, desks, supplies
- Backup of the infrastructure platform, operating system, data, and applications
- Copies of technical and operations manuals
- Test schedule and methods

Plan testing should occur on both a scheduled and as-needed basis. If natural disasters or other threats normally occur during a certain part of the year, testing before those seasons should be part of the routine plan. Testing should be realistic and progressive. The goal of each test is to find deficiencies, which are then resolved before moving on to the next test.

**Progressive Steps to Test Plans**

*(Move to the next step only when identified deficiencies have been resolved)*

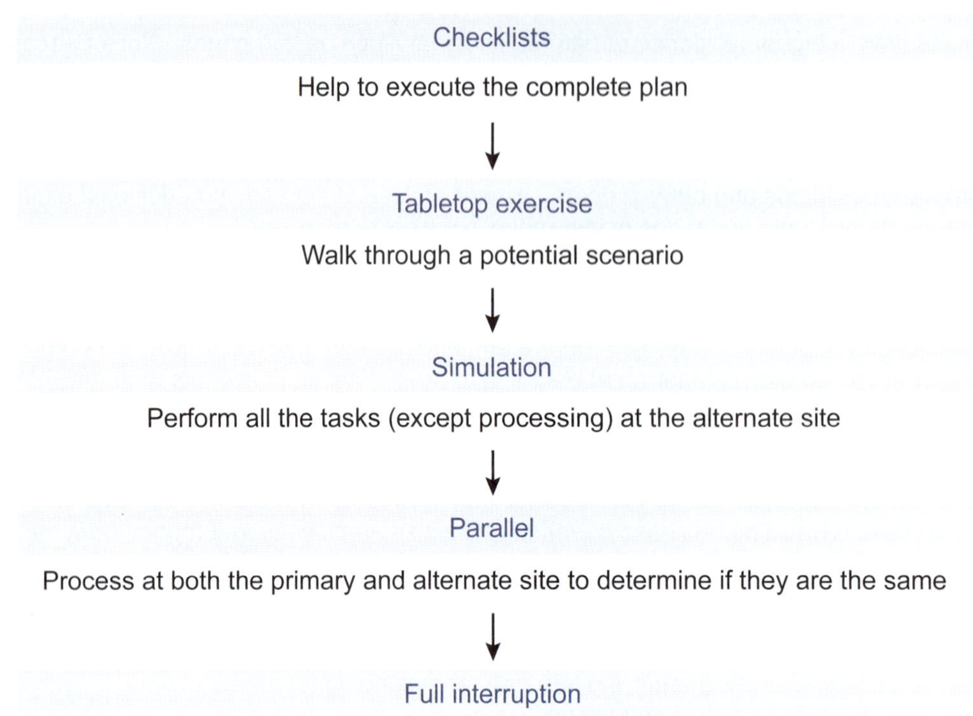


## Business Resilience

Business resilience goes beyond business continuity planning, with a more dynamic, strategic approach to risk management. It addresses not just physical risks but also those that affect the organization's vision, including operational, market, and brand reputation risks. **Resilience** is an organization's ability to expect and prepare for risk, while also having the flexibility to **adapt** to a quickly changing business environment. Resilient organizations devise actionable plans to survive, recover from, and even thrive in the wake of unforeseen events.

**Business Resilience**

Consider the sudden and unexpected COVID-19 pandemic of 2020, which caused many businesses to close because of government orders or a change in consumer appetites. Grocery stores, for example, had to expand their strategies to ensure the safety of in-store shoppers while also offering online ordering and contactless deliveries.

Many merchants, such as Walmart and Amazon, already had online sales platforms and delivery structures in place. They could quickly shift the focus of their workforce, respond to changing product demands, and create ad campaigns to accommodate unusual circumstances. Smaller grocers had to be agile, implementing new platforms to survive. When vaccines were developed and approved, many regional grocery stores with pharmacies negotiated to be the first in their communities to offer the shots, providing consumers an incentive to return to their stores.

## Business Resilience Planning

Business resilience planning focuses on a **long-term perspective** and complements business continuity planning, which is more short-term or situational. Management understands the details of each crisis and uses a well-rehearsed response to deal with problems as quickly as possible. To achieve effective resilience, organizations must strike a balance between six critical areas:

### Financial Resilience

A flexible capital position that allows the business to endure unexpected changes in costs or revenue.

### Operational Resilience

Operations that can adjust to changes in supply or demand without compromising quality. Businesses that are resilient continue to function normally under external pressures.

### Organizational Resilience

A positive work environment that values differences and encourages everyone to contribute their best. Resilient businesses minimize workforce changes, prioritize employee retention, and impose high performance expectations.

### Reputational Resilience

Actions that align with defined organizational values. Reputational resiliency includes communicating about, and being conscious of, societal expectations. Management must be open to making adjustments in response to constructive criticism.

### Business Model Resilience

An agile business strategy that quickly adjusts to technology, market trends, or regulatory changes.

### Technological Resilience

Infrastructure that can adapt to cyber threats while also keeping up with customer needs and competition. Utilize high-quality data. Establish continuity and disaster recovery plans.

## Benefits of Business Continuity and Resilience

Management plans that implement effective continuity and resilience can achieve positive outcomes in the face of adversity. Continuity and resilience, when combined, enable organizations to:

- Reduce the risk of loss
- Mitigate threats
- Recover from disruptions
- Improve reputation

## Disaster Recovery

Disaster recovery refers to regaining functions and access to IT infrastructure following an event, such as a natural disaster or cyberattack. Disaster recovery normally requires **data** and computer processing to be **duplicated** in a place that was not affected by the disaster.

Major components of a disaster recovery strategy include:

- **Disaster recovery team:** A group that develops, implements, and manages the disaster recovery effort. Plans should outline the roles and responsibilities of each team member, with alternates named in case a team member is not available.

  In case of a disaster, communication with other team members, employees, vendors, and customers is essential. The communication methods chosen should assume that phone and Internet services will not be available. The team should be trained, and the plan should be rehearsed.

- **Risk assessment:** Evaluate potential threats to the organization and their impact. Determine what steps and resources will be required to resume operations after each type of event. For example, how will the recovery team respond in case of a cyberattack versus a natural disaster?
- **Identification of critical assets:** A good disaster recovery plan outlines the systems, applications, and data that are most critical for business continuity, as well as the steps needed to recover data. The assets should be listed in order from the most critical to the least critical.
- **Backups:** Determine what data needs backup (or relocation), who will back it up, and how. Include a recovery point objective that specifies the backup frequency and a recovery time objective that limits disaster downtime. The disaster recovery plan is affected by how much downtime a business can tolerate and how regularly its data is backed up.
- **Tests and optimization:** The recovery team should regularly test and adjust its approach to accommodate changing threats and business needs.

### Key Disaster Recovery Objectives

**Recovery Point Objective (RPO) vs. Recovery Time Objective (RTO)**

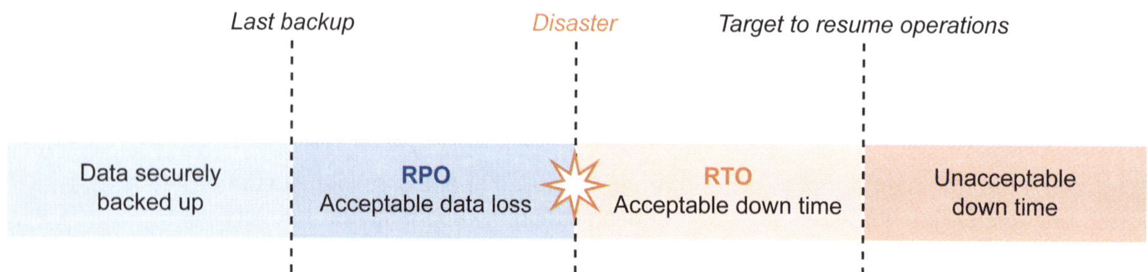


A disaster recovery plan includes essential parameters that specify the amount of data loss an entity can sustain and how long it can afford for its systems to remain down:

- **Recovery Point Objective (RPO):** RPO is the target that a business sets for the maximum *quantity of data* it can tolerate losing. This parameter's duration is measured in time, from the moment of failure to the most recent reliable data backup. For instance, the RPO is 24 hours if an organization currently has a failure, and the most recent full data backup was 24 hours ago.
- **Recovery Time Objective (RTO):** RTO is the target set by a business for the maximum time that should elapse between a system failure or data loss and the point when operations are fully restored.

The RTO and RPO should be lower (ie, nearer to zero) for critical applications. Note that the cost of setting up RTO and RPO for such applications can increase as the targets become stricter.

## Disaster Recovery Sites

A **disaster recovery site** is a secondary location used to restore an organization's IT infrastructure and critical operations when a disaster has affected its primary center. The disaster recovery site should be in a different geographical area to help ensure that a disaster hitting the first site will not also affect the second. Operations can continue at the secondary site until it is safe to return to the primary site or a new permanent location.

**Disaster Recovery Site Options**

| | Cold Site | Warm Site | Hot Site | Parallel Site |
|---|---|---|---|---|
| **Off-Site Location** | Yes | Yes | Yes | Yes |
| **Equipment at Location** | No | Yes | Yes | Yes |
| **Connectivity at Location** | No | Yes | Yes | Yes |
| **Active Before Disaster** | No | No | Yes | Yes |
| **Staff at Location** | No | No | Minimum | Maximum |
| **Recovery Time** | Weeks/months | Hours/days | Seconds/minutes | Seconds |
| **Cost Range** | $ Low | $$ Medium | $$$ High | $$$$ Very high |

**Cold site:** Cold sites are backup facilities **without hardware**. A cold site is an empty office with power, cooling, air conditioning, and communication equipment only. Cold locations are the **least expensive** recovery sites. Because a cold site has no preinstalled equipment, it **takes a long time** to set up infrastructure (ie, computers, loading of data) before operations can resume. In a disaster, IT staff must move and activate servers to take over the principal site's workload. If the disaster destroys the equipment, the business will have to buy new equipment and have it delivered to the cold site.

**Warm site:** Warm sites are the second least expensive type of disaster recovery site, falling between hot and cold. A warm site has **partial equipment** and network connectivity with no staff. It cannot perform as well as the primary site because it is not fully equipped or is not equipped with the same hardware. A warm site, therefore, has a lower operational capacity than a primary site. Daily or weekly data synchronization between the primary and secondary sites is needed, so there may be data loss or other issues if the primary site is damaged. A warm site is best suited to businesses that have **noncritical data**, where a brief downtime will not cause a major problem.

**Hot site:** Hot sites are backup facilities that **mimic the primary production core but are minimally staffed**. A hot site has the hardware, software, and network connectivity to execute a near-real-time backup or replication of sensitive data. The production workload can be transferred to a hot site within seconds or minutes, ensuring minimal downtime without data loss. To ensure data synchronization between sites, a hot site must be online and uninterruptible. Hot sites are **expensive** to support. To be effective, this form of disaster recovery site should be **far away from the production core**. This reduces the risk of a hot site suffering from the same disaster as the primary site.

**Parallel site (mirrored server):** A parallel or mirrored site has a **replicated server**, processes the same data as the production server, and has a **full staff**. The site runs in real time and can take over operations in a matter of seconds. The goal of a parallel site is to ensure the continuous delivery of **critical data or services**, such as those needed by government or medical applications. It is the **most expensive** disaster recovery choice.

**Mobile disaster recovery sites:** Mobile disaster recovery sites, often set up in trucks or trailers, are hot sites on wheels. Mobile units can be driven to (or away from) disaster areas and equipped with the technology needed to limit downtime.

**Cloud-based disaster recovery solutions:** In a cloud solution, the business outsources its disaster recovery resources to a vendor. All data is mirrored at the cloud provider, which manages the physical location and infrastructure. Cloud options can be inexpensive; however, as with any outsourced technology and services, management should require a service level agreement (SLA) and SOC or compliance examinations.

## Business Impact Analysis

**Representative Task (Remembering and Understanding):** Summarize steps in a business impact analysis.

A **business impact analysis (BIA)** is a systematic process for evaluating the potential consequences of a disruption in **critical business functions** caused by a disaster, accident, or emergency. A BIA is an essential part of any organization's business continuity plan.

Management should complete an impact analysis regularly and base it on the **worst-case scenario**. Using **outside consultants** is helpful to get an impartial perspective.

The **five phases** of a BIA are:

**Five Phases of Business Impact Analysis**

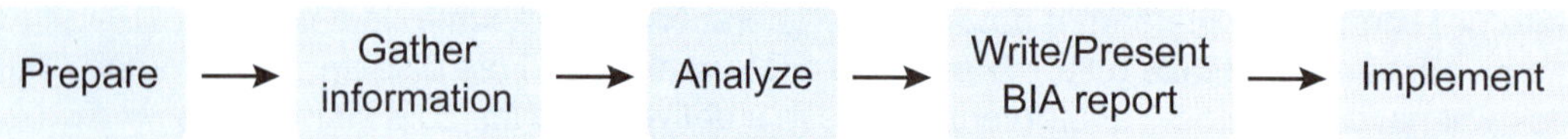


**Prepare:** Identify stakeholders, usually C-level executives, and secure their support. Define objectives and goals; this includes determining whether the BIA is for the entire organization or a particular department. Establish the BIA project team by involving internal staff and external consultants. Appoint a project manager and define the roles and responsibilities of the team members. Draft an initial project plan and review it with the stakeholders.

**Gather information:** The BIA team identifies key business processes and asks process leads/managers to fill out a survey, answer inquiries, or attend workshops. They should gather information about:

- Departments and physical locations
- Process names and descriptions
- All inputs and outputs of the process
- Maximum tolerable downtime
- Operational and financial impact

- Legal/regulatory compliance issues/fines
- History of prior disruptions and how they were managed

Once the survey responses are gathered, the BIA team combines them into tables and schedules for easy visualization and understanding.

**Analyze:** The BIA team analyzes each business process to figure out whether it is a **critical business function (CBF).**

- Rank business processes from the most critical to least critical.
- Identify the personnel and technology resources needed to recover and operate each process (at both normal and bare minimum capacities).
- Establish a baseline **RTO** to restore the business to an acceptable level.
- Identify both the upstream and downstream impact of the disruption.
- Quantify the process outage in terms of lost time and money.

**Write and present the BIA report:** The team should create the BIA report using a template, such as NIST SP 800-34. The BIA report document is based on the information gathered and analyzed to help management make implementation decisions.

A BIA report typically includes:

- Executive summary
- Objectives and scope
- Methods used to discover and analyze information
- Detailed findings for each department/process
  - Criticality ranking
  - Tolerable loss of downtime (ie, RTO)
  - Tolerable levels of loss (ie, RPO)
  - A comparison of the cost of loss against the estimated cost to recover the process
- Recommendations for a recovery plan (personnel, technology, and process)

The BIA report and key findings should be presented to management. This presentation usually addresses recovery time, costs/loss, and practices for mitigating major risks.

**Implementation, training, and testing:** The last step in the BIA process is to implement management's decisions. This includes training employees and performing tests to find out if there are any deficiencies. If a deficiency exists, the BIA team should reassess its recommendations, and amend the report.

**Benefits of Performing a Business Impact Analysis**

| | | |
|---|---|---|
| Provides a complete picture of business processes and their vulnerabilities in one place | Identifies and prioritizes critical business functions | Determines RTO and RPO |
| Serves as a reference guide to make and implement management's decisions | Quantifies the downtime in terms of costs | Provides solutions for disaster recovery |

# Mirroring, Replication, and Backup

**Representative Task (Remembering and Understanding):** Explain the objectives of mirroring and replication.

## Mirroring

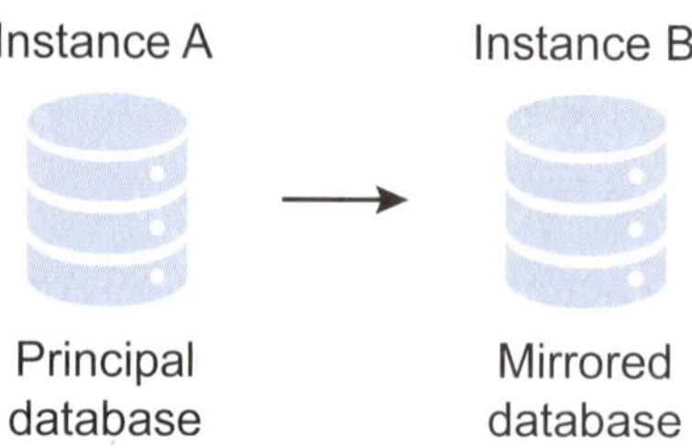


Mirroring, also known as shadowing, involves two copies of a database that are kept on **separate machines**. During mirroring, only one copy, the **principal database**, is available for use. Updates to the principal database are copied to the **mirrored database**. If a primary server fails or is offline for maintenance, the system can automatically **fail over** to the mirrored database.

Mirroring requires the immediate reperformance of update, insert, and delete operations in the mirrored database that have been committed in the principal database. A transaction cannot commit in fully secure mode until the log records for the transaction have been written to disk on the mirror. **Distributed databases are not supported** by mirroring. A distributed database is a database that stores data on multiple physical or virtual servers, possibly in different geographical locations.

## Replication

**Replicating Data and Data Objects**

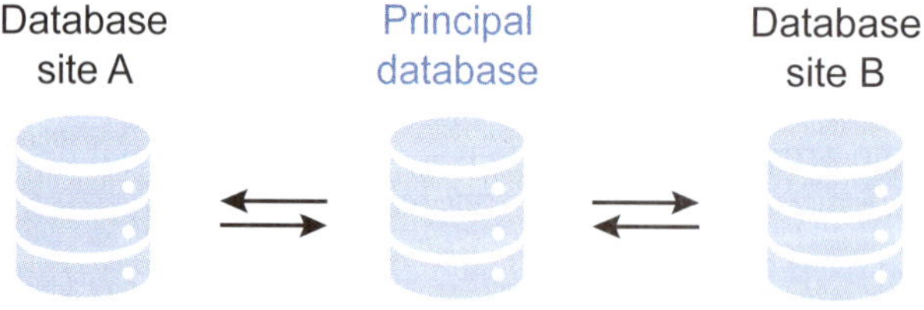


Replication involves maintaining multiple copies of **data and database objects** on different databases that may be located in multiple geographical regions. File servers are a classic example of replication because they are replicated across continents so that users can download a file from the closest location, thus avoiding network delays and slow response. Replication speeds up the execution of parallel commands and can support distributed databases.

**Mirroring vs. Replication**

| | Mirroring | Replication |
|---|---|---|
| **Definition** | Copy of a database on a separate machine | Multiple copies of data and database objects |
| **Target** | Entire database | Only data and database objects |
| **Location** | Different machine or site | Different databases |
| **Distributed Database** | Not supported | Supported |
| **Cost** | $$$ Very expensive | $ Inexpensive |

When a database is duplicated on a different machine, the original database is referred to as the principal database and the copied database is the mirror. Replication is the duplication of data and database objects in multiple locations to enhance the distribution database's performance. Replication was designed for distributed databases, while mirroring does not support distributed environments.

## Backup

Data backup, mirroring, and replication are often confused terms. These processes are related but not the same. Mirroring and replication focus on business continuity, which is the continuous operation of critical business functions following a disaster.

Backups, whether manual or automated, are performed regularly, creating **save points** for all data on the organization's production servers. In case of data loss, these save points can be restored, but the data generated between the save points can be lost. Data can be backed up on different devices and in separate places, both on premises and in the cloud. Certain physical media, such as disks or magnetic tapes, can be used for long-term data backup.

Data backups can take many hours; therefore, businesses schedule them at night or on weekends to minimize production system downtime. Backups are a useful approach to protecting data and are ideal for the **long-term storage** of **vast amounts** of **static data**. Many industries are required to keep long-term records in order to comply with mandatory **retention periods**.

The risk of data loss can be minimized by performing backups on a schedule and on different media. For example, under the **grandfather-father-son method**, backups are performed daily, weekly, and monthly using a mix of digital sources and media types.

**Grandfather-Father-Son Data Backup Method**

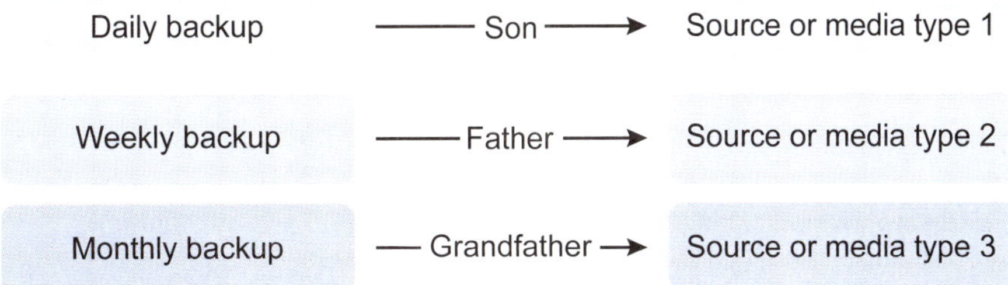


A process should be in place to monitor backups for errors. Management should establish criteria for determining whether personnel should restart the backup process or rerun it at the next scheduled time. A pattern of repeated backup errors may call for further investigation.

# Backup Types

**Representative Task (Application):** Determine the appropriateness of the organization's data backup types (eg, full, incremental, differential), including recovery considerations.

**Data Backup Types**

| Full | Incremental | Differential |
|---|---|---|

**Full backup:** Full backups are copies of an entire data set. This is the ideal backup strategy because it restores data quickly and easily. However, full backups are resource intensive and time-consuming compared with other data backup methods. Full backups require substantial space and could disrupt operations. For this reason, they are normally performed at scheduled intervals with incremental or differential backups in between.

| Full Backup Advantages | Full Backup Disadvantages |
|---|---|
| • Easy to store and manage<br>• Fastest restoration after a disaster | • Backups are slow<br>• Takes a lot of storage space<br>• Resource intensive<br>• If compromised, everything is lost (need additional safeguards) |

**Incremental backup:** In an incremental backup, only the data created or modified **since the last full or incremental backup** is saved. In contrast to using only full backups, which copy the entire data set to storage, an occasional full backup can be performed with incremental backups in between. If restoration is needed, the full backup is loaded first, followed by the incremental backups in the same order as they were saved.

**Incremental Backup Method**

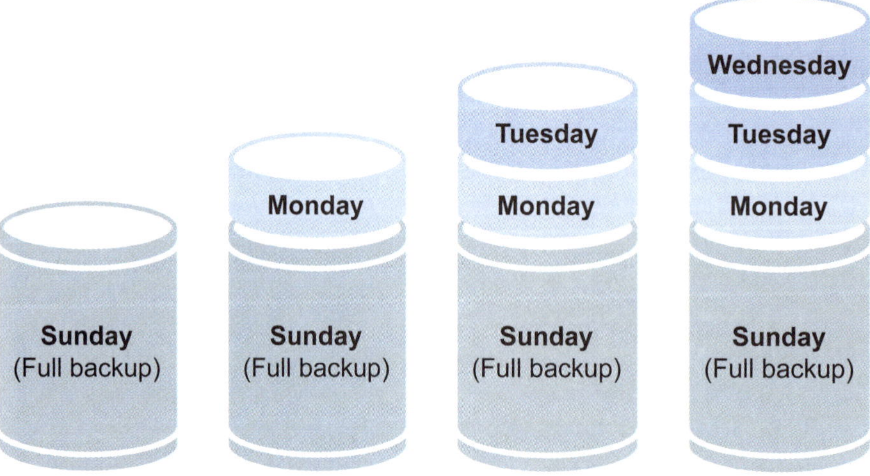


Restore = Full backup + Increments (in order added)

For example, one could perform a full backup once a week, perhaps on a Sunday when employees are using the fewest resources. Then any changes made to files on Monday through Saturday could be backed up incrementally.

| Incremental Backup Advantages | Incremental Backup Disadvantages |
| --- | --- |
| • Fast backup of increments | • Longer restore time |
| • Less storage needed | • Restore must be completed in correct order |
| • Can be run frequently | • Each increment must be backed up correctly |

**Differential backup:** A differential backup combines a full backup and incremental backup. Differential backups begin by functioning similarly to incremental backups. However, while an incremental backup contains only those files that have changed since the last increment, under the differential method each increment backs up all the changes since the last full backup. Thus, the differential method requires more storage than the incremental method.

**Differential Backup Method**

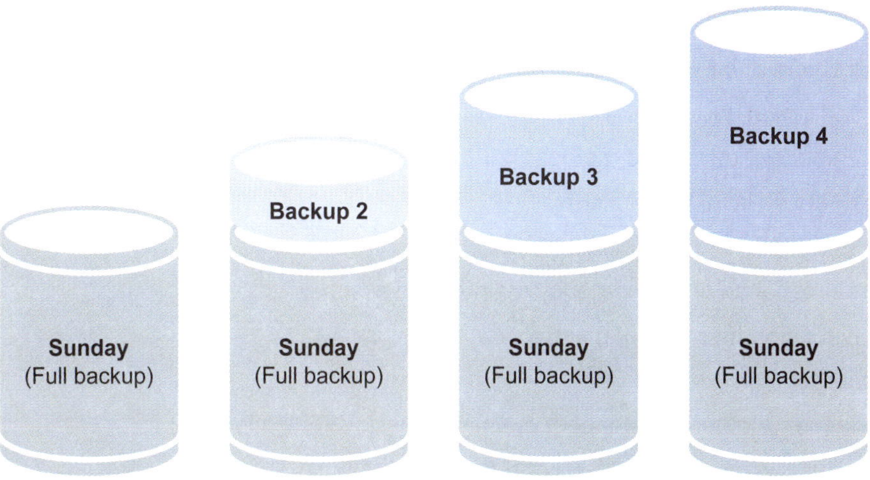


Restore = Full backup + Last differential

For example, on Monday, the backup may contain only the files that have changed since Sunday. On Tuesday, the backup would also include any files that have changed since Sunday (ie, both Monday and Tuesday), and so on until the next full backup.

| Differential Backup Advantages | Differential Backup Disadvantages |
| --- | --- |
| • Restoration is more efficient than incremental | • Longer restore time than full backup |
| • Less storage needed than performing full backups | • More storage than incremental backups |
| • Middle-ground solution | |

# System Availability

**Representative Task (Remembering and Understanding):** Recall measures of system availability (eg, agreed service time, downtime).

System availability refers to the ability of an IT service to perform its agreed function when required. Requirements regarding system availability are specified by business process owners (eg, management) or through contractual agreements (eg, service level agreements).

A **service level agreement (SLA)** defines the details of a service to be delivered by a third-party vendor (external SLA) or IT department (internal SLA). SLAs specify the expectations (eg, objectives, scope) for the availability, usage, and performance of the service, including concurrent users, capacity, processing, and storage requirements, the responsibilities of each party, and any penalties for not meeting service level requirements.

SLAs may address one or multiple services. Key components of an external SLA include:

- Description of the services provided
- Roles and responsibilities of the service provider
- Duration and scope of service
- Exceptions and limitations
- Definition of important terms and metrics
- Agreed upon service level targets/KPIs
- Support hours and contact methods
- Scheduled maintenance and emergency maintenance
- Criteria for evaluation (frameworks)
- Incident and problem management
- SOC, compliance, or other independent examinations or certifications
- Pricing models and charges
- Compensation for downtime

**Evaluating Availability in SLAs**

An examination of controls and evidence related to availability focuses primarily on management's description of its requirements, SLAs, or other contractual obligations.

It is the responsibility of management to ensure that contractual agreements, such as SLAs, meet the needs of the business. A helpful way of thinking about SLAs is to consider the four P's:

- **Promises:** What are the guarantees related to services provided by the service organization? Examples include uptime guarantees, support response time, and maintenance windows.
- **Provisioning:** Specify how servers, processing, storage, and other resources are allocated (ie, provisioned) and used. This helps provide guidance regarding how users interact with services, how those services integrate with other platforms, and the availability, security, and performance of service-provided data.

- **Penalties:** SLAs and contracts may outline specific penalties or reimbursements for loss of availability. For example, a cloud provider may offer 99.9% availability for their cloud platform, which equates to about 20 minutes of downtime per month. Downtime beyond that may involve credits toward service.
- **Processes:** The complexity of cloud-based arrangements means that both the level of control over the cloud environment (eg, private, hybrid, public) and the management of services provided must be considered. For example, availability considerations should include a process for managing services (ie, deciding on a maintenance window and change management processes) and managing contractual breaches or complaints.

The basic calculation for service availability, as defined by the Information Technology Infrastructure Library (ITIL), is:

**Availability percentage**

$$\text{Availability (\%)} = \frac{(\text{Agreed service time} - \text{Downtime})}{\text{Agreed service time}}$$

**Agreed service time:** The expected time the service will be in operation (ie, **uptime**). If an SLA specifies users must have access to a cloud-based system from 7:00 a.m. to 7:00 p.m. during the workweek, the agreed service time is 12 hours, or 43,200 seconds, per day. The SLA specifies the agreed service time measurement granularity (eg, hours, minutes, seconds).

**Downtime:** The time during the agreed service time that the service is not available. Customers usually receive compensation for downtime, either through time added to billing periods or monetary credits.

**Average downtime:** The mean amount of time a system is unavailable during downtimes.

**Outage occurrence rate:** The frequency at which unavailability occurs.

**Mean time to recover (MTTR):** The average time to restore after an outage.

Minor differences in availability percentages can make a significant difference in downtime. For example, with 99.999% availability, the downtime is 5 minutes. If availability drops below 99%, downtime can rise to 3 days per year. A system that is unavailable 3 days per year could cause a major disruption to operations. Vendors advertise (and customers require) SLAs with service uptime guarantees of 99.999% (referred to as "**five nines**").

Good availability statistics do not guarantee good customer outcomes. Beware of the "watermelon effect," where a service provider meets the measuring goal but cannot support consumer outcomes; the service metrics are positive (green), but despite that outward success, the underlying results are negative (red).

For example, an Internet streaming service may have 99.999% weekly availability (5 minutes of downtime). However, during a popular event like the Super Bowl game, even a downtime small enough to meet availability requirements could be upsetting for customers.

**System Availability: Watermelon Effect**

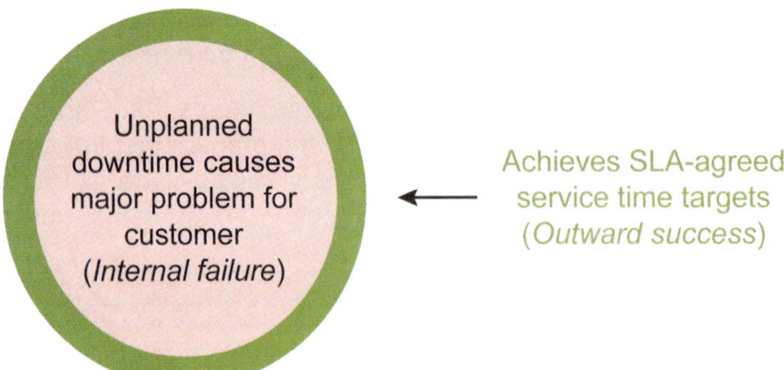


## Planned Downtime Controls

A certain amount of downtime is inevitable, but setting up informed downtime for planned maintenance can minimize the interruptions to system operations caused by unplanned downtimes. In addition, system or service unavailability is sometimes necessary, as a business may not have the resources to ensure continuous service delivery.

**High-availability services**, such as those associated with security or critical infrastructure, rely on an ability to continue operations even during planned downtime of equipment. Strategies to reduce unavailability during planned downtimes include:

- Staggering downtime among different processing nodes or facilities
- Running systems or processes on backup/redundant equipment

# SOC 2® Examination Procedures: Availability

**Representative Task (Analysis):** Detect deficiencies in the suitability of the design and deviations in the operation of controls related to a service organization's availability service commitments and system requirements in a SOC 2® engagement using the Trust Services Criteria.

**SOC 2® engagements were previously discussed in the SOC chapter. It would be helpful to review that content along with this representative task, which focuses on a service auditor's procedures to obtain sufficient appropriate evidence.**

When an organization **outsources** business functions or technology, it must have a governance and monitoring process in place to manage third-party risk. The organization may contractually require the vendor **(service organization)** to supply a **SOC 2® report** from an independent CPA. The contract or service level agreement (SLA) usually outlines the service organization's principal service commitments and system requirements. These are the promises and representations the service organization makes to its customers about its services.

As covered in the SOC chapter, SOC 2® examinations provide **reasonable assurance** about security, *availability*, processing integrity, confidentiality, or privacy. A user entity receiving a SOC 2® report must have **sufficient knowledge** to understand and assess its contents.

In a SOC 2® examination, **availability** refers to the **accessibility of information** used in the service organization's system, including the ability to provide products or services to customers. Of particular concern is whether the service organization's system includes **suitably designed controls** to keep the system available for operations, monitoring, and maintenance. In a SOC 2®, type 2 examination, the service auditor performs tests of controls to determine if the controls **operated effectively** throughout a period.

**Examples of Service Organizations That May Need a SOC2® Report for Availability**

| IaaS, PaaS, and SaaS providers | Cellular and Internet service providers | Website and email providers | Managed IT services |
|---|---|---|---|

## Detect Deficiencies in the Suitability of the Design of Controls

In all SOC 2® examinations, a service auditor must obtain evidence that the service organization's controls were suitably designed based on the **trust services criteria**. A service auditor evaluates the operating effectiveness of controls only in a type 2 examination.

When evaluating whether controls are suitably designed, the service auditor may consider each control individually or in combination with other controls. To assess the suitability of the design of controls in a SOC 2® examination, service auditors must:

- Understand management's process for identifying risks that threaten the achievement of the service organization's principal service commitments and system requirements
- Assess the completeness and accuracy of management's risk assessment
- Perform an independent risk assessment
- Evaluate the link between the identified risks and the controls stated in management's description of its system
- Determine whether management has implemented the controls

**Procedures** to evaluate the suitability of the design of controls normally include **reperformance, inquiries, inspection, observations, and walkthroughs**. When evaluating the suitability of the design, the service auditor should use professional judgment to **compare management's controls with identified risks** and the **trust services criteria**. Risks include both those identified by management and the service auditor. The trust services criteria serve as a benchmark for the outcome of controls.

When examining the availability trust services category, the service auditor should consider all relevant **common** and **supplemental** criteria, as well as the **additional category-specific criteria** for availability:

See the Trust Services Criteria exhibit in the Appendix for the detailed common and supplemental criteria, which are discussed further in the Security chapter.

- Common Criteria
  - **CC1 Control Environment**
  - **CC2 Communication and Information**
  - **CC3 Risk Assessment**
  - **CC4 Monitoring**
  - **CC5 Control Activities**
- Supplemental Criteria
  - **CC6 Logical and Physical Access Controls**
  - **CC7 System Operations**
  - **CC8 Change Management**

    *Additional Point of Focus for Availability*
    - **CC8.1** System resilience is considered when designing systems. Resilience is tested during development to help ensure the ability to respond to, recover from, and restore operations after significant disruptions.
  - **CC9 Risk Mitigation**
- Additional Category-Specific Criteria for Availability
  - **A1.1 Infrastructure and Capacity Controls**
    - Maintains, monitors, and evaluates current processing capacity and use of system components (infrastructure, data, and software) to manage capacity demand and to enable the implementation of additional capacity.
      - **Measures Current Usage:** Use of system components is measured to establish a baseline for capacity management and to monitor or evaluate the risk of impaired availability because of capacity constraints.
      - **Forecasts Capacity:** The expected average and peak use of system components is forecasted and compared to system capacity and tolerances. Forecasting considers system resilience and capacity in the event of the failure of system components.
      - **Makes Changes Based on Forecasts:** Change management processes are started when forecasted usage exceeds capacity tolerances.
  - **A1.2 Backup and Replication Controls**
    - Authorizes, designs, develops (or acquires), implements, operates, approves, maintains, and monitors environmental protections, software, data backup processes, and recovery infrastructure.
      - **Identifies Environmental Threats:** As part of risk assessment, management identifies environmental threats that could impair the availability of the system, including threats resulting from weather, failure of control systems, electrical discharge, fire, and water.
      - **Designs Detection Measures:** Implements detection measures to identify anomalies that could result from environmental threats.
      - **Implements and Maintains Environmental Protection Mechanisms:** Implements and supports environmental protection mechanisms to prevent and mitigate environmental events.
      - **Implements Alerts to Analyze Anomalies:** Implements environmental threat alerts that notify personnel to conduct analysis.
      - **Responds to Environmental Threat Events:** Procedures are in place to respond to environmental threat events, and those procedures are evaluated periodically. They include automatic mitigation systems (ie, uninterruptible power and generators).

- **Communicates and Reviews Detected Environmental Threat Events:** Detected environmental threat events are communicated and reviewed by personnel or vendors, and actions are taken when necessary.
- **Determines Data Requiring Backup:** Data is evaluated to determine whether backup is required.
- **Performs Data Backup:** Procedures are in place for backing up data, monitoring to detect backup failures, and taking corrective action when failures occur.
- **Addresses Offsite Storage:** Backup data is stored at a location far enough away from the principal storage location that it is unlikely a security or environmental event will threaten both sets of data.
- **Implements Alternate Processing Infrastructure:** Measures are implemented to migrate processing to alternate infrastructure if normal processing infrastructure becomes unavailable. Measures include geographic separation, redundancy, and failover capabilities.
- **Considers Data Recoverability:** Identifies threats to data recoverability (ie, ransomware attacks) that could impair availability of the system and related data. Implements mitigation procedures.

- **A1.3 Business Continuity and Backup Testing**
  - Tests recovery plan procedures supporting system recovery.
    - **Implements Business Continuity Testing:** Business continuity plans are tested periodically to test the ability to respond to, recover from, and resume operations after significant disruptions. Testing includes:
      - Development of test scenarios based on the likelihood and magnitude of threats
      - Consideration of system components and vendors that can impair availability
      - Scenarios that consider the potential lack of availability of key personnel or vendors
      - Continuity plans are revised based on test results
  - **Tests Integrity and Completeness of Backup Data:** The integrity and completeness of backup data is tested periodically.

In a SOC 2® engagement, a deficiency in the suitability of the design of controls means that the controls would not provide reasonable assurance of achieving the service organization's principal service commitments and system requirements because a particular control does not exist or the design is flawed; the only way to correct the deficiency is to add (or change) the control. Material deficiencies result in a report modification, such as a separate paragraph.

**A Deficiency in the Suitability of the Design of a Control Exists When...**

| The control does not exist | The control exists but would not achieve objectives even if performed as designed |
|---|---|

### Detect Deficiencies in the Suitability of the Design of Controls

An Internet service provider (ISP) sells Internet services to health care providers. Because of the nature of medical emergencies, the Internet service must have high availability to ensure the health care providers can access their cloud-based software and data.

Every six months, the ISP provides its users with a SOC 2® report to give assurance for the availability trust service category. Risk assessments performed by management and the service auditor have identified a risk that *"Planned downtimes interrupt the user entity's ability to connect to the Internet."*

A point of focus under A1.2 states: ***"Implements Alternate Processing Infrastructure:*** *Measures are implemented for migrating processing to alternate infrastructure in the event normal processing infrastructure becomes unavailable. Measures may include geographic separation, redundancy, and failover capabilities for components."*

To determine whether the planned downtime controls are suitably designed to achieve the ISP's principal service commitments and system requirements based on the availability trust services criteria, the service auditor performs the following procedures:

- **Inquiry:** The service auditor asks management to explain how planned downtimes are scheduled, their purpose, and how the customer's service is maintained.
- **Inspection:** The service auditor reviews the SLA, internal policy and procedure manuals, planned downtime logs, alerts, and the settings in the monitoring software.

According to the SLA, the ISP staggers planned downtimes between multiple geographic locations. When one system is down, that system automatically fails over to a redundant system in a different geographic location. The ISP uses software to monitor its primary and backup servers.

Upon evaluating the connection between the identified risks, controls, and the trust services criteria, the service auditor determines that the ISP's controls are suitably designed to achieve the ISP's principal service commitments and system requirements.

## Detect Deviations in the Operating Effectiveness of Controls

In a SOC 2®, type 2 examination, the service auditor performs tests of controls to determine whether controls operated effectively to achieve the service organization's principal service commitments and system requirements throughout a period. The service auditor's tests of controls and results are included in the report.

Note that the service auditor must first determine that a control is suitably designed. By definition, a control that is not suitably designed cannot operate effectively.

**A Deviation in the Operating Effectiveness of a Control Exists When...**

| The control is suitably designed but does not operate as expected | The person performing the control does not have authority or is not competent |
|---|---|

Evaluating the operating effectiveness of controls requires the service auditor to determine whether:

- The control operated effectively, and
- The evidence provided by the service organization is reliable.

Tests of controls include reperformance, inquiry, inspection, and observation. Walkthroughs may also be performed. The service auditor must use professional judgment to decide whether to test a sample or the entire population. Evidence is reliable if it is accurate, complete, precise, and detailed.

**Detect Deviations in the Operating Effectiveness of Controls**

In the scenario above, the ISP asked the service auditor to perform a type 2 engagement. To test the operating effectiveness of the ISP's controls regarding automatic failovers during planned downtimes, the service auditor performed the following additional procedures:

- **Inspection:** The service auditor obtained logs containing information about downtimes reported by customers. A sample of the customer outage reports was compared to the ISP's maintenance logs. The comparison was performed to determine if there was a correlation between planned downtime and customer loss of service.

While the service auditor found controls were suitably designed, many of the customer loss-of-service complaints corresponded with the dates and times of the ISP's planned downtimes. Upon further inquiry, the service auditor learned there was a communication problem in which customers' routers were not set up properly and the failover IP addresses were blocked by firewalls.

The ISP's description of its system listed several complementary user entity controls. One such complementary control is that the user entity is responsible for the setup of its own routers. Thus, although there were connectivity problems, they were not the result of a deviation in the operating effectiveness of the ISP's controls. The failure existed in the complementary user entity controls, so it does not affect the outcome of the ISP's SOC 2® report.

# 3.04 Change Management

## Overview

**Representative Task (Remembering and Understanding):** Explain the purpose of change management related to internal hardware and software applications, including the risks and the different types of documentation used (eg, system component inventory, baseline configuration).

As organizations and technologies develop, **changes to IT systems** are necessary. Such changes can be complex and may negatively affect an organization's operations or regulatory compliance if not authorized or managed effectively. Because IT system changes can involve the entire organization, change management requires collaboration across functional areas, including senior management and the board.

**Common IT System Changes**

| Additions | Deletions | Upgrades | Cloud transitions |
|---|---|---|---|
| Configuration changes | Code modifications | Updates or patches | Data modifications |

Management should design and implement a formal **IT change management process** to mitigate **risks**. Change management should be a *documented, repeatable, and auditable* process that protects the organization's production (ie, live) environment from unauthorized or inappropriate changes. All changes must go through a systematic process that includes authorization, use of different environments, segregation of duties, testing, and documentation.

## IT Change Risks

### General Risks

A poorly designed change management process may expose the organization to risks, such as unauthorized changes, downtime, security threats, and inefficient operations, as well as error prone reports or financial statements. This exposure can cause:

- Failure to meet organizational availability, capacity, reliability, and performance objectives
- Control deficiencies and unfavorable audit opinions
- Subpar or unstable changes that cause incidents or disruptions, hindering employee productivity and aggravating customers
- Security incidents that lead to compliance fines or lawsuits

## Patch-Related Risks

Patches may affect multiple system libraries and other coding used by application programs. Software, whether internally developed or acquired, may need **patches** to address new or previously undetected vulnerabilities. Such patches may be substantial and/or complex.

Outside of the normal change management process, vendors may automatically push patches. Although vendor-managed patches are helpful, they can also create risks, especially when the IT management team is not aware of the patch or its timing. Minor changes in configuration may have a ripple effect throughout other systems or applications.

## Emerging Risks

Besides managing changes within an on-site system, the change management process should also address **emerging technological risks** in the global environment. This includes deciding which team members oversee changes related to:

- Mobile device hardware, software, and applications, especially for "bring your own device" (BYOD)
- Third-party IaaS, PaaS, and SaaS cloud applications
- Automation, machine learning, and artificial intelligence solutions

## End-User Computing and User-Developed Applications

End-user computing and user-developed applications may complicate change management. Systems often allow users to create their own processing or ad hoc reporting applications through existing applications and tools (eg, Excel, SQL, data visualization). It may be difficult to design comprehensive controls around **customized solutions**. IT change personnel may overlook such systems because they are smaller in scale or there is no communication with the users.

## Third-Party/Vendor Risks

Services and technology can be bought from third-party vendors, ranging from SaaS applications to a private cloud that the organization will manage. The outsourcing of such services can make it difficult to figure out **which party is responsible** for the change management controls.

When a third-party vendor supplies services, a SOC report may be needed to understand the controls implemented by the vendor and any subservice organizations it uses. SOC reports also have a section that describes the **complementary controls** a user organization must implement in combination with the vendor.

A vendor's SOC report may or may not ensure that controls are effective. Management should understand the scope of the report and how to interpret it, and they should assess the risks. To recall, a **type 1 SOC report** pertains to a specified date and does not test the operating effectiveness of controls. Thus, an organization needs to understand that this report states only whether the vendor has fairly described its system and whether the controls are suitably designed. An organization should require a **type 2 SOC report** from an independent auditor who performs procedures to evaluate the operating effectiveness of controls throughout a period.

The organization should include specific language regarding SOC reporting, patches, and patch deployment notifications in all its contracts with third-party service and cloud providers. This helps the organization perform its governance duties over the change management process, both internally and externally.

## Compliance Risks

A strong change management process should meet **regulatory compliance** requirements. Systems and processes may need to be revised to align with new or updated laws or requirements. Many laws, such as HIPAA, require organizations to have a documented change management process.

## Change Management Plan Documentation

A **change management plan** is a document that outlines an organization's **policies and procedures** regarding requesting, approving, implementing, and monitoring changes to hardware, software, and firmware. It should detail the procedural steps, as well as the roles and responsibilities for internal personnel and/or external service providers.

**Change documentation** is critical, especially when a problem needs to be diagnosed. Part of the plan includes having a method to keep track of the **approval, status**, and **history of changes**. Thus, for effective change management, the organization must inventory all the components in its information system and document their configuration.

- **System component inventory:** All assets within an IT system should be inventoried and documented. The inventory should include all components with enough detail to allow for tracking and reporting. For example, the details may document the component name, date of receipt, cost, model, serial number, manufacturer, supplier information, component type, responsible personnel, and physical location. To prevent duplication, each component should have a unique identifier.

  The inventory should be updated whenever there is a new installation, removal, or system update. Organizations might use automated technologies to scan for components. Inventories help the organization to:

  - Map critical services to stakeholders and other related services
  - Identify assets related to the critical services
  - Identify which components need change
  - Determine a baseline configuration
  - Find unauthorized components connected to the system

- **Baseline configuration:** A baseline configuration is a formally reviewed and agreed-upon system specification recorded at a given moment in time; it serves as a reference point from which future builds, releases, and changes may be requested. It may also be used as a rollback (ie, restore) point if needed. Organizations can use automated tools to create a baseline configuration for tracking operating system or software version numbers, configuration settings, and patches. Baselines should be created for different environments such as development, testing, and operation (ie, production).

## Elements of IT Change Management

**Representative Task (Remembering and Understanding):** Explain the different environments used (eg, development, staging, production) and the types of tests performed (eg, unit, integration, system, acceptance).

In most organizations, the IT function has two key roles that are supported through change management processes and controls:

- Operate and maintain current services and commitments
- Offer new functions or security measures that help the organization achieve its objectives

**Elements of IT Change Management**

| | | | |
|---|---|---|---|
| Environments and migration | Types of change | Sources of change | Scope of changes |
| Change process | Change scheduling | Change management tools | Continuous monitoring |

## Environments

Changes to systems and applications are developed, evaluated, and made live in separate environments. An **environment** refers to an **infrastructure** set designated for a specific purpose.

Application or system changes migrate (ie, move) to the next environment as each team completes its phase of the work. The environments should be as similar as possible, having the same hardware, software versions, and patches. Similar environments help increase the probability that changes will work as expected in a live situation. The similarity also makes it easier to isolate problems by reducing the number of variables to consider.

**Migration through Environments**

- **Development environment:** Developers program (ie, code) new software or changes to existing systems and applications. Developers may be internal personnel or external vendors.
- **Testing environment:** Quality assurance engineers evaluate the changes and perform extensive tests on each component to detect problems.
- **Staging environment:** A small sample group of end users tries out the changes in a close-to-production environment before releasing them to all users.
- **Production environment:** The new software or changes go live for all users.

**Segregation of duties** is an important change control during **migration** and may be required by regulations. No single individual should have the authority to make code changes in a development environment, perform testing and staging, and implement the changes in a production environment. Segregation of duties is an internal control that helps the organization prevent, detect, and correct unauthorized changes and errors.

| | Change Management Roles and Responsibilities |
|---|---|
| **Change Requester** | • Requests a change by filling out a change request ticket<br>• Provides details about the requested change, including needs, risks, goals, and objectives |
| **Change Manager** | • Manages daily activities of the change management process<br>• Reviews and authorizes change requests<br>• Meets with Change Advisory Board (CAB) or Emergency Change Advisory Board (ECAB)<br>• Creates schedules and monitors progress<br>• Ensures policies and procedures are followed<br>• Performs post-implementation review |
| **Change Advisory Board (CAB)** | • Advises the Change Manager on major change requests, scheduling, and post-implementation review<br>• Advises on change process policies and procedure models |
| **Emergency Change Advisory Board (ECAB)** | • Subset of Change Advisory Board<br>• On call 24/7<br>• Advises Change Manager on declared emergency change requests |
| **Change Builder** | • Develops the change and plans for implementation, verification, and backout<br>• Updates change record |
| **Change Tester** | • Tests change for problems<br>• Updates change record |
| **Change Implementer** | • Manages the change rollout<br>• Communicates with all involved stakeholders<br>• Resolves cross-functional (departmental) issues<br>• Ensures consistent execution by following policies/procedures<br>• Updates change record |

## Types of Change

Change management processes differ based on the type of change requested. For example, management may reduce the steps in approval processes to quicken the response in emergency situations or may increase the approval requirements for high-risk changes. Changes can be classified based on their timing, urgency, frequency, and risk.

### Emergency changes

- Need to be implemented ASAP
- Immediate response to service disruptions or security incidents
- Must be approved by Change Manager and ECAB

### Preapproved standard changes

- Low-risk, routine changes
- Follow a repeated pattern, such as swapping minor equipment or creating a new instance in a database
- Preapproved by Change Manager and/or CAB

### Normal changes

- Medium to high-risk changes
- Must go through full change management process
- Changes that are not standard or repeated
- Hardware and software upgrades; changing data centers
- Must be approved by Change Manager and CAB

### Automated changes

- Low-risk, automated processes built into tools
- Vendor-driven patches
- Do not need human intervention to run
- Timing and changes must be monitored by Change Manager

## Sources of Change

The need for changes can stem from various internal and external factors. Organizations must balance any conflicting demands on their IT staff, as well as the costs of change. Management identifies sources of change during governance, risk assessment, operating, and monitoring activities.

Management may request IT changes related to:

- **Internal governance:** Changes to business risks, objectives, strategies, and processes, as well as changes to address known capacity issues or performance problems
- **Customer expectations:** IT systems changes that create positive customer experiences or fulfill promises made in service level agreements (SLAs)
- **External threats:** Pressures to keep up with competitive, social, and political conditions
- **Regulations:** New or amended regulations that require a change to IT systems in order to maintain compliance
- **Security threats/vulnerabilities/patches:** Changes made to mitigate new security threats
- **Audits:** IT changes to correct control or compliance weaknesses identified in an audit or risk assessment
- **Aligning with new vendors or partners:** Interfacing with other systems or creating new business processes may drive change to current IT systems

## Scope of Change

Configuration changes, as well as any other modifications to IT-based assets, are included within the scope of an efficient change management procedure. The following assets are subject to change management:

| Hardware | Software | Data | Security Controls |
|---|---|---|---|
| Servers, routers, switches, power, user computers, network printers, phones, mobile devices | Operating systems, middleware, applications | Complete database updates, individual file updates, data integration, data migration and conversion | Antivirus software, firewalls, intrusion protection/detection systems |

## Change Management Process

### Basic Process

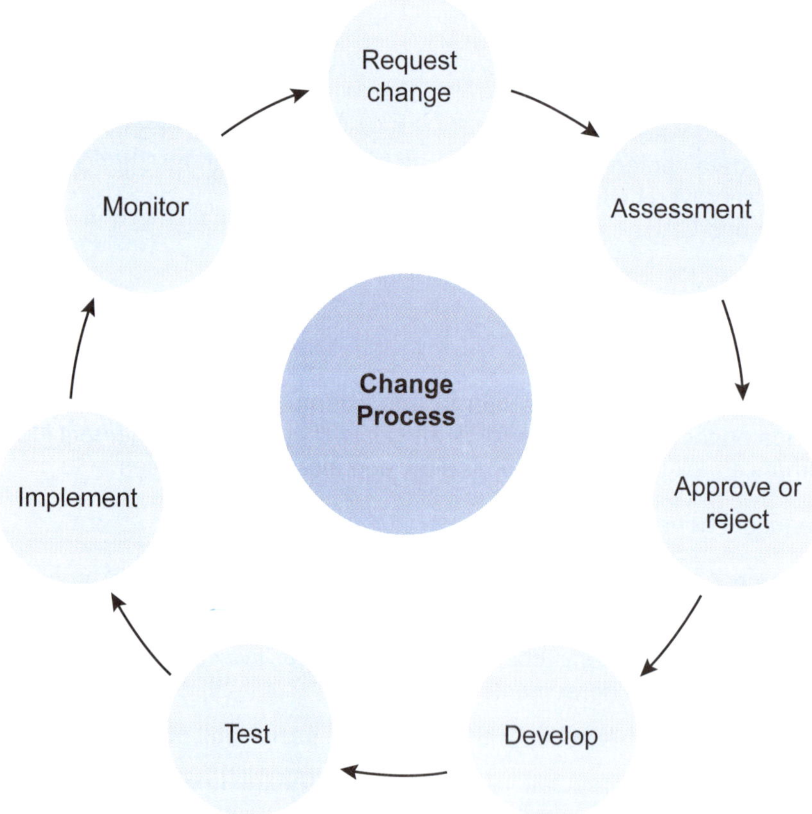


An organization's change management process must be tailored to fit its needs, but a common workflow is usually followed. The basic **change control process components** include:

- **Change requests:** As the first step in the change process, change requests may:
  - Come from parties within the existing system
  - Result from the failure of some aspect of the system
  - Seek experimentation to improve processes

- **Assessment:** Assessments of risk, impact, and cost are performed to give management the appropriate information for deciding whether to approve or reject the proposed change.
- **Approve or reject:** Based on the assessments and organizational objectives, management will determine if a change is justified and whether the benefits outweigh the costs. Then management allows the change to move forward, rejects the change, or sends it back for further assessment.
- **Develop:** Development planning starts with understanding the acceptance criteria. **Acceptance criteria** are the conditions or parameters a change must meet to be accepted by the end user. For example, what would a change to the design of a user interface look like, or how would it behave? If developers do not understand the acceptance criteria before they begin their work, the change may not be sufficient. Once the criteria are understood, the developers can start coding (ie, building) the change.
- **Test:** All changes should be tested prior to implementation. Both manual and automated testing methods allow for evaluating the function and performance of the change. When changes must be made quickly, as in an emergency, testing may not be possible. In that case, post-implementation review and monitoring may be necessary.
- **Implement:** Implementation includes:
  - The new processes or components, including development (ie, building) and testing
  - An indication of all aspects of the existing process and all personnel within the entity that will be affected
  - Design or modification of policies, procedures, forms, or reports
  - Training of those who are part of the system
  - A **backout plan** to reverse a failed change
- **Review and monitor:** Once a change is made, it will be monitored to determine whether it is properly executed and has the intended effects. Monitoring may be performed through technology, post-implementation reviews, or audits.

The organization should have a published **change schedule** to let all stakeholders know the planned implementation dates for all approved changes. This schedule must be updated regularly to avoid activity conflicts and to track the progress of changes.

## Detailed Change Management Process

| Change Process Steps, Roles, and Procedures | | |
|---|---|---|
| **Step in Change Process** | **Change Role** | **Change Procedures** |
| Request for change (RFC) | Change requester | Create a change request documenting details. |
| Assess/ authorize/reject | Change Manager/CAB | Assess RFC for impact, risks, costs. Approve or deny, documenting decision on RFC. |
| Build | Change builder | Understand acceptance criteria and build the change, implementation, verification, and backout plans. Periodically update change record. |
| Test | Change tester | Test the change, implementation, verification, and backout plans. Update change record. |

| Change Process Steps, Roles, and Procedures | | |
|---|---|---|
| **Step in Change Process** | **Change Role** | **Change Procedures** |
| Scheduling (go/no go) | Change Manager, change requester, change implementer | Examine the change schedule to make sure there are no conflicts with other scheduled changes. Update change record. |
| Implementation | Change implementer | Implement change and verification plan. Backout plan is implemented if there is a failed change. Update change record. |
| Review | Change Manager, change requester, change implementer | Verify the results of the change were as expected and act if there is a problem. Update change record. |
| Close | Change Manager | Ensure all information has been entered and close the change record. |

## Continuous Change Integration and Testing

Traditional development teams manually build, test, and deploy software. Modern development may encompass ongoing and automated code changes, testing, and monitoring by combining continuous integration (CI) with continuous delivery and/or continuous deployment (CD). Taken together, the entire process is known as the **CI/CD pipeline**.

In **CI**, a team of developers shares (ie, "commits") the changes it has built to the source code frequently, making sure the changes pass tests before deployment into the production environment. For example, code changes from multiple developers may be merged and tested daily. This helps to ensure that different developers' code changes do not conflict with each other.

The advantage of CI is that problems are found much earlier because the new or amended code is tested and validated in smaller increments. Because the changes are smaller, developers can feel more confident they are adding new code to a tested foundation, rather than diagnosing and fixing problems after a substantial change.

When CI is combined with **continuous delivery**, integrated code is automatically released into a repository (eg, GitHub), so it is ready to be released into production anytime. However, the deployment is triggered manually. When CI is combined with **continuous deployment**, the entire process—from committing the code to testing and deploying it into the production environment—is automated.

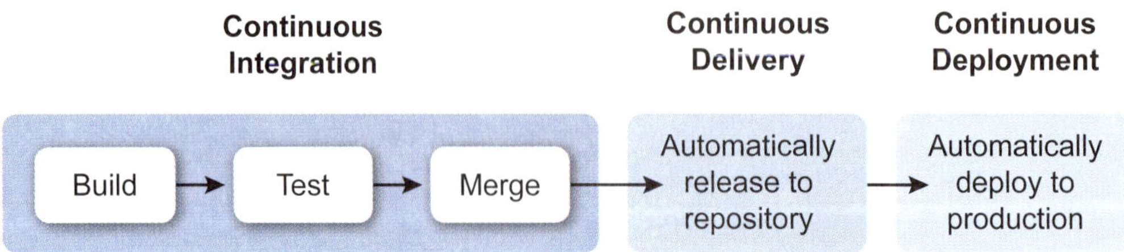

Four **functional tests**, whether manual or automated, may be performed in the following order:

- **Unit testing:** Initial, narrow tests performed on **individual components or functions**. For example, if a change affects three components, each is tested separately before they are put together (ie, integrated).
- **Integration testing: Multiple components** or functions are combined and **tested as a group**. The purpose of integration testing is to find out if a subset of parts behaves properly when put together.
- **System testing:** The entire system is tested as a whole to find defects. All components are integrated to make sure the complete system works properly.
- **Acceptance testing:** Final testing by **end users** (ie, user acceptance testing), to ensure that the changes meet **acceptance criteria**. The identity of the end users depends on the context of the change. For example, company employees would be the end users of an internal software program. However, for public-facing applications, the end users would include external customers. When development is outsourced, the third-party developer may send the changes to be tested by the customer for approval.

## System Conversions

**Representative Task (Remembering and Understanding):** Explain the approaches that can be used when converting to a new information system (eg, direct, parallel, pilot).

System conversions are migrations from an old system to a new system. Conversions may involve significant changes to hardware, software, databases, and business processes. This can be a complex process that requires more planning and testing (pre- and post-implementation) than normal changes. Firm controls must be in place to manage the risks associated with a system changeover. Risks include incompatibility problems, loss of functions or data, interruptions to operations, and user confusion because of a lack of training.

There are four common approaches to system conversions:

- **Direct conversion:** The old system is abandoned, and a new system takes over on a specific "conversion day," which may be during the weekend or overnight. After conversion, employees use only the replacement system. Direct conversion involves the highest risk because the old system will no longer be operational. It is theoretically the fastest method of conversion, assuming the implementation goes well.
- **Parallel conversion:** Both the old system and the new system operate at the same time. Parallel conversions are the safest strategy, as the old system can be used while any issues with the replacement system are addressed, and employees are trained. The replacement system outputs can also be cross-checked with the old system to ensure they are the same. However, running two systems takes more time, effort, and money. In addition, employees may be reluctant to transition to the replacement system if they can fall back on the familiar system.
- **Phased conversion:** The old system is converted to the new system gradually at designated times. Thus, the system implementation is staggered, such that some users are working with the new system while others are waiting for their part of the system to be converted. A phased approach has the advantage of focusing on one step at a time, rather than the complete system at once. The risks of the phased approach are incompatibility between systems and a slower rollout.
- **Pilot conversion:** The new system is used in one part of an organization, a certain department or geographic location, prior to implementing it across the entire organization. The pilot is a trial, taking a risk on a smaller scale to work out problems before the system is adopted in full. Because the pilot method takes more time to implement, the organization must choose the pilot carefully to make sure it is a representative sample.

**System Conversion Approaches**

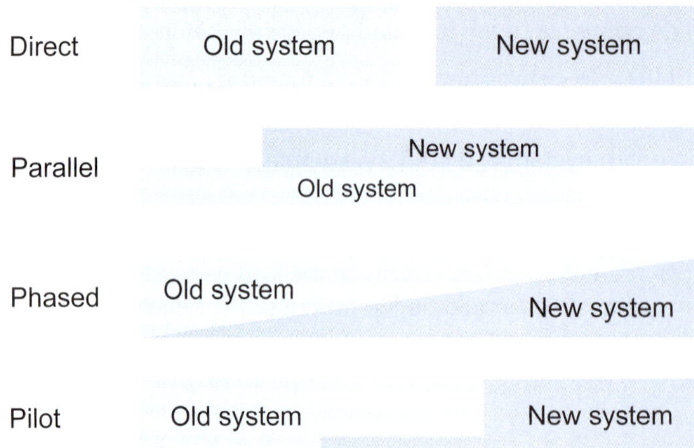


## Patch Management

**Representative Task (Remembering and Understanding):** Explain patch management.

Patches are modifications made to a system's firmware or software to fix a security flaw or a functional problem, or to introduce new features. Firmware is permanently installed in hardware memory and instructs the machine how to operate or interact with software. For example, a basic input/output system (BIOS) is necessary for computer hardware to boot an operating system, and drivers are necessary to send jobs to printers.

- **Patch management** focuses on ensuring software and systems are consistent and kept up to date. Patches are interim fixes for a specific problem (eg, bug, security gap, instabilities) and are added to existing software.
- **Release management** ensures that patches and system updates are compatible with existing processes and systems, and that changes are tested prior to installation and update rollout. Releases may be updates to new versions or comprise a service pack, which includes a series of patches and maintenance updates.

Patch management is crucial to **keep systems up to date** and to do so **without interrupting operations**. Out-of-date systems are vulnerable to security incidents, performance issues, or shutdown.

Typically, patch management involves both change management and configuration management processes:

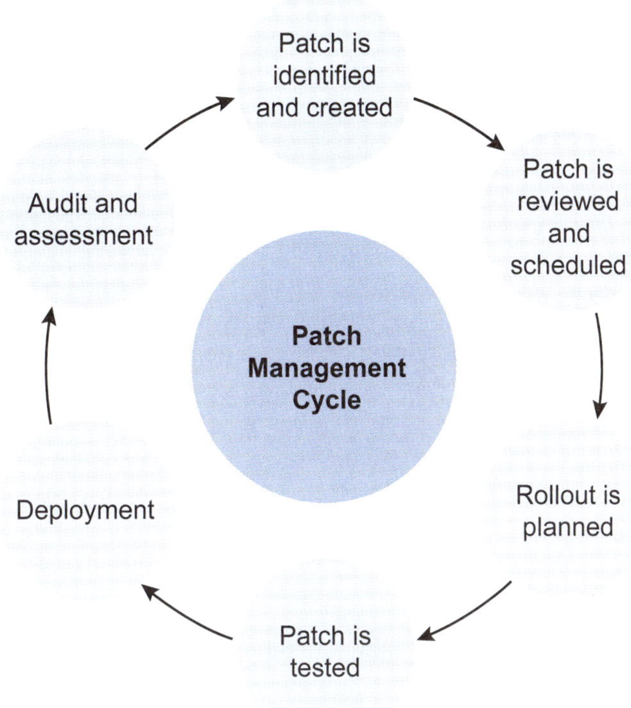


## Assessing Patch Risks

Unaddressed security flaws can put IT assets at risk; therefore, patches should be implemented as soon as possible. However, improperly planned patch installations also pose a risk. The organization should regularly **conduct risk assessments** that consider the impact and likelihood of problems related to inadequate or untimely patch installation. Patches should be classified as "critical" or "routine." Critical patches may be deployed, adhering to emergency change management procedures with a post-deployment review.

## Patch Schedule

Though patches are urgent, routine patch deployments should preferably take place during preproduction so that fixes can be fully tested in a **staging** or "**sandbox**" environment. Patches should be deployed as part of a **scheduled routine** at regular intervals (eg, Microsoft's Patch Tuesday) in all critical applications and devices. Defined timelines for fixes, as well as explicit responsibilities and standards for prioritizing security vulnerabilities, are also crucial. Rather than applying individual patches to different systems, organizations should develop a plan that **bundles patches and updates into releases**.

Vendors normally announce patches for commercially released software on their websites or through email notifications. Vendors can push patches and releases automatically if the customer agrees; therefore, IT management should take precautions to be aware of the date of the vendor's automatic deployment.

## Critical Security and Functionality Patches

Cybersecurity catastrophes may be caused by vulnerabilities that could have been avoided or fixed by available patches that were not yet installed. For instance, in the 2017 Equifax data breach, not patching a crucial system resulted in the compromise of 148 million individuals' personally identifiable information.

The **National Vulnerability Database** gives a **criticality score** to each patch, from 0 to 10. A score **above 7** shows a **substantial risk**. Organizations should prioritize critical security patches, especially those with a score of 9 or 10.

A **zero-day vulnerability** is one that has been identified in a system but for which the vendor has **not yet officially offered a patch**. Organizations may not have time to wait for a vendor to release the patch; therefore, they should have a plan to address such vulnerabilities and implement mitigation controls, especially if the threat is critical.

## Testing Change Management

**Representative Task (Application):** Test the design and implementation of change control policies (eg, acceptance criteria, test results, logging, monitoring) for IT resources (eg, applications, infrastructure components, configurations) in organizations, including those that have adopted continuous integration and continuous deployment processes.

**Representative Task (Analysis):** Perform a walkthrough of an organization's change management procedures and compare the observed procedure with the documented policy requirement.

As part of its **governance** responsibilities, management should design and implement **internal controls** within the change management process. Effective internal controls **prevent, detect, and correct errors and fraud**. Internal and external auditors evaluate the design and implementation of management's change controls through internal audits, financial audits, SOC examinations, and compliance audits.

### Preventive Controls

Preventive controls are an organization's first line of defense, as they **stop unauthorized changes before they occur**. Modern change management tools can automate preventive controls, applying them consistently without human participation. Automated preventive controls reject certain changes unless triggered otherwise by a specific action or defined criteria.

**Change Management Preventive Controls**

#### Communication

- Change management objectives, policies, roles, and responsibilities are communicated to internal and external parties
- System and process changes are communicated in a timely manner
- Changes are scheduled and the timing communicated prior to implementation

#### Risk Assessment

- Considers changes to the regulatory, economic, and physical environment
- Considers the impacts of new business lines and changes to existing business lines
- Considers changes in leadership and management philosophies
- Considers changes in the entity's systems and changes in the technological environment
- Considers changes resulting from relationships with third parties such as vendors and business partners
- Considers changes in internal and external threats to system components and the components' vulnerabilities

### Segregation of Duties

- Change approval and implementation duties are segregated
- Testing activities are segregated from development activities
- Detective and corrective controls are in place if segregation is not feasible

### Procedures

- Entity has a process for changes to systems and components
- Changes are appropriately authorized prior to design, development or acquisition, and configuration
- System changes are tested and approved prior to implementation
- Processes are in place to prevent unauthorized changes
- A process is in place for emergency changes
- A process is in place to back out or remediate failed changes
- Confidential and private information is protected during changes

### Documentation

- Change management policies are documented
- System changes and tests of changes are tracked and documented
- Change requests and approvals are documented

## Detective Controls

Although preventive controls are a crucial component of the overall approach, they are insufficient by themselves. Detective controls include continuous **monitoring for changes** and applying benchmarking **metrics** using technology and audits. The goal of detective controls is to determine whether any unwanted changes or unintended outcomes have occurred. Findings from monitoring activities supply the knowledge used to mitigate change control gaps.

**Detective Controls Monitor for Changes to...**

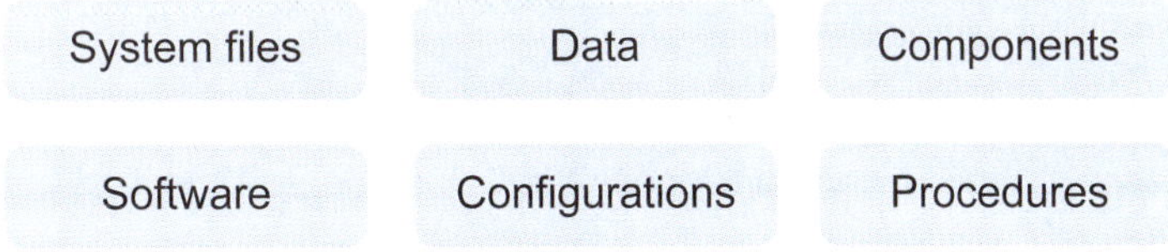


An internal IT function or outsourced **managed service provider** monitors the system for changes using various software programs or manual procedures, including:

- Antivirus and anti-malware programs
- Change detection programs
- Log monitoring
- Vulnerability scans
- Incident alerting

- Post-implementation reviews
- Internal IT audits
- External IT audits

**Metrics** provide a method for analyzing and benchmarking the effectiveness of change management policy and processes. Change management software may have built-in dashboards that display key performance indicators (KPIs), such as the number or percentage of:

**Change Management Key Indicators**

| Authorized changes | Changes implemented | Unauthorized changes | Emergency changes | Successful and failed changes |
|---|---|---|---|---|

### Corrective Controls

Corrective controls are actions taken to fix specific post-change conditions, such as **backout and system restore procedures**. Rollback procedures return the system to the configuration it was in prior to any changes.

### Outsourced Function Considerations

Organizations may outsource or co-source their IT services, including aspects of change management, such as development or monitoring. **SLAs** and **contracts** should clearly define the service organization's principal service commitments and system requirements. In addition, management should ensure that the contract requires the service organization to supply a SOC 2® report, or the contract language includes a "**right to audit**" clause.

## Testing Change Control Policies: General

Both internal and external CPAs evaluate the design and implementation of an organization's change control policies. The **design of controls** is tested to determine whether management has assessed and appropriately responded to risks. **Implementation** relates to whether the controls management designed were put into action. Neither designing nor implementing a control is enough to make it operate effectively. The effective operation of controls depends on human behavior, with the risk of errors or intentional circumvention.

**Tests of controls** include reperformance, inquiry, inspection, observation, and walkthroughs. Procedures to evaluate the design and implementation of change control policies for hardware and software may include:

### Inquiry

- What is the organization's change control process? Is it documented? Is it fully implemented?
- How does the organization decide which changes to make? Is there a documented risk assessment?
- Have there been any problems with the change control process? If so, what corrections have been made? How are process changes communicated?
- Does the organization use an electronic ticketing system and track change approvals?
- What are the roles and responsibilities of individuals charged with change control? Are outsourced services or technology used in the process?
- Are changes logged and tested prior to implementation? Are these processes automated or manual? What tests are performed? Who performs the tests? How do you determine if the acceptance criteria were met?

- How is the change control process monitored and by whom? What software is used? Are any audits performed by independent, external parties?
- Have there been any failed changes or outages? If so, what was the correction process?
- How often are operations disrupted by changes or patches?
- How do the authorization procedures differ for low-risk versus high-risk changes and standard versus emergency situations?
- Do the individuals who authorize changes also implement them? Do individuals working on development also test the changes or implement them in the production environment? How are duties segregated?
- Is there a formal process for patches? How many emergency patches were made in the past year and what process did they go through?
- How does the organization decide whether a change was successful? What do they do if it was not?
- What metrics does the organization regularly monitor?

## Inspection

- Read change control policy documents to obtain an understanding of the process and controls in place.
- Read the documentation of changes pushed by vendors.
- Review board minutes to find whether any major changes have occurred.
- Review change schedules to obtain an understanding of what changes are in progress or were implemented. Determine whether there are authorized change request tickets for a sample of the changes on the schedule.
- Review change logs, monitoring reports, and metrics.
- Obtain a sample of requests for change and determine whether the requests were properly approved and if the process was completed from initiation to close.Obtain access lists to determine whether any individuals have conflicting roles.
- Obtain a sample of emergency changes to determine whether the situations met the criteria for an emergency and whether there was a post-implementation review of the changes.

## Walkthrough

An auditor's walkthrough combines different tests of controls to understand the flow of a process. The auditor then documents the findings with written narratives and/or flowcharts/diagrams. The purpose is to understand the process that was implemented in comparison with the process documented in procedure manuals. Often, documented policies are found to be out of date or have not been followed. Walkthroughs help to find such situations and give a clearer picture of daily operations.

**Testing Manual Emergency Change Control Processes**

An organization that develops its own internal software engaged a CPA firm to provide risk advisory services. For this engagement, the firm was asked to review the organization's change management process and develop findings, conclusions, and recommendations.

The CPA firm first obtained an understanding of the organization and its change management process through oral inquiries and written checklists filled out by IT personnel. In summary, the CPA's questions were:

- Is there a documented change management policy?
- Are changes properly approved?
- Are changes tested before implementation?
- Is there a segregation of duties between change requesters and change approvers? Between developers, testers, and implementers?
- How often are emergency changes made and have they been approved?
- How are changes monitored after implementation?
- How often was there an outage or interruption to operations because of failed changes? Did these events result in any security breaches?

After receiving oral and written answers, the CPA firm performed a walkthrough to make sure they understood the process. The process, as explained by personnel assisting with the walkthrough, was documented using narratives and diagrams. The walkthrough process findings were compared with the written policy.

The CPA noted that there was a difference between the written policy for emergency change authorization and what personnel say they do in actual situations. The documented policy required *written* approval from both the Change Manager and the Emergency Change Advisory Board (ECAB) prior to implementation.

The CPA firm sampled 10% of the total number of emergency changes made in the last year. For each change, the firm asked for copies of the approval documentation. A substantial number of the approval documents had only an authorization from the Change Manager, with no documented approval from the ECAB.

When the firm inquired further, the Change Manager said that the ECAB was contacted in the middle of the night and the board members gave their approval orally through a conference phone call.

Based on these findings, the CPA firm could not conclude whether the emergency changes were properly approved. A recommendation was made to modify the policy to state that ECAB members should send an email within 8 hours to document such decisions. This would help prevent unauthorized emergency changes, and it would establish an audit trail, as outlined in the written change management policy.

## Testing Continuous and Automated Change Processes

CPAs may need to evaluate the design and implementation of controls in a **CI/CD process**, either as part of internal auditing or externally through risk advisory or attestation engagements, such as a SOC or compliance examination. Evaluating the design and implementation of controls in automated CI/CD processes may differ from a standard change management process.

No matter the model, strong change management controls are important because a failure to design or implement such controls can result in failed code changes, business disruption, reputational harm, or regulatory fines. For CI/CD, the primary risks are that:

- Unauthorized changes may be released into the production environment, and
- Deployed changes may function improperly or present security risks.

Testing the design and implementation of CI/CD change control policies involves the same tests of controls: reperformance, inquiry, inspection, observation, and walkthroughs. CI/CD testing may encompass both automated and manual controls, including:

| CI/CD Change Management Controls |
| --- |
| **Minimal Required Controls** |
| Changes are documented and tested with evidence of acceptable results retained prior to deployment in the production environment. |
| All changes are documented. Prior to deployment, change documentation must include, at a minimum:<br>• Description of the change<br>• Acceptable criteria<br>• Risk assessment/impact of the proposed change<br>• Rollback procedures<br>• Evidence of reviews and approvals by an independent party<br>• Evidence of testing and results |
| Developers cannot approve their own acceptable criteria. |
| All changes and test cases are reviewed by an individual other than the person who developed the change. |
| Test libraries are periodically reviewed for completeness, accuracy, and validity. |
| All changes and test cases must be deployed through an approved release platform, using approved release platform templates. |
| Pipeline templates are defined and periodically reviewed for integrity. |
| Segregation of duties is maintained between product and pipeline teams. |

| Potential Additional CI/CD Change Management Controls |
| --- |
| **Additional Controls for Consideration** |
| Business approval of proposed changes occurs prior to development activities. |
| Documentation of changes is stored in a central repository. |
| All dependencies are defined and documented prior to deployment of the change. |
| Supporting documentation, including procedures and user guidance, are updated prior to deployment. |
| Change documentation and test results are stored in accordance with relevant data retention policies. |
| Release content information is retained for a period required to meet relevant regulatory requirements. |

**Change policy documentation:** An organization's policies and procedures should describe the change process and the documented audit trail. The audit trail should show the reason for changes, as well as the progression and timeline of a change—from the request to risk assessment, approvals, testing, and deployment. Policies should also describe ticketing systems and the CI/CD tools that are acceptable for use. If a CI/CD tool makes automated decisions, each decision and the data used to make it should be recorded and automatically added to the change request ticket.

**CI/CD processes and acceptable criteria documentation:** CI/CD processes should be documented and applied consistently to ensure compliance. The criteria for allowing a change to progress automatically through each stage in the CI/CD pipeline must be clear, consistent, and well documented. Requirements for exception handling should also be documented and should include added approvals or testing. Emergency changes should be retroactively sent through the standard change management process to find the root cause of the emergency.

**Access control:** An automated CI/CD pipeline must still incorporate user authentication and segregation of duties. The tools used may help in setting up role-based access controls. For example, a code change should be tested by someone other than the developer who wrote it. In addition, developers should not be allowed to determine the acceptable criteria for testing their code changes.

**Logging and alerting:** All actions taken by the automated tool and the personnel involved in the CI/CD process should be documented. Controls must ensure that no actions can be hidden, and actions to change logs should be restricted. Alerts should be set up to notify appropriate personnel of changes that circumvent approved CI/CD processes.

**CI/CD component inventory and baseline configuration:** To be effective, the CI/CD environments and components must work together seamlessly. A complete and current inventory of all components should be maintained. Components include code, tests, and acceptance criteria. A baseline configuration also helps to establish a specified point from which all changes are made, as well as a rollback point if necessary.

**Monitoring infrastructure:** The CI/CD infrastructure should undergo security testing, such as vulnerability scans and penetration testing (ie, ethical hacking). Each environment must be secure.

**Monitoring acceptance criteria:** Management should determine the proper thresholds for moving through the CI/CD pipeline and provide documentation that explains how each acceptance criterion was decided upon and the consequences for noncompliance. Acceptance criteria should be monitored and updated as the CI/CD process matures.

**Testing Automated CI/CD Processes**

An internal IT auditor was examining the controls that pertain to the development and deployment of company intranet web-based applications. The company uses continuous integration (CI) and continuous deployment (CD) to automate the merging, testing, and deploying of code changes.

The IT auditor obtained an understanding of the CI/CD pipeline and related controls by performing inquiries and inspecting documentation. Specifically, the auditor's testing focused on understanding the:

- Organization's CI/CD policies and procedures, including whether they have been implemented
- Documentation and logs generated by the CI/CD process
- Use of different environments, their security, and their resemblance to the production environment
- User authentication and segregation of duties within the CI/CD pipeline
- Development and use of acceptance criteria
- Monitoring of code changes and alerts for unauthorized changes
- Process for emergency changes and exceptions
- Compliance with internal policies and external regulations

Once the auditor understood the process, it was diagrammed in a flowchart. The auditor performed a walkthrough by observing development and testing personnel during the process.

In addition, the auditor inspected the system-generated log files and tested the existence (ie, implementation) of automated controls through reperformance.

# ISC 4
# Data Management

# ISC 4: Data Management

# 4.01 Data Management

## Data Collection Methods and Techniques

**Data collection** is the formal process of accumulating information about a specific subject, account, process, or control. Organizations use multiple types of data collected from various sources to prepare reports, perform analyses, research problems, and make decisions.

Selecting the appropriate method of collecting data is important to ensure that the information will be complete, accurate, and relevant. If the collection method is problematic, the data may not be dependable and thus cannot be relied upon. **Data integrity** refers to the belief that the data is pure—that is, there has been no alteration during its collection, processing, transmission, or storage.

Data collection **methods and techniques** should be developed with consideration for the following factors:

- What types of data need to be gathered?
- What is the source of the information?
- Are there multiple sources of data?
- How is the data recorded in the system, when is it recorded, and by whom?
- What format is the information in, and can that format be analyzed?
- What controls can ensure the data is complete and accurate?
- How will the data be used and by whom?
- Is the method of data collection subject to laws or regulations?
- What is the timing of the data collection?

Critical enterprise data may stem from:

- **Transactional and operational (software) applications:** Upstream systems and processes that create, read, update, or delete **(CRUD)** data
- **Analytical applications / reporting tools:** Downstream systems or processes that import, manipulate, or consume data
- **Off-premises applications:** Third-party data that an organization uses independently or combines (ie, "mashes up") with internal data

The method of data collection depends on the complexity and size of the data, as well as the type of database used. Data may be structured, semistructured, or unstructured:

- **Structured:** Data that has a specific format or schema, such as tables with fields and records. Structured data can be created or stored in relational databases or spreadsheets that may have input masks to ensure the data is formatted correctly. Because structured data is predefined, it can be searched, sorted, and analyzed easily using SQL, Python, or other languages. Examples include information found in enterprise resource planning (ERP) systems, accounting information systems (AIS), and customer relationship management (CRM) systems.
- **Semistructured:** Data that has a partial structure but is not as defined as structured data. Semistructured data may contain metadata, or tags, which make it easier to organize than unstructured data. Examples include email, comma-separated values (CSV) files, Internet of Things (IoT) sensor data, web server logs, and HTML-, XML-, and XBRL-tagged text.
- **Unstructured:** Raw data that does not have a predefined format. It is free-form and difficult to search. Examples include text, PDFs, video, audio, and photos.

**Common Sources of Data**

| Internal software | Devices | External parties |
|---|---|---|
| ERP, AIS, and CRM systems, point of sale systems, industry-specific applications, mobile applications, chat systems, OCR software, manufacturing systems, application or system logs, testing, forms, private images, surveys, and research | IT hardware, mobile devices, IoT devices, cameras, sensors, security monitoring equipment, swipe cards, scanners, biometric devices, GPS tracking systems, industry-specific mechanical equipment | Website analytics, social media, shippers, outsourced service providers, government reports, industry reports, news, demographics, public images, and consumer research groups |

Organizations capture data from these sources through a wide variety of manual, electronic, and automated equipment and/or processes. These include:

- **Keying and forms:** Data can be manually keyed directly into a database or input using electronic forms. Such forms may be on paper or a part of desktop, web, and mobile applications.
- **File import:** Data stored in different databases or applications can be shared between them by extracting (ie, exporting) the data from one location, then importing (ie, loading) it into another.
- **Barcodes:** Barcodes can be applied to almost any object (eg, documents, equipment, inventory) and linked to software for tracking; the codes may be read by a laser reader or decoded using a mobile device application. For example, store checkout clerks use a scanning device to read UPC codes on products or ISBN codes on books. Barcodes are found on most personal identification cards, such as driver's licenses and passports, and are also used to track mail and shipped parcels.
- **QR codes:** Quick response (QR) codes are black and white squares that can be read by a device, such as a smartphone camera. QR codes are typically used for sharing URLs or other digital information. For example, when a user scans a QR code with their smartphone camera, a link to a website or mobile application will be generated. This is often seen in conjunction with restaurant menus or television streaming services. The QR code may also provide statistics about its use.
- **RFID tags:** Radio frequency identification (RFID) is a wireless, contactless technology that organizations use to track assets (eg, equipment, inventory, cargo shipments). This method is more advanced than barcoding, using a reader, tags, and an antenna to wirelessly transmit data to an application.
- **Character recognition:** Optical character recognition (OCR), optical mark reading (OMR), and intelligent character recognition (ICR) automatically capture and extract data from documents such as receipts, checks, forms, IDs, and contracts. This reduces the need for manual data entry. For example, a mobile device can scan business expense receipts; using OCR, the receipt information is uploaded

to the expense reporting application via the Internet. Magnetic ink character recognition (MICR) is used in the banking industry for checks and deposits. OCR captures typed information, while ICR can process handwritten documents. OMR captures marks made by humans on documents such as forms, surveys, and tests.

- **Digital signatures:** Digital signatures allow users to sign documents or approve workflows over the Internet via an application or email. A digital signature is encrypted, geolocated, and time-stamped to authenticate the signer's identity. Sensitive electronic documents may require a digital certificate issued by a third party, such as a bank or government entity, to supply proof of identity.
- **Swipe/chip/NFC cards:** Swipe cards may be credit cards or cards that allow users to enter restricted areas. Credit, debit, and prepaid cards may also use a chip for contact transactions or wireless near-field communication (NFC) technology for contactless payments.
- **Sensors:** Sensors can track data points that relate to weather or environmental conditions. For example, sensor or IoT devices may capture temperature, humidity, pressure, weight, water, gas, or chemical levels.
- **Image and video capture:** Image captures can be photos taken by a camera, graphics displayed on a monitor, or video tape recordings.
- **Voice capture:** Conversations or voice messages can be captured using cloud-based technology or on-site call-recording devices.
- **Web and screen scrapers:** Web scraping means using a tool or bot to extract content and data from a website. Screen scraping refers to copying information shown on a digital display so that it can be used for another purpose.
- **Electronic data interchange (EDI):** EDI is the computer-to-computer exchange of documents in a standard electronic format between business partners. For example, a business may use EDI to submit purchase orders to vendors, send invoices or shipping status notifications to customers, or confirm payment information.
- **Automated scripts:** Tasks can be performed using targeted software code. For example, an organization may perform calculations from data fields in its database using a script language such as SQL.
- **Robotic process automation (RPA):** Software technology may also be used to build, deploy, and manage software robots that automate manual tasks. For example, RPA could collect data by automatically opening a PDF invoice, extracting data (eg, invoice number, dollar amount, vendor name), and inserting the data into a relational database table.
- **Application programming interfaces (APIs):** APIs are software interfaces that allow two or more computer systems or software applications to communicate and share data. An API is an automated set of rules in computer code; fields from one system's database are either copied or extracted and are then imported into another system using the API. A common example is the interface between PayPal and web storefronts that allows customers to complete transactions using PayPal.
- **Artificial intelligence (AI):** Computer systems that can simulate human intelligence by making connections between data points, then using those connections to perform tasks such as visual perception, speech and facial recognition, and translation.
- **Machine learning:** A type of artificial intelligence in which computer systems learn and adapt without receiving explicit instructions, but instead by using algorithms and statistical models to analyze and draw inferences from patterns in data.

# Data Life Cycle

**Representative Task (Remembering and Understanding):** Summarize the data life cycle (ie, the span of the use of information, from creation through active use, storage, and final disposition).

**Data Life Cycle**

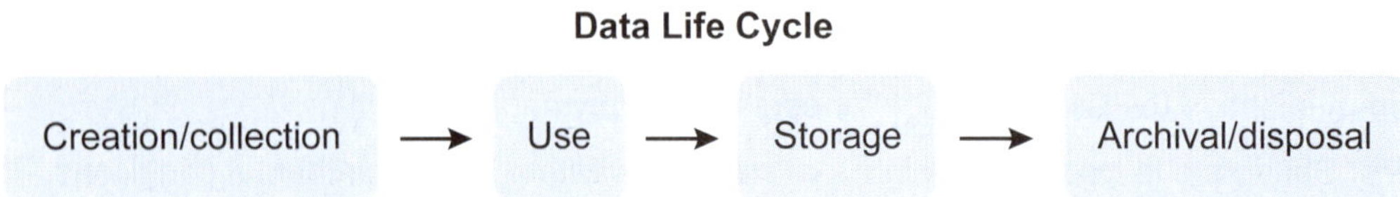


Organizations are responsible for the security, availability, processing integrity, confidentiality, and privacy of data while it is in their possession. The obligations regarding specific types of data may be imposed by internal governance, private contracts, and/or public regulations. For this reason, organizations should implement data loss prevention (DLP) processes that involve **classifying data types**, determining appropriate **access roles**, and **implementing controls**.

Certain types of data may require different procedures, and an organization's data handling procedures may be subject to external audit by regulators or independent CPAs. For example, an organization that processes financial transactions may need a SOC 1® examination. A data center may need a SOC 2® examination for security. Health care professionals may be subject to a Health Insurance Portability and Accountability Act (HIPAA) examination. Websites collecting information in the European Union are subject to the General Data Protection Regulation (GDPR), and credit card processors must follow Payment Card Industry Data Security Standard (PCI DSS) standards.

The **data life cycle** consists of four general phases:

## Creation/Collection

As discussed in the previous task, data can be created or collected from various devices and sources. Organizations may gather structured, semistructured, or unstructured data during manual or electronic processes. Controls should be implemented to ensure that the collected data is **standardized** and has **minimal errors**.

Regulations may specify the types of data that can be collected, as well as the **rights of data subjects**, such as consent. While collecting data for analysis is helpful for gaining insight, organizations should be careful to collect only the data necessary to achieve their **legitimate and lawful** purposes. Collection methods should be reliable, fair, transparent, and legal.

## Use

Data use encompasses **actions** such as viewing data on a screen, reporting, analysis, processing, and transmission. One of the primary considerations is that the data should be accessed and disclosed only for a permitted purpose and only by those **authorized** to do so. Organizations should implement controls to prevent unauthorized access or disclosure of data by internal and external parties. Controls should also ensure that data is used only for the intended purposes within the parameters of what is legally allowed by consent or regulation.

## Storage

During the storage phase, data may be held on hard drives, media, or a database server. An organization's data may be kept in different databases around the world, whether on premises or in the cloud. The data infrastructure may be owned by the organization or outsourced to an external infrastructure as a service (IaaS) or platform as a service (PaaS) provider. The type of database used depends on the nature of the items stored. Structured data is typically stored in a relational database, while unstructured data may need a NoSQL (not only SQL) database.

Data should be stored for only as long as necessary, with a formal retention plan in place based on data classifications. The organization should implement controls to make sure stored data is not lost, stolen, corrupted, or accessed without authorization. Infrastructure should be assessed for security vulnerabilities; processes such as encryption can safeguard data from unauthorized access or use when it is "at rest." Data redundancy practices, including disaster recovery, backup, and restore plans, can help an organization recover from weather-related events or cybersecurity attacks.

## Archival/Disposal

The archival/disposal phase involves archival, deletion, and destruction. Data is archived when it is no longer *actively* needed for operations or decisions but still must be kept for reasons such as complying with mandatory retention periods. **Archiving** does not duplicate data but simply puts it in long-term storage in case it needs to be accessed again later. Archived data is typically stored on less expensive physical media, such as magnetic tapes. Cloud storage is also popular because it may transfer some risk to a third party.

When data has been flagged for permanent disposal, it should be deleted, and the storage device must be altered in such a way that the data is no longer accessible. Deletion and destruction are not the same: **Deletion** may remove a file, but unlike destroyed data, the file can remain on the device. For example, hitting "delete" on a personal computer sends the file to the recycle bin rather than permanently removing it. Even after the recycle bin is emptied, a file continues to exist until it is overwritten by new data or the hard drive is destroyed. Data flagged for disposal should be sanitized (ie, redacted or anonymized) with more extreme measures that render the storage devices unreadable.

**Destruction** methods may include shredding papers, overwriting files, degaussing (ie, demagnetizing a device), or the physical destruction of storage media. Because partial destruction could leave data on a device and data disposal is a critical security concern, organizations may hire an external provider that specializes in the destruction of data and devices. Remote data-wiping may also be used for the factory resetting of smartphones, tablets, and other mobile and Internet-connected devices.

Organizations should have strong policies and procedures relating to the disposal of data. Improper handling could lead to a data breach, resulting in lawsuits, loss of revenue, and fines.

# Data Storage and Database Schemas

**Representative Task (Remembering and Understanding):** Define the various types of data storage (eg, data warehouse, data lake, data mart) and database schemas (eg, star, snowflake).

**Data Lake, Data Warehouse, and Data Mart**

SQL database
NoSQL database
Flat file data
Data sources

Unstructured, semistructured, & structured data
Data lake

Transformation

Structured data
Data warehouse

HR
Marketing
Sales
Data mart

The significant amounts of data an organization collects from multiple sources may be in different formats (eg, structured versus unstructured) and intended for different purposes (eg, transaction processing, analysis). The differences rarely accommodate a "one size fits all" approach, so organizations must assess their needs and decide how to **structure** their **storage architecture**. Ideally, the chosen **data management** method(s) should keep the data available when needed while also being secure and cost effective.

## Types of Data Storage

Whether using **on-premises** or **cloud** storage solutions, organizations must consider:

- How much data needs to be stored?
- What kinds of data are involved?
- Where does the data come from?
- When does the data need to be accessed and by whom?
- What technology best fits each type of data and its intended use?
- What are the long-term storage costs and risks?

Four common storage options include relational databases, data lakes, data warehouses, and data marts. Relational databases may have both read and write capabilities to collect, process, and store short-term data. However, data lakes, warehouses, and marts are typically read-only as they are primarily used for long-term storage and analytical purposes that require protecting the data from alteration.

**Relational database:** Organizations use relational databases to hold **current, structured data**. Organized into a series of tables, the database is like a spreadsheet with columns (ie, attributes) and rows (ie, records). Associations between the data in different tables create relationships. For example, a Sales table is related to a Customer table because every sale must have a customer.

Relational databases are the foundation of business applications, such as ERP systems and AIS, and may be used for **online transactional processing (OLTP).** Relational databases built using **Structured Query Language (SQL)** can hold billions of rows of data. Forms can be made for easy data input, and queries help to filter results or generate outputs (eg, reports, dashboards).

**Data lake:** Unlike a database, a data lake can hold **diverse types of data**, whether structured, semistructured, or unstructured. Data may come from both internal and external sources, with the data lake serving as a **central repository** to store massive amounts of data in its **original (ie, raw and native) format** until it is needed. The purpose may be to perform deep, multidimensional analysis or simply to hold large amounts of data inexpensively.

Data **does *not* need to be transformed** into a uniform structure to be housed in a data lake. While more complex than relational databases, data lakes support **online analytical processing (OLAP).** OLAP can analyze different data types to find patterns that otherwise might not be discovered. For example, an analyst or artificial intelligence (AI) using OLAP to examine retail sales may discover that the sales of one product are highly correlated with the sales of another product. This finding could influence product placement decisions to increase sales. The products may be placed physically near each other in a store or recommended as an additional item to an online shopper.

**Data warehouse:** Data warehouses are designed to collect and store large amounts of **historical, structured data** from **multiple databases**. Because a data warehouse stores data from different sources, its main purpose is to be a **central repository** supporting **business intelligence (BI) activities**, particularly querying and analytics.

Data **must be transformed** into a uniform structure to be housed in a data warehouse. **ETL or ELT processes** are essential to put information into the correct format. ETL is a **data integration** process that includes three steps: extraction, transformation, and loading. ETL systems extract raw data directly from individual databases or a data lake, transform it into a uniform structure, then load it into a data warehouse. ELT is a similar data integration process that includes the same three steps, but in a different order: extraction, loading, and then transformation. ELT systems extract raw data directly from individual databases or a data lake, load it into a data warehouse, and then transform it into a uniform structure.

**Data marts:** Data marts are smaller (mini) versions of a data warehouse intended for a specific business purpose. For example, the sales department could use a data mart as a **focused repository** to hold **historical, structured** sales-related information. By narrowing the scope of the data, a data mart helps the business unit avoid sorting through unnecessary information (eg, HR data), thus improving both **security and speed**.

| | Data Lake | Data Warehouse | Data Mart |
|---|---|---|---|
| **Data Scope** | General, raw | General, structured | Focused, structured |
| **Prior Processing** | None to light | Moderate to high | Very high |
| **Analysis Limitations** | Input sources | Data transformation methods | Data topic focus |
| **Ease of Navigation** | Hard | Moderate | Easy |

## Database Schemas

A database schema is a blueprint of the **database's** underlying **structure**. Typically presented as a **diagram**, schemas show the tables, attributes, primary keys (PK), and relationships (ie, associations) in a database. The schema is used to design (ie, model) the database and help administrators or auditors understand its foundation. For example, an administrator may use a schema to understand how to integrate data or design queries. An auditor can use the schema to obtain an understanding of the database and decide whether reports based on queries are complete and accurate.

There are three broad types of schemas used to create databases:

**Conceptual:** A conceptual model, used in the initial phases of design, is the "big picture" view of a database. This model is not specific to any hardware, software, or type of database but is simply a representation of the tables in the database, the contents of those tables, and the relationships between them. Relationships are notated as multiplicities, which are the minimum and maximum number of times a class of data can participate in a relationship. Diagrams of conceptual models may be referred to as **unified modeling language (UML)** diagrams or **entity relationship diagrams (ERD).**

**Logical:** Once the type of database (eg, relational) is known, the conceptual model can be converted into a logical model, even if the specific software is unknown. A logical model shows the attributes and primary keys that will be included for each table. It does not show the relationships between the tables other than listing foreign keys (FK), which are the primary keys of a different table. For example, if a database has two tables—Sales and Customer—the Sales table might list the sales ID#, date, and amount. It would be helpful to add an attribute to relate a customer to the sale. The customer is a foreign key (ie, the information that stems from a different table).

**Physical:** A physical model is used to implement the logical model once the type of software is known. For example, many Microsoft subscriptions include Access, a program that can be used to make simple databases, forms, and SQL queries.

Conceptual, logical, and physical schemas would appear as follows:

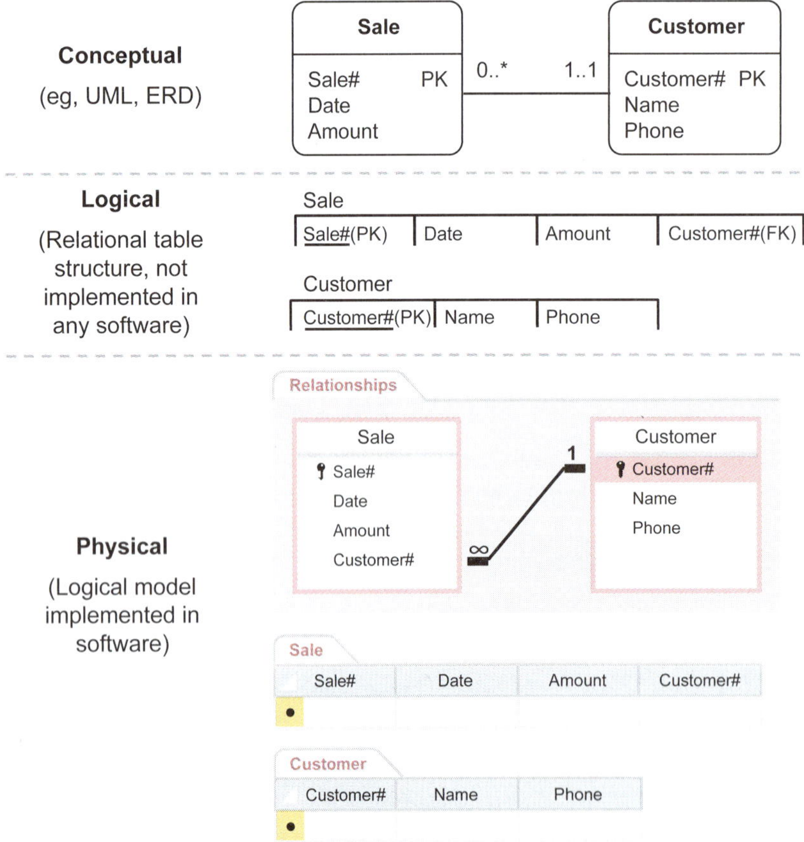

Database schemas become essential for organizational productivity as the amount of data grows. Poorly managed and documented relational models are difficult to support and create operational problems for users as well as the organization.

**Advantages** of schemas include:

- **Access and security:** Database schema design separates data into entities (ie, classes), making it easier to exchange a schema between databases. Database permission controls can further secure sensitive data.
- **Organization and communication:** Database schema documentation improves internal stakeholder organization and communication. By supplying a shared source of truth, it helps users understand logical restrictions and aggregation across tables.
- **Integrity:** Organization and communication assure data validity, allowing administrators to avoid data duplication and thus control the normalization operations.

Two other approaches to logical and physical schemas are the **star** and **snowflake**.

**Star:** The star model is a **basic schema for data warehouses** and **data marts**. The model is shaped like a star because it uses a **central fact table** and **associated dimension tables** (points of the star). The goal of a star schema is to separate numerical "fact" data from descriptive dimensional data, which simplifies data organization and enhances query performance.

For example, a central fact table may hold numerical data such as product ID#, cost, quantities, or unit of measure. Dimension tables might store descriptive data such as product name, buyer name, vendor name, or vendor location. Centralizing the numerical data in a fact table links it to the dimension tables, which provide descriptive information. These relationships reduce the number of joins required for queries and facilitate data aggregation.

Star tables are best used for simple joins (ie, one-to-one relationships). The fact table is connected to dimension tables via a foreign key relationship to the primary key of each dimension table.

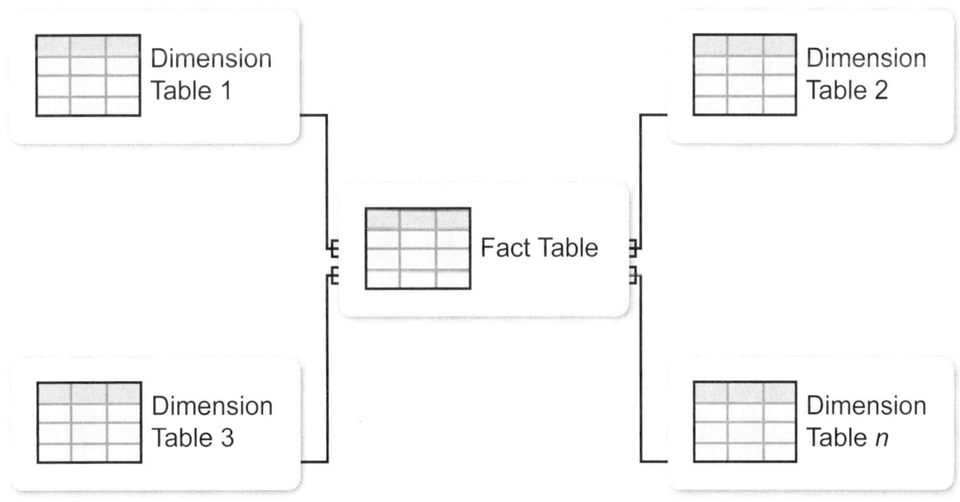


**Snowflake:** The snowflake schema is a variant of the star schema in that it also has a central fact table and associated dimension tables. However, this schema is expanded because the dimension tables are divided into multiple smaller tables. Each dimension is further divided until it is normalized, resulting in no repetition of values in the dimensional tables. This subdivision creates a more detailed and structured description, which is helpful for data analysis "drill down" (eg, navigating from summary data to more detailed data).

Because snowflake schemas are more detailed and contain more tables, they take up a lot of storage space and may cause performance problems. Snowflake schemas are best for situations in which the organization needs to perform complex queries or advanced analysis.

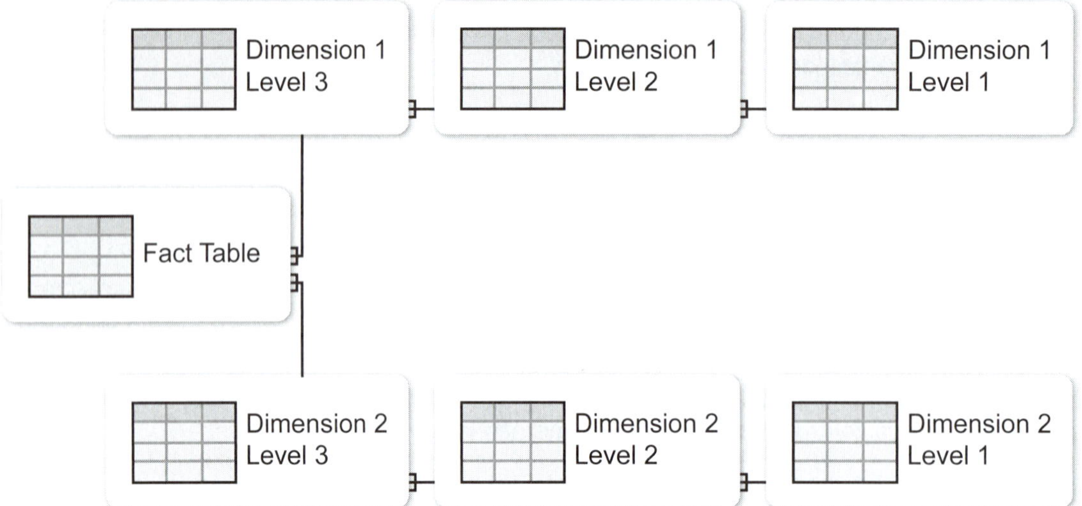


## Relational Database Structure

**Representative Task (Application):** Examine a relational database's structure to determine whether it applies data integrity rules, uses a data dictionary, and normalizes the data.

### Overview

CPAs may perform internal audits or external engagements to evaluate **data reliability** (ie, quality). For example, a university's **internal audit** department might perform data integrity audits to ensure proper governance over the data that must be given to government organizations as a condition of receiving special project funding. In addition, an organization may engage a CPA to **attest** to the integrity of data as a condition of a service contract or business sale. CPAs may also perform **advisory** services to help organizations reduce data errors and improve the quality of their business intelligence.

Evaluating data structures typically involves considering the following factors:

| Factor | Determines |
|---|---|
| **Accuracy** | Is the data correct? |
| **Validity** | Is the data in the correct format, data type, and value range? |
| **Completeness** | Does the data have all the elements it should? |
| **Consistency** | Is the data the same across multiple systems? |
| **Uniqueness** | Are records or fields duplicated? |
| **Timeliness** | Is the data current? |
| **Relevance** | Does the data meet the needs it is intended for? |

| Factor | Determines |
|---|---|
| **Accessibility** | Do end users have access to the data they need? |
| **Security** | Is the data protected from unauthorized access or modification? |
| **Protection** | Is the data backed up? |

A CPA's **procedures** include **examining the database's structure** (ie, schema or design) and related **documentation** to figure out if data integrity rules are applied, a data dictionary is used, and the data is normalized:

- **Data integrity rules:** The rules and constraints built into a database's design to ensure data integrity.
- **Data dictionary:** Metadata that supplies a detailed description of data design elements, such as the type, size, and constraints of the data, as well as its relationships to other data.
- **Data normalization:** A series of design rules (ie, normal forms) used to break complex data structures down into smaller parts and thus reduce data redundancy and anomalies.

## Relational Database Elements

To recall, a relational database is a collection of structured data in which certain data points are associated (ie, related) to one another. The basic elements of a relational database are as follows:

- **Table:** A table in a relational database is like a spreadsheet, with columns and rows. The columns describe field attributes, and each row is an individual record. Tables hold information about a specific entity or an association between entities. An **entity** is a **group** of objects with similar characteristics; an association is a related link between two tables.

  For example, AIS are relational databases that may follow a REA (resources, events, and agents) pattern, where entities represent resources (material items that are given and received, such as inventory and cash), events (things that happen, such as sales and cash receipts), and agents (internal and external parties who participate in events, such as sales personnel and customers).

- **Attribute:** Attributes are the column fields in a relational database table; they hold detailed information the organization wants to keep about an entity or association. The attributes function like column headers in a spreadsheet. For example, in a table for sales, attributes may include the sales ID#, date of the sale, and the sale's dollar amount.
  - **Primary key:** Each table must have at least one attribute that uniquely identifies an individual record. The primary key should be data about a record that cannot be duplicated and will not change. If there is no naturally occurring unique data, the primary key may be system generated (eg, customer ID, employee ID). Every record must have a primary key so that it can be linked to other tables. Some tables may have primary keys that are a combination of multiple fields. Such a combination is referred to as a **composite primary key**.
  - **Foreign key:** A table's primary key, which is added to another table, creating an association. For example, consider a Sales table with a primary key of Sale# and a Customer table with a primary key of Customer#. The Sales table would include the foreign key field Customer# to associate the sale with a specific customer.

- **Record:** A record is a row in a table, representing a single entry or instance.
- **Association:** Tables in a database may be related by different associations. Three of the fundamental relationships are:

| Relationship | Example |
|---|---|
| One to one (1:1) | For every department, there is only one manager. |
| One to many (1:M) | For every manager, there are many employees. |
| Many to many (M:M) | Many employees assist many customers. |

To associate tables in a relational database, the primary key of one table is added to another table and then the two tables are **joined**. Joins are created differently depending on the software. For example, some programs create a join by dragging a line from the primary key on one table to the corresponding foreign key on another.

In conceptual **entity relationship diagrams (ERD)** and **unified modeling language (UML) diagrams**, associations are described in terms of their **multiplicities** (ie, cardinalities), which are the minimum and maximum number of times an entity (ie, class in a UML diagram) can be associated with another entity. Associations may be optional or mandatory. Relationships may occur zero, one, or multiple times.

For example, a customer (agent) could hypothetically participate in no sales, one sale, or many sales (event). This would be expressed as "0..*" to show that the minimum number of times a customer could participate in a sale is zero (optional) and the maximum could be many times. Each sale must have at least one customer but *only* one customer, which would be expressed as "1..1"; in other words, both the minimum and maximum number of customers participating in a sale is 1.

A conceptual database schema would look like this:

**Conceptual Schema—UML Diagram**

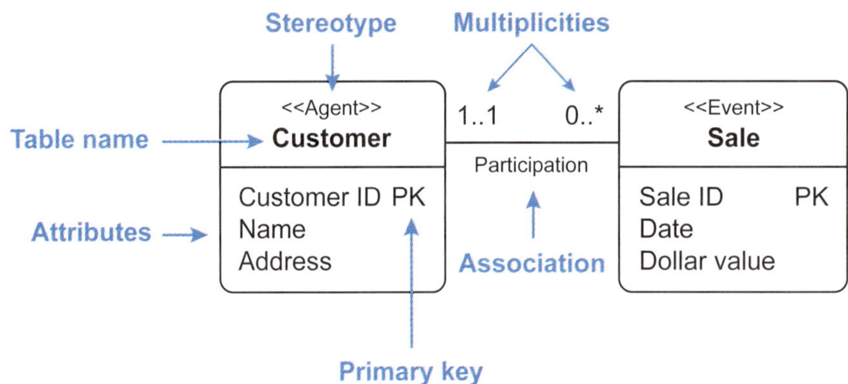


## Data Integrity Rules

Data integrity is an umbrella term that describes all the factors discussed earlier, such as accuracy, validity, consistency, etc. It means that data is input correctly during collection and has no unauthorized changes (unintentional or intentional) throughout its life cycle.

Data integrity primarily focuses on the physical and logical integrity of a database.

**Physical integrity:** Physical integrity refers to protecting data from access or modification arising from external threats such as power outages, natural disasters, and malicious actors. Environmental and security hardware and software controls protect the physical aspects of data.

**Logical integrity:** When CPAs examine the structure of a database, they are mostly concerned with what predefined rules (ie, automated constraints or controls) have been built into the database's design to make sure that the data is correct, formatted properly, and protected from unauthorized changes. A database may have built-in constraints that are automatically, consistently, and routinely applied to all data to reduce errors.

Constraints define the properties of an attribute and reject values that do not follow the rules. This is necessary to prevent errors and inconsistent formatting. For example, humans can recognize that "mm/dd/yyyy" is the same as "Month, Day, Year," but a computer may not.

Common constraints include:

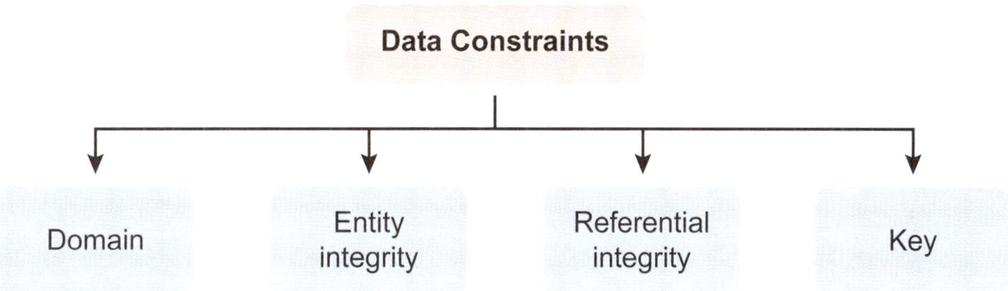


**Domain constraint:** In this context, a domain is the set of acceptable values that a field can hold. A domain constraint restricts what values can be input into a field by defining a valid set of values or data types for a table attribute. The constraint may require the attribute to be a number, character, date, time, string, etc. For example, a domain constraint may require that the month on a date field is limited to valid months of the year, 01–12, or a name field may contain only 50 characters.

**Entity integrity constraint:** Primary keys are essential for ensuring data integrity and creating table relationships. An entity integrity constraint requires that the primary key field is not null (ie, blank). For example, a SQL database coding should contain the specific language that the primary field has a "not null" constraint. When that is coded, any attempt to leave the primary key field blank or delete the contents will be rejected.

**Referential integrity constraint:** Referential integrity requires that foreign key values entered in a related table must first exist in the primary table. For example, if a Sales table has the Customer# field as a foreign key, the Customer# entered must first exist in the Customer table. Referential integrity reduces errors but does not completely prevent them because an incorrect Customer# is still valid as long as it exists in the Customer table. In addition, the database will accept a null value unless the Customer# field also has an entity integrity constraint.

**Key constraint:** A key constraint requires that the primary key be unique. Primary keys identify a specific record and cannot be duplicated. The key constraint would ensure that there is no redundancy in the primary key field.

## Data Dictionary

A data dictionary (ie, data definition matrix or data catalogue) is where the **data type** and **properties of fields** in a database table are set, including constraints. The data dictionary contains attribute information such as titles, descriptions, and formats. This hidden data is referred to as **metadata** (ie, data about data).

It is easier to design, update, report, or integrate a database when the attributes are clearly defined. The definitions also help ensure the development and communication of consistent data across the organization.

The data type describes the kind of data an attribute holds. Data type names may vary between database software vendors but still have a similar meaning. For example, a data dictionary and data types may appear as:

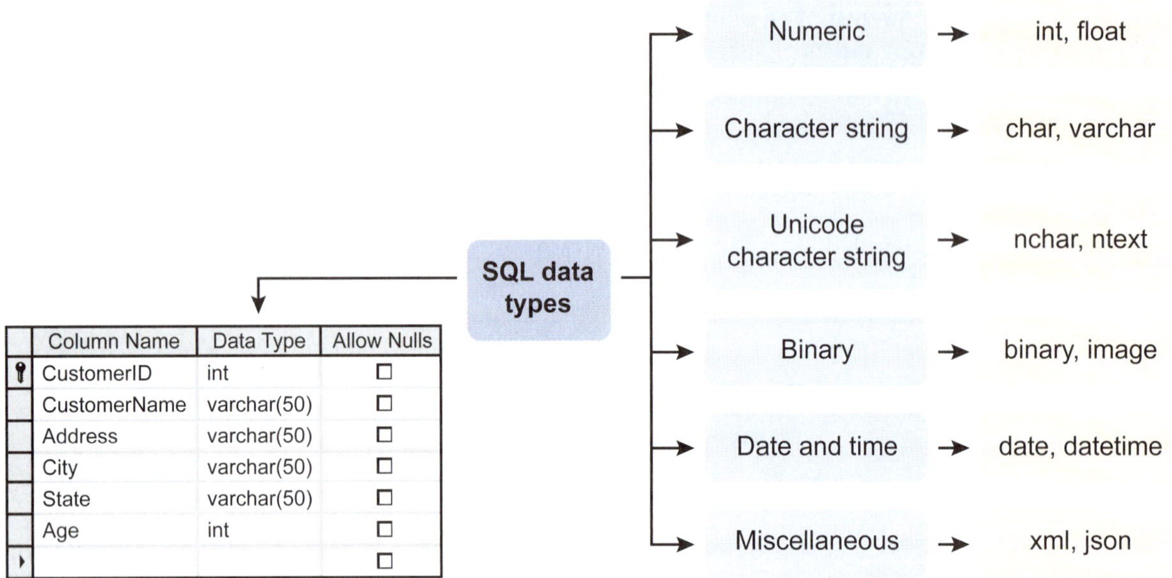


| Column Name | Data Type | Allow Nulls |
|---|---|---|
| CustomerID | int | ☐ |
| CustomerName | varchar(50) | ☐ |
| Address | varchar(50) | ☐ |
| City | varchar(50) | ☐ |
| State | varchar(50) | ☐ |
| Age | int | ☐ |
| | | ☐ |

Depending on the software used, other attribute properties might be found in a data dictionary. For example, in Microsoft Access the data dictionary might specify the following additional information:

- **Field size:** For text, the field size is the number of characters the field can contain (eg, up to 255 characters). For numbers or currency, it is the type of number (ie, integer or decimal)
- **Format:** How the field is displayed. For example, dates may appear as mm/dd/yyyy
- **Input mask:** The required pattern for inputting data. For example, phone numbers may have an input mask of (###) ###-#### so that all phone numbers have the same number of digits and are formatted consistently
- **Caption:** The help text that appears to users so that they understand what information a field is asking for
- **Default value:** The value that is automatically entered into a field. For example, the default value of a date field might be the current date
- **Validation rule:** A constraint that limits the value that can be entered into a field
- **Validation text:** The error message that appears to users when the validation rule is violated
- **Required:** A constraint that ensures the field will not be left blank (ie, not null constraint)
- **Indexed:** Whether the field can be sorted and searched

## Data Normalization

Data normalization is the process of **organizing a database** logically to reduce redundancy (ie, data duplication) and inconsistent dependencies. Redundant data uses more storage space, increases costs, and makes inserting, deleting, and updating data more difficult. Inconsistent dependencies make data difficult to query (ie, filter, sort, and analyze) and can cause errors. For example, if tables and relationships are properly organized, updating data in one place should update it in all places. Without proper organization, data may update in some places but not in others, causing inconsistencies.

Therefore, normalization is important to the **structural design** of a database. It involves creating tables and relationships based on a **series of rules** known as **normal forms**. Each normal form builds upon the one before, subdividing large tables into smaller tables that are associated by primary and foreign keys. If only the first rule is used, the database is in "first normal form." If the first three rules are used, the database is in "third normal form." Although there are other levels of normalization, the third normal form is sufficient for most applications.

**Unnormalized Form (0NF)** *(Database that has not been structured according to any rules)*

| Product ID | Description | Cost | Quantity on Hand | Warehouse |
|---|---|---|---|---|
| 101 | Textbook | $100 | 200 | Texas, Vermont |
| 102 | Laptop | $800 | 40 | Florida |
| 103 | Calculator | $50 | 300 | Indiana, New York, Colorado |

**First Normal Form (1NF)**

To use the first normal form:

- Each record should have a primary key (PK).
- Repeating groups should be eliminated.
- Each cell should hold a single piece of data.

| Product ID | Description | Cost | Quantity on Hand | Warehouse |
|---|---|---|---|---|
| 101 | Textbook | $100 | 120 | Texas |
| 101 | Textbook | $100 | 80 | Vermont |
| 102 | Laptop | $800 | 40 | Florida |
| 103 | Calculator | $50 | 100 | Indiana |
| 103 | Calculator | $50 | 100 | New York |
| 103 | Calculator | $50 | 100 | Colorado |

### Second Normal Form (2NF)

To use the second normal form:

- The database must be in the first normal form.
- Separate tables should be created for sets of values that apply to multiple records.
- These tables must be related with a foreign key (FK).

| Product ID (PK) | Description | Cost |
|---|---|---|
| 101 | Textbook | $100 |
| 102 | Laptop | $800 |
| 103 | Calculator | $50 |

| Warehouse ID (PK) | Warehouse | Product ID (FK) | Quantity on Hand |
|---|---|---|---|
| W1 | Texas | 101 | 120 |
| W2 | Vermont | 101 | 80 |
| W3 | Florida | 102 | 40 |
| W4 | Indiana | 103 | 100 |
| W5 | New York | 103 | 100 |
| W6 | Colorado | 103 | 100 |

### Third Normal Form (3NF)

To use the third normal form:

- The database must be in the second normal form.
- Fields that do not depend on the key should be eliminated.

Data is fully normalized once all attributes in a table are dependent on the primary key, the entire primary key, and only the primary key.

| Product ID (PK) | Description |
|---|---|
| 101 | Textbook |
| 102 | Laptop |
| 103 | Calculator |

| Product ID (PK) | Cost |
|---|---|
| 101 | $100 |
| 102 | $800 |
| 103 | $50 |

| Warehouse ID (PK) | Warehouse | Product ID (FK) | Quantity on Hand |
|---|---|---|---|
| W1 | Texas | 101 | 120 |
| W2 | Vermont | 101 | 80 |
| W3 | Florida | 102 | 40 |
| W4 | Indiana | 103 | 100 |
| W5 | New York | 103 | 100 |
| W6 | Colorado | 103 | 100 |

# SQL Database: Data Flow Diagram and Queries

**Representative Task (Application):** Examine a SQL query (common commands, clauses, operators, aggregate functions, and string functions) to determine whether the retrieved data set is relevant and complete.

**Representative Task (Analysis):** Investigate a business process model (eg, flowchart, data flow diagram, business process model and notation [BPMN] diagram) to identify potential improvements.

During an engagement, a CPA may ask the organization to supply reports or other outputs by **retrieving underlying data** from its databases. **SQL** is the most common standard programming language for **relational databases**. Although SQL can create, update, insert, and delete data, this blueprint task is focused solely on queries.

A **query** is a question, specifically a request for information. Queries are entered into a database engine using the same programming language as the database. SQL queries use a SQL sub-language known as **data query language (DQL).**

CPAs need to read a SQL query to understand whether the **output** is **relevant and complete**. Without understanding the parameters used to fetch data, a CPA cannot rely on any outputs as **sufficient appropriate evidence** (eg, in a SOC examination). For this reason, auditors may observe a query as it is entered, save a screenshot, or request some documentation that evidences the exact SQL statement used to run the query, which produced an output. CPAs may also obtain data sets from a client and create their own custom queries to extract data.

## Sample Database

SQL queries are most easily learned by example. The first step when examining queries is to obtain an understanding of the data structure. It is important to understand the tables, attributes, and relationships that are available to be queried. One of the ways to obtain this understanding is to review diagrams of conceptual, logical, and physical schemas.

Review the following narrative, data flow diagram, and ERD to become familiar with the structure of the sample database. Use this information to understand the query examples that follow.

### Narrative

During a risk advisory engagement, a CPA evaluated the data integrity of an office supply retailer's accounting information system (AIS). The retailer's AIS is a relational database. The database structure follows the REA ontology (ie, resources, events, and agents).

The auditor is currently focused on the retailer's revenue cycle. For simplicity, assume all sales are in cash and are tax exempt.

A sale involves:

- **Resources:** Inventory and cash
- **Events:** Sales and cash receipts

- **Agents:** Internal sales representative and cashier; external customer
- **Associations:**
  - **Stockflow** to record the decrease in Inventory (credit) and the increase in Cost of Goods Sold (debit)
  - **Duality** to record the increase in Sales (credit) and Cash Receipts (debit)
  - **Participation** to show the agents who take part in events

The tables, fields (ie, attributes), primary keys, and relationships between the data can be found in the entity relationship diagram (ERD). The ERD was printed from the software's relationship tool. Note that the stockflow and duality tables use composite primary keys, meaning that more than one primary key is necessary to establish the proper relationships between tables.

The following data flow diagram was provided by the retailer to show the business process and data flow:

**Cash Sale Data Flow Diagram**

Sales rep
Customer
Inventory
Sales journal
Cash receipts journal
Remove stock
Quantity sold
1. Advise customer
2. Pick goods
3. Ring sale
4. Collect cash payment
Cashier

## Entity Relationship Diagram (ERD)

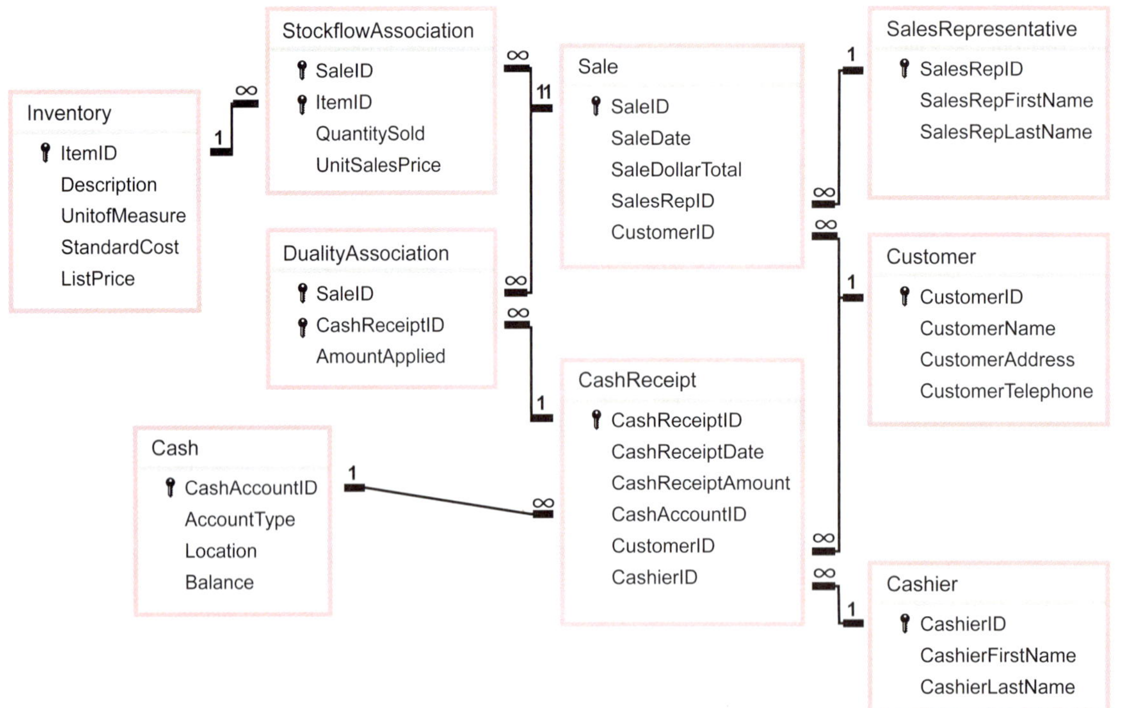

## SQL Commands and Clauses

SQL uses a standard syntax for queries used to retrieve data (ie, select queries):

**SELECT** attribute name(s)
**FROM** table name(s)
**WHERE** conditions/criteria are met;

The SELECT and FROM clauses are *required*; however, the WHERE clause is *optional*. Although these words are capitalized here for easier understanding, they are not case sensitive. Note that there is a semicolon at the end of the last clause. This lets the computer know it has reached the end of that individual query, as multiple queries could be entered sequentially.

- **SELECT** (required): Specifies the **columns** (ie, attributes or fields) from which the query will retrieve data.
- **FROM** (required): Specifies the **table(s)** that hold the data to be included in the query answer.
- **WHERE** (optional): Specifies the criteria that **rows** must meet to be included in the query answer. WHERE clauses can hold multiple criteria. If no criteria are needed, the WHERE clause is omitted.

Consider the following examples for the **Sales Representative** table:

| SalesRepID | SalesRepFirstName | SalesRepLastName | HourlyRate | Location |
|---|---|---|---|---|
| E23 | Charles | Jones | $25.50 | Location 1 |
| E26 | Karen | Green | $25.50 | Location 2 |
| E30 | Marie | Nelson | $32.00 | Location 3 |
| E32 | Samuel | Adams | $32.00 | Location 1 |
| E35 | Timothy | Bell | $41.00 | Location 1 |

**Basic SELECT-FROM Statement**

**Desired output:** List of all sales representatives, including first and last name.

**SQL query:**

**SELECT** SalesRepFirstName, SalesRepLastName
**FROM** SalesRepresentative;

**Output:**

| SalesRepFirstName | SalesRepLastName |
|---|---|
| Charles | Jones |
| Karen | Green |
| Marie | Nelson |
| Samuel | Adams |
| Timothy | Bell |

To determine whether this query is relevant and complete, an auditor would examine the syntax and see that there are no WHERE clauses that would filter out results. The table and fields correspond to the relationship diagram and the data dictionary. The count and details can be compared with other source documents such as HR records to make sure they are complete.

Note that the results of the query are not in alphabetical order. To specify how the query results are **sorted**, the **ORDER BY** clause would be added to the statement. When the ORDER BY clause is used, it must be followed by the column name(s) to be sorted. If multiple columns are to be sorted, the ORDER BY clause should state each column name in the preferred reporting order, separated by a comma (eg, Location, SalesRepLastName).

The sorting order must be ascending or descending. If ascending is desired, nothing needs to be added; however, **DESC** should be added if **descending order** is preferred.

**ORDER BY to Sort Ascending/Descending**

**Desired output:** List of all sales representatives, including first and last name, in ascending order by last name.

**SQL query:**

```
SELECT SalesRepFirstName, SalesRepLastName
FROM SalesRepresentative
ORDER BY SalesRepLastName;
```

Note that **ASC** could have been added to the ORDER BY clause, but it was omitted because the default sort is ascending order.

**Output:**

| SalesRepFirstName | SalesRepLastName |
|---|---|
| Samuel | Adams |
| Timothy | Bell |
| Karen | Green |
| Charles | Jones |
| Marie | Nelson |

**Desired output:** List of all sales representatives, including first and last name, in descending order by last name.

**SQL query:**

```
SELECT SalesRepFirstName, SalesRepLastName
FROM SalesRepresentative
ORDER BY SalesRepLastName DESC;
```

**Output:**

| SalesRepFirstName | SalesRepLastName |
|---|---|
| Marie | Nelson |
| Charles | Jones |
| Karen | Green |
| Timothy | Bell |
| Samuel | Adams |

Note that the column names appear as they do in the database. Often, names in a database may be long and have no spaces. This prevents duplication of column names throughout an extensive database. To make the report more user friendly, the **column** names can be **renamed** on the output using the **AS** clause. Renaming is referred to as creating an **alias**.

### AS to Rename Column Header

**Desired output:** List of all sales representatives, including first and last name, in ascending order by last name. Column headers should use the aliases (ie, be changed to) "First" and "Last."

**SQL query:**

**SELECT** SalesRepFirstName **AS** First, SalesRepLastName **AS** Last
**FROM** SalesRepresentative
**ORDER BY** SalesRepLastName;

**Output:**

| First | Last |
|---|---|
| Samuel | Adams |
| Timothy | Bell |
| Karen | Green |
| Charles | Jones |
| Marie | Nelson |

When reviewing an output, it is important to understand that the column names on the output may not be the same as in the database. Look for the AS clause to figure out if it has been renamed.

In the earlier examples, the SELECT statement included only two of the attributes in the Sales Representative table. If desired, an asterisk (*) placed after SELECT will retrieve all attributes (ie, columns) in a table. Depending on the size of the table, an auditor may prefer that the SQL query use the asterisk to ensure the retrieved data is complete.

### SELECT * to Retrieve All Data in a Table

**Desired output:** List of all data in the Sales Representatives table.

**SQL query:**

**SELECT** *
**FROM** SalesRepresentative;

**Output:**

| SalesRepID | SalesRepFirstName | SalesRepLastName | HourlyRate | Location |
|---|---|---|---|---|
| E23 | Charles | Jones | $25.50 | Location 1 |
| E26 | Karen | Green | $25.50 | Location 2 |
| E30 | Marie | Nelson | $32.00 | Location 3 |
| E32 | Samuel | Adams | $32.00 | Location 1 |
| E35 | Timothy | Bell | $41.00 | Location 1 |

By default, SQL will retrieve duplicate information in a data table. It is important to distinguish between a true duplicate and information that can legitimately be the same. For example, compare the following tables:

| SalesRepID | SalesRepFirstName | SalesRepLastName | HourlyRate | Location |
|---|---|---|---|---|
| E23 | Charles | Jones | $25.50 | Location 1 |
| E26 | Karen | Green | $25.50 | Location 2 |
| E30 | Marie | Nelson | $32.00 | Location 3 |
| E32 | Samuel | Adams | $32.00 | Location 1 |
| E35 | Timothy | Bell | $41.00 | Location 1 |

| SalesRepID | SalesRepFirstName | SalesRepLastName | HourlyRate | Location |
|---|---|---|---|---|
| E23 | Charles | Jones | $25.50 | Location 1 |
| E26 | Karen | Green | $25.50 | Location 2 |
| E30 | Marie | Nelson | $32.00 | Location 3 |
| E32 | Samuel | Adams | $32.00 | Location 1 |
| E35 | Timothy | Bell | $41.00 | Location 1 |
| E40 | Marie | Nelson | $32.00 | Location 3 |

In the first example, some of the hourly rates and locations are the same. However, none of the ID#s or names are the same. This table does not have duplicates.

In the second example, one salesperson's name, hourly rate, and location appear to be duplicated. However, the SalesRepID (primary key) is different. An inquiry would need to be made to determine whether this is a true duplicate or not.

If it is a true **duplicate**, the **DISTINCT** clause can remove it from the query output only. A different command would be needed to delete the record from the database. Because that command is not a query command, it is not shown here.

**SELECT DISTINCT to Remove Duplicate from Query Output**

**Initial output:**

| SalesRepFirstName | SalesRepLastName |
|---|---|
| Samuel | Adams |
| Timothy | Bell |
| Karen | Green |
| Charles | Jones |
| Marie | Nelson |
| Marie | Nelson |

**Desired output:** List of all sales representatives, including first and last name, in ascending order by last name. Do not show duplicate records.

**SQL query:**

```
SELECT DISTINCT SalesRepFirstName, SalesRepLastName
FROM SalesRepresentative
ORDER BY SalesRepLastName;
```

**Revised output:**

| SalesRepFirstName | SalesRepLastName |
|---|---|
| Samuel | Adams |
| Timothy | Bell |
| Karen | Green |
| Charles | Jones |
| Marie | Nelson |

## Logical Operators

Logical operators are **Boolean search terms** used to specify which records should be included in the query result. Common logical operators are AND, OR, and NOT. **AND** will include only those records that match *all* criteria. **OR** will include records that match *at least one criterion*. **NOT** includes records that *do not match* the specified criteria.

The following examples use the Inventory table:

| ItemID | Description | UnitofMeasure | StandardCost | ListPrice |
|---|---|---|---|---|
| CASE1 | Laptop Case | Each | $50.00 | $65.00 |
| CELL1 | Mobile Phone | Each | $400.00 | $500.00 |
| CLP1 | Binder Clips | Box of 24 | $7.00 | $9.00 |
| COMP1 | Monitor | Each | $75.00 | $125.00 |
| COMP2 | Desktop Comp | Each | $445.00 | $650.00 |
| PAP1 | Copy Paper | Box of 5 | $25.00 | $40.00 |
| PAP2 | Copy Paper | Box of 10 | $50.00 | $75.00 |
| PEN1 | Ink Pens | Box of 6 | $8.00 | $10.00 |
| PEN2 | Pencils | Box of 6 | $5.00 | $8.00 |
| TAB1 | Tablet | Each | $235.00 | $295.00 |

### WHERE AND to Retrieve Data that Meets Multiple Criteria

**Desired output:** List of all inventory where the unit of measure is "Each" and the cost is over $300.

**SQL query:**

```
SELECT ItemID, Description, UnitofMeasure, StandardCost, ListPrice
FROM Inventory
WHERE UnitofMeasure='Each' AND StandardCost>300;
```

**Output:**

| ItemID | Description | UnitofMeasure | StandardCost | ListPrice |
|---|---|---|---|---|
| COMP2 | Desktop Comp | Each | $445.00 | $650.00 |
| CELL1 | Mobile Phone | Each | $400.00 | $500.00 |

**WHERE OR to Retrieve Data that Meets at Least One Criteria**

**Desired output:** List of all inventory where the standard cost or list price is above $200. Include the ItemID, description, cost, and list price.

**SQL query:**

```
SELECT ItemID, Description, StandardCost, ListPrice
FROM Inventory
WHERE StandardCost>200 OR ListPrice>200;
```

**Output:**

| ItemID | Description | StandardCost | ListPrice |
|---|---|---|---|
| COMP2 | Desktop Comp | $445.00 | $650.00 |
| TAB1 | Tablet | $235.00 | $295.00 |
| CELL1 | Mobile Phone | $400.00 | $500.00 |

**WHERE NOT to Retrieve Data that Does Not Meet Specified Criteria**

**Desired output:** List of all inventory where the list price is *not* $100 or more. Include the ItemID, description, cost, and list price.

**SQL query:**

```
SELECT ItemID, Description, StandardCost, ListPrice
FROM Inventory
WHERE NOT ListPrice>100;
```

**Output:**

| ItemID | Description | StandardCost | ListPrice |
|---|---|---|---|
| CASE1 | Laptop Case | $50.00 | $65.00 |
| PEN1 | Ink Pens | $8.00 | $10.00 |
| PEN2 | Pencils | $5.00 | $8.00 |
| PAP1 | Copy Paper | $25.00 | $40.00 |
| PAP2 | Copy Paper | $50.00 | $75.00 |
| CLP1 | Binder Clips | $7.00 | $9.00 |

## Comparison Operators

Queries may apply **comparison operators** to numeric, text, and date fields using the **WHERE** clause. In numeric and date fields, the application is easy—based on which numbers are **lower**, **higher, or equal**. However, SQL has a special order for text values, ranking them in the order they appear in the English alphabet. Thus "a" will be a lower value than "z." A is equal to 1 and Z is equal to 26. Words that begin with the same letter are ranked in order by their second letter; if the second letter matches, the ranking moves to the third letter, and so forth.

Other comparison operators include BETWEEN, NULL, and LIKE. **BETWEEN** retrieves records in a range, and it includes the end points in the range. For example, if a query includes a range of 1 to 10, then 10 records will be returned, not eight. **NULL** means that a field is empty (ie, it has no data). Note that null does not mean zero because zero itself is a value. **LIKE** finds records that fit a pattern, such as those with a similarity in field value.

| Operator | Query Output |
|---|---|
| **Equal to (=)** | Records for which a field's value equals the specified value |
| **Less than (<)** | Records for which a field's value is less than a specified value |
| **Less than or equal to (<=)** | Records for which a field's value is equal to or less than a specified value |
| **Greater than (>)** | Records for which a field's value is greater than a specified value |
| **Greater than or equal to (>=)** | Records for which a field's value is greater than or equal to a specified value |
| **Not equal to (<>) or (!=)** | Records for which a field's value does not equal a specified value |
| **BETWEEN X and Y,** *where X and Y are endpoints in a range of values (>=X and <=Y)* | Records for which a field's value falls within a specified range, including the end points of the range |
| **IS NULL** | Records for which a field's value is empty (ie, null) |
| **EXISTS or IS NOT NULL** | Records for which a field has a value (ie, is not blank) |
| **LIKE** | Records that match a pattern<br>The LIKE operator may include wildcard symbols, such as the following:<br>* will find any number of extra characters (eg, "A*" will find A1, A12, A123)<br>? will find one extra character per ? (eg, "A?" will find only A1, A2, A3)<br>% will match any character (eg, "A%" will find A1, A12, 1A, 12A) |

The following examples use the **Sales** table:

| SaleID | SaleDate | SaleDollarTotal | SalesRepID | CustomerID |
|---|---|---|---|---|
| S001 | 12/01/2024 | $1,100.00 | E23 | C2323 |
| S002 | 12/06/2024 | $3,050.00 | E26 | C4731 |
| S003 | 12/08/2024 | $2,100.00 | E23 | C2323 |
| S004 | 12/14/2024 | $2,205.00 | E23 | C2323 |
| S005 | 12/16/2024 | $1,865.00 | E35 | C2831 |
| S006 | 12/18/2024 | $3,250.00 | E32 | C6125 |
| S007 | 12/23/2024 | $875.00 | E30 | C4731 |
| S008 | 12/26/2024 | $4,150.00 | E23 | C2323 |
| S009 | 12/28/2024 | $650.00 | E26 | C4731 |
| S010 | 12/30/2024 | $2,800.00 | E30 | C6125 |

**WHERE =, <, <=, >, >=, <> to Filter Records**

**Desired output:** List of all sales where the SalesRepID is E23.

**SQL query:**

```
SELECT SaleID, SaleDate, SaleDollarTotal, SalesRepID, CustomerID
FROM Sale
WHERE SalesRepID='E23';
```

**Output:**

| SaleID | SaleDate | SaleDollarTotal | SalesRepID | CustomerID |
|---|---|---|---|---|
| S001 | 12/01/2024 | $1,100.00 | E23 | C2323 |
| S003 | 12/08/2024 | $2,100.00 | E23 | C2323 |
| S004 | 12/14/2024 | $2,205.00 | E23 | C2323 |
| S008 | 12/26/2024 | $4,150.00 | E23 | C2323 |

**Desired output:** List all sales where the dollar amount of the sale is less than or equal to $1,000.

**SQL query:**

```
SELECT SaleID, SaleDate, SaleDollarTotal, SalesRepID, CustomerID
FROM Sale
WHERE SaleDollarTotal<=1000;
```

**Output:**

| SaleID | SaleDate | SaleDollarTotal | SalesRepID | CustomerID |
|---|---|---|---|---|
| S007 | 12/23/2024 | $875.00 | E30 | C4731 |
| S009 | 12/28/2024 | $650.00 | E26 | C4731 |

**Desired output:** List all sales where the dollar amount of the sale is greater than $4,000.

**SQL query:**

```
SELECT SaleID, SaleDate, SaleDollarTotal, SalesRepID, CustomerID
FROM Sale
WHERE SaleDollarTotal>4000;
```

**Output:**

| SaleID | SaleDate | SaleDollarTotal | SalesRepID | CustomerID |
|---|---|---|---|---|
| S008 | 12/26/2024 | $4,150.00 | E23 | C2323 |

**WHERE BETWEEN to Filter Records**

**Desired output:** List of all sales between 12/25/24 and 12/31/24. Report should include only the SaleID, date, and dollar amount.

**SQL query:**

```
SELECT SaleID, SaleDate, SaleDollarTotal
FROM Sale
WHERE SaleDate BETWEEN '12/25/2024' AND '12/31/2024';
```

**Output:**

| SaleID | SaleDate | SaleDollarTotal |
|---|---|---|
| S008 | 12/26/2024 | $4,150.00 |
| S009 | 12/28/2024 | $650.00 |
| S010 | 12/30/2024 | $2,800.00 |

### WHERE NULL to Find Fields Without Data

Assume that a power outage forcibly caused the computer to shut down. The auditor would like to find out if there was any data loss.

**Desired output:** List of any sales where a field is empty.

**SQL query:**

```
SELECT SaleID, SaleDate, SaleDollarTotal, SalesRepID, CustomerID
FROM Sale
WHERE SaleID IS NULL OR SaleDate IS NULL OR SaleDollarTotal IS NULL OR SalesRepID
IS NULL OR CustomerID IS NULL;
```

**Output:**

| SaleID | SaleDate | SaleDollarTotal | SalesRepID | CustomerID |
|---|---|---|---|---|
| S005 | 12/16/2024 | | E35 | C2831 |
| S007 | 12/23/2024 | $875.00 | | C4731 |

### WHERE LIKE to Find a Pattern

**Desired output:** List of all sales made to a CustomerID beginning with the letter and number C4. Include in the report the SalesID, date, dollar amount, and CustomerID.

**SQL query:**

```
SELECT SaleID, SaleDate, SaleDollarTotal, CustomerID
FROM Sale
WHERE CustomerID LIKE 'C4*';
```

**Output:**

| SaleID | SaleDate | SaleDollarTotal | CustomerID |
|---|---|---|---|
| S002 | 12/06/2024 | $3,050.00 | C4731 |
| S007 | 12/23/2024 | $875.00 | C4731 |
| S009 | 12/28/2024 | $650.00 | C4731 |

## Aggregate Functions (Vertical Calculations)

Aggregate functions are vertical calculations performed on a column. These functions include **average, sum, minimum, maximum, and count**. All aggregate functions follow the pattern of SELECT AVG (field name), SELECT MIN (field name), etc.

| Aggregate Function | Query Output |
|---|---|
| **AVG** | Computes the average of a column of data |
| **SUM** | Add all the values in a column (ie, foot the column) |
| **MIN** | Find the smallest value in a column |
| **MAX** | Find the largest value in a column |
| **COUNT** | Count the number of records (ie, rows) in a column |

The following examples use the **Cash Receipts** table:

| CashReceiptID | CashReceiptDate | CashReceiptAmount | CashAccountID | CustomerID | CashierID |
|---|---|---|---|---|---|
| CR101 | 12/01/2024 | $1,100.00 | Ca789125 | C2323 | E222 |
| CR102 | 12/06/2024 | $3,050.00 | Ca123501 | C4731 | E111 |
| CR103 | 12/08/2024 | $2,100.00 | Ca123501 | C2323 | E111 |
| CR104 | 12/14/2024 | $2,205.00 | Ca789125 | C2323 | E222 |
| CR105 | 12/16/2024 | $1,865.00 | Ca123501 | C2831 | E111 |
| CR106 | 12/18/2024 | $3,250.00 | Ca351327 | C6125 | E111 |
| CR107 | 12/23/2024 | $875.00 | Ca351327 | C4731 | E111 |
| CR108 | 12/26/2024 | $4,150.00 | Ca789125 | C2323 | E222 |
| CR109 | 12/28/2024 | $650.00 | Ca123501 | C4731 | E111 |
| CR110 | 12/30/2024 | $2,800.00 | Ca123501 | C6125 | E111 |

**SELECT AVG *(field name)* to Find the Average of a Column**

**Desired output:** Find the average of all cash receipts.

**SQL query:**

```
SELECT AVG(CashReceiptAmount) AS AvgOfCashReceiptAmount
FROM CashReceipt;
```

**Output:**

| AvgOfCashReceiptAmount |
|---|
| $2,204.50 |

### SELECT SUM *(field name)* to Find the Total of a Column

**Desired output:** Total all cash receipts.

**SQL query:**

```
SELECT SUM(CashReceiptAmount) AS SumOfCashReceiptAmount
FROM CashReceipt;
```

**Output:**

| SumOfCashReceiptAmount |
|---|
| $22,045.00 |

### SELECT COUNT *(field name)* to Find the Number of Records in a Column

**Desired output:** Count the number of cash receipts.

**SQL query:**

```
SELECT COUNT(CashReceiptAmount) AS CountOfCashReceiptAmount
FROM CashReceipt;
```

**Output:**

| CountOfCashReceiptAmount |
|---|
| 10 |

When using **aggregate functions**, it is often helpful to compute **subtotals** within the column data. For example, within the Cash Receipts table it may be helpful to show subtotals by bank account, dates, or cashier. To create subtotals, the **GROUP BY** clause must be added to the statement. The table will be grouped by the field chosen in the query, and any aggregate function will apply to the subgroup. To group records by multiple fields, list the field names, separated by commas, in the preferred order.

When **criteria** are added to an **aggregate function**, the **HAVING** clause is used. For example, the cash receipts could be subtotaled by cashier, but only for cash receipts above or below a certain amount.

### GROUP BY to Perform an Aggregate Function on a Subgroup

**Desired output:** Subtotal cash receipts by cashier.

**SQL query:**

```
SELECT SUM(CashReceiptAmount) AS SumOfCashReceiptAmount, CashierID
FROM CashReceipt
GROUP BY CashierID;
```

**Output:**

| SumOfCashReceiptAmount | CashierID |
|---|---|
| $14,590.00 | E111 |
| $7,455.00 | E222 |

### HAVING to Perform an Aggregate Function on a Subgroup with Criteria

**Desired output:** Subtotal cash receipts above $3,000 by cashier.

**SQL query:**

```
SELECT SUM(CashReceiptAmount) AS SumOfCashReceiptAmount, CashierID
FROM CashReceipt
GROUP BY CashierID
HAVING SUM(CashReceiptAmount)>3000;
```

**Output:**

| SumOfCashReceiptAmount | CashierID |
|---|---|
| $6,300.00 | E111 |
| $4,150.00 | E222 |

This is a prime example of why CPAs need to be able to read SQL query syntax. There is no way to tell, by looking at the output, how the calculation is performed. One might assume that it is the sum of all cash receipts; however, examining the query shows that filters have been added.

### HAVING to Perform an Aggregate Function on a Subgroup with Criteria Combined with the WHERE Clause for a Range

**Desired output:** Subtotal cash receipts above $3,000 by cashier in the last two weeks of the year.

**SQL query:**

```
SELECT SUM(CashReceiptAmount) AS SumOfCashReceiptAmount, CashierID
FROM CashReceipt
WHERE CashReceiptDate BETWEEN '12/16/2024' AND '12/31/2024'
GROUP BY CashierID
HAVING SUM(CashReceiptAmount)>3000;
```

**Output:**

| SumOfCashReceiptAmount | CashierID |
|---|---|
| $3,250.00 | E111 |
| $4,150.00 | E222 |

Again, without seeing the actual query, it is impossible to know what parameters were used to perform this computation. Note how the HAVING clause is used to restrict the output based on a sum (ie, an aggregate function). However, the WHERE clause is used for criteria that is not based on an aggregate function.

## Expressions (Horizontal Calculations)

An expression is the horizontal calculation of two fields (ie, columns) in a record (ie, row). In order to create the expression, a new column must be added to the output.

The following examples use the **Stockflow Association** table for the first half of the month:

| SaleID | ItemID | QuantitySold | UnitSalesPrice |
|---|---|---|---|
| S001 | CELL1 | 2 | $500.00 |
| S001 | PAP1 | 2 | $40.00 |
| S001 | PEN1 | 2 | $10.00 |
| S002 | COMP2 | 4 | $650.00 |
| S002 | COMP1 | 3 | $125.00 |
| S002 | PAP2 | 1 | $75.00 |
| S003 | CELL1 | 4 | $500.00 |
| S003 | PAP1 | 2 | $40.00 |
| S003 | PEN1 | 2 | $10.00 |
| S004 | TAB1 | 7 | $295.00 |
| S004 | CASE1 | 1 | $65.00 |
| S004 | PAP2 | 1 | $75.00 |

### Horizontal and Vertical Calculations

**CPA procedure:** For the first half of the month, verify that total sales amounts shown in the Stockflow Association table match the amounts shown in the Sales table.

**Step 1:** Multiply (ie, extend) the quantity sold by the unit sales prices in the Stockflow Association table.

**SQL query:**

```
SELECT SaleID, ItemID, QuantitySold, UnitSalesPrice, [QuantitySold]*[UnitSalesPrice] AS SaleExtension
FROM StockflowAssociation;
```

**Output:**

| SaleID | ItemID | QuantitySold | UnitSalePrice | SaleExtension |
|---|---|---|---|---|
| S001 | CELL1 | 2 | $500.00 | $1,000.00 |
| S001 | PAP1 | 2 | $40.00 | $80.00 |
| S001 | PEN1 | 2 | $10.00 | $20.00 |
| S002 | COMP1 | 3 | $125.00 | $375.00 |
| S002 | COMP2 | 4 | $650.00 | $2,600.00 |
| S002 | PAP2 | 1 | $75.00 | $75.00 |
| S003 | CELL1 | 4 | $500.00 | $2,000.00 |
| S003 | PAP1 | 2 | $40.00 | $80.00 |
| S003 | PEN1 | 2 | $10.00 | $20.00 |
| S004 | CASE1 | 1 | $65.00 | $65.00 |
| S004 | PAP2 | 1 | $75.00 | $75.00 |
| S004 | TAB1 | 7 | $295.00 | $2,065.00 |

**Step 2:** Subtotal each sale.

**SQL query:**

**SELECT** SaleID, **SUM**([QuantitySold]*[UnitSalesPrice]) **AS** Sale Extension
**FROM** StockflowAssociation
**GROUP BY** SaleID;

**Output:**

| SaleID | SaleExtension |
|---|---|
| S001 | $1,100.00 |
| S002 | $3,050.00 |
| S003 | $2,100.00 |
| S004 | $2,205.00 |

**Step 3:** Query the Sales table to determine the sales amounts during the first half of the month.

**SQL query:**

**SELECT** SaleID, SaleDollarTotal
**FROM** Sale
**WHERE** SaleDate **BETWEEN** '12/1/2024' **AND** '12/15/2024';

**Output:**

| SaleID | SaleDollarTotal |
|---|---|
| S001 | $1,100.00 |
| S002 | $3,050.00 |
| S003 | $2,100.00 |
| S004 | $2,205.00 |

**Step 4:** Compare the results of both queries to determine if the sales amounts recorded in the two tables agree.

**Stockflow Association Table**

| SaleID | SaleExtension |
|---|---|
| S001 | $1,100.00 |
| S002 | $3,050.00 |
| S003 | $2,100.00 |
| S004 | $2,205.00 |

**Sales Table**

| SaleID | SaleDollarTotal |
|---|---|
| S001 | $1,100.00 |
| S002 | $3,050.00 |
| S003 | $2,100.00 |
| S004 | $2,205.00 |

## Joining Tables

If the **data** to be included in a query is in **multiple tables**, a **JOIN** must be performed. Recall that a relationship between tables is created by posting the primary key of one table as a foreign key in the other table, or by posting the primary keys of both tables to a separate table (eg, an association table).

Four **JOIN types** are possible:

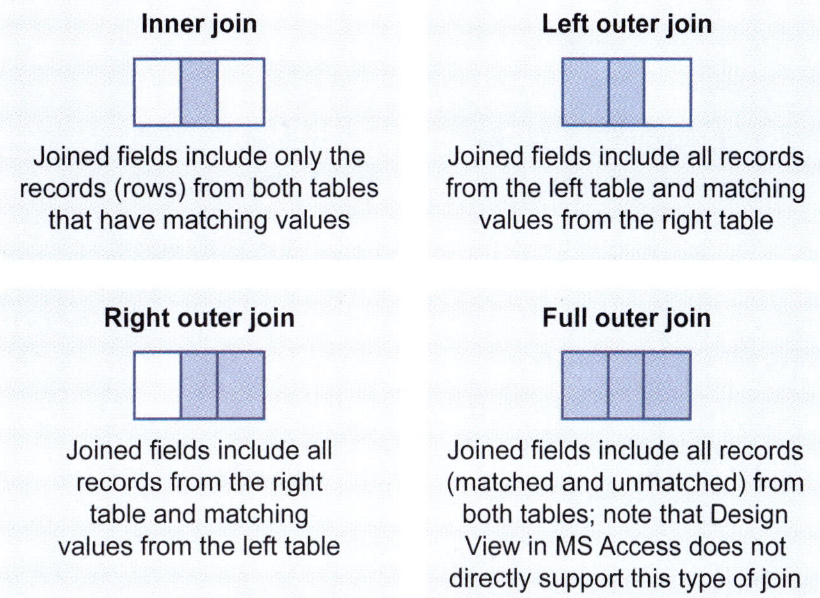


The following examples use the Inventory table, as well as the Stockflow Association table from the previous example (first half of the month only):

| ItemID | Description | UnitofMeasure | StandardCost | ListPrice |
|---|---|---|---|---|
| CASE1 | Laptop Case | Each | $50.00 | $65.00 |
| CELL1 | Mobile Phone | Each | $400.00 | $500.00 |
| CLP1 | Binder Clips | Box of 24 | $7.00 | $9.00 |
| COMP1 | Monitor | Each | $75.00 | $125.00 |
| COMP2 | Desktop Comp | Each | $445.00 | $650.00 |
| PAP1 | Copy Paper | Box of 5 | $25.00 | $40.00 |
| PAP2 | Copy Paper | Box of 10 | $50.00 | $75.00 |
| PEN1 | Ink Pens | Box of 6 | $8.00 | $10.00 |
| PEN2 | Pencils | Box of 6 | $5.00 | $8.00 |
| TAB1 | Tablet | Each | $235.00 | $295.00 |

| SaleID | ItemID | QuantitySold | UnitSalesPrice |
|---|---|---|---|
| S001 | CELL1 | 2 | $500.00 |
| S001 | PAP1 | 2 | $40.00 |
| S001 | PEN1 | 2 | $10.00 |
| S002 | COMP2 | 4 | $650.00 |
| S002 | COMP1 | 3 | $125.00 |
| S002 | PAP2 | 1 | $75.00 |
| S003 | CELL1 | 4 | $500.00 |
| S003 | PAP1 | 2 | $40.00 |
| S003 | PEN1 | 2 | $10.00 |
| S004 | TAB1 | 7 | $295.00 |
| S004 | CASE1 | 1 | $65.00 |
| S004 | PAP2 | 1 | $75.00 |

**INNER JOIN**

**SQL query:**

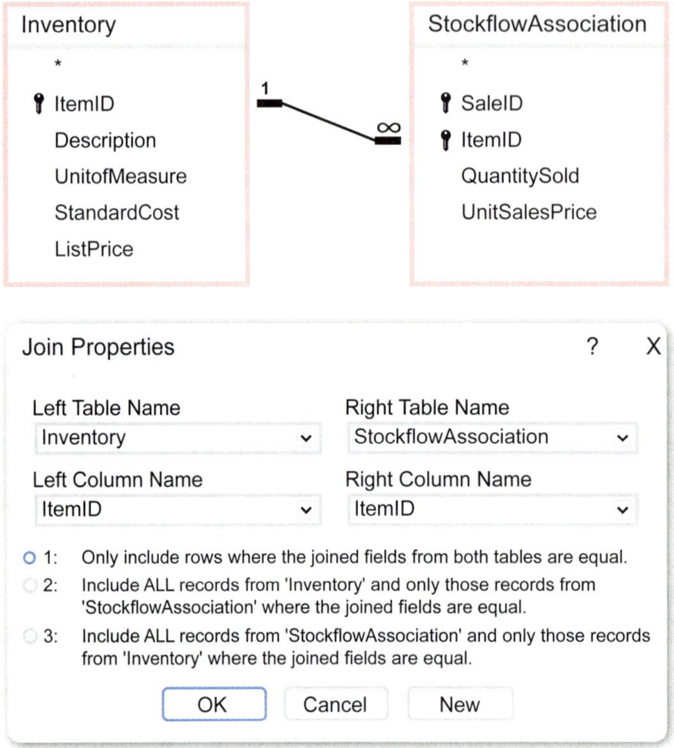


**SELECT** Inventory.ItemID, StockflowAssociation.ItemID
**FROM** Inventory **INNER JOIN** StockflowAssociation **ON** Inventory.ItemID = StockflowAssociation.ItemID
**GROUP BY** Inventory.ItemID, StockflowAssociation.ItemID;

**Output:**

| Inventory.ItemID | StockflowAssociation.ItemID |
|---|---|
| CASE1 | CASE1 |
| CELL1 | CELL1 |
| COMP1 | COMP1 |
| COMP2 | COMP2 |
| PAP1 | PAP1 |
| PAP2 | PAP2 |
| PEN1 | PEN1 |
| TAB1 | TAB1 |

Note that the inner join provides only results that match both tables. The Binder Clips and Pencils were not included in the results because there were no sales of those items in the data set (ie, no stockflow association for those items).

## LEFT JOIN

**SQL query:**

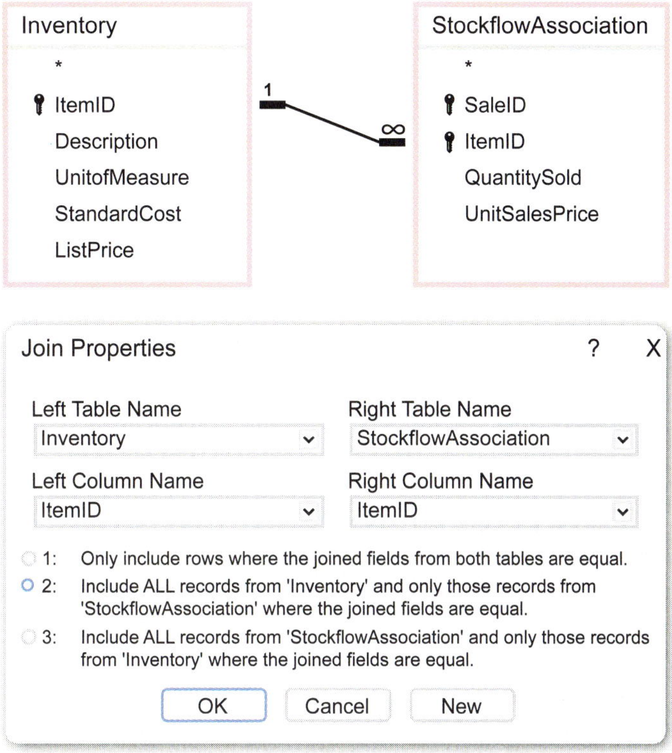


**SELECT** Inventory.ItemID, StockflowAssociation.ItemID
**FROM** Inventory **LEFT JOIN** StockflowAssociation **ON** Inventory.ItemID = StockflowAssociation.ItemID
**GROUP BY** Inventory.ItemID, StockflowAssociation.ItemID;

**Output:**

| Inventory.ItemID | StockflowAssociation.ItemID |
|---|---|
| CASE1 | CASE1 |
| CELL1 | CELL1 |
| CLP1 | |
| COMP1 | COMP1 |
| COMP2 | COMP2 |
| PAP1 | PAP1 |
| PAP2 | PAP2 |
| PEN1 | PEN1 |
| PEN2 | |
| TAB1 | TAB1 |

Note that left join includes all the items in Inventory, even if there was not a sale (ie, no stockflow association).

**RIGHT JOIN**

**SQL query:**

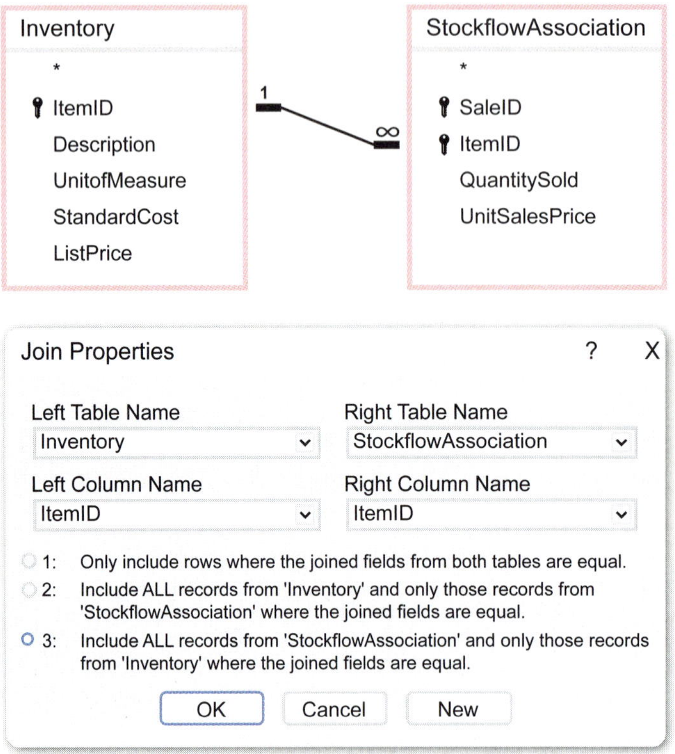


**SELECT** Inventory.ItemID, StockflowAssociation.ItemID
**FROM** Inventory **RIGHT JOIN** StockflowAssociation **ON** Inventory.ItemID = StockflowAssociation.ItemID
**GROUP BY** Inventory.ItemID, StockflowAssociation.ItemID;

**Output:**

| Inventory.ItemID | StockflowAssociation.ItemID |
|---|---|
| CASE1 | CASE1 |
| CELL1 | CELL1 |
| COMP1 | COMP1 |
| COMP2 | COMP2 |
| PAP1 | PAP1 |
| PAP2 | PAP2 |
| PEN1 | PEN1 |
| TAB1 | TAB1 |

Note that the right join returned the same results as the inner join. This will not always be the case, depending on the data set.

**FULL OUTER JOIN**

**SQL query:**

**SELECT** Inventory.ItemID, StockflowAssociation.ItemID
**FROM** Inventory **FULL OUTER JOIN** StockflowAssociation **ON** Inventory.ItemID = StockflowAssociation.ItemID
**GROUP BY** Inventory.ItemID, StockflowAssociation.ItemID;

**Output:**

| Inventory.ItemID | StockflowAssociation.ItemID |
|---|---|
| CASE1 | CASE1 |
| CELL1 | CELL1 |
| CLP1 | |
| COMP1 | COMP1 |
| COMP2 | COMP2 |
| PAP1 | PAP1 |
| PAP2 | PAP2 |
| PEN1 | PEN1 |
| PEN2 | |
| TAB1 | TAB1 |

Note that the full outer join included all products that were in either table.

## Order of Execution

When examining an SQL statement, it is important to understand the order of execution (ie, order of operations). SQL queries are performed in a specific order, like mathematical computations. An understanding of the order enables users to write better queries, avoid syntax errors, and identify errors.

Note how the order of executing an SQL query differs from the order in which the query is written. If a clause has not been included in the written statement, that operation will be skipped during execution.

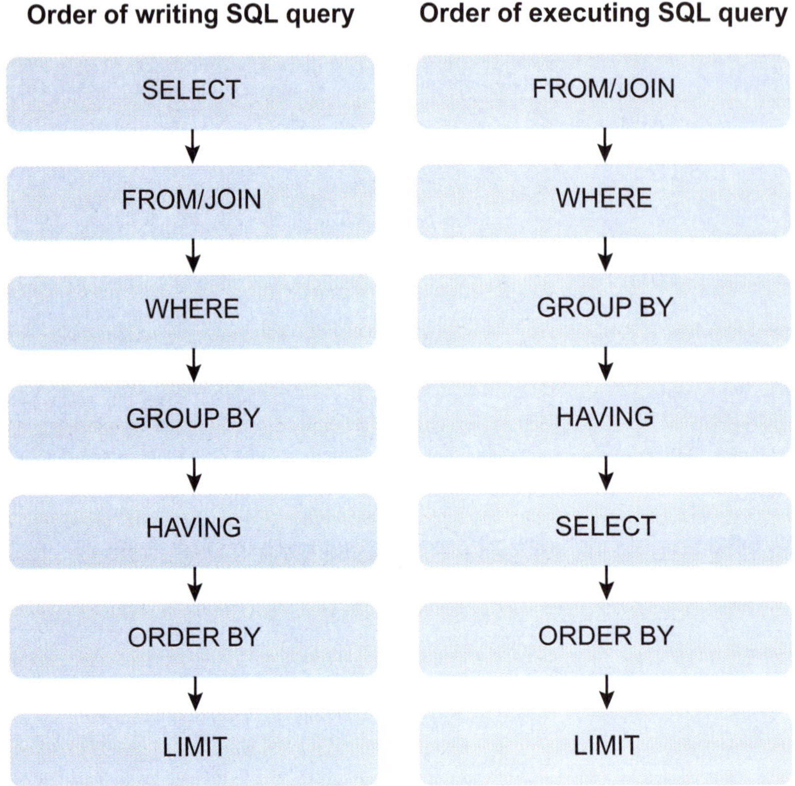


The **LIMIT** clause simply specifies the maximum number of rows (ie, records) to be included in a query's output (eg, report, display). Additional rows that meet the query criteria beyond the specified maximum are not included. The LIMIT clause can improve reporting speed when querying large data sets. It can also be used to select an audit sample.

The order of execution can be explained as follows:

| Order of executing SQL query | What the operation entails |
|---|---|
| FROM/JOIN | Selects the table(s) from which the data should be extracted |
| ↓ WHERE | Specifies the criteria rows must meet to be included in query results |
| ↓ GROUP BY | Determines if the query requires aggregating (eg, group, subtototal) |
| ↓ HAVING | Specifies aggregate functions (eg, sum, average) and criteria to be applied to the group (requires the GROUP BY clause) |
| ↓ SELECT | Selects the fields/columns that should be included in the query results |
| ↓ ORDER BY | Specifies how the query results should be sorted |
| ↓ LIMIT | Restricts the number of rows that should be included in the query results |

Recall that a SQL query is required to contain a SELECT clause and a FROM clause, at minimum. Thus, those operations will always be part of the order of execution. All the remaining clauses are optional and would only be executed if specifically included in the query.

## Analysis

### CPA Analysis

After reviewing the data flow diagram, the ERD, and the results of the queries, the auditor realized there was an internal control deficiency: cashiers were accepting cash receipts from customers while also making deposits into bank accounts. This represents a lack of a segregation of duties.

The CPA found this deficiency by reviewing the database tables. There is a relationship between the cashiers and the bank accounts. The data flow diagram provided by the client did not detail the last step in the process, which is making bank deposits. Had that step been included in the diagram, a line would have appeared from the cashier, bringing attention to the dual duties.

The CPA advised the client that the business process should be changed such that a different employee makes bank deposits. The accounting department should reconcile the bank deposits to the cash receipts journal.

# Data Integration

**Representative Task (Analysis):** Integrate the data available from different data sources to provide information necessary for financial and operational analysis and decisions.

**Representative Task (Remembering and Understanding):** Identify data extraction methods and techniques.

## Overview

In the earlier tasks, individual databases were discussed in terms of their structure and the relationships between the data. However, organizations typically have **multiple sources of data** for different uses or processes. These sources of data may be internal or external, on-premises or cloud-based.

To be useful for **financial and operational analysis** or decision-making, data from multiple sources must be connected, combined, and delivered in such a way that end users can consume the data. For example, an organization may want to understand how its social media advertising campaigns relate to sales. This will involve connecting to databases to extract data, **combining** multiple data sets, and **delivering** the combined data in a single, unified view that an analyst can **consume**.

Data integration may be performed on a large-scale, enterprise-wide basis, using data lakes and data warehouses to store massive amounts of data streamed from web or mobile applications in real time. Or the integration can be as simple as end users combining data from various sources, using spreadsheets or data visualization software. For example, CPAs commonly use self-service software tools such as spreadsheets, computer assisted audit tools, data analytics software, and data visualization applications.

## Data Integration Technologies

Data integration can occur through **manual or automated** processes. Both types involve **extracting** (ie, exporting) data from sources and **loading** (ie, importing) it into a target. Because the data may be in different formats or have errors or anomalies, it may need to be **cleaned, joined, and transformed** for use.

**Manual processes** may be sufficient for smaller, ad hoc projects that use **historical data**. However, such processes do not satisfy information needs when:

- The same data integration must be performed routinely
- The format of the data sources is not the same
- Only part of a data set is needed
- Extensive data sets must be evaluated
- Real-time information is important

With technologies such as the Internet, mobile devices, software as a service (SaaS) applications, social media, and IoT, even moderate-sized organizations can collect billions of rows of data. "**Big data**" allows for **real-time** reporting, analysis, and decision-making, but only when organizations are able to harness it and put it into a digestible format. Because this is now a widespread concern, newer technologies have been developed to **connect data and automate integrations**.

Modern methods of data integration rely on IT architectures and software that are designed to connect, combine, and deliver data. Examples include the following:

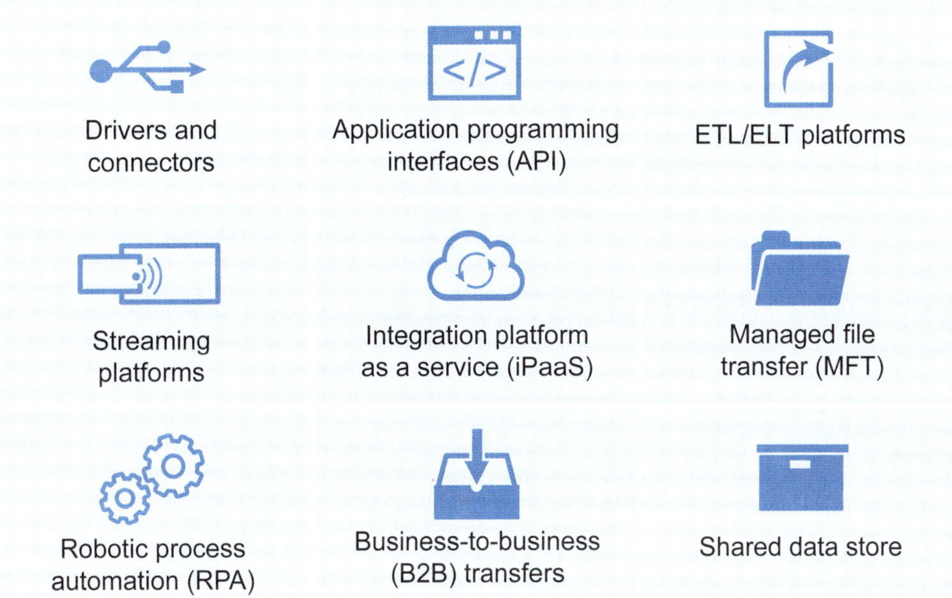


- **Drivers and connectors:** Many products such as Microsoft Excel and Power BI come with a list of sources to which users can connect to import data. The connections may be through the vendor's application and database product lines or through third parties. Once imported, the data sources can be integrated and transformed inside the product.
- **Application programming interfaces (API):** An API is a connection that allows two applications to share data in real time without human intervention. For example, most data analysis and visualization tools come with prebuilt API connections to common ERP, CRM, email, and social media applications. An API connection requires a key. Once it is set up, information flows easily between the two programs to do things like update databases or create dashboards.
- **ETL/ELT platforms:** ETL and ELT tools help to *extract* data from multiple sources, *transform* the data to refine it for quality, and *load* it into a central repository such as a database, data lake, or data warehouse. Although coding can be done manually, ETL tools make the process of moving data more efficient. In addition, ETL and ELT tools improve data integrity through transformations that include:
    - **Cleansing:** Resolving inconsistencies and null values
    - **Standardization:** Putting all data in a similar format
    - **Duplicate removal:** Excluding or discarding duplicate data
    - **Anomaly removal:** Flagging or removing outliers
    - **Sorting:** Organizing data

  In the ETL process, data is transformed before it is loaded into the destination. In ELT, data is transformed after the loading. There is also another process known as reverse ELT, where data is transformed before it is extracted.

- **Streaming platforms:** Streaming platforms allow for the continuous flow of data through a pipeline in which the data is extracted, transformed, and loaded in real time. For example, on websites that track the stock market or weather sensors, information that is only minutes old may already be useless. Streaming data allows for the instant updates most web- and mobile-based users have become accustomed to.
- **Integration platform as a service (iPaaS):** Integration platforms sold as an iPaaS help organizations connect on-premises legacy systems to cloud-based applications. Such platforms use connectors to extract data from SaaS applications and a second method to access on-premises data that is behind a firewall.

- **Managed file transfer (MFT):** Transferring files internally or externally can be risky from a compliance standpoint. MFT helps organizations securely transfer and integrate unstructured data like PDFs and other documents. Regulations such as HIPAA and GDPR or industry standards like PCI DSS require that organizations encrypt, transmit, monitor, and store sensitive data through secure methods.
- **Robotic process automation (RPA):** RPA, which can be either stand-alone or API-controlled, uses robotics to automate repetitive tasks and business processes. An RPA application (ie, bot) uses a script to replicate the same actions or clicks that a human would perform. In data integration, RPA allows for screen scraping to gather, transform, or move data. For example, RPA can automatically extract information from an email, put it in the correct format, and then upload it to a database.
- **Business-to-business (B2B) transfers:** Business to business data transfers are useful for coordinating business processes and data sharing between two or more parties, such as vendors, customers, and transaction processors. B2B transfer platforms help organizations integrate business processes and format electronic data interchanges (EDI). The platform collects data from sources, transforms it into a standardized format, and then transmits it to the proper destinations among business partners. Standardization may include data mapping, encryption, and validation processes to ensure data is recognized and managed appropriately on both ends of the transfer.
- **Shared data store:** A data store is a central repository for structured data (eg, relational databases) and unstructured data (eg, document files). The data store may be used by an organization, business unit, or business partners that need to share data. Through integration, the store can be used as a place to hold data that will then be extracted by users. For example, a shared data store might include a list of all the data types a user can select to import into data analytics or visualization software.

## Data Integration Purposes

As discussed earlier, data integration can help an organization bring information together to perform analysis and make decisions. It refers to the **transfer of data for consumption** by machines or humans. Situations where data integration is necessary include:

- **Aggregating data:** Data from multiple applications are copied into a central repository for analysis and processing. Data warehouses, data lakes, and data marts are examples of repositories. Data aggregation is useful for creating dashboards, analyzing information from two different applications, and migrating data from on-premises databases to the cloud.

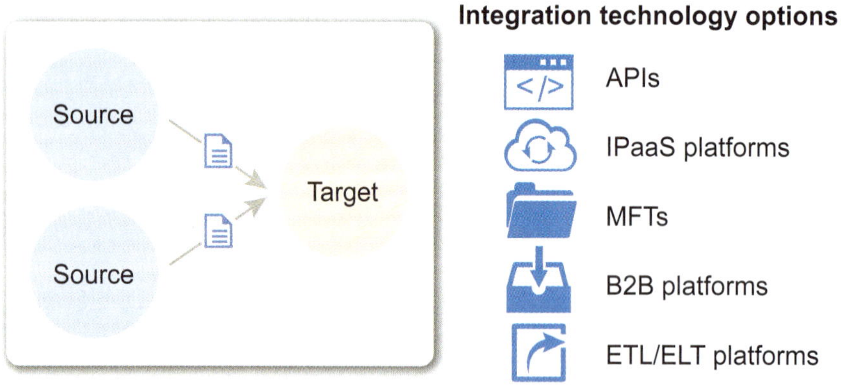


- **Ingesting streaming data:** Websites, point of sale systems, and sensors are just a few of the applications and devices that send real-time data to other applications, which then integrate the information. For example, a point of sale system can be used when integrating real-time information with inventory levels and sales data. Website visits, ad clicks, and visitor demographics are updated in real time on advertising platforms such as Google Ads by using widgets (ie, code snippets inserted into the website HTML). IoT devices can send data to security systems and applications for real-time alerts.

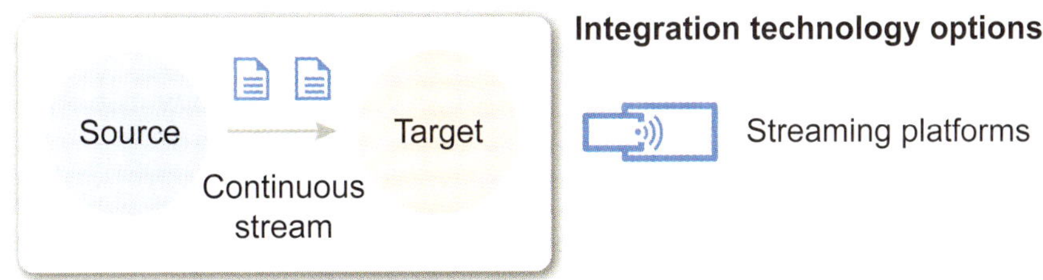


- **Syncing data between multiple applications:** Business processes often rely on more than one application, such as when the timing of data sync is crucial because the data is needed in near real time. For instance, creating a new customer account in CRM software may instantly update the customer records in a separate AIS system, or vice versa.

- **Sharing data with external partners:** Organizations often share data with outsourced service providers, business partners, suppliers, and government agencies. For example, an organization may send electronic purchase orders to its suppliers, electronically file tax returns, transmit data as required by regulations, or use an outsourced organization to process transactions.

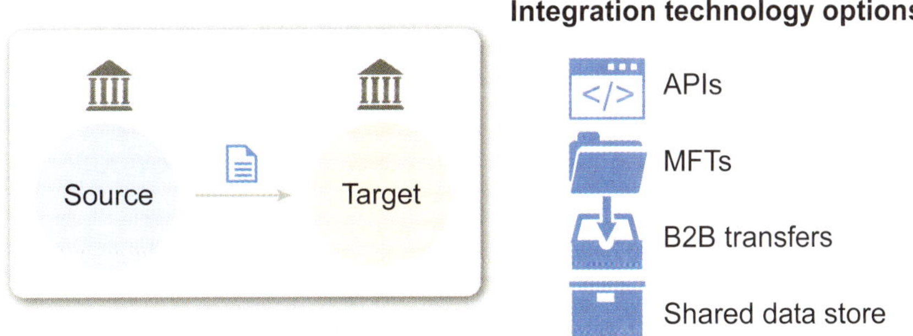


- **Broadcasting events:** Events typically refer to notifications about a change in status or alerts from a warning system. For example, an event can be as simple as notifying a customer about the status of a shipment or it may be an alert received about a possible cybersecurity attack.

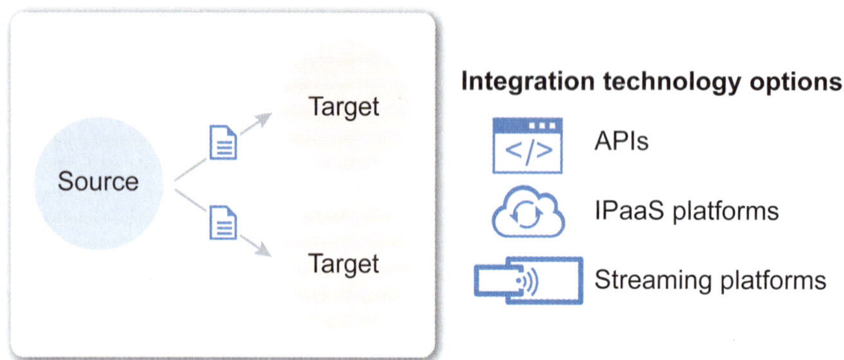


- **Moving bulk/batch data:** While many uses of integration require real-time data, in many other instances data is integrated in batch. For example, transactions from multiple applications may be batched nightly or for integration with financial systems. Data may also be migrated in bulk. Historical information spanning long time periods may be integrated in batch for analysis.

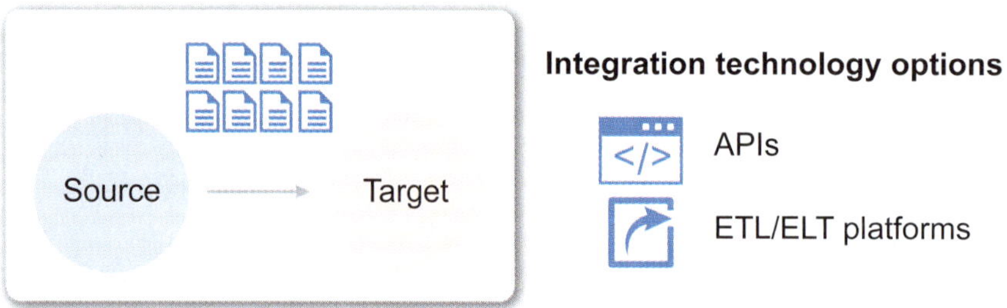


- **Processing synchronous data requests:** End users may trigger data integration by requesting data from a system. In a synchronous data transfer, the user makes a request, then waits for the information to be returned. For example, when an end user tries to make a report or searches for information, data from different data sources may be called up and integrated. This is especially common when end users need information from a third-party system (eg, a doctor wants to review the prescriptions a patient has filled at any pharmacy).

- **Processing asynchronous events:** Asynchronous data transfers, known as "fire and forget" events, happen when information is sent without an expectation of confirmation or action on the other end. For example, when an organization emails a customer, there may be little or no expectation of a response. Automated workflows are similar; if an expense is waiting for approval, the system takes no action until the approval is received, whether that occurs immediately, within days or weeks, or never.

- **Creating user interfaces and mash-ups:** Information may be integrated into a central repository for consumption by human users. Intranets, the Internet, public websites, search engines, and mobile apps are all examples of platforms where data is integrated for use by humans. The term mash-up is often used in reference to data analytics and visualization: Data from one source is "mashed up" with data from a different source for comparison or to find patterns.

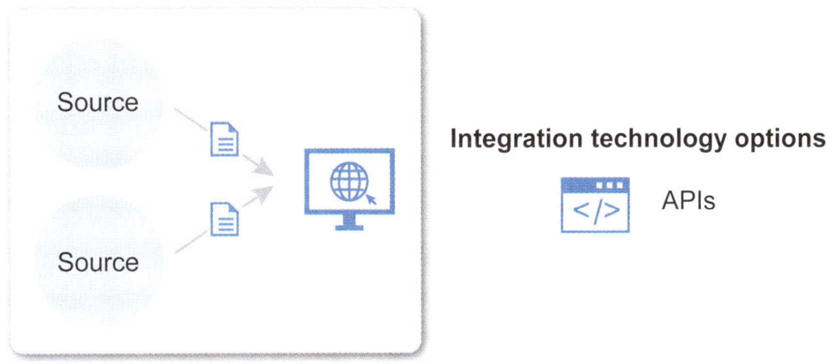


## Data Transformations

Data cleaning and standardization are an important step in integrating data. Data cleaning means removing or correcting extracted data that is incomplete, inaccurate, irrelevant, or duplicated. Data standardization involves merging the formats of data from different systems into one format.

Such transformations can occur in different stages during integration, depending on the type of architecture and software used. As an example, transformation during an ETL process may include:

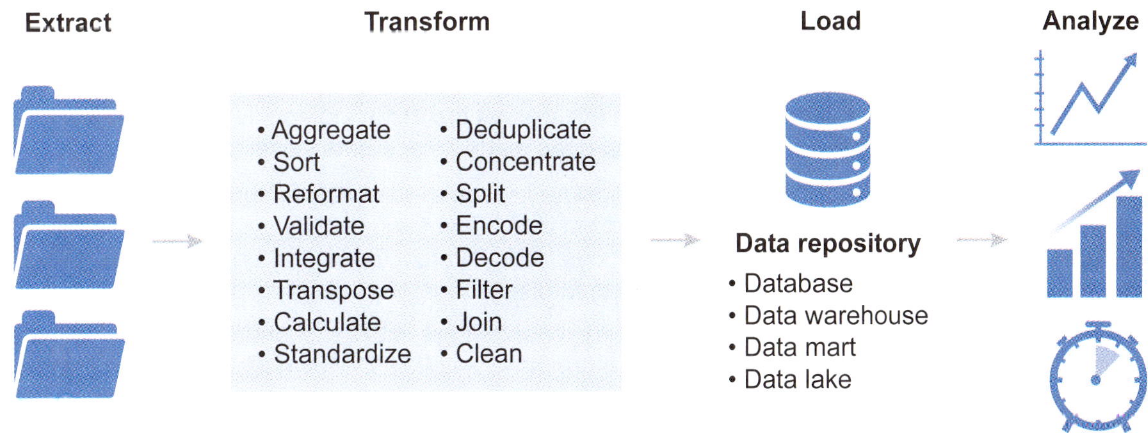

Common data transformations in data integration processes include:

- **Cleaning leading zeros and removing nonprintable characters:** Leading and trailing zeros and nonprintable characters should be removed where appropriate as they can cause problems with data analysis. Nonprintable characters include white spaces, page breaks, line breaks, or tabs; these characters most often appear when numbers or dates have been stored as text in the source files but need to be analyzed as numeric values.
- **Encoding data:** Encoding means assigning free-form values to data to make it compatible with the target database. Examples include changing NULL values to 0 or changing "M" to "male" and "F" to "female."
- **Decoding data:** Decoding involves standardizing the codes for data. One source system may represent customer status as "AC" for active or "IN" for inactive, while another system may represent the same customer status as 1 (active) or 0 (inactive). In the transformation phase, the data would be decoded and then recoded for a consistent format.
- **Renaming attributes:** Renaming assigns each data element one standard name with one standard definition. For example, one data source may assign the header CUST_NUM to a customer number, while another system might assign the header ACCOUNT_NUM. During the transformation phase, a standard name for customer number would be decided.
- **Splitting data:** Data splitting divides data into separate fields or columns, as when a column with employees' full names is split into two columns to separate the first and last names. Proper data structures should follow the "one fact, one place" rule; a full name is an example of multiple facts in one place.
- **Filtering data:** Filtering involves removing extraneous fields and records. For example, if the source data has three columns (eg, job code, age, salary), then the target database may accept only two fields (eg, job code and salary), or the target could ignore those records where salary is not present (salary is null).
- **Transposing data:** Transposing means to disconnect rows and columns. For example, columns and rows could be switched or the data pivoted by turning multiple columns into multiple rows, or vice versa.
- **Joining data:** Joining refers to connecting multiple data points by a common field. For example, weather data from online sources and internal sales data might be joined by zip code.
- **Calculations and extensions:** These involve calculating new values based on existing data. For example, new variables may be created that calculate total cost, profit margin, or total sales.
- **Removing redundant data:** Redundant data is deleted by finding and removing duplicate records or columns.
- **Grouping:** Data may be summarized into groups or subgroups (eg, summarizing total sales by store or region).
- **Removing headers or subtotals:** This involves removing headers or subtotals if they aren't necessary in the target database.
- **Sorting data:** Sorting means rearranging the data into a useful order (eg, ascending, descending, custom).
- **Validating the data:** Validation is performed to ensure that the extracted data is accurate. For example, it may need to be verified that a postal code in the source data exists.
- **Standardizing the data:** This involves formatting data into tables to match the format of the target database. For example, a field in one source system may be numeric, and the same column in the target system may be text. The extracted source data could be in different formats for each data type; thus, all the extracted data should be converted into a standardized format. Specific formatting issues include:
  - **Date/time conversion:** There are many issues regarding dates because there are many date and time formats. For example, one source may store dates as MM/DD/YYYY, while another system uses Month, DD, YYYY.

- **Numbers:** Numbers can be misinterpreted, particularly if entered manually with a mix of numerals and words (eg, 7 or seven). Negative numbers may need to be reformatted. Also, any data with accounting characters should be reformatted to show the data in raw form (eg, 123.45, not $123.45).
- **International characters and encoding:** When working with source data from a different country, it may have accent marks, special characters, or invisible computer characters (eg, line breaks, tabs, returns). These characters may need to be removed before analysis.
- **Languages and measures:** Like international characters, certain words or measures may be stated differently in data elements although they have the same meaning (eg, cheese or fromage, ketchup or catsup). When analyzing the data, such words and measures must be made uniform for consistency.

### Data Integration and Transformation

A CPA was engaged to perform an agreed-upon procedures attest engagement to integrate data from multiple sources, then perform an analysis to determine whether a county property tax appraiser's valuations are comparable to arm's length sales in compliance with state law. The overall property tax just values are required to be "reasonable," which state law defines as no more than 15% below the average qualified sale values. The 15% allowance accounts for the costs of selling the property, such as broker fees and closing costs.

The CPA interviewed personnel from the appraiser's office to determine the potential sources of data. The appraiser personnel stated that the following data could be supplied:

- Value data is sorted in the county's tax system by property ID number. The same information is shown on the appraiser's public website, as required by law.
- The county receives a spreadsheet from the county clerk's office that contains data for all property transfers in date order. Transfers may be qualified or unqualified. A qualified sale is between two unrelated parties for market value and may be used for tax valuation. An unqualified sale may be one between related parties or a sale under market value in situations such as foreclosures. Unqualified sales may not be used for tax assessments. The transfer data is integrated into the assessor's data and website within 45 days.

The CPA requested that the appraiser's office provide an extract of all the value data from its system, as well as the transfer spreadsheet from the clerk's office showing all sales for the last calendar year. Both files were provided in a comma-separated values (CSV) format. The appraiser's data had 80,000 records and the clerk's data had 15,000 records. Each data source contained the following fields:

**County Appraiser Value Data**

| Property ID | Property Address | Property Type | Just (Market) Value | Assessed Value | Taxable Value |
|---|---|---|---|---|---|

**County Clerk's Transfer Data**

| Date of Sale | Property ID# | Property Address | Qualified Sale (Y/N) | Sale Amount |
|---|---|---|---|---|

The CPA performed the analysis using the following procedures

- Each CSV file was loaded into a separate spreadsheet.
- Each spreadsheet was first manually scanned for blanks or obvious outliers. Then the columns were sorted to see the highs and lows. The CPA noticed a problem in which the clerk had sales marked as qualified, but they were for less than $5,000. This alerted the CPA to the fact that the Qualified Sale (Y/N) field might not be accurate, which was confirmed by the appraiser's office.
- Because the clerk's data contained errors, the CPA determined that criteria would have to be added to the analysis. Sales that were marked unqualified or less than $5,000 were deleted. By law, the unqualified sales could not be used for tax valuation purposes, and the incorrectly marked qualified sales would skew the analysis too much.
- The CPA also noted that some of the sale dates were in December of the previous year and in January of the year after. These records were also deleted because they did not pertain to the analysis.
- The appraiser data contained three value fields: Just (Market) Values, Assessed Value, and Taxable Value. The analysis was concerned only with the just value and assessed value. Taxable value was not needed as it represented the amount taxed after various valid exemptions; thus, the Taxable Value field was deleted.
- Once satisfied that the data did not contain significant errors, outliers, or extraneous information, the CPA loaded both CSV files into a computer assisted audit tool (CAAT). The CAAT tool was used to:
  - Perform analysis in read-only mode for assurance that no further changes to the data would be made
  - Join the two data files using Property ID# as the primary key
  - Perform the following CAAT functions:
    - Calculate statistics on the entire data set, including count, sum, average, maximum, minimum, and standard deviation.
    - Classify on the field Property Type to create groups. Statistics were also run for every group.
    - Stratify the group data to determine counts for ranges of valuations (ie, 0 to 100,000, 100,001 to 200,000)
- After performing the functions in the CAAT tool, the CPA used data visualization software, which had a built-in connector to import the data. The data visualization software allowed for validating the numerical results of the CAAT software (ie, determining if both programs' calculations were the same), and interactive graphs were made. The interactive graphs would give report users the ability to click on parts of the tables and graphs so that they could "drill down" and see the actual data for themselves.
- The CPA issued a written and electronic report with the finding that the property appraiser's valuations exceeded the 15% allowed difference between just values and sales values.

# ISC

## Security, Confidentiality and Privacy

# ISC 5
# Regulations, Standards, and Frameworks

# ISC 5: Regulations, Standards, and Frameworks

# 5.01 Regulations, Standards, and Frameworks

## Overview

This chapter discusses various regulations, standards, and frameworks that organizations may use to develop their systems and controls. In addition, external CPAs may use them in risk advisory or attestation engagements, such as SOC 2®+, SOC for Cybersecurity, or compliance audits. It is important to understand the nature of the regulations, standards, and frameworks, and how they are applied.

**Regulations:** Regulations, which may also be called rules or administrative laws, have the **legal force of law**. Organizations must follow regulations or face negative consequences. Government bodies and agencies in the U.S. issue regulations to implement (ie, administer) laws approved by the legislative branch, which includes city, county, state, and federal legislatures. Organizations with operations in regions outside the U.S. must also follow the laws of those jurisdictions.

Two examples of regulations are:

- **HIPAA:** Health Insurance Portability and Accountability Act
- **GDPR:** General Data Protection Regulation

**Standards: Private-sector** entities establish standards that may be used by private or public organizations. Unlike the rule of law, standards are voluntary or contractually required. Standards are agreed-upon criteria for quality or reporting that provide reliable, explicit, repeatable, comprehensive, and comparable requirements. Most standards focus on the public interest, independence, and adherence to rules (ie, due process).

Two examples of standards are:

- **PCI DSS:** Payment Card Industry Data Security Standard
- **CIS Controls:** Center for Internet Security (CIS) Controls

**Frameworks:** Frameworks provide a **structure** that may be used, in the absence of defined standards, for presenting common concepts. A framework can be viewed as a set of **guiding principles** that convey ideas but are not requirements.

Examples of frameworks include:

- COSO Internal Control–Integrated Framework
- COSO Enterprise Risk Management (ERM)
- NIST Cybersecurity Framework (CSF)
- NIST Privacy Framework
- NIST SP 800-53
- COBIT® 2019

# Health Insurance Portability and Accountability Act (HIPAA)

**Representative Task (Remembering and Understanding):** Recall the covered entities and permitted uses and disclosures of the HIPAA Security and Privacy Rules.

The **Health Insurance Portability and Accountability Act (HIPAA)** is a U.S. federal law that mandates the creation of national standards to prevent the use or disclosure of sensitive **protected health information (PHI)** without the patient's consent. The intent of HIPAA **regulations** is to protect the **privacy** of patients.

To implement HIPAA, the U.S. Department of Health and Human Services (HHS) developed the Privacy Rule, Security Rule, and Breach Notification Rule.

**Privacy Rule:** The Privacy Rule addresses how covered entities use or disclose PHI obtained orally, in writing, or electronically. It sets the standard that patients have the right to know and control how their health information is used. The goal of the rule is to ensure that PHI is appropriately protected while permitting the exchange of information required to deliver health care.

**Security Rule:** The Security Rule applies only to electronic protected health information (ePHI). ePHI includes all individually identifiable health information that a covered entity creates, receives, maintains, or transmits electronically. It does not include oral or written information. The goal of the Security Rule is to ensure the confidentiality, integrity, and availability of ePHI, as well as to protect against threats and unauthorized uses or disclosures.

**Breach Notification Rule:** This rule sets the notification requirements that covered entities must follow in case of a security or privacy breach. In this context, a breach is the unauthorized access, use, or disclosure of PHI. Covered entities must notify individuals when their data has been exposed in a breach. The Breach Notification Rule explains the timing, content, and methods to notify individuals, the media, HHS, and law enforcement.

The HIPAA Security and Privacy Rules are contained in 45 CFR Part 164. The CPA exam covers §164.103 to §164.530, excluding Implementation Specifications and Compliance Dates. Selected sections are included in this chapter.

## Covered Entities

Subpart A, §164.104, states that HIPAA applies to covered entities, including **health care providers**, **health plans**, and **health care clearinghouses**. Covered entities may be individuals, organizations, or institutions.

Business associates who provide services to covered entities are also subject to the same HIPAA regulations. A **business associate** is a **third-party vendor** who supplies services (eg, utilization review, billing, claims processing) to a covered entity. After signing a **business associate agreement**, the covered entity may disclose protected health information to help carry out its health care functions. Business associates may also use **subcontractors** to fulfill aspects of their service. For example, a business associate that provides a software application may house ePHI with a third-party cloud data center. The business associate must take measures to ensure their subcontractors also follow HIPAA rules (eg, HIPAA-compliant storage).

Examples of covered entities include the following:

| Health Care Providers | Health Plan Providers | Health Care Clearinghouses |
|---|---|---|
| • Doctors<br>• Dentists<br>• Nursing homes<br>• Pharmacies<br>• Outpatient care practices<br>• Home health agencies<br>• Hospitals | • Self-administered health plans<br>• Health insurance companies<br>• PPOs and HMOs<br>• Government programs<br>  ○ Medicare<br>  ○ Medicaid<br>  ○ Military and veterans' health care programs | Entities that process nonstandard health information into a standardized format (eg, converting paperwork to electronic records) on behalf of another entity |

## Security Standards

Subpart C, §164.302 to §164.318, sets forth security standards for protecting ePHI. This subpart includes four categories: security standards, administrative safeguards, physical safeguards, and technical safeguards.

- **§164.306 Security Standards: General Rules**
  - **General requirements:** Covered entities and business associates must:
    - Ensure the confidentiality, integrity, and availability of all ePHI that they create, receive, keep, or transmit
    - Protect against threats to the security or integrity of ePHI
    - Protect against uses or disclosures of ePHI that are not permitted under the Privacy Rule
    - Ensure that their workforce follows the HIPAA rules
  - **Maintenance:** Covered entities and business associates must review and change security measures as needed to continue to protect ePHI.
- **§164.308 Administrative Safeguards:** Covered entities and business associates must implement policies and procedures for:
  - **Assigned security responsibility:** Identifying the security official who is responsible for the development and implementation of policies and procedures
  - **Security management process:** Preventing, detecting, containing, and correcting security violations
  - **Workforce security:** Ensuring that only appropriate members of their workforce have access to ePHI and preventing unauthorized access
  - **Information access management:** Authorizing access to ePHI consistent with the Privacy Rule
  - **Security awareness training:** Requiring all members of their workforce (including management) to complete a security awareness training program
  - **Security incident procedures:** Establishing an incident response plan to identify and respond to security incidents
  - **Contingency plan:** Having business continuity, disaster recovery, and data backup plans to respond to emergencies or other occurrences (eg, fire, vandalism, system failure, natural disaster) that may damage systems containing ePHI
  - **Evaluation:** Monitoring and testing security policies and procedures

- **§164.310 Physical Safeguards:** Covered entities and business associates must implement policies and procedures for:
  - **Facility access controls:** Limiting physical access to facilities and ensuring that electronic information systems are accessed only by authorized individuals
  - **Workstation use:** Specifying the functions and physical surroundings of workstations that can access ePHI
  - **Workstation security:** Restricting physical interaction with workstations that access ePHI
  - **Device and media control:** Managing the receipt and removal of hardware and electronic media that hold ePHI
- **§164.312 Technical Safeguards:** Covered entities and business associates must implement policies and procedures for:
  - **Access controls:** Allowing access to software programs only to those who have been granted access rights
  - **Audit controls:** Using hardware, software, or procedures to record and examine activity in information systems that hold ePHI
  - **Integrity:** Protecting ePHI from unauthorized changes or destruction
  - **Authentication:** Verifying the identity of each person or entity seeking access to ePHI
  - **Transmission security:** Using technical security measures to guard ePHI transmitted over an electronic network

## Privacy Standards

Subpart E, §164.500 to §164.534, sets forth the rules about **permitted and required uses and disclosures** of PHI (ie, oral, written, or electronic health records) by covered entities and business associates. It also addresses the circumstances in which consent is needed, along with prohibited uses and disclosures.

- **§164.502 Uses and Disclosures of PHI:** General Rules: Covered entities and business associates may not use or disclose PHI except as permitted or required by the privacy standards:
  - **Covered entities:** Permitted uses and disclosures: A covered entity may use or disclose PHI as follows:
    - Disclosure to the individual (including parents and legal guardians of minors)
    - Use for treatment, payment, or health care operations
    - Use allowed by the individual (eg, request approved to send medical records to another physician)
  - **Covered entities:** Required disclosures: A covered entity must disclose PHI to the individual when requested and to HHS when needed to investigate HIPAA compliance.
  - **Business associates:** Permitted uses and disclosures: A business associate may use or disclose PHI only according to the terms of its business associate contract. It may not use PHI for any purpose that would be a violation if performed by a covered entity.
  - **Business associates:** Required disclosures: A business associate must disclose PHI to the covered entity, to the individual when requested, and to HHS when needed to investigate HIPAA compliance.
  - **Prohibited uses and disclosures:** A covered entity or business associate may *not* use or disclose:
    - Genetic information for health insurance underwriting purposes (ie, eligibility, computation of premium, pre-existing condition exclusions, or policy renewal)
    - PHI for sales (ie, receiving a payment for PHI), except as permitted for public health, research, treatment, or payment purposes

- **Minimum necessary:** When PHI is used or disclosed to another covered entity or a business associate, only the minimum information necessary to accomplish the intended purpose should be included. This does not apply to disclosures for treatment or disclosures to the individual.
- **Disclosures to business associates:** A covered entity may disclose PHI to a business associate if the covered entity receives assurances that the business associate will safeguard the information. A business associate may disclose PHI to a subcontractor if the business associate receives assurances that the subcontractor will safeguard the information. These assurances must be in writing, through a contract or other agreement.
- **Personal representatives:** A covered entity may disclose PHI to the personal representative of a deceased individual, adult, or emancipated minor.

Examples of scenarios in which a covered entity is permitted to disclose PHI without patient authorization include:

| Scenario | Description |
|---|---|
| Disclosure for treatment, payment, and health care operations | If a patient needs a service that requires a referral to a different covered entity (eg, lab services, imaging), the referring covered entity should disclose PHI to the referred entity so that it can provide treatment and conduct health care operations (eg, a doctor can send PHI to an outpatient lab, enabling it to conduct patient services without requesting patient consent/authorization). |
| Disclosure that benefits the public interest | In the case of a pandemic or instances where PHI contains information that would be of benefit to the public interest, disclosure is allowed to entities such as public health agencies or law enforcement. While this disclosure is discretionary according to HIPAA, states may mandate disclosures in specific circumstances (eg, child abuse reporting, workers' comp claims). |
| Limited data sets for health research, public health, or health care operations | Data mining is used for a broad range of purposes within medical research, particularly as it relates to public health and health care operations. PHI use is allowed for data mining provided that direct identifiers of individuals have been removed (ie, anonymized PHI), and that the entity or researcher agrees to appropriate PHI safeguards. |

- **§164.520 Notice of Privacy Practices**
  - **Right to notice:** Except as provided in the privacy standards, each individual has a right to adequate notice of the covered entity's **uses and disclosures** of PHI, the individual's **rights**, and the covered entity's **legal duties**.
  - **Individual rights:** The notice must explain the individual's rights and describe how to exercise those rights. Individual rights include:
    - Requesting restrictions on certain uses and disclosures of PHI
    - Receiving confidential communications of PHI
    - Inspecting and copying PHI
    - Amending PHI
    - Receiving an accounting of disclosures of PHI
    - Obtaining a paper copy of the notice
  - **Complaints:** The notice must explain that the individual can complain to the covered entity or HHS if they believe their privacy rights have been violated. A statement must be included saying that the individual will not be retaliated against for filing a complaint.

# General Data Protection Regulation (GDPR)

**Representative Task (Remembering and Understanding):** Recall the scope of the GDPR and the six principles and key concepts for personal data.

The **General Data Protection Regulation (GDPR)** is a law that sets forth principles and rules about the processing of personal data of individuals located within the European Union (EU). It is a goal of the **European Parliament** to *"respect the rights and freedoms of natural persons, whatever their nationality or place of residence, including the right to the* ***protection of personal data****."* The GDPR is also meant to ensure the **free movement of personal data** between EU member states. It details the rights of data subjects and the obligations of those who process personal data (by manual or automated means), including those who monitor or enforce compliance.

The EU includes many countries. The current list of member states can be found on the Internet, and the list changes from time to time. It does not include all countries in Europe.

The GDPR defines personal data as *"any information…related to an identified or identifiable natural person (data subject)."* Data subjects can be identified by reference to their:

- Basic identity information: Name, address, and ID numbers
- Web data: Location data, IP address, username, cookie data, and radio-frequency identification (RFID) tags
- Physical, physiological, genetic, and mental health information
- Economic, cultural, or social background

## Scope

GDPR applies to the processing of personal data by a controller or processor who operates:

- In the EU, even if the processing takes place outside the EU
- Outside the EU, if the processing involves personal data subjects in the EU and is related to the offering of goods/services or monitoring the subjects' behavior
- Outside the EU, but where EU law applies because of public international laws

In the GDPR, "**processing**" refers to collecting, recording, organizing, structuring, storing, altering, retrieving, using, disclosing, disseminating, restricting, erasing, or destroying personal data. A **controller** is a person, public authority, agency, or other body that determines the purposes and means of processing personal data. A **processor** processes personal data on behalf of the controller.

The following flowchart is helpful for understanding whether an organization is subject to the GDPR:

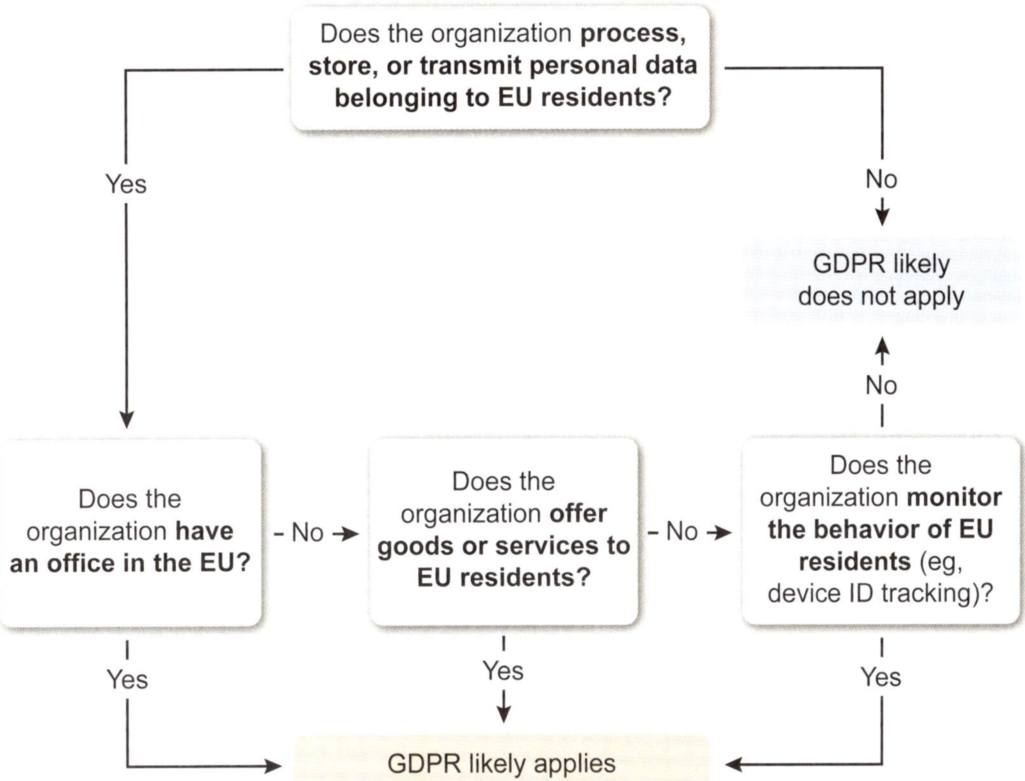


## Principles

Before processing any personal data, an organization must obtain the data subject's explicit permission (**consent**). Regulations expressly prohibit the use of legal jargon, so hiding permissions information under the organization's terms and conditions or its privacy policy will not suffice. The GDPR clearly states that any entity managing private or sensitive data must obtain permission **every time** it wants to access the data. Every time data is used for a **new purpose**, a **new consent** request is required.

Whenever a new project, change, or product is introduced, a **data protection impact assessment** should be performed to determine the impact of the action. Employees must be educated about GDPR standards and trained regularly. When an organization is large enough and processes significant amounts of personal data, it should appoint a **data protection officer**. The data protection officer would oversee advising the company on how to comply with EU GDPR requirements. GDPR compliance requires businesses to **notify** all data subjects of a security **breach within 72 hours** of discovering the breach.

GDPR legislation targets both **transparency and accountability** related to the collection and use of consumer data. These two precepts are reinforced through the **six privacy principles**:

| Six Privacy Principles of the GDPR | |
|---|---|
| **1. Processed lawfully, fairly, and in a transparent manner** | Entities need to provide a clear indication of:<br>• What personal data is collected<br>• Why that data is collected<br>• How that data is used |
| **2. Collected for specified, explicit, and legitimate purposes** | Entities are not allowed to sell personal information to third parties without consent.<br>• Personal data must be collected for a specific purpose<br>• Separate consent is required for any additional purpose |
| **3. Adequate, relevant, and limited to what is necessary** | Entities should process only the specific personal data they need to achieve the stated purpose. |
| **4. Accurate** | Entities must have processes in place to keep information accurate and up to date. |
| **5. Kept for no longer than necessary** | Personal data should be kept only as long as required to meet the collection purpose.<br>• Statutory limits supersede this requirement, as with, for example, regulations involving contracts or legal records<br>• Data must be deleted, destroyed, or sufficiently anonymized when it is no longer needed. |
| **6. Protected against unauthorized processing and damage** | Security measures must be in place to protect personal data against unauthorized or unlawful processing, accidental loss, destruction, or damage |

- **Lawfulness of processing**
  - Processing is lawful only if one of the following applies:
    - The data subject has given consent to the processing for a specific purpose.
    - The processing is necessary:
      - For the performance of a contract to which the data subject is a party,
      - For a controller to fulfill a legal compliance obligation,
      - To protect the vital interests of the data subject or another natural person, or
      - For a task being conducted in the public interest.
- **Conditions for consent**
  - When processing is based on consent, the controller must be able to supply evidence of the data subject's consent.
  - Data subjects may withdraw consent.
  - Regarding children, parental consent is needed if a minor is under 16 years old.

- **Special categories of personal data**
  - Processing of personal data that reveals racial or ethnic origin, political opinions, religious or philosophical beliefs, trade union membership, genetic data, biometric data, health data, or sexual orientation is **prohibited unless** the data subject has given consent or other criteria are met.
- **Information to be provided when personal data is collected from the data subject**
  - The controller should provide the data subject with notice of the:
    - Controller's identity and contact information
    - Purpose and legal basis for the personal data processing
    - Period for which the personal data will be stored
    - Right to request access to the personal data
    - Right to request correction, restriction, or erasure (ie, "right to be forgotten") of personal data
    - Right to withdraw consent
    - Right to make a complaint to authorities
    - Right to reject automated decision making, including profiling
- **Controller responsibilities**
  - Taking risks into consideration, the controller must implement appropriate technical and organizational measures to protect the security of personal data.
  - The controller must ensure that only personal data necessary for a specific purpose is collected, processed, and stored.
  - The controller must ensure all processors provide sufficient guarantees (ie, assurances) that they will take appropriate technical and organizational measures to protect the security of personal data and ensure the rights of the data subject.
  - The controller must maintain a record of processing activities under its authority.
  - Within 72 hours of discovering a breach, the controller must notify the supervisory authority and the data subject.
- **Processor responsibilities**
  - Provide sufficient guarantees (ie, assurances) that appropriate technical and organizational measures will be taken to protect both the security of personal data and the rights of the data subject. Measures may include encryption and other data obfuscation techniques.
  - The processor must not contract with another processor without the written authorization of the controller.
  - Processing shall be performed subject to a contract with the controller that sets forth the duration, nature of processing, types of personal data, and the obligations of both the processor and controller.
  - The processor must be able to restore availability and access to the personal data in the event of a disaster or security incident.
  - The processor must have a process for regularly testing, assessing, and evaluating the effectiveness of security measures to prevent accidental or unlawful destruction, loss, modification, unauthorized disclosure, and unauthorized access to the personal data transmitted or stored.
  - The processor must notify the controller of any personal data breach.

## Payment Card Industry Data Security Standard (PCI DSS)

**Representative Task (Remembering and Understanding):** Recall the requirements of the PCI DSS.

**PCI DSS** is a **global security standard** to prevent the *"theft and use of* ***personal consumer financial information*** *from* ***payment card*** *transactions and processing systems."* It covers any payment card or device that has the logo of one of the founding members of the PCI Security Standards Council (PCI SSC): American Express, Discover Financial Services, JCB International, MasterCard, or Visa, Inc. This includes **credit, debit, and prepaid cards**, whether used for in-person, mobile, telephone, or online payments.

The standard sets forth minimum controls and operational requirements for *all* entities that **store, process, or transmit** cardholder data and/or authenticate sensitive data. Vulnerabilities may stem from:

- Point-of-sale (POS) devices
- Servers, computers, and mobile devices
- Wireless hotspots
- Web-based shopping applications
- Paper-based storage
- Transmission of cardholder data
- Remote access

Besides the payment card brands, PCI DSS standards also apply to **software and device manufacturers**, as well as service providers and acquirers. A **service provider** is a third-party organization that processes, stores, or transmits cardholder data on behalf of another entity, such as a brand. Such managed services may include firewalls, intrusion detection systems, or hosted environments. An **acquirer**, also referred to as a merchant bank, is a third-party financial institution that processes payment card transactions on behalf of merchants. The institution can thus supply a payment gateway, and it is subject to the rules of payment brands that name it as an acquirer.

**Entities That Store, Process, or Transmit Cardholder Data**

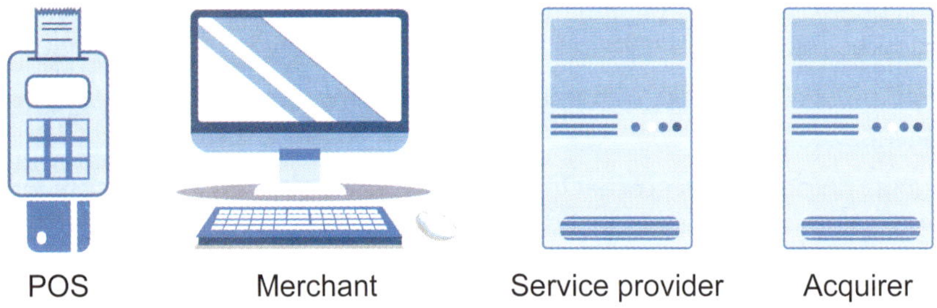


Adhering to the PCI DSS standards involves a continuous process of assessing risk, repairing vulnerabilities, and reporting on compliance:

- **Assess:** Finding every location where cardholder data is stored, inventorying IT assets and business processes, and looking for vulnerabilities that may expose cardholder data.
- **Repair:** Fixing known vulnerabilities, safely erasing unused cardholder data in storage, and implementing secure business processes.
- **Report:** Documenting assessment and remediation details, as well as providing compliance reports to the acquiring bank and card brands. Service processors may also need to complete other reporting requirements, such as a SOC 2® report.

**PCI DSS Compliance Process**

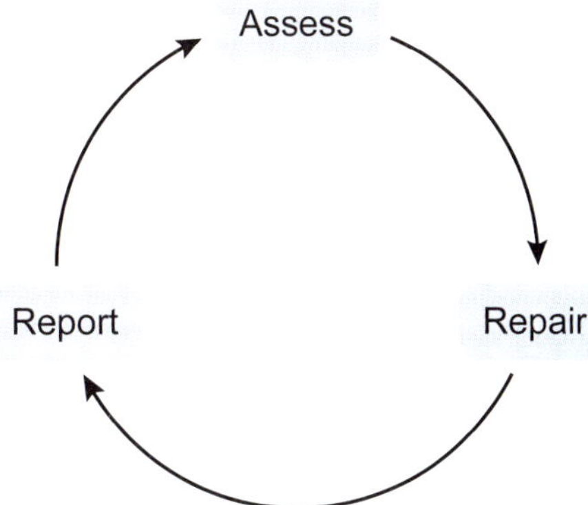


The PCI SSC manages security standards. Enforcement is conducted by American Express, Discover, JCB, MasterCard, and Visa. Each payment card brand has its own tools for assessing compliance and enforcement. The 12 specific requirements for PCI DSS are:

**PCI DSS Requirements**

| | |
|---|---|
| Build and maintain a secure network and systems | 1. Install and maintain a firewall configuration to protect cardholder data<br>2. Do not use vendor-supplied defaults for system passwords and other security parameters |
| Protect cardholder data | 3. Protect stored cardholder data<br>4. Encrypt transmission of cardholder data across open, public networks |
| Maintain a vulnerability management program | 5. Protect all systems against malware and regularly update anti-virus software or programs<br>6. Develop and maintain secure systems and applications |
| Implement strong access control measures | 7. Restrict access to cardholder data according to a business's need-to-know<br>8. Identity and authenticate access to system components<br>9. Restrict physical access to cardholder data |
| Regularly monitor and test networks | 10. Track and monitor all access to network resources and cardholder data<br>11. Regularly test security systems and processes |
| Maintain an information security policy | 12. Maintain a policy that addresses information security for all personnel |

CPAs may perform risk advisory services, security assessment reports, or attestation services related to PCI DSS, either separately or as part of a SOC engagement. Such services often include:

- Compliance assessments
- Self-assessment questionnaires
- Policy and procedure development
- Vulnerability scans
- Penetration tests

## Center for Internet Security (CIS) Controls

**Representative Task (Remembering and Understanding):** Recall the overview of each CIS Control.

The **Center for Internet Security (CIS)** is an international group of individual volunteers and organizations that share information about attacks/attackers, root causes, tools, and defensive actions. Based on the collected information, the CIS has suggested **18 IT security controls** every organization should implement.

It is important to understand each CIS security control and why it is critical:

| CIS Controls | |
|---|---|
| 1. Inventory and control of enterprise assets | 10. Malware defenses |
| 2. Inventory and control of software assets | 11. Data recovery |
| 3. Data protection | 12. Network infrastructure management |
| 4. Secure configuration of enterprise assets and software | 13. Network monitoring and defense |
| 5. Account management | 14. Security awareness and skills training |
| 6. Access control management | 15. Service provider management |
| 7. Continuous vulnerability management | 16. Applications software security |
| 8. Audit log management | 17. Incident response management |
| 9. Email and web browser protection | 18. Penetration testing |

1. **Inventory and Control of Enterprise Assets**

   **Overview:** Inventory, track, and manage all devices so that the organization understands the totality of assets that need to be monitored and protected. Such assets include end-user devices (tablets and cell phones), network devices, noncomputing/Internet of Things (IoT) devices, and servers connected through physical, virtual, or remote access. This control also helps the organization find unauthorized or unmanaged assets that need to be removed or remediated. Organizations may use asset discovery tools to search their networks and create inventory lists.

**Why is it critical?** Proper asset management is necessary for security monitoring, incident response, and backup and recovery operations. Without a complete inventory of IT assets, the organization cannot know what it should be defending or where its critical data resides. Hackers search for assets that are not properly configured or patched, leaving an open vulnerability. Incident response may be delayed when an attack focuses on an asset that the organization is not aware of.

2. **Inventory and Control of Software Assets**

   **Overview:** Inventory, track, and manage all operating systems and applications used by the organization to ensure that only properly authorized software is on the system. This includes detecting unauthorized software and preventing its installation or execution. Organizations may use automated inventory tools to find such software or use allow lists to prevent the execution of unauthorized scripts.

   **Why is it critical?** Having a complete and accurate inventory of software is an important part of preventing attacks. Attackers may look for vulnerable versions of software to exploit. Controls such as updates, patches, and the monitoring of threat lists will be less effective if the organization is not managing all the software in its ecosystem. Other considerations include ensuring that the organization uses only software that is properly licensed and needed for business purposes.

3. **Data Protection**

   **Overview:** Use processes and technical controls to manage data. Controls should encompass all steps in the data life cycle, from creation/collection to use, storage, and archival/disposal.

   **Why is it critical?** Managing data becomes more difficult when it is no longer contained within an organization's four walls. Cloud-based systems, mobile devices, and outsourced relationships add complexity and vulnerability. Organizations that hold data subject to regulations (eg, HIPAA, GDPR) can face serious negative consequences in case of a breach. Data theft can occur on a network or it may result from a physical attack such as device theft. To protect data, an organization should understand where it is located and monitor outflows.

4. **Secure Configuration of Enterprise Assets and Software**

   **Overview:** Set up and maintain secure configurations for all hardware and software. Configuration updates should be approved and tracked to create a record that can be used for compliance, incident response, and audits.

   **Why is it critical?** Hardware and software bought from a vendor or service provider often come with default configurations to allow for quick deployment by the user. For example, network hardware may have a default password. Applications like operating systems may also include unnecessary software (ie, bloatware). If defaults are left in place, they can create a vulnerability because hackers are aware that users normally forget or neglect to change the configurations. Configurations should be continuously managed, with changes made to improve security or address additional security concerns.

5. **Account Management**

   **Overview:** Utilize processes and tools to ensure that only authorized individuals can grant credentials to user, administrator, and service accounts. Account inventories, logging, and monitoring should be included in an overall identity access management (IAM) program.

   **Why is it critical?** Threat actors do not always use hacking to penetrate an enterprise setting; it is more common for unauthorized persons to access a company's resources using legitimate user credentials. Weak or compromised passwords, accounts left open after an employee's termination, and unused test accounts are all valid means used by hackers to gain entry to a system. Accounts with administrative rights are high-value targets because they can be used by attackers to create new accounts or make changes that leave the door open for future attacks.

6. **Access Control Management**

   **Overview:** Practice access control management by using processes and tools to create, assign, manage, and revoke user access. The principle of least privilege should be followed (ie, allow only the minimum access needed for each role). Other, granular recommendations include multifactor authentication (MFA) for administrative access, remote network access, and access control that is centralized or role-based.

   **Why is it critical?** Internal and external threats are likely when users have access beyond what is essential to their job. For example, the sales department does not need access to the applications used by the accounts payable department. Unnecessary access rights create avenues for data loss or theft, either from the inside or outside. In the example above, not only could a sales department employee access accounts payable without a valid reason, but an external attacker could gain access to the sales department's user privileges.

7. **Continuous Vulnerability Management**

   **Overview:** Develop a plan to evaluate and track the vulnerabilities of all assets in the infrastructure, which will reduce an attacker's window of opportunity. Monitor public and private industry sources for information on emerging threats and vulnerabilities.

   **Why is it critical?** In order to defend against cyberattacks, organizations must have current information about software updates, patches, security advisories, and threat intelligence. With those security resources in hand, the IT environment must include ongoing monitoring to find and address problems before attackers can exploit the same resources to cause harm. For example, if there is a known issue with a software program, a threat exists until the vendor supplies a patch. During the interim, the organization must watch its systems and rely on other controls to prevent an attack. Vulnerability testing may also be performed to check for known insecure assets.

8. **Audit Log Management**

   **Overview:** Establish a standard audit log management process to collect, review, and retain audit logs. The logs track user events, such as when a user logged in and out, accessed files, or shared files. In contrast, system logs show system process start/end times and crashes.

   **Why is it critical?** Regular audit log reviews identify activity baselines and operational trends. This data is useful for quickly detecting unusual system activity and responding to it. If log files are not kept up to date and monitored, an attack could continue long term without being discovered. Log files can show how and when an attack occurred, what information was accessed, and if data was taken. Audit records may also be needed internally for incident response or used by external forensic analysts connected to cybersecurity insurance claims.

9. **Email and Web Browser Protection**

   **Overview:** Use controls to protect against or detect threats from emails or web vectors that allow attackers to manipulate users. Blocking malicious URLs and file types is one of the most important technical controls for securing email servers and web browsers. The controls also include anti-malware protection for email servers and limiting the use of unauthorized and unnecessary email client and browser extensions. Providing a "report spam" button allows users to notify the organization of suspicious activity.

   **Why is it critical?** Email and web browsers allow attackers to interact with users and trick them into supplying information, which leads to unauthorized access. One type of social engineering attack is phishing, where an attacker sends a legitimate-looking email so that users may believe they are sharing information with a trusted source when they are not.

10. **Malware Defenses**

    **Overview:** Prevent the installation, spread, and execution of malicious code or applications. Installing malware defenses at all entry points, automating updates, and centralizing anti-malware management are examples of specific actions an organization can take to combat malware.

**Why is it critical?** Malicious software (eg, worms, viruses, Trojans) is a major threat associated with Internet use. Malware attacks can capture user credentials, steal data, find other targets, and encrypt or destroy data. Many organizations have been attacked with ransomware, which prevents them from using their system until the attacker is paid money. Malware can come from many sources, including devices, email, web browsers, cloud services, or other media. A system can be infiltrated when an unsuspecting user clicks on a link, opens an email attachment, installs software, or uses USB drives.

### 11. Data Recovery

**Overview:** Employ consistent data backup and recovery practices to restore systems after an incident.

**Why is it critical?** One model for data security is the CIA triad (confidentiality, integrity, and availability). Confidentiality relates to controls aimed at preventing unauthorized use or disclosure of confidential or personal information. Integrity involves controls that ensure against unauthorized modifications to files or configurations. Availability refers to controls that ensure an organization can access its data in a timely manner. Data backups help an organization recover quickly from attacks, disasters, and other unplanned outages. In certain situations, such as air traffic control, a loss of availability can be dangerous. A loss of integrity results in data that cannot be trusted. A loss of confidentiality can lead to regulatory sanctions and fines, as well as reputational damage. The ability to restore systems from consistent backups is a fundamental control.

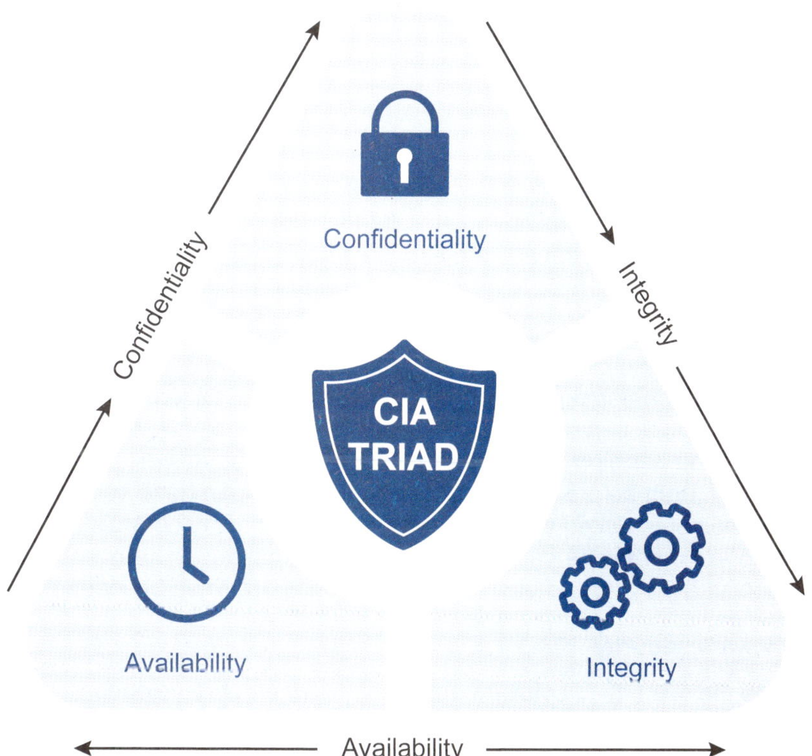


### 12. Network Infrastructure Management

**Overview:** Manage network devices through tracking, monitoring, and reporting. Network devices, such as gateways, routers, switches, wireless access points, and firewalls, should be monitored. Default passwords and configurations on new equipment should be changed.

**Why is it critical?** Attackers search networks for vulnerabilities and exploit them to gain access, redirect traffic, and intercept data. Vulnerabilities may stem from new network devices when configurations, passwords, unneeded software, and ports are left at default settings. Organizations should also ensure their network infrastructure software is current through patch and release management or by replacing outdated equipment. Other actions include making a diagram of the network, using secure communication protocols, using VPNs for remote devices, and having dedicated computing resources for administrative work.

13. **Network Monitoring and Defense**

    **Overview:** Use processes and technical tools to monitor networks and defend against internal and external threats. Examples include implementing network and host-based intrusion detection systems, centralizing security event alerts, capturing network traffic flow logs, and deploying port-level access control.

    **Why is it critical?** Security tools are effective only when combined with continuous monitoring. Monitoring helps find and respond to threats before they can have a significant effect on the organization. It is a part of a broader situational awareness in which the network is constantly scanned to prevent, detect, and respond to attacks. Understanding activity metrics also supplies insight for improving security response strategies and regulatory compliance.

14. **Security awareness and skills training**

    **Overview:** Encourage security-conscious behavior by requiring employees and contractors to take part in security awareness training programs.

    **Why is it critical?** Even the best security program will be insufficient without an adequately trained workforce. Human vulnerabilities, whether intentional or unintentional, are the greatest cause of security incidents, such as those that result from mishandling data, losing devices, using weak passwords, or clicking on email attachments. Training makes employees and contractors aware of security risks and their responsibility to prevent or report suspicious activity.

15. **Service provider management**

    **Overview:** Develop processes to evaluate whether service providers who hold sensitive data, supply IT platforms, and manage services have implemented security controls. Vendor management practices include keeping a list of approved service providers, establishing outsourced services policies, requiring written contracts and service level agreements (SLAs), and assessing service providers through internal or external audits.

    **Why is it critical?** Most organizations use third parties such as service providers, freelancers, and vendors. Connected third parties pose a security risk to an organization's infrastructure, networks, and data. Vendor management is part of an organization's governance, risk, and compliance processes. Management handles the decision of whether to outsource or not, as well as any consequences that stem from outsourcing. Both before and after the agreement to purchase services, organizations should ensure that their outsourced vendors have adequate security controls and follow regulations. Post-agreement monitoring may be carried out through internal audits or external attestation engagements, such as SOC and compliance examinations performed by independent CPAs.

16. **Applications software security**

    **Overview:** Manage the security of software applications, whether developed in-house, hosted, or purchased from a third party. This management includes preventing, detecting, and remediating security weaknesses.

    **Why is it critical?** Managing a software's security life cycle is critical for discovering and fixing security vulnerabilities. Software can hold sensitive data, control system operations, or allow access. Attackers can exploit poor design, coding errors, and untested applications to cause harm. Organizations should have processes for addressing known vulnerabilities in software as well as finding those that were not previously known; the processes will differ based on how the software was obtained. For example, the method of evaluating security for an in-house developed program will be different from the method used for a purchased cloud-based SaaS application.

17. **Incident response management**

    **Overview:** Develop and maintain incident response management (eg, policies, plans, procedures, defined roles, training, communications) to detect and respond to an attack.

**Why is it critical?** Despite threat detection and prevention processes, security breaches are inevitable. Having a predefined and tested incident response plan reduces attack-to-response time. The goal is to detect threats and stop their spread before they cause harm. Incident response management includes having a comprehensive plan that results from the coordination of internal and external stakeholders. It should be tested at least annually with adjustments made for new threats or newly found vulnerabilities.

18. **Penetration testing**

    **Overview:** Conduct penetration tests to find the control weaknesses an attacker may exploit or to confirm security controls. Penetration tests simulate an attack by using the same tools and techniques as attackers do. The goal is to determine how far an attack might extend and what business processes or data might be affected. These tests may be performed internally or by an external party, such as a CPA firm providing risk advisory services.

    **Why is it critical?** Without testing, the organization will not know how its security controls may perform in an actual situation. Having the tests performed by an external party supplies an independent assessment, which may provide additional insight. Testing is an opportunity to find gaps and remediate them, as well as verify the effectiveness of current controls.

## NIST Cybersecurity Framework (NIST CSF)

**Representative Task (Remembering and Understanding):** Recall the three parts of the NIST CSF (Core, Tiers, Organizational Profiles).

### Overview

The United States Congress passed the Cybersecurity Enforcement Act of 2014 (CEA) to encourage **voluntary** public-private partnerships focused on improving cybersecurity practices, research, and education. As a result of the CEA, the **National Institute of Standards and Technology (NIST)** created the **Cybersecurity Framework (CSF)** to help organizations manage and reduce their cybersecurity risks.

The CSF can be used by organizations of all sizes in all sectors (eg, industry, government, nonprofit), whether adopted voluntarily or mandated through contracts or regulations. This framework can help organizations improve their cybersecurity risk management programs by assessing their current cybersecurity posture, prioritizing risk responses, and communicating with internal and external parties.

The framework comprises three parts:

- **CSF Core:** A set of suggested broad activities and outcomes (ie, controls) an organization may consider in its approach to cybersecurity. The CSF Core consists of functions, categories, and subcategories.
- **CSF Tiers:** Tiers that describe how sophisticated (ie, rigorous) an organization's cybersecurity risk management program is, ranging from Tier 1 (partial implementation, informal, reactive) to Tier 4 (adaptive, formal, and proactive).
- **CSF Profiles:** The organization compares its Current Profile with its Target Profile, adding CSF Core categories and subcategories to mitigate control gaps. The Profiles represent the level of the organization's current and desired CSF Core functions based on its current and desired CSF Tiers.

NIST also has a CSF website that provides informative references and implementation examples. Informative references help organizations map the CSF to other prominent frameworks and regulations.

## CSF Core

The CSF Core consists of a hierarchy of connected functions, categories, and subcategories:

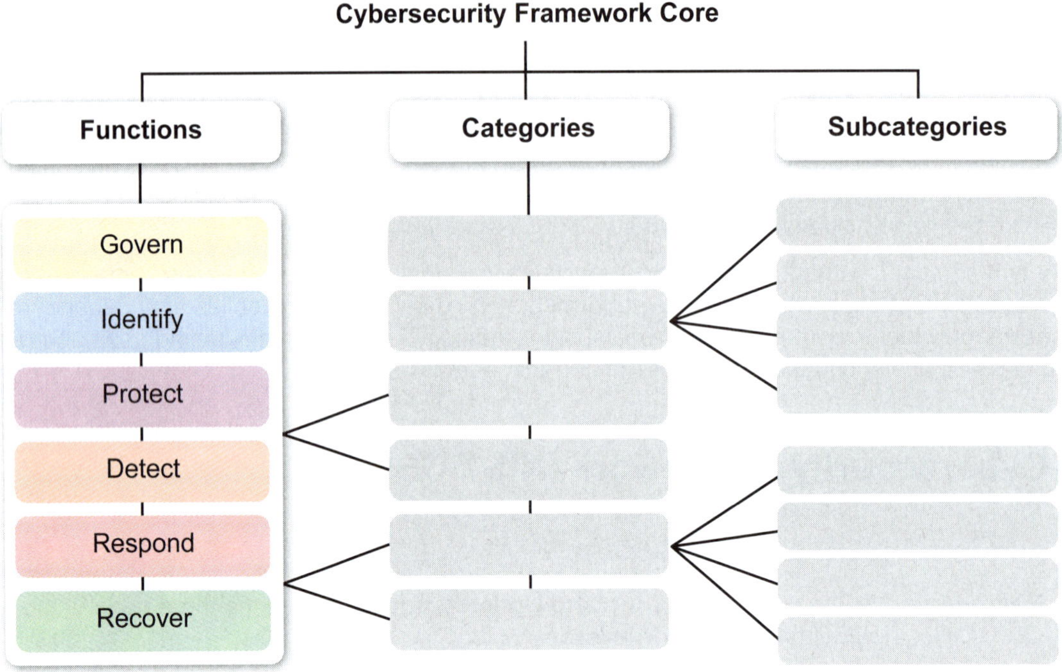


- **Functions:** Functions are the highest level of organizing cybersecurity outcomes within the CSF Core. The six functions are:

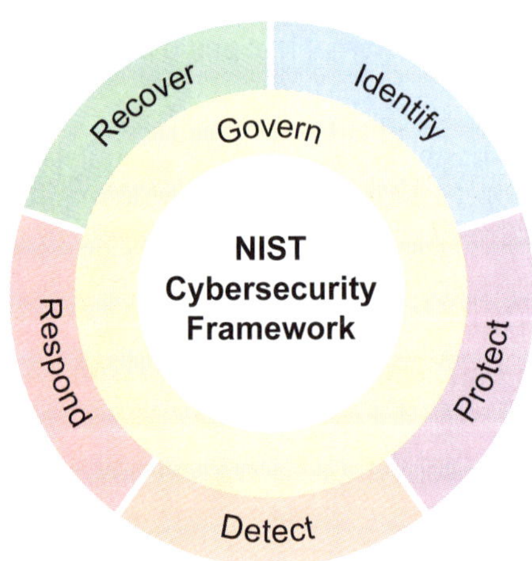

According to the NIST, the functions are defined as follows:

- **Govern:** Develop the organization's cybersecurity risk management strategy, expectations, and policies. The govern function helps organizations prioritize the five other functions. It includes roles, responsibilities, authorities, policies, and oversight.
- **Identify:** Inventory the organization's assets (eg, data, hardware, software, systems, facilities, services, people, suppliers). Assess cybersecurity risks and opportunities for improvement.
- **Protect:** Implement the appropriate safeguards to secure assets. The goal of this function is to avoid or reduce the likelihood and impact of adverse cybersecurity incidents.
- **Detect:** Enable the timely discovery and analysis of anomalies or indications that a cybersecurity incident is occurring.
- **Respond:** Apply the appropriate activities to take action and contain a detected cybersecurity incident.
- **Recover:** Support the timely restoration of normal operations to reduce the effects of cybersecurity incidents.

- **Categories:** Each function is subdivided into categories, which are a collective group of cybersecurity outcomes related to a particular function. For example, Asset Management is one of the outcome categories in the Identify function.
- **Subcategories:** Each category is further subdivided into specific outcomes for technical and management activities. For example, the Identify function Asset Management category includes a subcategory, "Inventories of hardware managed by the organization are maintained."

Appendix A to the NIST CSF document has a table listing all the Core functions, categories, and subcategories:

**Excerpt from NIST CSF Appendix A**

**IDENTIFY (ID):** The organization's current cubersecurity risks are understood

- **Asset Management (ID.AM):** Assets (e.g., data, hardware, software, systems, facilities, services, people) that enable the organization to achieve business purposes are identified and managed consistent with their relative importance to organizational objectives and the organization's risk strategy
  - **ID.AM-01:** Inventories of hardware managed by organization are maintained

*Source: The NIST Cybersecurity Framework (CSF) 2.0*

The categories related to the six CSF Core functions are:

**CSF Core Function and Category Names**

| Function | Category |
|---|---|
| Govern (GV) | • Organizational Context<br>• Risk Management Strategy<br>• Roles, Responsibilities, and Authorities<br>• Policy<br>• Oversight<br>• Cybersecurity Supply Chain Risk Management |
| Identify (ID) | • Asset Management<br>• Risk Assessment<br>• Improvement |
| Protect (PR) | • Identity Management, Authentication, and Access Control<br>• Awareness and Training<br>• Data Security<br>• Platform Security<br>• Technology Infrastructure Resilience |
| Detect (DE) | • Continuous Monitoring<br>• Adverse Event Analysis |
| Respond (RS) | • Incident Management<br>• Incident Analysis<br>• Incident Response Reporting and Communication<br>• Incident Mitigation |
| Recover (RC) | • Incident Recovery Plan Execution<br>• Incident Recovery Communication |

## CSF Tiers

**CSF Tiers** help organizations to:

- Determine their Current and Target CSF Profiles
- Develop governance strategies and processes based on risk appetite and available resources

NIST separates the four CSF Tiers in terms of the sophistication and rigorousness of an organization's **cybersecurity risk governance** (ie, Govern) and **cybersecurity risk management** (ie, Identify, Protect, Detect, Respond, and Recover). Tier 1, Partial, represents the least rigorous cybersecurity stature and is not recommended. Tier 4, Adaptive, is the most sophisticated and hard to achieve. NIST recommends that any organization assessing itself in Tier 1 should increase its efforts to reach Tier 2 at a minimum.

**CSF Tiers**

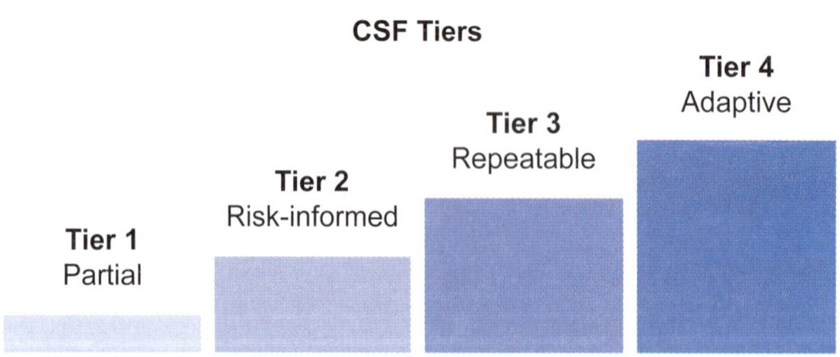

**Tier 1: Partial (Weakest—not recommended)**

- **Cybersecurity risk governance:** Informal and limited cybersecurity risk governance and management. The organization's cybersecurity posture is reactive and managed in an ad hoc manner. Cybersecurity practices are random and not based on objectives, threats, or business requirements.
- **Cybersecurity risk management:** Limited cybersecurity risk awareness. Cybersecurity is managed on an irregular, case-by-case basis. Information is not communicated internally on an organization wide basis or externally. The organization is unaware of all its cybersecurity risks.

**Tier 2: Risk-Informed**

- **Cybersecurity risk governance:** Risk governance and management practices exist, but not as a formal organization-wide policy. Cybersecurity outcomes are prioritized by risk objectives, threats, and business needs.
- **Cybersecurity risk management:** Awareness of cybersecurity risk exists in some areas of the organization, and information is shared internally and informally. Cyber risk assessment on internal and external assets is performed but is not repeatable or reoccurring. The organization may receive information from other entities and can generate its own information, but rarely shares it with others. The organization may be aware of cybersecurity risks, but it does not respond to those risks consistently.

**Tier 3: Repeatable**

- **Cybersecurity risk governance:** Risk governance and management is documented in a formal, organization-wide policy. Risk-informed policies, processes, and procedures are defined, implemented, and reviewed. Policies are routinely updated based on changes to business needs and threats.
- **Cybersecurity risk management:** There is an organization-wide approach to cybersecurity. Consistent methods are in place to monitor and respond to risk changes. Personnel have the appropriate knowledge and training to perform their roles and responsibilities. Cybersecurity risk is communicated and monitored through all lines of operation. The organization understands its role in the cybersecurity ecosystem, and it shares information with other entities. Cybersecurity practices, including monitoring external partners, are incorporated into written agreements and governance structures.

**Tier 4: Adaptive (Strongest)**

- **Cybersecurity risk governance:** There is an organization-wide approach to cybersecurity that uses risk-informed policies, processes, and procedures to address potential cybersecurity incidents. Cybersecurity practices are based on past, present, and predictive factors. The organization practices continuous improvement, leverages advanced technologies, and adjusts quickly to respond to complex threats. The organizational budget is based on the current and predicted risk environment and risk tolerance. Cybersecurity risk management is a part of the organization's culture.
- **Cybersecurity risk management:** The organization adapts cybersecurity practices based on lessons learned and predictive indicators. Real-time information is used to understand and act on cybersecurity risks. The organization shares information with internal and external parties. All formal documents (eg, contracts, SLAs) and informal communications (eg, media releases) proactively address cybersecurity threats and support the entity's relationships with customers, vendors, and partners.

## CSF Profiles

A **CSF Profile** describes an organization's cybersecurity posture based on the CSF Core functions and CSF Tiers. To decide how to improve its cybersecurity risk management program, an organization should establish its Current Profile and then compare that profile with its Target Profile.

- **Current Profile:** The outcomes the organization is achieving (or attempting to achieve) based on its current CSF Tier.
- **Target Profile:** The outcomes the organization would like to achieve in the future based on its desired CSF Tier.

An organization may take the following steps to improve its cybersecurity practices, using the CSF Profiles:

**Steps for Creating and Using a CSF Profile**

Govern
Identify
Protect
Detect
Respond
Recover
NIST Cybersecurity Framework
1 Scope the profile
2 Gather needed information
3 Create the profile
4 Analyze gaps and create an action plan
5 Implement action plan and update profile
Repeat

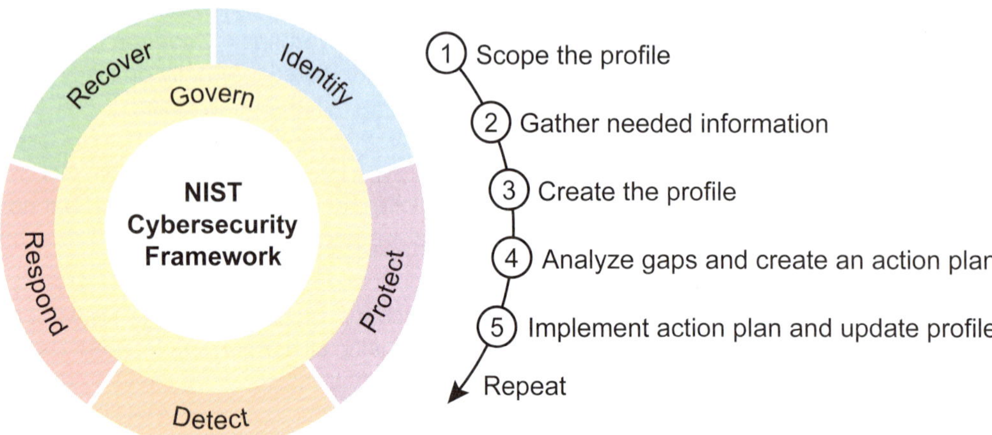

In the fourth step, the Current Profile and Target Profile should be compared based on the CSF Tiers. A list should be made of the CSF Core outcomes (ie, categories and subcategories) needed to **mitigate gaps** between the two profiles. The resulting gap list creates an action plan for management to prioritize cybersecurity improvements based on the costs (eg, equipment, labor, services) and benefit (ie, decreased risk).

Such a comparison of CSF Profiles may appear as follows:

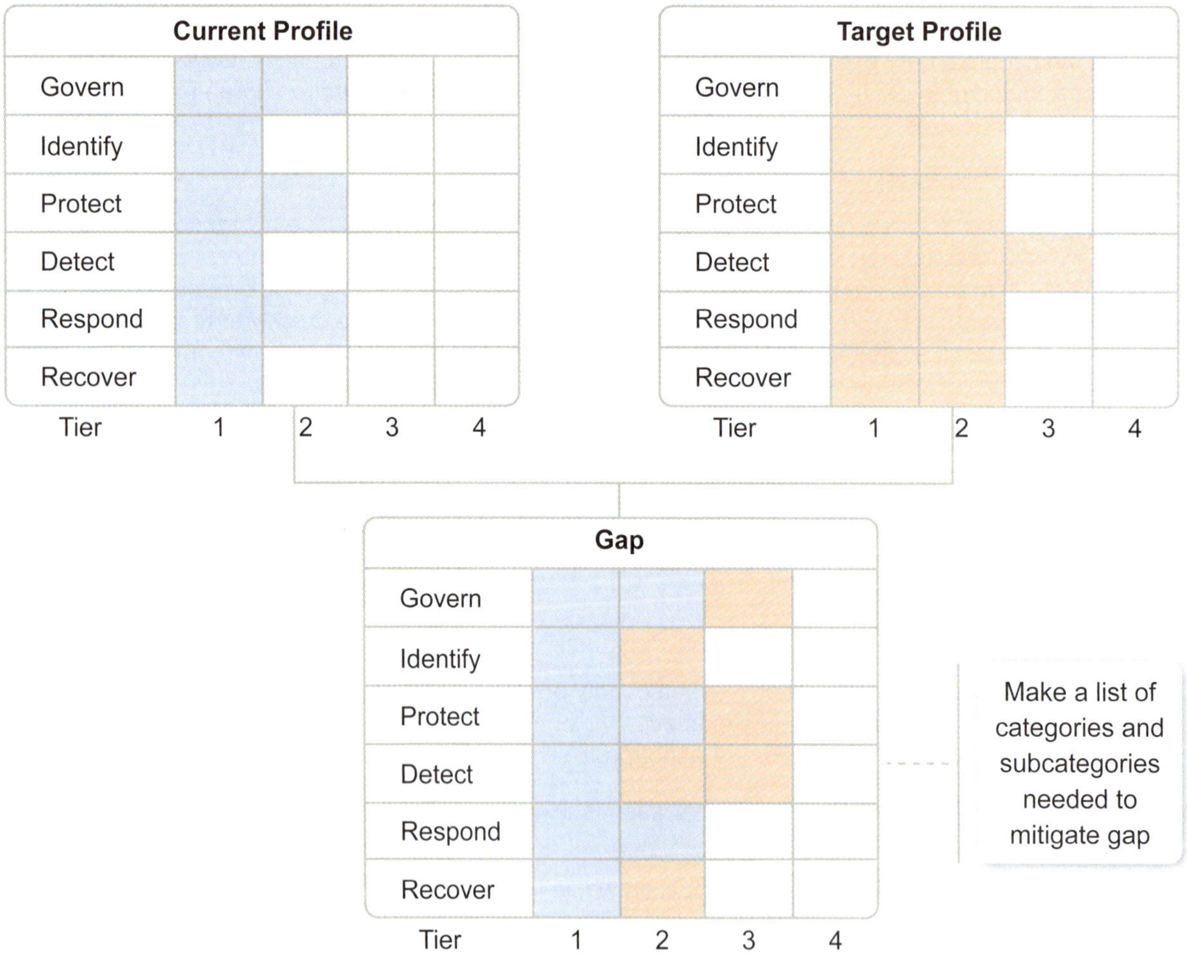

Current Profile
Govern
Identify
Protect
Detect
Respond
Recover
Tier 1 2 3 4
Target Profile
Govern
Identify
Protect
Detect
Respond
Recover
Tier 1 2 3 4
Gap
Govern
Identify
Protect
Detect
Respond
Recover
Tier 1 2 3 4
Make a list of categories and subcategories needed to mitigate gap

## NIST Privacy Framework

**Representative Task (Remembering and Understanding):** Recall the three parts of the NIST Privacy Framework (Framework Core, Framework Profiles, Framework Implementation Tiers).

Organizations that have implemented the NIST CSF may have a robust security program, but this does not mean **privacy risk** is appropriately managed. Recognizing this, NIST developed the **Privacy Framework**. This **voluntary** framework follows the **same structure as the CSF**, making it simple for businesses to align the two. Together, the Privacy Framework and the CSF improve consumer privacy, streamline compliance, and give businesses a comprehensive enterprise risk management tool.

**Cybersecurity and Privacy Risk Relationship**

| Cybersecurity risks | Overlap | Privacy risks |
|---|---|---|
| **Cybersecurity risks** associated with cybersecurity incidents arising from loss of confidentiality, integrity, or availability | Cybersecurity related privacy events | **Privacy risks** associated with privacy events arising from data processing |

The Privacy Framework considers privacy events that may cause problems for individual data subjects. To help organizations manage privacy risks, this framework:

- Suggests privacy controls that may be incorporated into the design and deployment of all systems, products, and services related to information about individuals
- Communicates privacy practices
- Strengthens collaboration between different organizational departments

Like the CSF, the NIST Privacy Framework consists of three parts:

- **Privacy Core:** A set of suggested privacy protection activities and outcomes (ie, controls) that the organization may consider. The core consists of functions, categories, and subcategories. While the tables in the Privacy Framework do not show the maps to other implementation guidance, NIST maintains a web page where the Privacy Framework is crosswalked to regulations and other frameworks.
- **Privacy Tiers:** Tiers that describe how sophisticated an organization's privacy risk management program is, ranging from Tier 1 (partial implementation that is informal and reactive) to Tier 4 (adaptive implementation that is formal and proactive).
- **Privacy Profile:** The list of framework outcomes (ie, categories and subcategories) that the organization has prioritized and selected based on its business needs, the type of data processing, and the data subjects' privacy needs. The organization compares its Current Profile with its Target Profile, adding Framework Core functions, categories, and subcategories as needed to transition to the target.

## Privacy Core

The core consists of three types of elements that work together to manage **privacy risk from data processing:** functions, categories, and subcategories.

- **Functions:** Five broad privacy activities that an organization should perform continuously and concurrently. These functions—Identify-P, Govern-P, Control-P, Communicate-P, and Protect-P—are the main part of the framework and the highest level of structuring basic privacy risk management practices. Because some of the function names are the same as those in the CSF, the suffix "-P" denotes that they refer to the Privacy Framework.

  According to the NIST *Privacy Framework: A Tool for Improving Privacy Through Enterprise Risk Management* V1.0, the functions are defined as follows:
  - **Identify-P:** Develop the organizational understanding needed to manage the privacy risk for individuals that arises from data processing.
  - **Govern-P:** Develop and implement an organizational governance structure that enables an ongoing understanding of the organization's risk management priorities, informed by privacy risk.
  - **Control-P:** Develop and implement appropriate activities that enable organizations or individuals to manage data with sufficient granularity for managing privacy risks.
  - **Communicate-P:** Develop and implement appropriate activities that enable organizations and individuals to have a reliable understanding and discussion about data processing and the associated privacy risks.
  - **Protect-P:** Develop and implement appropriate data processing safeguards.
- **Categories:** Each function is subdivided into categories, which are groups of privacy outcomes. For example, one of the outcome categories in the Identify-P function is Inventory and Mapping.
- **Subcategories:** Each category is subdivided into subcategories that are specific outcomes for technical and/or management activities (ie, controls). For example, the Inventory and Mapping category includes a subcategory, "Systems/products/services that process data are inventoried."

Appendix A to the Privacy Framework document has a table listing all the Framework Core elements:

**Excerpt from NIST Privacy Framework Appendix A**

| Function | Category | Subcategory |
|---|---|---|
| **IDENTIFY-P (ID-P):** Develop the organizational understanding to manage privacy risk for individuals arising from data processing. | **Inventory and Mapping (ID.IM-P):** Data processing by systems, products, or services is understood and informs the management of privacy risk. | **ID.IM-P1:** Systems/products/services that process data are inventoried.<br><br>**ID.IM-P2:** Owners or operators (eg, the organization or third parties such as service providers, partners, customers, and developers) and their roles with respect to the systems/products/services and components (internal or external) that process data are inventoried.<br><br>**ID.IM-P3:** Categories of individuals (eg, customers, employees or prospective employees, consumers) whose data are being processed are inventoried.<br><br>**ID.IM-P4:** Data actions of the systems/products/services are inventoried. |

*Source: Privacy Framework: A Tool for Improving Privacy Through Enterprise Risk Management V1.0*

Although the NIST CSF covers all cybersecurity events, some functions can be added to the Privacy functions to address cybersecurity-related privacy events. For example, the **CSF functions Detect, Respond, and Recover** are pertinent to both cybersecurity and privacy.

**Using Functions to Manage Cybersecurity and Privacy Risks**

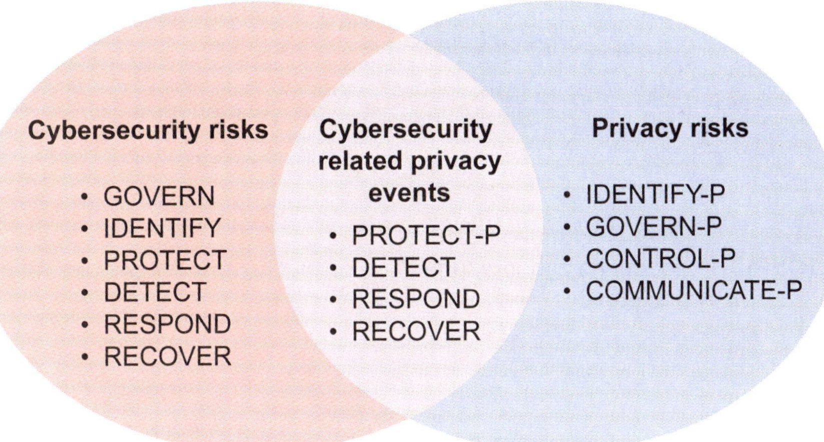


With these added functions, the management of cybersecurity risks and privacy risks would be interrelated as shown:

| Function | Description | Categories |
|---|---|---|
| **Identify-P** | How does data processing affect privacy risk? | • Inventory and mapping<br>• Business environment<br>• Risk assessment<br>• Data processing ecosystem risk management |
| **Govern-P** | How does the organization govern organization-wide privacy risks? | • Governance policies, processes, and procedures<br>• Risk management strategy<br>• Awareness and training<br>• Monitoring and review |
| **Control-P** | What control activities manage data privacy risks? | • Data processing policies, processes, and procedures<br>• Data processing management<br>• Disassociated processing |
| **Communicate-P** | What techniques communicate data processing and associated privacy risks? | • Communication policies, processes, and procedures<br>• Data processing awareness |

| Function | Description | Categories |
|---|---|---|
| **Protect-P** | What techniques can protect personal data? | • Data protection policies, processes, and procedures<br>• Identity management, authentication, and access control<br>• Data security<br>• Maintenance<br>• Protective technology |
| **Detect (CSF)** | What techniques can identify a cybersecurity incident? | • Anomalies and events<br>• Security continuous monitoring<br>• Detection processes |
| **Respond (CSF)** | What techniques can contain a detected cybersecurity incident? | • Response planning<br>• Communications<br>• Analysis<br>• Mitigation<br>• Improvements |
| **Recover (CSF)** | What techniques can restore capabilities or services impaired by a cybersecurity incident? | • Recovery planning<br>• Improvements<br>• Communications |

## Privacy Tiers

Implementation tiers offer a benchmark for measuring how effectively an organization has perceived its privacy risk and assessed the systems and personnel in place to manage that risk. Tiers represent a progression from informal, reactive responses to agile, risk-informed responses.

To use the tiers, organizations first assess their current tier. Next, they consider the desired tier based on threats, regulatory requirements, and the organization's business needs, which include protecting the privacy of data subjects. The organization should weigh the costs and benefits of progressing to the next tier, as well as the actions that would be needed to do so. NIST recommends that any organization assessing itself in Tier 1 increase its efforts to at least Tier 2.

The implementation tiers for the Privacy Framework are the same as the CSF's. To recall, NIST separates the four implementation tiers in terms of the sophistication of an organization's:

- Risk management process
- Integrated risk management program
- External participation

| | |
|---|---|
| **Tier 1 (Partial)** | No systematic risk management processes or programs<br>Understanding of risks is incomplete and does not extend to third parties |
| **Tier 2 (Risk-informed)** | Incomplete risk management processes<br>Underdeveloped risk management programs<br>Partial understanding of internal and external data processing risks |
| **Tier 3 (Repeatable)** | Well-established risk management processes<br>Robust risk management programs<br>Complete understanding of internal and third-party data processing risks |
| **Tier 4 (Adaptive)** | Dynamic and responsive risk management processes<br>Risk management programs respond and adapt to changing business environment<br>Interactive data processing risk identification with internal and external stakeholders |

## Privacy Profiles

When deciding how to improve its privacy risk management program, an organization should establish its **Current Profile** and then **compare** it with a **Target Profile**. Just as with the CSF, the difference between the Current and Target Profiles will allow an organization to identify gaps, design a mitigation strategy, and estimate the resources (eg, staffing, finance, technology) needed to meet the desired privacy outcomes.

Functions, categories, and subcategories are added to mitigate the gap between the Current Profile and Target Profile. This analysis will be subjective, based on the organization's internal risk assessment priorities, regulatory requirements, and other privacy priorities. For example, if an organization wants to be in Implementation Tier 3, its Target Profile would need to be adjusted to reflect the additional activities required. Successful use of the Privacy Framework is based on achieving the Target Profile, not the desired implementation tier.

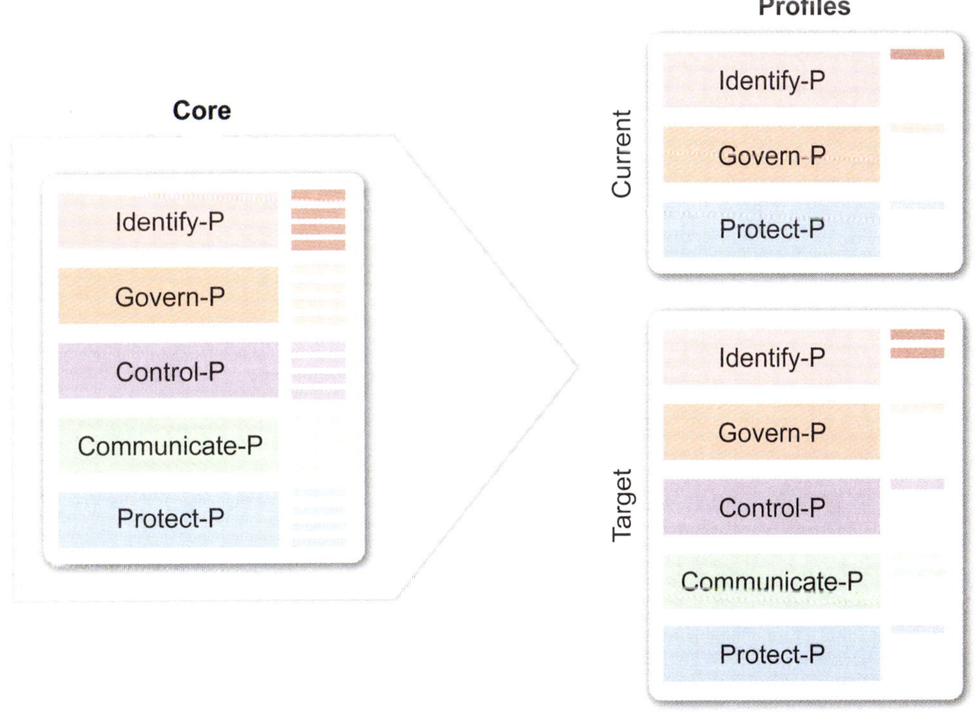

# NIST SP 800-53

**Representative Task (Remembering and Understanding):** Recall the purpose, applicability, target audience, and organizational responsibilities of NIST SP 800-53.

## Purpose

*NIST Security and Privacy Controls for Information Systems and Organizations* (NIST SP 800-53) is a **compliance standard** developed by the U.S. Department of Commerce and NIST. The main purpose is to help organizations **identify the security and privacy controls** necessary to mitigate risks as required by various federal regulations. This framework is also mandatory for **federal information systems**. According to NIST, *"Security controls are the safeguards or countermeasures employed within a system or an organization to protect the confidentiality, integrity, and availability of the system and its information and to manage information security risk. Privacy controls are the administrative, technical, and physical safeguards employed within a system or an organization to manage privacy risks and to ensure compliance with applicable privacy requirements."*

NIST SP 800-53 has three goals:

- Offer a **comprehensive and customizable list of controls** for present and future defense based on developing technology and threats
- Lay the foundation to evaluate the techniques and processes for **determining control effectiveness**
- Improve cross-organizational **communication** by developing a **common terminology** for discussing risk management concepts

## Applicability

All U.S. federal information systems must follow the NIST SP 800-53 standard, except systems pertaining to national security. However, any organization using an information system with regulated or sensitive data can adopt the standard's guidelines.

The Federal Information Processing Standards (FIPS) require companies to establish a minimal baseline of security measures as outlined in NIST SP 800-53. The standard also helps firms comply with the Federal Information Security Modernization Act (FISMA), which sets security and privacy standards for federal programs.

## Target Audience

The standard is aimed at a wide range of information system and information security professionals, including:

- Individuals in charge of information system management, security, and/or risk management and oversight (eg, chief information officers, information system managers)
- Individuals with responsibility for information system development (eg, program managers, system designers and developers)
- Individuals with information security implementation and operational responsibilities (eg, system administrators, information system security officers)
- Individuals responsible for monitoring and assessing information security (eg, auditors, system evaluators)
- Commercial enterprises that manufacture information technology products and systems, develop information security technologies, and provide information security services

## Organizational Responsibilities

- Clearly state security/privacy specifications and criteria
- Design and develop information technology products using current best practices
- Maintain reliable standards and procedures to integrate systems and security products into the existing systems
- Continuously monitor information systems to determine both the ongoing effectiveness of security controls and any changes in the systems or the operational environment
- Ensure that systems comply with legislation, directives, policies, and standards
- Maintain comprehensive information security planning and system development life cycle management

## Security and Privacy Controls

The security and privacy controls discussed in NIST SP 800-53 are like those found in other frameworks, standards, and regulations. The standard includes the following "control families":

| NIST 800-53 Security and Privacy Control Families | | | |
|---|---|---|---|
| **ID** | **Family** | **ID** | **Family** |
| AC | Access control | PE | Physical and environmental protection |
| AT | Awareness and training | PL | Planning |
| AU | Audit and accountability | PM | Program management |
| CA | Assessment, authorization, and monitoring | PS | Personnel security |
| CM | Configuration management | PT | PII Processing and transparency |
| CP | Contingency planning | RA | Risk assessment |
| IA | Identification and authentication | SA | System and services acquisition |
| IR | Incident response | SC | System and communications protection |
| MA | Maintenance | SI | System and information integrity |
| MP | Media protection | SR | Supply chain risk management |

Families of controls contain **base controls**, **discussions**, and **control enhancements**. Discussions provide additional information about a base control or control enhancement. Control enhancements either add functionality or specificity to a base control or increase its strength.

# Control Objectives for Information and Related Technology (COBIT® 2019)

**Representative Task (Remembering and Understanding):** Recall the governance system principles, governance framework principles, and the components of a governance system according to COBIT® 2019.

**ISACA** (formerly known as the Information Systems Audit and Control Association) has developed a framework, referred to as **C**ontrol **Ob**jectives for **I**nformation and Related **T**echnology (COBIT®), for the governance and management of enterprise IT. The **COBIT®** framework is business oriented because it provides a systematic way of integrating IT with business strategy and risk management.

COBIT® has become a central framework for any organization seeking to develop enterprise governance for IT (EGIT), based on two core concepts: **governance system principles** and **governance framework principles**.

## Governance System Principles

COBIT® 2019 is based on **six governance system principles** that describe the core requirements of an enterprise information and technology governance system.

**Governance System Principles**

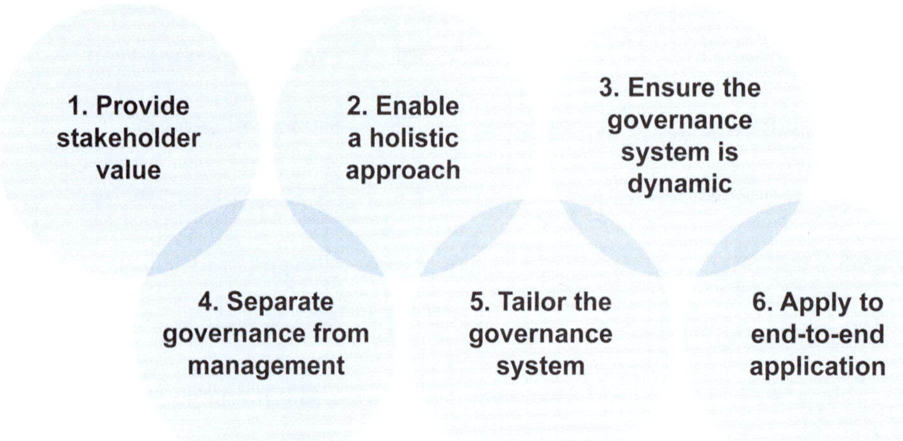


1. **Provide stakeholder value**

   The objective of an entity is to bring value to stakeholders by addressing their needs and generating a financial return or public service. Stakeholders' needs are met by transforming their requirements into actionable strategies. To accomplish this, ISACA suggests the use of a "**goal cascade**," comprising four steps:

   **Stakeholder drivers and needs:** First, identify factors affecting stakeholder needs.

   **Enterprise goals:** Second, translate stakeholder needs into the generic goals of the entity. COBIT® 2019 suggests 13 enterprise goals that fall into categories aligned with the four balanced scorecard dimensions.

**Enterprise Goals**

**Financial**

- Portfolio of competitive products and services
- Managed business risk
- Compliance with external laws and regulations
- Quality of financial information

**Internal**

- Optimization of internal business process functionality
- Optimization of business process costs
- Staff skills, motivation, and productivity
- Compliance with internal policies

**Customer**

- Customer-oriented service culture
- Business service continuity and availability
- Quality of management information

**Growth**

- Managed digital transformation programs
- Product and business innovation

**Alignment goals:** Third, align all business IT efforts with enterprise goals. COBIT® 2019 suggests using alignment goals that translate the enterprise goals into an IT balanced scorecard. For example, the enterprise goal of "managed business risk" becomes the alignment goal of "managed *IT-related risk*."

**Governance and management objectives:** Finally, use the alignment goals to develop what COBIT® 2019 refers to as the **components of a governance system** (described later in this chapter).

2. **Enable a holistic approach**

   COBIT® 2019 is considered a single integrated framework because it aligns with other relevant standards and frameworks. Rather than having many isolated frameworks that address strategic components independently, COBIT® 2019 ensures that the IT impact and initiatives generated by using other frameworks align with management goals across an organization. This holistic approach ensures business initiatives are clearly connected to an overarching strategy. Many other frameworks, including the Trust Services Criteria, have maps showing the connections to/similarities with COBIT®.

3. **Ensure the governance system is dynamic**

   COBIT® 2019 uses design factors (eg, enterprise goals and strategy) to influence the design of an enterprise's governance system. When there is a change in a design factor, the impact of the changes should be considered and the governance system should be updated as necessary.

4. **Separate governance from management**

   COBIT® 2019 distinguishes between governance and management objectives:

| Governance (EDM) | Management (APO, BAI, DSS, MEA) |
|---|---|
| • *Evaluates* strategic options based on stakeholders' needs<br>• *Directs* management on strategies chosen<br>• *Monitors* management's achievement of strategies | To achieve strategy set by the governing body, management:<br>• *Aligns, plans, and organizes* IT activities<br>• *Builds, acquires, and implements* IT solutions<br>• *Delivers, services, and supports* IT services<br>• *Monitors, evaluates, and assesses* IT performance in accordance with internal targets, internal control objectives, and external requirements |

**COBIT® 2019 Core Model**

5. **Tailor the governance system**

   COBIT® 2019 provides guidance to help businesses in different industries create a governance system that can meet their specific needs. The primary method of tailoring a governance system to a business is through the selection and use of **design factors**. Design factors are used to assess an enterprise's technology capabilities and growth objectives, select framework components that will meet those objectives, and identify **focus areas** that target specific governance needs.

**Governance System Examples**

| Design Factors | Focus Areas |
|---|---|
| • Enterprise size, strategy, and goals | • Cybersecurity |
| • Risk profile | • Digital transformation |
| • Threat landscape | • Cloud computing |
| • Compliance requirements | • Privacy |
| • Role of IT and IT-related issues | • Software development operations |
| • Sourcing model for IT | • IT architecture |
| • IT implementation methods | • Centralization (or decentralization) |
| • Technology adoption strategy | • Project and resource management |

6. **Apply to end-to-end application**

   COBIT® 2019 enables a business to apply IT governance across the organization. Thus, systems put in place for the governance and management of IT should apply to all information processing components, not just the IT function.

## Governance Framework Principles

To maximize the benefits of EGIT, the six system principles must work in tandem with the **three governance framework principles**.

**Governance Framework Principles**

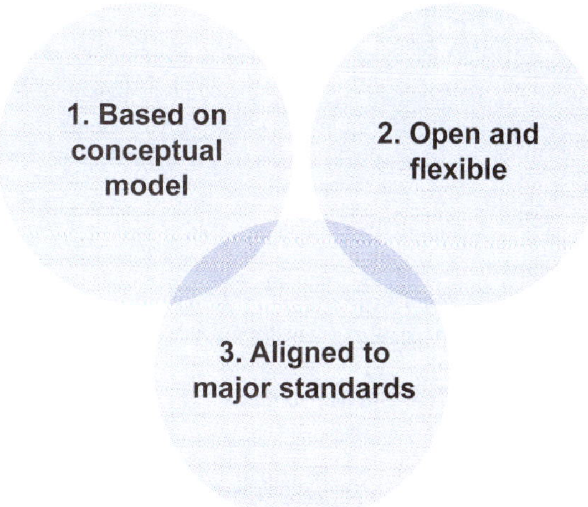


In the current version of the COBIT® framework, the three identified framework principles are:

1. Based on a conceptual model
2. Open and flexible
3. Aligned to major standards

## Components of a Governance System

Components are factors that influence the organizational governance and management system over IT. The components are distinct and interact with one another to achieve governance and management goals. There are **seven components**:

**COBIT® 2019 Components of a Governance System**

**Processes:** A well-organized set of practices and activities that produce specific outcomes in order to achieve the goals.

**Organizational structures:** Key decision-making entities within the enterprise.

**Principles, policies, and procedures:** Transforming desired behavior into practical day-to-day management guidance.

**Information:** All information essential for the effective functioning of the enterprise's governance system is pervasive across the organization.

**Culture, ethics, and behavior:** Applicable for both individuals and organizations and essential for proper governance and management activities.

**People, skills, and competencies:** Requiring good decision making, course correction when needed, and successful completion of all activities.

**Services, infrastructure, and applications:** IT processing provided to the governance and management system.

# ISC 6
# Security

# ISC 6: Security

# 6.01 Threats and Attacks

## Threat Agents

**Representative Task (Remembering and Understanding):** Classify the different types of threat agents (eg, internal or external, nation or non-nation-state sponsored, adversary, threat actors, attacker, or hacker).

Cybersecurity threats and risks exist anytime network-connected IT resources access, transmit, or store data. While noncommercial attacks are common, businesses and critical infrastructure (eg, power grids) are also highly vulnerable.

An effective defense requires a detailed understanding of the "enemy," including their intentions and goals. Cybersecurity professionals may refer to the enemy as a threat actor, threat agent, adversary, or hacker. A threat agent is a person, group, or other entity that **initiates** all or part of an **incident** intended to compromise the **security** of an organization.

**Types of Cyber Threat Agents**

| | Motivation | Character | Sophistication | Cyber Activities |
|---|---|---|---|---|
| **Nation-States** | Geopolitical | State-sponsored threat agents working for political units | Most advanced, with dedicated resources, global personnel, and extensive planning and coordination | Stealing funds, sensitive information, or intellectual property; espionage; disrupting critical infrastructure; influencing public discourse |
| **Cybercriminals** | Financial | Individuals who target cash-rich or data-rich businesses | Advanced, with planning and support functions besides specialized technical capabilities | Ransomware, a type of malicious software that prevents access to a computer system until a fee is paid |
| **Hacktivists** | Ideological | Individuals who focus on creating awareness or exposing secrets | Less sophisticated, relying on readily available tools that do not require expertise | Gaining access to confidential information or data to share publicly |
| **Cyberterrorists** | Ideological violence | Individuals or criminal organizations spreading fear, unrest, and conflict throughout the world | Advanced, with ability to target nations, large companies, and critical services | Interruption to vital infrastructure and systems |
| **Insiders** | Discontent | Disgruntled employees or external spies who have infiltrated an organization | Dangerous because they have been granted access to bypass externally facing security perimeters | System disruption, stealing or corrupting data |

# Cybersecurity Attacks

**Representative Task (Remembering and Understanding):** Identify types of attacks (eg, physical, distributed denial of service, malware, social engineering, web application attacks, mobile device attacks).

**Representative Task (Remembering and Understanding):** Identify techniques used in a cyberattack (eg, buffer overflow, mobile code, cross-site scripting, SQL injections, race conditions, covert channel, replay, and return-oriented attack).

## Cyberattack Types and Techniques

Cyberattacks involve the **illegal** use of computers or other technologies to gain **unauthorized access** to data, systems, or networks. The attack may target an individual or multiple systems, devices, or components.

**Possible Outcome of Cyberattacks**

| Unauthorized access | Unauthorized modification of data | Unauthorized use of data | Destruction of physical or digital assets | Extortion of financial assets | Denial of service |
|---|---|---|---|---|---|

Types of cyberattacks include:

- **Physical attacks:** Theft, vandalism, and unauthorized access are primary examples of physical attacks by threat agents who may be insiders (eg, disgruntled employees) or external parties.

  Physical attacks may include:

| Tailgating/piggybacking | Door propping | Pass-backs | Lost/stolen access credentials |
|---|---|---|---|
| Individual with physical access permissions is followed through a door by an unauthorized person. | Doors are left unlocked and/or open or doors are weak and easily broken through. | An individual with physical access permissions gives their access card or keys to an unauthorized person. | Due to error or theft, an individual with access permissions loses their badge, keys, or codes, which are then used by an unauthorized person. |

  Controls against physical attacks include:

  - Access controls, such as keyed locks, badges, and badge access reviews
  - Surveillance cameras and alarm systems
  - Visitor management and escort policies
  - Perimeter security, such as fences, walls, or fences
  - Security guards

- Clean desk policies
- Awareness programs
- Log-on and log-off policies

- **Denial of service (DoS)/Distributed denial of service (DDoS):** In a DoS attack, a network is flooded with so many requests that regular traffic is slowed or completely interrupted. A DDoS attack is a type of DoS attack in which multiple machines are used to attack a single target. DDoS attacks can be extremely powerful, sending a massive number of requests to the target simultaneously. Using multiple machines makes attributing the attack difficult because its true origin is hard to pinpoint. Attackers may use botnets, which are groups of machines rented to conduct DDoS attacks.

**Distributed Denial of Service (DDoS) Attack**

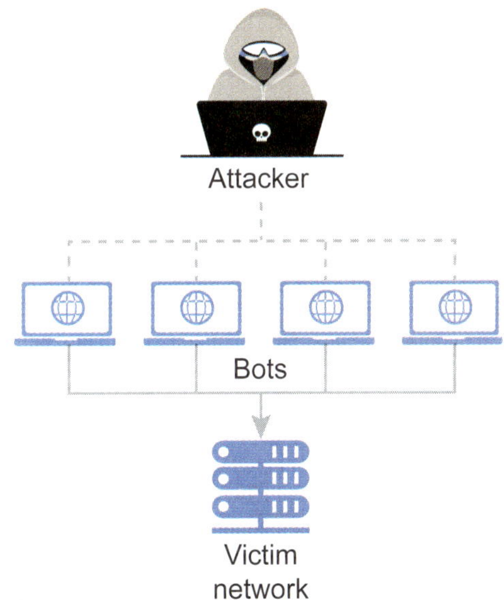


Controls against DoS/DDoS attacks include:

- Hardware, software, and network protections such as firewalls, VPNs, anti-spam software, traffic filtering, and computing optimization
- Incident response plans

- **Malware:** An application that infiltrates a system to gain unauthorized access to data and/or disrupt operations. Malware may be spread using worms sent through various methods such as email or instant messaging, Trojan horses on websites or files, or viruses in downloaded files. A worm is a virus that self-propagates and can use up all a computer's resources so that it stops functioning. Trojan horses are hidden viruses or malicious files. Malware enters systems when it is downloaded and executed by users who believe they are accessing legitimate software or files.

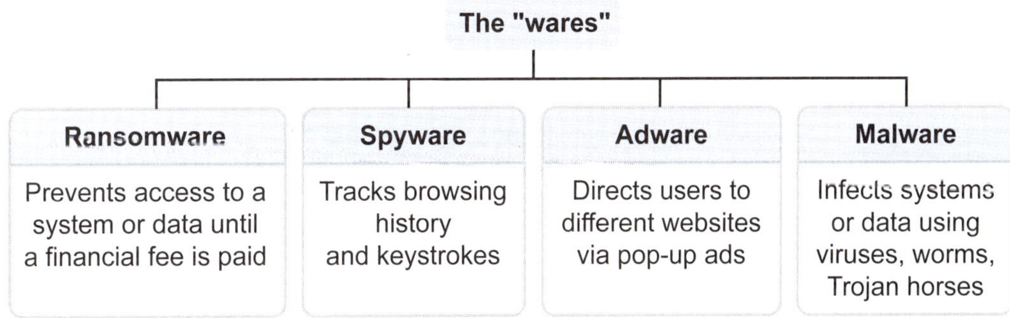

Controls against malware include:

- Ensuring security software, patches, and updates are current
- Ensuring patches are from a trusted source and are implemented, tested, and monitored
- Implementing proper network segmentation and configuration
- Using firewalls, encryption, and anti-malware/anti-ransomware software
- Using authentication, access controls, and automated logoffs
- Removing unused software and disabling unused features
- Auditing and reviewing access logs for failed log-in attempts, file share access, and remote access
- Documenting and testing incident response plans

- **Social engineering:** Attacks that exploit a user's trust or lack of technical knowledge. By using psychological manipulation, social engineering tricks people into sharing sensitive information or performing specific actions. Such attacks may originate with emails, direct messages, or phone calls. The attacker conveys a message that combines a level of urgency (eg, your account has been compromised) with seeming authority or authenticity (eg, an email that looks like it is from the relevant business, using its logo and signature), instructing the victim to take a compromising action (eg, log onto a website, download a malicious program). The attacker may attach a file that has malicious code or an invoice for payment due.
  - **Phishing:** Uses social engineering techniques that trick internal users into opening malicious attachments or embedded links in emails. The attack is masked as a legitimate request from a trusted source. Phishing is the most widely used form of social engineering attack. Besides emails, phishers may use scam phone calls (vishing) or text messages (smishing). Their techniques may be automated and often involve spoofing (ie, using an email address, phone number, or web address that appears legitimate).
  - **Spear phishing:** Attacks that target a specific individual or organization. In contrast to broad, unsophisticated phishing attacks, spear phishing uses information gathered from social media and other publicly available online sources to disguise the attacker as a friend, colleague, vendor, or company department (eg, help desk). Whaling is spear phishing that targets high-ranking individuals within an organization.

**Social Engineering: Phishing Attacks**

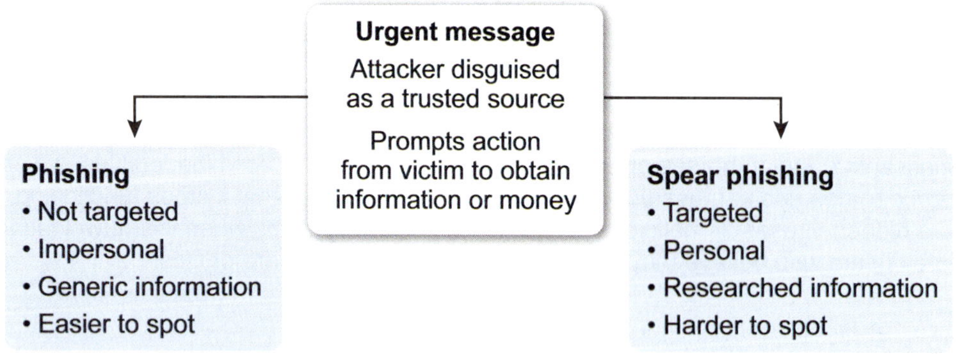

**Urgent message**
Attacker disguised as a trusted source
Prompts action from victim to obtain information or money

| Phishing | Spear phishing |
|---|---|
| • Not targeted | • Targeted |
| • Impersonal | • Personal |
| • Generic information | • Researched information |
| • Easier to spot | • Harder to spot |

Controls against phishing attacks include:

- Avoiding unknown or suspicious links, emails, and applications
- Requiring annual security awareness training for employees and contractors
- Scanning downloads for viruses
- Configuring systems to allow downloads only from trusted sources
- Using an application to screen or block unknown phone numbers or robocalls

- **Web application attacks:** Exploits vulnerabilities in web-based applications (eg, employee portals, intranets, websites) to inject malicious code into communications between the web user interface and servers.
    - **Cross-site scripting (XSS):** An attacker can use XSS to deliver a malicious script to an unsuspecting user's browser. The browser executes the script because it appears to be from a trusted source. Once executed, the malicious script can access and use any data stored by the browser, including cookies, and may completely change the HTML page content. XSS is mitigated by sanitizing user inputs to block scripts or executable programs that do not originate from within the web application.
    - **SQL injection:** An attacker inserts (injects) a SQL query or command in an application through a data entry input field (eg, username), typically to execute predefined SQL code commands. SQL injection is mitigated by input sanitization and treating anything entered into a form field as untrusted data.
    - **Clickjacking:** Hiding or masking inputs or web interface actions to trick users into clicking a malicious link or initiating an unintended action. The attacker "hijacks" clicks intended by the user for a certain page and diverts them to another page, often by using iframes (ie, invisible frames). Clickjacking can be mitigated through client-side and server-side measures that either disallow frames on a website or ensure that the frame has the same origin as the website.

  Controls against web application attacks include:
    - Requiring security awareness training for all employees and contractors
    - Performing security reviews during the system development life cycle
    - Penetration testing
    - Requiring strong passwords and authentication in development tools

- **Wireless network attacks:** Wireless networks are not as secure as wired connections and may be exploited to gain unauthorized access to an organization's network. Besides performing malicious acts, such as stealing data, attackers can use a wireless network to slow processes or even crash a system.

  Controls against wireless network attacks include:
    - Using the newest hardware with upgraded encryption protocols
    - Deploying a wireless intrusion detection system (WIDS)
    - Keeping software up to date
    - Ensuring proper configurations and network passwords
    - Establishing multifactor authentication
    - Setting up a separate guest Wi-Fi
    - Ensuring Wi-Fi does not extend outside the building
    - Encrypting network data
    - Enabling media access control (MAC) address filtering

- **Mobile device attacks:** Most digital fraud now occurs on mobile devices, including phishing frauds and password thefts. Apps may collect data without the user's consent. When a user connects to an open, password-free Wi-Fi network, anyone nearby can easily spy on the user's online activity. Common mobile security threats include network spoofing (eg, free airport Wi-Fi), phishing attacks, spyware, malicious apps, and broken cryptography.

  Controls against mobile device attacks include:
    - Protecting mobile devices and SIM cards from theft or loss
    - Avoiding public Wi-Fi networks
    - Using a VPN on mobile devices

- Logging out of websites
- Removing permissions on unused apps/limiting permissions on used apps
- Avoiding suspicious emails, texts, and notifications
- Reading reviews and researching developers prior to installing apps
- Keeping apps updated
- Using security software on mobile devices
- Using remote locking services

Other cyberattack techniques include:

| Buffer overflow attack | Malicious mobile code | Race condition attack |
|---|---|---|
| Writes data to hardware beyond its buffer memory capacity | Executed automatically via a web browser | Exploits gaps in time between sequential operations |
| **Covert channel** | **Replay attack** | **Return-oriented programming attack** |
| Unauthorized intra-system channel that adds secret data | Eavesdrops on secure messages and resends them to trick a user into action | Changes return addresses within existing executable memory instruction sequences |

- **Buffer overflow attacks:** Attacks that target the processing or memory limitations of hardware in order to overwrite data, reset the hardware configurations to an easy-to-attack default setting, or disrupt services with system crashes. These attacks exploit vulnerabilities in an application or system code or use complex, unexpected user interactions to overwhelm a system or device. Buffer overflow attacks are primarily mitigated through regular code testing, updates and security patches, and operating system protections like data execution prevention.
- **Malicious mobile code (MMC):** Software that is downloaded from remote computers, sent over a network, and then executed on a local device without the recipient explicitly installing or running it. Mobile code is not an application installed on a computer or phone; it is executed automatically via a web browser. Examples include JavaScript for Minecraft or PDF documents. Developers of mobile software have little to no control over the environment in which their code will run. Mobile code running alongside other, potentially malicious, code is a major threat.
- **Race condition attacks:** A race condition (also known as a time-of-check-to-time-of-use condition) occurs when a device or system tries to perform two or more operations at once, yet because of its nature, must complete those operations in the proper sequence. For example, a security system might request a user's log-in and password before checking them against a database and permitting access. In any such sequence, there is a brief period when the system has completed the first task but has not begun the second. If that period is long enough, an attacker may fool the system into performing unauthorized actions.
- **Covert channel:** An unauthorized intra-system channel that sends data in small pieces across existing channels or networks. Covert channels add data to a data stream without influencing the main stream. This lets a covert receiver extract data without leaving a data trail. Detection is difficult because a single packet may have only one or two bits of secret data. It takes clever programming to create a covert channel, and access to the file system at the source end of the communication is required. This means that a covert channel can be started only by a virus or by someone with administrative or other authorized access to the system programming.

- **Replay attacks:** Attacks that take place when a threat agent monitors a secure network connection, intercepts a message, and then purposefully delays or resends that message to trick the recipient into doing what the agent wants. Replay attacks pose an additional risk because a hacker, with no special knowledge, can easily decrypt a communication after grabbing it from the network; by simply transmitting it again, the attacker can be successful. The user receives the message twice in a replay attack, hence the name. The key to thwarting such an attack is using the proper encryption technique (eg, session key) and/or time stamp for the original data.
- **Return-oriented programming attacks:** Attacks that exploit existing code to perform certain malicious functions. When data execution prevention (DEP) is used, a threat agent cannot directly execute buffered instructions because the buffer's memory is nonexecutable. To bypass DEP, a return-oriented programming attack manipulates return addresses instead of injecting harmful instructions. Thus, rather than executing the malicious code directly, the attacker has mixed the sequences of "good" instructions by altering stored return addresses; the code will then be flagged as executable, making a conventional DEP approach defenseless against this attack.

**Threat Vectors**

Mediums that may be exploited in a cyberattack

| User log-ins | Web applications | System networks |
|---|---|---|
| Email systems | Mobile devices | Remote access |

## Cyberattack Phases

**Representative Task (Remembering and Understanding):** Explain the stages in a cyberattack (eg, reconnaissance, gaining access, escalation of privileges, maintaining access, network exploitation, covering tracks).

**Attacks** using advanced computer technology can hide inside a network for **months or years** before being discovered. An attacker may have a long time to gather sensitive information and run a covert operation. Although the specifics of attacks vary, the following sequence is common:

**Stages in a Cybersecurity Attack**

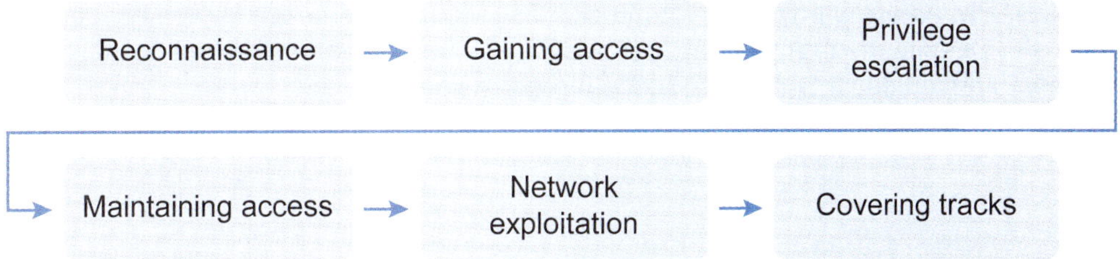


- Reconnaissance: During this early stage, attackers conduct research (ie, **scanning**), followed by the identification and listing (ie, **enumeration**) of vulnerable targets. The attackers obtain information from publicly accessible sources (eg, company websites, social media). To protect its information, an entity should implement **security awareness training** so that employees and contractors understand what should and should not be published, including confidential documents, customer lists, event participants, and job duties and responsibilities (eg, using particular security technologies inside the organization).

- Gaining access (intrusion): An attack breaches the system perimeter (ie, network boundary separating internal business systems and data from the wider Internet) and gains access to the environment. To prevent this, an entity should ensure full visibility of all traffic in and out of the environment; use address filtering to protect against perimeter breaches; install antivirus software; detect any malware; and deploy automatic defenses to stop attacks.
- Escalation of privileges: Once inside the system perimeter, attackers try to compromise additional servers, systems, and user accounts (ie, **lateral movement**). Intruders can use tools to steal credentials, gain access to the administrator account, and then get into any system on the network that the administrator account can access. Prevention strategies include **penetration testing, zero trust security**, and closing lateral network access points. An organization may hire an **ethical hacker** to stress-test their network security by penetrating as deeply as possible without detection. Many CPA firms offer penetration testing (ie, ethical hacking) as part of their risk advisory services.
- Maintaining access: After establishing lateral movement and privilege escalation, attackers have unrestricted access to the target network. The next step is sustainment (staying in place quietly). The attackers maintain access to the environment by installing various malware backdoor variants or gaining entry to remote access services like business VPNs. Mitigation strategies include anomaly detection systems, security information and event management (SIEM) systems, and reviews of user permissions.
- Network exploitation: At this stage, the attackers have complete control and will act on the motivation to accomplish their goal. Their goal could be data exfiltration, destroying critical infrastructure, interrupting business operations, or instilling fear as a means of extortion. Mitigation may include using network-based intrusion detection systems (IDS) and other traffic analysis tools.
- Covering tracks (obfuscation): Attackers try to conceal the source/origin of their efforts to avoid being caught. In addition, by covering their tracks, they make it harder to understand the scope of the data breach. For successful obfuscation, attackers may use spoofing, log cleaning, zombie accounts, and Trojan commands. Mitigation may focus on log analysis to detect tampering, file integrity monitoring (FIM), and forensic analysis.

## Cybersecurity Risks: Cloud Platforms

**Representative Task (Remembering and Understanding):** Identify the cybersecurity risks related to cloud environments, platforms, and services.

Cloud computing delivers IT resources via the Internet, with pay-as-you-go pricing. Instead of purchasing, owning, and supporting physical data centers and servers, an entity can use a cloud service provider (CSP) to access technology services such as computing power, storage, applications, and databases on an as-needed basis. Typically, an entity pays only for the cloud services used, which lowers the cost and supplies economies of scale. Despite the many benefits, moving a company's workloads to a publicly hosted cloud service exposes it to added security threats. These threats include:

| | |
|---|---|
| **Data Leakage** | Data theft could result in the loss of intellectual property, a product road map, or some other sensitive information. A company's weak cloud security controls, such as data storage without encryption or a failure to implement multifactor authentication for access, are common reasons for data leakage. |
| **Data Loss** | Natural disasters (eg, earthquakes), malicious attacks, or service providers' data wipes can all result in the loss of data kept on cloud servers. This could be devastating if there were no recent backups. Reviewing the CSP's terms of service and backup policies is vital to data longevity. |
| **Insecure APIs** | Application programming interfaces (APIs) enable consumers to customize cloud services. To allow this customization, API documentation is provided on the Internet. Cyberattackers can take advantage of the readily available documentation to identify potential methods for accessing and exfiltrating sensitive data from an organization's cloud environment. |
| **Malware Attacks** | Cloud services can be used as a channel for data exfiltration. For example, attackers can encrypt code and upload it to YouTube; after that, the malware releases sensitive data a few characters at a time. |
| **Insider Abuse (End-User Control)** | When a company doesn't address the risk posed by its employees' use of cloud services, the employees may inappropriately share confidential documents or use unauthorized services (ie, shadow IT). |
| **Legal and Regulatory Compliance Violations** | Most businesses are governed by a regulatory agency (eg, HIPAA for medical patient records, FERPA for student records). Noncompliance with any regulatory body can pose serious threats to the company. |
| **Contract Breaches** | Contracts limit how business partners or clients use and access data. When employees transfer restricted data onto their cloud accounts without receiving authorization from the appropriate authorities, they put the company and themselves in danger of legal action. |
| **Data Sovereignty/ Residence/Control** | Most CSPs have several data centers spread across the country or world. This improves the accessibility and performance of cloud-based services while also serving as a backup in the event of business-disrupting events such as natural disasters, power outages, etc. However, organizations storing data in the cloud do not always know where the data is located in the CSP's data centers, and this could result in cybersecurity risks. |
| **Poor Visibility and Incident Response** | Many companies have thorough internal cybersecurity response plans. When a company owns its network infrastructure and has internal security, visibility is sufficient to identify an incident's scope and undertake remedies to contain the attack. In contrast, a cloud-based infrastructure limits visibility, rendering standard processes and security tools inefficient. |

# Cybersecurity Risks: Internet of Things (IoT)

**Representative Task (Remembering and Understanding):** Identify the cybersecurity risks related to the Internet of Things (IoT).

**The Internet of Things (IoT)** is a network of physical objects ("things") with embedded sensors, software, and other technologies for connecting and exchanging data with other devices and systems via the Internet. IoT devices range from common domestic items (eg, smart thermostats) to high-tech industrial equipment (eg, machine power sensors). These devices may have inadequate security requirements and serve as a gateway for attackers to gain access to the larger network.

Because IoT is a collection of **gadgets**, security risks associated with individual gadgets (eg, mobile device risks) also apply to IoT. Common attack types include distributed denial of service (DDoS), physical attacks, brute force attacks (trying multiple passwords to connect), application-based attacks, and malware. Other attack types that are relatable to IoT include:

**Man in the Middle**

- Attack intercepts data transmission between two devices
- Passive attack: attacker records data without altering it
- Active attack: attacker modifies data

**Radio Frequency Jamming**

- Attacker disrupts communications by interfering with radio signals
- Devices called "RF jammers" emit a high-powered signal on the same frequency as receiving device
- Receiving device is overwhelmed and cannot decode the signal

Common IoT cybersecurity risks include:

- **Poor data protection:** IoT devices often connect a secure network to devices that are not secure. When connected devices are breached, information can be leaked or attackers can gain unauthorized access. IoT devices rarely have enough power to support encryption but can access shared networks through wired or wireless connections.
- **Limited security integration:** IoT device integration into security systems can be difficult because of their diversity and scale.
- **Open-source code vulnerabilities:** Firmware for IoT devices often incorporates open-source software, which is susceptible to bugs and exploitation.
- **Poor security testing:** Most IoT developers do not prioritize security and thus may not conduct adequate vulnerability testing to uncover IoT system weaknesses.
- **Unpatched vulnerabilities:** IoT devices may have known security vulnerabilities. This could be because patches are not available or are hard to install.
- **Weak passwords:** Consumers often forget to update the default passwords provided with their IoT devices, which gives cybercriminals easy access. In other instances, users create weak, discoverable passwords.

**Weak Passwords**

- Running numbers: 123456, 111111, 654321
- Clustered keys: qwerty, asdfgh, 1q2w3e
- Common phrases: letmein, trustno1, admin
- Password: password1, strongpassword, wrongpassword
- Using personal name, company name, or family member's names
- Curse words

- **Vulnerable APIs:** APIs are often used as entry points to attack command-and-control centers.
- **Poor visibility:** IoT devices are often used by employees without the knowledge of their employer's IT department, making it difficult to have a complete inventory of the assets that need to be protected and monitored.
- **Excessive data volume:** More devices will generate more data. A large volume of data makes monitoring, management, and security challenging.
- **Increased attack surface area:** The **attack surface** refers to the sum of all potentially exposed network areas (ie, weaknesses) that an attacker could use to gain access to a system. For example, a customer portal is one part of an organization's attack surface as it may be compromised, allowing access to an attacker. Endpoint devices may also be included because associated vulnerabilities, such as weak passwords or unpatched software, can be exploited by an attacker.

**Attack Surface Area**

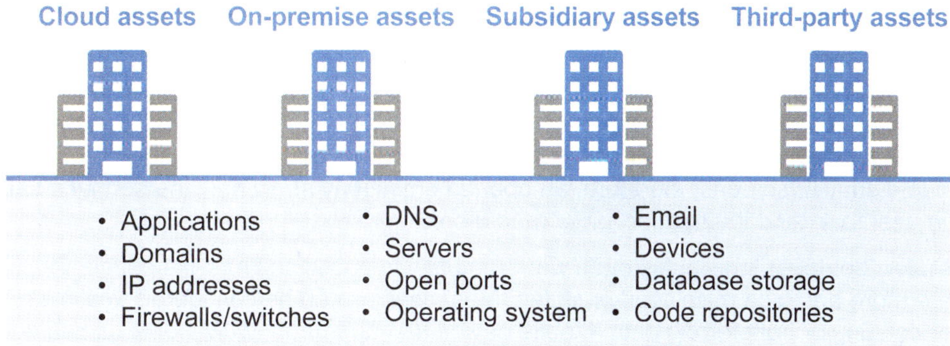

# Cybersecurity Risks: Mobile Technologies

**Representative Task (Remembering and Understanding):** Identify the cybersecurity risks related to mobile technologies.

Consumers and businesses use mobile devices more than computers. Although most mobile devices are cell phones or tablets, others such as laptops, USB drives, and external hard drives also pose a security risk.

Cybersecurity risks related to mobile technologies include:

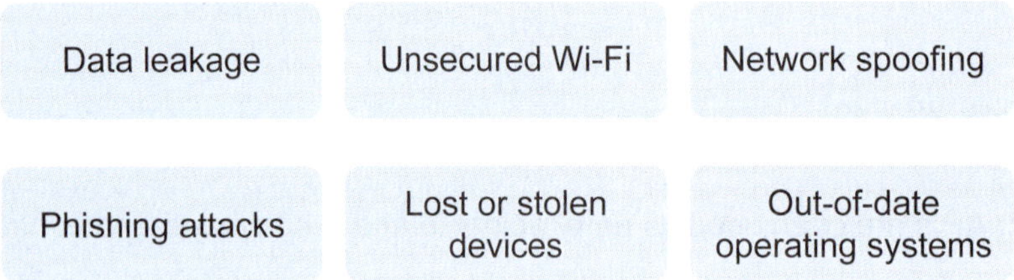


- **Data leakage:** Data leaks may result from mobile app security breaches. Apps are a major concern because mobile users might give permissions without understanding their security. Apps, which may be installed for free through official stores (eg, Apple, Google), send a user's personal and business data to a remote server. To avoid data leakage, the user should grant each app only the permissions it requires for proper functioning.
- **Unsecured Wi-Fi:** Free, public wireless Internet networks are typically not secure. Therefore, free Wi-Fi (ie, unknown network) usage should be minimized and is never proper for accessing sensitive data (eg, financial information).
- **Network spoofing:** Network spoofing refers to hackers setting up fake access points in high-traffic public places like coffee shops, libraries, and airports. Cybercriminals give these access points labels like "Free Airport Wi-Fi" or "Coffeeshop" to lure users, who may be required to start an account before accessing the free service. When users register with an email address and/or password they also use for other accounts, the hacker gains the information needed to access those accounts.
- **Phishing attacks:** Many mobile devices, such as phones, are always on, so most phishing attacks (fake emails) target them. Mobile users are particularly exposed as they are more likely to open and read each email as it arrives. In addition, email apps for mobile devices display less information to accommodate smaller screens; therefore, an opened email may show only the sender's name at first, forcing the user to extend the header bar to read more.
- **Lost or stolen devices:** Individuals often work remotely in public settings like coffee shops, where devices are more apt to be misplaced or stolen. Most devices can be configured to allow remote access for deleting or transferring data. Mobile device management (MDM) tools can safeguard, encrypt, or delete important enterprise data from a lost or stolen device.
- **Out-of-date operating systems:** Mobile device security, like other data security measures, requires the ongoing work of identifying and patching vulnerabilities that could be exploited by threat agents.

In addition, weak passwords, improper or lack of multifactor authentication (MFA), improper session handling, and poor cryptographic controls increase the risk related to mobile device usage. Mobile device security **controls** include Find My Device, screen locks after x minutes of no activity or n number of password attempts, disabling removable storage, blocking USB ports, and wiping data remotely.

# Threat Modeling and Landscape

**Representative Task (Remembering and Understanding):** Explain threat modeling and threat landscape.

## Threat Landscape

The **threat landscape** refers to **all** the **potential** cybersecurity **threats** that may target user groups, organizations, and industries. The threat landscape **changes daily** as new cyber threats appear.

The following elements may influence the threat landscape:

- Release of updated software
- Creation of new hardware architectures
- Introduction of novel data processing techniques (eg, edge computing, use of cloud services)
- Emerging vulnerabilities that allow cybercriminals to launch fresh attacks
- Sudden, unexpected changes that force an organization to adapt to a new infrastructure framework (eg, COVID-19 and working from home)

**Threat landscape analysis** enables the identification of potential information security issues facing a specific entity. A **preemptive approach** should then be taken to implement **preventive** measures.

## Threat Modeling

Businesses use **threat modeling** to identify the sources, targets, and potential effects of attacks. Threats are analyzed from the attacker's perspective. This helps security teams figure out what assets or resources would make attractive targets and whether the organization's IT hardware and systems are vulnerable. The risks are then communicated to management. Threat modeling considers the effects of an attack on software, applications, systems, networks, mobile devices, Internet of Things (IoT) devices, and business processes.

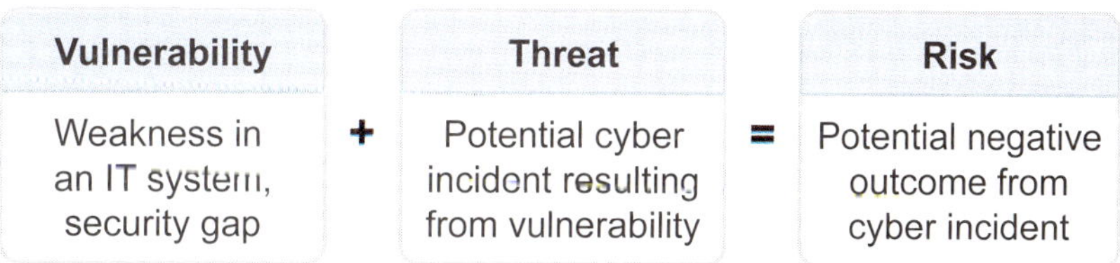


Threat modeling helps evaluate risk by quantifying the likelihood of an adverse event (eg, cyberattack rendering network unusable) and the resulting impact (ie, lost time, resources, or business). The extent and priority of the risk can then be established.

## Threat Modeling Process

**Define Security Requirements**

Identify high-value and critical assets.

**Diagram**

Break down application or system functionalities to understand how they interact with internal and external users/endpoints; map to examine data flows and business processes.

**Identify Threats**

Determine internal and external threats. A threat model such as Microsoft STRIDE (spoofing, tampering, repudiation, information disclosure, denial of service, and elevation of privilege) may be used.

**Rank and Document**

Assess the likelihood and impact of threats on a layer-by-layer basis (eg, application, server, network). Document threats for reporting and monitoring purposes.

**Mitigate**

Implement security controls to mitigate risk and limit damage.

**Validate**

Perform tests to ensure that threats are mitigated.

# Third Party Cybersecurity Risk Assessment

**Representative Task (Application):** Determine the specific cybersecurity threats in an organization's connections with customers, vendors, and partner organizations.

An organization's **cybersecurity risk management program** must include analyzing threats in its connections with customers, vendors, and business partners. Often, vendors and business partners store, process, or transmit sensitive information on the organization's behalf.

As discussed in the SOC chapter, the AICPA defines an entity's cybersecurity risk management program as:

> *"The set of* ***policies, processes, and controls*** *designed to* ***protect information and systems from security events*** *that could compromise the achievement of the entity's cybersecurity objectives and to detect, respond to, mitigate, and recover from, on a timely basis, security events that are not prevented."*

Organizations should have an internal process for assessing cybersecurity risks associated with their relationships with external parties. Organizations that have a SOC for Cybersecurity examination must describe their system using the DC 100 *Description Criteria for Management's Description of an Entity's Cybersecurity Risk Management Program*. Management's description should discuss the organization's **risk assessment process**. The Description Criteria includes "DC12: *The process for identifying, assessing, and managing the risks associated with vendors and business partners*." An organization's governance process should include the same risk assessment regardless of whether a third party examination is performed.

**Outsourcing** business processes or technology to third parties poses greater risk and requires the organization to obtain an understanding of the **vendor's system and controls**. Risks also stem from a vendor's use of subservice organizations, which creates a long chain of cybersecurity vulnerabilities **(the "nth" party risk).**

Risk assessment processes that an organization may have in place include:

| Third party risk management | Vendor risk assessments | Threat modeling |
|---|---|---|

- **Third party risk management:** The organization's legal department should have input into contracts with third parties and customers. The department should draft public notices (eg, privacy notices) with input from management and the IT department. Management, IT, and legal should review contracts and service level agreements (SLAs) from vendors and partner organizations, such as subsidiaries. Contracts should address:
  - Scope and nature of services
  - Hardware, software, and other IT requirements
  - Responsibilities of each party
  - IT security and exception handling requirements
  - Ability to perform independent internal control audits
  - Requirement to obtain an attestation report from an independent CPA (ie, SOC2®, SOC for Cybersecurity, or other compliance examinations)
  - Confidentiality and privacy agreements
  - Vendor or business partner cybersecurity insurance requirements

- **Vendor risk assessments:** Internal and external assessments or audits to understand the effectiveness of policies and procedures regarding the selection and monitoring of vendors. Vendor oversight includes ensuring that contractual and SLAs are met. Annual reviews should be performed to:
  - Evaluate the services and any cybersecurity threats or vulnerabilities. Perform reviews that may include security questionnaires, interviews, walkthroughs, site visits, and IT scanning and testing.
  - Consider whether assessed risks are being addressed by contractual agreements.
  - Decide whether the oversight is consistent with laws, regulations, industry standards, and accepted practices.
- **Threat modeling:** Interactions with customers, vendors, and business partners should be included in structured processes for threat modeling. This helps to quantify and address cybersecurity risks within third party relationships.

### Third Party Cybersecurity Threat Modeling

A university is concerned about protecting its systems and data from cyberattacks. The university's IT security team performs an annual risk assessment, including consideration of risks associated with students, vendors, and business partners. Part of the annual review includes threat modeling:

1. **Identify high-value and critical assets that are externally dependent (ie, involve interaction with students, vendors, and business partners that an attacker may target).** Examples include websites, database servers, networks, and security software, such as firewalls.
2. **Decompose (ie, break down) applications and diagram all interactions with external parties.**
   - Create use cases or perform walkthroughs to understand external dependencies and interactions.
   - Understand availability requirements.
   - Identify data flows and table relationships.
   - Identify data that is confidential or private.
   - Identify entry and exit points an attacker may target.
   - Identify access rights (ie, trust levels) that are granted to external parties.
3. **Determine specific cybersecurity threats in the university's connections with students, vendors, and partner organizations.**

   Threats and controls are categorized using the Microsoft STRIDE model:

| Threat Type | Threat Description | Controls |
|---|---|---|
| **Spoofing** | Accessing and using another's credentials | Authentication |
| **Tampering** | Maliciously modifying data at rest and in transit | Integrity |
| **Repudiation** | Performing prohibited operations that are not traceable | Non-repudiation |
| **Information Disclosure** | Reading a file without authorization | Confidentiality |
| **Denial of Service** | Denying access to valid users by making the system inaccessible | Availability |
| **Elevation of Privilege** | Gaining unauthorized privileged access to compromise a system | Authorization |

4. **Rank and document threats by impact, likelihood, and ease of exploitation, considering operational significance and the sensitivity of data.**

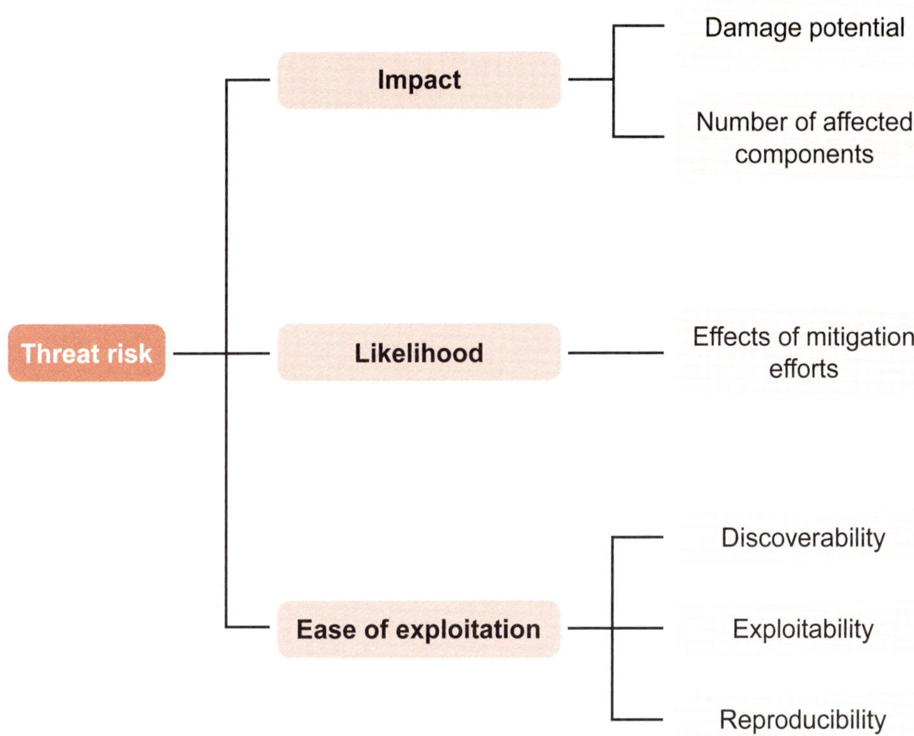


***Example:***

**Threat:** Attacker gaining access to confidential student information

**Threat type:** Spoofing

**Risk assessment (1–10):**

- Damage potential: Reputation, legal, and financial risks (10)
- Affected users: All users (10)
- Likelihood: Moderate (6)
- Discoverablllty: Easily found out (10)
- Exploitability: Requires a compromised router (7)
- Reproducibility: Fully reproducible (10)
- **Score (10 + 10 + 6 + 10 + 7 + 10)/6 = 8.83 (high risk)**

5. **Establish policies and procedures to mitigate risks.**
   - Authentication controls:
     - Credentials are encrypted both in transit and at rest
     - Enforced character types and lengths are used for passwords
     - Periodic password changes are required
     - Password resets do not reveal hints
     - Passwords are stored with hashes
   - Audit and logging controls
   - Exception management controls
   - Input validation controls
6. **Validate that controls work properly by performing penetration tests.**

## Internal Cybersecurity Risk Assessment

**Representative Task (Application):** Determine the specific cybersecurity threats to an organization's on-premises and cloud-based applications, networks, and connected devices (eg, mobile and Internet of Things (IoT) devices).

Like third party risk assessments, an internal risk assessment is a necessary part of an effective cybersecurity risk management program. Such an assessment includes finding threats to applications, networks, and connected devices.

Risk management is primarily aimed at internal governance, but an organization may also be required to disclose its assessment processes to customers and regulators, as well as to CPAs during attestation engagements. For example, in a SOC for Cybersecurity examination, the AICPA's DC 100 *Description Criteria for Management's Description of an Entity's Cybersecurity Risk Management Program* states that an organization must describe its processes for *"identifying cybersecurity risks and environmental, technological, organizational and other changes that could have a significant effect on the entity's cybersecurity risk management program"* and for *"assessing the related risks to the achievement of the entity's cybersecurity objectives."*

Therefore, it is important for CPAs to understand how an organization analyzes threats. The AICPA's DC 100 Description Criteria supply a framework of the steps organizations should incorporate into their cybersecurity risk assessment process. According to DC 11, internal risk assessment should include:

- Maintaining a detailed inventory of all IT system assets, including hardware, software, and networking equipment
- Assigning roles of accountability for assets as well as risk assessment
- Considering the types of threats, along with their likelihood and potential effects. Threats may include:
  - Errors (unintentional) and fraud (intentional)
  - Internal acts associated with different employee roles (eg, finance, operations, IT, sales)
  - External acts by customers, vendors, business partners, or other threat agents

- Considering vulnerabilities and control deficiencies
- Obtaining threat and vulnerability information from government (eg, National Vulnerability Database) and other cybersecurity information sources
- Identifying changes that would alter or add risks

**Internal Cybersecurity Risk Assessment**

The same university as in the previous example determines its cybersecurity risk by maintaining a detailed inventory of its IT assets. Assets are prioritized based on how critical they are to operations. Designated departments are accountable for the safeguarding of certain assets, including the classification, security, storage, and retention of data. Hardware and software are subject to policies for purchase, maintenance, security, and disposal.

The IT team annually performs a risk assessment to identify internal and external cyber threats and vulnerabilities. Risks are scored based on their likelihood and potential impact. Assessment includes determining risks associated with external parties. Specific policies are in place to assess and manage relationships with students, vendors, and business partners.

Management reviews the results of the risk assessment against internal parameters to decide if existing protections are still needed and if extra protections should be added. Internal audit conducts periodic cybersecurity risk assessments and reviews security policies. An external party performs quarterly vulnerability scans and penetration tests to find technical threats and vulnerabilities.

# 6.02 Mitigation

## Secure Remote Access

**Representative Task (Remembering and Understanding):** Identify ways to protect networks and devices used to access the network remotely (eg, isolation and segmentation, virtual private network (VPN), wireless network security, endpoint security, system hardening, intrusion prevention and detection systems).

Remote access allows users to connect to a service, application, machine, or data from anywhere in the world. Distributed network access requires added network and device security protections beyond conventional measures. **Secure remote access** encompasses a variety of policies, processes, devices, and applications implemented to **prevent unauthorized network access**.

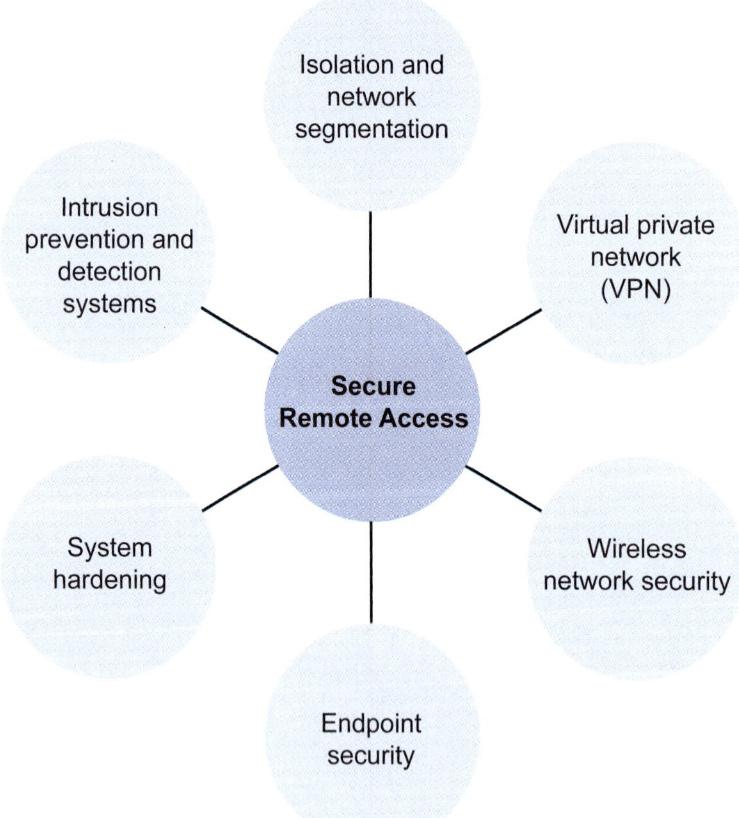

**Isolation and network segmentation:** Segmentation controls how traffic flows among the parts of the network, either by stopping data transmissions altogether or by limiting data transmissions by type, source, destination, or other attributes. For example, if a company has remote sales offices, it can limit data communication and access to core systems from those locations by using firewalls. **Firewalls** control and allow users and data at network access points. A firewall can be a physical device (hardware) or a computer program (application) that blocks the transmission media being used.

**Virtual private network (VPN):** A VPN allows users to establish a direct link with a trusted network zone from a remote location in an untrusted zone (eg, public Internet). A **secure communication channel** is established using cryptographic keys that identify a user's machine as a trusted device and **encrypt traffic** to thwart data snooping and interception efforts.

**Wireless network security:** Wi-Fi security keeps devices and networks safe when they are connected wirelessly. Without Wi-Fi security, anyone with a computer or mobile device within range of the router's wireless signal can access a network and steal personal data. Changing the default passwords, as well as setting up security protocols that use encryption, are common protective mechanisms against security risks.

**Endpoint security:** Any device that connects to the corporate network from outside the firewall is considered an endpoint. Laptops, cell phones, tablets, etc., are all considered endpoint devices. Security is critical because any remote endpoint can be a point of entry for an attack. Endpoint protection solutions offer a centralized management console to monitor, protect, investigate, and respond to security events or incidents.

**System hardening:** Hardening refers to a set of tools, techniques, and practices for reducing vulnerability in technology applications, systems, and infrastructure. System hardening reduces security risk by eliminating attack vectors and reducing the attack surface. When unnecessary programs, account functions, applications, ports, permissions, and access points are deleted, attackers and malware are less likely to infiltrate your IT ecosystem.

**Intrusion prevention and detection systems:** Boundary protection systems protect **external network access points**, which are any connections by which data flows into or out of a company's internal network (eg, intranet). The process of delineating an information system's boundary includes considering where data is stored, the source and destination of data flows, and critical system dependencies (eg, an application that supplies the data interface, network components that transmit the data).

| Intrusion Detection System (IDS) | Intrusion Prevention System (IPS) |
|---|---|
| Installed on user's device | Installed on a network between the external Internet and internal intranet |
| Identifies suspicious data requests and network activity:<br>• Notifies the user<br>• Alerts administrators | Identifies suspicious data requests and network activity:<br>• Notifies network administrators<br>• Prevents data transmission |
| Does not prevent suspicious activity | Prevents suspicious activity through behavioral signatures (eg, common malicious patterns) and artificial intelligence (AI) modeling |
| False positives are low-impact:<br>• Network activity is not interrupted<br>• Functional service impact is limited to a single device | False positives are high-impact:<br>• Network activity is interrupted<br>• Service impact may affect large parts of the organization |

- **Intrusion detection systems (IDS):** Installed on a user's device, an IDS identifies suspicious data requests and network activity and notifies the user. The system provides a frontline service that detects anomalies and alerts administrators through a security information and event management (SIEM) system. However, an IDS does not block an attack. There are different types of IDS, each focusing on a specific IT area:
  - **Network-based:** IDS that examine all traffic on the network through two methods:
    - ***Wireless:*** Monitors and analyzes wireless network traffic and protocols. Commonly used within an organization's wireless network or in locations where unauthorized access may occur
    - ***Network behavior analysis (NBA):*** Identifies threats that generate unusual traffic (eg, distributed denial of service [DDoS], botnets, malware) and policy violations (eg, a device providing unauthorized network services to other systems)

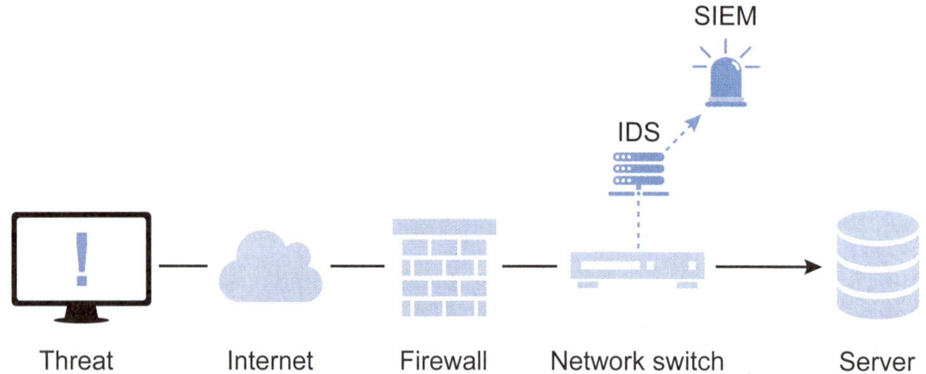


  - **Host-based:** IDS that inspect outgoing data from a host device and check for missing or misplaced system files
  - **Protocol-based:** IDS that primarily protect web servers by examining data going to and from a user front end (eg, website, cloud-based app)
  - **Application protocol-based:** IDS that protect internal application servers by inspecting traffic sent by the application and traffic between application servers

- **Intrusion prevention systems (IPS):** Installed on a company's network between the external Internet and the intranet, an IPS is used to detect suspicious activity, alert network administrators, and prevent the data transmission

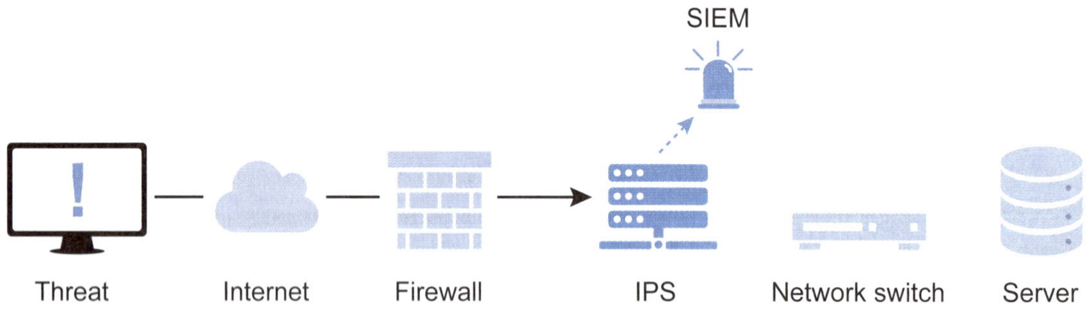

# Vulnerability Management

**Representative Task (Remembering and Understanding):** Recall the definition and purpose of vulnerability management.

Vulnerabilities are points of weakness in a system that an attacker can exploit to gain unauthorized access and disrupt processes or operations. **Vulnerability management** is a **continuous** process of detecting, assessing, reporting, managing, and remediating cyber vulnerabilities across endpoints, applications, and systems.

When combined with other security measures, vulnerability management **prioritizes** potential threats while **minimizing** their **attack surface**. A security team may use a vulnerability management solution to **automate** the process.

**Vulnerability Management Cycle**



The vulnerability management cycle has **five sequential stages**:

- **Assess:** The first step in the vulnerability management cycle is to **identify at-risk assets**. To do this, legacy systems may use vulnerability management tools to scan the network. Because an asset cannot be detected under that approach unless it is connected to the network, sensors (ie, agents) may be placed on the individual assets. The scan produces a report showing which assets need patches or remediation. A modern approach is to use a cloud-based solution that allows for continuous scanning of all endpoints and provides dashboards with real-time information. Cloud-based solutions may also be easier to integrate with multiple systems

- **Prioritize:** Once vulnerable assets are identified, **assign a value to prioritize investigation** and assess risk. Such values should reflect risk levels researched using threat intelligence information gathered from both internal and external sources. Cloud-based solutions integrate up-to-date threat information gathered from government and external security organizations
- **Act:** After prioritizing risks, **decide what action to take**. Three options may be to:
    - **Accept the risk** if the assets are noncritical or the threat is low
    - **Mitigate** using strategies or techniques that reduce the possibility of exploitation by attackers. This action does not remove the vulnerability but may reduce risk
    - **Remediate** the vulnerability by patching or upgrading the asset. This is the preferred option when the asset is critical and exposed to high risk
- **Reassess:** Rescan the system to determine whether the mitigation/remediation action fixed the vulnerable asset. Reassessment may identify other issues as well
- **Improve:** Identify underlying causes and strengthen the system. Continuously evaluate metrics to look for areas of weakness

## Layered Security and Defense-in-Depth

**Representative Task (Remembering and Understanding):** Explain the concepts of layered security and defense-in-depth.

### Layered Security

Layered security assumes that the **individual components** of a system can **never be completely secure**. It aims to create overlapping layers of protection so that attackers must defeat **multiple security measures** at once. If one protection fails, deeper layers will still stop or slow down an attack. The goal is to stop a single security flaw from making the entire system vulnerable.

Effective layering involves a variety of security measures, each of which defends against a separate attack vector. Layered security *does not* mean implementing the same defense multiple times.

Layered security supports secure networks, routers, computers, and servers. Typically, sensitive data is segregated in its own section of a network so that hacked systems cannot access it. This risk-based approach focuses on both the sources of threats (eg, persons, Internet, software) and categories of attack (eg, ransomware, denial of service).

When creating a security policy, management considers the target asset and the operating environment to identify the affected levels of security. For example, when securing a server in a company building, consider physical access, network connections, server operating systems, and the value of any applications, databases, or other data on the server.

### Defense-in-Depth

Defense-in-depth works under the premise that **systems** can **never be completely secure**. Defense-in-depth relies on strategic plans to:

- **Broaden controls:** The major benefit of a defense-in-depth strategy is its built-in, multifaceted approach, which includes three types of controls:
    - **Physical controls:** Security measures that protect IT systems from physical harm

- ○ **Technical controls:** Hardware and applications that protect a system (eg, layered security)
- ○ **Administrative controls:** Policy and procedures put in place by an organization to control access to the system and train employees

- **Assume active intrusions:** Deception is an often-used technique in defense-in-depth; misleading clues guide the attacker to a dedicated server where no sensitive data is stored. This will frustrate the attacker and slow down the attack's progression

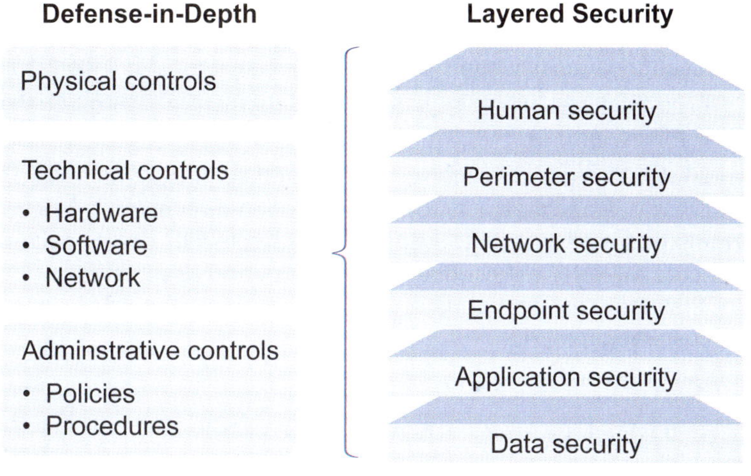


## Access Controls

**Representative Task (Remembering and Understanding):** Define the concepts of least privilege, zero trust, whitelisting, and the need-to-know principle.

**Access controls** are procedures and controls that **limit or detect access** to critical information resources. Access controls can apply to both **physical controls** (over actual pedestrian foot traffic in buildings) and **logical controls** (over access to virtual data).

There are four key questions when considering access controls:

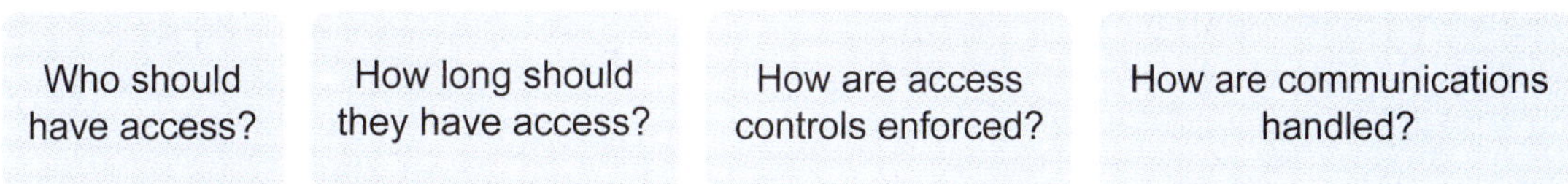


- **Principle of least privilege:** Only the **minimum level of access** necessary to perform an operation should be granted, and **for the minimum time** necessary. The purpose of the principle of least privilege is to safeguard the organization's assets from both internal and external threats by **reducing the attack surface area**. Other benefits include increased system stability, providing audit readiness, and achieving regulatory compliance

- **Zero trust:** This model is a widely used network architecture framework for intrusion detection systems that treats **all network data** communication as **suspicious or untrusted**. It requires **all users**, whether **internal or external**, to be **verified, approved, and continually validated** for security configuration and posture prior to gaining or maintaining access to applications and data. The network IDS tracks endpoint behavior, monitors data flows in real time, checks for anomalies, and alerts administrators if an issue is detected
- **Whitelisting:** This practice involves using **pre-approved lists** of rules, policies, or other verification processes to determine whether a user may access data, an application may be installed, or an IP address may transmit or receive network data. Users can access only the restricted set of features the system administrator considers safe. Whitelisting is a strict lockdown technique, although it can prevent many cybersecurity attacks when used correctly. However, it is inconvenient and frustrating for end users. It also requires careful implementation and ongoing administration, even though it is not a foolproof barrier to attacks
- **Need-to-know principle:** This principle states that, regardless of security clearance level or other approvals, a user should have access only to the information that their job function requires. A user requires both **permissions *and* a need to know**. For example, HR personnel do not need access to finance department data to perform their jobs. Data access and associated controls must be regularly reviewed to ensure that users are appropriately allowed (or denied) access based on their current role, position, or data access requirements

## Acceptable Use Policies

**Representative Task (Remembering and Understanding):** Recall the purpose and content of a technology acceptable use policy, including considerations specific to mobile technologies and bring-your-own-device (BYOD).

A technology **acceptable use policy** is a documented policy that establishes guidelines and permissions for the use of an organization's assets (eg, hardware, software, networks, Internet). The purpose of acceptable use policies is to **safeguard** the confidentiality, availability, and integrity of **data**. For example, **acceptable use agreement (AUA)** policies warn employees against intentionally or unintentionally storing data insecurely on a mobile device or transmitting data over an insecure network.

Prior to using a device, employees must sign an **AUA** and acknowledge the terms of the policy. The AUA helps to ensure that both the user and IT keep devices safe.

An AUA may contain policies related to:

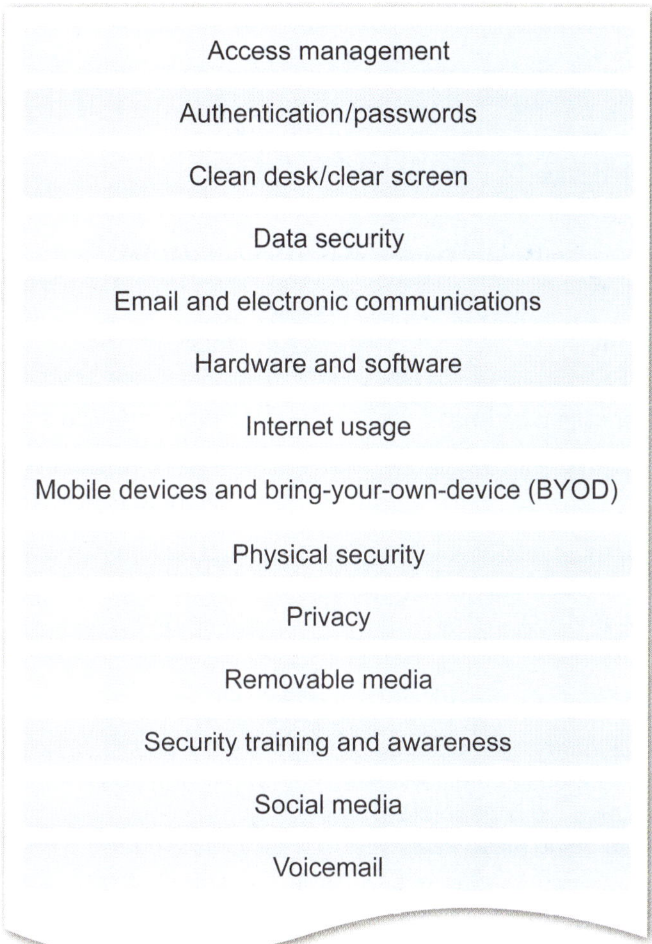


## Mobile Computing

In computing, "mobile" refers to portable or transportable equipment. Tablets, cell phones, laptops, USB drives, and digital cameras are examples of common mobile devices. Mobility makes implementing logical (virtual) and physical access controls more difficult.

The vulnerabilities, threats, and risks associated with mobile computing include:

- **Poor wireless network security:** Information traveling across mobile networks is often less secure. This vulnerability may allow a malicious outside threat, resulting in a loss of sensitive information
- **Lack of perimeter control:** Mobility allows the use of devices outside the enterprise boundaries, thus removing security controls. Malware crossing boundaries and network perimeters may get into the enterprise network. Risks include data leakage, corruption, or unavailability
- **Unencrypted information stored on a device:** Unencrypted data can be read and used by a malicious outsider who intercepts data in transit, steals a device, or finds a lost device
- **Loss of employee productivity:** Portable mobile devices can be lost or stolen. Data stored on these devices is not always backed up, causing a loss of confidential or private information
- **Device location discovery:** Bluetooth can enable hackers to identify the location of the device and launch an attack. Risks include device corruption and the potential loss or exposure of sensitive data

- **Poor mobile device management (MDM) strategy:** Without a proper device management strategy, employees might bring their own devices, which lack the necessary security controls. Risks include data exposure and data loss if the device is lost or stolen
- **Unsecure third party applications:** Devices that allow third party applications can carry malware (ie, propagation of Trojans or viruses). This can be a gateway for intrusion into the enterprise network

**Controls** reduce the risk that sensitive data stored on mobile devices will be exposed. **MDM** systems and/or **secure containers** enforce controls. Secure containers are areas of a mobile device that are separately authenticated and encrypted. The intent is to store critical business data in a manner that differs from personal data storage on the device.

**Mobile Device Management (MDM)**

**Device management**

- All business-approved mobile devices should be registered in a database.
- Devices owned by the user should be marked.
- Organizations can push updates to only authorized devices, excluding personally owned mobile devices.

**Data storage**

- Only store necessary content on the mobile device.
- With remote server access, local data storage is usually not needed.
- Data should be regularly backed up to shared folders on the organization's file server.

**Physical security**

- If the device is stationary, use a cable locking system or a motion detector with an alarm so a sound is generated when the device is being taken away.

**Tagging**

- If a device is misplaced, a physical asset ID tag could help in its return.
- Company name should not appear on tag.

## Bring-Your-Own-Device (BYOD)

Employees may be allowed to use their personal electronic devices for work purposes if the employee and management agree in writing ahead of time. There are both advantages and risks to BYOD policies.

Advantages include:

- Increased productivity, convenience, and employee satisfaction
- Cost savings because the organization does not have to buy and maintain the devices and related applications

Disadvantages include:

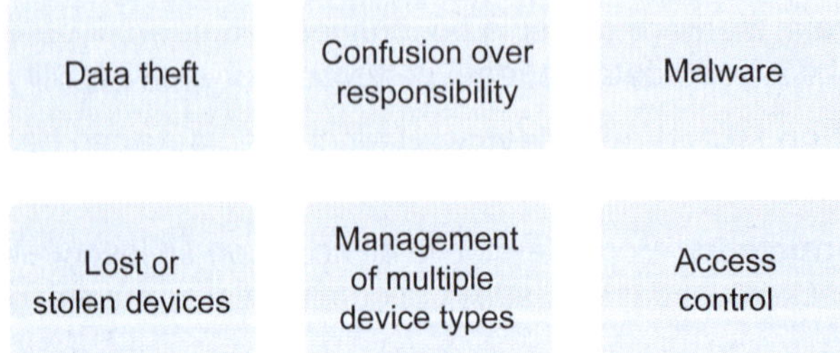

AUA language related to **company-owned mobile devices** or **BYOD** may include the following provisions:

- IT may refuse to allow the connection of mobile devices to the network infrastructure, both physically and virtually
- All mobile devices must be registered with IT
- Devices must have updated software, antivirus software, and a firewall
- All mobile devices must be protected by a strong password. Employees must agree to never disclose their passwords to anyone
- Employees may not make modifications to the organization-owned hardware or installed software without the approval of IT
- Employees must follow data removal procedures to erase entity-specific data from devices that are no longer needed
- If a mobile device is lost or stolen, it is the user's responsibility to tell IT right away. IT will remotely erase all the data
- The organization may seize a device for legal reasons
- IT can and will establish audit trails, which may be accessed or used without notification

## COSO ERM Framework and Cyber Risk

**Representative Task (Remembering and Understanding):** Explain how the COSO frameworks can be used to assess cyber risks and controls.

The **COSO Enterprise Risk Management (ERM) Framework** provides guidance to help organizations **strategically manage risks** that threaten the achievement of the entity's objectives. Benefits of the ERM Framework include:

- Promoting identification and management of organization-wide risks
- Increasing identification of opportunities by comparing the pros and cons of possibilities
- Reducing the cost of negative events and maximizing positive outcomes
- Managing performance risks to reduce disruption and increase opportunity
- Prioritizing and maximizing allocation of resources
- Enhancing resilience (ie, the ability to expect and respond to change)

New technologies, such as artificial intelligence, blockchain, cloud computing, and machine learning, introduce additional risks. Increased digital reach, especially when organizations share data with external parties such as outsourced service providers, adds the risks of complexity, unpredictability, and dependence on a noncontrollable infrastructure.

Cyber attackers are constantly developing and discovering new ways to exploit vulnerabilities. While major enterprises may be attractive targets for disruption and pursuing illicit gains, small businesses and local governments are easier to exploit. No organization is safe from the threat of cyber attacks. Because the risk cannot be avoided, it must be managed.

Developing a **cyber risk management program** requires identifying the organization's most critical data, developing security strategies, and employing risk mitigation techniques to protect the **confidentiality, integrity, and availability** of information. The COSO ERM Framework contains five components and 20 principles to help organizations think strategically about cyber risks:

| Governance and Culture | Strategy and Objective Setting | Performance | Review and Revision | Information, Communication, and Reporting |
|---|---|---|---|---|
| **Mission, Vision, and Core Values** | **Strategy Development** | **Business Objective Formulation** | **Implementation and Performance** | **Enhanced Value** |
| 1. Exercises board risk oversight<br>2. Establishes operating structures<br>3. Defines desired culture<br>4. Demonstrates commitment to core values<br>5. Attracts, develops, and retains capable individuals | 6. Analyzes business context<br>7. Defines risk appetite<br>8. Evaluates alternative strategies<br>9. Formulates business objectives | 10. Identifies risks<br>11. Assesses severity of risks<br>12. Prioritizes risks<br>13. Implements risk responses<br>14. Develops portfolio view | 15. Assesses substantial change<br>16. Reviews risk and performance<br>17. Pursues improvement in ERM | 18. Leverages information systems<br>19. Communicates risk information<br>20. Reports on risk, culture, and performance |

**Governance and culture:** Governance and culture serve as the **foundation** for all other ERM components. Governance sets up the entity's **tone**, emphasizes the importance of cyber vigilance, institutes operating structures, and shows a **commitment to core values** (ie, attracts, develops, and retains cybersecurity-certified employees or advisors).

Board governance includes **oversight** of the organization's cyber strategy, execution, and monitoring. It also includes benchmarking activity against other industry members and the management of required disclosure of breaches. Assessment and oversight of third party vendors may be accomplished through independent SOC or other compliance reports.

Management should reinforce a strong cyber culture through security awareness and training programs. A formal cyber risk management program would document policies, standards, communications, expectations, and accountability.

A good example of the information to be included in an organization's cyber risk management program is the AICPA's DC 100, *Description Criteria for Management's Description of the Entity's Cybersecurity Risk Management Program*, found in the SOC chapter.

**Strategy and objective setting:** When strategy and business objectives are established, cyber risk management is integrated into the entity's strategic plan. The organization analyzes the **business context** (eg, trends, relationships), defines **risk appetite** (ie, cost versus benefit), evaluates alternative strategies, and plans **business objectives**. Business objectives enable the strategy to be implemented and shape the entity's day-to-day operations and compliance priorities.

Strategy and objective setting include taking an inventory of critical assets, identifying risks, and determining where vulnerabilities exist, considering the organization's risk appetite. Needs should be communicated to stakeholders who make decisions about technology investments. The board should weigh the financial and reputational damage of breaches against the cost and complexity of cyber defense technology.

Recognized cybersecurity frameworks, such as those from the NIST and the AICPA, aid in setting up proper strategies and objectives. The chosen framework should coincide with business operations, control structures, contract terms, industry standards (eg, PCI DSS), and regulatory obligations (eg, HIPAA, GDPR).

**Performance:** Cyber risk assessment begins with taking an inventory of critical assets. This determination of critical assets should include consideration of the organization's objectives, such as regulatory compliance. Certain industries, like health care and financial services, may face stiffer consequences from an attack.

An organization that seeks to protect everything may not put enough resources into key areas. It is important to focus efforts on the most critical systems and the most severe threats. Identified risks should be assessed for **severity** and prioritized based on risk appetite. **Continuous assessment and prioritization** through monitoring help the organization anticipate attacks that are likely to occur in its industry and how to mitigate the risk of those attacks. The greater the possibility of a severe attack, the higher the organization should prioritize the risk.

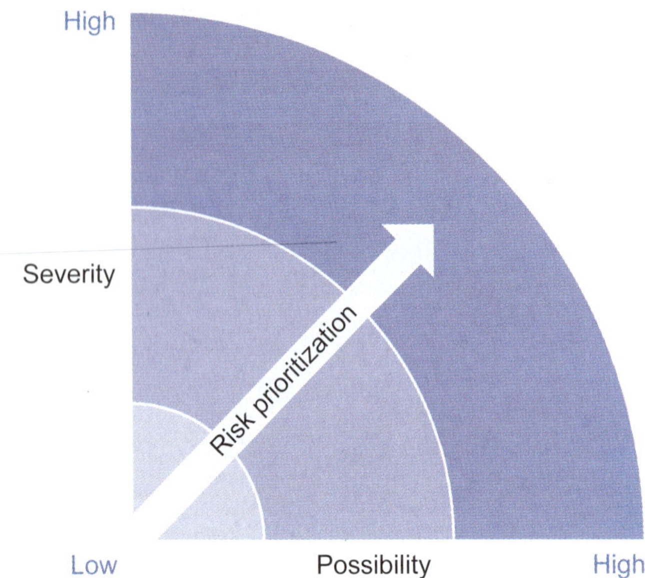


Risk responses may include accepting the risk, transferring it to third parties, or designing controls to mitigate the risks. Such responses create a **portfolio view** of the level of risk the entity has taken on to pursue its strategy and entity-level business objectives.

**Review and revision:** As changes occur in an organization's internal and external environments, cyber risk assessment processes are iterative. Each change must be evaluated to determine its impact on the enterprise and how to best manage the cyber risk. Such evaluation should be ongoing and assessed against performance targets.

For external review of its cyber risk management program, the organization may seek a **risk advisory consulting** engagement with a CPA or a **SOC for Cybersecurity examination**. In a risk advisory engagement, CPAs review the program and make suggestions for improvement. A SOC for Cybersecurity assurance examination provides an independent CPA's opinion in the form of a report the organization may share with customers, investors, and business partners.

**Information, communication, and reporting:** The organization leverages information systems to support ERM decisions related to its strategic and operational objectives. **Complete, accurate, and relevant information** is important to sound decision making, especially during an attack. **Reliability of data** and **reporting speed** affect response to the attack and any resulting damage.

**Governance, risk, and compliance (GRC) software** applications may include rule sets for particular cybersecurity frameworks. These applications help the organization establish appropriate policies and provide a method for internal audit. Intrusion detection tools such as **security information and event management (SIEM) systems** provide alerting and reporting. Monitoring may also be performed through third party **managed service providers**.

Organizations need to think about the criteria for **disclosing cyber event information** to consumers, other businesses, law enforcement, and regulatory bodies. Failure to make proper disclosures could result in severe fines and sanctions or a loss of reputation and income. Communication should be incorporated into incident response plans and managed by experts, such as public relations firms.

# Preventive, Detective, and Corrective Controls

**Representative Task (Application):** Determine the common preventive, detective, or corrective controls (eg, intrusion prevention systems, device and software hardening, log analysis, intrusion detection systems, virus quarantining, patches) to mitigate the risk of cyber attacks for an organization.

To mitigate the risk of cyber attacks, organizations deploy **controls** for their physical and virtual assets. **Physical assets** encompass network components and hardware, while **virtual assets** include data and cloud services. **Processes** covered in other chapters, such as incident response, change management, and patches, are also control techniques.

There are three general classifications of controls:

| Preventive | Detective | Corrective |
|---|---|---|
| Stop errors or fraud before they occur | Find errors or fraud after they have occurred | Remedy detected errors or fraud after they occur |

## Preventive Controls

Preventive controls prevent an action or process from occurring. Such controls could involve preventing access to data or systems, preventing data from being updated or changed, or preventing data transmission.

**Preventive Controls**

- Authentication
- Authorization
- Antivirus software
- Anti-malware tools
- Firewalls
- Awareness training
- Intrusion prevention systems
- Device and software hardening

- **Authentication:** The goal of authentication controls is to ensure that persons using credentials are who they claim to be. Multifactor authentication controls, such as added credentials, temporary PINs, security questions, and biometrics, could be used for authentication
- **Authorization:** While authentication checks the identity of a user (eg, Roger) before allowing access, authorization controls what the user can do after entering (eg, view sales information). Both authentication and authorization controls are necessary because an attacker can steal a user ID and password to access the system. **Access control lists (ACLs)** identify which users or services have access to a specific digital environment. Access control is achieved by enforcing **allow or deny rules** based on each user's authorization level. For example, an ACL may deny access to standard users who try to change their security settings. However, administrators are authorized to modify security settings; thus, the ACL will allow them to do so

- **Antivirus and anti-malware:** Viruses are malicious code designed to replicate and spread from one system to another, corrupting the way computers work. Viruses are classified as "infectious" malware (**mal**icious + soft**ware**). **Antivirus software** scans files and quarantines or removes malicious files based on configuration, but it may be limited to detecting and removing only infectious malware. **Anti-malware tools** detect, remove, or quarantine a wider range of malware (eg, viruses, worms, Trojan horses, backdoors, spyware, rootkits). Anti-malware applications can be **host based** (runs on a specific host), **network based** (runs on a firewall or IPS), or **cloud based**
- **Firewalls:** Firewall technology mitigates unauthorized external access and other external threats. Typically, firewalls can be configured in several ways to filter traffic and define connectivity rules. For example, an organization may create a demilitarized zone (DMZ) where users of its public-facing website or other resources on the Internet cannot access internal private networks. Another issue with firewalls is that malicious activity is often conducted by insiders (eg, employees, contractors). Networks perceive anyone inside the entity as a trusted source because they have valid login credentials. To provide greater control over who has access to vital systems, a second firewall should be installed between the network and back-end systems
- **Cybersecurity awareness training:** Security awareness training programs increase employees' and contractors' security knowledge and awareness, and provide a model for their behavior
- **Intrusion prevention systems:** An intrusion prevention system (IPS) is a device that examines traffic to detect potential threats. If an intrusion is detected, the IPS stops the traffic from reaching its destination and sends an alert through the organization's security information and event management (SIEM) system
- **Device and software hardening:** Hardening, in a security context, refers to adding controls and protections to reduce or eliminate vulnerabilities. For devices, this means adding physical protections such as biometric scanners (eg, fingerprint scanners, face recognition); operating system protections, including remote wipe and administration capabilities; and robust access controls (ie, two-factor authentication). For software, hardening primarily relies on data compartmentalization and encryption, as well as code analysis and review. Both device and software hardening rely on monitoring processes to ensure the continued effectiveness of security protections

## Detective Controls

Detective controls are used to log and identify suspected malicious activity **after it has occurred**. If potential malicious behavior is detected, these controls may start other processes, such as quarantine. Detective controls include:

| Detective Controls |
|---|
| • Intrusion detection systems<br>• Log analysis |

- **Intrusion detection systems (IDS):** An IDS is a hardware or software application that monitors a network for malicious activity or policy violations. When deployed at strategic points on a network, an IDS analyzes passing traffic and matches it to a library of known attacks. If the IDS detects an attack or abnormal activity, the administrator receives a notification. IDS monitoring may result in false alarms, so there should be a balance for security versus alarm fatigue
- **Log analysis:** Log analysis detects errors or exceptions in computer-generated log files. Logs establish an **audit trail** and chain of custody, as well as support monitoring and debugging activities. Besides monitoring and troubleshooting, logs also help predict issues and provide business intelligence, particularly for Internet interactions (eg, website engagement, conversion rates, site referrals)

  Log files can be generated from a wide variety of resources, including network assets (eg, routers, firewalls), user devices (eg, workstations, printers), entry points (ie, badge scanners), software, and monitoring systems. The files may be semistructured data that must be standardized (ie, normalized) before it can be analyzed. Applications such as a SIEM can automate the collection and normalization of logs that are generated by multiple systems or assets

### Log File Types

#### Event Logs

Network traffic and usage such as login attempts, failed password attempts, application events

#### Server Logs

Activities for a specific server

#### System Logs

Operating system events, including startup, system changes, shutdown, errors, and warnings

#### Access Logs

List of users or bots accessing files or applications

#### Change Logs

Chronological list of changes made to application or files

#### Availability Logs

System performance, uptime, downtime

#### Resource Logs

Connectivity and capacity limits

#### Threat Logs

List of activities that match predefined security rules

## Corrective Controls

Corrective controls are used to restore or reinstate data and processes after an error, intrusion, or other disruption. Such controls include monitoring and recovery procedures to restore data and ensure that business processes can continue.

**Corrective Controls**

- Virus quarantining
- Patch management
- Vulnerability management
- Incident response plans

- **Virus quarantining:** Antivirus and anti-malware applications use **quarantine** to **isolate** infected data on a computer. The software can find files that contain viruses and worms, as well as infected system files. These programs ask the user whether they want to quarantine, clean, or remove infected files. If the quarantine option is selected, the infected file is placed under the control of the antivirus/anti-malware program, preventing it from causing further damage to the user's system. If the file is a system file infected with malware, removing it altogether may cause problems; in such cases, cleaning the file is a better option
- **Patch and vulnerability management:** As discussed in other chapters
- **Incident response plans:** As discussed in other chapters

### Cybersecurity and CPA Firms

Besides providing cybersecurity consulting and assurance services to their clients, CPA firms must also consider the threats to their own practice. A hacker may view a CPA firm as a high-value target because it provides a single point of access to sensitive information for all the firm's clients.

Because CPAs are legally responsible for maintaining the confidentiality of client information, they must design and implement controls that prevent, detect, and correct cyber incidents. Just as with any other organization, common controls to mitigate a CPA firm's risks include:

- **Authentication:** Strong passwords and multifactor authentication controls, as well as immediate removal of terminated employees. Multifactor authentication controls send a notification to a mobile device to confirm the requested login. Staff are automatically logged out and their screens are locked after a period of inactivity. Only registered and validated users/devices may connect to the firm's network within designated hours
- **Authorization:** Staff are granted access only to the clients they work with, and only for the time necessary for the engagement. Staff do not have access to administrative tools or the ability to change a client's permanent files and related workpapers. Administrative privileges are minimized
- **Antivirus and anti-malware:** All firm servers, workstations, laptops, and mobile devices have antivirus and anti-malware software installed. Automated scans are performed weekly, and records are reviewed by IT personnel. Flash drives are not allowed; clients' files must be transferred through secure email or private portals. Files are scanned prior to download
- **Firewalls and intrusion prevention systems:** Two firewalls are used to filter traffic. A perimeter firewall monitors traffic to and from the firm's network. An internal firewall exists between the network and back-end systems. An intrusion prevention system is used to identify and block malicious traffic
- **Hardening:** Video cameras are monitored 24/7 by an outsourced security alarm company. Client and staff areas are separated by locked doors that require an access code. Onsite servers and network equipment are in an unmarked, locked room. Only IT personnel have access to rooms with hardware. Cloud storage is used where appropriate. Workstations and laptops are encrypted. Staff must sign an acceptable use agreement for all firm devices and BYOD devices. The firm maintains accurate records of hardware inventory and has procedures for proper disposal. Operating systems for all equipment are kept up to date with the latest patches. Data is backed up daily
- **Staff screening and training:** All firm employees must submit to a background check prior to employment. During employment, all firm employees must attend security awareness and incident response training annually. IT personnel send routine emails containing security information, such as how to avoid phishing attempts. Employees also receive training on confidentiality requirements for CPAs and compliance regulations applicable to their duties
- **Reporting:** IT personnel maintain and review log files. The firm uses a SIEM to monitor systems and networks. The SIEM application provides a dashboard to monitor key metrics and activity
- **Testing:** Annually, the firm hires an independent consultant to perform penetration testing. The consultant also performs quarterly vulnerability scans
- **Incident response and disaster recovery plans:** The firm has formal incident response and disaster recovery plans, which are reviewed and tested at least annually

# Identification and Authentication

**Representative Task (Application):** Determine the appropriate identification and authentication techniques and technologies (eg, password management, single sign-on (SSO), multifactor authentication, personal identification number (PIN) management, digital signatures, smart cards, biometrics) in a specific scenario.

Identification is the ability to identify a user of a system or an application running within the system. Authentication is the ability to confirm that users are who they say they are, and applications are what they claim to be.

## Identity Access Management

**Identity access management (IAM)** involves verifying information to authenticate the identity of an individual user. IAM specifies how a user is identified (eg, username, email, employee number); how roles are managed and assigned to different users or groups; what level of access is granted; and which assets are restricted based on a user's role, group, and level. There are three primary types of IAM:

| Single Sign-On (SSO) | Multifactor Authentication (2FA) | Privileged Access Management (PAM) |
|---|---|---|
| • Allows one set of user login credentials to access multiple applications such as username, email, employee numbers<br>• Easier on user to remember one set of login information<br>• Risk of violating principle of least privilege when a user gains access to systems that are not needed | • Two-factor authentication requires two different identification methods to gain access<br>• Examples include answering security questions, receiving a PIN number on a mobile device or through email, or biometric scans (fingerprint, retinal scans)<br>• Secure, but expensive to maintain due to technical requirements | • Restricts and monitors access to critical systems, using highly granular permissions to satisfy compliance standards<br>• Creates a detailed audit trail and alerts administrators of unusual activity<br>• Most expensive and complex identification method because of the amount of IT resources and management required to operate/maintain |

## User Authentication

End users often misunderstand authentication, authorization, and logical access control concepts. Such concepts may be perceived as one composite function, but it is crucial to recognize their differences when establishing a security framework.

**Authentication** verifies user identities. This verification technique usually involves a login and password, but it may also use PIN numbers, fingerprint scans, smart cards, and other methods. To begin the authentication process, the user must have an account in the system so that the authentication mechanism can query that account. Alternatively, a new account may be created during the procedure.

Authentication may rely on:

- **User IDs** and **passwords** authenticate users (ie, they are who they say they are) and prevent others from accessing the system. Password policies may include:
  - Password length is more important than password complexity
    - Enforcing complex passwords that have uppercase and lowercase letters, numbers, and special characters works in theory, but falls short in practice
    - Use pass phrases and allow for password lengths of at least 64 characters
  - Do not enforce regular password resets
    - Enforcing a reset usually results in a minimal modification to the original password
    - Frequent resets may result in the use of predictable password patterns
  - Screen all new passwords against lists of commonly used and compromised passwords
  - Implement two-factor authentication
  - Limit the number of failed password attempts before account lockout (eg, three failed logins should lock out a user)
- **Personal identification number (PIN):** The most common example is a four- or five-digit number that is used with a bank debit card. PINs are widely used in identity authentication in endpoint devices, including cell phones and tablets, as well as IoT devices (ie, smart thermostats)
- **Biometric identification:** Biometric identity authentication identifies users based on a unique biological feature of a human. Common examples include fingerprint and hand/palm scans, iris or eye scanners, or voice and facial recognition. Biometric authentication is the strongest authentication control
- **Smart cards:** The most widely recognized smart card is the little chip in a credit or debit card that holds identity and authorization information. Cell phone SIM cards, public transit cards, and corporate ID badges use this technology as a method of SSO authentication
- **Digital signatures:** Digital signatures are created using data encryption to record a unique identifier and other information, such as date, location, or an associated organization or affiliation. Digital signatures provide a method to confirm the authenticity and integrity of data (eg, DocuSign)

## Password Management Systems

Password management systems help organizations manage credentials for multiple IT systems and enforce password best practices by reducing the end user's reliance on memorization. Enterprise password management systems have the following features:

| Encrypted 2FA vault | Endpoint password management | Access controls for BYOD |
|---|---|---|
| Password best practice enforcement | Reporting tools | Remote management |

### Data Center Identification and Authentication Techniques

A data center relies on several layers of security to prevent unauthorized access to its facilities, equipment, and data. Identification and authentication security measures begin long before an individual is granted physical access to the data center.

For example, a technician who repairs servers may go through the following layers of security:

- Like all employees and contractors, the technician must provide proof of attending security awareness training and have a background check prior to being granted access credentials
- A badge with a smart chip is made once the technician passes the training and background check
- The technician's retina is scanned and stored in a secure database
- Upon arriving at the data center facility, the technician must stop at a security gate to show their badge. The guard checks the badge and other identification against a pre-approved list of individuals allowed to enter the fenced-in area
- Upon arrival, the technician enters a waiting area. To go through the doors into the operations center, the technician must pass a retinal scan and touch their badge against a wall-mounted reader. Only one person at a time may walk through a doorway
- Once in the operations center, the retinal scan and badge reading is required to go through every door
- To log in to the system, the technician must enter a username and password. Passwords must be of a certain length, contain certain types of characters, and be changed frequently. Multifactor authentication sends a code to the technician's mobile device to confirm that the activity is valid and approved
- During the entire visit, the data center's security system tracks the technician's whereabouts, using video surveillance and creating an auditable record

# Authorization Models and Controls

**Representative Task (Application):** Determine the appropriate authorization model (eg, discretionary, role-based, mandatory) and the controls (eg, access control list, account restrictions, physical barriers) used to implement the model in a specific scenario.

**Authorization** relates to the system resources a user or object may access **after authentication** and entry. Access control policies are a set of rules that define the conditions necessary to **grant permissions** to system resources, such as files. **IAM** policies can be application-specific or may pertain to a set of user actions within the context of an organizational unit or across organizational boundaries.

Administrators must determine the appropriate type of **authorization model** for setting up user credentials and assigning authority to manage them. Different applications or processes within an organization may use different models. For example, an employee **(subject/owner)** who creates a spreadsheet **(object)** may have discretion to choose who to share it with. However, authorization within the organization's accounting information system (AIS) may be under the control of only the system administrator. In that situation, individuals within the accounting department could not choose or change access rights to perform functions, such as recording journal entries. The decision often depends on the sensitivity or criticality of the data or process.

**IT Objects**

- Devices
- Files
- Records
- Tables
- Fields
- Programs
- Domains
- Directories
- Physical facilities
- Processes

Authorization models include:

| Discretionary access control (DAC) | Role-based access control (RBAC) | Mandatory access control (MAC) | Rule-based access control (RuBAC) | Policy-based access control (PBAC) | Risk-adaptive access control (RAdAC) |
|---|---|---|---|---|---|

- **Discretionary access control (DAC):** DAC leaves access control at the discretion of the object's owner or anyone else allowed to control access to the object. The owner has the authority to decide who has access to an object and what the access rights are. Most desktop applications (eg, spreadsheets) use DAC as the default access control mechanism. DAC's advantages include its being user friendly, simple to administer, and flexible. Disadvantages include a low level of data protection, lack of centralized access management (poor visibility), and permission conflicts (overlay of privileges)

**Discretionary Access Model (DAC)**

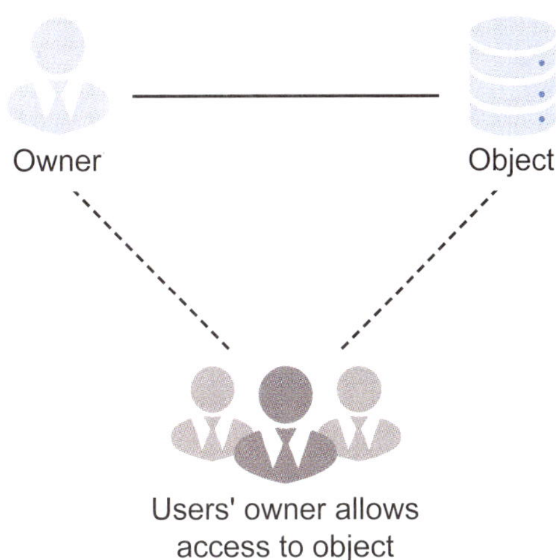


Under DAC, all subjects and objects that have been granted access to information in the system can:

- Pass that information to other subjects or objects
- Grant privileges to other subjects
- Change security attributes on subjects, objects, information systems, or system components
- Choose the security attributes to be associated with newly created or revised objects
- Change the rules governing access control

- **Role-based access controls (RBAC):** Role-based access control systems are determined by different user job titles within an organization. Access control varies based on an individual's role in the organization, taking into consideration their authority, responsibility, and job competency. The major disadvantage of RBAC is the lack of customization; the model's advantages are that it is simple to implement, user friendly (eg, all IT technicians have a small level of access within the organization), and little of the administrator's time is needed to manage the controls. In addition, just as in a manual system, RBAC supports the proper **segregation of duties** in the IT environment. Duties should be segregated between authorization, recording, custody, and comparison tasks. For example:
    - **Authorization:** Development of new programs and changes to existing programs should be performed by **systems analysts** and **programmers**. These personnel should not be involved in the supervision of computer operations or the control and review of output
    - **Recording: Data input clerks** and **computer operators** have the role of entering information into the computer and running the programs, respectively. These personnel should not have access to program code that would enable them to change programs, nor should they control the output
- **Mandatory access controls (MAC):** In contrast to DAC, permissions to objects in the MAC model are determined by settings configured by only the system administrator. MAC is used in environments where sensitive information is held, such as government. Resource objects are given a security label that includes a classification (eg, top secret, confidential) and a category defining the department or role that may be granted access. When a user tries to access an object, the operating system checks the user's permissions against the object's security label. MAC is the most secure model but also the most expensive to maintain because object labels and account permissions must be continuously updated

**Mandatory Access Model (MAC)**

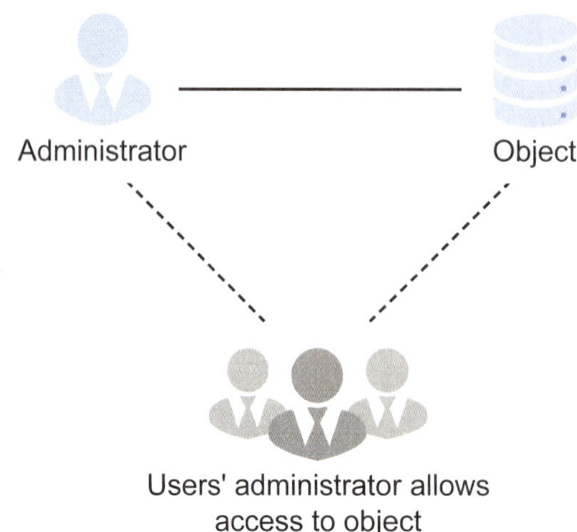


- **Rule-based access controls (RuBAC):** RuBAC governs access to locations, devices, or databases based on a predetermined set of rules or access rights, regardless of a user's position or role within the organization. The major advantage of this model is that it **gives clarity** (detail) on what is permitted and it is **flexible**, allowing any individual access if they follow the rules. The biggest disadvantage is that the model requires a significant amount of administrative work to set up, monitor, and adjust. RuBAC systems can vary based on the rules that are set. Examples include:
  - No access during nonbusiness hours
  - No access if a user tries to log in outside of designated locations or IP addresses
  - Certain individuals have read-only access rights to files
- **Policy-based access controls (PBAC):** PBAC **combines** the business **roles** of users with **policies** (rules) to define what access capabilities each role should have. This model is a combination of the role- and rule-based access control models. For example, a manager's role can apply to multiple users across several departments. Policies can then be established to define the specific systems or data access attached to the manager's role. Policies (ie, broad principles) are more flexible than rules (which tend to be strict and/or narrow in scope) and can encompass many types of parameters (eg, role, identity, risk, operational need, data-driven decisions). PBAC allows organizations to be **constantly developing** and implementing more **robust and adaptive techniques** for keeping up with the development of data consumption. For example:
  - Branch managers (role) can view the client basic profile, bank accounts, and card data of clients in the same line of business (LoB) and location as themselves (policy)
  - A physician (role) can view all patient medical records pertaining to that physician's specialty (policy)
- **Risk-adaptive access control (RAdAC):** Besides user identity, the risk-adaptive approach for determining and enforcing access controls considers security metrics such as the physical location of the connection, the strength of the authentication method (eg, two-factor authentication, SSO), and the type of security associated with the session transmission (eg, VPN, public key/private key encryption). RAdAC is a more robust form of access control but also expensive, as it combines the elements of user identity and role with more sophisticated device and contextual data in making the decision to allow or deny access

## Role-Based Access Control (RBAC)

As part of an IT audit, an internal auditor reviewed the user permissions in the organization's cloud-based software as a service (SaaS) accounts payable system to determine whether they matched the organizational hierarchy and job duties. The application used a RBAC managed by the organization's CFO.

To perform the audit, the auditor inspected the following:

- Organizational chart
- Job descriptions
- Permissions report generated from the system

**Organizational Chart**



### Job Descriptions

***CFO***

- Serve as accounts payable system administrator
- Enter bills
- Authorize payments
- Schedule payments
- Record journal entries
- Sync accounts payable to the general ledger
- Manage user account access permissions

***Accountant***

- Record journal entries
- Sync accounts payable to the general ledger

***Clerk***

- Enter bills

***Approver***

- Approve bills

***Payer***

- Schedule payments

***Internal Auditor***

- Perform internal operating and IT audits, with read-only access to the accounts payable system

**Accounts Payable System Permissions**

| Role | Read Only | Permissions | |
|---|---|---|---|
| **CFO** | ☐ | ☑ Enter bills<br>☑ Authorize payments<br>☑ Schedule payments | ☑ Record journal entries<br>☑ Sync<br>☑ Manage user access |
| **Accountant** | ☐ | ☐ Enter bills<br>☐ Authorize payments<br>☐ Schedule payments | ☑ Record journal entries<br>☑ Sync<br>☐ Manage user access |
| **Clerk** | ☐ | ☑ Enter bills<br>☐ Authorize payments<br>☐ Schedule payments | ☐ Record journal entries<br>☐ Sync<br>☐ Manage user access |
| **Approver** | ☐ | ☐ Enter bills<br>☑ Authorize payments<br>☐ Schedule payments | ☐ Record journal entries<br>☐ Sync<br>☐ Manage user access |
| **Payer** | ☐ | ☐ Enter bills<br>☐ Authorize payments<br>☑ Schedule payments | ☐ Record journal entries<br>☐ Sync<br>☐ Manage user access |
| **Internal Auditor** | ☑ | ☐ Enter bills<br>☐ Authorize payments<br>☐ Schedule payments | ☐ Record journal entries<br>☐ Sync<br>☐ Manage user access |

The internal auditor matched the job descriptions to the permissions and did not find any discrepancies. As a last step, the auditor asked for a log of all new, modified, or deleted user accounts to determine who made changes. The CFO, who is the designated system administrator, made all changes.

Based on the testing and findings, the internal auditor concluded that the role-based user access controls were suitably designed and operating effectively. Had there been any discrepancies, the internal auditor would have performed further procedures, notified the CFO of any discrepancies, and requested evidence of remediation.

# 6.03 Testing

## Testing: Security Awareness Training

**Representative Task (Application):** Perform procedures to obtain an understanding of how the entity communicates information to improve security knowledge and awareness and to model appropriate security behaviors to personnel through a security awareness training program.

CPAs **perform procedures** during engagements in which they give an **opinion** with a level of **assurance**, such as attestation examinations that provide reasonable assurance. The phrase "obtain an understanding" is normally associated with the **planning** phase of an audit, specifically **risk assessment**. According to AT-C 205, auditors performing an examination must obtain an understanding of a subject matter to:

- Identify risks and assess the risk of material misstatement
- Design and perform further procedures to respond to the identified risks
- Obtain reasonable assurance to support their opinion

The auditor must obtain an understanding of the design of controls and figure out whether controls have been implemented. Procedures may include a combination of **reperformance, inquiry, inspection, and observation**. The auditor may conduct a **walkthrough**, which typically involves inquiry but must also include at least one of the other procedures.

AT-C 205 further states that obtaining an understanding provides a frame of reference to exercise **professional judgment** throughout an examination, such as when the auditor:

- Considers the characteristics of a subject matter
- Assesses the suitability of criteria
- Determines the factors significant to directing the engagement team's efforts, including any special considerations (eg, a need for specialized skills or the work of a specialist)
- Establishes and evaluates the appropriateness of quantitative materiality levels and considers qualitative materiality factors
- Designs and performs procedures
- Evaluates evidence, including the reasonableness of the written representations

Most regulations, standards, and frameworks include **security awareness training** as a recommended or required control. External auditors often need to perform procedures to ensure that an organization has a security awareness training program and that it is sufficient. For instance, an organization may undergo a **HIPAA regulatory compliance** examination, which requires proof of a security awareness training program. An entity's contract with an outsourced vendor may require that the vendor's employees complete such training, which is evaluated during a **SOC 2®** engagement. Another organization may have a **SOC for Cybersecurity** examination to provide assurance about its cybersecurity risk management program.

Security awareness training is a **preventive control** used to **educate employees** and **model behavior** so they can understand the importance of security measures, the organization's policies, and how to report suspected incidents. The contents of the training may come from regulation requirements or may be suggested by the framework used as the foundation for the organization's cybersecurity risk management program.

Effective security awareness training has the following characteristics:

- All employees and contractors must attend the training at least annually
- Training materials should be relevant to the roles and responsibilities of attendees
- Attendees should be evaluated for knowledge retention as part of the training
- Training attendance should be documented

When performing procedures to obtain an understanding of an organization's security awareness program, the auditor may make inquiries, inspect policy manuals and **course materials/attendance records**, observe a training class, or walk through the process from start to finish. The auditor needs to know whether there is a security awareness program, what it entails, which employees attend it, and how records are kept. The auditor needs information that explains and evidences the *who, what, where, when, and why* of the organization's security awareness program.

The following example shows the steps an auditor may take to obtain an understanding of the program:

**Testing: Security Awareness Training**

During a SOC for Cybersecurity engagement, an auditor performed procedures to obtain an understanding of a manufacturer's cybersecurity risk management program. The criteria used to prepare management's description of the program was the AICPA's DC 100 *Description Criteria for Management's Description of an Entity's Cybersecurity Risk Management Program* (description criteria). The criteria used to evaluate whether controls within the cybersecurity risk management program were effective to achieve the entity's cybersecurity objectives were the criteria for security, availability, and confidentiality set forth in TSP section 100, *2017 Trust Services Criteria for Security, Availability, Processing Integrity, Confidentiality, and Privacy* (AICPA, Trust Services Criteria) (control criteria).

The purpose of obtaining the understanding was to assess risk and plan further procedures. Besides other items, management presented the following information in its description of the program, as required by the DC 100 description criteria:

- **DC10:** The process used to hire and develop competent individuals and contractors and to hold those individuals accountable for their cybersecurity responsibilities
- **DC13:** The process for internally communicating relevant cybersecurity information necessary to support the functioning of the entity's cybersecurity risk management program, including (1) objectives and responsibilities for cybersecurity and (2) thresholds for communicating identified security events that are monitored, investigated, and determined to be security incidents requiring a response, remediation, or both
- The key security policies and processes implemented and operated to address the entity's cybersecurity risks, including those addressing:
  - Prevention of intentional and unintentional security events
  - Detection of security events, identification of security incidents, development of a response to those incidents, and implementation activities to mitigate and recover from identified security incidents

Trust Services Criteria CC2, which stems from Principle 14 of the COSO Internal Control–Integrated Framework, says, *"The entity internally communicates information, including objectives and responsibilities for internal control, necessary to support the functioning of internal control."* A point of focus under CC2.2 further states, *"Communicates Information to Improve Security Knowledge and Awareness-The entity communicates information to improve security knowledge and awareness and to model appropriate security behaviors to personnel through a security awareness training program."*

Risk assessment procedures such as inquiry, inspection, and observation help an auditor obtain an understanding of an entity's cybersecurity risk management program and related controls. Controls should provide reasonable assurance of achieving the entity's cybersecurity objectives.

To obtain an understanding of how the manufacturer provides security awareness training to its personnel and what is required from contractors, the auditor performed the following procedures:

- **Inquiry:** Ask management and other personnel:
  - How are policies and procedures developed? Who prepares them, and who needs to approve them? How often are these policies and procedures updated?
  - How is leadership involved in the security awareness training development and deployment process?
  - Who develops the training content? What is done to ensure the training content is timely and relevant? How often is the content updated?
  - How is training material deployed? How is the target audience determined? How is training attendance tracked?
  - How is an employee's comprehension and knowledge evaluated?
  - How is training quality and effectiveness monitored?
  - What training must contractors receive? Is that formalized in a contract?
  - How is contractor training monitored?
- **Inspection:** Obtain and review the following documents:
  - Policies and procedures documentation
  - Evidence of leadership approval of training programs, including meeting minutes, project charter, etc.
  - Security awareness training materials (eg, slides, handouts), including approval of training materials by a responsible and knowledgeable party within the organization
  - Security awareness training attendance records
  - Evidence of post-training knowledge test and results, and the training team's assessment of those results
  - Evidence of updates to training materials
  - Contracts with contractors
  - Documentation of contractor security awareness training
- **Observation:** Attend at least one internal security awareness training session.

*Note: While the above example relates to a SOC for Cybersecurity examination, security awareness training-related procedures also apply to other attestation engagements, such as HIPAA, GDPR, PCI DSS, and SOC 2®.*

# Testing: Walkthrough of IT Security Procedures

**Representative Task (Analysis):** Perform a walkthrough of an organization's procedures relevant to IT security (eg., IT risk management, human resources, training, and education) and compare the observed procedure with the documented policy requirement.

A **walkthrough** is a combination of audit procedures used to understand and document a process from start to finish. The procedures include tests of controls performed through reperformance, inquiry, inspection, and observation. An auditor may create diagrams (eg, flowchart, Business Process Model and Notation [BPMN]) of processes during a walkthrough.

Walkthroughs are helpful to confirm the:

- Auditor's understanding of processes and procedures
- Design of controls
- Implementation of controls
- Effectiveness of controls

**Testing: Security Awareness Training Walkthrough**

The auditor in the previous example conducted a walkthrough to compare the manufacturer's documented employee security awareness training policies with the observed process. The auditor had already performed inquiries, inspected documents, and attended a training session, so the walkthrough and creating a diagram of the entire process would be the last steps in obtaining an understanding of the program.

According to management's description:

- Security awareness training courses should assist employees in recognizing and responding to social engineering attacks as well as avoiding unsecure practices (eg, writing down passwords, leaving sensitive material unattended)
- Training courses are developed by third-party cybersecurity experts, who provide the electronic course materials that the Training manager uploads to the manufacturer's learning management system (LMS) after the IT manager first approves of the course content. The LMS tracks attendance and successful completion
- Upon being hired and thereafter annually, all employees must successfully complete a basic security awareness training course. Employees are not provided access to the manufacturer's network until the course has been completed
- Employees who have access to customer and employee data must take additional courses in incident management and data protection
- IT personnel, IT management, and internal auditors must meet minimum requirements for cybersecurity risk management training and continuing education each year
- Human Resources assesses security awareness training attendance and successful completion on a semiannual basis
- Internal Audit periodically assesses employees' awareness of corporate policy by attempting to tailgate into buildings, sending simulated phishing emails, and performing desk sweeps, among other tactics. Internal Audit also periodically performs a review to determine whether any employees are allowed access to the network prior to taking the required security awareness training courses

The auditor met separately with the manufacturer's Human Resources manager, Training manager, IT manager, and Internal Audit manager to hear each one's explanation of the process and get more detailed information. Because there were no differences reported, the auditor made the following BPMN diagram to document the process in the workpapers:

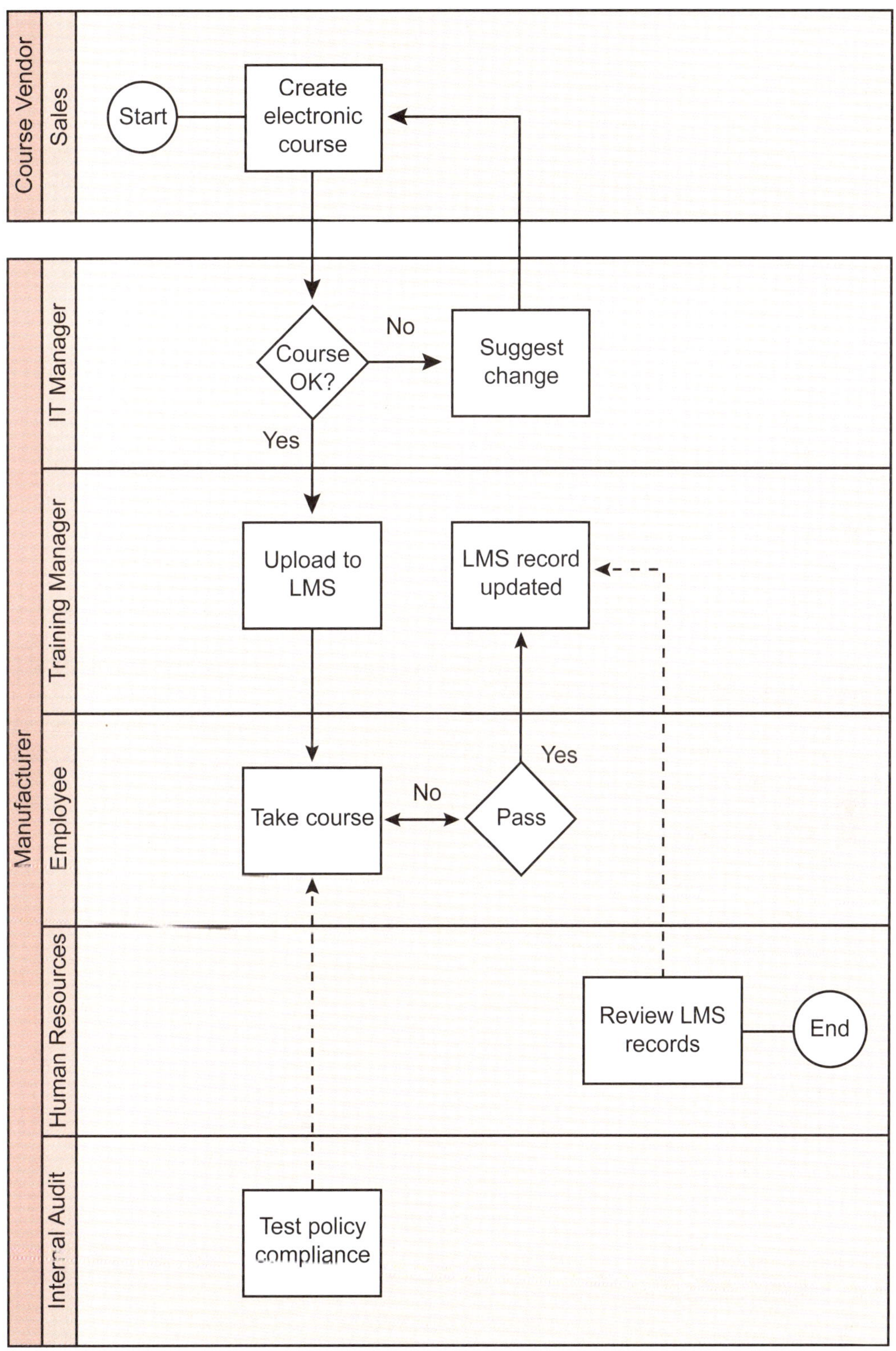

# Testing: Security Assessment Report

**Representative Task (Application):** Provide input into a security assessment report by documenting the issues, findings, and recommendations identified while performing tests of controls.

CPAs may perform **security assessments** as part of **risk advisory services**. According to CS 100, *Statement on Standards for Consulting Services*, **consulting services** are professional services that apply the CPA's technical skills, education, experience, knowledge, and observations. Advisory services, one of the six different consulting services referenced in the standards, are defined as professional services in which the CPA's function is to "**develop findings, conclusions, and recommendations** for client consideration and decision making."

A CPA firm may be engaged to perform security assessments as part of an organization's internal ERM program or due to a required contractual or regulatory obligation. For example, covered entities subject to HIPAA must have a third party security assessment. Organizations subject to PCI DSS arrangements may also need a security assessment.

The scope of a **security assessment report (SAR)** depends on the reason for the service and the extent of testing. The purpose is to evaluate the effectiveness of controls, the quality of risk management processes, and the strengths/weaknesses of systems. By proactively testing the security of the system, the CPA can present the client with findings and recommend controls to correct deficiencies before an incident occurs. The assessment also provides proof of compliance with contracts or regulations.

SARs normally involve **vulnerability scans** and **penetration testing**, which find critical flaws that might allow a breach. To recall, vulnerability scans are automated, high-level tests that locate weaknesses in hardware, software, and networks. A person (ie, **ethical hacker**) performs a penetration test (ie, pen test) to not only find security weaknesses but also to circumvent controls and exploit those weaknesses. Other manual **tests of controls**, such as reperformance, inquiry, inspection, and observation, may also be performed in a security assessment. For example, inquiries may be made of IT personnel, or system documentation may be inspected.

The **contents of a SAR** may include:

- Identification of the CPA who performed the assessment
- Identification of the organization for whom the report was prepared
- Introduction and purpose
  - Applicable laws, regulations, and standards
  - Scope
- System overview
  - System description
  - Purpose of system
- Executive summary
  - Summary of findings
  - Summary of recommendations
- Detailed findings report and table

- Infrastructure vulnerability scans
- Operating system and database vulnerability scans
- Web application vulnerability scans
- Penetration test report

**Testing: Security Assessment Report (SAR)**

An organization that processes cardholder data was required to have an annual security assessment, according to the PCI DSS standards. Besides reviewing quarterly vulnerability scans, the engaged CPA firm performed manual tests of controls. One set of tests was directed at figuring out whether the organization changed the vendor-supplied default passwords on network-connected devices and applications.

The CPA firm interviewed personnel, examined documents, and reperformed log-ins using the default passwords. The SAR prepared by the CPA firm regarding this specific testing reported the following:

**Issue:** Attackers may find default device and application passwords in manufacturers' user manuals or on the Internet. An attacker could then use the default password to gain unauthorized access.

**Risk level:** Moderate exploitation of the vulnerability may significantly affect the confidentiality, integrity, and/or availability of systems or data.

**Affected systems:** Any Internet- or network-connected system using password authentication would be affected.

**Tests performed:** Interviewed personnel and examined procedural documentation to verify that default passwords are changed before a device or application is connected to the network and that any unnecessary default passwords are removed or disabled. The client supplied a list of devices and applications used. For a sample, manually attempted to log on with default passwords to verify that they had been changed, removed, or disabled. If the default password did not work, also attempted to log on using blank credentials, common phrases such as "admin," and information found on device stickers, such as serial numbers and media access control (MAC) addresses. Default passwords were obtained from vendor manuals and Internet resources.

**Findings:** Found 10 instances of end-user installed applications that could be logged into using default passwords. Six of the instances related to vendor demonstration software where the default password was found in online training materials, as well as emails from the vendor. The remaining four instances related to specialty applications shared by a group of users in violation of the organization's policies. The default password for one wireless router was found by testing the numbers found on a sticker on the back of the device.

**Recommendations:** Communicate policies and train personnel about the sharing of software and the use of vendor demonstration software, including the requirement to immediately change default passwords. Establish policies and approval procedures for vendor demonstration software. Establish policies and procedures to ensure that devices are installed only by IT department staff, who must change the default passwords.

# SOC 2® Examination Procedures: Security

**Representative Task (Analysis):** Detect deficiencies in the suitability of the design and deviations in the operation of controls related to a service organization's security service commitments and system requirements in a SOC 2® engagement using the Trust Services Criteria.

**SOC 2® engagements were previously discussed in the SOC chapter. It would be helpful to review that content along with this representative task, which focuses on a service auditor's procedures to obtain sufficient appropriate evidence.**

## Overview

When an organization **outsources** business functions or technology, it must have a governance and monitoring process in place to manage third-party risk. The organization may contractually require the vendor **(service organization)** to provide a **SOC 2® report** from an independent CPA. The contract or service level agreement (SLA) usually outlines the service organization's principal service commitments and system requirements, which are the promises and representations the organization makes to its customers about its services.

To recall, SOC 2® examinations provide **assurance** about *security*, availability, processing integrity, confidentiality, or privacy. A user entity receiving a SOC 2® report must have **sufficient knowledge** to understand and assess its contents.

According to the Trust Services Criteria, **the Security trust services category** pertains to a service organization's ability to protect against unauthorized access, unauthorized disclosure of information, and damage to systems that could compromise the availability, integrity, confidentiality, and privacy of information or systems and affect the entity's ability to achieve its principal service commitments and system requirements.

The Trust Services Criteria state that security refers to protecting:

- Information during its collection or creation, use, processing, transmission, and storage, as well as
- Systems that use electronic information to process, transmit or transfer, and store information to enable the entity to meet its objectives.

Security controls prevent or detect improper segregation of duties; system failures; incorrect processing; theft or other unauthorized removal of data or system resources; misuse of software; and improper access to or use of, alteration, destruction, or disclosure of information.

All SOC 2® examinations include the Security trust services category. Other trust services categories (Availability, Processing Integrity, Confidentiality, or Privacy) may be added as requested by the engaging party. Compliance examinations or other attest services may also be added to a SOC 2® engagement for efficiency and effectiveness. Often, the subject matter of a SOC 2® examination overlaps with compliance requirements; when this occurs, the dual-purpose examinations are referred to as SOC 2®+ engagements.

The service auditor may consider controls suitably designed either individually or when combined with other controls. To assess the suitability of the design of controls in a SOC 2® examination, the service auditor must:

- Understand management's process for identifying risks that threaten the achievement of the service organization's principal service commitments and system requirements
- Assess the completeness and accuracy of management's risk assessment
- Perform an independent risk assessment
- Evaluate the link between identified risks and the controls stated in management's description of their system
- Determine whether management has implemented the controls

**Procedures** to evaluate the suitability of the design of controls normally include **reperformance, inquiries, inspection, observations, and walkthroughs**. During the evaluation, the service auditor should use professional judgment, **comparing management's controls with the identified risks** and the **Trust Services Criteria**. Risks include those identified by either management or the service auditor. The Trust Services Criteria serve as a **benchmark** for the outcome of controls.

When examining the Security trust services category, the service auditor should consider all relevant **common** and **supplemental criteria**. To recall, these criteria are aligned with the 17 principles outlined in the **COSO Internal Control–Integrated Framework**. There are no additional criteria specific to the Security category.

Because all SOC examinations include the Security trust services category, the common and supplemental criteria are summarized in this chapter. See the Trust Services Criteria exhibit in the Appendix for all the detailed points of focus.

The additional category-specific criteria for availability, processing integrity, confidentiality, and privacy are discussed in their respective chapters. Note that some of the common and supplemental criteria have additional points of focus for specific categories, especially the Confidentiality and Privacy categories.

| Criteria Type | TSC Series | TSC Category | TSC Criteria | COSO Component | COSO Principles |
|---|---|---|---|---|---|
| Common | CC1 | All | Control Environment | Control Environment | 1–5 |
| | CC2 | All | Information and Communication | Information and Communication | 13–15 |
| | CC3 | All | Risk Assessment | Risk Assessment | 6–9 |
| | CC4 | All | Monitoring of Controls | Monitoring Activities | 16–17 |
| | CC5 | All | Control Activities | Control Activities | 10–12 |
| Supplemental | CC6 | All | Logical and Physical Access Controls | Control Activities | 12 |
| | CC7 | All | System Operations | Control Activities | 12 |
| | CC8 | All | Change Management | Control Activities | 12 |
| | CC9 | All | Risk Mitigation | Control Activities | 12 |

## Common Criteria

- **CC1 Control Environment**
  - **CC1.1** (COSO Principle 1): Demonstrates a commitment to integrity and ethical values.
  - **CC1.2** (COSO Principle 2): Board of directors is independent from management and exercises oversight over internal control.
  - **CC1.3** (COSO Principle 3): Management creates structures, reporting lines, authorities, and responsibilities to achieve its objectives (principal service commitments and system requirements in a SOC 2® examination).
  - **CC1.4** (COSO Principle 4): Demonstrates commitment to attract, develop, and retain competent personnel and outsourced service providers.
  - **CC1.5** (COSO Principle 5): Individuals are held accountable for their internal control responsibilities.
- **CC2 Information and Communication**
  - **CC2.1** (COSO Principle 13): Obtains/generates and uses relevant, quality information to support internal control.
  - **CC2.2** (COSO Principle 14): Information is communicated internally to support internal control.
  - **CC2.3** (COSO Principle 15): Information is communicated with external parties to support internal control.
- **CC3 Risk Assessment**
  - **CC3.1** (COSO Principle 6): Objectives (principal service commitments and service requirements in a SOC 2® examination) are specified with enough clarity to identify and assess internal and external risks.
  - **CC3.2** (COSO Principle 7): Risks that threaten the achievement of objectives (principal service commitments and service requirements in a SOC 2® examination) are identified and analyzed as a basis for determining how they should be managed.
  - **CC3.3** (COSO Principle 8): Risk assessment includes consideration of the potential for fraud.
  - **CC3.4** (COSO Principle 9): Changes that could significantly affect internal control are identified and assessed.
- **CC4 Monitoring Activities**
  - **CC4.1** (COSO Principle 16): Ongoing and separate evaluations are performed to determine whether the components of internal control are present and functioning.
  - **CC4.2** (COSO Principle 17): Internal control deficiencies are evaluated and communicated to the parties responsible for taking corrective action, including senior management and the board of directors, in a timely manner.
- **CC5 Control Activities**
  - **CC5.1** (COSO Principle 10): Control activities are selected and developed to mitigate risks that threaten the achievement of objectives (principal service commitments and service requirements in a SOC 2® examination).
  - **CC5.2** (COSO Principle 11): General control activities over technology are selected and developed to support the achievement of objectives (principal service commitments and service requirements in a SOC 2® examination).
  - **CC5.3** (COSO Principle 12): Control activities are deployed through policies that establish what is expected and procedures that put the policies into action

All supplemental criteria (CC6–CC9) expand on COSO Principle 12. See the Trust Services Criteria exhibit in the Appendix for the detailed points of focus.

## Supplemental Criteria

- **CC6 Logical and Physical Access Controls**
  - **CC6.1:** Logical access security software, infrastructure, and architectures are implemented to protect information assets from security events and meet objectives (principal service commitments and system requirements in a SOC 2® examination).
  - **CC6.2:** Prior to issuing system credentials and granting system access, new internal and external users are registered and authorized. User system credentials are removed when the access is no longer authorized.
  - **CC6.3:** Access to data, software, functions, and other information assets is authorized, modified, or removed based on roles, responsibilities, or system design and changes, with consideration for the concepts of least privilege and segregation of duties.
  - **CC6.4:** Physical access to facilities and information assets (ie, data centers, backup storage, and other sensitive locations) is restricted to authorized personnel.
  - **CC6.5:** Logical and physical protections over physical assets are discontinued only after the ability to read or recover data and software from those assets has been diminished and such protections are no longer needed to meet objectives (principal service commitments and system requirements in a SOC 2® examination).
  - **CC6.6:** Logical security measures protect against threats from sources outside of system boundaries.
  - **CC6.7:** The transmission, movement, and removal of information is restricted to authorized internal and external users or processes. Information is protected during transmission, movement, and removal.
  - **CC6.8:** Controls are implemented to prevent, detect, and act upon unauthorized malicious software.
- **CC7 System Operations**
  - **CC7.1:** Uses detection and monitoring procedures to identify changes to configurations that result in new vulnerabilities, as well as susceptibility to such vulnerabilities.
  - **CC7.2:** Monitors system components and the operation of components for anomalies that indicate malicious acts, natural disasters, or errors affecting the ability to meet objectives (principal service commitments and system requirements in a SOC 2® examination). Anomalies are analyzed in order to decide whether they are security events.
  - **CC7.3:** Security events are evaluated to determine whether they could have or did result in failing to meet objectives (principal service commitments and system requirements in a SOC 2® examination); if so, actions are taken to prevent or address such failures.
  - **CC7.4:** Executes a defined incident response plan to understand, contain, remediate, and communicate security incidents.
  - **CC7.5:** Identifies, develops, and implements activities to recover from identified security incidents.
- **CC8 Change Management**
  - **CC8.1:** Authorizes, designs, develops or acquires, configures, documents, tests, approves, and implements changes to infrastructure, data, software, and procedures.
- **CC9 Risk Mitigation**
  - **CC9.1:** Identifies, selects, and develops mitigation activities for risks that may cause business disruptions.
  - **CC9.2:** Assesses and manages risks associated with vendors and business partners.

In a SOC 2® engagement, a **deficiency in the suitability of the design of controls** means that a control would not achieve the service organization's principal service commitments and system requirements because the control either does not exist or the design is flawed. The only way to correct a deficiency is to change (or add) the control. Material deficiencies result in a **report modification**, such as a separate paragraph.

**A Deficiency in the Suitability of the Design of a Control Exists When...**

| The control does not exist | The control exists but would not achieve objectives even if performed as designed |
|---|---|

### Detect Deficiencies in the Suitability of the Design of Controls

A fintech company is undergoing its first SOC 2®, type 2 examination. The organization has a robust Internal Audit team that performs ongoing and separate IT audits throughout the year. At the end of each internal audit, a report is provided to management and the audit committee. The audit report outlines the Internal Audit team's procedures, findings, and recommendations.

During the risk assessment phase of the examination, the service auditor determined there is a risk that *"management does not track whether internal control deficiencies identified in internal evaluations were remediated in a timely manner."* A point of focus under CC4.2 (COSO Principle 17) states, *"Monitors Corrective Action: Management tracks whether deficiencies are remediated on a timely basis."*

The service auditor performed the following procedures to understand how management tracks corrective actions for internal control deficiencies:

**Inquiry:** The service auditor interviewed members of senior management and the Internal Audit department. Management said that all internal audit reports are read and discussed. Sometimes they agree with the internal audit findings, and other times they do not. When they agree, they consider the recommendations in the report but may devise and implement other plans that they believe will correct the problem. Management further stated that these decisions are sometimes shared with the Internal Audit team, and sometimes they are not. Other than internal emails, there is no formal tracking process in place.

The Internal Audit team said they have oral and email conversations with management about findings and recommendations. Sometimes they are made aware of corrections, but not always. If they are made aware and the change is significant, a follow-up review is performed within a reasonable period. However, for minor or moderate corrections, the follow-up is just incorporated into the next normally scheduled internal audit related to the issue.

**Inspection:** The service auditor reviewed a sample of internal audit reports, email communications with management after the report's issuance, and the list of internal audits performed during the examination period. The service auditor asked to read any policies and procedures regarding roles and responsibilities after an internal audit. Both management and Internal Audit confirmed that there were no written policies or procedures to that effect.

After performing the inquiry and inspection procedures, the service auditor's professional judgment was that both management's and the Internal Audit team's tracking and monitoring of corrective actions were too lax. The service auditor attributed this to a lack of defined policies and procedures. Thus, in evaluating the organization's risks and controls considering CC4.2, the service auditor opined that there was a material deficiency in the suitability of the design of controls. The deficiency related to the suitability of design because the control did not exist.

## Detect Deviations in the Operating Effectiveness of Controls

In a SOC 2®, type 2 examination, the service auditor performs tests of controls to determine whether controls operated effectively to achieve the service organization's principal service commitments and system requirements throughout a period. The service auditor's tests of controls and results are included in the report.

Note that a service auditor must first determine that a control is suitably designed. By definition, a control that is not suitably designed cannot operate effectively.

**A Deviation in the Operating Effectiveness of a Control Exists When...**

| The control is suitably designed but does not operate as expected | The person performing the control does not have authority or is not competent |
|---|---|

Evaluating the operating effectiveness of controls requires the service auditor to determine whether:

- The control operated effectively, and
- The evidence provided by the service organization is reliable.

Tests of controls include reperformance, inquiry, inspection, and observation. Walkthroughs may also be performed. The service auditor must use professional judgment to decide whether to test a sample or the entire population. Evidence is reliable if it is accurate, complete, precise, and detailed.

### Detect Deviations in the Operating Effectiveness of Controls

In an alternative to the scenario above, the service organization might have a written policy and procedure saying that, within 30 days of receiving an internal audit report, senior management provides a written response detailing a remediation plan and setting a target implementation date. Further, management informs the Internal Audit team when implementation is completed.

Management has designed a spreadsheet to track corrective actions for control deficiencies identified through internal audits and deficiencies reported by other personnel. The spreadsheet includes an overview of the remediation plan, target implementation date, and actual implementation date.

The spreadsheet is always available on a shared drive accessible by the Internal Audit team. The Internal Audit team performs follow-up reviews to ensure that the corrective actions are appropriate and completed in a timely manner.

The service auditor performed the following procedures to determine whether the controls operated effectively:

**Inspection:** A sample of the internal control deficiencies found during the examination period was selected from management's tracking spreadsheet. For deficiencies reported in an internal audit, the service auditor obtained and read the original audit report to compare the Internal Audit team's recommendation with the corrective action taken. The service auditor then performed other procedures such as inquiry, inspection, and walkthroughs to determine whether the control deficiencies were in fact remediated. Part of the inspection included reading any related emails and the Internal Audit team's follow-up audit reports.

After performing the procedures, the service auditor was convinced that management's controls over the monitoring of corrective actions operated effectively. Corrective action was taken promptly and confirmed through a follow-up internal audit.

# ISC 7
# Confidentiality and Privacy

# ISC 7: Confidentiality and Privacy

# 7.01 Confidentiality and Privacy

**Representative Task (Remembering and Understanding):** Explain encryption fundamentals, techniques, and applications.

## Encryption

**Encryption** is a common technique to protect the confidentiality and privacy of data, whether on premises or in the cloud. In encryption, algorithms transform data so that it cannot be read without entering a string of characters referred to as a **cryptographic key**. Encryption can be applied when data is at rest (in storage) or in transit (during transmission). Once the data is locked (encrypted), only someone with the right cryptographic key can open (decrypt) it.

### Fundamentals

Encryption changes human-readable **plaintext** into incomprehensible **ciphertext**. Although encrypted data appears random, **algorithms** follow a logical process to encrypt on one end and decrypt at the other. The key must be unique and unpredictable so that an unauthorized person or device cannot guess it.

- **Plaintext:** Unencrypted data that anyone can easily read, use, and interpret. Such data may include words, scripts, or common coding languages
- **Ciphertext:** Plaintext that has been encrypted according to an algorithm. Ciphertext can be turned back into plaintext only by parties who know the encryption algorithm and have a key that allows the data to be decrypted
- **Key:** The fundamental part of the algorithm that encrypts and decrypts the data. There are two primary types of keys:
  - **Private/secret key:** A cryptographic key including letters and numbers shared only between the user who generates the key and the user allowed to decrypt the data. In symmetric encryption, data is both encrypted and decrypted using a private key; this enhances confidentiality and speeds transmission. Thus, a private key is useful for encrypting large amounts of data
  - **Public key:** In asymmetric encryption, the message sender uses a public key to encrypt data. A public key can be widely published or safely transmitted. It is paired with a private key held by an authorized receiver to decrypt the ciphertext. Because public keys are slower and less confidential, they are primarily used for brief messages like website certificates, digital signatures, and private communications
  - **Algorithm:** A mathematical formula used to generate a key and change plaintext into an encrypted or decrypted state; also known as a cipher

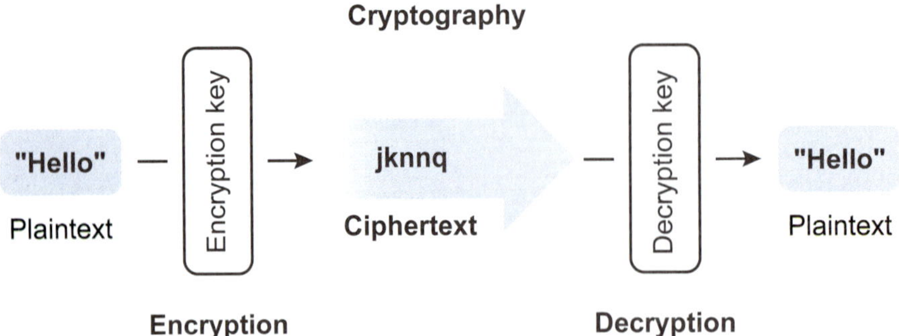


## Techniques

The two primary encryption methods, symmetric and asymmetric, use a different technique to transform plaintext into ciphertext:

- **Symmetric cryptography:** Encryption and decryption using the same private key. The most common symmetric cryptography algorithm is the **Advanced Encryption Standard (AES)**, created by NIST. It is a **block cipher** that generates a minimum key size of 128 bits (16 bytes). Block ciphers encrypt data by transforming (ie, substituting, shifting, or mixing) fixed blocks of plaintext into fixed blocks of ciphertext. The algorithm repeats the transformations multiple times, creating a **round function** that adds a unique key. Applications requiring stronger security, such as those for banking or government, may use 192-bit or 256-bit AES.

  The goal of using longer encryption blocks and increased rounds is to make it more difficult for supercomputers to "crack the code" through brute-force attacks (ie, checking all potential key combinations until the correct one is found). More bits exponentially increase the number of combinations an attacking computer would have to try. There are very few successful attacks on 128-bit or higher AES, which is why businesses use this standard.

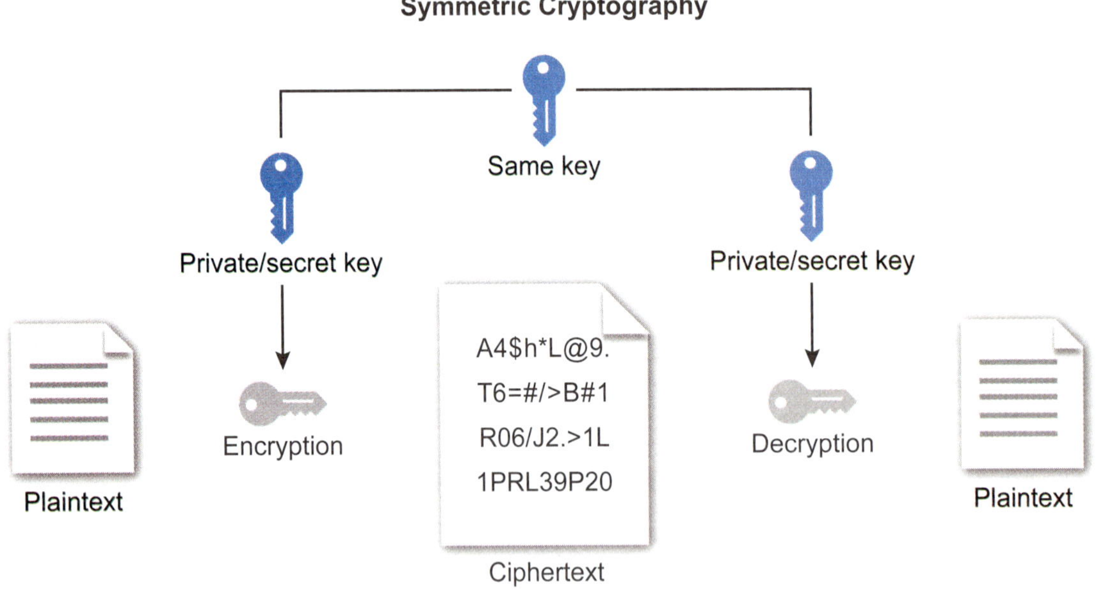


- **Asymmetric cryptography:** Requires **paired keys**—encryption using a **public key** and decryption using a **private/secret key** that is known and available only to an authorized recipient. The most common asymmetric algorithm is **RSA (Rivest-Shamir-Adleman)**, which uses 1024-bit keys and can expand to 4096 bits. A level below 2048 bits is not currently considered safe because computers can solve the equations. With RSA, the public key consists of **two numbers**, one resulting from the multiplication of two large **prime numbers** and the other being a **random number**. The private key has the correct prime numbers to solve the factorization equation.

**Asymmetric Cryptography**

Different keys

Public key

Private/secret key

Plaintext

Encryption

A4$h*L@9.
T6=#/>B#1
R06/J2.>1L
1PRL39P20

Ciphertext

Decryption

Plaintext

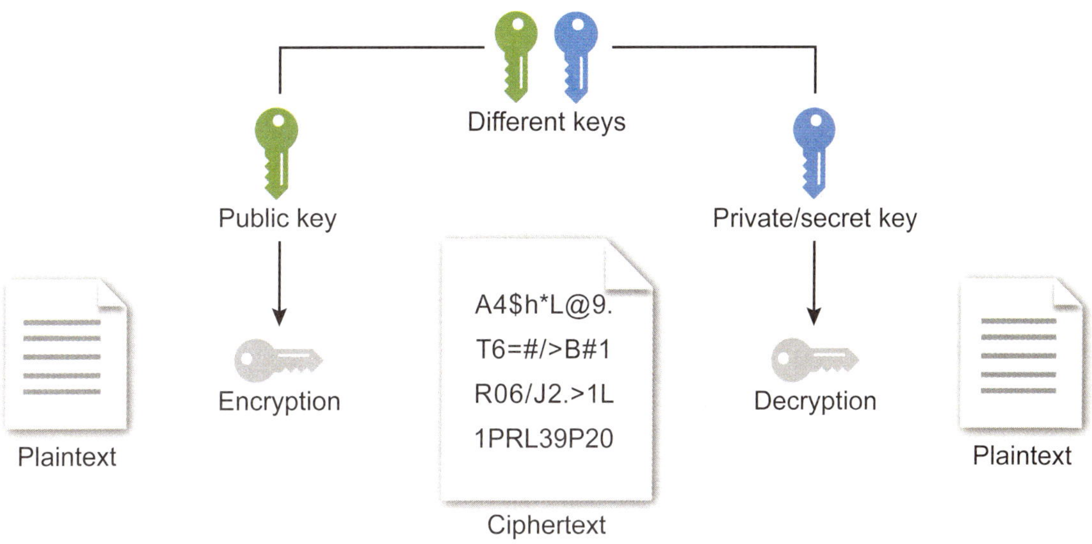

## Applications

Both symmetric and asymmetric encryptions are widely used and may be combined. Each method has its own advantages and disadvantages.

- **Symmetric** cryptography (eg, AES) is used for encrypting data at rest and in transit. It is fast, secure, and supported. AES use is common in cases involving:
  - Corporate systems
  - Financial institutions, such as banks and payment card companies
  - Cloud storage
  - Wireless security
  - Password management
  - Government data, including "top secret" documents
  - Data stored (ie, at rest) on a device such as a computer (eg, Microsoft BitLocker)
  - Data used in software testing environments
- **Asymmetric** cryptography (eg, RSA) is used for data transmission, secure connections, and digital signatures. It is slower than symmetric cryptography. RSA use is common in cases involving:
  - **Digital signatures:** Verifying identity for someone to sign a document
  - **Blockchain:** Verifying identity to approve cryptocurrency transactions
  - **Public key infrastructure (PKI):** Regulating encryption keys via the creation and administration of digital certificates
- **Combinations:** Many use cases combine symmetric and asymmetric cryptography to improve both speed and security. Such cases include:
  - **Web browsing:** Through asymmetric cryptography, a single-use symmetric encryption key is created and then used to encrypt/decrypt the contents of an Internet browsing session
  - **Mobile chat systems:** Using asymmetric cryptography, the identities of participants are verified at the start of a conversation. The conversation's ongoing contents are then encrypted through symmetric cryptography

### Basic Encryption Applications:

- **Secure socket layer (SSL):** An encryption-based network security protocol designed to protect data transmissions between web browsers and web servers
- **Transport layer security (TLS):** A protocol designed to replace or enhance SSL and protect data communications over a network between two endpoints (eg, email servers, endpoints for voice over Internet protocol [VOIP] or instant messaging)
- **Secure/multipurpose Internet mail extension (S/MIME):** Provides an added layer of security for email; primarily used by Microsoft products (eg, Outlook, Exchange)
- **Internet protocol security (IPSec):** A suite of protocols that authenticates and encrypts data packets sent between two devices over a network
- **Virtual private networks (VPNs):** Used to encrypt communication over a public network by setting up an encrypted connection to a device behind a network boundary (ie, firewall)

## Confidentiality versus Privacy

**Representative Task (Remembering and Understanding):** Recall the differences between confidentiality and privacy.

| Privacy | vs. | Confidentiality |
|---|---|---|
| State of being away from public attention | | State where certain information is kept secret |
| Is about individuals | | Is about information |
| Personal choice | | Professional obligation |
| Pertains to rights | | Pertains to agreements |
| Restricts the public from accessing personal data | | Restricts unauthorized people from accessing proprietary data |

**Privacy** applies to personal information about **people**, while **confidentiality** encompasses diverse types of **restricted or proprietary** information. Information is confidential if the custodian is required by law or a contractual agreement to limit access to the information or restrict its use, retention, or disclosure. Proprietary information, trade secrets, and legal settlement agreements are examples of confidential information.

Private information is personal data that could identify an individual (eg, name, Social Security number, date of birth, ID number, email address, username). **Sensitive personal data** goes a step further and relates to a person's race, ethnicity, physical or mental health, political or religious beliefs, sexual orientation, etc. The collection, use, retention, access to, disclosure, or disposal of sensitive personal data may be subject to **laws** and **contractual agreements** requiring informed consent. For **informed consent**, a person is told what information is being requested and why and is asked if they agree to provide the information. Legislation and regulations involving privacy, such as the **General Data Protection Regulation (GDPR)** and the **Health Insurance Portability and Accountability Act (HIPAA)**, protect individuals from entities (eg, researchers, businesses) that might try to collect data using unethical or poorly controlled practices. Privacy laws also provide protections for specific populations or vulnerable groups (eg, minors, mental health patients).

Consider the following questions about customer information in an accounting information system:

**Privacy Concerns**

- Why is the data being collected?
    - Does the collection have a specific, relevant purpose?
- What data is collected?
    - Is the data linked to a specific individual?
    - Is the data relevant to the stated purpose of the collection?
- How is the data collected?
    - Does the person know their data is being collected?
    - Can they refuse the data collection?

**Confidentiality Concerns**

- Where can the data be accessed?
    - Can the data be accessed from anywhere using any device?
- Who can access the data?
    - Can only specific individuals access the data?
    - Does the accessor have a "need to know"?
- Where is the data stored?
    - If electronically, how is the data protected from disclosure (eg, copying, emailing)?
    - If physically (ie, a paper file), who has access to the storage space?

Businesses may be required to follow different privacy laws and regulations, based on the **jurisdictions** in which they operate. Also, different regulations may define **personally identifiable information (PII)** differently, so organizations must understand each applicable regulation to understand what the definition of PII is in a given situation. Examples of privacy laws and regulations include the following:

- **General Data Protection Regulation (GDPR):** GDPR is a regulation that requires businesses to protect the personal data and privacy of European Union citizens when conducting transactions within EU member states. It also addresses transfers of personal data outside the EU
- **Children's Online Privacy Protection Act (COPPA):** COPPA safeguards children's privacy by placing certain restrictions on website operators and granting parents tools to help them control what information is collected about their children online
- **Gramm-Leach-Bliley Act:** Financial institutions—and businesses that provide consumers with financial products or services like loans, investment advice, or insurance—must disclose to their clients how they share customer information and protect sensitive data
- **Family Educational Rights and Privacy Act (FERPA):** FERPA is a federal law enabling parents to request both access to and amendment of their children's educational records, as well as some control over the disclosure of PII from those records. Every school that receives funding from a relevant U.S. Department of Education program is subject to this law
- **Health Insurance Portability and Accountability Act (HIPAA):** HIPAA provides measures of data security and privacy to protect individuals' medical information/records

# Protecting Confidential Data During Application Development

**Representative Task (Remembering and Understanding):** Identify methods for the protection of confidential data during the design, development, testing, and implementation of applications that use confidential data (eg, data obfuscation, tokenization).

The design, development, testing, and implementation of applications that use (or will use) confidential data carry heightened risks of unauthorized data disclosure. For example, application testing and implementation personnel do not need to know an individual's personal health information to evaluate the operation of an application.

**Data obfuscation** methods **change or mask data** into a unique form to protect sensitive or personal information. These techniques make the data useless (or less useful) to an attacker while still supporting the functionality of systems. Restoring the data later to its original state may or may not be possible, depending on the obfuscation technique.

Organizations use data obfuscation methods to meet compliance goals, reduce risks related to data transmission, and prevent (or reduce the risk of) data tampering and leakage during application development and testing.

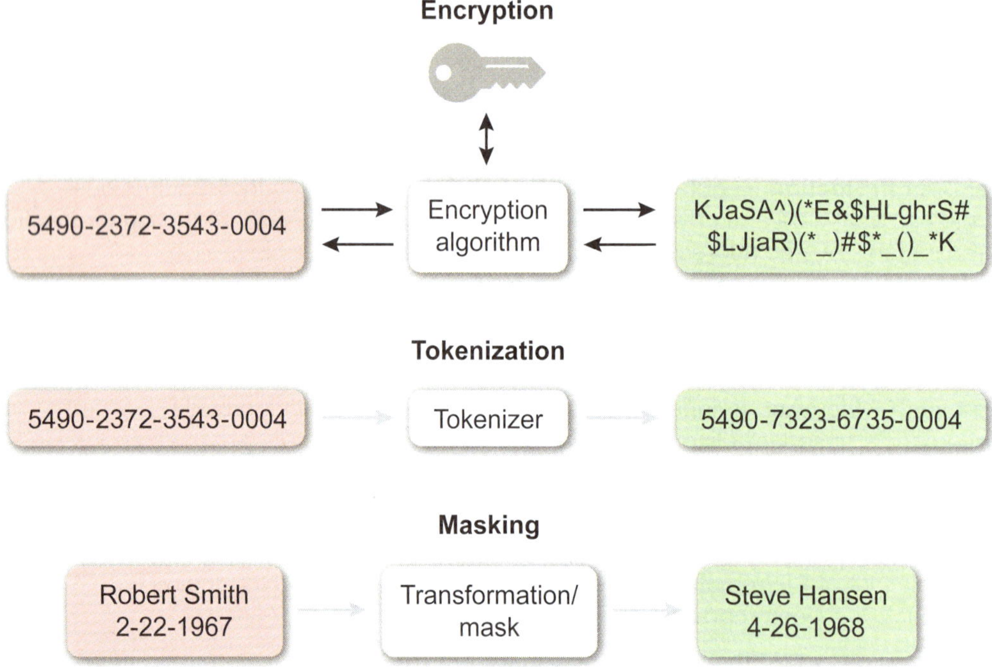


The three most common data obfuscation techniques are encryption, tokenization, and masking. These techniques change or mask data using different algorithms. Both encryption and tokenization are reversible because it is possible to derive the original values from the obfuscated data. If data masking is conducted appropriately, it is irreversible.

- **Encryption:** As stated earlier, encryption uses an algorithm to encode plaintext data into ciphertext that cannot be easily decrypted without a key. The more complex the data encryption algorithm, the less vulnerable the data is to unauthorized access. The advantage is that encryption does not destroy the underlying data and can be used on any type of data (structured or unstructured). In addition, while developing the encryption key can be computationally expensive, the actual process of encrypting and decrypting data requires a minimal amount of computer resources. This makes applying encryption to enormous amounts of data inexpensive in terms of resource usage. The disadvantage is that data cannot be manipulated or analyzed when encrypted
- **Tokenization:** Similar to encryption, tokenization replaces sensitive information with a meaningless value (ie, token); however, the token can be mapped to the original data. Tokenized data enables operations such as processing a credit card payment without showing the credit card number. The actual data never leaves the organization and cannot be viewed or decrypted by a third-party processor
- **Masking:** Data masking substitutes realistic but misleading data for original data to ensure privacy. The primary advantage is that testing, training, development, or support teams can work with a data set using masked data without compromising real data. However, once false data has replaced actual data, there is no algorithm to restore it. Masking examples include:
  - **Data replacement:** Replacing personally identifying details and names with other symbols and characters (eg, replacing Social Security numbers with # symbols)
  - **Data substitution:** Fully replacing the underlying data with alternate false data that seems legitimate (eg, John replaced with Bill)
  - **Data shuffling or randomization:** Data shuffling techniques mix data attributes while keeping the logical connections. The shuffled data is from a data set within either a single attribute (eg, zip code) or a set of attributes (eg, date of birth and city)
  - **Data sanitization:** Permanent removal of personally identifiable information (PII) from sensitive data

Service organizations that develop applications for user entities may need a SOC 2® examination. Trust Services Criteria 8.1, which relates to change management, has an additional point of focus for the confidentiality trust services category. It says, "*The entity protects confidential information during system design, development, testing, implementation, and change processes to support the achievement of the entity's objectives* (eg, principal service commitments and system requirements)." A similar point of focus relates to privacy. **Note that this representative task has almost the same language as the trust services criteria for both confidentiality and privacy**.

## Data Loss Prevention

**Representative Task (Remembering and Understanding):** Explain data loss prevention (DLP).

**Data loss prevention (DLP)** involves policies and processes that prevent the unauthorized disclosure of data outside of an organization. The risks related to data loss (eg, data breaches) are significant. Loss of confidential or private data may lead to brand damage, loss of customers, regulatory fines, and litigation.

DLP solutions are part of an organization's governance and risk response. To protect against the loss of confidential and private information, DLP includes the following components:

- Design data classification, data flow, backup, and incident response policies
- Search, find, classify, and inventory sensitive data throughout the organization
- Log, monitor, and control the movement of sensitive data across networks and endpoints
- Improve compliance with laws and regulations
- Optimize data storage and transmission

An organization's data may exist in a multitude of places and statuses. DLP focuses on data protections in three states: **data at rest, data in transit, and data in use.**

| State | Locations | Functional Areas |
|---|---|---|
| **Data at Rest** | • Cloud or on-premises databases<br>• Local computers<br>• Internal websites (intranet)<br>• Archived data (eg, email)<br>• Mobile devices<br>• USB drives/CDs/DVDs<br>• Fax machines/copiers/scanners | • Physical endpoint security<br>• Host device encryption<br>• Mobile device protection<br>• Network/Internet storage<br>• Physical media (storage)<br>• Disposal and destruction |
| **Data in Transit** | • Email (business and personal)<br>• Web/Internet<br>• File transfers<br>• Data sharing<br>• Social media (eg, Facebook, LinkedIn)<br>• Instant messaging | • Perimeter security<br>• Network monitoring<br>• Internet access control<br>• Data collection and exchange<br>• Information messaging<br>• Remote access/virtual private network (VPN) |
| **Data in Use** | • Workstation<br>• Server<br>• Mobile device/endpoint | • Restricted user monitoring<br>• Access/permissions<br>• Data obfuscation<br>• Export/save controls |

Implementing a DLP program involves the following steps and actions:

| Steps | Actions |
|---|---|
| **Identify** and inventory all data assets | • Inventory all structured and unstructured data<br>• Identify where and how data is stored |
| **Classify** and prioritize data according to its sensitivity and importance | • Classify protected data—personally identifiable information (PII), protected health information (PHI), or payment card information (PCI)<br>• Identify and prioritize the organization's confidential and private data |
| **Create** data usage policies | • Define who has a "need to know," and create/implement access controls<br>• Define who can create, read, update, and delete (CRUD) data<br>• Define how and under what circumstances data can be transmitted, copied, or shared |
| **Monitor** access to critical data | • Create and monitor robust logs and audit trails that document when data assets were accessed or changed<br>• Monitor data transmissions between parties within and outside the organization |
| **Educate** employees and stakeholders | • Implement data security awareness and incident response training programs |

The pervasiveness of data across a wide variety of devices, coupled with the considerable number of threats against various systems and network architectures, has resulted in a need to implement DLP in multiple ways. The most common DLP architectures are:

- **Endpoint:** Protects against data loss on devices, including computers, laptops, tablets, and cell phones. This is done through the operating system, using data encryption and device policies that monitor activities (eg, uploading, copying, printing) and interactions (eg, plugging in a USB drive, connecting a Bluetooth device).
- **Network:** Monitors data transmissions to prevent accidental data loss and keep malicious actors (eg, disgruntled employees, unauthorized users) from exfiltrating data. The monitoring is typically done through a firewall or network device that inspects network data packets and allows or blocks those packets based on defined policies.
- **Cloud:** Depending on the cloud service model, an organization may have data stored in a cloud that it does not directly control. A cloud DLP helps the organization to identify and classify cloud-based data and to implement security, access, and transmission policies. For example, DLP applications can "crawl" through data, looking for information based on user-defined settings or predefined rules based on common regulations. In addition, cloud DLP may help with the "de-identification" of data, which is important in a setting where multiple entities may share the same hardware or data storage devices.

## Implications of Data Breaches

**Representative Task (Remembering and Understanding):** Identify financial and operational implications of a data breach.

Data is highly valuable to businesses. It is also valuable to cybercriminals, competitors, and disgruntled employees who may use it for fraudulent purposes. Data breaches can affect an organization's finances, reputation, operations, valuation, and staff morale. Different data classifications have varying levels of risk. Depending on its industry, an organization may collect and store the following data:

- **Personally identifiable information:** Names, dates of birth, Social Security numbers, or contact information
- **Financial information:** Financial statements, transactions, payroll data, or bank accounts
- **Health information:** Medical records
- **Intellectual property:** Product drawings/specifications, scientific formulas, custom software, and other material that the business has developed
- **Customer/sales data:** Current and target customer lists, pricing, volume, or quotas
- **Legal information:** Merger and acquisition details, litigation, or regulatory rulings
- **Information technology/security:** Software source code, usernames and passwords, and encryption keys

Depending on the type and extent of data loss, an organization may suffer financial and operational effects. The costs for discovering and responding to a data breach include:

- **Detection and escalation:** Processes and activities that enable a company to identify and notify the proper personnel of a data breach in a timely manner. Examples include forensic and investigative activities, assessment and audit services, crisis team management, and communications to top management
- **Post-data breach response:** Processes related to communication between the company and persons affected by a data breach, as well as any related expenditures for grievance and reparation. Examples include cash payments, help desk activities, issuing new credit cards, product discounts, credit monitoring, legal expenditures, and regulatory fines
- **Notification costs:** Activities conducted to notify individuals affected by the breach. Examples include emails, letters, and/or telephone calls for notification, and communication with regulators
- **Lost business cost:** Customer loss, business disruption, and system downtime. Examples include revenue losses from system downtime, loss of customers, and diminished goodwill

## Confidential and Private Data Management

**Representative Task (Application):** Determine controls and data management practices to securely collect, process, store, transmit, and delete confidential data or data subject to privacy regulations.

Protecting confidential and private data is important to an organization's **governance, risk, and compliance (GRC)**. GRC includes assessing **risks** and designing/implementing **controls** that respond to those risks. Data security control activities include organizational and technological protections that ensure data is not created, accessed, used, or changed in an unauthorized manner. Best practice is for management to develop controls that incorporate recognized **regulations, standards,** and **frameworks.**

Because the regulations, standards, and frameworks often address the same topics, **mappings** (ie, crosswalks) show the connections between them. For example, the AICPA maps its Privacy Management Framework to the Trust Services Criteria and GDPR regulations. The Trust Services Criteria are also mapped to NIST Cybersecurity Framework (CSF), NIST 800-53, GDPR, and ISACA's Control Objectives for Information and Related Technologies (COBIT). NIST **crosswalks** its Privacy Framework to its CSF and NIST 800-53. The U.S. Department of Health and Human Services (DHHS) has mappings between HIPAA, COBIT, NIST CSF, and NIST 800-53.

Management, internal auditors, and external auditors evaluate an organization's data management practices and controls during:

- Strategic planning and resource allocation
- Risk assessment and diagnostic evaluation
- Implementation of systems, procedures, and processes
- Monitoring and reporting
- Internal audits of security, privacy, and controls
- External risk advisory consulting engagements
- External audits such as SOC 2®, SOC for Cybersecurity, and compliance examinations

**Confidential versus Private Data Management**

Managing confidential data and private data is similar, but not exactly the same. While improper handling of either may have negative consequences, the scope is different. For example, the leak of a new product diagram might give secret information to competitors, resulting in a loss of market advantage. However, a breach of patient information might expose an individual's sensitive medical history, causing harm to that patient (ie, an innocent third party). The first situation has negative consequences only for the organization. The second has negative consequences for both the affected individual and the regulated organization.

## General Data Security Controls

Organizations with confidential or private data should implement the following IT security controls:

- Management of IT asset inventory
- IT risk assessment
- Restriction and monitoring of logical access
- Restriction and monitoring of physical access
- Environmental controls
- Authentication and authorization controls
- Audit/log records
- Network controls and monitoring
- Antivirus and anti-malware software
- Vulnerability scans and penetration testing
- Segregation of duties
- Normalization and inventory of data structures
- Documentation of data flows
- Encryption in transit and at rest; protection of encryption keys
- Backups and data restores
- Change management, patch, and systems development policies
- Incident response and business continuity/disaster recovery plans

## Management of Confidential Data

- The handling of internal and external confidential data follows internal procedures, contractual terms, and regulations, where applicable
- Systems are configured to match confidential data definitions and technical specifications
- The data is classified as confidential when received or created
- The accuracy, completeness, and relevance of confidential data is protected from the point of collection to destruction
- Errors are monitored and investigated
- Only qualified employees and contractors may handle confidential data

- Third parties (eg, contractors, business partners) have appropriate contracts and service level agreements requiring controls and independent examinations
- Employees and contractors receive training related to the security of confidential information
- Confidential data is used only for its intended purpose
- Confidential data is kept for only the time necessary and based on retention policies, unless a law or regulation requires otherwise
- Confidential information is protected from being erased or destroyed during the retention period
- Procedures are in place to identify confidential data for which the retention periods are ending
- The data related to requests for deletion are captured, identified, and flagged for destruction according to policies and procedures
- Destruction policies require anonymization, redaction, and approved destruction methods

## Management of Data Subject to Privacy Regulations

As discussed earlier, controls for private data are more stringent because those controls are regulated and affect innocent third parties (eg, customers, users, patients). An organization and its management can face dire consequences for **unauthorized access or use** of personal information. Regulations for every jurisdiction in which the organization operates must be understood and strictly followed.

**Consequences** for not protecting personal data subject to privacy regulations may include:

- Mandatory regulatory audits
- Orders to stop processing data
- Fines and, in some countries, criminal prosecution
- Loss of revenue, customers, and employees
- Litigation
- Reputational damage
- Operational burdens

Two privacy regulations discussed earlier include **HIPAA** (United States) and **GDPR** (European Union). The specific rules for these regulations are not the same because they deal with different subject matters and come from different governing bodies. Other guidance related to privacy can be found in the **NIST Privacy Framework**, as well as the **Trust Services Criteria**.

The following is a summary of **privacy controls**, not specific to any one regulation:

- **Policies and procedures**
  - Privacy agreements, notices, and communications with data subjects
  - Collection, creation, use, retention, and disposal
  - Viewing, accessing, and changing of data
  - Disclosing and transmitting to external parties
  - Security controls during collection, processing, storage, and deletion
  - Preserving and confirming data quality and integrity
  - Monitoring through continuous and separate examinations
- **Governance processes**
  - Structures establishing responsibility for oversight, monitoring, and compliance
  - Privacy awareness training programs for internal employees and external contractors

  - Qualifications required for internal employees and external contractors
  - Evaluating and responding to changes in regulations
  - Reviewing contracts for consistency with privacy policies and regulations

- Data classification, risk assessment, monitoring, and incident response
  - Classifying personal information according to applicable regulations
  - Assessing risks related to unauthorized access or use for each data classification
  - Assessing risks related to vulnerabilities and cybersecurity threats
  - Establishing a formal incident response plan, including breach notifications
  - Performing ongoing and separate examinations of the design and operating effectiveness of privacy and security controls, and identifying deviations and deficiencies

**HIPAA Compliance Audit Risk Assessment Procedure**

A CPA firm was engaged to perform a HIPAA regulatory compliance audit on a retail pharmacy chain, which was a covered entity because it electronically transmitted patients' personal health information (ePHI) to health plans.

The auditor first needed to determine the controls the pharmacy put in place to collect, process, store, transmit, and delete ePHI. Risk assessment procedures helped the auditor obtain an understanding of the pharmacy's system and controls.

Prior to arriving at the audit location, the auditor sent the following Request for Information, asking the pharmacy's management to provide explanations (*inquiry audit procedure*) and/or documentation (*inspection audit procedure*) about its HIPAA compliance efforts:

| HIPAA Compliance Audit Request for Information | |
|---|---|
| **Please provide explanations and/or documentation for the following:** | **File name** |
| Prior HIPAA audit reports, evaluations, or assessments | |
| Guidance used to develop policies and procedures | |
| Entity-level risk assessments | |
| Risk assessments for systems that house ePHI, including vulnerability scans and network penetration testing | |
| Risk management policies | |
| Organizational chart | |
| Inventory of all information systems and networks, including diagrams | |
| Data groups according to the criticality and sensitivity | |

| HIPAA Compliance Audit Request for Information | |
|---|---|
| **Please provide explanations and/or documentation for the following:** | **File name** |
| Information security policies that outline security management practices and processes, such as access control, data protection, password management, acceptable use policies, workstation security, workforce/HR security, and sanction procedures | |
| Patch management policies and procedures | |
| Incident management and business continuity/disaster recovery plans | |
| Most recent disaster recovery plan tests and results | |
| Data backup and recovery procedures | |
| Physical security policies and procedures | |
| Data destruction and media reuse procedures | |
| Procedures for disposal of media and devices | |
| Role-based access, including job and level of ePHI access; log of employees based on ePHI access type | |
| Encryption and decryption policies and procedures | |
| List of software used to manage and control access to the Internet | |
| Mechanisms to ensure data integrity during transmission | |
| Policies and procedure for use of wireless networks | |
| IT monitoring systems, policies, and procedures | |
| System-generated listing for all users with access to systems housing ePHI and for new hires within last year; procedures for establishing user access for new employees | |
| Listing of contractors with access to ePHI, including copies of business associate agreements | |
| User authentication policies and procedures | |
| Termination of employee and contractor access | |
| Privacy policies and notice of privacy practices | |
| Privacy practices, including use and disclosure; right to request information; right to request protection of PHI; individual access to ePHI; denial of access to PHI; amendment of ePHI; ePHI disclosures and accounting of disclosures; and administrative requirements | |

| HIPAA Compliance Audit Request for Information | |
|---|---|
| **Please provide explanations and/or documentation for the following:** | **File name** |
| Employee background checks and confidentiality agreements | |
| Employee privacy practices/security awareness training documentation | |
| Complaint handling policies and procedures | |
| Complaints over privacy practices in the last year | |
| Employee sanction and disciplinary policies for privacy violations | |
| Mitigation policies and procedures in a breach | |
| Whistleblower anti-intimidation/anti-retaliation policies | |

***Source:*** *Centers for Medicare and Medicaid Services (CMS), Office of E-Health Standards and Services, Sample—Interview and Document Request for HIPAA Security Onsite Investigations and Compliance Reviews*

## Walkthrough Procedures: Confidentiality and Privacy

**Representative Task (Analysis):** Perform a walkthrough of an organization's procedures relevant to confidentiality and privacy (eg, IT risk management, human resources, training, and education), and compare the observed procedure with the documented policy requirement.

A **walkthrough** is a combination of audit procedures used to understand and document a **process** from start to finish. The audit procedures include tests of controls such as reperformance, inquiry, inspection, and observation. An auditor may create diagrams (ie, flowchart, Business Process Model and Notation [BPMN]) of processes during a walkthrough.

Walkthroughs are helpful to confirm the:

- Auditor's understanding of processes and procedures
- Design of controls
- Implementation of controls
- Effectiveness of controls

## HIPAA Compliance Audit Walkthrough Procedure

The pharmacy chain in the previous example provided the requested information to the auditor. The auditor reviewed the responses and documentation.

While at the pharmacy's headquarters, the auditor conducted a walkthrough to compare the pharmacy's documented employee onboarding policies with the observed process. The auditor previously determined that the stated policies aligned with the HIPAA regulations.

As part of the walkthrough, the auditor performed inquiry, inspection, and observation procedures:

- **Inquiry:** In order to obtain a further understanding of the processes related to employee onboarding, the following personnel were interviewed:
  - HIPAA compliance officer
  - Systems security manager
  - IT personnel responsible for administration and monitoring of systems that store, transmit, or access ePHI
  - Physical security manager
  - Human resources manager
  - Director of training
- **Inspection:** The following documents were inspected to further understand the processes related to onboarding and HIPAA standards:
  - Risk assessments regarding employee onboarding
  - New employee onboarding flowchart
  - New employee background check policies
  - New employee confidentiality agreements
  - New employee security awareness training materials
  - Policies and procedures for granting user access for new employees
  - Policies and procedures for monitoring user access
  - Communications about employee sanction policies and procedures
  - HIPAA training course materials
  - Human resource records
  - User access audit logs
  - HIPAA Security Rule §164.306 Security standards*
  - HIPAA Security Rule §164.308 Administrative safeguards*
  - HIPAA Security Rule §164.310 Physical safeguards*
  - HIPAA Security Rule §164.312 Technical safeguards*
  - HIPAA Privacy Rule §164.530 Administrative requirements*
- **Observation:** The following processes were observed to determine if they matched the documented policies:
  - HIPAA training course and documentation procedures
  - Establishment of new user access

**Refer to the Regulations, Standards, and Framework chapter to review the specific requirements under HIPAA.*

The administrative requirements in HIPAA Privacy Rule §164.530 mandate that every employee of a covered entity (ie, the pharmacy chain) receive security and privacy training. New employees should receive this training within a "reasonable period" after joining the pharmacy's workforce. In addition, the pharmacy must document this training in a written or electronic format. Training documentation must be kept for six years.

During the walkthrough, the auditor observed the training course presentation and found it was acceptable. According to the pharmacy's documented policies and procedures, new hires are required to attend the course within the first week of employment, prior to being granted user access to information systems. When the course was over, the auditor asked for hard copy of the sign-in sheet. The auditor then compared the attendance record with human resource records and user access logs to determine:

- How many employees are new hires?
- What were the new hires' starting dates?
- Was the training course taken within the first week?
- Were any of the new hires granted user access prior to completing the course?

The auditor found that one employee was given immediate access to the pharmacy's system upon hire and prior to taking the training course. To follow up, additional inquiries were made to determine the reason for this, and further procedures were performed to find out if it was an isolated or frequent deviation.

## SOC 2® Examination Procedures: Confidentiality and Privacy

**Representative Task (Analysis):** Detect deficiencies in the suitability of the design and deviations in the operation of controls related to a service organization's confidentiality and privacy service commitments and system requirements in a SOC 2® engagement using the Trust Services Criteria.

**SOC 2® engagements were previously discussed in the SOC chapter. It would be helpful to review that content along with this representative task, which focuses on a service auditor's procedures to obtain sufficient appropriate evidence.**

### Overview

When an organization **outsources** business functions or technology, it must have a governance and monitoring process in place to manage third-party risk. The organization may contractually require the vendor **(service organization)** to provide a **SOC 2® report** from an independent CPA. The contract or service level agreement (SLA) usually outlines the service organization's principal service commitments and system requirements, which are the promises and representations the organization makes to its customers about its services.

To recall, SOC 2® examinations provide **assurance** about security, availability, processing integrity, confidentiality, or privacy. A user entity receiving a SOC 2® report must have **sufficient knowledge** to understand and assess its contents.

**Confidentiality** refers to an organization's ability to protect confidential (ie, sensitive) information, from the time of its collection or creation to final disposal. According to the trust services criteria, information is confidential if "*the **custodian** of the information is **required to limit its access, use, and retention and restrict its disclosure** to defined parties (including those who may otherwise have authorized access within its system boundaries).*" Information may be deemed confidential through contracts or laws and regulations; it may include proprietary information, such as trade secrets or information in legal nondisclosure agreements. When included in an engagement, a CPA can examine a service organization to determine whether it achieved its principal service commitments and system requirements regarding the *confidentiality* **trust services category.**

Whereas confidentiality applies to diverse types of sensitive information, **privacy** refers only to "**personal information** that is collected, used, retained, disclosed, and disposed of." When included in an engagement, a CPA can examine a service organization to determine if it achieves its principal service commitments and system requirements regarding the *privacy* **trust services category**.

Because both confidentiality and privacy practices may stem from laws or regulations, an examination of such practices may be combined with a compliance or certification audit. In that case, the audit would be a **SOC 2®**+ engagement. The **security** trust services category would also be examined, as it is included for all SOC 2® engagements.

**Examples of Service Organizations that May Need a SOC 2® Report for Confidentiality or Privacy**

- IaaS, PaaS, and SaaS providers
- Managed IT services
- Health care technology services
- Third-party administrators
- Data centers
- Secure communication service providers
- Transaction processors
- Website and Internet service providers

## Detect Deficiencies in the Suitability of the Design of Controls

In all **SOC 2® examinations**, a service auditor must obtain evidence that the service organization's controls were suitably designed based on the **trust services criteria**. A service auditor evaluates the operating effectiveness of controls only in a type 2 examination.

The service auditor may consider controls suitably designed either **individually or in combination** with other controls. To assess the suitability of the design of controls in a SOC 2® examination, the service auditor must:

- Understand management's process for identifying risks that threaten the achievement of the service organization's principal service commitments and system requirements
- Assess the completeness and accuracy of management's risk assessment
- Perform an independent risk assessment
- Evaluate the link between the identified risks and the controls stated in management's description of its system
- Determine whether management has implemented the controls

**Procedures** to evaluate the suitability of the design of controls normally include **reperformance, inquiries, inspections, observation, and walkthroughs**. When evaluating the suitability of the design, the service auditor should use professional judgment, **comparing management's controls with the identified risks and the trust services criteria**. Risks include those identified by management as well as the service auditor. The trust services criteria serve as a **benchmark** for the **outcome of controls**.

When examining either the confidentiality or privacy trust services category, the service auditor should consider all relevant **common, supplemental**, and category-specific **additional criteria**. Both confidentiality and privacy have their own set of criteria. The two are not the same.

See the Trust Services Criteria in the appendix for the detailed common and supplemental criteria, which will be discussed further in the Security chapter. Some common and supplemental criteria have added points of focus specifically related to confidentiality and/or privacy engagements. Also see the appendix for a full list of the additional criteria specific to the confidentiality and privacy categories. The following list is a summary.

- Common Criteria
  - **CC1 Control Environment**

    *Additional Points of Focus for Privacy*

    - CC1.3 Structures, reporting lines, and authorities support compliance with legal and contractual privacy requirements.
    - CC1.5 Takes disciplinary action when an employee violates privacy policies or causes a privacy incident.
  - **CC2 Communication and Information**

    *Additional Points of Focus for Confidentiality*

    - CC2.3 Communicates objectives related to confidentiality and changes to those objectives.

    *Additional Points of Focus for Privacy*

    - CC2.2 Communicates information to improve privacy knowledge and awareness.
    - CC2.2 Communicates the process for employees to report a privacy incident.
    - CC2.3 Communicates objectives related to privacy and changes to those objectives.
    - CC2.3 Communicates incident reporting methods to user entities, subservice organizations, third parties, and data subjects.
  - **CC3 Risk Assessment**
  - **CC4 Monitoring**
  - **CC5 Control Activities**
- Supplemental Criteria
  - **CC6 Logical and Physical Access Controls**

    *Additional Points of Focus for Confidentiality*

    - CC6.1 Restricts logical access to and use of confidential information to identified purposes.

    *Additional Points of Focus for Privacy*

    - CC6.1 Restricts logical access to and use of personal information to authorized personnel who require access to fulfill the identified purpose.
  - **CC7 System Operations**

    *Additional Points of Focus for Confidentiality*

    - CC7.3 Detected security events are evaluated to determine whether they could or did result in the unauthorized disclosure or use of confidential information.
    - CC7.3 When an unauthorized disclosure or use of confidential information occurs, the affected information is identified, actions are taken to prevent recurrence, and control failures are addressed.

    *Additional Points of Focus for Privacy*

    - CC7.3 Detected security events are evaluated to determine whether they could or did result in the unauthorized disclosure or use of personal information.
    - CC7.3 When an unauthorized disclosure or use of personal information occurs, the affected information is identified, actions are taken to prevent recurrence, and control failures are addressed.

- CC7.4 Breach response procedures are defined and applied in a confirmed privacy incident.
- CC7.4 Privacy incidents that resulted in the unauthorized use or disclosure of personal information are communicated to data subjects, legal and regulatory authorities, and others as required.
- CC7.4 Individuals or organizations involved in the unauthorized use or disclosure of personal information are evaluated and sanctioned if appropriate.

- **CC8 Change Management**

  *Additional Points of Focus for Confidentiality*

  - CC8.1 Confidential information is protected during system design, development, testing, implementation, and change processes.

  *Additional Points of Focus for Privacy*

  - CC8.1 Personal information is protected during system design, development, testing, implementation, and change processes.
  - CC8.1 Privacy requirements are considered in the design of systems and processes; collection and processing of personal information is limited to only what is necessary.

- **CC9 Risk Mitigation**

  *Additional Points of Focus for Confidentiality*

  - CC9.2 Obtains confidentiality commitments from vendors and business partners.
  - CC9.2 Periodically assesses confidentiality compliance by vendors and business partners.

  *Additional Points of Focus for Privacy*

  - CC9.2 Obtains privacy commitments from vendors and business partners.
  - CC9.2 Periodically assesses privacy compliance by vendors and business partners.

- **Additional Category-Specific Criteria for Confidentiality**
  - **C1.1 Identification and Maintenance of Confidential Information**
    - Policies and procedures are in place to define, identify, and designate confidential information when it is received or created.
    - Retains confidential information for no longer than necessary.
    - Policies and procedures are in place to protect confidential information from erasure or destruction during the specified retention period.
  - **C1.2 Disposal of Confidential Information**
    - Policies and procedures are in place to identify confidential data that needs to be destroyed at the end of the retention period.
    - Policies and procedures are in place to automatically or manually destroy confidential information identified for destruction.

- **Additional Category-Specific Criteria for Privacy**
  - **P1 Notice and Communications**
    - P1.1 Provides data subjects a notice of privacy practices.
      - Privacy notices include the following information:
        - Purpose for collecting personal information
        - Choice and consent
        - Types of personal information collected
        - Methods of collection
        - Use, retention, and disposal

            - Access
            - Disclosure to third parties
            - Security
            - Quality, including data subject's responsibilities
            - Monitoring and enforcement
        - Privacy notices are provided to data subjects before personal information is collected, when there is a change in privacy practices, or when personal information is used for a new purpose.
- **P2 Choice and Consent**
    - P2.1 Communicates choices for collection, use, retention, disclosure, and disposal.
        - Data subjects are informed of choices available, and that implicit or explicit consent is required unless a law or regulation says otherwise.
        - Data subjects are informed of the consequences of denying, refusing, or withdrawing consent.
        - Consent is obtained when personal information is collected or when it is used for a new purpose.
        - Consent is obtained before personal information is transferred to or from an individual's endpoint device.
- **P3 Collection**
    - P3.1 Collection of personal information.
        - Collection is limited to only personal information that is necessary.
        - Management reviews methods of collection before they are implemented to make sure they are fair and lawful.
        - Information obtained from third parties is fair and lawful.
        - Data subjects are informed if additional information is acquired.
    - P3.2 Communicates need for consent and consequences for failure to consent.
- **P4 Use, Retention, Disposal**
    - P4.1 Limits use of personal information to intended purposes for which there is consent.
    - P4.2 Securely retains personal information for no longer than necessary.
    - P4.3 Securely disposes of personal information.
- **P5 Access**
    - P5.1 Grants data subjects the ability to access their information and provides copies.
    - P5.2 Corrects, amends, or appends personal information when requested.
- **P6 Disclosure and Notification**
    - P6.1 Disclosures to third parties are made after obtaining consent from the data subject.
    - P6.2 Creates and retains a complete, accurate, and timely record of authorized disclosures.
    - P6.3 Creates and keeps a complete, accurate, and timely record of detected or reported unauthorized disclosures (including breaches).
    - P6.4 Obtains privacy commitments from vendors and third parties with access to personal information; periodically assesses compliance.
    - P6.5 Obtains commitments from vendors and third parties with access to personal information to provide notification in event of actual or suspected unauthorized disclosure.
    - P6.6 Provides notice of breaches and incidents to data subjects, regulators, and others.
    - P6.7 Provides data subjects an accounting of the personal information held and disclosure upon request.

- **P7 Quality**
  - P7.1 Personal information is accurate, up-to-date, complete, and relevant.
- **P8 Monitoring and Enforcement**
  - P8.1 Implements a process for handling inquiries, complaints, and disputes from data subjects. Promptly makes corrections.

In a SOC 2® engagement, a deficiency in the suitability of the design of controls means that a control would not achieve the service organization's principal service commitments and system requirements because the control either does not exist or the design is flawed. The only way to correct a deficiency is to change (or add) the control. Material deficiencies result in a report modification, such as a separate paragraph.

**A Deficiency in the Suitability of the Design of a Control Exists When...**

| The control does not exist | The control exists but would not achieve objectives even if performed as designed |
|---|---|

**Detect Deficiencies in the Suitability of the Design of Controls**

The pharmacy chain in the previous examples uses a cloud-based SaaS e-prescribing application to receive prescriptions electronically from physicians. The business associate agreement signed by the SaaS provider (service organization) requires an annual SOC 2®+ examination by an independent CPA firm to provide assurance that the provider:

- Meets principal service commitments and system requirements regarding the security and privacy trust services categories and
- Follows HIPAA regulations.

The SaaS application stores personal information at a third-party data center (subservice organization). Risk assessments performed by the SaaS provider's management identified a risk that "*Data subjects and regulators will not be notified of data breaches in the manner prescribed by HIPAA regulations if they are not reported by third-party vendors.*"

A point of focus under Trust Services Criteria P6.4 states, "***Obtains Commitments to Report Unauthorized Disclosures:*** *A process exists for obtaining commitments from vendors and other third parties to report to the entity actual or suspected unauthorized disclosures of personal information.*" Further, HIPAA §164.502(e)(1) provides, "*A business associate may disclose protected health information to a business associate that is a subcontractor and may allow the subcontractor to create, receive, maintain, or transmit protected health information on its behalf, if the business associate obtains satisfactory assurances…that the subcontractor will appropriately safeguard the information.*" HIPAA §164.502(e)(2) states, "*The satisfactory assurances required by paragraph (e)(1) of this section must be documented through a written contract or other written agreement or arrangement with the business associate.*"

The service auditor performed the following procedures to understand the processes the SaaS provider uses to ensure that the third-party data center commits to reporting unauthorized disclosures of the patients' personal information:

**Inquiry:** The service auditor asked management to explain its written agreements with the data center and its vendor risk management program. The service auditor inquired whether there had been any actual or suspected breaches and, if so, whether notifications were received promptly. Last, the service auditor asked if the data center provides a SOC 2® or HIPAA compliance examination report because it is carved out of the SaaS provider's examination.

**Inspection:** The service auditor reviewed the contract between the SaaS provider and the data center. In addition, the service auditor reviewed the SaaS provider's incident response plan to figure out if it addressed breach notifications by third parties and also reviewed the data center's latest SOC 2® report.

Upon inspection, the contract between the SaaS provider and data center had the following terms modeled from the HHS Sample Business Associate Agreement:

- "Both Parties are committed to complying with all federal and state laws governing the confidentiality and privacy of health information."
- "Both Parties intend to protect the privacy and provide for the security of Protected Health Information disclosed to Data Center under this Agreement, HIPAA, and other applicable laws."
- "Data Center will annually provide SaaS Provider a SOC 2® report and HIPAA compliance report from examinations performed by independent CPAs."
- "Data Center will report to SaaS Provider in writing any use or disclosure of PHI not supported by this agreement of which it becomes aware, and Data Center agrees to report to SaaS Provider any security incident affecting Electronic PHI of SaaS Provider of which it becomes aware. Data Center agrees to report any such event within five (5) business days of becoming aware of the event."
- "Data Center will notify SaaS Provider in writing promptly upon the discovery of any Breach of Unsecured PHI no later than thirty (30) calendar days after discovery of a Breach. Data Center will reimburse SaaS Provider for any costs incurred by it in following the requirements of Subpart D of 45 CFR §164 that are imposed on SaaS Provider because of a Breach committed by Data Center."
- "Data Center will provide an accounting of all disclosures within ten (10) days after written request by SaaS provider."
- "Data Center will inform SaaS provider of any changes to its privacy practices within ten (10) days."

Upon evaluating the connection between the identified risks, the controls, and the trust services criteria, the service auditor's professional judgment was that the SaaS provider's controls were suitably designed to achieve their principal service commitments and system requirements.

## Detect Deviations in the Operating Effectiveness of Controls

In a SOC 2®, type 2 examination, the service auditor performs tests of controls to determine whether controls operated effectively to achieve the service organization's principal service commitments and system requirements throughout a period. The service auditor's tests of controls and results are included in the report.

Note that a service auditor must first determine that the control is suitably designed. By definition, a control that is not suitably designed cannot operate effectively.

**A Deviation in the Operating Effectiveness of a Control Exists When...**

| The control is suitably designed but does not operate as expected | The person performing the control does not have authority or is not competent |
|---|---|

Evaluating the operating effectiveness of controls requires the service auditor to determine whether:

- The control operated effectively and
- The evidence provided by the service organization is reliable.

Tests of controls include reperformance, inquiry, inspection, and observation. Walkthroughs may also be performed. The service auditor must use professional judgment to decide whether to test a sample or the entire population. Evidence is reliable if it is accurate, complete, precise, and detailed.

### Detect Deviations in the Operating Effectiveness of Controls

In the same examination, the SaaS provider asked the service auditor to perform a type 2 engagement. The auditor performed tests of controls related to the Trust Services Criteria P6.4 point of focus, "*Evaluates Third Party Compliance with Privacy Commitments: The entity has procedures in place to evaluate whether third parties have effective controls to meet the terms of the agreement, instructions, or requirements.*"

**Inquiry:** The service auditor asked management to explain its vendor risk management controls. Management responded that controls include obtaining independent SOC 2®, type 2 and HIPAA compliance examination reports for any vendor classified as a subservice organization. The policy is for management, the legal team, and the chief information officer (CIO) to review these reports. In addition, for vendors where there is a significant risk of sensitive data breaches, the SaaS provider requests copies of the vendor's incident response plan, security awareness training materials, and accounting of PHI disclosures.

**Inspection:** The service auditor reviewed reports from the SaaS provider's vendor risk management application to determine how much time had passed since the vendor last submitted the required documentation, as well as which SaaS personnel reviewed it and when.

The service auditor found that many of the SaaS provider's vendor records showed documentation received dates that were more than a year old. Management was asked to explain and said that the documents were received but had not been entered into the vendor risk management application yet. The service auditor performed further procedures to determine whether it was truly a data entry issue or if the documents had not been received. Upon further inspection, the service auditor found that most of the documents were being held by the legal department awaiting review. Thus, the service auditor concluded that, while the controls were suitably designed, they did not operate as expected because personnel were not following prescribed processes.

The service auditor's opinion included a separate paragraph to describe the deviation in the operating effectiveness of controls.

# ISC 8
# Incident Response

# ISC 8: Incident Response

# 8.01 Incident Response

## Events and Incidents

**Representative Task (Remembering and Understanding):** Recall the differences between security/cybersecurity events and incidents.

**Incident response** refers to an organization's policies and procedures outlining the actions that should be taken when a security or cybersecurity event or incident occurs. While an *event* and an *incident* may sound synonymous, in a security context, there is a difference between them. It is important to understand and use the proper terms because an incident might trigger required **reporting or disclosures** according to contracts or regulations, whereas an event may not.

| Event | Incident |
|---|---|
| Observable occurrence in a network or system | Event that negatively impacts an organization |

An **event** is a **singular occurrence** of a change in a system or network. The change may come from inside or outside the organization and can result from a normal operation, error (unintentional), or fraud (intentional). For example, a successful or unsuccessful login attempt would be an event. The attempt may be benign, such as an authorized user simply mistyping their password. However, it could also be indicative of a brute force attack, which is an incident.

**Incidents** are events that violate security policies, procedures, or acceptable use policies. An incident may jeopardize the data in a network or system that processes, stores, or transmits data. Unlike a mere event, an incident requires action by administrators or business personnel to protect the system. For example, if an intrusion prevention system identifies, isolates, and removes a malicious file before it can compromise any systems, the occurrence is an event. If the file executes code and gains unauthorized access to data, the occurrence is a security/cybersecurity *incident*. A **breach** is an incident involving confirmed, unauthorized access to data or disclosure of that data.

Incidents have the potential to:

- Cause damage to systems
- Result in the theft or destruction of assets
- Impair the confidentiality, integrity, or availability of information or systems
- Violate security policies, security procedures, or acceptable use policies

**Incident Examples**

- Violation of security policy
- Attempt to gain security access
- Denial of service
- Unauthorized use
- Unauthorized modification
- Loss or disclosure of confidential or private information

## Cybersecurity Insurance

**Representative Task (Remembering and Understanding):** Explain the use of insurance as a strategy for mitigating a security incident or data breach.

Security incidents and data breaches can be expensive in terms of loss to the organization, compensation to consumers, and regulatory fines. A **cybersecurity insurance** policy allows management to **transfer the risk of loss** to a third party (ie, the insurance company) in exchange for money (ie, premiums). General liability insurance does not cover cyber losses, so a cybersecurity policy must be added to an existing business policy or bought separately.

To apply for, obtain, and renew cyber insurance, organizations must first demonstrate to the insurer that they have suitable risk management policies, cybersecurity controls, and incident response plans. The underwriting process motivates management to assess the vulnerabilities of their security systems and engage in ongoing improvements to obtain an affordable policy and keep the premiums low.

Key factors considered by cybersecurity insurance providers are:

- Existing security strength of the organization (eg, systems, people, policies)
- Industry standards and regulations (eg, COSO, NIST, COBIT, ISO) used by the organization
- Risk tolerance of the organization (as communicated by management)
- Risk tolerance of the insurer
- Premium costs (what the organization will pay)
- Number of customers, types of information, and revenue
- Prior claims history
- Coverage limits and deductibles
- Geographical location and political exposure
- Frequency and depth of security audits
- Use of third party service providers

Cybersecurity insurance may cover losses to both first and third parties. **First party losses** are costs incurred directly by the organization. **Third party losses** are liabilities owed to external individuals (eg, customers) or organizations. A cybersecurity insurance company adjusts (ie, manages) the claim and may provide a legal defense (ie, attorney).

The following table describes first party and third party losses commonly covered by cybersecurity insurance policies:

| First Party Losses |
|---|
| **Business Interruption/Loss of Income** |
| • Recovery and replacement of lost or stolen data<br>• Legal counsel to understand regulatory and notification obligations<br>• Notification of affected individuals, call centers, crisis management, and public relations<br>• Forensic investigation services to confirm and identify the incident or breach<br>• Credit protection services<br>• Financial payments for ransom demands<br>• Financial payments made due to social engineering, such as phishing<br>• Financial reimbursement for payments made for fines and penalties |
| **Third Party Losses** |
| • Compensatory payments to affected individuals<br>• Claims and settlement expenses due to lawsuits, disputes, or regulatory actions |

Cybersecurity insurance **does not** cover:

- Claims made (and possibly reported) outside of policy effective dates
- Claims or defense costs related to criminal proceedings or grand jury investigations
- Loss or transfer of money or securities not related to a cyber incident or breach
- Interruptions of utility services such as electricity, gas, or water
- Claims where the organization had prior knowledge
- Business interruption related to systems owned by outsourced service providers, unless the organization also purchased dependent systems failure coverage
- Property damage and bodily injury claims
- Professional liability and employment claims

Besides coverage, insurance policies may include cybersecurity education, software, and resources to assist an organization both before and after an incident. Pre- and post-loss control and risk management solutions establish and improve cybersecurity controls and incident response processes.

| Pre-Incident Services | Post-Incident Services |
|---|---|
| • Self-assessments<br>• Training and education<br>• Legal summaries<br>• Incident response plan templates<br>• Software protections<br>• Consultations<br>• Preferred professional service vendors | • Post-incident forensic reviews<br>• Claims adjusting<br>• Legal defense<br>• Call centers, customer notification, customer credit monitoring, and identity restoration<br>• Crisis management, public relations |

## Incident Response Plans

**Representative Task (Remembering and Understanding):** Summarize contents commonly included in incident response plans (eg, roles, responsibilities, methods, steps, timelines).

As discussed in the **Availability** chapter, organizations need to assess their IT systems and make plans for multiple types of contingencies. **Incident response plans** provide a systematic method of handling **substantial non-disaster-related risks** such as application errors, problems with hardware installations, coding bugs, security and cybersecurity incidents, communication errors, data transfer errors, and other IT-specific risks.

While preventative measures may reduce the number of incidents, organizations should have a documented and tested plan in place to **act quickly** should one occur. The goals of an incident response plan are to:

| | | |
|---|---|---|
| Detect incidents | Mitigate weaknesses | File proper reports |
| Minimize loss | Restore IT services | Prevent future incidents |

A complete incident response process involves the following steps:

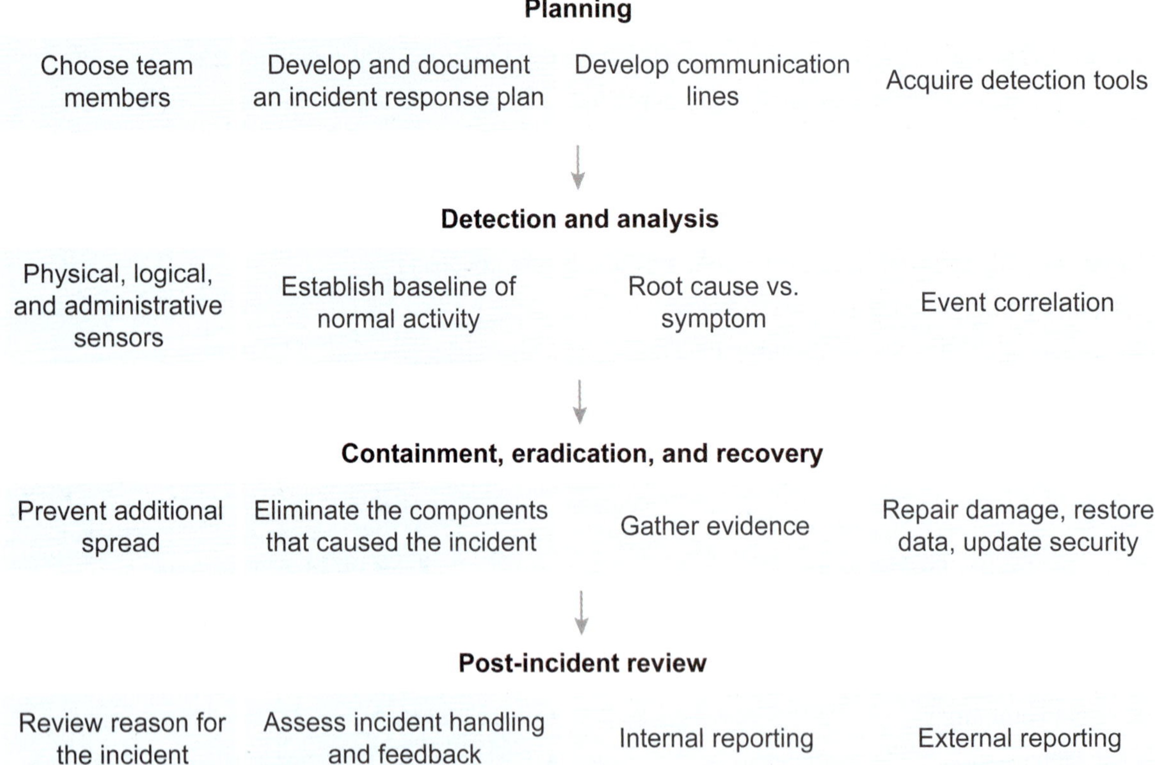

## Incident Response Plans

Incident response plans begin with a risk strategy or policy designed by senior management. The "**tone at the top**" governs the definition of an incident, the organizational structure of incident response teams, prioritization of incidents, procedures, performance measures, and reporting responsibilities.

Management selects the individuals who will make up the incident response team. Organizations may use three different staffing models to design, document, and execute incident response plans:

- **In-house/employees:** The organization conducts all incident response activities internally, with no guidance or intervention from external parties. The advantage of this model is that management controls the entire process. The primary disadvantages are cost and lack of technical ability. Incident response tools (eg, forensic analysis, secure storage) and licenses are expensive. Internal team members may need additional and ongoing training.
- **Partially outsourced:** Specific components of incident response are outsourced to an external party, typically a managed security service provider (MSSP). Outsourcing can involve forensic investigation, legal services, and communication or public relations activities. A hybrid approach offers a balance between operational control and the cost of maintaining specialized incident response systems and personnel.
- **Fully outsourced:** The organization outsources all elements of its incident response to one or more MSSPs. This may be the cheapest option, as the services may be used only on rare occasions but still must be available 24/7. Full outsourcing eliminates the need to train employees or buy/maintain incident response systems (eg, advanced intrusion detection sensors) and infrastructure (eg, firewalls). Management and IT staff would communicate with the service provider and approve plans.

The organization should use a cross-departmental approach to address all aspects of planning for and responding to incidents. Internal roles and responsibilities may include:

| Incident Response Roles and Responsibilities | |
|---|---|
| **Management** | • Establish incident response policy, budget, and staffing<br>• Responsible for efficiency and effectiveness of incident response |
| **IT Department** | • Prevention, containment, eradication, and recovery activities<br>• Coordinate response with third party service providers |
| **Legal Department** | • Review incident response plans, policies, and procedures to ensure compliance with laws and minimize liability |
| **Risk Management** | • Manage claims and lawsuits<br>• Contact insurance companies |
| **Public Affairs** | • Communicate with the media and public |
| **Human Resources** | • Coordinate internal awareness training<br>• Communicate when incident exposes employee data<br>• Oversee disciplinary actions if incident caused by an employee |
| **Physical Security/ Facilities Management** | • Provide access to facilities if needed after normal operating hours |
| **Internal Audit** | • Review systems to ensure compliance with contracts and regulatory obligations<br>• Review systems to ensure compliance with internal policy and procedures |

Once established, the team should develop and document a detailed incident response plan. The plan should include:

- Definitions of an "event" and an "incident"
- Roles and responsibilities of both internal and external members of the team
- Contact information and order of contact for team members
- Cybersecurity insurance policy information and contacts
- Third party service providers and contacts (eg, Internet service provider, cloud service provider, web hosting provider, software vendors)
- Incident response framework outlining the required steps in each phase and response times
- Containment strategies for common types of incidents
- Policies for communicating with external parties such as law enforcement and the media
- Documentation of:
  - Logging, altering, and monitoring activities
  - Incident response checklists
  - Required external reporting times and guidelines (eg, PCI DSS, HIPAA, GDPR, federal and state authorities)
  - Communications with customers (eg, letters, email, phone call scripts)
  - Incident response plan testing requirements and schedules
  - Training and incident response awareness programs
  - Post-incident review requirements

**Incident Response Plan**

### Definitions

#### Event

Any observable occurrence in a system, network, environment, process, or workflow. Events may or may not be negative.

#### Incident

A potential or actual violation of computer security policies, acceptable use policies, or standard security procedures that jeopardizes the confidentiality, integrity, or availability of IT resources or operations. Security incidents may have one or more of the following characteristics:

- Violation of a security policy
- Attempts to gain unauthorized access
- Denial of service
- Unauthorized use of IT resources
- Unauthorized modification of IT resources
- Loss or disclosure of confidential or protected information

## Contact Information

| Name | Title | Role | Phone # |
|---|---|---|---|
| | Information Security Manager | IR Manager | |
| | Chief Information Officer | CIO | |
| | IT Security Staff | IRT Member | |
| | Communications Manager | IHT Member | |
| | Legal Counsel | IHT Member | |
| | Risk Manager | IHT Member | |
| | HR Manager | IHT Member | |
| | Physical Security Manager | IHT Member | |
| | Internal Audit Manager | IHT Member | |
| | Third Party Vendors / Service Providers | External | |
| | Cybersecurity Insurance Company | External | |
| | Regulatory / Governmental Reporting Agencies | External | |

## Roles and Responsibilities

### Incident Handling Team (IHT)

- Advise and act on elements of incident response plan relevant to individual's area of expertise
- Maintain an understanding of the plan and policies
- Ensure incident response complies with contractual and regulatory requirements
- Participate in tests of the incident response plan and procedures

### Chief Information Officer (CIO)

- Obtain executive management approval for the incident response plan
- Ensure that service level agreements with service providers define incident response requirements
- Review service provider SOC 2® and other compliance examination reports
- Ensure incident response plan and policies are current and meet objectives
- Ensure the Incident Response (IR) Manager has necessary authorities
- Approve the closing of moderate and severe incidents
- Coordinate with Risk Manager to ensure that cybersecurity insurance is adequate

### Incident Response Team (IRT)

Comprised of IT Management and experienced technical staff. The role of the IRT is to respond to an incident so that containment, investigation, recovery, and reporting occur quickly. Third party vendors are part of the IRT, as necessary. The IRT is also responsible for issuing advisories and creating company-wide education or awareness programs.

### Incident Response Manager (IR Manager)

Oversees and coordinates all IRT activities, including the detection, analysis, and containment of the incident.

- Communicate incident response requirements to the CIO, IHT, and other stakeholders
- Declare when an incident has occurred
- Contact and supervise the work of the IRT
- Ensure IRT members are trained in incident handling
- Test the incident response plan at least annually
- Update the incident response plan as necessary
- Ensure incident response complies with contractual and regulatory requirements
- Ensure evidence gathering, chain of custody, and preservation
- Understand vendor service level agreements and obligations
- Maintain awareness of cybersecurity insurance policy terms
- Take corrective action when the incident response plan is not followed

### Incident Response Team Members

Technical staff who work directly on the affected information system. The IRT includes IT staff, subject matter experts (SMEs), outsourced service providers, and forensic experts.

- **Subject Matter Expert/Tech-Lead**
  - Assist the IR Manager
  - Assign duties to IRT technical staff
  - Understand incident response plan and procedures
  - Configure tools to trigger event and incident alerts
  - Analyze network traffic for signs of an incident
  - Review log files for unusual activity
  - Monitor business applications for signs of an incident
  - Collect and analyze all evidence, determine root cause, and implement rapid recovery
  - Ensure evidence gathering, chain of custody, and preservation
- **Network Personnel**
  - Analyze network traffic
  - Run tracing tools
  - Look for and record network incident evidence
  - Contact Internet service provider when needed for incident response
  - Block traffic from the intruder
- **Operating System Personnel**
  - Ensure patches are current
  - Ensure backups are run and are current
  - Examine system log and record unusual activity
- **Recorder**
  - Appointed by the IR Manager to document the incident

## Incident Response Framework

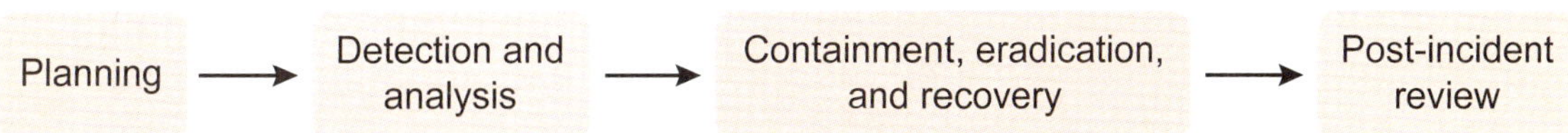


### Phase I–Planning

- Establish IHT and IRT
- Develop an incident response plan, listing procedures and workflows for the IHT and IRT
- Ensure that all parties are aware of incident response procedures and workflows
- Ensure IHT and IRT receive proper training
- Ensure the IRT has adequate tools and equipment
- Establish reporting methods, documentation, timelines, and checklists
- Maintain network and asset inventories and diagrams
- Review penetration tests and remediation efforts
- Review vulnerability reports and remediation efforts
- Establish proper authorities and system credentials
- Ensure cybersecurity insurance policy is in place and provides adequate protection

### Phase II–Detection and Analysis

#### Detection

If an employee, external party, or tool detects a suspicious event, a ticket should be submitted to the Help Desk. IT Security, Help Desk personnel, or the IRT should quickly decide whether the reported concern is an event or an incident. Incident handling should follow this plan. The following may be symptoms of an incident:

- Alert from an incident response tool
- Suspicious entries in system or network logs
- Repetitive unsuccessful login attempts within a brief time
- Unexplained new accounts or files
- Unexplained modifications or deletions of data or system file names or dates
- Denial or disruption of services
- Inability to log on to system
- System crashes
- Poor system performance
- Unauthorized changes to user permissions

#### Analysis

The IR Manager should immediately activate the IRT to investigate an identified incident. This investigation should include analyzing the category (root cause) of the incident, its scope, and its potential impact. The Recorder should begin formal documentation of the incident. Record all incidents in the Incident Handling and Assessment Log, as well as the Incident Reporting Form.

**Category:** Describe the type of attack (eg, phishing, network sniffing, man in the middle, denial of service)

**Scope:** Consider the following factors to determine the potential impact of the incident:

- Systems affected
- Confidential or protected information involved
- Entry point (eg, Internet, network, physical)
- Potential damage
- Estimated time to recover
- Resources needed to manage the incident

**Impact:** The severity of the incident will determine the IRT and IHT response. The IR Manager must review all incident reports. Functional and information impacts are categorized as follows:

| Functional Impact | Description |
|---|---|
| None | No effect on the ability to provide services to all users |
| Limited | Can still provide critical services to all users, but less efficiently |
| Moderate | Unable to provide a critical service to some users |
| Critical | Unable to provide critical services to all users |

| Information Impact | Description |
|---|---|
| None | No information was accessed, changed, or deleted |
| Integrity loss | Public or nonsensitive data was accessed, changed, or deleted |
| Proprietary breach | Internal information was accessed, changed, or deleted |
| Privacy breach | Confidential or private information was accessed, changed, or deleted |

### Phase III–Containment, Eradication, and Recovery

Containment, eradication, and recovery activities focus on regaining control, limiting damages, eliminating malicious components, and restoring normal system operations.

#### Containment

Containment focuses on regaining control and limiting damage. Predetermined strategies for common incidents are contained in the Appendix. To minimize the impact of the incident on operations, the IR Manager should collaborate with management and the IHT. Third parties, such as service providers, may need to be notified. If law enforcement involvement is necessary, all efforts should be made to preserve data and maintain a chain of custody. Actions may include:

- Stop the attacker by disabling accounts, resetting connections, changing passwords, and implementing firewalls
- Isolate compromised systems from the network
- Perform system backup
- Change passwords
- Identify critical systems that must remain operational

- Do not let the attacker know you are aware of their presence
- Collect system and network logs
- Create a memory image of the affected systems
- Take photographs of physical locations
- Review security camera footage
- Monitor communication channels
- Notify interested parties and subject matter experts

### Eradication

Eradication eliminates all the components the attacker used in the incident. Actions may include:

- Use a separate administrative tool instead of system tools
- Disable breached user accounts
- Mitigate vulnerabilities used by the attacker
- Install a clean version of affected operating systems and applications
- Apply security patches
- Disable unnecessary services
- Install/update antivirus software
- Change all account passwords
- Verify eradication is complete

### Recovery

Recovery involves restoring the system to normal operation. If possible, restore the system in a test environment. Network monitoring should continue because the attacker may return. Actions may include:

- Restore systems from a clean backup
- Replace corrupted data from a clean backup
- Restore network connections and access rules
- Communicate added security measures
- Increase monitoring activities

## Phase IV–Post-Incident Review and Reporting

Once the system has been restored, a review should be completed to improve security and incident response procedures. All internal and external reporting should be completed within required time periods.

### Review

The IRT should meet with relevant parties (management, legal, communications, risk management, vendors) to discuss the root causes of the incident and to gain an understanding of how to prevent similar recurrences. Amend incident response procedures based on lessons learned during the process. Consideration should be given to:

- Effectiveness of detection and incident response
- Whether the incident response plan and procedures were followed
- Problems with the process
- Proposed improvements to tools, systems, policies, procedures, training, and communication
- Proposed improvements to increase the speed of response

#### Documentation

The incident should be documented. Documentation retention time is based on factors such as possible legal action, regulatory compliance, and forensic analysis. Documentation may include:

- System events (logs, audit records)
- Sequence of actions taken, including dates, times, and individuals' names
- Detection method
- Root cause, attack category, and scope
- Impact assessments
- Evidence gathered
- Internal and external communications
- Justification for deviations from the incident response plan and procedures
- Recommendations for additional measures or plan changes

#### Reporting and Communication

Internal and external reporting must be completed in a timely manner based on contractual, legal, or regulatory requirements. The IR Manager, CIO, or other IHT member should manage communications with law enforcement. All information is confidential. External communications may include customers, media, regulatory agencies, service providers, forensic analysts, and the cyber insurance company.

### Plan Review and Testing

This incident response plan must be reviewed and tested at least annually. The IR Manager, IRT, IHT, and CIO must take part in training and simulated incidents at least annually.

### Appendix

- Incident response checklist
- Media statement template
- Customer letter template
- Incident response organizations
- Containment strategies
- Cybersecurity insurance policy information
- Third party service agreements information
- Regulatory information and reporting requirements

*Sources: Adapted from NIST SP 800-61 Computer Security Incident Handling Guide and the AICPA Incident Response Plan*

## Incident Management Tools

Besides traditional security controls, an organization may use dedicated tools to manage its incident response. Detecting incidents is difficult because they may come from a wide variety of systems and attack vectors. For example, incidents may originate from networks, external USB drives, email, authentication mechanisms, websites, web-based applications, or file sharing systems. Tools can monitor all systems simultaneously (full-stack observability) and provide visual analytics.

Incident management tools may be on premises or cloud based, and the processes used can be manual, automated, or a combination of the two. Manual incident intervention may involve intrusion detection systems that alert administrators. Automated tools can lock accounts or block network traffic upon detecting a threat.

Incident response tools may be purchased from private software vendors or obtained through open exchanges. Tool integration can be described in terms of the OODA loop:

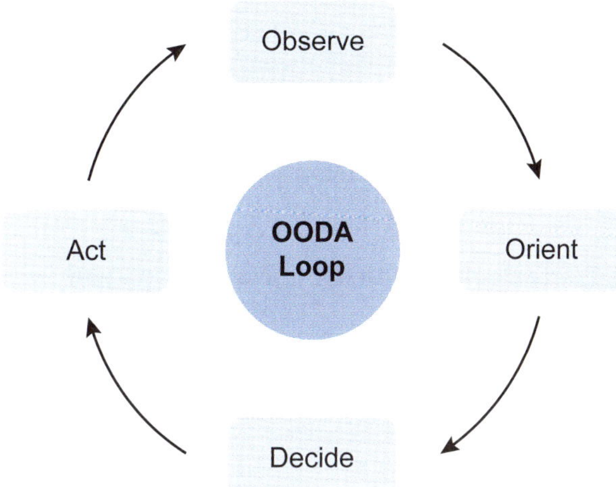


**Observe: Use Security Monitoring to Identify Events that Might Require Investigation**

**Security Information and Event Management (SIEM)**

Gathers and analyzes logs and files from systems throughout the organization, including hardware, applications, networks, and security devices (eg, firewalls, antivirus filters). Provides alerts for security incidents (eg, malware activity, log-in attempts) and any activity that conflicts with existing security rules or policies.

**Intrusion Detection System (IDS)**

Scans for attack signatures (ie, behaviors that look suspicious according to defined patterns, like an email from an unknown sender with an attachment) to identify either known attacks or suspicious activity on a server or network.

**Network Analyzers**

Examine network traffic across edge systems (eg, gateways, firewalls) and internal network devices (eg, routers, switches) to track specific instances of an activity and the protocols used. This determines which digital assets are communicating between each other on the network in order to identify suspicious communication activity or changes in volume.

**Vulnerability Scanners**

Isolate potential areas of risk, assess the attack surface (eg, a single workstation, the whole network) of the organization for known weaknesses, and provide remediation instructions. Vulnerabilities may be caused by misconfiguration, software bugs, or components that require updates.

**Availability Monitoring**

Monitors, logs, and reports on both the uptime and availability of infrastructure components (eg, network hardware, bandwidth availability) and applications (eg, SaaS, webservice apps), as well as administrative performance that is outside an acceptable threshold.

**Web Proxies**

Restrict access to websites and log which systems are accepting or initiating communication with external sources. Web proxies log remote IP addresses and are used for tracking threats (from known or suspicious IP address ranges) and forensics (ie, determining where an attack originated).

**Orient: Evaluate Organization's Assets Against Current Threat Landscape**

**Asset Inventory**

Understanding an organization's critical systems, networks, and applications helps prioritize events and incidents. An automated asset discovery and inventory program can update lists and detect changes.

**Security Research**

Security research allows an organization to understand the global threat landscapes and how they affect assets.

**Decide: Make Quick Decisions to Minimize Damage and Speed Recovery**

**Organization's Security Policies**

Policies should be in place to determine when an event is classified as an incident, based on a violation of security policies and procedures.

**Containment Strategies**

Predetermined strategies for dealing with common or known threats can provide consistency and speed in decision-making. Containment strategies can be tested prior to an incident in order to strengthen processes and educate incident response teams on dealing with an emergency.

**Act: Implement Incident Response Procedures to Contain, Eradicate, and Recover**

**Incident Response Forensic Tools**

Examine memory, databases, and networks in order to identify, preserve, and analyze incident evidence, thus creating a legal audit trail.

**System Backup and Recovery Tools**

Restore the system to a safe point prior to the incident and reduce data loss.

**Patch Management Tools**

Provide system and application updates, based on new threats, in order to close security vulnerabilities.

## Incident Response Timeline

The incident response timeline encompasses activities involving internal and external stakeholders, resources, and processes. Besides the recovery of systems and data, incident response teams need to consider and draft notices to business partners, customers and affected individuals, regulators, and consumer reporting agencies, where required by laws or contractual agreements.

Incident response timelines vary based on incident type, forensic analysis, and the organization's specific contractual and regulatory reporting requirements. However, a sample timeline might be:

**Incident Response Timeline**

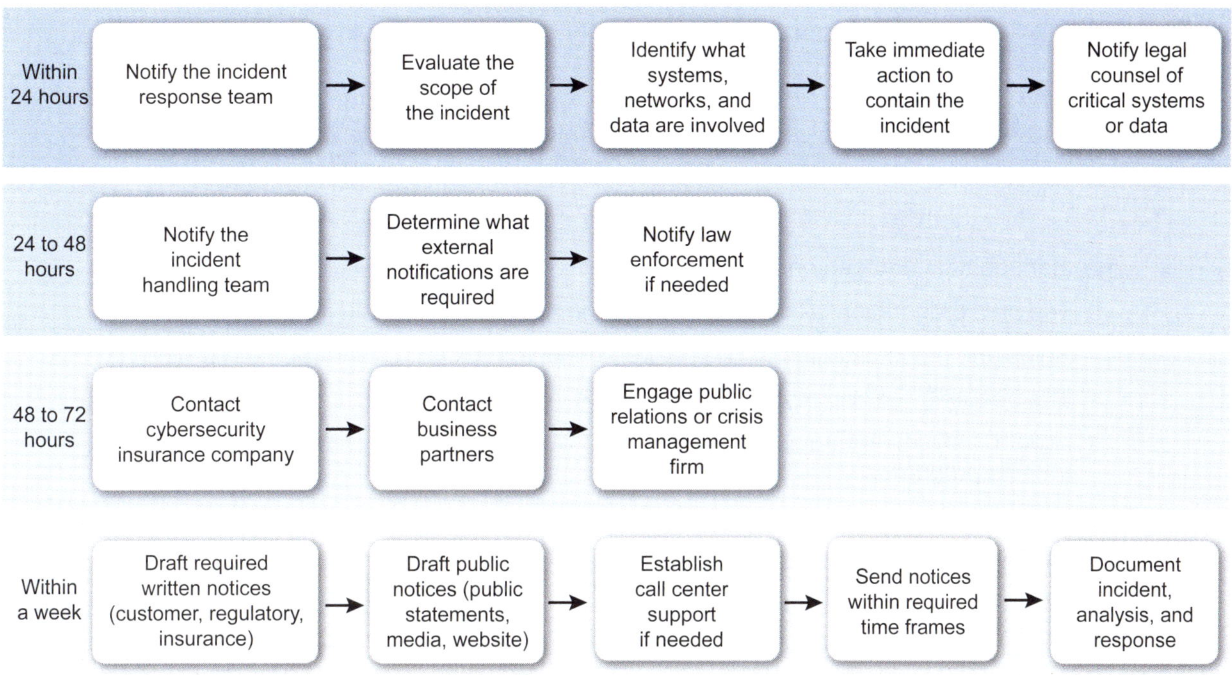


## Post-Incident Review

**Representative Task (Application):** Perform procedures to test whether the entity responded to cybersecurity incidents in accordance with the incident response plan.

After an actual incident (post-mortem), it is important to determine whether the incident response plan was followed. CPAs may perform this testing as part of an internal audit, an external risk advisory engagement, or an external attestation engagement such as a compliance, SOC 2®, or SOC for Cybersecurity examination.

Internal purposes for such testing are to understand deviations from the plan, identify weaknesses, and make suggestions for improvement. An external CPA may also perform procedures to test adherence to incident response plans during an attestation engagement required by contractual or regulatory compliance obligations.

Procedures to determine whether the entity responded in accordance with a documented incident response plan require an auditor to obtain an understanding of both the plan and the response. Procedures for a test of controls may include reperformance, inquiry, inspection, or observation. For example:

**Tests of Controls: Incident Response Plans**

**Inquiry**

Ask management and personnel questions about:

- The plan preparation process, including when it was last revised
- Roles and responsibilities of internal personnel and external vendors
- The frequency of plan review and simulated drills performed
- How employees are trained on the plan, as well as security awareness training programs
- Use of incident response tools
- Metrics such as number of incidents, average downtime, time to recover
- Control and reporting obligations to third parties (ie, customers, vendors, regulators)
- Explanations for plan deviations
- Known plan deficiencies
- Corrective actions taken in response to an incident

**Inspection**

Review the following documents:

- Incident response plan
- Annual testing documentation
- Applicable regulations and contractual obligations
- Human resource job descriptions
- Evidence and records maintained for an incident
- Internal and external communications for an incident
- Output from help desk ticketing systems and incident response tools
- Output from system backups and recovery solutions
- Documentation of availability metrics
- Employee incident response training materials and attendance records
- Notices to customers and regulators
- Call center activity reports
- Documentation of lawsuits and regulatory actions against the organization
- SOC 2® and compliance examination reports for the organization or vendors
- Law enforcement reports
- Cybersecurity insurance claims documentation

Using the above information, an auditor can compare the documented incident response plan with the actual incident response. If there are discrepancies between the documented plan and actual performance, the auditor should make additional inquiries of management or appropriate personnel. Depending on the type of engagement, the auditor may provide suggestions for plan improvements or issue an opinion that addresses adherence to the incident response plan.

Comparisons should also be made against frameworks, contracts, or regulatory requirements to decide if the plan itself is sufficient. For example, in a SOC for Cybersecurity examination, an independent auditor issues an opinion about an organization's cybersecurity risk management program, which includes incident response. In a SOC for Cybersecurity examination, the organization may choose to use the Trust Services Criteria or other designated criteria, such as from NIST; in a SOC 2® examination, only the Trust Services Criteria may be used. An organization subject to HIPAA, GDPR, or PCI DSS will also have specific requirements. Thus, auditors should consider the adequacy of the plan itself, considering all the factors affecting the organization.

# ISC

## Appendices

# Appendix A
# Trust Services Criteria

# Appendix A: Trust Services Criteria



*Source: TSP Section 100 2017 Trust Services Criteria for Security, Availability, Processing Integrity, Confidentiality, and Privacy (with Revised Points of Focus – 2022)*

# Common Criteria

## Control Environment

| | COSO Principle 1 | COSO Principle 2 | COSO Principle 3 |
|---|---|---|---|
| | Demonstrates a commitment to integrity and ethical values. | Board of directors demonstrates independence from management and exercises oversight. | Management establishes, with board oversight, structures, reporting lines, and appropriate authorities and responsibilities. |
| | CC1.1 | CC1.2 | CC1.3 |
| **Specific to COSO** | • Sets tone at top<br>• Establishes standards of conduct<br>• Evaluates adherence<br>• Addresses deviations timely | • Establishes oversight<br>• Applies relevant expertise<br>• Operates independently | • Considers all entity structures<br>• Establishes reporting lines<br>• Defines, assigns, and limits authorities and responsibilities |
| **Trust Services Modification** | • Considers contractors and vendor employees in demonstrating commitment | • Supplements board expertise through use of subcommittees and consultants | • Considers TSC in defining authorities and responsibilities<br>• Considers interactions with external parties<br>**Only when using the TSC for privacy:**<br>• Establishes structures, reporting lines, and authorities to support compliance with legal and contractual privacy requirements |

| | COSO Principle 4 | COSO Principle 5 |
|---|---|---|
| | Demonstrates a commitment to attract, develop, and retain competent individuals. | Entity holds individuals accountable for their internal control responsibilities. |
| | CC1.4 | CC1.5 |
| **Specific to COSO** | • Establishes policies and procedures<br>• Evaluates competence and addresses shortcomings<br>• Attracts, develops, and retains individuals<br>• Plans and prepares for succession | • Enforces accountability through structures, authorities, and responsibilities<br>• Establishes performance measures, incentives, and rewards<br>• Evaluates performance measures, incentives, and rewards for ongoing relevance<br>• Considers excessive pressures<br>• Evaluates performance and rewards or disciplines individuals |
| **Trust Services Modification** | • Considers individual's background<br>• Considers individual's technical competency<br>• Provides training to maintain technical competencies | **Only when using the TSC for privacy:**<br>• Takes disciplinary actions when an employee violates privacy policies or causes a privacy incident |

# Communication and Information

<table>
<tr><th></th><th>COSO Principle 13<br>Obtains, generates, and uses relevant information to support internal control.</th><th>COSO Principle 14<br>Internally communicates internal control objectives and responsibilities.</th><th>COSO Principle 15<br>Entity communicates with external parties regarding internal control matters.</th></tr>
<tr><td></td><td>CC2.1</td><td>CC2.2</td><td>CC2.3</td></tr>
<tr><td>Specific to COSO</td><td>• Identifies information requirements<br>• Captures internal and external data<br>• Processes and transforms data<br>• Maintains quality through processing</td><td>• Communicates internal control information<br>• Communicates with Board of Directors<br>• Provides whistle-blower hotlines<br>• Selects communication methods</td><td>• Communicates to external parties<br>• Enables inbound communications<br>• Communicates with Board of Directors<br>• Provides separate communication lines<br>• Selects communication methods</td></tr>
<tr><td>Trust Services Modification</td><td>• Documents data flow<br>• Documents data assets<br>• Classifies data<br>• Uses data that is complete, accurate, current, and valid<br>• Manages the location of data assets</td><td>• Communicates responsibilities<br>• Communicates reporting failures, incidents, and concerns<br>• Communicates objectives and changes<br>• Communicates information to improve security knowledge and awareness<br>Only when performing engagement at system level:<br>• Communicates information about system operation and boundaries<br>• Communicates system objectives<br>• Communicates system changes<br>Only when using the TSC for privacy:<br>• Communicates information to improve privacy knowledge and awareness<br>• Communicates incident reporting methods</td><td>Only when performing engagement at system level:<br>• Communicates information about system operation and boundaries<br>• Communicates system objectives<br>• Communicates system responsibilities<br>• Communicates reporting failures, incidents, and concerns<br>Only when using the TSC for confidentiality:<br>• Communicates confidentiality objectives and changes to external parties<br>Only when using the TSC for privacy:<br>• Communicates privacy objectives and changes to external parties<br>• Communicates incident reporting methods</td></tr>
</table>

# Risk Assessment

| | COSO Principle 6 | COSO Principle 7 | COSO Principle 8 |
|---|---|---|---|
| | Specifies objectives with sufficient clarity to identify and assess risks. | Identifies and analyzes risk as a basis for determining how to manage risk. | Entity considers potential for fraud in assessing risks. |
| | CC3.1 | CC3.2 | CC3.3 |
| **Specific to COSO** | **Operations Objectives:**<br>• Reflects management's choices<br>• Considers tolerance for risk<br>• Includes operations and financial performance goals<br>• Forms a basis for committing resources<br>**External Financial Reporting Objectives:**<br>• Complies with accounting standards<br>• Considers materiality<br>• Reflects entity activities<br>**External Nonfinancial Reporting Objectives:**<br>• Complies with external frameworks<br>• Considers required level of precision<br>• Reflects entity activities<br>**Internal Reporting Objectives:**<br>• Reflects management's choices<br>• Considers the required level of precision<br>• Reflects entity activities<br>**Compliance Objectives:**<br>• Reflects external laws and regulations<br>• Considers tolerances for risk | • Includes entity, subsidiary, division, operating unit, and functional levels<br>• Analyzes internal and external factors<br>• Involves appropriate levels of management<br>• Estimates significance of identified risks<br>• Determines how to respond to risks | • Considers various types of fraud<br>• Assesses incentives and pressures<br>• Assesses opportunities<br>• Assesses attitudes and rationalizations |
| **Trust Services Modification** | • Establishes sub-objectives for risk assessment related to trust services categories | • Identifies threats to objectives<br>• Identifies vulnerability of system components<br>• Analyzes threats and vulnerabilities from vendors, business partners, and other parties<br>• Assesses the significance of risks | • Considers risk related to IT use and access to information |

| | COSO Principle 9<br>Identifies and assesses changes that could significantly impact the system of internal control. |
|---|---|
| | CC3.4 |
| **Specific to COSO** | • Assesses changes in the external environment<br>• Assesses changes in the business model<br>• Assesses changes in leadership |
| **Trust Services Modification** | • Assesses changes in systems and technology<br>• Assesses changes in vendor and business partner relationships<br>• Assesses changes in threats and vulnerabilities |

## Monitoring Activities

| | COSO Principle 16<br>Performs ongoing and/or separate evaluations to determine if components of internal control are present and functioning. | COSO Principle 17<br>Evaluates and communicates internal control deficiencies in a timely manner to those responsible for corrective action. |
|---|---|---|
| | CC4.1 | CC4.2 |
| **Specific to COSO** | • Considers a mix of ongoing and separate evaluations<br>• Considers rate of change in business processes<br>• Establishes a baseline understanding<br>• Uses knowledgeable personnel<br>• Integrates ongoing evaluations into business processes<br>• Adjusts the scope and frequency of separate evaluations based on risk<br>• Evaluates feedback objectively | • Assesses the results of ongoing and separate evaluations<br>• Communicates deficiencies to those responsible for corrective action<br>• Monitors corrective action |
| **Trust Services Modification** | • Uses different types of ongoing and separate evaluations, including penetration testing, independent certification, and internal audits | |

# Control Activities

| | COSO Principle 10 | COSO Principle 11 | COSO Principle 12 |
|---|---|---|---|
| | Selects and develops control activities that mitigate risk to an acceptable level. | Selects and develops general control activities over technology. | Deploys control activities through policies that establish what is expected and procedures that put policies into action. |
| | CC5.1 | CC5.2 | CC5.3 |
| **Specific to COSO** | • Integrates with risk assessment<br>• Considers entity-specific factors<br>• Determines relevant business processes<br>• Evaluates a mix of manual and automated control activity types<br>• Considers at what level control activities are applied<br>• Addresses segregation of duties | • Determines dependency between use of technology in business processes and technology general controls<br>• Establishes relevant technology infrastructure control activities<br>• Establishes relevant security management process control activities<br>• Establishes relevant technology acquisition, development, and maintenance control activities | • Establishes policies and procedures to support deployment of management's directives<br>• Establishes responsibility and accountability for control activities<br>• Performs control activities in a timely manner<br>• Takes corrective action<br>• Performs control activities using competent personnel<br>• Reassesses policies and procedures |

# Supplemental Criteria

## Logical and Physical Access Controls

| | Extending COSO Principle 12 | Extending COSO Principle 12 | Extending COSO Principle 12 |
|---|---|---|---|
| | Implements logical access security software, infrastructure, and architectures over protected information assets. | Entity registers and authorizes new internal and external users. Users are removed when access is no longer authorized. | Entity authorizes, modifies, or removes access to data, software, and functions based on roles and responsibilities. |
| | CC6.1 | CC6.2 | CC6.3 |
| **Trust Services Supplement** | • Identifies, classifies, and manages the inventory of information assets<br>• Assesses new architectures<br>• Restricts logical access<br>• Identifies and authenticates users<br>• Considers network segmentation<br>• Manages points of access<br>• Restricts access to information assets<br>• Manages identification and authentication<br>• Manages credentials for infrastructure and software<br>• Uses encryption to protect data<br>• Protects cryptographic keys | • Controls access credentials to protected assets<br>• Reviews validity of access credentials<br>• Prevents use of credentials when no longer valid | • Creates or modifies access to protect information access<br>• Removes access to protected information assets<br>• Uses access control structures<br>• Reviews access roles and rules |
| **Trust Services Modification** | **Only when using the TSC for confidentiality:**<br>• Restricts access to and use of confidential information to authorized personnel<br>**Only when using the TSC for privacy:**<br>• Restricts access to and use of personal information to authorized personnel | | |

| | Extending COSO Principle 12<br>Restricts physical access to facilities and protects information assets.<br>CC6.4 | Extending COSO Principle 12<br>Discontinues logical and physical protections only after the ability to read or recover data and software is no longer required.<br>CC6.5 | Extending COSO Principle 12<br>Implements logical access security measures to protect against threats outside system boundaries.<br>CC6.6 |
|---|---|---|---|
| **Trust Services Supplement** | • Creates or modifies physical access<br>• Removes physical access<br>• Recovers physical devices<br>• Reviews physical access | • Removes data and software for disposal | • Restricts access<br>• Protects identification and authentication credentials<br>• Requires additional authentication or credentials<br>• Implements boundary protection systems |

| | Extending COSO Principle 12<br>Restricts the transmission, movement, and removal of information to authorized internal and external users.<br>CC6.7 | Extending COSO Principle 12<br>Implements controls to prevent, detect, and act upon the introduction of unauthorized or malicious software.<br>CC6.8 |
|---|---|---|
| **Trust Services Supplement** | • Restricts the ability to perform transmission<br>• Uses encryption technologies or secure communication channels to protect data<br>• Protects removal media<br>• Protects endpoint devices | • Restricts application and software installation or modification<br>• Detects unauthorized changes to software and configuration parameters<br>• Uses a defined change control process<br>• Uses antivirus and anti-malware software<br>• Scans information assets from outside the entity for malware and other unauthorized software |

# System Operations

| | Extending COSO Principle 12<br>Uses detection and monitoring procedures to identify changes to configurations and susceptibilities to newly discovered vulnerabilities.<br>CC7.1 | Extending COSO Principle 12<br>Monitors system components for anomalies that are indicative of malicious acts, natural disasters, and errors.<br>CC7.2 | Extending COSO Principle 12<br>Evaluates security incidents and takes action to prevent or address such failures.<br>CC7.3 |
|---|---|---|---|
| **Trust Services Supplement** | • Uses defined configuration standards<br>• Monitors infrastructure and software<br>• Implements change detection mechanisms<br>• Detects unknown or unauthorized components<br>• Conducts vulnerability scans | • Implements detection policies, procedures, and tools<br>• Designs detection measures<br>• Implements filters to analyze anomalies<br>• Monitors detection tools for effective operation | • Responds to security incidents<br>• Communicates and reviews detected security events<br>• Develops and implements procedures to analyze security incidents<br>**Only when using the TSC for confidentiality:**<br>• Assesses the impact on confidential information<br>• Determines if confidential information has been used or disclosed<br>**Only when using the TSC for Privacy:**<br>• Assesses the impact on personal information<br>• Determines if personal information has been used or disclosed |

| | Extending COSO Principle 12<br>Responds to security incidents by executing a defined incident response program. | Extending COSO Principle 12<br>Identifies, develops, and implements activities to recover from security incidents. |
|---|---|---|
| | CC7.4 | CC7.5 |
| **Trust Services Supplement** | • Assigns roles and responsibilities<br>• Contains and responds to security incidents<br>• Mitigates ongoing security incidents<br>• Resolves security incidents<br>• Restores operations<br>• Develops and implements communication protocols for security incidents<br>• Obtains understanding of incident and determines containment strategy<br>• Remediates identified vulnerabilities<br>• Communicates remediation activities<br>• Evaluates the effectiveness of incident response<br>• Evaluates incidents<br>**Only when using the TSC for privacy:**<br>• Applies breach response procedures<br>• Communicates unauthorized use and disclosure<br>• Applies sanctions | • Restores the affected environment<br>• Communicates information about the incident<br>• Determines the root cause of the incident<br>• Implements changes to prevent and detect recurrences<br>• Improves response and recovery procedures<br>• Implements incident recovery plan testing |

# Change Management

## Extending COSO Principle 12

Authorizes, designs, develops or acquires, configures, documents, tests, approves, and implements changes to infrastructure, data, software, and procedures.

### CC8.1

**Trust Services Supplement**

- Manages changes throughout the system life cycle
- Authorizes changes
- Designs and develops changes
- Documents changes
- Tracks system changes
- Configures software
- Tests system changes
- Approves system changes
- Deploys system changes
- Identifies and evaluates system changes
- Identifies changes in infrastructure, data, software, and procedures to remediate incidents
- Creates baseline configuration of IT technology
- Provides for changes necessary in emergency situations
- Manages patch changes

**Only when using the TSC for availability:**

- Considers system resilience

**Only when using the TSC for confidentiality:**

- Protects confidential information

**Only when using the TSC for privacy:**

- Protects personal information
- Considers privacy requirements in the design of systems and processes and limits the collection and processing of personal information to what is necessary for the identified purpose

# Risk Mitigation

| | Extending COSO Principle 12<br>Identifies, selects, and develops risk mitigation activities for risks arising from potential business disruptions. | Extending COSO Principle 12<br>Assesses and manages risks associated with vendors and business partners. |
|---|---|---|
| | CC9.1 | CC9.2 |
| **Trust Services Supplement** | • Considers mitigation of risks of business disruption<br>• Considers the use of insurance to mitigate financial impact risks | • Establishes requirements for vendor and business partner engagements<br>• Identifies vulnerabilities<br>• Assesses vendor and business partner risks<br>• Assigns responsibility and accountability for managing vendors and business partners<br>• Establishes communication protocols for vendors and business partners<br>• Establishes exception handling procedures from vendors and business partners<br>• Assesses vendor and business partner performance<br>• Implements procedures for addressing issues identified during vendor and business partner assessments<br>• Implements procedures for terminating vendor and business partner relationships<br>**Only when using the TSC for confidentiality:**<br>• Obtains confidentiality commitments from vendors and business partners<br>• Assesses compliance with confidentiality commitments of vendors and business partners<br>**Only when using the TSC for privacy:**<br>• Obtains privacy commitments from vendors and business partners<br>• Assesses compliance with privacy commitments of vendors and business partners |

# Additional Criteria

## Availability

| | A1.1 | A1.2 | A1.3 |
|---|---|---|---|
| | Maintains, monitors, and evaluates processing capacity and use of system components to manage capacity demand. | Implements, operates, approves, maintains, and monitors environmental protections, software, backup, and recovery infrastructure. | Tests recovery plan procedures supporting system recovery. |
| **Trust Services Supplement** | **Only when using the TSC for availability:**<br>• Measures current usage<br>• Forecasts capacity<br>• Makes changes based on forecasts | **Only when using the TSC for availability:**<br>• Identifies environmental threats<br>• Designs detection measures<br>• Implements and maintains environmental protection mechanisms<br>• Implements alerts to analyze anomalies<br>• Responds to environmental threats<br>• Communicates and reviews detected environmental threats<br>• Determines data requiring backup<br>• Performs data backup<br>• Addresses offsite storage<br>• Implements alternate processing infrastructure<br>• Considers data recoverability | **Only when using the TSC for availability:**<br>• Implements business continuity plan testing<br>• Tests integrity and completeness of backup data |

## Confidentiality

| | C1.1 | C1.2 |
|---|---|---|
| | Identifies and maintains confidential information. | Disposes of confidential information. |
| **Trust Services Supplement** | **Only when using the TSC for confidentiality:**<br>• Defines and identifies confidential information<br>• Retains confidential information<br>• Protects confidential information from destruction | **Only when using the TSC for confidentiality:**<br>• Identifies confidential information for destruction<br>• Destroys confidential information |

# Processing Integrity

| | PI1.1 | PI1.2 | PI1.3 |
|---|---|---|---|
| | Obtains or generates, uses, and communicates relevant, quality information related to processing. | Implements policies and procedures over system inputs, including controls over completeness and accuracy to result in products, services, and reporting. | Implements policies and procedures over system processing to result in products, services, and reporting. |
| **Trust Services Supplement** | **Only when using the TSC for processing integrity:**<br>• Identifies functional and nonfunctional information specifications<br>• Defines data necessary to support a product, service or reporting obligation | **Only when using the TSC for processing integrity:**<br>• Defines characteristics of processing inputs<br>• Evaluates processing inputs<br>• Creates and maintains records of system inputs | **Only when using the TSC for processing integrity:**<br>• Defines processing specifications<br>• Defines processing activities<br>• Detects and corrects production errors<br>• Records system processing activities<br>• Processes inputs |

| | PI1.4 | PI1.5 |
|---|---|---|
| | Implements policies and procedures to make available or deliver output completely, accurately, and timely in accordance with specifications. | Implements policies and procedures to store inputs, items for processing, and outputs completely, accurately, and timely in accordance with specifications. |
| **Trust Services Supplement** | **Only when using the TSC for processing integrity:**<br>• Protects output<br>• Distributes output only to intended parties<br>• Distributes output completely and accurately<br>• Creates and maintains records of system output activities | **Only when using the TSC for processing integrity:**<br>• Protects stored items<br>• Archives and protects system records<br>• Stores data completely and accurately<br>• Creates and maintains records of system storage activities |

# Privacy – P1.0 Notice and Communication

| | |
|---|---|
| P1.1 | Provides notice to data subjects about privacy practices. Notice is updated and communicated to data subjects in a timely manner for changes to privacy practices. |
| **Trust Services Supplement** | **Only when using the TSC for privacy:**<br>• Provides notice to data subjects regarding the collection and use of personal information<br>• Provides notices of changes to policy practices or before information is used<br>• Covers entities and activities in notice<br>• Uses clear and conspicuous language<br>• Presents current privacy notice in location easily found by data subjects<br>• Reviews privacy notice<br>• Communicates changes in privacy notice<br>• Retains prior notices |

# Privacy – P2.0 Choice and Consent

| | |
|---|---|
| P2.1 | Communicates choices available regarding the collection, use, retention, disclosure, and disposal of information of data subjects and the consequences of each choice. |
| **Trust Services Supplement** | **Only when using the TSC for privacy:**<br>• Informs data subjects about choices available to them and what consent is required<br>• Communicates consequences of denying or withdrawing consent<br>• Obtains implicit or explicit consent<br>• Documents and obtains consent for new purposes and uses<br>• Obtains explicit consent for sensitive information<br>• Obtains consent for data transfers |

# Privacy – P3.0 Collection

| | P3.1 | P3.2 |
|---|---|---|
| | Personal information is collected consistent with the entity's objectives related to privacy. | Communicates the need for explicit consent as well as the consequences of a failure to provide consent. Obtains consent prior to collection. |
| **Trust Services Supplement** | **Only when using the TSC for privacy:**<br>• Limits the collection of personal information<br>• Collects information by fair and lawful means<br>• Collections information from reliable resources<br>• Informs data subjects when additional information is acquired | **Only when using the TSC for privacy:**<br>• Informs data subjects of consequences for failure to provide consent<br>• Documents explicit consent to retain information |

# Privacy – P4.0 Use, Retention, and Disposal

| | P4.1 | P4.2 | P4.3 |
|---|---|---|---|
| | Limits the use of personal information to identified purposes. | Retains personal information consistent with objectives. | Disposes of personal information, securely and consistent with objectives. |
| **Trust Services Supplement** | **Only when using the TSC for privacy:**<br>• Uses personal information for intended purposes | **Only when using the TSC for privacy:**<br>• Retains personal information for no longer than necessary<br>• Protects personal information from erasure or destruction | **Only when using the TSC for privacy:**<br>• Captures, identifies, and flags requests for deletion<br>• Disposes of, destroys, and redacts personal information<br>• Erases or destroys personal information |

# Privacy – P5.0 Access

| | P5.1 | P5.2 |
|---|---|---|
| | Grants identified and authenticated data subjects the ability to access their stored personal information. | Corrects, amends, or appends personal information based on information provided by data subjects and communicates such information to third parties as required. |
| **Trust Services Supplement** | **Only when using the TSC for privacy:**<br>• Responds to data controller requests<br>• Authenticates data subject's identity<br>• Permits data subjects access to their personal information<br>• Provides understandable personal information within reasonable time<br>• Informs data subjects if access is denied | **Only when using the TSC for privacy:**<br>• Responds to data controller requests<br>• Communicates denial of access requests<br>• Permits data subjects to update or correct personal information<br>• Communicates denial of correction requests |

# Privacy – P6.0 Disclosure and Notification

| | P6.1 | P6.2 | P6.3 |
|---|---|---|---|
| | Discloses personal information to third parties with the prior and explicit consent of data subjects. | Creates and retains a complete, accurate, and timely record of authorized disclosures of personal information. | Creates and retains a complete, accurate, and timely record of detected or reported unauthorized disclosures (including breaches) of personal information. |
| **Trust Services Supplement** | **Only when using the TSC for privacy:**<br>• Communicates privacy policies to third parties<br>• Discloses personal information only when appropriate<br>• Discloses personal information only to appropriate third parties<br>• Discloses information to third parties for new purposes and uses only with data subject's consent | **Only when using the TSC for privacy:**<br>• Creates and retains a record of authorized disclosures | **Only when using the TSC for privacy:**<br>• Creates and retains records of detected or reported unauthorized disclosures |

| | P6.4 | P6.5 | P6.6 |
|---|---|---|---|
| | Obtains privacy commitments from vendors and other third parties who have access to personal information. Assesses compliance. | Obtains commitments from vendors and other third parties with access to personal information to notify the entity of actual or suspected unauthorized disclosures. | Provides notification of breaches and incidents to affected data subjects, regulators, and others. |
| **Trust Services Supplement** | **Only when using the TSC for privacy:**<br>• Evaluates third-party compliance with privacy commitments<br>• Remediates misuse of personal information by third-parties<br>• Obtains commitments to report unauthorized disclosures | **Only when using the TSC for privacy:**<br>• Remediates misuse of personal information by third party<br>• Reports actual or suspected unauthorized disclosures | **Only when using the TSC for privacy:**<br>• Identifies reporting requirements<br>• Provides notice of breaches or incidents |

| | P6.7 |
|---|---|
| | Provides data subjects with an accounting of personal information held and disclosure of personal information upon request. |
| **Trust Services Supplement** | **Only when using the TSC for privacy:**<br>• Responds to data controller requests<br>• Identifies types of personal information and handling process<br>• Captures, identifies, and communicates requests for information |

## Privacy – P7.0 Quality

| | Collects and maintains accurate, up-to-date, complete, and relevant personal information. |
|---|---|
| | P7.1 |
| **Trust Services Supplement** | **Only when using the TSC for privacy:**<br>• Ensures accuracy and completeness of personal information<br>• Ensures relevance of personal information |

## Privacy – P8.0 Monitoring and Enforcement

| | Implements a process for receiving, addressing, resolving, and communicating the resolution of inquiries, complaints, and disputes from data subjects. |
|---|---|
| | P8.1 |
| **Trust Services Supplement** | **Only when using the TSC for privacy:**<br>• Communicates to data subjects or data controllers<br>• Addresses inquiries, complaints, and disputes<br>• Documents and communicates dispute resolution and recourse<br>• Documents and reports compliance review results<br>• Documents and reports instances of noncompliance<br>• Performs ongoing monitoring |

# Appendix B
# SOC 1®, Type II
# Report

# Appendix B: SOC 1®, Type II Report

# Section 1 — Independent Service Auditor's Report

## Independent Service Auditor's Report

To: Management of ABC Company

*Scope*

We have examined ABC Company's ("ABC") description of its system, entitled "ABC Company Description of the System" for processing of the accounting transactions for user entities utilizing Microsoft Dynamics 365 throughout the period October 1, Year 1, to September 30, Year 2 (description), and the suitability of the design and operating effectiveness of ABC Company controls included in the description to achieve the related control objectives stated in the description, based on the criteria identified in "ABC Company Management Assertion" (assertion). The controls and control objectives included in the description are those that management of ABC Company believe are likely to be relevant to user entities' internal control over financial reporting, and the description does not include those aspects of the processing of accounting transactions for user entities that are not likely to be relevant to user entities' internal control over financial reporting.

ABC Company uses the cloud-based Microsoft Dynamics 365 accounting system and Microsoft Azure for creating and storing off-site backups. The description includes only the control objectives and related controls of ABC Company and excludes the control objectives and related controls of the subservice organizations. The description also indicates that certain control objectives specified by ABC Company can be achieved only if complementary subservice organization controls assumed in the design of ABC Company controls are suitably designed and operating effectively, along with the related controls at ABC Company. Our examination did not extend to controls of the subservice organizations, and we have not evaluated the suitability of the design or operating effectiveness of such complementary subservice organization controls.

The description indicates that certain control objectives specified in the description can be achieved only if complementary user entity controls assumed in the design of ABC Company controls are suitably designed and operating effectively, along with related controls at the service organization and the subservice organizations. Our examination did not extend to such complementary user entity controls, and we have not evaluated the suitability of the design or operating effectiveness of such complementary user entity controls.

*Service organization's responsibilities*

In section 2, ABC Company has provided an assertion about the fairness of the presentation of the description and suitability of the design and operating effectiveness of the controls to achieve the related control objectives stated in the description. ABC Company is responsible for preparing the description and its assertion, including the completeness, accuracy, and method of presentation of the description and the assertion, providing the services covered by the description, specifying the control objectives and stating them in the description, identifying the risks that threaten the achievement of the control objectives, selecting the criteria stated in the assertion, and designing, implementing, and documenting controls that are suitably designed and operating effectively to achieve the related control objectives stated in the description.

*Service auditor's responsibilities*

Our responsibility is to express an opinion on the fairness of the presentation of the description and on the suitability of the design and operating effectiveness of the controls to achieve the related control objectives stated in the description, based on our examination.

Our examination was conducted in accordance with attestation standards established by the American Institute of Certified Public Accountants. Those standards require that we plan and perform the examination to obtain reasonable assurance about whether, in all material respects, based on the criteria in management's assertion, the description is fairly presented and the controls were suitably designed and operating effectively to achieve the related control objectives stated in the description throughout the period October 1, Year 1, to September 30, Year 2. We believe that the evidence we obtained is sufficient and appropriate to provide a reasonable basis for our opinion.

An examination of a description of a service organization's system and the suitability of the design and operating effectiveness of controls involves the following:

- Performing procedures to obtain evidence about the fairness of the presentation of the description and the suitability of the design and operating effectiveness of the controls to achieve the related control objectives stated in the description, based on the criteria in management's assertion
- Assessing the risks that the description is not fairly presented and that the controls were not suitably designed or operating effectively to achieve the related control objectives stated in the description
- Testing the operating effectiveness of those controls that management considers necessary to provide reasonable assurance that the related control objectives stated in the description were achieved
- Evaluating the overall presentation of the description, suitability of the control objectives stated in the description, and suitability of the criteria specified by the service organization in its assertion

We are required to be independent and to meet other ethical responsibilities in accordance with relevant ethical requirements related to the examination engagement.

*Inherent limitations*

The description is prepared to meet the common needs of a broad range of user entities and their auditors who audit and report on user entities' financial statements and may not, therefore, include every aspect of the system that each individual user entity may consider important in its own particular environment. Because of their nature, controls at a service organization may not prevent, or detect and correct, all misstatements in processing or reporting transactions. Also, the projection to the future of any evaluation of the fairness of the presentation of the description, or conclusions about the suitability of the design or operating effectiveness of the controls to achieve the related control objectives, is subject to the risk that controls at a service organization may become ineffective.

*Description of tests of controls*

The specific controls tested and the nature, timing, and results of those tests are listed in Section 4.

*Opinion*

In our opinion, in all material respects, based on the criteria described in ABC Company's management assertion:

a. The description fairly presents the ABC Company's system for processing of the accounting transactions for user entities utilizing Microsoft Dynamics 365 that was designed and implemented throughout the period October 1, Year 1, to September 30, Year 2.
b. The controls related to the control objectives stated in the description were suitably designed to provide reasonable assurance that the control objectives would be achieved if the controls operated effectively throughout the period October 1, Year 1, to September 30, Year 2, and subservice organizations and user entities applied the complementary controls assumed in the design of ABC Company controls throughout the period October 1, Year 1, to September 30, Year 2.

c. The controls operated effectively to provide reasonable assurance that the control objectives stated in the description were achieved throughout the period October 1, Year 1, to September 30, Year 2, if complementary subservice organization controls and user entity controls assumed in the design of ABC Company controls operated effectively throughout the period October 1, Year 1, to September 30, Year 2.

*Restricted use*

This report, including the description of tests of controls and results thereof in Section 4, is intended solely for the information and use of ABC Company, user entities of ABC Company's system during some or all of the period October 1, Year 1, to September 30, Year 2, and their auditors who audit and report on such user entities' financial statements or internal control over financial reporting and have a sufficient understanding to consider it, along with other information, including information about controls implemented by user entities themselves, when assessing the risks of material misstatement of user entities' financial statements. This report is not intended to be and should not be used by anyone other than these specified parties.

*[City, State]*

*[Date of Report Issuance]*

*[Service Auditor Firm Information]*

# Section 2 — ABC Company Management Assertion

## ABC Company Management Assertion

We have prepared the description of ABC Company's ("ABC") system for processing of the accounting transactions for user entities utilizing Microsoft Dynamics 365 system entitled "ABC Company Description of the System" for processing of the user entities' transactions throughout the period October 1, Year 1, to September 30, Year 2 (description), for user entities of the system during some or all of the period October 1, Year 1, to September 30, Year 2, and their auditors who audit and report on such user entities' financial statements or internal control over financial statement reporting and have a sufficient understanding to consider it, along with other information, including information about controls implemented by the subservice organizations and user entities of the system themselves, when assessing the risks of material misstatements of user entities' financial statements.

ABC Company uses the cloud-based Microsoft Dynamics 365 accounting system and Microsoft Azure for creating and storing off-site backups. The description includes only the control objectives and related controls at ABC Company and excludes the control objectives and related controls of the subservice organizations. The description also indicates that certain control objectives specified by ABC Company can be achieved only if complementary subservice organization controls assumed in the design of ABC Company controls are suitably designed and operating effectively, along with the related controls at ABC Company. The description does not extend to controls of the subservice organization.

The description indicates that certain control objectives specified in the description can be achieved only if complementary user entity controls assumed in the design of ABC Company controls are suitably designed and operating effectively, along with related controls at the service organization. The description does not extend to controls of the user entities.

We confirm, to the best of our knowledge and belief, that:

1. The description fairly presents the processing of the accounting transactions for user entities utilizing Microsoft Dynamics 365 system during some or all of the period October 1, Year 1, to September 30, Year 2, for processing their transactions as it relates to controls that are likely to be relevant to user entities' internal control over financial reporting. The criteria we used in making this assertion were that the description:

   i. Presents how the system made available to user entities of the system was designed and implemented to process relevant user entity transactions, including the following, if applicable:

      (1) The types of services provided, including, as appropriate, the classes of transactions processed

      (2) The procedures, within both automated and manual systems, by which those services are provided, including, as appropriate, procedures by which transactions are initiated, authorized, recorded, processed, corrected as necessary, and transferred to the reports and other information prepared for user entities of the system

      (3) The information used in the performance of the procedures, including, if applicable, related accounting records, whether electronic or manual, and supporting information involved in initiating, authorizing, recording, processing, and reporting transactions; this includes the correction of incorrect information and how information is transferred to the reports and other information prepared for user entities

      (4) How the system captures and addresses significant events and conditions other than transactions

      (5) The process used to prepare reports and other information for user entities

*ABC Company*

*Report on ABC Company Description of the System and on the Suitability of Design and Operating Effectiveness of Controls for the Period October 1, Year 1, to September 30, Year 2*

(6) The services performed by a subservice organization, if any, including whether the inclusive method or the carve-out method has been used in relation to them

(7) The specified control objectives and controls designed to achieve those objectives, including, as applicable, complementary user entity controls and complementary subservice organization controls assumed in the design of the service organization's controls

(8) Other aspects of our control environment, risk assessment process, information and communications (including the related business processes), control activities, and monitoring activities that are relevant to the services provided

ii. Includes relevant details of changes to the ABC Company system during the period covered by the description

iii. Does not omit or distort information relevant to the service organization's system, while acknowledging that the description is prepared to meet the common needs of a broad range of user entities of the system and their user auditors and may not, therefore, include every aspect of the system for processing of the accounting transactions for user entities utilizing ABC Microsoft Dynamics 365 system that each individual user entity of the system and its auditor may consider important in its own particular environment

2. The controls related to the control objectives stated in the description were suitably designed and operating effectively throughout the period October 1, Year 1, through September 30, Year 2, to achieve those control objectives if the subservice organizations and user entities applied the complementary controls assumed in the design of ABC Company controls throughout the period October 1, Year 1, to September 30, Year 2. The criteria we used in making this assertion were that:

   i. The risks that threaten the achievement of the control objectives stated in the description have been identified by management of the service organization

   ii. The controls identified in the description would, if operating effectively, provide reasonable assurance that those risks would not prevent the control objectives stated in the description from being achieved

   iii. The controls were consistently applied as designed, including whether manual controls were applied by individuals who have the appropriate competence and authority

*ABC Company*

# Section 3 — ABC Company Description of the System

## Description of the System

ABC Company was formed in 1989 to provide outsourced accounting services and financial statement preparation to emerging midsize companies. Industries include manufacturing, medical practices, life sciences, automotive, construction, energy, and nonprofit.

ABC Company's full line of services includes the following:

- Accounting and general ledger setup in Dynamics 365
- Managed accounts receivable and accounts payable
- Financial statement preparation and reporting

## The Control Environment

### Control Environment

The ABC control environment is reflected in the organizational structure, hiring practices, and information and communication throughout ABC Company. The following is a description of the key controls that are an integral part of the ABC internal control environment.

### Organization and Management

Executive Management has the ultimate responsibility for overseeing the business policies of ABC Company. Executive Management meets at least once a quarter to discuss matters pertinent to ABC's operations and review financial results. The Audit Committee meets quarterly and is responsible for reviewing financial results, litigation, and significant events affecting current or future growth.

Management is responsible for activities associated with developing, maintaining, and supporting critical data-processing systems. The organization structure of this group provides for the segregation of duties among user entity provided services, accounting, human resources, IT, and computer operations.

### Human Resource Involvement

ABC's Human Resources Department provides the following services:

- HR generalist support
- Recruitment
- Employee relations
- Payroll and reporting
- Benefits

### Information and Communication Activities

ABC Company's information system obtains, captures, processes, analyzes, and reports relevant, appropriate, timely, current, and accurate user entity information. The system identifies and captures financial and nonfinancial information relating to internal and external events and activities that are relevant to managing the user entities of ABC Company. This information is communicated to individuals to allow them to carry out risk management, operations, financial reporting, compliance, and other responsibilities. ABC Company also communicates with its user entities on a routine basis via phone, letter, and email.

### Monitoring

Internal controls are continuously evaluated and monitored by department managers and owners. Executive Management monitors and reports on department functions and compliance with laws and regulations. Executive Management meets on a regular basis to review performance against plan, growth plans, initiatives, and operational issues and to communicate these to the CFO on a routine basis.

Executive Management consists of the President and Chief Operating Officer, Chief Financial Officer, Chief Information Officer, and their direct reports. They meet on a regular basis to review performance against plan, growth plans, initiatives, and operational issues. These initiatives may result in projects.

Management designates personnel to monitor selected projects during design and implementation to consider the impact on the control environment prior to implementation. Recommendations by both internal and external auditors regarding internal controls are given appropriate consideration.

### Risk Assessment

Risk management identifies risks and ranks them based on probability and severity, with those high in either or both categories receiving the most preparation and higher priority to resolve. On a monthly basis, management meets to discuss the risks that the business is facing. These include various aspects of financial and technological risks. In addition, management meets with the staff on a regular basis to discuss any outstanding issues pertaining to the functioning of the company.

### Monitoring of the Subservice Organizations

Subservice organizations are monitored as part of ABC's system for processing accounting transactions for user entities utilizing Microsoft Dynamics 365.

- Cloud-based Microsoft Dynamics 365 system: ABC uses the Microsoft Dynamics 365 cloud-based system to process accounting transactions and prepare financial statements for user entities. ABC monitors the usage of the cloud-based Microsoft Dynamics 365 system through the review of its SOC 1® Type II report as well as through the daily usage of the accounting system.
- Microsoft Azure backups: ABC monitors the usage of Azure for backups and off-site storage through the daily interaction of the systems by the IT Department by performing daily backups and monitoring the success/failure of those backups.

## Description of Processing Accounting Transactions

### User Entity Accounting Setup

The signed Agreement is obtained and reviewed by the ABC Contracts Department prior to the new client being set up on Microsoft Dynamics 365. The ABC Accounting Department sets up the new property upon receiving an email with the new client setup parameters from the Controller. The general ledger (GL) structure is agreed to with the client in writing, the setup of the GL and beginning balances are entered by the Accounting Department, and the Contracts Department verifies the completeness and accuracy of the setup in Microsoft Dynamics 365 to the agreed client GL requirements. Also, the GL and adjusting journal entries (AJE) to book the beginning balances are reviewed and approved by the ABC Controller.

### Accounts Receivable Process

Customers of the user entities are set up in Dynamics by the ABC Accounts Receivable (AR) Team upon receipt of the Signed Contract and Payment Schedule. The customer setup is reviewed for completeness and accuracy by the Controller. Copies of customer invoices are faxed or emailed to ABC Company, which then enters and posts them into the respective company account in Dynamics. When customer payments are received by the client, copies of the receipts are sent to ABC Company, which then posts the payments into the Microsoft Dynamics 365 system. Monthly AR Aging Reports are prepared for each user entity, reviewed by the ABC Controller, and emailed to the user entities' Controller.

AR write-offs are initiated by the user entity's Controller. The user entity's Controller completes the Write-Off Form and has their CFO approve the Form. The Form is then emailed to the ABC Accounting Department, which enters the write-off into Microsoft Dynamics 365 for the respective company. The ABC Controller then reviews the write-off entry with the supporting documentation and, if approved, posts the write-off. Accounts receivable reconciliations are reviewed and approved by the ABC Accounting Manager to verify that monies received were completely and accurately posted to the GL.

### Accounts Payable Process

When a new vendor is needed for a user entity in Dynamics, a New Vendor Request Form is completed by the user entity with attached supporting documentation (eg, W-9, invoice, etc.) and submitted to the ABC Payables Department. Once the form is completed with applicable supporting documents, a review is performed for completeness and accuracy by the ABC Controller. When approved, the Payables Department sets up the new vendor in Dynamics, and the Controller reviews the setup in Dynamics against the initial request to verify the completeness and accuracy of the Dynamics setup. The new vendor setup in the ABC Microsoft Dynamics 365 system can only be done by the ABC Accounting Department. The Controller does not have access to set up new vendors.

Invoices received for services incurred or goods received by the user entities are approved by the user entities' Controller or CFO and submitted to the ABC Accounting Department. Prior to issuance, prepared payments (ACH or Check) are reviewed against supporting vendor invoices for accuracy prior to release to the vendors.

The Microsoft Dynamics 365 system has automated configuration controls in place to prevent duplicate invoices or duplicate payments being made to vendors.

Monthly AP Aging Reports are prepared for each user entity, reviewed by the ABC Controller, and emailed to the user entities' Controller or CFO.

### Financial Statement Preparation and Distribution

Members of the Accounting Department are assigned to respective user entity companies within Microsoft Dynamics 365. The first step in the process is the generation of the Trial Balance for each user entity from Dynamics. The second step is that adjusting entries are made for items such as wages payable, accumulated depreciation, and prepaid office supplies. After adjusting entries have been made by the Accountant, the adjusted Trial Balance is generated. The third step is that the Accountant generates the Income Statement, Balance Sheet, Statement of Retained Earnings, and Cash Flow Statement directly from Dynamics.

Month-end checklists are completed by the Accountant for each user entity and signed off by the reviewer (either the Controller or another Accountant without access to that user entity in Dynamics) prior to issuing the financial package to the user entities.

The financial statement package is then distributed to each user entity by the 10th business day of every month via the ABC client portal.

# Description of Information Technology Controls

## Logical Access

### Windows Network and Microsoft Dynamics 365:

*Granting Access*

System access includes Windows for workstation and laptop authentication and email as well as Microsoft Dynamics 365 for accounting of user entity transactions and reporting. All new hires are granted access to Microsoft Network to log into their workstations or laptops for email. If the new hires are part of the Accounting Department and need access to Dynamics 365, the hiring manager completes the New Hire and Job Modification Form. The form outlines the new hire's name, date, title, and responsibilities as they relate to specific user entity access (XYZ Company, MNP Company, etc.) and specific roles within each company (AP, AR, view only for reporting). When the form is completed, it is emailed to IThelpdesk@ abccompany.com with an approval from the ABC Controller via email or on the request. Access is granted by IT per the request into Microsoft Dynamics 365.

*Revoking Access*

An email from HR or the department manager is sent to IThelpdesk@abccompany.com. The IT Department is responsible for disabling Windows Active Directory access and Microsoft Dynamics 365. The IT Department lead is responsible for collecting all the equipment, including the workstation or laptop. If equipment is not collected by the termination date, then IT is instructed to wipe the workstation or laptop and disable the access to the machine prior to or on the termination date.

### IT Administrators:

Administrator access privileges to the Windows network environment and Microsoft Dynamics 365 are granted to Windows Domain Administrators only. Administrators do not have access to enter data, modify data, or process data in Dynamics 365; they only have access to set up access permissions for users.

System access roles and privileges to Windows and Microsoft Dynamics 365 are reviewed semiannually by the Controller or CFO. Any necessary changes as a result of these reviews are sent to the IT Department to modify the access permissions.

### Unique User IDs:

There are unique IDs for Windows and Microsoft Dynamics 365. The unique user ID is the first initial and last name.

### System Password Requirements:

*Windows:* The Windows local network passwords, including Administrator passwords, are changed every 90 days, maintain a password history of 10 passwords, require a minimum of eight characters, and have complexity enabled, which means each password should include one capital letter, one lower case letter, and one special character.

*Microsoft Dynamics 365:* The Microsoft Dynamics 365 password requirements, including Administrator passwords, require a minimum of eight characters, have complexity enabled, and must contain one upper case letter and one number. The passwords are enforced to be changed every 90 days.

## Backups

**Backup Schedule and Backup Results:**

Microsoft Dynamics 365 data are backed up daily to a separate virtual server located in the cloud at Microsoft Azure. The daily backup results are reviewed by the IT Department for success and failure. Any backup processing problems are investigated and resolved within 24–48 hours. If the backup failure cannot be resolved within 48 hours, then the issue is escalated to the CIO. Any changes to the backup schedule are approved by the CIO via email.

## Control Objectives and Related Controls

ABC Company Organization has specified the control objectives and identified the controls that are designed to achieve the related control objectives. The specified control objectives, related controls, and complementary user entity controls are presented in Section 4, "Description of ABC Company Control Objectives and Related Controls, and Independent Service Auditor's Description of Tests of Controls and Results" and are an integral component of ABC Company's description of its system.

## Complementary Subservice Organization Controls

The Company's controls related to the system for processing of the accounting transactions for user entities utilizing the ABC Microsoft Dynamics 365 system cover only a portion of the overall internal control for each user entity of the Company. It is not feasible for the control objectives related to the system for processing of the accounting transactions for opt-in clients, utilizing either user entities' accounting system or the ABC Microsoft Dynamics 365 accounting system and the supporting general computer controls, to be achieved solely by Company. Therefore, each user entity's internal control over financial reporting must be evaluated in conjunction with the Company's controls and the related tests and results detailed in Section 4 of this report, taking into account the related complementary subservice organization controls expected to be implemented at the subservice organizations as described below.

| | Complementary Subservice Organization Controls | Related Control Objectives (CO) |
|---|---|---|
| | **Microsoft Dynamics 365: ABC utilizes the cloud-based Microsoft Dynamics 365 accounting system for processing accounting transactions for user entities.** | |
| 1 | Microsoft Dynamics 365 is responsible for ensuring that any changes to the application are evaluated, tested in a separate test environment, and approved prior to being moved into production. | CO 4 |
| | **Microsoft Azure: ABC utilizes Azure for creating and storing off-site Windows backups.** | |
| 1 | Microsoft Azure is responsible for securely storing ABC daily Microsoft Dynamics 365 data backups. | CO 6 |

## Complementary User Entity Controls

ABC Company controls related to the system for processing of the accounting transactions for user entities utilizing the ABC Microsoft Dynamics system cover only a portion of overall internal control for each user entity of the Company. It is not feasible for the control objectives related to the System to be achieved solely by the Company. Therefore, each user entity's internal control over financial reporting should be evaluated in conjunction with ABC Company's controls and the related tests and results detailed in Section 4 of this report, considering the related complementary user entity controls identified under each control objective, where applicable. For user entities to rely on the controls reported on herein, each user entity must evaluate its own internal control to determine whether the identified complementary user controls have been implemented and are operating effectively.

*ABC Company*

*Report on ABC Company Description of the System and on the Suitability of Design and Operating Effectiveness of Controls for the Period October 1, Year 1, to September 30, Year 2*

# Section 4 — Description of ABC Company Control Objectives and Related Controls, and Independent Service Auditor's Description of Tests of Controls and Results

This report, when combined with an understanding of the controls at user entities, is intended to assist auditors in planning the audit of user entities' financial statements or user entities' internal control over financial reporting and in assessing control risk for assertions in user entities' financial statements that may be affected by controls at ABC Company. Our examination was limited to the control objectives and related controls specified by ABC Company in Sections 3, "ABC Company Description of the System," and 4 of the report, and did not extend to controls in effect at user entities.

It is the responsibility of each user entity and its independent auditor to evaluate this information in conjunction with the evaluation of internal control over financial reporting at the user entity in order to assess total internal control. If internal control is not effective at user entities, ABC Company's controls may not compensate for such weaknesses.

ABC Company's internal control represents the collective effect of various factors on establishing or enhancing the effectiveness of the controls specified by ABC Company. In planning the nature, timing, and extent of our testing of the controls to achieve the control objectives specified by ABC Company, we considered aspects of ABC Company's control environment, risk assessment process, monitoring activities, and information and communications.

The following table clarifies certain terms used in this section to describe the nature of the tests performed:

| Test | Description |
|---|---|
| **Inquiry** | Inquiry of appropriate personnel and corroboration with management |
| **Observation** | Observation of the application, performance, or existence of the control |
| **Inspection** | Inspection of documents and reports indicating performance of the control |
| **Reperformance** | Reperformance of the control |

When using information produced by ABC Company, which includes, but is not limited to, management's reports used in the performance of tools and reports generated to facilitate testing of control populations, the audit firm evaluated whether the information was sufficiently reliable for our purposes, including, as necessary, obtaining evidence about the completeness and accuracy of the information and evaluating whether the information was sufficiently precise and detailed for our purposes.

*ABC Company*

*Report on ABC Company Description of the System and on the Suitability of Design and Operating Effectiveness of Controls for the Period October 1, Year 1, to September 30, Year 2*

| Controls Specified by ABC Company | Tests of Controls | Results of Tests |
|---|---|---|
| **Control Objective 1: User Entity Accounting Setup**<br>Controls provide reasonable assurance that new user entities are set up in the Microsoft Dynamics 365 system accurately and completely. | | |
| 1.1 The ABC Accounting Department sets up the new user entity in Dynamics 365 upon receiving an email with the new client setup parameters and the signed Agreement from the Controller. | For a selection of new user entity setups, inspected a sample of setups in Dynamics 365 to determine whether the setups were performed by the ABC Accounting Department per the signed Agreement and the client setup parameters as sent from Controller. | No exceptions noted. |
| 1.2 The general ledger structure is agreed to with the client in writing, the setup of the GL and beginning balances are entered by the Accounting Department, and the Contracts Department verifies the completeness and accuracy of the setup in Microsoft Dynamics 365 to the agreed client GL requirements. | For a selection of new user entity setups, inspected a sample in Dynamics 365 to determine whether the general ledger structure as agreed to with the client in writing, the setup of the GL and beginning balances were entered by the Accounting Department, and the Contracts Department verified the completeness and accuracy of the setup in Microsoft Dynamics 365 to the agreed client GL requirements. | No exceptions noted. |
| 1.3 The general ledger setup and adjusting journal entries (AJE) to book the beginning balances are reviewed and approved by the ABC Controller for completeness and accuracy. | For a selection of new user entity setups, inspected a sample of setups in Dynamic 365 to determine whether the general ledger setup and adjusting journal entries (AJE) to book the beginning balances were reviewed and approved by the ABC Controller for completeness and accuracy. | No exceptions noted. |

**Complementary User Entity Controls**

None

*ABC Company*

*Report on ABC Company Description of the System and on the Suitability of Design and Operating Effectiveness of Controls for the Period October 1, Year 1, to September 30, Year 2*

| Controls Specified by ABC Company | Tests of Controls | Results of Tests |
|---|---|---|
| **Control Objective 2: Accounts Receivable Process**<br>Controls provide reasonable assurance that accounts receivable payments received are posted accurately and completely. | | |
| 2.1 Customers of the user entities are set up in Dynamics by the ABC Accounts Receivable Team upon receipt of the Signed Contract and Payment Schedule. The setup is reviewed for completeness and accuracy by the Controller. | For a selection of new receivable setups for user entities, inspected a sample of new customer setups to determine whether the customers of the user entities are set up in Dynamics by the ABC AR Team upon receipt of the Signed Contract and Payment Schedule and the setup was reviewed for completeness and accuracy by the Controller. | No exceptions noted. |
| 2.2 Copies of these customer invoices are faxed or emailed to ABC Company, which then enters and posts them into the respective user entity account in Dynamics by the ABC Accounting Department. Another member of the ABC Accounting Department reviews the setup against the invoices to verify it was set up completely and accurately. | For a selection of receivable invoices, inspected a sample of customer invoices to determine whether the customer invoices were faxed or emailed to ABC Company, entered, and posted into the respective user entity account in Dynamics by the ABC Accounting Department and another member of the ABC Accounting Department reviewed the setup against the invoices to verify it was set up completely and accurately. | No exceptions noted. |
| 2.3 When customer payments are received by the client, copies of the receipts are sent to ABC Company, which then posts the payments into the Microsoft Dynamics 365 system. Another member of the ABC Accounting Department reviews the invoice posting to verify that all invoices were posted completely and accurately. | For a selection of receivable invoices, inspected a sample of customer payments for user entities to determine whether the copies of the receipts were sent to ABC Company, which then posted the payments into the Microsoft Dynamics 365 system, and another member of the ABC Accounting Department reviewed the invoice postings to verify that all invoices were posted completely and accurately. | No exceptions noted. |
| 2.4 Monthly AR Aging Reports are prepared for each user entity, reviewed by the ABC Controller, and emailed to the user entities' Controller. | For a selection of months and user entities, inspected a sample of monthly AR Aging Reports to determine whether they were prepared for each user entity, reviewed by the ABC Controller, and emailed to the user entities' Controller. | No exceptions noted. |

| Controls Specified by ABC Company | Tests of Controls | Results of Tests |
| --- | --- | --- |
| 2.5 The ABC Controller reviews the write-off entries with the supporting documentation and, if approved, posts the write-off in Dynamics 365. | For a selection of write-offs, inspected a sample of monthly write-offs by user entity to determine whether the ABC Controller reviewed the write-off entries with the supporting documentation and, if approved, posted the write-off in Dynamics 365. | No exceptions noted. |
| 2.6 Accounts receivable reconciliations are reviewed monthly and approved by the ABC Accounting Manager to verify that monies received were completely and accurately posted to the GL. | For a selection of user entities, inspected a sample of monthly accounts receivable reconciliation to determine whether they were reviewed and approved by the ABC Accounting Manager to verify that monies received were completely and accurately posted to the GL. | No exceptions noted. |

**Complementary User Entity Controls**

1. The user entities are responsible for providing the services or goods to their customers as well as preparing invoices received in their respective systems.
2. The user entities are responsible for collections of all customer accounts.
3. The user entities are responsible for approving all write-off amounts prior to sending to ABC Company.
4. The user entities are responsible for submitting receivable invoices to ABC Company timely.

| Controls Specified by ABC Company | Tests of Controls | Results of Tests |
| --- | --- | --- |
| **Control Objective 3: Accounts Payable Process**<br>Controls provide reasonable assurance that accounts payables for user entity customers are authorized and updated completely and accurately into Microsoft Dynamics 365. | | |
| 3.1 A New Vendor Request Form is completed by the user entity with attached supporting documentation (W-9, invoice, etc.) and submitted to the ABC Payables Department. Once approved, the Payables Department sets up the new vendor in Dynamics, and the Controller reviews the setup in Dynamics against the initial request to verify the completeness and accuracy of the Dynamics setup. | For a selection of new vendor setups, inspected a sample of completed New Vendor Request Forms with supporting documentation to determine whether the Payables Department set up the new vendor in Dynamics per the request and the Controller reviewed the setup in Dynamics against the initial request to verify the completeness and accuracy of the Dynamics setup. | No exceptions noted. |

*ABC Company*

*Report on ABC Company Description of the System and on the Suitability of Design and Operating Effectiveness of Controls for the Period October 1, Year 1, to September 30, Year 2*

| Controls Specified by ABC Company | Tests of Controls | Results of Tests |
|---|---|---|
| 3.2 Access to set up new vendors is restricted to the Payables Department. | Inspected the permissions in Dynamics 365 to determine whether access to set up new vendors is restricted to the Payables Department. | No exceptions noted. |
| 3.3 Invoices received for services incurred or goods received by the user entities are approved by the user entities' Controller or CFO and submitted to the ABC Accounting Department. | For a selection of invoices for services incurred or goods received by the user entities, inspected a sample of invoices to determine whether they were approved by the user entities' Controller or CFO and submitted to the ABC Accounting Department. | No exceptions noted. |
| 3.4 Prior to issuance, prepared payments (ACH or Check) are reviewed against supporting vendor invoices for accuracy prior to release to the vendors. | For a selection of payments for vendor invoices, inspected a sample of prepared ACH or Check payments to determine whether the payments were reviewed against supporting vendor invoices for accuracy prior to release to the vendors. | No exceptions noted. |
| 3.5 The Microsoft Dynamics 365 system has automated configuration controls in place to prevent duplicate invoices or duplicate payments being made to vendors. | Inspected the Microsoft Dynamics 365 configurations for payables to determine whether automated configuration controls are in place to prevent duplicate invoices or duplicate payments being made to vendors. | No exceptions noted. |
| 3.6 Monthly AP Aging Reports are prepared for each user entity, reviewed by the ABC Controller, and emailed to the user entities' Controller or CFO. | For a selection of user entities, inspected a sample of monthly AP Aging Reports to determine whether the Reports were reviewed by the ABC Controller and emailed to the user entities' Controller or CFO. | No exceptions noted. |

**Complementary User Entity Controls**

1. The user entities are responsible for notifying the ABC Company timely of any new vendors prior to submitting invoices for payment.
2. The user entities are responsible for approving invoices received for services incurred or goods received by the user entities' Controller or CFO.

*ABC Company*

*Report on ABC Company Description of the System and on the Suitability of Design and Operating Effectiveness of Controls for the Period October 1, Year 1, to September 30, Year 2*

| Controls Specified by ABC Company | Tests of Controls | Results of Tests |
|---|---|---|
| **Control Objective 4: Financial Statement Preparation and Distribution**<br>Controls provide reasonable assurance that preparation of monthly financial statements are accurate, complete, and distributed timely. | | |
| 4.1 On a monthly basis, the Accounting Department generates the Trial Balance for each user entity, makes adjusting journal entries, and generates the Adjusted Trial Balance. | For a selection of months, inspected a sample of Adjusted Trial Balance Reports for user entities to determine whether the Accounting Department generated the Trial Balance for each user entity and made adjusting journal entries. | No exceptions noted. |
| 4.2 On a monthly basis, the Accounting Department generates the Income Statement, Balance Sheet, Statement of Retained Earnings, and Cash Flow Statement directly from Dynamics. A review of the reports is performed by the ABC Controller on a month-end checklist. | For a selection of months, inspected a sample of user entities to determine whether the Accounting Department generated the Income Statement, Balance Sheet, Statement of Retained Earnings, and Cash Flow Statement directly from Dynamics as well as inspected the completed month-end checklist to verify that the review of the reports by the ABC Controller was performed. | No exceptions noted. |
| 4.3 Month-end checklists are completed by the Accountant for each user entity and signed off by the reviewer prior to issuing the financial package to the user entities. | For a selection of months, inspected a sample of user entities to determine whether month-end checklists are completed by the Accountant for each user entity and signed off by the reviewer prior to issuing the financial package to the user entities. | No exceptions noted. |
| 4.4 The financial statement package is then distributed to each user entity by the 10th business day of every month via the ABC client portal. | For a selection of months, inspected a sample of user entities to determine whether the financial statement package was distributed to each user entity by the 10th business day of every month via the ABC client portal. | No exceptions noted. |

**Complementary User Entity Controls**

The user entities are responsible for providing supporting documentation to ABC for journal entries requested by the user entities for ABC to make in the Microsoft Dynamics 365 system.

*ABC Company*

*Report on ABC Company Description of the System and on the Suitability of Design and Operating Effectiveness of Controls for the Period October 1, Year 1, to September 30, Year 2*

| Controls Specified by ABC Company | Tests of Controls | Results of Tests |
|---|---|---|
| **Control Objective 5: Logical Access**<br>Controls provide reasonable assurance that logical access to the Windows Network and Microsoft Dynamics 365 is restricted to authorized users. | | |
| 5.1 Access privileges to the Windows network and Microsoft Dynamics 365 are granted based on business need as directed by HR or the hiring manager and granted by IT. | For a selection of new hires or job role changes, inspected a sample to determine whether user access was granted to the Windows network environment and Microsoft Dynamics 365 based on business need as directed by HR or the hiring manager and granted or revoked by IT. | No exceptions noted. |
| 5.2 Access privileges to the Windows network and Microsoft Dynamics 365 are disabled as directed by HR or the hiring manager and revoked by IT upon notification of the termination. | For a selection of terminations, inspected a sample to determine whether user access was revoked from the Windows network environment and Microsoft Dynamics 365 by IT upon notification of the termination. | No exceptions noted. |
| 5.3 Administrator access privileges to the Windows network environment and Microsoft Dynamics 365 are granted to Windows Domain Administrators only. | For a selection of Windows Domain Administrators, inspected a sample to determine whether Administrator access privileges to the Windows network environment and Microsoft Dynamics 365 were granted to Windows Domain Administrators only. | No exceptions noted. |
| 5.4 Users are assigned a unique ID for the Windows network and Microsoft Dynamics 365. | Inspected the user listing for the Windows network and Microsoft Dynamics 365 to determine whether all users are assigned a unique ID. | No exceptions noted. |
| 5.5 Passwords for the Windows network are a minimum of eight characters with complexity enabled and a forced change of passwords every 90 days. | Inspected the password configuration settings to determine whether the passwords for the Windows network are a minimum of eight characters in length with complexity enabled and changed every 90 days. | No exceptions noted. |
| 5.6 Passwords for Microsoft Dynamics 365 are a minimum of eight characters with complexity enabled and a forced change of passwords every 90 days. | Inspected the password configuration settings to determine whether the passwords for Microsoft Dynamics 365 are a minimum of eight characters in length with complexity enabled and changed every 90 days. | No exceptions noted. |

| Controls Specified by ABC Company | Tests of Controls | Results of Tests |
|---|---|---|
| 5.7 System access roles and privileges to the Windows network and Microsoft Dynamics 365 are reviewed semiannually by the Controller or CFO. Any necessary changes because of these reviews are sent to the IT Department to modify the access permissions. | Inspected a sample of semiannual access permission reviews to determine whether the Windows network and Microsoft Dynamics 365 are reviewed semiannually by the Controller or CFO and any changes because of the review are sent to the IT Department to modify the access permissions. | No exceptions noted. |

**Complementary User Entity Controls**

None

| Controls Specified by ABC Company | Tests of Controls | Results of Tests |
|---|---|---|
| **Control Objective 6: Backups**<br>Controls provide reasonable assurance that Microsoft Dynamics 365 data files are backed up. | | |
| 6.1 Microsoft Dynamics 365 data are backed up daily to a separate virtual server located in the cloud at Microsoft Azure. The daily backup results are reviewed by the IT Department for success and failure. | For a sample of days, inspected the backup results to determine whether the Microsoft Dynamics 365 data were backed up daily to a separate virtual server located in the cloud at Microsoft Azure and the daily backup results were reviewed by the IT Department for success and failure. | No exceptions noted. |
| 6.2 Any backup processing problems are investigated and resolved within 24–48 hours. If the backup failure cannot be resolved within 48 hours, then the issue is escalated to the CIO. | For a sample of backup failures for Microsoft Dynamics 365 data, inspected the resolutions to determine whether the backup processing problems were investigated and resolved within 24–48 hours; and if the backup failure could not be resolved within 48 hours, then the issue was escalated to the CIO. | No exceptions noted. |

**Complementary User Entity Controls**

None

# Appendix C
# SOC 2®, Type II Report

# Appendix C: SOC 2®, Type II Report

# Section 1 — Assertion of Service Organization's Management

## Assertion of ABC Company's Management

We have prepared the accompanying description of ABC Company's Network Operations Management system, titled "ABC Company's Description of Its System," throughout the period October 1, Year 1, to September 30, Year 2 (description), based on the criteria for a description of a service organization's system in DC Section 200, *2018 Description Criteria for a Description of a Service Organization's System in a SOC 2® Report* (AICPA, *Description Criteria*) (description criteria). The description is intended to provide report users with information about the Network Operations Management system that may be useful when assessing the risks arising from interactions with ABC Company's system, particularly information about system controls that ABC Company has designed, implemented, and operated to provide reasonable assurance that its service commitments and system requirements were achieved based on the trust services criteria relevant to Security and Confidentiality (applicable trust services criteria) set forth in TSP Section 100, *2017 Trust Services Criteria for Security, Availability, Processing Integrity, Confidentiality or Privacy* (AICPA, *Trust Services Criteria*).

ABC Company uses the following subservice organization: Amazon Web Services (AWS) for encryption, cloud storage, and retrieval of backups for restoring systems and data. The description indicates that complementary subservice organization controls that are suitably designed and operating effectively are necessary, along with controls at ABC Company, to achieve ABC Company's service commitments and system requirements based on the applicable trust services criteria. The description presents ABC Company's controls, the applicable trust services criteria, and the types of complementary subservice organization controls assumed in the design of ABC Company's controls. The description does not disclose the actual controls at the subservice organization.

The description indicates that complementary user entity controls that are suitably designed and operating effectively are necessary, along with controls at ABC Company, to achieve ABC Company's service commitments and system requirements based on the applicable trust services criteria. The description presents ABC Company's controls, the applicable trust services criteria, and the complementary user entity controls assumed in the design of ABC Company's controls.

We confirm, to the best of our knowledge and belief, that:

1. The description presents ABC Company's system that was designed and implemented throughout the period October 1, Year 1, to September 30, Year 2, in accordance with the description criteria.
2. The controls stated in the description were suitably designed throughout the period October 1, Year 1, to September 30, Year 2, to provide reasonable assurance that ABC Company's service commitments and system requirements would be achieved based on the applicable trust services criteria, if its controls operated effectively throughout the period and if the subservice organization and user entities applied the complementary controls assumed in the design of ABC Company's controls through that period.
3. The controls stated in the description operated effectively throughout the period October 1, Year 1, to September 30, Year 2, to provide reasonable assurance that ABC Company's service commitments and system requirements were achieved based on the applicable trust services criteria, if the complementary subservice organization controls and complementary user entity controls assumed in the design of ABC Company's controls operated effectively throughout that period.

*ABC Company*

# Section 2 — Independent Service Auditor's Report

## Independent Service Auditor's Report

To: Management of ABC Company

*Scope*

We have examined ABC Company's accompanying description of its Network Operations Management system, titled "ABC Company's Description of Its System" throughout the period October 1, Year 1, to September 30, Year 2 (description), based on the criteria for a description of a service organization's system in DC Section 200, *2018 Description Criteria for a Description of a Service Organization in a SOC 2® Report* (AICPA, *Description Criteria*) (description criteria) and the suitability of the design and operating effectiveness of ABC Company's controls, stated in the description throughout the period October 1, Year 1, to September 30, Year 2, to provide reasonable assurance that ABC Company's service commitments and system requirements were achieved based on the trust service criteria relevant to Security and Confidentiality (applicable trust services criteria) set forth in TSP Section 100, *2017 Trust Services Criteria for Security, Availability, Processing Integrity, Confidentiality or Privacy* (AICPA, *Trust Services Criteria*).

ABC Company uses the following subservice organization: Amazon Web Services (AWS) for encryption, cloud storage, and retrieval of backups for restoring systems and data. The description indicates that complementary subservice organization controls that are suitably designed and operating effectively are necessary, along with controls at ABC Company, to achieve ABC Company's service commitments and system requirements based on the applicable trust services criteria. The description presents ABC Company's controls, the applicable trust services criteria, and the types of complementary subservice organization controls assumed in the design of ABC Company's controls. The description does not disclose the actual controls at the subservice organization. Our examination did not include the services provided by the subservice organization, and we have not evaluated the suitability of the design or operating effectiveness of such complementary subservice organization controls.

The description indicates that complementary user entity controls that are suitably designed and operating effectively are necessary, along with controls at ABC Company, to achieve ABC Company's service commitments and system requirements based on the applicable trust services criteria. The description presents ABC Company's controls, the applicable trust services criteria, and the complementary user entity controls assumed in the design of ABC Company's controls. Our examination did not include such complementary user entity controls, and we have not evaluated the suitability of the design or operating effectiveness of such controls.

*Service Organization's Responsibilities*

ABC Company is responsible for its service commitments and system requirements and for designing, implementing, and operating effective controls within the system to provide reasonable assurance that ABC Company's service commitments and system requirements were achieved. ABC Company has provided the accompanying assertion, titled "Assertion of ABC Company's Management" (assertion), about the description and the suitability of design and operating effectiveness of controls stated therein. ABC Company is also responsible for preparing the description and assertion, including the completeness, accuracy, and method of presentation of the description and assertion; providing the services covered by the description; selecting the applicable trust services criteria and stating the related controls in the description; and identifying the risks that threaten the achievement of the service organization's service commitments and system requirements.

*Service Auditor's Responsibilities*

Our responsibility is to express an opinion on the description and on the suitability of design and operating effectiveness of controls stated in the description, based on our examination. Our examination was conducted in accordance with attestation standards established by the American Institute of Certified Public Accountants. Those standards require that we plan and perform our examination to obtain reasonable assurance about whether, in all material respects, the description is presented in accordance with the description criteria and the controls stated therein were suitably designed and operating effectively to provide reasonable assurance that the service organization's service commitments and system requirements were achieved based on the applicable trust services criteria. We believe that the evidence we obtained is sufficient and appropriate to provide a reasonable basis for our opinion.

An examination of the description of a service organization's system and the suitability of the design of and operating effectiveness of controls involves the following:

- Obtaining an understanding of the system and service organization's service commitments and system requirements
- Assessing the risks that the description is not presented in accordance with the description criteria and that controls were not suitably designed or did not operate effectively
- Performing procedures to obtain evidence about whether the description is presented in accordance with the description criteria
- Performing procedures to obtain evidence about whether controls stated in the description were suitably designed to provide reasonable assurance that the service organization achieved its service commitments and system requirements based on the applicable trust services criteria
- Testing the operating effectiveness of controls stated in the description to provide reasonable assurance that the service organization achieved its service commitments and system requirements based on the applicable trust services criteria
- Evaluating the overall presentation of the description

Our examination also included performing such other procedures as we considered necessary in the circumstances.

We are required to be independent and to meet our other ethical responsibilities in accordance with relevant ethical requirements relating to the examination engagement.

*Inherent Limitations*

The description is prepared to meet the common needs of a broad range of users and may not, therefore, include every aspect of the system that individual users may consider important to meet their informational needs. There are inherent limitations in the effectiveness of any system of internal control, including the possibility of human error and the circumvention of controls. Because of their nature, controls may not always operate effectively to provide reasonable assurance that the service organization's service commitments and system requirements are achieved based on the applicable trust services criteria. Also, the projection to the future of any conclusions about the suitability of the design and operating effectiveness of controls is subject to the risk that controls may become inadequate because of changes in conditions or that the degree of compliance with policies or procedures may deteriorate.

*Description of Tests of Controls*

The specific controls we tested and the nature, timing, and results of those tests are presented in Section 4.

*Opinion*

In our opinion, in all material respects:

a. The description presents ABC Company's Network Operations Management system that was designed and implemented through the period October 1, Year 1, to September 30, Year 2, in accordance with the description criteria.

b. The controls stated in the description were suitably designed throughout the period October 1, Year 1, to September 30, Year 2, to provide reasonable assurance that ABC Company's service commitments and system requirements would be achieved based on the applicable trust services criteria, if its controls operated effectively throughout that period and if the subservice organization and user entities applied the complementary controls assumed in the design of ABC Company's controls throughout that period.

c. The controls stated in the description operated effectively throughout the period October 1, Year 1, to September 30, Year 2, to provide reasonable assurance that ABC Company's service commitments and system requirements were achieved based on the applicable trust services criteria if complementary subservice organization and complementary user entity controls assumed in the design of ABC Company's controls operated effectively throughout that period.

*Restricted Use*

This report, including the description of tests of controls and results thereof in Section 4, is intended solely for the information and use of ABC Company, user entities of the ABC Company's Network Operations Management system during some or all of the period October 1, Year 1, to September 30, Year 2, business partners of ABC Company subject to risks arising from interactions with the Network Operations Management system, practitioners providing services to such user entities and business partners, prospective user entities and business partners, and regulators who have sufficient knowledge and understanding of the following:

- The nature of the service provided by the service organization
- How the service organization's system interacts with user entities, business partners, subservice organizations, and other parties
- Internal control and its limitations
- Complementary user entity controls and complementary subservice organization controls and how those controls interact with the controls at the service organization to achieve the service organization's service commitments and system requirements
- User entity responsibilities and how they may affect the user entity's ability to effectively use the service organization's services
- The applicable trust services criteria
- The risks that may threaten the achievement of the service organization's service commitments and system requirements and how controls address those risks

This report is not intended to be, and should not be, used by anyone other than those specified parties.

*[City, State]*

*[Report Date]*

*[Service Auditor Firm Information]*

# Section 3 — Service Organization's Description of Its System

## ABC Company's Description of Its System

### Overview of Operations

ABC Company is based in Dallas, Texas. ABC provides managed IT services and network operation center services to local businesses throughout the US. It offers 24/7 support from experienced Network Engineers for small- and medium-size businesses.

### Principal Service Commitments and System Requirements

ABC's network and systems supporting the ABC Company system are protected with technical, physical, and administrative security and confidentiality controls that enable ABC's customers to be confident in the security of the system and safeguarding of confidential data.

### Components of the System Used to Provide the Service

#### Boundaries of the System

The scope of this SOC 2® report is solely around the ABC Company system as operated and managed by the ABC team. The ABC Company system includes the ABC network and information technology infrastructure and the client portal used to report support issues.

#### Infrastructure

ABC's offices continually replicate all internal company files between its three offices. These files are backed up on-premises using a network-attached storage (NAS) server, while AWS services are used to create and store encrypted off-site backups for these systems.

#### Software

ABC's Network Operations Management system consists of key applications: network operations software and related dashboards, client portal and the related database, and AWS to back up and encrypt client files.

### People

#### Contract Administration

The Contract Administration team ensures that client relationships are set up to ensure that service commitments and system requirements are clearly communicated in contractual agreements.

#### Information Systems

The Information Systems team supports the Network Operations Management system through the execution and monitoring of information technology systems, as well as providing IT support for ABC employees.

#### Human Resources

Human Resources works with Information Services to arrange for the onboarding and offboarding of employees supporting the Network Operations Management system.

### Management

ABC's management is composed of seasoned asset and portfolio management and network operations professionals. The Company is led by the Chief Executive Officer. The management team also includes the following:

- **President**, who has an extensive background in network operations and system security industries and who is responsible for overseeing ABC's contract management and technical services teams
- **Chief Financial Officer**, who has finance and accounting experience across varying industries and companies and who is responsible for the management of ABC's finance, accounting, and tax functions
- **Vice President of Information Technology**, who has experience in systems security and network operations centers and who is responsible for the management of ABC's information technology network, infrastructure, systems, operations, support, and security
- **Director of Operations**, who has experience in the network operations and hosted data centers and who is responsible for managing the Operations team and services
- **Director of Human Resources**, who has experience in human resources and people management for several industries, including tech companies

## Procedures

### Physical Security

Physical access to company facilities is controlled through access key card systems and limited to appropriate individuals. Provisioning and deprovisioning of physical access is completed as part of the new hire and termination process.

### Logical Security

*Employee Authentication and Authorization*

Logical security for all systems in scope for this report use Active Directory (AD) Security Groups to authenticate and are governed by the password configurations within AD. Therefore, password configuration settings for the ABC systems are in alignment with the ABC Company Password Policy. This policy includes requirements for password length, history, expiration, and complexity, as well as the threshold for automatic lockout and setting for lockout duration.

*Access Provisioning*

New logical access provisioning for newly hired employees and incremental logical access provisioning for existing employees each go through a similar process to document the request, approval, and provisioning via the ticketing system.

*Access Removal*

As part of the employee offboarding process, logical access to in-scope systems and data is timely removed for terminated employees, including badge access. Additionally, periodic user access review includes verification that all terminated employee accounts have been completely disabled.

*Privileged Access*

Privileged access at ABC is both restricted to authorized individuals and periodically reviewed. Specifically, Active Directory Domain Administration accounts are restricted to IT personnel who require privileged access to perform their roles and responsibilities.

*Boundary Protections*

The Company's information technology resources and systems are protected behind firewalls with restricted ports.

### Network Security

Employee remote access to the corporate network is controlled through the use of a virtual private network (VPN) tunnel with two-factor authentication.

## Change Management

### Application Change Management

Changes to ABC systems are documented, communicated, tracked, tested, and approved prior to movement into production. In-scope applications have dedicated environments for development, testing, and production. Any changes affecting the clients are communicated through the client portal.

## Vulnerability Management

Vulnerability management includes antivirus software, as well as quarterly external network vulnerability scans. Antivirus software is configured to update virus definitions automatically in real time and push these definitions to all connected devices. Antivirus software is installed on all PCs and servers. On a quarterly basis, management performs external network vulnerability scans and penetration tests. Results are reviewed, and if applicable, remediation is tracked.

## Incident Management

The Breach Response Guide provides employees guidance on how to identify a security incident, notification steps, and IT steps for assessing and resolving the security incident. This document includes definitions, a checklist for the first 24 hours of response, and the data breach response plan.

## Data Management

### Data in Transit

Data is protected in a variety of ways when in transit to, from, and within the ABC network. This protection is data segmentation, so that clients may only access their own data in ABC-provided systems. Also, in-scope systems require the use of secure protocols when transmitting information over public networks. Use of these secure protocols protects data on its way into or out of the ABC network.

### Data at Rest

Encryption is used to encrypt data at rest and system backups, including encryption software installed on all company laptops and tablets using 256-AES (Advanced Encryption Standard).

### Data Destruction

Confidential information is retained in compliance with the Company's Customer Data Retention policy. When required by the policy, the Company appropriately disposes of customer data. Additionally, ABC follows an asset disposal policy that outlines the required steps to be performed when disposing of endpoints, servers, and other technology equipment. The execution of this policy for applicable assets is documented as part of the asset inventory tracking.

## Backups and Recovery

### Backup Strategy

For data hosted on-premises, automated backups for ABC-hosted production system data are scheduled to run at predefined intervals. Status of backups is monitored on a weekly basis. Any issues identified are investigated and resolved by the IT team or escalated as appropriate.

## Data

Client and company data are protected through technical, administrative, and physical controls covered in the Procedures section of this report.

## Subservice Organization

The Company uses the following subservice organization and monitors its provided services and controls.

### Amazon Web Services (AWS)

The Company uses AWS for the encryption, cloud storage, and retrieval of backups for restoring systems and data for systems. AWS is responsible for accuracy, completeness, timeliness, and security of its backup creation, encryption, cloud storage, and retrieval services for restoring data and systems. The Company monitors AWS's provided services through obtaining and reviewing the SOC 2® report and the IT team's daily and weekly verification checklists.

## Control Environment

The control environment is shaped primarily through the Company's established workplace conduct standards. New employees are required to read and formally acknowledge the established workplace conduct standards as part of the new hire process. Background checks are also performed for new hires. During the new vendor and contractor onboarding process, confidentiality contract terms or nondisclosure agreements are drafted and signed by vendors and contractors.

## Risk Assessment and Mitigation

ABC management performs a risk assessment annually using an industry-accepted risk-management framework and includes the following:

a. Determining business objectives
b. Evaluating the effect of environmental, regulatory, and technological changes on ABC's system security
c. Analyzing risks associated with the threats
d. Identifying threats to operations, including security threats
e. Determining a risk-mitigation strategy
f. Communication of annual risk assessment results and risk mitigation strategy

## Trust Services Criteria and Related Control Activities

Management selects, implements, and manages control activities through Policies and Procedures. Refer to the above Procedures section for the Company's relevant control activities.

## Trust Services Criteria Not Applicable to the In-Scope System

All the underlying trust services criteria related to Security and Confidentiality are applicable to the system.

## Information and Communication

### Internal Communications

A Company organizational chart is established and documents reporting lines and authorities as well as helps with communication among the various departments of the organization.

Upon hire, employees are provided a copy of their job description and are required to read and acknowledge receipt of the job description. For all existing employees, job descriptions that define user responsibilities and required qualifications/experience exist for all key positions. The descriptions are used as part of the annual performance evaluations, which are formally conducted by employees' supervisors to ensure that performance feedback is communicated and documented. Also, as part of the foundation of communicating expectations and requirements, policies are formally documented and annually reviewed for key IT, operational, and security domains. All employees are required to participate in annual Security Awareness Training.

On a bimonthly basis, each department outlines its goal achievement, client-related issues and commitments, and system and operational issues and reports them to Senior Management. Monthly, Senior Management outlines and discusses ABC's goal achievement, client-related issues and commitments, and system and operational issues with the Company owner.

### External Communications

In addition to internal communication, ABC follows established customer onboarding procedures to ensure all clients are consistently set up for Asset Management servicing. An Onboarding Checklist is required to be filled out for each new client's site to ensure that all required contracts, documents, and information are obtained from the client and entered into ABC's systems. During the new client onboarding process, commitments and responsibilities are communicated and agreed to in the terms and conditions of the client contract with ABC. To use the client portal, users of the Company's portal are required to acknowledge and accept the user terms and conditions as a condition of accessing the system. The Portal User Guide is documented to aid in the operation and use of the portal application for clients.

## Monitoring Activities

### Ongoing Monitoring

There are daily, weekly, monthly, quarterly, or annual tasks performed, and results are documented in the Daily Verification Checklist. Key weekly tasks or procedures include the following:

- Identify and address system anomalies
- Review system access privileges and use
- Track and control the implementation of patching
- Review and validate logical access modifications due to new hires, terminations, transfers, or general access changes

Additionally, on an annual basis, IT Management performs a privileged access review to ensure that privileged access is restricted to appropriate IT personnel. Issues noted are discussed and resolved with Management.

### Separate Evaluations

Third-party penetration testing is performed to identify potential external threats and exposures. Results are reviewed and tracked until remediation.

*ABC Company*

*SOC 2 Report Relevant to Trust Services Criteria for Security and Confidentiality*
*October 1, Year 1, to September 30, Year 2*

## Complementary Subservice Organization Controls

The Company relies on the following services and complementary controls at the subservice organization as part of its controls in meeting the following trust services criteria:

| TSC Series # | Applicable Subservice Organization | Complementary Subservice Organization Controls |
|---|---|---|
| CC6.7, CC7.2, C1.1, C1.2 | AWS | AWS is responsible for encryption, off-site storage, and retrieval of backups for restoring systems and data. |

## Complementary User Entity Control Considerations

The Company's description and its described controls in Section 4 are designed to achieve the Trust Services Security and Confidentiality Categories and Criteria, with the assumption that certain controls would be implemented by user entities. This section describes some of the controls that should be in operation to complement the controls at the Company. User auditors should determine whether user entities have established controls to provide assurance of the following:

| TSC Series # | Complementary User Entity Controls |
|---|---|
| CC2.2, CC2.3, CC6.1, CC6.2, CC6.3, CC6.6 | Users of the Company's portal are required to sign an online acknowledgment form of the acceptance of the Company's terms and conditions to access and use the client portal. |
| CC6.1, CC6.6 | Users of the Company's portal are required to use the provided portal access ID and password to obtain access to use the portal and control knowledge and use of their ID and password. Users of the portal are required to protect their user ID and password and not share it with others. |

*ABC Company*

*SOC 2 Report Relevant to Trust Services Criteria for Security and Confidentiality*
*October 1, Year 1, to September 30, Year 2*

# Section 4 — Trust Services Category, Criteria, Related Controls, and Tests of Controls

## Tests Of Operating Effectiveness

Our tests of the operational effectiveness of controls were designed to cover a representative number of transactions throughout the period of October 1, Year 1, to September 30, Year 2, for each of the controls listed in this section, which are designed to meet the applicable trust services criteria. In selecting particular tests for the operational effectiveness of controls, we considered (a) the nature of the items being tested, (b) the types of available evidential matter, (c) the nature of the audit objectives to be achieved, (d) the assessed level of control risk, and (e) the expected efficiency and effectiveness of the test.

| Test | Description |
|---|---|
| **Inquiry** | Made inquiries of appropriate personnel and corroborated responses with management |
| **Observation** | Observed application or existence of specific controls |
| **Inspection** | Inspected documents and reports indicating performance of the control |
| **Reperformance** | Reperformance of the control |

## Procedures For Assessing Completeness And Accuracy Of Information Provided By The Entity (IPE)

For tests of controls requiring the use of IPE (eg, controls requiring system-generated populations for sample-based testing), we perform a combination of the following procedures where possible, based on the nature of the IPE, to address the completeness, accuracy, and data integrity of the data or reports used: (1) inspect the source of the IPE, (2) inspect the query, script, or parameters used to generate the IPE, (3) tie data between the IPE and the source, and/or (4) inspect the IPE for anomalous gaps in sequence or timing to determine that the data is complete, is accurate, and maintains its integrity. In addition to the above procedures, for tests of controls requiring Management's use of IPE in the execution of the controls (eg, periodic reviews of user access listings), we inspect Management's procedures to assess the validity of the IPE source and the completeness, accuracy, and integrity of the data or reports.

*ABC Company*

*SOC 2 Report Relevant to Trust Services Criteria for Security and Confidentiality*
*October 1, Year 1, to September 30, Year 2*

## Trust Services Categories and Criteria

| TSC Series # | Trust Services Criteria | ABC Company Control Activity Numbers |
|---|---|---|
| | **Security (Common and Supplemental Criteria)** | |
| CC1.1 - Control Environment | COSO Principle 1: The entity demonstrates a commitment to integrity and ethical values. | CE-1, CE-2, CE-3, CE-7 |
| CC1.2 - Control Environment | COSO Principle 2: The Board of Directors demonstrates independence from management and exercises oversight of the development and performance of internal control. | CI-4 |
| CC1.3 - Control Environment | COSO Principle 3: Management establishes, with board oversight, structures, reporting lines, and appropriate authorities and responsibilities in the pursuit of objectives. | CE-4, CE-5 |
| CC1.4 - Control Environment | COSO Principle 4: The entity demonstrates a commitment to attract, develop, and retain competent individuals in alignment with objectives. | CE-2, CE-6, CE-7 |
| CC1.5 - Control Environment | COSO Principle 5: The entity holds individuals accountable for their internal control responsibilities in the pursuit of objectives. | CE-5, CE-6 |
| CC2.1 - Communication and Information | COSO Principle 13: The entity obtains or generates and uses relevant, quality information to support the functioning of internal control. | CI-1, CI-4, MA-1 |
| CC2.2 - Communication and Information | COSO Principle 14: The entity internally communicates information, including objectives and responsibilities for internal control, necessary to support the functioning of internal control. | CI-4 |
| CC2.3 - Communication and Information | COSO Principle 15: The entity communicates with external parties regarding matters affecting the functioning of internal control. | CE-3, CI-3, CI-2 |
| CC3.1 - Risk Assessment: Operations Objectives | COSO Principle 6: The entity specifies objectives with sufficient clarity to enable the identification and assessment of risks relating to objectives. | CI-4, RA-1, MA-1 |
| CC3.2 - Risk Assessment | COSO Principle 7: The entity identifies risks to the achievement of its objectives across the entity and analyzes risks as a basis for determining how the risks should be managed. | CI-4, RA-1, MA-1, MA-2 |
| CC3.3 - Fraud Risk Assessment | COSO Principle 8: The entity considers the potential for fraud in assessing risks to the achievement of objectives. | CE-1, CE-5, MA-1 |

*ABC Company*

*SOC 2 Report Relevant to Trust Services Criteria for Security and Confidentiality*
*October 1, Year 1, to September 30, Year 2*

| TSC Series # | Trust Services Criteria | ABC Company Control Activity Numbers |
|---|---|---|
| CC3.4 - Assessing Changes in Risk | COSO Principle 9: The entity identifies and assesses changes that could significantly affect the system of internal control. | RA-1 |
| CC4.1 - Monitoring Activities: Periodic Evaluations | COSO Principle 16: The entity selects, develops, and performs ongoing and/or separate evaluations to ascertain whether the components of internal control are present and functioning. | CI-4, MA-1, MA-2 |
| CC4.2 - Monitoring Activities: Exception Monitoring | COSO Principle 17: The entity evaluates and communicates internal control deficiencies in a timely manner to those parties responsible for taking corrective action, including Senior Management and the Board of Directors, as appropriate. | RA-1, MA-1, MA-2, CA-1 |
| CC5.1 - Control Activities: Risk Mitigation | COSO Principle 10: The entity selects and develops control activities that contribute to the mitigation of risks to the achievement of objectives to acceptable levels. | CI-4, RA-1, MA-1, MA-2, CA-1, CA-2 |
| CC5.2 - Control Activities: IT General Controls | COSO Principle 11: The entity also selects and develops general control activities over technology to support the achievement of objectives. | CI-4, MA-1, MA-2, CA-1, CA-2 |
| CC5.3 - Control Activities: Polices/Procedures | COSO Principle 12: The entity deploys control activities through policies that establish what is expected and in procedures that put policies into action. | CE-5, CE-6, |
| CC6.1 - Logical and Physical Access Controls | The entity implements logical access security software, infrastructure, and architectures over protected information assets to protect them from security events to meet the entity's objectives. | CI-3, MA-1, MA-2, MA-3, LA-1, LA-2, LA-3, LA-4, SO-1, SO-2, SO-3 |
| CC6.2 - Logical and Physical Access Controls: User Provisioning | Prior to issuing system credentials and granting system access, the entity registers and authorizes new internal and external users whose access is administered by the entity. For those users whose access is administered by the entity, user system credentials are removed when user access is no longer authorized. | CI-3, MA-1, MA-3, LA-4, LA-5, LA-6 |
| CC6.3 - Logical and Physical Access Controls: User Provisioning | The entity authorizes, modifies, or removes access to data, software, functions, and other protected information assets based on roles, responsibilities, or the system design and changes, giving consideration to the concepts of least privilege and segregation of duties, to meet the entity's objectives. | CI-3, LA-5, LA-6, MA-1, LA-6 |

*ABC Company*

*SOC 2 Report Relevant to Trust Services Criteria for Security and Confidentiality*
*October 1, Year 1, to September 30, Year 2*

| TSC Series # | Trust Services Criteria | ABC Company Control Activity Numbers |
|---|---|---|
| CC6.4 - Logical and Physical Access Controls: Physical Access | The entity restricts physical access to facilities and protected information assets (for example, data center facilities, backup media storage, and other sensitive locations) to authorized personnel to meet the entity's objectives. | LA-7 |
| CC6.5 - Logical and Physical Access Controls: Data Destruction | The entity discontinues logical and physical protections over physical assets only after the ability to read or recover data and software from those assets has been diminished and is no longer required to meet the entity's objectives. | LA-1 |
| CC6.6 - Logical and Physical Access Controls: User Authentication | The entity implements logical access security measures to protect against threats from sources outside its system boundaries. | CE-1, CE-3, CE-7, CI-3, LA-3, LA-4, SO-1, SO-2, C-2 |
| CC6.7 - Logical and Physical Access Controls: Data In Transit | The entity restricts the transmission, movement, and removal of information to authorized internal and external users and processes and protects it during transmission, movement, or removal to meet the entity's objectives. | LA-4, LA-7, SO-1, SO-2, SO-3, SO-5 |
| CC6.8 - Logical and Physical Access Controls: Unauthorized/ Malicious Software | The entity implements controls to prevent or detect and act on the introduction of unauthorized or malicious software to meet the entity's objectives. | MA-1, MA-2, SO-4, LA-2 CM-1 |
| CC7.1 - System Operations: Configuration Standards | To meet its objectives, the entity uses detection and monitoring procedures to identify (1) changes to configurations that result in the introduction of new vulnerabilities and (2) susceptibilities to newly discovered vulnerabilities. | MA-1, MA-2, CA-1 CM-1 |
| CC7.2 - System Operations: Security Events | The entity monitors system components and the operation of those components for anomalies that are indicative of malicious acts, natural disasters, and errors affecting the entity's ability to meet its objectives; anomalies are analyzed to determine whether they represent security events. | MA-1, MA-2, RA-1, SO-4 |
| CC7.3 - System Operations: Security Incidents | The entity evaluates security events to determine whether they could result or have resulted in a failure of the entity to meet its objectives (security incidents) and, if so, takes actions to prevent or address such failures. | MA-2, CM-1, RM-1 |

*ABC Company*

*SOC 2 Report Relevant to Trust Services Criteria for Security and Confidentiality*
*October 1, Year 1, to September 30, Year 2*

| TSC Series # | Trust Services Criteria | ABC Company Control Activity Numbers |
|---|---|---|
| CC7.4 - System Operations: Incident Response | The entity responds to identified security incidents by executing a defined incident response program to understand, contain, remediate, and communicate security incidents, as appropriate. | MA-2, SO-3, SO-4, CM-1, RM-1 |
| CC7.5 - System Operations: Incident Recovery | The entity identifies, develops, and implements activities to recover from identified security incidents. | CI-4, CA-2, SO-3, SO-4, CM-1, RM-1 |
| CC8.1 - Change Management | The entity authorizes, designs, develops or acquires, configures, documents, tests, approves, and implements changes to infrastructure, data, software, and procedures to meet its objectives. | CE-1, CE-3, CE-7, MA-1, MA-2, LA-2, SO-1, CM-1, CM-2, RM-1 |
| CC9.1 - Risk Mitigation | The entity identifies, selects, and develops risk-mitigation activities for risks arising from potential business disruptions. | RA-1 |
| CC9.2 - Third-Party Risk Management | The entity assesses and manages risks associated with vendors and business partners. | RA-1, CE-3 |
| | **Confidentiality (Additional Criteria)** | |
| C1.1 - Identify/Maintain Confidential Information | The entity identifies and maintains confidential information to meet the entity's objectives related to confidentiality. | CE-3, C-1, C-2 |
| C1.2 - Data Disposal | The entity disposes of confidential information to meet the entity's objectives related to confidentiality. | CI-1, C-1 |

*ABC Company*
*SOC 2 Report Relevant to Trust Services Criteria for Security and Confidentiality*
*October 1, Year 1, to September 30, Year 2*

## ABC Company's Internal Controls and Service Auditor's Tests of Controls

Below represents the key internal controls identified by (service organization) to meet the (criteria in scope) trust services criteria and the related auditor testing procedures and results.

| ABC Company Control Activity | Test Procedures Performed | Results of Tests |
|---|---|---|
| | **Security (Common Controls)** | |
| **Control Environment (CE)** | | |
| CE-1: The Company has established workplace conduct standards. New employees are required to read and formally acknowledge the established workplace conduct standards. | Inspected Company standards and policies to determine that it has implemented workplace conduct standards.<br>For a sample of new employees, inspected signed acknowledgments to determine that they read and formally acknowledged the workplace conduct standards. | No exceptions noted. |
| CE-2: As part of the new hire process, background checks are performed for new hires. | For a sample of new hires during the audit period, inspected supporting records to determine that a background check was performed as part of the hiring process. | No exceptions noted. |
| CE-3: During the new vendor or contractor onboarding process, confidentiality contract terms or nondisclosure agreements are drafted and signed. | For a sample of new vendors and contractors, inspected signed contracts with confidentiality terms or nondisclosure agreements to determine that confidential agreements are in place and signed. | No exceptions noted. |
| CE-4: A Company organizational chart is established and documents reporting lines and authorities. | Inspected the Company organizational chart to determine that a Company organizational chart is established and documents reporting lines and authorities. | No exceptions noted. |
| CE-5: Upon hire, employees are provided a copy of their job description and are required to read and acknowledge receipt. | For a sample of newly hired employees, inspected the employees' job description and their signed acknowledgment to determine that job descriptions are documented and newly hired employee are required to read and acknowledge receipt. | No exceptions noted. |
| CE-6: Annual performance evaluations are formally conducted by employees' supervisors to ensure that performance feedback is communicated and documented. | For a sample of current employees, inspected completed assessments to determine that annual performance evaluations are formally conducted by employees' supervisors to ensure that performance feedback is communicated and documented. | No exceptions noted. |

*ABC Company*

*SOC 2 Report Relevant to Trust Services Criteria for Security and Confidentiality*

*October 1, Year 1, to September 30, Year 2*

| ABC Company Control Activity | Test Procedures Performed | Results of Tests |
|---|---|---|
| CE-7: Employees are required to participate in annual Security Awareness Training. | For a sample of current employees, inspected support of attending the annual Security Awareness Training to determine that they participated. | No exceptions noted. |
| **Communication and Information (CI)** | | |
| CI-1: An Onboarding Checklist is required to be filled out for each new client's site to ensure that all required contracts, documents, and information are obtained from the client and entered into ABC's systems. | For a sample of new clients' sites, inspected the completed Customer Onboarding Checklist to determine that required steps were completed to ensure that all required contracts, documents, and information are obtained from the client and entered into ABC's systems. | No exceptions noted. |
| CI-2: The Portal User Guide is documented to aid in the operation and use of the portal application. | Inspected the Portal User Guide to determine that formal documentation is provided to customers for the operation and use of the portal application. | No exceptions noted. |
| CI-3: Users of the Company's portal are required to acknowledge and accept the user terms and conditions as a condition of accessing the system. | For a sample of new portal users, inspected tracked online acknowledgments and acceptance of the terms and conditions for users of the portal. | No exceptions noted. |
| CI-4: On a bimonthly basis, each department outlines its goal achievement, client-related issues and commitments, and system and operational issues and reports them to Senior Management. | For a sample of two-month periods, inspected bimonthly report packages to the Senior Management to determine that goal achievement, client-related issues and commitment, and system and operational issues and risks are communicated. | No exceptions noted. |
| **Risk Assessment (RA)** | | |
| RA-1: ABC Management performs a risk assessment annually using an industry-accepted risk-management framework. | Inspected ABC Management's risk-assessment approach, completed assessment, communication of results, and risk-mitigation strategy to determine that it was performed annually and used an industry-accepted risk-management framework. | No exceptions noted. |

*ABC Company*

*SOC 2 Report Relevant to Trust Services Criteria for Security and Confidentiality*
*October 1, Year 1, to September 30, Year 2*

| ABC Company Control Activity | Test Procedures Performed | Results of Tests |
|---|---|---|
| **Monitoring Activities (MA)** | | |
| MA-1: IT Verification Reviews are performed on a set schedule to monitor IT and security control activities and processes. Each task within the reviews is documented in the Daily Verification Checklist. | For a sample of weeks, inspected the completed IT Verification Reviews to determine that each task was performed and documented in the Daily Verification Checklist. | No exceptions noted. |
| MA-2: Third-party penetration testing is performed to identify potential external threats and exposures. Results are reviewed and tracked until remediation. | Inspected the third-party penetration test report and tracking support to determine that the testing was performed and results were reviewed and tracked until remediation. | No exceptions noted. |
| MA-3: On an annual basis, a user access review is performed for in-scope applications to determine that employee access is commensurate with job responsibilities. | For each in-scope application, inspected the annual user access review to determine that a user access review is performed for in-scope applications to determine that employee access is commensurate with job responsibilities. | No exceptions noted. |
| **Control Activities (CA)** | | |
| CA-1: On a quarterly basis, management performs external network vulnerability scans. Results are reviewed, and, if applicable, remediation is tracked. | For a sample of quarters, inspected vulnerability scanning results, Management's reviews, and remediation trackers to determine that Management performs quarterly external network vulnerability scans, reviews the results, and, if needed, tracks remediation tasks. | No exceptions noted. |
| **Logical and Physical Access Controls (LA)** | | |
| LA-1: Active Directory Domain Administration accounts are restricted to IT personnel who require privileged access to perform their roles and responsibilities. | Inspected the listing of Domain Administrator accounts to determine that access is restricted to IT personnel who require privileged access to perform their roles and responsibilities. | No exceptions noted. |
| LA-2: Password configuration settings are configured in accordance with ABC Security Guidelines. | Inspected the password configurations to determine that the configurations are aligned with the ABC Security Guidelines. | No exceptions noted. |

*ABC Company*
*SOC 2 Report Relevant to Trust Services Criteria for Security and Confidentiality*
*October 1, Year 1, to September 30, Year 2*

| ABC Company Control Activity | Test Procedures Performed | Results of Tests |
|---|---|---|
| LA-3: Employee remote access to the corporate network is controlled through the use of a virtual private network (VPN) tunnel with two-factor authentication. | Inspected configuration of the VPN to determine that two-factor authentication is required. | No exceptions noted. |
| LA-4: New hire access to in-scope systems and data require Management approval prior to provisioning. | For a sample of new hires, inspected help-desk tickets to determine that the access request was documented and authorized by Management prior to provisioning. | No exceptions noted. |
| LA-5: Logical access to in-scope systems and data is timely removed for terminated employees. | For a sample of terminated employees, inspected help-desk tickets and updated access listings to determine that access was timely removed through the disabling of the user account. | No exceptions noted. |
| LA-6: Encryption software is installed on all Company laptops and tablets. | For a sample of employees, inspected their Company-provided laptop and tablet to determine that encryption is installed. | No exceptions noted. |
| LA-7: Physical access to Company facilities is controlled through access key card systems and limited to appropriate individuals. | Observed the existence of locked perimeter doors and access card scanners to determine that physical access to Company facilities is controlled through access key card systems.<br>Inspected access listing to Company facilities to determine that access was appropriate. | No exceptions noted. |
| **System Operations (SO)** | | |
| SO-1: The Company's information technology resources and systems are protected using firewalls. | Inspected the Company's network diagrams to determine that firewalls are stationed at the boundary of the network.<br>Inspected the firewall configurations to determine that the Company's systems are protected through the use of firewalls. | No exceptions noted. |
| SO-2: Clients may only access their own data in Company-provided systems. | Inspected the data segmentation configurations to determine that clients may only access their own data. | No exceptions noted. |
| SO-3: Data and system backups are encrypted. | Inspected configuration of the backup system to determine that data and system backup files were encrypted. | No exceptions noted. |

*ABC Company*
*SOC 2 Report Relevant to Trust Services Criteria for Security and Confidentiality*
*October 1, Year 1, to September 30, Year 2*

| ABC Company Control Activity | Test Procedures Performed | Results of Tests |
|---|---|---|
| SO-4: Antivirus software is configured to update virus definitions automatically in real time and push these definitions to all connected devices. Antivirus software is installed on all PCs and servers. | Inspected the antivirus configurations to determine that vendor updates are being automatically downloaded in real time and then pushed to all connected devices. | No exceptions noted. |
| SO-5: Automated backups for Company-hosted production system data are scheduled to run at predefined intervals. Status of backups is monitored on a weekly basis. | For a sample of weeks, inspected the backup monitoring line item on the Validator Checklist to determine that the status of backups was proactively being monitored. | No exceptions noted. |
| **Change Management (CM)** | | |
| CM-1: Application and system changes are documented, tested, and approved. | Inspected a sample of application and system changes to determine that they were documented, tested, and approved. | No exceptions noted. |
| CM-2: In-scope applications have dedicated environments for development, testing, and production. | Observed the existence and use of separate development, testing, and production environments for each in-scope application. | No exceptions noted. |
| **Risk Mitigation (RM)** | | |
| RM-1: The Breach Response Guide provides employees guidance on how to identify a security incident, notification steps, and IT steps for assessing and resolving the security incident. | Inspected the Breach Response Guide to determine that the document outlines how to identify a security incident, notification steps, and IT steps for assessing and resolving the security incident. | No exceptions noted. |
| | **Confidentiality** | |
| C-1: Confidential information is retained in compliance with the Company's Customer Data Retention policy. When required by the policy, the Company appropriately disposes of customer data. | Inspected the Customer Data Retention policy for data retention and disposal requirements.<br>For a sample of client data-deletion requests, inspected documentation to determine that data disposal followed steps required by the Company's Customer Data Retention policy. | No exceptions noted. |
| C-2: In-scope systems require the use of secure protocols when transmitting information over public networks. | Inspected Transport Layer Security (TLS) settings for in-scope systems to determine that in-scope systems require the use of secure protocols when transmitting information over public networks. | No exceptions noted. |